# SAP® Change and Transport Management

SAP PRESS and the SAP Technical Support Guides are issued by Bernhard Hochlehnert, SAP AG

Thomas Schneider
SAP Performance Optimization Guide
4th Ed. 2006, 522 pp., ISBN 1-59229-069-8

Sigrid Hagemann, Liane Will
SAP R/3 System Administration
2nd Ed. 2003, 520 pp., ISBN 1-59229-014-0

Helmut Stefani
Archiving Your SAP Data
A comprehensive guide to plan and execute archiving projects
2003, 360 pp., ISBN 1-592229-008-6

Bert Vanstechelman, Mark Mergaerts
The SAP OS/DB Migration Project Guide
SAP PRESS Essentials 5
2005, 88 pp., ISBN 1-59229-056-6

Vanstechelman, Mergaerts, Matthys
mySAP ERP Upgrade Project Guide
SAP PRESS Essentials 16
2006, approx. 120 pp., 1-59229-090-6

Achim Kösegi, Rainer Nerding

# SAP® Change and Transport Management

SAP PRESS is an imprint of Galileo Press,
Fort Lee (NJ), USA
Bonn, Germany



**Translation** Lemoine International, Inc., Salt Lake City, UT
**Copy Editor** Nancy Etscovitz, UCG, Inc., Boston, MA
**Cover Design** Silke Braun, Galileo Press, Germany
**Printed** in Germany

**ISBN 1-59229-059-0**
Second edition, revised and expanded

# Foreword to the series of books

At SAP AG, our first priority is to ensure that the SAP software solutions in your enterprise run successfully and at a minimal cost. This "Lowest Cost of Ownership" is achieved with fast and efficient implementation, together with optimal and dependable operation. SAP Active Global Support is actively and consistently there to help you, with the new SAP Solution Management strategy. Throughout the entire lifecycle of a solution, SAP offers customers all necessary services, first-class support, a suitable infrastructure, and the relevant know-how. The new strategy is backed up by three powerful support programs: *Safeguarding*, or, in other words, risk management; *Solution Management Optimization*, which aims to optimize the customer's IT solution; and *Empowering*, which ensures a targeted, effective transfer of knowledge from SAP to the customer.

The imparting of knowledge is also one of the key aims of this book—part of the line of *SAP Technical Support Guides*. This series gives you a detailed overview of technical aspects and concepts for managing SAP software solutions. The topics dealt with in these books range from a technical implementation project to running a software system and the relevant database system.

Whether you are new to SAP system management or wish to gain further qualifications, you will benefit from the wealth of practical experience and first-hand information contained in these books. With this line of books, SAP also endeavors to help prepare you for qualification as a "Certified Technical Consultant". Please note, however: These books cannot replace, nor do they attempt to replace, personal experience gained from working with the various SAP solutions! Rather, the authors offer suggestions to help in your day-to-day work with the software. Innovation in SAP solutions always brings with it new challenges and solutions for system management. The demands made on the customer's own or external support organizations also increase. The expertise and knowledge of these organizations can be a great help in avoiding problems when using the software. Therefore, one of the core tasks of this series of books is to teach problem-solving skills.

Even in this Internet age, books prove to be an ideal medium for imparting knowledge in a compact form. Furthermore, their content complements the new service and support platform, the SAP Solution Manager, and other new services offered by SAP. The series provides background knowledge on the operation and functioning of new SAP solutions and contributes to customer satisfaction.

**Gerhard Oswald**
Member of the executive board of SAP AG

**Dr. Uwe Hommel**
Senior Vice President at SAP AG
SAP Active Global Support

Rot, March 2006

# Contents

# Part 2 Technical Tasks

## 7 Transport Setup Activities at Installation 175



## 8 Setting Up the TMS 207

## 11 Managing Customizing Changes 335



## 12 Promoting Change Requests 373

# Introduction

mySAP ERP 2004 is the SAP solution around the successor of SAP R/3—SAP ECC 5.0—which provides even more functionality by using additional software components to meet the requirements of enterprises and organizations of any size. Although this functionality is built into the software, it must be configured during its implementation to meet the specific needs of an organization. This process, known as *Customizing*, uses special SAP adaptation tools. A customer's SAP adaptation may also require *development* work; that is, the customer must program new or modified functionality using SAP's ABAP programming language.

In general, mySAP ERP 2004 resembles most other business software installations in that its implementation requires:

- Configuration and/or development work
- A carefully planned realization of business needs in the software
- The realization of an appropriate technical infrastructure in the system landscape
- Project management that controls the scope of what is to be implemented and defines the roles and responsibilities of the people on the implementation team
- Thorough testing and validation of the changes achieved through Customizing or development
- Training for end users
- Future expansion of the software's initially implemented functionality and usage

To provide an infrastructure that fulfills these implementation needs, SAP recommends implementing the different software instances with three strictly separate environments:

- A development environment for Customizing and development work
- A quality assurance environment for testing business functionality using representative test data
- A production environment for normal business operations, which is secure from changes made in other environments until those changes have been verified and are ready for transfer into the production environment

These three environments are realized through *systems* and *clients*, which are logical divisions within an SAP system. The collection of clients and systems required for an SAP implementation forms the *system landscape*.

Figure 1 depicts the standard three-system landscape used to support ECC 5.0 (or previous versions) and recommended by SAP. The development system is an SAP system for Customizing and development efforts. The quality assurance system is then used to test and verify Customizing and development work. Once Customizing and development changes have been validated and approved, they are delivered to the production system.

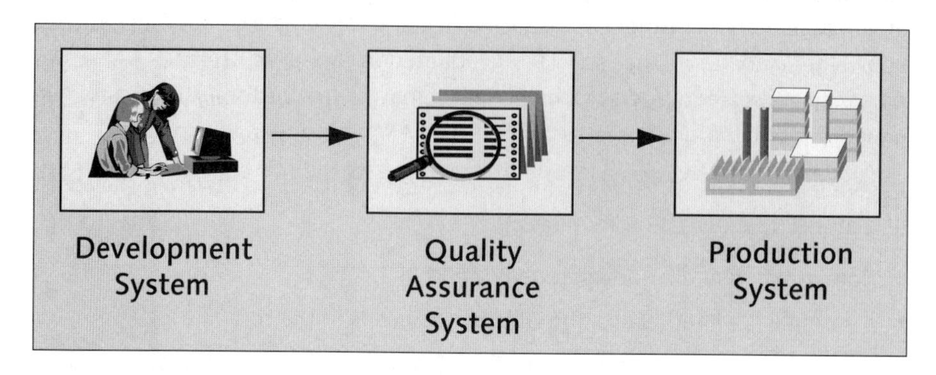


**Figure 1** The standard three-system landscape

To manage changes created during Customizing and development, and to ensure that applications remain consistent across multiple ECC systems, changes are recorded and organized in *change requests* and are *transported* to different clients and ECC systems within the system landscape. The process of transporting requires the *releasing* and *exporting* of the change requests from the development system and then *importing* them into another ECC System. The techniques for change and transport management are also known as *software logistics*—the process of moving or transporting changes made to the SAP software.

Implementing change and transport management includes the following tasks:

- Setting up a system landscape
- Regulating the systems and clients in which Customizing and development changes are made
- Recording Customizing and development changes to change requests during the initial implementation of SAP *and* during any subsequent improvement of the production environment
- Managing the transport of changes to all clients and SAP systems within the system landscape
- Testing, validating, and approving changes using the quality assurance system
- Maintaining the production system over time by applying SAP Support Packages and upgrades

Although the main goal of a particular mySAP ERP 2004 implementation is to fulfill your business requirements, this can be realized only if you ensure system stability and data validity through correct change and transport management.

Many aspects of change and transport management are technical in nature, but the procedures you define to implement it will affect all staff members. The business knowledge required to perform Customizing and test SAP systems is possessed mainly by the staff in the corresponding functional departments, and it is they who perform Customizing and testing. Therefore, not just technical staff, but all people involved in an SAP implementation need to understand change and transport management and the structure of the system landscape. Those who actually make the changes to the SAP system need additional expert knowledge of the relevant tools and procedures.

## How This Book Is Organized

The information in this book is organized into three parts, each aimed at people involved in this procedure at different levels. **Part 1**, "The Big Picture," provides a basic explanation of how changes are made and distributed. It enables those managing the SAP implementation to develop a valid change and transport management strategy.

**Part 2**, "Technical Tasks," is essential reading for technicians coordinating the setup of the technical infrastructure or performing, for example, SAP system administration tasks.

**Part 3**, "Tools," is the how-to section, providing detailed information on the tools described in Part 1. This part is also a reference section for those requiring in-depth knowledge. The first three chapters of Part 3 will be of particular use to anyone performing Customizing or development work during an SAP implementation.

Chapters 13 and 14 are indispensable for those responsible for importing changes. Chapters 15 and 16 contain information about maintenance and the change of release in a mySAP ERP system landscape. These chapters are relevant to system administrators and technical consultants who need to perform these tasks. Project managers can also obtain an overview of necessary activities and efficient procedures in maintenance or upgrade projects. Chapter 17 describes new functionalities of SAP Solution Manager in the area of software change management. In particular, customizing synchronization within an SAP system landscape and change request management are discussed. Chapter 18 contains additional information about transports in Java by supporting the SAP NetWeaver Development Infrastructure (NWDI), which is primarily used for distributing developments via using SAP Web Dynpro in the SAP Enterprise Portal. In future, the NWDI will enable and control further changes within mySAP ERP—particularly contents and roles that are also required in the SAP Enterprise Portal.

The information in this book pertains primarily to the ABAP instances of SAP NetWeaver '04 and the software components based thereon, like ECC 5.0. Other SAP products—parts of mySAP ERP2004 as well as other SAP solutions—use the same technology because they are all based on the technology of SAP NetWeaver '04. There can be slight differences, however; for example, not all SAP products use the same client concept as ECC 5.0, and some SAP products have extended the standard functionality for their purposes. In those cases, the menu paths shown in this book might not be directly reproducible. However, the essential basics and the tools for operating these products are still of value in that they will enable you to understand the principles of change and transport management. Additionally, you should consult the specific product documentation.

Chapter 18 contains additional information about transports in Java by supporting the SAP NetWeaver Development Infrastructure (NWDI), which is primarily used for distributing developments using SAP Web Dynpro in the SAP Enterprise Portal. In the future, the NWDI will enable and control additional changes within mySAP ERP—particularly contents and roles that are also required in the SAP Enterprise Portal.

# Part 1
# The Big Picture

During customer activities in the SAP ECC system such as development and Customizing, changes are made to the software. Change and transport management consists of special procedures for distributing these changes across your system landscape. The need for logistics or coordination of changes arises from three main facts:

- To ensure data consistency, the changes may need to be limited to some or all clients, in some or all systems. Where, how, and when these changes are introduced must be regulated.
- The customer's production system must be protected from changes that have not been fully tested. This means Customizing, development, and testing of changes should be performed in systems outside the production system.
- A number of people may be making different kinds of changes at the same time or at different times. This means that objects and settings must be protected, changes must be documented, and a change history must be made available.

*Software logistics* is the logistics of managing these changes and the corresponding requirements on the system landscape. To establish software logistics during your R/3 implementation, you need to:

- Set up change management
- Implement a transport strategy
- Build a system landscape that allows you to make and test all the required changes while preventing inconsistencies and protecting the integrity of your production system

In Part 1, this procedure is explained in more detail, and you are encouraged to use SAP-recommended standards. The specific topics covered in Part 1 include:

- An introduction to the components of the system landscape.
- An introduction to the realization of business requirements through Customizing and development efforts.
- An explanation of clients and client roles used in an implementation.
- Guidelines for setting up and maintaining a system landscape.
- An introduction to the relevant SAP tools. These tools receive more extensive coverage in Part 2 and Part 3.

# 1 SAP ECC Architecture and Data Components

SAP ECC architecture is shaped by its use of client/server technology—that is, the way it distributes the software services needed by users over multiple servers. SAP ECC system administration and performance optimization require a detailed understanding of this client/server technology. In contrast, change and transport management, which is implemented by configuring the SAP ECC system appropriately, focuses mainly on a specific element within the architecture, namely the database. Change and transport is concerned with:

- The role the database plays in the architecture
- The architecture of the database itself, in terms of the data components and clients

The database stores the SAP ECC software. An important part of this software is the *SAP ECC Repository*, which provides the runtime environment for the various business applications. The database also contains the various data components, such as the business data that is required for or generated by day-to-day business transactions.

Data can be isolated by assigning it to one of several separate "containers" in the SAP ECC Repository. These containers are called *clients*. When a user logs on, they log on to a particular client and can display or change only the data corresponding to that client. Data that can be displayed or changed from only one client is called *client-dependent data*. Data that can be accessed from all clients is called *client-independent data* or *cross-client data*.

To ensure the success of your change and transport management strategy, the people performing Customizing or development during SAP ECC system implementation need to understand:

- The different data components in the database
- Which data is client-dependent and which is client-independent

After a brief look at client/server architecture, this chapter describes the SAP ECC database, clients, and the various data components, and explains which data is client-dependent and which data can be accessed by all clients.

For information on how to create and maintain the various data components, see Chapter 2.

## 1.1 Client/Server Architecture in Brief

SAP recognized early on that to provide a scalable and global business software package to meet a wide range of customer needs, the way to go was client/server technology. Client/server technology distributes different applications and system services across multiple hardware servers. Servers may contain a combination of services, and run on different hardware platforms. SAP's use of multilayer client/server computing maximizes performance and provides flexibility in management and hardware options.

The client/server architecture of SAP ECC consists of three types of services:

- A database service for storing and retrieving business data
- An application service for running business processes
- A presentation service for the graphical user interface (GUI)

From a hardware perspective, these three layers—the database, application, and presentation layers—can run separately on different servers or all together on the same server. A typical installation supporting numerous SAP users uses multiple presentation servers. To increase system performance, the application layer can be distributed over multiple servers. This is depicted in Figure 1.1, where a database server and multiple application and presentation servers support an SAP ECC system.

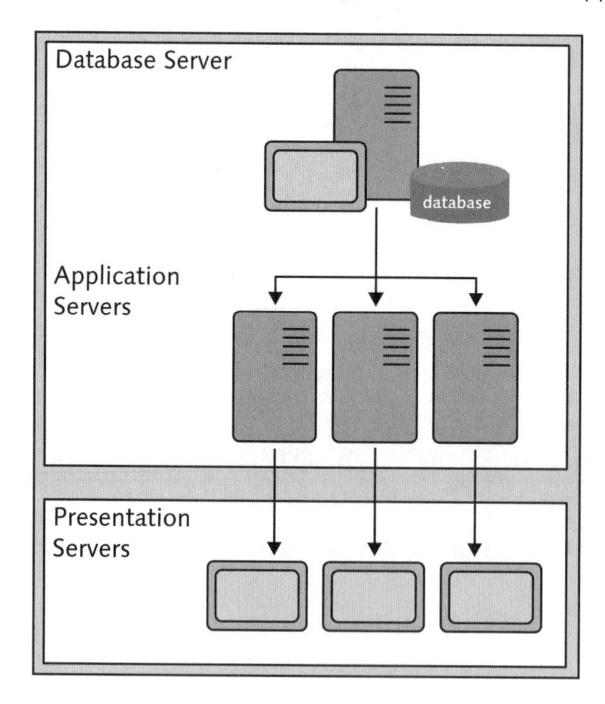


**Figure 1.1** The three-layer architecture of SAP ECC

Regardless of the number of application and presentation servers, each SAP ECC system has only one database. It is the number of databases (one for each SAP ECC system) in which changes originate or to which changes must be transported that is of central importance for change and transport management.

**Example: SAP ECC Client/Server Technology in Practice**

A medium-sized distribution firm purchases a Hewlett-Packard server for running the Windows XP Server operating system. An Oracle database is chosen because the company is already using Oracle for other applications. Both the Oracle database and the SAP ECC applications run on the Hewlett-Packard server. The presentation servers are PCs using SAP's graphical user interface (SAP GUI) or a Web browser running SAP Enterprise Portal to connect to SAP ECC's database and application processes.

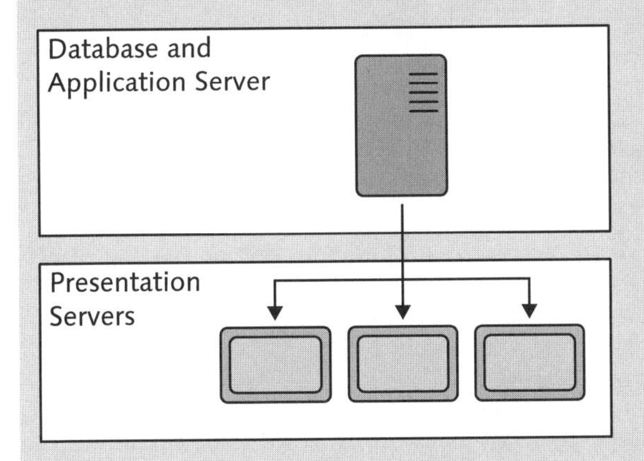


**Figure 1.2** Integrated database and application server

After some time, significant growth in the data volume and the number of users reduces system performance. Therefore, two additional Hewlett-Packard servers are purchased and added to the SAP ECC system as application servers. The only service running on the original server is the Oracle database.

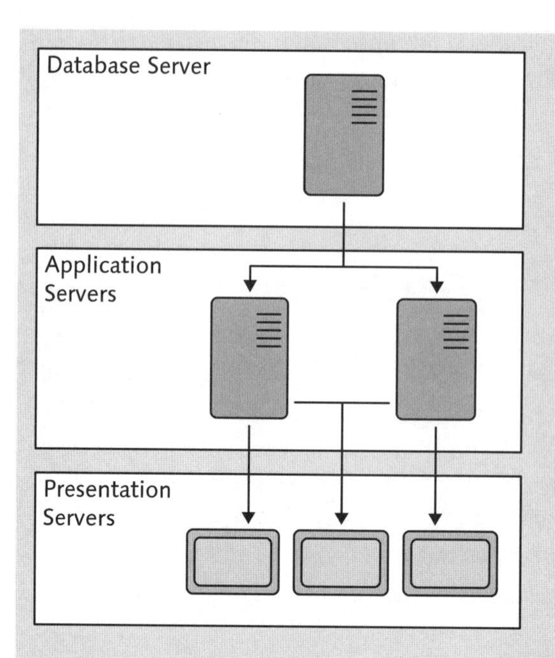


**Figure 1.3** One database server with additional application servers

Thus, an SAP ECC system may have a single server that provides both application and database services. Alternatively, the application layer can be distributed over multiple computers. In any case, the SAP ECC system has only one database.

## 1.2 The SAP ECC Database

In many software packages, the actual software is considered to be separate from the data that is entered or created using the software. The term *software package* is synonymous with *program* or *executable*, and the data is stored external to this software in a file. When you print a spreadsheet, for example, you require both a software executable and a spreadsheet file.

Unlike other software packages, SAP ECC software is not separate from its data. Both application functionality and business data are stored together in the database, along with SAP ECC documentation and performance statistics. The database contains almost everything the users can see: transaction data, program source code, text, menu options, screens, and even printer and fax definitions. In other words, the database contains virtually all system-related components. Only a few system-related files reside outside the database—for example, the kernel.

The database can be divided into two logical components: the *Repository* and *customer data*.

### 1.2.1 The Repository

The Repository provides the data structures and programs you need to maintain data in the SAP ECC system.

The central part of the Repository is the *ABAP Dictionary*, which contains descriptions of the structure and the relationships of all data. These descriptions are used by SAP ECC to interpret and generate the application objects of the runtime environment—for example, programs or screens. Such objects are referred to as *Repository objects.*

During SAP ECC implementation, you may wish to perform development work in the system to adapt the Repository to meet specific requirements. Using the tools in the *ABAP Workbench*, you can create or modify Repository objects, thus adding or changing table structures or programs. The result of such development work is one or both of the following:

- New customer Repository objects are added to the Repository.
- Standard SAP objects in the Repository are modified.

**Warning** SAP recommends that you do not modify standard SAP objects in the Repository. See Chapter 2.

### 1.2.2 Customer Data

In addition to the Repository, the other logical component of the database is customer data. This customer data consists of any kind of data entered into the system by the customer—the organization or company that purchased and uses the SAP software—either during SAP ECC implementation or during day-to-day business processing. Customer data includes:

- Customizing data
- Application data
- User master data

*Customizing data* is generated when SAP ECC is configured to meet the particular needs of the customer through Customizing. *Application data*, also known as *business data*, is the data required for or generated by day-to-day business processing in the system. *User master data* is the records of SAP users' passwords and authorizations.

To return to the analogy of the spreadsheet application, the data in the spreadsheet file is the equivalent of the customer data. Of this data, the application data is the data entered to fill the cells of the spreadsheet. The Customizing data is the formatting data—for example, the data specifying bold characters or colored cells in the spreadsheet. The equivalent of the Repository objects is the spreadsheet application itself, with its menu options, macros, and screens.

### 1.2.3 Technical Implementation

SAP ECC requires a database that has a relational database management system (RDBMS) such as Oracle, MS SQL Server, MAX DB, and DB2 databases. The chosen database system is system-neutral until it is populated with the Repository during the installation process.

The name of the relational database and the name of the SAP ECC system are frequently the same, and consist of three uppercase alphanumeric characters. Examples of SAP ECC system names include DEV, P11, or STO. Some names, such as the system identifier **SAP**, are reserved by SAP and may not be used as system names. (See Chapter 7.)

**Note** The abbreviation SID, for system identification, is often used as a placeholder for any SAP ECC system name.

## 1.3 SAP ECC Clients

An SAP ECC system has only one Repository, which provides the runtime environment where you create and maintain customer data. Within this single Repository, you can set up subdivisions called *clients* that help separate customer data into different groups.

When you log on to the system, you must log on to a specific client and can read or change only the data of that particular client. This data is client-dependent. Each client has its own data, but accesses the same Repository objects.

Most customer data is client-dependent. More precisely, application data is entirely client-dependent, while some Customizing data is shared by all clients and thus is client-independent. Figure 1.4 shows a database with multiple clients containing client-dependent data, and sharing all client-independent Customizing data and all Repository objects. These Repository objects provide the runtime environment.

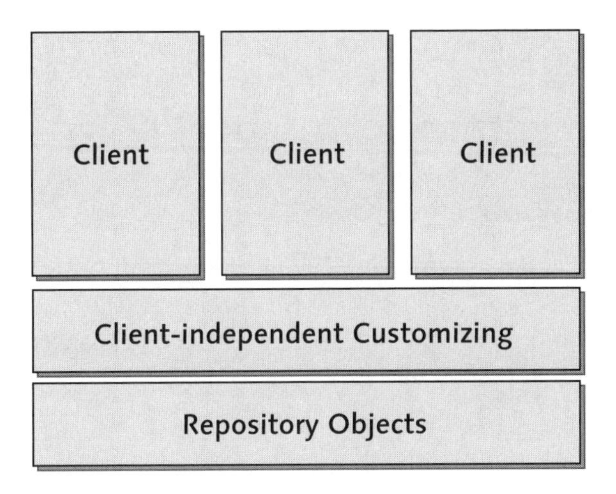


**Figure 1.4** A database contains separate SAP ECC clients that share client-independent Customizing data and Repository objects.

### 1.3.1 Technical Implementation

To protect customer data created in different clients, when you log on to an SAP System, you must log on to a specific client within that system. The client-dependent data you can access from this client is restricted to the data assigned exclusively to that client. Once you are in that client, the client-dependent data of all other clients in the SAP ECC system is inaccessible. You can still access all client-independent Customizing data and Repository objects.

Clients are technically identified by a three-digit number, the client ID. SAP uses the client ID as a key field in all tables that contain client-specific data. The data in these tables can be displayed or changed only if you log on to a specific client.

**Example: Client-Dependent Data**

The clients of an SAP ECC system are simply logical constructs within the database of that SAP system. Tables for client-dependent data have the client ID as the first key column. This column is always called MANDT, from the German word *Mandant*, meaning "client."

An example of a client-dependent SAP table is VBAP, which contains detailed line-item information for all sales documents created in the SAP ECC system. This table contains over 200 columns, of which the first 3 columns are unique for each row, thus enabling the database to uniquely identify the relevant sales document item.

In the table VBAP, the first three columns are MANDT (client ID), VBELN (sales document number), and POSNR (sales document item number). All other columns, for example MATNR (material number), are used to specify the details of the sales document item.

Here is an example of the kind of data stored in the table VBAP:

| MANDT | VBELN | POSNR | MATNR |
|---|---|---|---|
| 400 | 0000006398 | 000010 | C-1100 |
| 400 | 0000006401 | 000010 | CCS-99 |
| 400 | 0000006401 | 000020 | CCS-80 |
| 400 | 0000006403 | 000010 | C900 |
| 520 | 0000000844 | 000010 | C-1100 |
| 520 | 0000000844 | 000020 | C-2000 |
| ... | ... | ... | ... |

Although the table VBAP stores data from both client 400 and client 520, you cannot access the sales document data associated with client 520 when you are logged on in client 400. This is because table VBAP contains the column MANDT as its first key column, making the table's data client-dependent. To display or change any data in table VBAP, you must log on in the SAP ECC client indicated in the column MANDT.

### 1.3.2 Data Components

The data components of an SAP ECC client are the types of data that a user can access after logging on to a particular client (see Figure 1.3). As mentioned above, these include:

- **Customizing data**
  This is the configuration data that results from Customizing, and is a mandatory task during SAP ECC implementation. Most Customizing data is client-dependent; some is client-independent.
- **Application data**
  This is the sum of business data including *transaction data*, which is generated by individual sales or other transactions, and *master data*, which is a prerequisite for entering day-to-day transactions. Application data is the main source of database growth and eventually occupies the most space in the database. All application data is client-dependent.

- **User master data**
  This is data specifying which users can work in the system and which transactions they are authorized to use. All user master data is client-dependent.

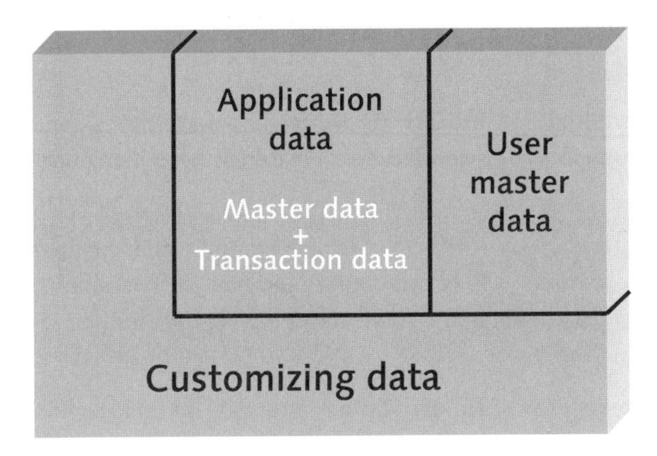


**Figure 1.5** Data components of an SAP ECC client

### Customizing Data

Customizing data is generated when the customer configures the required parameters and settings during Customizing, thus enabling SAP ECC to meet the customer's specific business requirements. Customizing data defines what kind of application data can be generated and how this data will look. Examples of Customizing data include:

- Organizational units such as companies, plants, and sales organizations
- A specific purchase order process flow
- Distribution requirements for production planning
- Multiple-language text for reports

Most Customizing is client-dependent. Some Customizing, however, is client-independent. This includes adjustments to global settings that affect all clients and the creation of or changes to Repository objects. A global setting may be technical in nature, such as the setting defining a printer, or more business-related, such as the setting specifying a company's factory calendar. More complicated customizing efforts may require the creation of a table to house data and configuration settings. Such a table structure is client-independent because it is a Repository object. For example, to configure your pricing strategy for a given product, you are required to create a table that specifies discounting criteria and amounts. This Customizing change, unlike the definition of the sales organization, is a client-independent change.

#### Application Data

Application data is the sum of all SAP ECC business data, and comprises both master data and transaction data. Application data is affected by Customizing settings, which determine what kind of application data can be generated and how this data will look. Application data is client-dependent.

Master data is the prerequisite for processing day-to-day transactions, and includes lists of approved vendors, supplier addresses, materials used in production, and purchaser data.

Transaction data is generated by day-to-day business operations, and includes customer orders, production orders, debits and credits, and payroll transactions. Transaction data is frequently accessed and is the fastest growing data in the SAP ECC system.

While application data is logically a construct of both master data and transaction data within the system, there is no formal distinction between the two. In other words, it is not possible to separate master data and transaction data.

#### User Master Data

SAP ECC's user and authorization concept is an essential part of system security. Information about users, known as user master data, is recorded in the system to authenticate users at logon and check their authorization for particular transactions.

When the user logs on to a client, the system authenticates whether there is a user ID in the user master data that matches the entered password. As the user triggers each new transaction they wish to use in SAP ECC, the system checks whether one of the authorization profiles assigned to that user in their user master data contains the necessary authorization for that transaction.

User IDs and authorization profiles are client-dependent, and therefore are valid only in the client in which the corresponding user master data records were created. User master records contain, for example, the user's logon name, assigned authorizations, and other attributes such as address and user type.

### 1.3.3 Standard SAP ECC Clients

SAP delivers SAP ECC with three standard clients:

- Client 000
- Client 001
- Client 066

Client 000 is reserved by SAP to enable the maintenance of the standard Repository objects and the baseline Customizing settings in the system. For example, during upgrades, new functions are supplied to this client and subsequently transported to the other clients in the system. Client 000 contains the basic Customizing settings with organizational structures and business parameter settings that are legally required for German organizations in regard to, for example, payment and tax structures. Even if you are not implementing SAP ECC in Germany, these settings provide helpful examples for your own Customizing. Due to its special role in the system, client 000 may not be modified or deleted by the customer. It contains no application data.

Client 001 is simply a copy of client 000, including the sample organizational structure and configuration, except that customers can modify Client 001. There is no application data in client 001.

Client 066 is reserved for SAP accesses to its customers' system to perform remote services such as EarlyWatch® and GoingLive™ Check. Almost no data exists in this client; it simply serves as a mechanism to allow remote access for the purpose of system monitoring without compromising the security of your system. This client should not be modified or deleted.

To create new clients in SAP ECC, you can use the technique known as *client copy*, which creates a copy of an existing client (see Chapter 9). To perform Customizing and development in SAP ECC, you should use client 001 or create a new client with a client copy. Normally, a copy is made of client 000. This copy is then used to realize company-specific business processes.

## 1.4 Questions

1. Which of the following components indicate that SAP ECC is a client/server system?

   **A.** Multiple databases

   **B.** A database server

   **C.** Three separate hardware servers—a database server, an application server, and a presentation server

   **D.** A database service, an application service, and a presentation service

2. Which of the following is NOT contained in the SAP ECC database?

   **A.** The Repository

   **B.** The kernel

   **C.** Customer data

   **D.** Transaction data

E. Customizing data

F. The ABAP Dictionary

3. Which of the following statements is correct in regard to SAP clients?

   A. An SAP client has its own customer data and programs, which are not accessible to other clients within the same SAP system.

   B. An SAP client shares Customizing and application data with other clients in the same SAP system.

   C. An SAP client shares all Repository objects and client-independent Customizing with all other clients in the same SAP system.

   D. An SAP client enables you to separate application data from Customizing data.

4. Which of the following statements is correct in regard to SAP's client concept?

   A. All Customizing settings are client-independent.

   B. A client has a unique set of application data.

   C. A client has its own Repository objects.

   D. All Customizing settings are client-dependent.

# 2 Realizing Business Processes in SAP ECC

The software SAP delivers to its customers is referred to as the *SAP standard*. It contains over 1,000 business process chains and their associated functions. Before working with SAP ECC, you not only have to install the software, you must also *implement* it. To meet the specific requirements of your company, you need to make decisions about *which* business processes and associated functions and settings you require, and possibly even create new programs or functions. To effect the implementation of these decisions, SAP ECC offers two main techniques:

- Customizing
- Development

Customizing involves using the *Implementation Guide* (IMG), and development is performed using the *ABAP Workbench*. Development is further divided into three methods:

- Creation of new Repository objects
- Enhancements
- Modifications

Figure 2.1 shows the SAP ECC software resulting from the implementation process. The software, represented by the horizontal bar, consists of the SAP ECC business applications and customer programs. The techniques used to add to, configure, and change the SAP standard are shown as arrows.

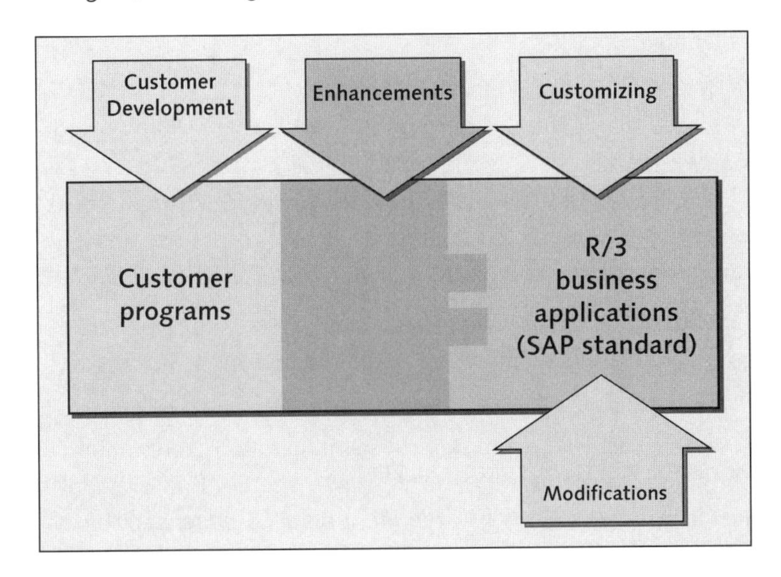


**Figure 2.1** Methods of adding to and changing the SAP standard

## 2.1 Customizing

Customizing is a mandatory activity during an SAP ECC implementation. When performing Customizing, you use the IMG (Transaction SPRO) to select the SAP ECC business processes your company requires, and to adjust all associated settings, such as those used to specify units of measurement and relevant business concepts. Customizing alterations adapt the SAP-standard solution for different branches of industry and company types, as well as for multiple languages and country-specific characteristics.

The Customizing procedure basically adds customer-specific data to the tables corresponding to SAP-standard objects. Therefore, Customizing is often thought of as table maintenance. These tables are later read by the programs that comprise the different business workflows.

**Example: Business Transactions That Are Set Up through Customizing**

An international company manufacturing bicycles begins installing its new SAP ECC system. To meet the company's specific needs, the following business processes and features are selected and set up during Customizing:

- **Sales organizations and distribution channels:**
  To enable wholesale customers to place orders for bicycles, SAP ECC is customized to recognize the sales organization responsible for the order, and the distribution channel used in getting the order to the customer.
- **Production planning:**
  The SAP ECC application module Production Planning is customized to enable orders to be filled on time.
- **Materials management:**
  The SAP ECC application module Materials Management is customized so that all required materials, such as tires and chains, are recognized and can be made available during the manufacture of all types of bicycles.
- **Billing and cost-allocation processes:**
  Customizing in this area sets up invoicing by defining pricing structures and applicable taxes.

As this simple example shows, Customizing covers numerous features of business processes. The people performing Customizing, whether they are company employees or external consultants, require a detailed understanding of the company's business processes.

### 2.1.1 SAP ECC Reference Model

In addition to the IMG (discussed in the next section), another SAP ECC tool that is helpful for Customizing is the *SAP ECC Reference Model* accessed in the *Business Navigator* (Transaction SB09). The Reference Model is a collection of modeling tools that provides configuration recommendations by offering different business scenarios to help you map out your company's business requirements.

The Reference Model enables you to model all essential elements of a company, such as organizational units, business processes, business objects, and the applications that use these business objects.

Subsections of the SAP ECC Reference Model include:

- SAP ECC process model
- Data model and object model
- Organization model
- Distribution model

The SAP ECC Reference Model and its various graphical tools act as a bridge between a company's everyday business needs and the actual implementation of its SAP ECC System (see Figure 2.2). Using the SAP ECC Reference Model to determine and model the scope of the SAP ECC implementation makes it easier to perform Customizing activities using the IMG.

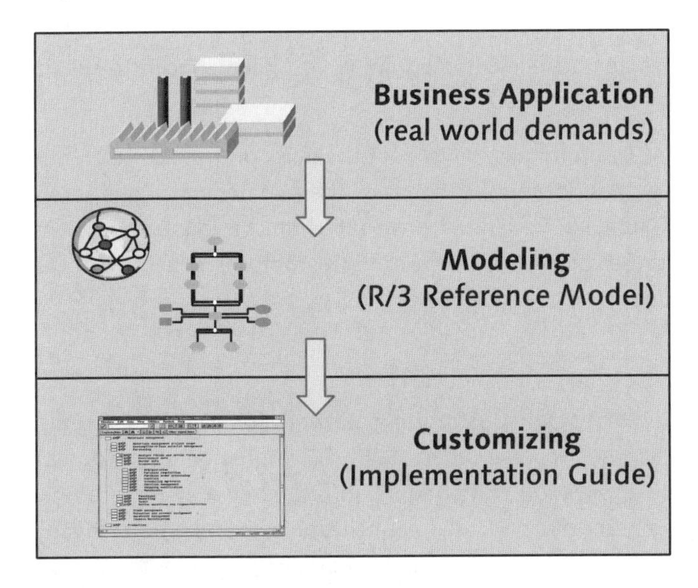


**Figure 2.2** Modeling business needs to facilitate Customizing

### 2.1.2 Implementation Guide (IMG)

To simplify Customizing, the IMG (Transaction SPRO) guides you through the various Customizing stages and procedures. In addition, the *project management* function within the IMG enables you to set up and manage Customizing projects, complete with planned and actual deadlines, resources, and activity completion status.

To start Customizing in the IMG, access the *SAP Reference IMG* (from the initial screen of Transaction SPRO, choose **Implement. projects • SAP Reference IMG**). The SAP Reference IMG is a tree structure in which you drill down to specific Customizing activities (see Figure 2.3). The nodes of the tree structure that you see first are organized to reflect the different SAP ECC application modules such as Financial Accounting, Sales and Distribution, Materials Management, and Plant Maintenance. Drilling down within (or expanding each branch of) the tree structure ultimately reveals lists of Customizing activities that are arranged in the order these activities should be performed.

Figure 2.3 shows some sample Customizing activities in the typical IMG tree structure. Clicking the icons beside each Customizing activity name enables you to access:

- The screen where you perform the Customizing activity
- Relevant SAP ECC documentation
- The screen where you can document why and how you perform this Customizing activity
- The relevant project management data (assuming you have chosen to set up the project management functionality)

The preliminary task for Customizing is to filter out the parts of the SAP Reference IMG that your company does not require, and save the remainder as your *Enterprise IMG*. You can then divide your Enterprise IMG into various subdivisions called *Project IMGs*, representing groups of related Customizing activities. These various IMGs are explained in more detail below.

#### Enterprise IMG

The SAP Reference IMG contains the Customizing activities for all SAP ECC application modules and functions. However, many SAP ECC implementations do not need all of the available application components; in fact, they may require only specific modules implemented for particular countries. For example, a company may initially wish to implement the Human Resources (HR) module to support only North American countries. To simplify Customizing, you generate an Enterprise IMG that contains only those parts of the SAP Reference IMG that are relevant to your implementation.

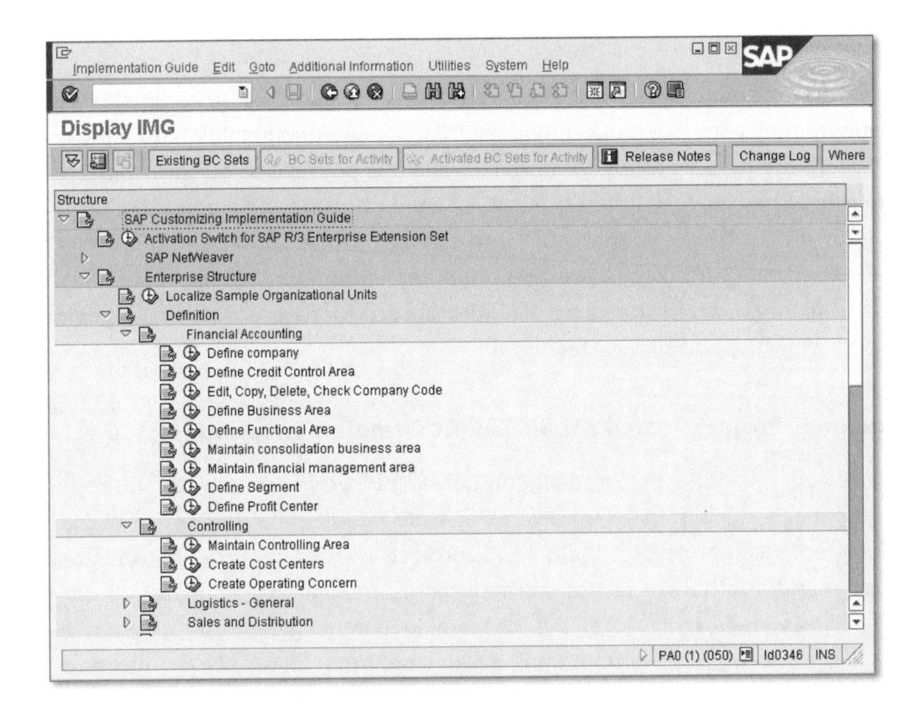


**Figure 2.3** A sample IMG tree structure

To generate an Enterprise IMG, from the initial screen of Transaction SPRO, choose **Basic functions • Enterprise IMG • Generate**. Select the relevant countries and deselect all application components except the components you require. Save your work to generate the Enterprise IMG. (See Chapter 11.)

One Enterprise IMG can be generated for each SAP ECC system. If you subsequently need to implement additional countries or more business application components, you can regenerate the Enterprise IMG. Regeneration does not affect the existing documentation or project management information.

Beginning with R/3 Release 4.6, the Enterprise IMG will no longer be used. SAP will deliver the SAP Reference IMG, and from this IMG, you will create Project IMGs only.

Generally, we recommend that you implement SAP software via using SAP Solution Manager. With SAP Solution Manager, not only the planning of processes and their implementation can be extensively supported. By using the data and process steps contained in the SAP Solution Manager system, the most diverse activities and their associated costs can be saved in further actions of the lifecycle of the implemented SAP software. Examples of this are the setup of system monitoring and the automatic generation of test plans.

### Project IMGs

Customizing requires expertise from different areas of business. In addition, most implementations are rolled out in phases; that is, new functionality is added over time by different user groups. Therefore, while it is possible to perform Customizing from either the SAP Reference IMG or the Enterprise IMG, a useful alternative is to divide the Enterprise IMG into subsets. These subsets, called Project IMGs, reflect the various business areas and implementation stages, and make it possible to organize Customizing activities according to the different types of business expertise and project teams.

**Example: Project Teams for an SAP ECC Implementation**

Before beginning SAP ECC implementation at a bicycle company, the responsible manager decides to set up several teams to handle different aspects of the implementation project. Initially, two project teams are formed: one for Finance and another for Logistics. These teams are again subdivided into different areas of expertise. The Finance team splits into one group for Controlling and one for Accounting. Similarly, the Logistics team divides into two teams: one for Production Planning and another for Materials Management. Thus, a total of four project teams emerge. After creating an Enterprise IMG tailored to the company's needs, four Project IMGs are created. Each team can begin Customizing in the respective Project IMG.

One year later, the management decides to extend its use of SAP ECC to include Human Resources. A new implementation phase is created. The Human Resources team is divided into two sections, one for Payroll and one for Personnel Management. The Enterprise IMG is regenerated and two additional Project IMGs are created, and Customizing for Human Resources is started.

**Tip** To coordinate the efforts of the various implementation teams, SAP recommends that you perform all Customizing activities from within a Project IMG.

Beginning with Release R/3 4.6C, you can also integrate the transport control via projects. Therefore, you gain the ability to plan and transport your developments and customizing activities in project structures. Changes that do not depend on each other can be structured in separate projects and imported to the follow-on systems independently. This is advisable, for example, when different projects are used at different times in the production operation, or to make assignments regarding contents. For this purpose, you must first create an Implementation

Guide (IMG) project in the IMG project management and then activate a related Change and Transport System (CTS) project.

Note that the settings assigned in a specific Customizing activity may affect one or more application components. Therefore, cross-application activities may appear in a Project IMG, even though the second application was not selected when the Project IMG was generated. For example, a Project IMG for Production Planning contains activities relating to Production Planning and Controlling.

Project IMGs provide project management functions to enable you to:

- Maintain status and resource information
- Maintain project documentation in SAP Office folders using either a standard text editor or Microsoft Word
- Transfer data between a Project IMG and Microsoft Project

**Note** The Enterprise IMG and Project IMGs are cross-client. In other words, the Enterprise IMG and Project IMGs, and their documentation and project data, are all accessible from any client within the system.

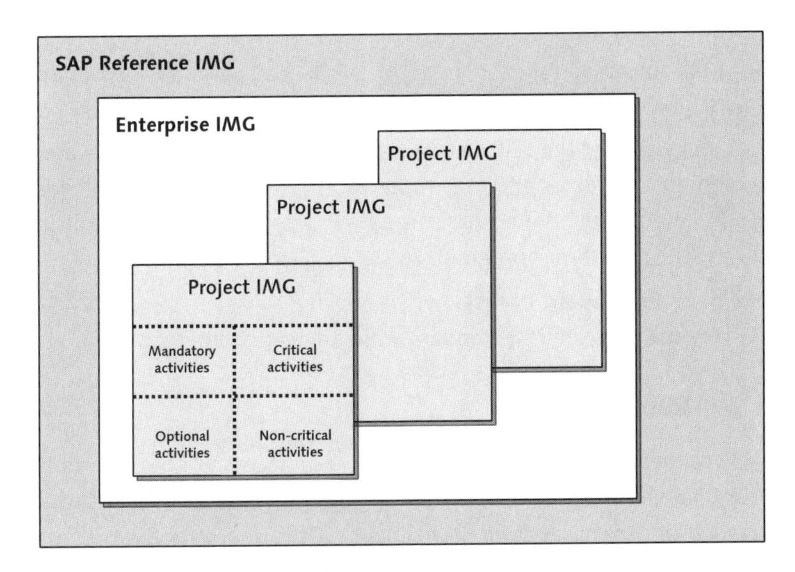


**Figure 2.4** The different views of Customizing activities

To organize your Customizing activities more effectively, Project IMGs can be filtered into views based on priority (see Figure 2.4). This helps you decide which Customizing activities are critical or mandatory and should be tackled first, and which activities can wait until a later time. You can create the following views when generating a Project IMG:

- Critical activities
- Mandatory activities
- Non-critical activities
- Optional activities

## 2.2 Development

The SAP ECC system creates the runtime environment by drawing on the Repository, which contains object definitions, user interfaces, and business transactions. These Repository objects are configured through Customizing, which normally satisfies all business requirements. When this is not the case, you can use the ABAP Workbench to develop new Repository objects or modify existing ones. Development can take the following forms:

- **Creation of new Repository objects:**
  The customer develops new Repository objects, such as new reports, screens, and tables.
- **Enhancements:**
  These are customer-developed objects that are anticipated in the standard SAP software; that is, they are referenced by SAP-standard objects. Such development does not really change the SAP standard; it only "enhances" the software. For example, certain SAP tables are constructed so that you can append fields to them without modifying them, and some SAP programs contain built-in "branches" to possible customer programs.
- **Modifications of SAP-standard objects:**
  These are changes made to an SAP-standard object in a customer system.

### 2.2.1 ABAP Workbench

From the ABAP Workbench (Transaction S001), you can access all the SAP tools required for ABAP development work. You can create your own Repository objects and enhance or modify existing SAP objects. Thus, if a business process that is vital for your company is not contained in the standard SAP System, you can use the ABAP Workbench to build an appropriate solution. The ABAP Workbench includes the following tools:

- *ABAP Dictionary Maintenance* (Transaction SE11) is used for development work on table descriptions and their interrelationships.
- The *ABAP Editor* (Transaction SE38) is used to modify ABAP programs.

- The *Function Builder* (Transaction SE37) is used to develop, maintain, test, and document function modules, and contains a function library, which serves as a central storage facility for all function modules.
- The *Menu Painter* (Transaction SE41) is the tool for creating the user interface of an ABAP program. You can use it to create or modify screen titles, menu bars, the standard toolbar, the application toolbar, and function keys.
- The *Screen Painter* (Transaction SE51) is the tool for creating dialog boxes and the underlying flow logic. The Screen Painter can be run in either a graphical or an alphanumeric mode.

**Note** ABAP stands for Advanced Business Application Programming and is SAP's proprietary programming language. It is designed to support the development of data processing applications in distributed systems, and handles multiple currency and multilingual issues. ABAP also contains a special set of commands for database operations called *Open SQL*, which allows R/3 to be programmed independently of the database system and operating system.

#### SSCR for Developers

SAP Software Change Registration (SSCR) is a procedure that registers all developers of Repository objects. Before creating or modifying Repository objects using the ABAP Workbench, developers must register and obtain an access key from SAP's Online Service System (OSS). The SSCR access key for a developer needs to be entered into the SAP system only once; that is, during the developer's subsequent attempts to create or change Repository objects, the SAP system will not request the SSCR access key.

### 2.2.2 Customer-Developed Repository Objects

Customer-developed Repository objects include programs, screens, menus, function modules, and data structures. These objects are created by an SAP customer using the ABAP Workbench to satisfy business needs beyond the scope of the SAP standard.

**Example: A Possible Customer Development**

The head of Sales at a bicycle company wishes to obtain some sales order statistics based on a nonstandard type of user input, and to simplify the screens where the orders are entered by the end users. The order-entry screen in the SAP standard is replaced with a new screen, created by the company's developer using the SAP Screen Painter. Using the ABAP Editor, this developer then attaches the new screen to an ABAP program that reacts to user input and performs the required statistical analysis. Finally, a further program is created, which displays the results in multiple currencies.

Not all customer-developed objects are completely unique. The new objects may have SAP-standard objects incorporated in their design. A customer-developed ABAP program may include, for example, SAP-standard function modules, such as user input validation routines.

Customer-developed Repository objects are not completely isolated from the existing SAP-standard objects, but like the SAP standard, are contained in the Repository. Therefore, to distinguish SAP-standard Repository objects from customer-developed objects, SAP requires you to heed the following precautions:

- All customer-developed Repository objects must be assigned to a customer *development class*. Development classes are used to group similar business objects, and every Repository object is assigned to a development class. SAP-standard Repository objects are all assigned to SAP development classes.
- New Repository objects must be given a unique name that falls within the *customer name range*. In SAP ECC, the name range of customer-developed objects typically begins with Y or Z.
- In larger, decentralized SAP ECC implementations, Repository objects may also be assigned to a *namespace*. A namespace is a name field that provides an integrated validation that checks for allowed object names. Namespaces provide a method by which objects for specific development can be created without the risk of creating objects with the same names. All objects belonging to this namespace start with this prefix: */CUSTOMER/*. This unique namespace must be requested from the SAP Service Marketplace. For example, this ensures that developments from SAP software partners do not collide with other developments and that your own developments are not overwritten.

### 2.2.3 Enhancements

SAP-standard programs that have been designed to allow enhancements can call customer-developed Repository objects. Enhancements also exist for data dictionary objects. To be enhanced, SAP objects must have one of the following:

- **User exits:**
  Points in an SAP program from which a customer's own program can be called
- **Program exits (also known as function module exits):**
  Predefined function module calls in the standard system for accessing customer-developed function modules

- **Menu exits:**
  Predefined placeholders in the graphical user interface for customer-developed menu options
- **Dynpro exits:**
  Predefined places in dynpros where customers can insert a dialog box they have created
- **Table appends:**
  Placeholders in ABAP Dictionary tables or structures for customer-defined fields external to the table or structure
- **Field exits:**
  Fields on screens that trigger processing of the field contents by customer-developed function modules
- **Text enhancements:**
  Enhancements in SAP data elements that allow customers to replace SAP-specified text with customer-defined keywords or documentation
- **BAdIs:**
  Enhancement technique based on ABAP Objects. Provides interface definitions used for enhancing ABAP sources, screens, GUI elements, and tables without modification. The upwards compatibility of the BAdI interface is ensured; registering in SSCR is not necessary.

User exits, program exits, menu exits, field exits, and screen exits enable customers to extend SAP applications by adding their own processing logic at predefined points. These types of customer exits are inactive when delivered. For the exit to call an enhancement developed by the customer using the ABAP Workbench, the exit must be activated. Customer exits provide you with a predefined interface between SAP programs and customer-developed programs.

Enhancements to tables and structures in the ABAP Dictionary are realized using append structures and text enhancements.

Appends are placeholders in SAP standard tables that refer to an append structure external to the table. By adding fields to the append structure, you are adding fields to the table without changing the table itself. Once the new fields have been added and the table has been activated, these fields can be referred to in ABAP programs just as normal table fields.

The merit and purpose of SAP enhancements are to enable you to add functionality to SAP-standard objects by creating new objects rather than modifying the SAP-standard objects. Customers who avoid modifying SAP-standard objects enjoy three benefits:

- They can receive customer support from SAP more easily.
- They have fewer problems applying SAP's periodic corrections to its software in the form of *Support Packages*.
- They can perform Release upgrades more quickly.

SAP guarantees that when you use enhancement techniques, you will not lose the functionality provided by your enhancement at the time of an Release upgrade or when applying a Support Package. SAP encourages the use of enhancement techniques as they reduce the periodic effort required to update your system—a reduction that is particularly significant in the long term.

User exits do in fact change an SAP-standard object—specifically, an INCLUDE module (see example in the next section). However, SAP guarantees that functionality provided by user exits will not be lost as long as the customer performs a modification adjustment for the INCLUDE module during upgrades.

### 2.2.4 Modifications

The benefit of enhancement technologies, such as program exits and append structures, is that they do not require the customer to modify SAP-standard objects. SAP does not recommend making modifications to SAP-standard objects other than the user exit modifications described above. In general, modifications are not guaranteed to work after an Release upgrade or the application of Support Packages. This means more support is required for updates to modified systems.

**Warning** SAP also recommends avoiding modifications to the standard code because this may have unwanted effects or cause errors in other parts of an application. SAP cannot ensure error-free system operation after customers make modifications.

Apart from activating user exits, customers usually perform modifications to their SAP systems for one of two reasons:

- To adjust functionality to meet a business need that SAP does not provide or provides differently
- To manually apply a correction to fix a known programming error as described by SAP in an *SAP Note*. However, if SAP Notes are implemented using the SAP Note Assistant tool, these corrections are not marked as modifications (Chapter 15).

Instead of modifying SAP objects, SAP recommends using Customizing, customer developments, or enhancements. If modifications are unavoidable, consult SAP.

**Example: The Most Common Modification: the User Exit**

The Sales and Distribution application has a wide variety of user exits that can be used to enhance existing functionality. You can implement a user exit by changing the INCLUDE module MV75AFZ1 to define a more complex sort procedure for contracts. This module is an SAP-standard object, and, prior to the customer's changes, looks like this:

```
Include MV75AFZ1
1
2  form user_sort using u_rcode.
3   clear u_rcode.
4  * Sort rules
5  * u_rcode = 4.
6  endform.
7
```

This INCLUDE module is called by another SAP-standard program, SAPMV75A, which lists contracts:

```
Program SAPMV75A
1  *-----------------------------------------
2  * Central Report to Display Contracts
3  *-----------------------------------------
...   ...   ...   ...   ...   ...   ...   ...   ...
...   ...   ...   ...   ...   ...   ...   ...   ...
222  * customer modifications
223  include mv75afz1.
224  include mv75afz2.
225  include mv75afz3.
226
```

Inserting sort criteria to MV75AFZ1 is a customer modification. SAP guarantees that it will continue to support the use of this module and its call from program SAPMV75A in future SAP ECC Releases. Therefore, while the program SAPMV75A may change from one SAP ECC Release to another, the customer version of MV75AFZ1 will remain effective after the modification adjustment process.

**Note** During an R/3 upgrade, you are given the opportunity to check whether you still require previously created user exits, and to allow those exits no longer needed to be overwritten.

### Modification Adjustments

An important reason for not making modifications is to avoid *modification adjustments* during Release upgrades or when applying Support Packages, also known as *patches*, from the SAP Service Marketplace, SAP's online support services formerly known as SAP's Online Service System (OSS). Modification adjustments are adjustments to SAP objects that ensure previous modifications remain implemented in the system after upgrade. Depending on the number and scope of modifications, the adjustment process may make an Release upgrade or application of Support Packages a complex and time-consuming process, requiring developers to have extensive application knowledge.

As of R/3 Release 4.5, the *Modification Assistant* tool guides you when making modifications and when subsequently performing modification adjustments. The Modification Assistant structures the way changes are made to SAP standard objects and logs all changes, providing you with a detailed overview that is easy to read and that drastically reduces the amount of effort needed to upgrade your system.

Even with the advent of the Modification Assistant, you should keep the number of modifications you make to an absolute minimum. Extensive background knowledge of application structure and process flow is indispensable for deciding whether modifications are avoidable, and if not, what kind of modifications should be made and how they should be designed.

See Chapter 15 for more information on Support Packages from the SAP Service Marketplace.

### Modifications Recommended in SAP Notes

The SAP Notes in the SAP Service Marketplace provide you with a database of task- or problem-oriented recommendations regarding SAP software and the applicable hardware. These recommendations sometimes provide solutions that require the customer to perform modifications to SAP objects—for example, manual programming corrections for Repository objects.

To eliminate the need for manually keying in such corrections, SAP offers Support Packages, or patches, to replace the objects affected by the error with improved versions. Support Packages are not customer modifications because the objects modified by Support Packages are overwritten during an Release upgrade, and there is no need to make modification adjustments.

If there is no Support Package available for solving your problem, you may have to make a manual change to the SAP-standard object based on SAP Notes. Before starting work, however, you need to confirm that the SAP Note is applicable to your Release, and that the symptoms it describes actually match those in your system. If you aren't sure, please contact SAP or use the SAP Note Assistant, which automatically checks these criteria before implementing notes and notifies you, if necessary, of any other dependent notes.

**Tip** Because modifications can subsequently entail modification adjustments during R/3 Release upgrades or when applying Support Packages, you should fully document the modification to accelerate modification adjustment. In your documentation, include the SAP Note number and the Release dependencies.

### SSCR for Modifications

Before making a modification, you must be registered as a developer in the SAP Software Change Registration (SSCR) in SAPNet. In addition, you must register each SAP-standard object you intend to modify. After registering an SAP-standard object, you receive an SSCR access key that must be applied to that object. Once the SSCR access key has been applied, it remains stored in the database so that subsequent changes to that object at the current Release level do not require additional SSCR registration.

By requiring this type of registration, SAP is made aware of the frequency of changes to the different Repository objects, and can respond by creating more enhancement technologies. Knowing which objects a customer has modified also makes it easier for SAP to provide quality customer support.

## 2.3 Questions

1. Which of the following strategies enables SAP customers to avoid making modifications to SAP-standard objects?

   A. Using enhancement technologies such as program exits and menu exits

   B. Modifying SAP delivered programs

   C. Changing SAP-standard functionality using the Implementation Guide (IMG)

   D. Performing Customizing to provide the required functionality

2. Which of the following statements are correct in regard to the Implementation Guide (IMG)?

   A. The IMG consists of a series of Customizing activities for defining a company's business processes.

   B. The IMG is an online resource providing the necessary information and steps to help you implement SAP application modules.

C. The IMG is client-independent.

D. All of the above.

3. Which of the following strategies enables an enterprise to meet its business needs by changing or enhancing SAP functionality?

   A. Maintaining application data using the various SAP business transactions in the SAP standard

   B. Using the ABAP Workbench to create the required Repository objects

   C. Using Customizing to modify programs after obtaining an access key from SAP's Online Support Services (OSS)

   D. Using customer exits to enhance the functionality of existing SAP-standard objects

4. Which of the following statements are correct in regard to modifications?

   A. A modification is a change to an SAP-standard object.

   B. A modification must be registered through SAP Software Change Registration (SSCR).

   C. SAP recommends modifications only if the customer's business needs cannot be met by Customizing, enhancement technologies, or customer development.

   D. All of the above.

5. Which of the following statements is correct in regard to Customizing?

   A. Customizing enables SAP application processes to be set to reflect a company's business needs.

   B. Customizing can be performed only from within a Project IMG.

   C. Customizing is necessary because SAP ECC, for example, is delivered without business processes.

   D. None of the above.

6. Which of the following statements are correct in regard to Repository objects?

   A. Customers can develop new Repository objects using the tools in the ABAP Workbench.

   B. Customer-developed Repository objects reside in the Repository alongside SAP-standard objects.

   C. Customers can create and assign new Repository objects to a development class.

   D. All of the above.

# 3 The mySAP ERP System Landscape

Your system landscape consists of the SAP systems and clients required to take you from the first stages of an mySAP ERP installation, through realization of your business needs within the software, to the start of R/3 production activities. Once in production, your system landscape will need to support continuous changes to the software—due to corporate demands for additional business functionality as well as updates in the form of Release upgrades or SAP Support Packages. So, the objective of a system landscape is to provide an implementation environment where:

- ▶ You can perform Customizing and make development changes without affecting the production environment.
- ▶ You can validate business processes before using them in the production environment.
- ▶ You can simulate and test Release upgrades and the application of Support Packages before they impact the production environment.
- ▶ You can work on Customizing and development to meet future business requirements without influencing the current production environment.

To meet the needs of your software implementation and to ensure smooth production operation, your system landscape must contain multiple clients and multiple systems. Clients provide isolated environments in which changes can be developed, tested, and then rolled into production. At least one client is needed for each step in this process; that is, every SAP ECC implementation requires at least three clients. In addition, due to the immediate impact of client-independent changes on all clients within the same SAP ECC system, SAP recommends that an SAP ECC implementation also have more than one SAP ECC system. Although every implementation will have a unique system landscape, SAP provides some recommended system landscapes and methods for setting up and maintaining landscapes. This chapter will present the different system landscapes and explain their advantages and disadvantages.

## 3.1 SAP ECC Client Roles

Access to SAP ECC is always in the context of a specific client number. In other words, when you log on to an SAP system, you log in to a specific client within that SAP system. Because different clients have different roles, your SAP ECC implementation needs several clients. For example, one client is required for Customizing and development, another for quality assurance testing, and yet another for end users to record business transactions and build production data.

Often, SAP implementations acquire clients over time that no longer have a purpose or value for the implementation. Each client uses database space, which equates to hardware resources. Even more costly are the organizational efforts necessary to keep and maintain the client over time. Such maintenance efforts include managing user access and ensuring that the client receives the latest Customizing and development changes. To ensure optimal performance, your SAP implementation should have only enough clients to fulfill your specific needs.

### 3.1.1 Critical Client Roles

To begin SAP ECC implementation efforts, one client is required. However, as the implementation progresses, this single client will no longer suffice. Other separate clients will be necessary, each devoted to a particular task. To function properly, an implementation requires a minimum of three clients. The critical client roles needed to fulfill the basic requirements of your SAP ECC implementation include the following:

- Customizing and development
- Quality assurance
- Production

**Note** Clients are technically represented in the SAP system with three digits. For example, the three standard clients delivered by SAP and explained in Chapter 1 are client 000, client 001, and client 066. However, to promote consistency and ease of reading, three abbreviations will be used throughout this book to represent the three standard SAP ECC client roles: **CUST** for the Customizing-and-development client, **QTST** for the quality assurance client, and **PROD** for the production client.

#### The Role of CUST

In the Customizing-and-development client (CUST), you adapt SAP ECC to meet your specific needs. In other words, this is where you perform Customizing and development work with the ABAP Workbench. All changes performed in this client are documented and recorded in *change requests*, so they can be promoted to all other clients in the system landscape. A change request is an important mechanism for recording, documenting, and transporting changes throughout the system landscape (see Chapter 4).

While it is technically possible to perform Customizing in different clients and then merge these Customizing efforts in a third client using change requests, SAP does not recommend this procedure. The end result is neither predictable nor retractable. If functionality that works in the original client does not work in the merged client, you will have problems tracking down the conflict responsible for the disrupted functionality. It is much more efficient for the people customizing your SAP system to work together in one central location, the CUST client.

**Tip** To meet your implementation needs, Customizing SAP ECC should be performed in and distributed from a single client.

### The Roles of QTST and PROD

The quality assurance client (QTST) provides the environment for testing and verifying new as well as existing Customizing settings and business application functionality. Application data can be added and manipulated for quality assurance testing. The production client (PROD) is needed for all production activities; in other words, this is where your company's business is carried out. This client harbors the production data.

It is important to remember that the effects of Customizing changes on application behavior are similar to those involved in changing a program; that is, the effect is immediate and, if incorrect, may negatively impact existing data. As a result, changes should first be performed in a Customizing-and-development client. It is only after Customizing and development are carefully tested in the QTST client that the changes are promoted to the PROD client. This ensures disruption-free production operation and the availability of valid functionality.

**Tip** SAP recommends avoiding Customizing and development work in the QTST and PROD clients.

The roles the required clients play during SAP ECC implementation are comparable to the operation of an assembly line (see Figure 3.1). Assembly lines require a well-defined procedure with different mandatory steps performed at different yet linear stages to arrive at a final deliverable result. Similarly, each change made to your SAP system starts at the beginning of the implementation process (CUST), moves on to testing (QTST), and, once the change is verified, makes its way into production (PROD). Making all changes originate from a single client ensures all of the following:

- The changes all follow the same testing procedures.
- The associated documentation is centralized, and is therefore easier to manage.

▶ Customizing settings and Repository objects in your system landscape remain consistent.

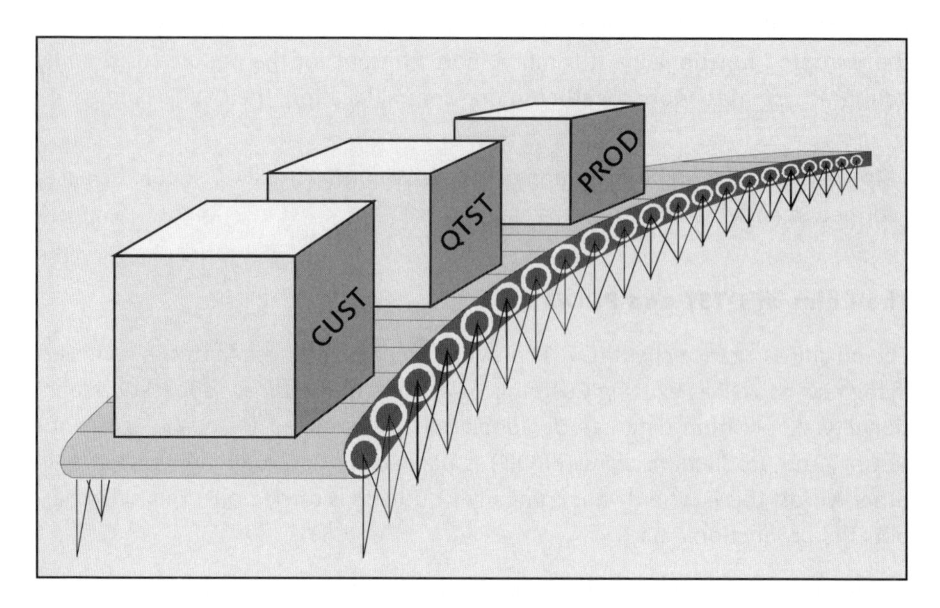


Figure 3.1 The assembly line for SAP ECC implementation

### 3.1.2 Additional Client Roles

To function properly, your SAP implementation requires the three standard clients mentioned above. However, you may find it necessary to define additional clients to fulfill certain needs. These alternative client roles can include any of the following:

▶ Unit test client

▶ Specialized development client

▶ Sandbox client

▶ End-user training client

#### Unit Test Clients

Before you promote Customizing and developments to the quality assurance client, SAP recommends that you perform *unit testing*. Unit testing is the lowest level of testing, where the program or transaction is tested and evaluated for faults. It is normally a part of the development phase and focuses on the inner functions of the program rather than on integration. For example, after configuring a new sales document type, you should test it and see whether you can create a sales order using that document type. Or perhaps you have written a report to analyze plant utilization. You should run this report several times to verify the results and achieve the desired layout. This requires a cyclical combination of Customizing and development and then testing to get the desired results.

Unit testing of SAP ECC functionality requires application data—more specifically, transaction data and master data. For example, to create a sales document, you need to have a customer number and materials (both master data). The result of the test is a new sales order, which is transaction data. To be able to provide results, most reports require some set of transaction data. Therefore, to unit test your Customizing and developments, you require sample application data and the ability to create new application data.

You can perform unit testing in the client CUST. However, SAP recommends setting up a unit test client to keep CUST free of application data. There are two reasons for this:

- Over time, unit testing causes a client to be cluttered with "bad" data—that is, data that is no longer suitable for unit tests. Inappropriate data does not allow for predictable test results.
- Application data is tightly coupled to Customizing settings. A Customizing change may not be possible because application data is already associated with the present Customizing settings. In fact, some settings, such as the configuration of your organization structure, cannot be changed once application data is associated with it. To enable such a change, you would have to delete all application data associated with the original setting. This is a very tedious task.

**Example: Application Data Associated with Customizing**

When Customizing the application Sales and Distribution, a project team creates the required sales organizations within their company. In addition, the team configures all possible distribution channels that are used by the different sales organizations. For example, the Canadian sales organizations distribute only to retail centers, whereas the American sales organizations distribute to retail centers and wholesalers, and by mail order.

The team assigns the sales organizations to the appropriate distribution channels and verifies the combinations through testing with different types of sales orders. During the first round of user acceptance testing, it becomes obvious that the mail order business is not really valid for the American sales organizations. Because mail order sales already exist for the American sales organizations, the team cannot simply delete this Customizing assignment. Before eliminating it, they must first delete all related sales orders—that is, the application data.

To avoid such complications, you can create another client that contains the necessary application data for unit testing. This unit test client provides an environment for maintaining a variety of application data separate from the Customizing environment. It is here that people performing Customizing can test transactions and developers can test reports and programs. (See also Chapter 6.)

**Note** For the sake of consistency and ease of reading, the abbreviation **TEST** will represent the unit test client throughout this book.

If your developers have diverse testing requirements for special programs, such as data conversion routines or interfaces to other computer systems, you may wish to provide them with their own unit test client. This allows for a unique set of business data that can be manipulated by the developers without impacting Customizing tests. In more complex SAP ECC implementations, you may need a *development unit test client* to test reports, screens, and other new functionality.

**Note** CUST is the client in which all Customizing, both client-dependent and client-independent, and developments are performed. TEST enables people performing Customizing to test the contents of their tasks and change requests. It also provides an environment for maintaining application data separate from the Customizing environment.

### Specialized Development Client

SAP recommends that both Customizing and development be performed in the same client. It is more efficient to have changes and documentation supporting an SAP implementation originate from a single source.

However, developers often demand a separate client in which they can develop their programs in isolation from the Customizing environment. They want a more stable client where the Customizing does not change every hour. Because each additional client in your system landscape requires you to make more administrative efforts to ensure that all clients are updated regularly with the latest Customizing efforts, other alternatives should be tried first. First, you should try a single CUST client. If that does not suffice, try using a combination of two TEST clients, one for Customizing and one for development. Only when these alternatives do not provide your developers with satisfactory results should you consider creating a unique development client.

### Other Common Client Roles

In addition to clients for Customizing and development (CUST), unit testing (TEST), quality assurance testing (QTST), and production (PROD), two clients commonly found within a system landscape include the following:

- **Sandbox client:**
  This client is a playground for people who are Customizing SAP ECC and want to test their efforts before actually impacting the Customizing-and-development client.
- **End-user training client:**
  This is an environment for training end users who will be using SAP ECC to supply and access production data.

> **Note** For the sake of consistency and ease of reading, the following abbreviations will be used throughout this book when representing the additional clients: **SAND** for a sandbox or playground client and **TRNG** for the end-user training client.

## 3.2 Defining an SAP Client

An SAP client is defined by its unique client settings. When you first create a client—for example, using *client maintenance* (Transaction SCC4)—you select the client's ID number and provide a short description. In addition, you make selections for all of the following parameters:

- The client's default currency
- The client role, such as Production, Test, or Customizing
- The client-dependent change option
- The client-independent change option
- The client protection and restrictions—for example, protecting the client against overwrites and upgrades

The last four settings allow only approved activities to take place in that particular client. It is your responsibility to see that the correct role, restrictions, and change options have been chosen for each client in your system landscape. These settings are established when the client is created, but you can change the settings for a client at any time. For more details on creating a client and selecting the appropriate settings, see Chapter 9.

The critical client settings are the client-dependent change option and the client-independent change option. They will be explained in more detail below.

### 3.2.1 Client-Dependent Change Options

The most critical client setting used to define a client is its client-dependent change option. This option determines whether changes are permitted in a client and whether the changes are going to be recorded automatically to change requests (see Figure 3.2).

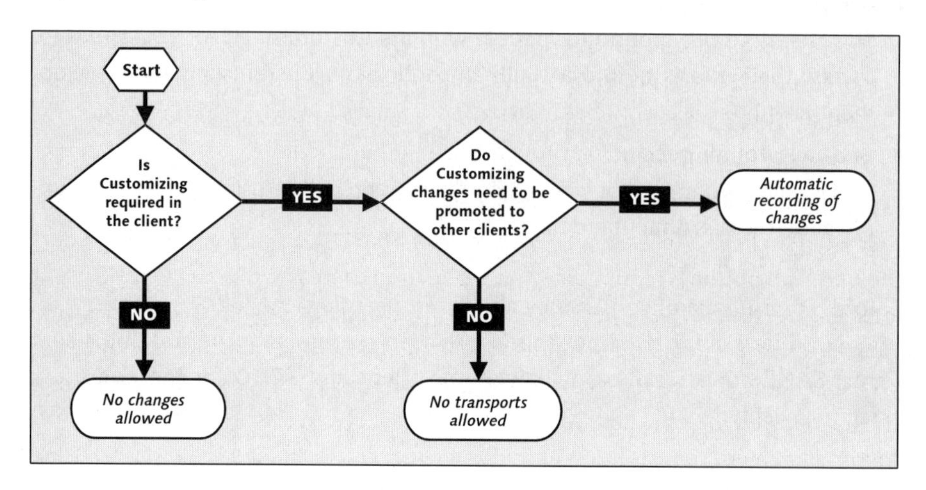


**Figure 3.2** The path for determining the appropriate client-dependent change option

Because repository objects are client-independent, they are not affected in this case. For repository objects, the client-independent changeability discussed in the next chapter is relevant. The client change options for client-dependent attributes include:

- **Changes without automatic recording:**
  This setting allows changes to client-dependent Customizing, but does not automatically record or include the changes in change requests. Customizing changes can be manually included in change requests for promotion to other clients and systems at any time. However, because it is difficult to keep track of changes and then manually record them, SAP does not recommend this option for any client in your system landscape. This setting will be useful only if you need a client from which certain selective changes will be promoted.
- **Automatic recording of changes:**
  This setting allows changes to client-dependent Customizing settings and automatically includes them in a change request. This enables their promotion and distribution to all other clients within your system landscape. This option should be assigned to your Customizing-and-development client (CUST).
- **No changes allowed:**
  This setting prevents all users from making client-dependent Customizing

changes from within the client. This option is useful for those clients in which Customizing changes do not take place—that is, clients that are used for testing and training purposes as well as production activities. Most clients in your system landscape, including TEST, QTST, TRNG, and PROD, should have this option.

- **No transports allowed:**
  This setting allows client-dependent Customizing changes that will not be promoted either manually or automatically to other clients. This option can be used to isolate a sandbox client (SAND), where Customizing settings are sampled, but do not need to be moved to any other client.

As mentioned above, SAP recommends setting the **No changes allowed** option for your PROD client. An alternative option for the PROD client is **No transport allowed**. This option is required for the production client if you also use the **Current settings** function. When special Customizing changes, known as data-only Customizing changes, need to be carried out in a production client without being saved to change requests, the **No changes allowed** setting is no longer valid. An example of data involved in such change is currency exchange rates, which may require frequent adjustment in SAP ECC. To avoid having to use change requests for these changes, SAP has introduced the **Current settings** function (see Chapter 11).

### 3.2.2 Client-Independent Change Options

The client change options for client-independent attributes protect both client-independent Customizing and Repository objects (see Figure 3.3). Repository objects and cross-client Customizing are categorized separately and can therefore be protected against changes either together or individually. The client-independent change options are as follows:

- Changes to Repository and client-independent Customizing allowed
- No changes to client-independent Customizing objects (Changes to Repository objects are still allowed.)
- No changes to Repository objects (Changes to client-independent Customizing are still possible.)
- No changes to Repository and client-independent Customizing objects

All clients in your system landscape—except for the Customizing-and-development client (CUST)—should be assigned the last client-independent change option, **No changes to Repository and client- independent Customizing objects**. The CUST client needs the setting **Changes to Repository and client-independent Customizing allowed**.

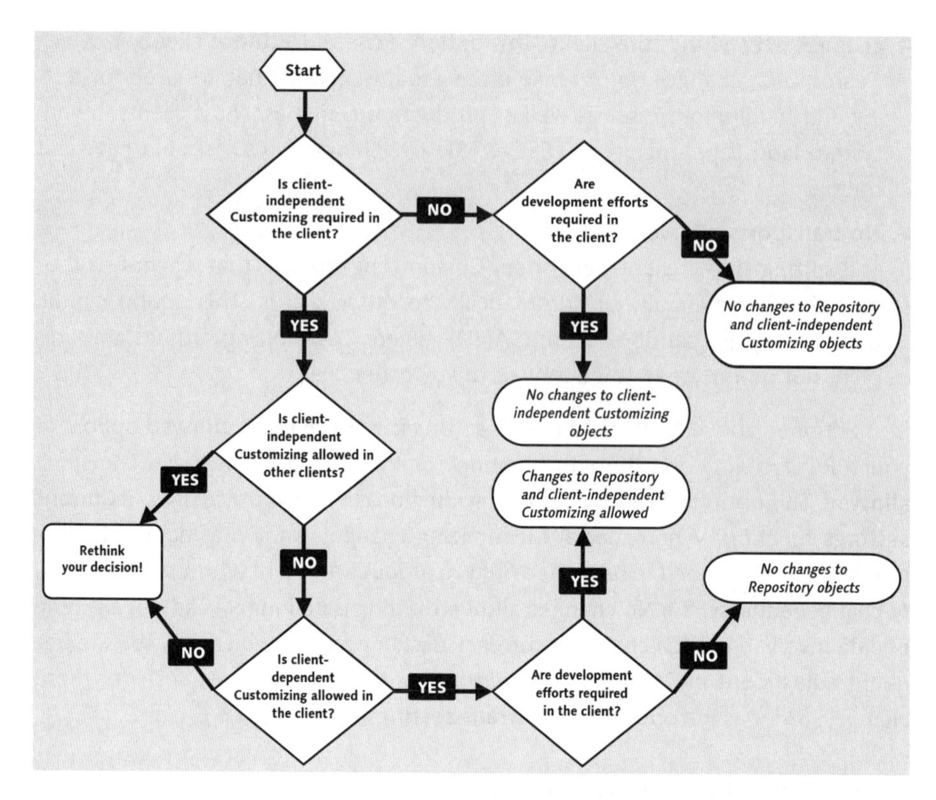


**Figure 3.3** The path for determining the appropriate client-independent change option

Technically, the client-dependent and client-independent change options are two different settings. Logically, the two settings are linked with regard to Customizing changes. Customizing changes rely and build upon other Customizing changes regardless of whether they are client-dependent or client-independent. For this reason, all Customizing activities should take place in a single client, the CUST client. Although a second client such as the sandbox client (SAND) may allow for client-dependent Customizing changes, client-independent Customizing should not be performed in this client.

**Tip** If client-independent Customizing takes place in a client, that client should also be used for client-dependent Customizing. Only one client within an SAP system should allow for both client-dependent and client-independent Customizing.

## 3.3 Multiple Clients in an SAP ECC System

An client is used to keep the application data of one client isolated and completely independent from another client. This is not necessary for all SAP products, because in an SAP Enterprise Portal, for example, users log on to the portal only once and then can call any other SAP system, even with different clients, and log on to it. Systems based on SAP Business Information Warehouse (SAP BW) have only one client as well. Because development, quality assurance, and production tasks each require different sets of application data, each area is provided with a different client. Based on the uniqueness of application data in each client, one might assume that any number of independent clients could operate in the same SAP system. With regard to hardware costs and required system maintenance, such a setup (one SAP system with all required clients) makes financial and organizational sense. The multiple-client concept for the SAP system does have certain limitations that are both functional and technical in nature.

### 3.3.1 Functional Limitations

Standard functions of the SAP system are implemented as programs in the Repository. The client independence of the entire Repository—with all its program objects and Dictionary objects—is a fundamental characteristic of the system. Customizing provides the finishing touches to the standard SAP functionality that supplies you with an operational client.

The SAP ECC system provides full multiple-client capability at the application data level; that is, all data created in a client is visible for only that one client and cannot be changed or even displayed by other clients. The vast majority of Customizing settings are also client-dependent. These *client-specific* Customizing settings are valid for only that one client. However, some IMG Customizing activities are client-independent; they create globally valid settings (such as decimal places for currencies) or result in the generation of programs and Dictionary elements. Because client-independent Customizing and all Repository objects are always accessible from every client, they provide a potential source of conflict. Customizing and Repository changes in one client could accidentally change, overwrite, or conflict with the needs of another client. An even worse scenario involves clients that do not detect changes to client-independent settings and objects that affect them.

To deal with these functional limitations, SAP recommends that you have only one client in an SAP system where changes to client-independent Customizing and Repository objects are allowed. This helps ensure the integrity of each client in a multiple-client system. Using the appropriate client-change options ensures that client-independent changes are made only in a single client within the SAP system.

SAP also recommends that only "like" clients reside in the same SAP system. For example, test or training clients can be in the same SAP system. This does not cause problems because these clients are generated as a copy of an existing Customizing-and-development client. The similar clients are based on the same Customizing and the same developments. Thus, such clients are not self-sufficient Customizing environments, but simply derivatives of the Customizing client that require the same client-independent objects and settings.

### 3.3.2 Technical Limitations

At a technical level, a client ID is the primary key field in the Customizing and application tables of the database. An database can house as many clients as you wish—up to a total of 1,000 clients. The required database resources and hardware performance are largely derived from the number of active users and not from the number of clients used.

You need to consider the influence of the number of clients in a system with regard to performance under the following technical concepts of the system:

- More clients require additional main memory for the system buffers. As a general rule, an additional 10MB is required for each client.
- Because each client occupies entries in database tables, more clients in a system may lead to higher database access times. This is especially true when accessing tables with a full table scan.
- The runtime of an Release upgrade depends on the number of clients. The more clients that have been defined in a system, the greater the import effort will be, as new entries have to be distributed to all clients within the system. Although the runtimes of an upgrade will always increase with each additional client, note that a major portion of the upgrade time is spent delivering new Repository objects and not client-dependent data. Therefore, the increased effort in upgrading a system with more clients is not directly proportional. For example, the upgrade of a four-client system will not take twice as long as the upgrade of a two-client system.
- Only limited technical maintenance is possible due to increased availability requirements. Multiple clients within an SAP system will have different roles and therefore different end-user demands. Technical maintenance, such as reorganizing the database or making an offline backup, requires the SAP system to be down and unavailable. Scheduling of system unavailability is more difficult if the end-user audience has varying demands.

**Note** For more information on the database requirements of a standard SAP client, see SAP Note 118823 in the SAP Service Marketplace.

### 3.3.3 Protective Measures for Multiple-Client Operations

SAP provides you with the following protective measures to prevent inadvertent changes from being made from a client within a multiple-client system and to ensure the successful coexistence of multiple clients in the same physical system:

- **Client-change options:**
  Changes to client-independent Customizing and Repository objects can be restricted to a specific client using the appropriate client-change options.
- **User authorizations:**
  Special user authorizations must be assigned for client-independent maintenance.
- **Special popups:**
  Whenever you perform client-independent Customizing activities or maintain a client-independent table, an warning message informs the user that the changes made will affect all clients throughout the SAP system.

> **Note** For more information on the limitations of multiple clients in a single SAP System, see SAP Note 31557 in the SAP Service Marketplace.

## 3.4 The SAP Three-System Landscape

The clients provide an environment where application data can be isolated while sharing a common Repository and client-independent Customizing. Because of the functional and technical limitations of multiple clients in a single SAP system including the sharing of a common Repository, SAP recommends you distribute the critical clients among several SAP systems. The three standard systems in this distribution are as follows:

- Development system
- Quality assurance system (sometimes referred to as the *test* or *consolidation system*)
- Production system

The recommendation for building a three-system landscape is not only valid for the SAP ECC system. If, for example, an SAP Enterprise Portal has common business processes with this system, the Portal system should dispose of a parallel three-system landscape as well. Otherwise, it is not possible to build and verify sensible test cases in the quality assurance system.

### 3.4.1 Standard SAP Systems

Customizing and development take place in the *development system*. All changes made in the development system are recorded to change requests and then promoted to quality assurance for validation. This system contains the CUST client.

In the *quality assurance system*, the functionality is tested without affecting the production environment. A quality assurance system enables you to integrate Customizing and developments and to check the validity and consistency of transported changes before moving the changes into the production environment. This system contains the QTST client.

All changes imported into the quality assurance system are then delivered to the *production system*. In this system, your business data will be collected and accessed. The system contains the PROD client.

**Note** For the sake of consistency and ease of reading, the following abbreviations will be used throughout this book to represent the different SAP systems: **DEV** for the Customizing-and-development system, **QAS** for the quality assurance system, and **PRD** for the production system. Each system needs a unique three-character alphanumeric system ID. For all purposes, the above-mentioned abbreviations can be considered the system IDs.

### 3.4.2 Distribution of Client Roles

As explained above, each required client is housed in its own SAP system. Additional client roles should then be distributed accordingly within the system landscape:

- The sandbox client (SAND), where sampling of client-dependent Customizing takes place, should be in the development environment. After testing Customizing settings in the sandbox client, the person performing the Customizing can go into the CUST client and implement the changes.
- The unit test client (TEST) must be in the same SAP system as the CUST client. Customizing changes and development changes are tested in the unit test client. Once unit tested, changes can then be promoted to the QTST client.
- Since the quality assurance system is more stable than the development system, the end-user training client (TRNG) is often found in the quality assurance system, where it will not impact the production system.

To meet the needs of your software implementation and to ensure smooth production operation, your system landscape should therefore contain at least three systems, the required clients, and any additional clients that are necessary and advantageous for your implementation. Figure 3.4 shows the standard system landscape and the distribution of required and other commonly used client roles.

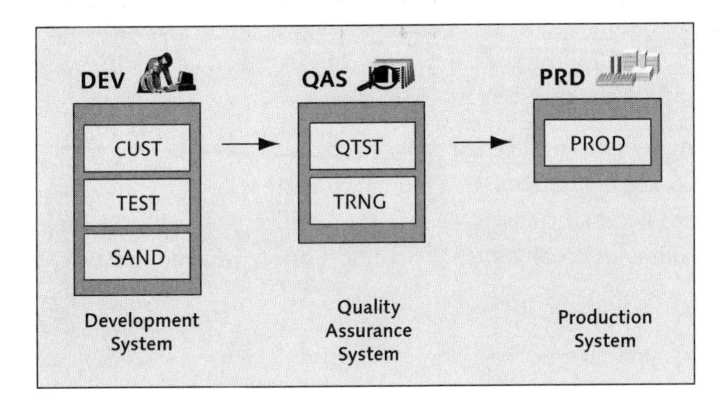


**Figure 3.4** The SAP standard three-system landscape with its client distribution

The three distinct systems and the clients recommended by SAP benefit your implementation in the following ways:

- For reasons of testing, security, and system performance, all Customizing and developments are separate from production activities.
- A quality assurance system enables you to integrate Customizing and development and to check the validity and consistency of transported changes before they are delivered to the production system.
- Upgrades and application of SAP Support Packages can be simulated and tested before applying them to the production system.

**Example: Derivation of SAP's Recommended Three-System Landscape**

A large chemical firm decided to implement SAP ECC with the objective to move all manufacturing and distribution processes from an existing, antiquated system to SAP ECC. This also required migrating historical data from the legacy system to SAP ECC at the start of production activities.

Initially, the company began its implementation using the three-system landscape SAP recommends with the following clients:

- CUST client 100, TEST client 200, and SAND client 400 in the development system (DDV)
- QTST client 100 and TRNG client 300 in the quality assurance system (DQA)
- PROD client 100 in the production system (DPR)

It immediately became obvious that testing data conversion routines with the legacy system was interfering with the testing of Customizing changes. To alleviate this problem, two new clients were created—client 210 in DDV for the unit testing of data conversion routines and client 210 in the quality assurance system (DQA) to support stress testing of conversion routines.

Also, because training sessions for end users occurred on a weekly basis, a master training client 310 was created in DQA. From this master client, the training client 300 in DQA was generated each week. This ensured a base level of application data and default user accounts for the support of each training session.

The company's system landscape looked like this:

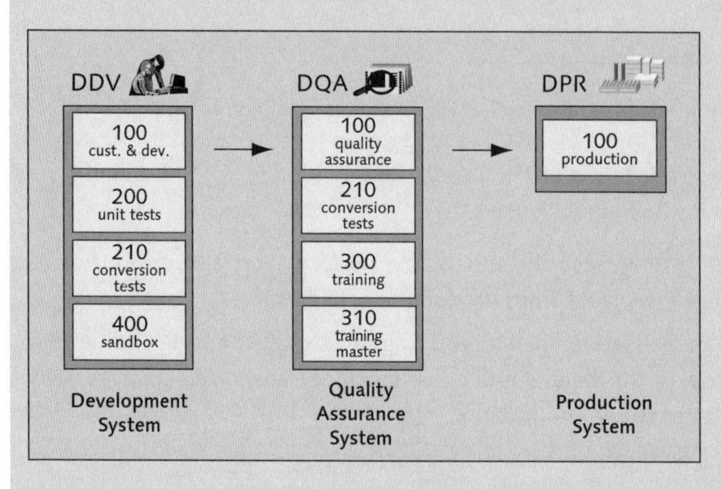


**Figure 3.5** System landscape example

Once the system was in production and the legacy system was eliminated, the company no longer required the data conversion clients. Therefore, client 210 in DDV and client 210 in DQA were deleted.

## 3.5 Alternative System Landscapes

SAP's recommended three-system landscape is simply a template from which you can build your system landscape. However, many customers have specific or temporary client needs that are added to the system landscape. Other customers see the need for additional SAP systems—for example, a system that may be used solely for end-user training. Some customers may have constraints that require them to implement a one-system or two-system landscape. Or, a customer may begin with the three-system implementation recommended by SAP, but over time require more SAP systems due to the need to introduce more functionality while still providing support changes to the production system.

Regardless of your environment, it is important to note that more clients and also additional SAP systems pose certain costs to your implementation:

- More hardware resources are needed.
- Managing the distribution of Customizing and development changes becomes more difficult.
- Support for Release upgrades and the application of SAP Support Packages has additional complications.
- The administrative responsibilities with regard to user access and authorization increase.

When designing your system landscape, you need to compare these costs with the necessity for providing environments in which Customizing and development can take place without impacting other implementation efforts, such as quality assurance testing and production activities. You should carefully weigh the limitations and disadvantages against the advantages the different system landscapes can provide to meet your specific needs.

### 3.5.1 One-System Landscape

A one-system landscape consists of a single SAP system used for Customizing and development as well as for quality assurance testing and production activities. A single SAP system for implementation requires that all clients share the same hardware, the Repository, and client-independent Customizing. Sharing these resources results in the following limitations for a one-system landscape:

- Changes to Repository objects are client-independent and immediately affect the runtime environment; therefore, changes are tested in the runtime environment of your production system, and there is a danger of production data loss as a result of inconsistencies or incorrect changes.
- The Customizing-and-development client as well as the quality assurance client can affect production performance.
- System availability is required for production activities at all times, not allowing opportunities for unique development and quality assurance demands.
- Production data security is compromised. For example, developers can create reports that access production data from another client.
- The system administrator cannot perform upgrades on a nonproduction system before upgrading the production system.

As a consequence of these limitations, no further development is possible after production work has started. Changes to Repository objects can be made only when production operations are stopped for development and testing. For these reasons, SAP does not recommend using a one-system landscape.

### 3.5.2 Two-System Landscape

A small, uncomplicated SAP ECC implementation may need only two systems. This two-system landscape is able to support an SAP ECC implementation with standard business functionality and limited customer development needs.

A two-system landscape allows development and production to be performed in two separate environments. However, this landscape has its weaknesses. Because development and quality assurance testing both occur in the development system, the stability of central resources during actual quality assurance testing may be jeopardized. Therefore, changes to Repository objects or client-independent Customizing cannot be made while quality assurance testing is in progress.

Change management also presents a problem for the two-system landscape. Complex development projects often involve transporting partial functionality, sometimes without taking dependencies into account. Change requests and the functionality in the change requests are not fully tested until after the changes have been imported. In addition, a change request upon import may result in an error due to dependencies on other change requests or problems within the change request itself. Therefore, in a two-system landscape, the transport of a change request cannot be fully tested before it is imported into production. This can cause inconsistencies and affect the production system.

Figure 3.6 depicts a two-system landscape. In this landscape, the development system has four different clients. Customizing and development activities occur in client CUST. Unit testing takes place in client TEST before being delivered to the quality assurance client (QTST). End-user training also takes place in this system in the client TRNG. The production system is reserved solely for production activities in the client PROD.

A three-system landscape provides a unique environment dedicated to quality assurance testing and, just as importantly, allows for the testing of transported change requests. The two-system landscape, in contrast, does not offer this option. This means the two-system landscape is viable only for environments where very few complex Customizing and development changes have to be promoted to production after the start of production activities.

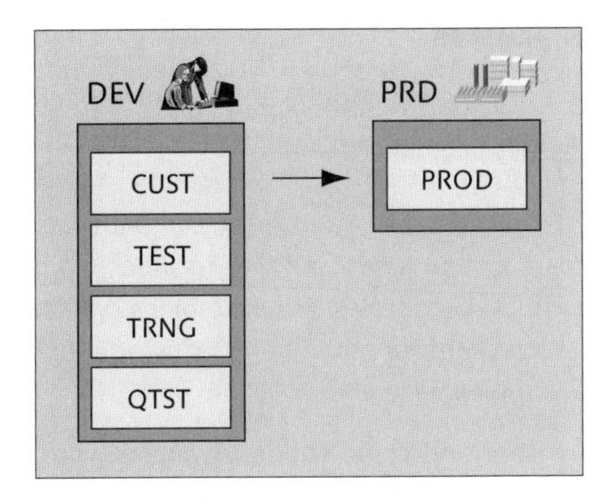


**Figure 3.6** A two-system landscape

### 3.5.3 Four-System Landscape

The SAP-recommended system landscape requires three SAP systems. These three systems house the critical roles for the SAP ECC implementation. However, customers frequently include more systems in their landscape to support a variety of testing demands or training needs. Noncritical clients, such as the sandbox client, the training client, or an additional testing client, are then isolated on their own SAP ECC system, extending the landscape to a four-system landscape. Such a system landscape is valid as long as the additional system provides long-term value for the implementation plan. It will require the latest copy of Customizing and development changes. An example of such a system is a training environment that is isolated from quality assurance activities (see Figure 3.7).

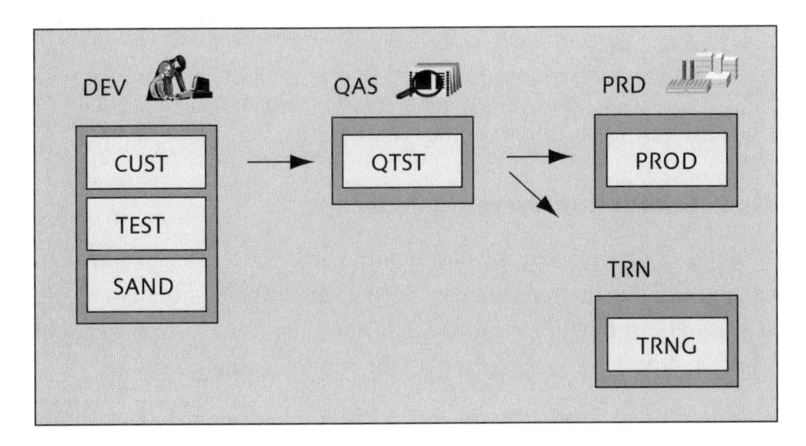


**Figure 3.7** A four-system landscape with a special training environment

## 3.6 Complex System Landscapes

Some customers require implementations that go beyond the SAP-recommended system landscape—for example, a large, multinational implementation. Such customers may need a *complex system landscape*—that is, an environment that extends beyond the standard three-system landscape. More specifically, you can think of a complex system landscape as a system landscape that includes more than one client playing any one of the critical client roles. For example, a system landscape that has two different production clients or two different Customizing-and-development clients is considered complex.

Because of its complexity, this type of system landscape requires strong management efforts and centralized coordination that still allows for localizing particular implementation tasks. It may also require the use of special SAP tools for the support of Customizing and development as well as the distribution and/or sharing of application data. The most important tool in this context is again SAP Solution Manager. You can use this tool for an intelligent distribution of the Customizing in complex landscapes via Customizing distribution, or for the sole usage of BC Sets in Solution Manager projects.

There are several kinds of complex system landscapes. To reflect the most common customer issues, this book will focus on the following three types:

- A *multiple production system landscape* has a single development system that supports many production systems.
- A *phased system landscape* is used to support the introduction of new business functionality to an existing production system. Customizing and development changes are made in two different clients, but all changes ultimately support the same production system.
- A *global system landscape* has multiple production and development systems sharing some common Customizing and developments.

### 3.6.1 Multiple Production System Landscape

A multiple production system landscape has multiple production data clients with similar Customizing and development needs. Such a landscape is shown in Figure 3.8. Since the multiple production systems stem from just one Customizing and development system, you may find yourself asking the following questions:

- If the data and business needs of the production environments are similar enough to share the same Customizing and developments, why isn't a single production system enough?

- Once in production, what happens if the different production systems have different Customizing and development demands that can no longer be served by a single development system?
- Different production systems require multiple production data environments. How do these different production systems share business data, such as master and transaction data?

The first two questions regarding the need for and support of multiple production systems are addressed in this chapter. A discussion regarding the management of business data across multiple SAP ECC systems is highlighted in Chapter 4.

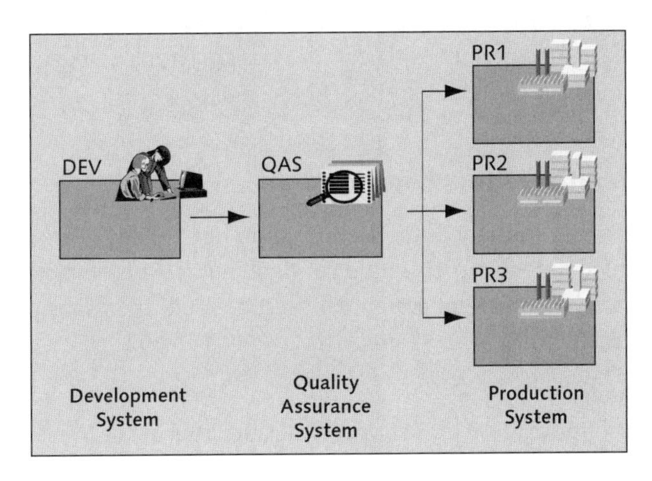


**Figure 3.8** A system landscape with multiple production systems

### Company Codes versus Multiple Production System Landscapes

Some organizations divide their SAP implementation and production data among different subsidiaries. In such an organization, one subsidiary may demand that its production data be in a separate SAP system (or even a separate client) from the production data of the other. The subsidiary could be accommodated by implementing a multiple production system landscape. However, this would impair the parent organization's ability to view all its subsidiaries' business data from within a single client.

A more fitting alternative for sharing business functionality and business data between different organizations can be provided by using *company codes*. Company codes in SAP ECC define the smallest organizational element for which a complete, self-contained set of accounts can be drawn up for external reporting. Company codes are either separate legal entities, as in the case of a second company, or part of the same legal entity, as in the case of two subsidiaries that report to a parent organization. One client in an SAP system can support several company codes. The standard clients 000 and 001 delivered by SAP already have a company code 0001, which is set up for Germany. This company code can be adapted or copied during Customizing.

Using company codes in conjunction with user authorizations, you can integrate several companies or subsidiaries in a single client. The SAP authorization concept enables the parent company to access all subsidiaries for report purposes, while subsidiary-specific data is protected against access from other subsidiaries through company code definition.

**Tip** To meet the needs of different companies within a parent organization, SAP recommends that customers first consider using company codes within a single production client rather than using multiple production clients.

### Specific Scenarios for Multiple Production Systems

When the use of company codes and user authorizations does not provide a large organization with the production requirements it demands, a multiple production system landscape is necessary. This type of system landscape would then satisfy the following requirements:

- **Unique language demands:**
  By using the Unicode technology, SAP ECC supports all languages of the Western and Eastern industrial world. In addition to Unicode, the system can be used in one non-Unicode codepage such as Latin-I, for example. You can also upgrade from an R/3 system that does not yet use the Unicode codepage. However, if multiple codepages need to be used, as is often the case in multinational corporate groups, you should definitely no longer consider using the Multiple Display, Multiple Processing (MDMP)—a technique using several non-Unicode codepages in parallel. Apart from the increased complexity of maintaining the different codepages, you also should be aware of the increased effort required if you want to migrate this system to a Unicode-enabled system at a later stage. The use of portals when accessing these MDMP systems can also result in such difficulties as risking data inconsistencies. Unicode solves all of these problems with slightly increased hardware requirements.
- **Performance concerns:**
  SAP ECC's client/server technology and newer hardware technologies allow for the distribution of many active users across multiple application servers. This distribution of resources typically meets the needs of even our largest customers. However, some customers have performance needs, networking concerns, and varying end-user demands that go beyond what one production system can provide. These customers require the multiple production system landscape.

**Example: A Multiple Production System Landscape to Meet Specific Language Requirements**

A multinational distribution company has facilities spanning the globe, from its headquarters in North America to distribution centers in Eastern Europe and its subsidiaries in Korea and China. The organization uses SAP ECC to manage corporate sales and financial data. However, due to the inherent cultural differences and autonomy of many of the Asian subsidiaries, the Board decides that all business data must be maintained in its local language. In other words, not only is the SAP GUI presentation interface for the end-user community in the local language, data is also entered in the respective languages. The language support for Korean and Chinese or Polish and Chinese in a single SAP system is not possible using one standard codepages. Therefore, either servers in the respective codepages or a Unicode system need to be installed. The following is a list of the required systems without Unicode support:

The respective end-user communities use production systems with the following system IDs:

- PNA supports North America by providing English.
- PEE supports Eastern Europe by providing Czech, English, Polish, and German.
- PCH supports China by providing Simplified Chinese and English.
- PKO supports Korea by providing Korean and English.

### Customizing and Development in Multiple Production Systems

A multiple production system landscape depends on the fact that all production systems have the same Customizing settings and Repository objects. After the initial start of production activities, Customizing and development activities continue in the development system to support production activities, enhance existing functionality, and introduce new business processes. Although many of these changes are created to satisfy a specific need of one production system, the changes still have to be distributed to all clients and systems to ensure consistent Customizing and development.

However, once in production, there is more reluctance to introduce changes into a production system, especially if there is no apparent benefit for the production activities. Therefore, over time, as the multiple production systems in a multiple system landscape become more autonomous, such landscape-wide Customizing and development transports become a hindrance. In this case, the multiple production system landscape may need to expand to become more like a global system landscape, which is explained in more detail below.

**Note** Support for a multiple production system landscape requires centralized Customizing and development that are rolled out to all production systems.

### 3.6.2 Phased System Landscape

Customers often implement mySAP ERP in different phases to meet varying business objectives within a specific time frame and to deal with management constraints and resource limitations. The first phase might be used to start up certain production plants or to install a particular application module such as Financial Accounting. The next phase then adds either additional plants or even a new module, such as Human Resources. A further phase could be an upgrade to the latest Release. (See also Chapter 6.) To support a multiple-phased implementation and to provide an environment in which new business processes can be introduced while current production activities are supported, SAP recommends using a *phased system landscape*.

Note that the word "phase" is used to represent a customer's need for implementing new functionality in its production system. This functionality may or may not be an Release upgrade. The implementation phase is often the introduction of new business processes through additional configuration. For example, Phases 1 through 3 may be the rollout of all company codes, plants, and financials. Phase 4 may be an upgrade of the SAP software, and Phase 5 may be the introduction of Internet functionality. The phased system landscape is designed to support both the rollout of new Customizing to address business needs and SAP Release upgrades.

#### Requirements of a Phased System Landscape

A phased system landscape requires resources to support production while at the same time providing an environment for new Customizing and development. To realize these goals, the following systems need to be added to the SAP-recommended three-system landscape:

- **Production support system:**
  This is a Customizing and development environment that closely resembles the production system; that is, its Customizing data and Repository objects are identical to those in the production system. This client is used for making changes or corrections demanded by production while the next phase of the implementation is being planned and tested in the DEV and QAS systems.

- **Final quality assurance system:**
  This is a quality assurance environment that closely resembles the production system and includes sample or complete production data. This client is used for testing and verifying any changes demanded by production—that is, those changes made in the production support system. This testing, also known as *regression testing*, is necessary so that the changes will not have an adverse affect on production data after import; that is, the new functionality will not negatively impact existing business functionality.

### Realizing a Phased Implementation

With the addition of these two new systems, the phased system landscape recommended by SAP should have five systems. As in the case of the three-system landscape, each critical environment required for the implementation has its own SAP system.

Figure 3.9 depicts the standard client roles and SAP systems for a phased system landscape. The notation **Phase N** represents the phase currently in production. Phase N+1 represents the next phase of the implementation to be brought into production at a later date and time. Phase **N+1** is the introduction of a new module or an R/3 Release upgrade.

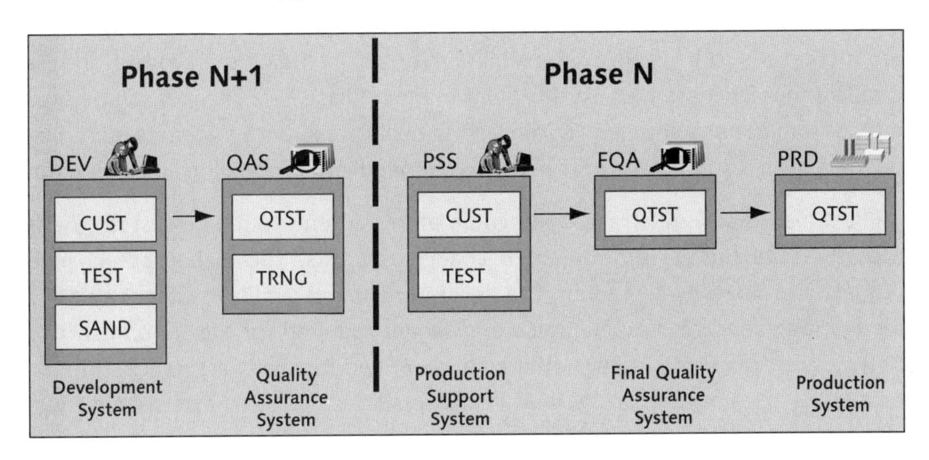


**Figure 3.9** The SAP-recommended phased system landscape

In a phased system landscape, Phase N changes are only those changes required to immediately support production. These take place in the production support system (in Figure 3.9, the SAP system PSS). All other Customizing and developments are part of the next phase and take place in the original development system. Phase N+1 functionality is unit tested in the development system (DEV) and then promoted to the quality assurance system (QAS) for validation.

Figure 3.10 shows the next step, the promotion of Phase N+1 functionality into production. SAP recommends first applying the changes to the final quality assurance system (in Figure 3.10, the R/3 System FQA). This provides an opportunity to perform business integration testing on a system most like a production system. During this final quality assurance testing, if any changes are required for the new phase, they must originate from the development system (DEV). The production support system (PSS) then remains consistent with production and can provide any needed production support in the meantime.

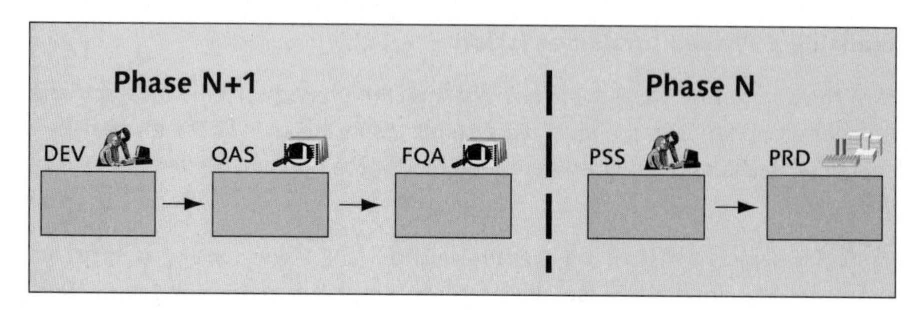


**Figure 3.10** The procedure for promoting changes in a phased system landscape

After validation of Phase N+1 on the final quality assurance system (FQA), all of these changes are applied to the production system (PRD) and eventually to the production support system (PSS). All SAP systems, including the production system, are then at Phase N+1. At this point in time, Phase N+2 changes can be promoted from the development system to the quality assurance system to start preparing for the testing of the next phase to be rolled into production at a later date.

If Phase N+1 is a new Release, an upgrade of the systems to the newest release is a prerequisite for the promotion of change requests. This is because change requests are Release-dependent. The development and quality assurance systems are first upgraded to the new Release. Changes required for the support of this Release are then made in development and verified in quality assurance. Prior to promoting the changes to the final quality assurance system, that system must also be upgraded to the new Release. Likewise, the production system will first need the upgrade before the change requests from Release N+1 can be applied and the production can be moved from Release N to Release N+1.

### Multiple Customizing-and-Development Clients

An initial rule with regard to client and system strategies is that Customizing and development originate from a single client. Customizing is the configuring of the SAP software and requires changes that are both client-dependent and client-independent. Customizing changes also build upon one another, creating dependencies that cannot be separated and are often hidden from those performing the Customizing. Development work then depends on the Customizing settings.

A phased system landscape requires that this rule be discounted, and Customizing and development take place in two different systems. For supporting the production system in Phase N, you need a development system with an identical repository, as well as client-dependent and client-independent Customizing. In other words, if a problem with the setup of a plant needs to be corrected in production, the production support environment cannot have undergone any changes to that plant or changes that may impact that plant.

Likewise, if a report is not working properly in production, a developer needs to modify the same version of the report in the production support environment—not a newer version of the report. Therefore, Customizing and development support for Phase N requires a constant environment, not one in which new business processes are being added. Accordingly, Phase N production support and configuration of Phase N+1 functionality must be in separate environments.

Any changes made to support Phase N production activities need to be part of the Phase N+1 rollout, and must be realized in the Phase N+1 development system, as shown in Figure 3.11. For example, if a Production Planning scheme is adjusted to support production needs, the required change must also be made in the development system. SAP recommends that these changes be manually applied to avoid conflicts with the current configuration in the Phase N+1 environment.

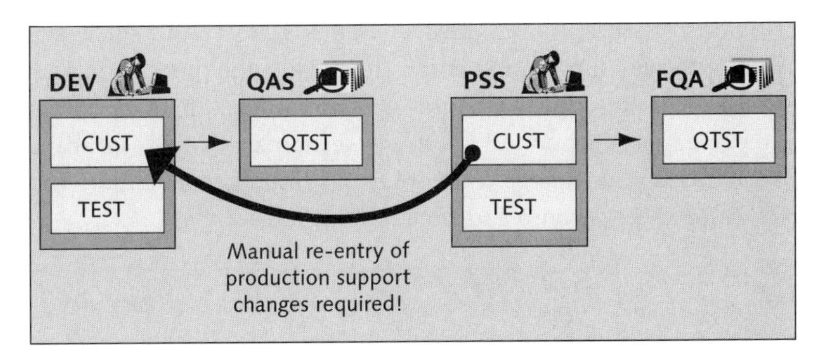


**Figure 3.11** Ensuring consistency between DEV and PSS

SAP provides several tools that help manage Customizing and development changes in multiple clients. These tools are explained in more detail below in the section "Global System Landscape."

### Alternative Phased System Landscape

Often, phased implementations that are small and uncomplicated do not require five SAP systems to maintain a stable production environment while also introducing new functionality. Based on the stability of your production system, the extent of customer developments, and the aggressiveness of your phased implementation, you may find that a four-system landscape suffices for a phased implementation. However, this option does have its limitations.

This four-system landscape functions without the final quality assurance system (FQA). The quality assurance system (QAS) is used in its place. First and foremost, the quality assurance system serves Phase N by providing immediate support for production. This is depicted in Figure 3.12.

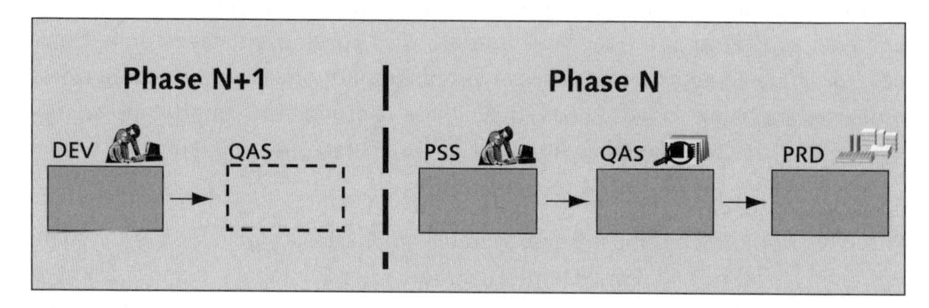


**Figure 3.12** The role of QAS in a four-system phased landscape prior to testing Phase N+1

When the time comes to begin thorough testing of Phase N+1, the quality assurance system supports Phase N+1 as shown in Figure 3.13. At this time, any changes required for the support of production are made in the production support system, unit tested there, and then transported into production without true quality assurance validation. As pointed out in the section about two-landscape systems, when the transport of changes cannot be fully tested before import into production, inconsistencies may arise and affect production.

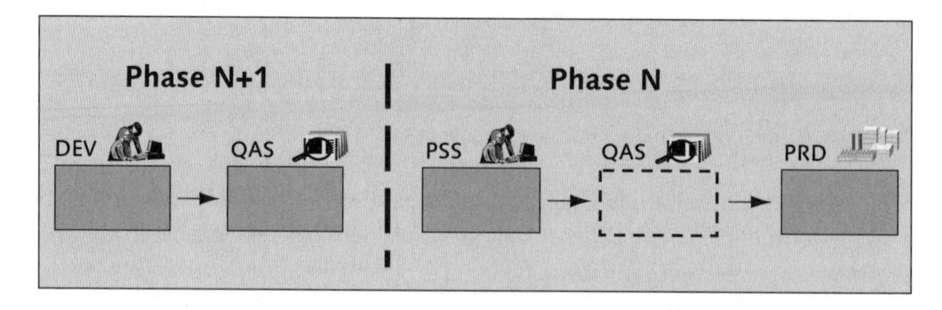


**Figure 3.13** The role of QAS in a four-system phased landscape while testing Phase N+1

Therefore, there should be a restrictive assessment of the requested changes for PRD. For important corrections that are necessary for solving problems inhibiting production, this phase should have an emergency plan ready as well.

### 3.6.3 Global System Landscape

Many enterprises today are implementing mySAP ERP on a worldwide scale and coordinating their efforts centrally. The demands of many subsidiaries and different legal and financial marketplaces require unique implementations. To maximize the benefits of a company's global business, such a global implementation has to provide all of the following:

- Core business processes on a global basis while coping with local and legal regulations
- Universal user access using different types of interfaces and supplying interfaces in local languages
- Global data consistency

While a global organization may wish to implement mySAP ERP globally from a centralized production system or perhaps using a multiple production system landscape, local requirements may not be addressed with such approaches. Therefore, many organizations centrally define their SAP organizational standards and default business processes, and then implement unique systems worldwide. To do so, a central corporate office supplies multiple subsidiaries with a set of Customizing and developments, which the subsidiaries use as a baseline when configuring mySAP ERP to meet their local requirements. This procedure is often referred to as a *rollout strategy*. The resulting environment is considered a *global system landscape*.

#### Realizing a Global System Landscape

Figure 3.14 shows a global system landscape where different subsidiaries accept Customizing and developments from their corporate headquarters. This Customizing and development package, referred to as the *global template*, is created in the corporate development system and tested in its quality assurance system. The global template is then passed on to the individual subsidiaries, which continue to customize and develop the SAP systems to meet their specific needs. This procedure takes place in each subsidiary's unique system landscape, which can be a standard three-system landscape or any of the alternatives mentioned above. Ultimately, all subsidiaries are in production with similar settings and functionality, while unique requirements are fulfilled. This forms a system landscape with decentralized yet loosely coupled production systems.

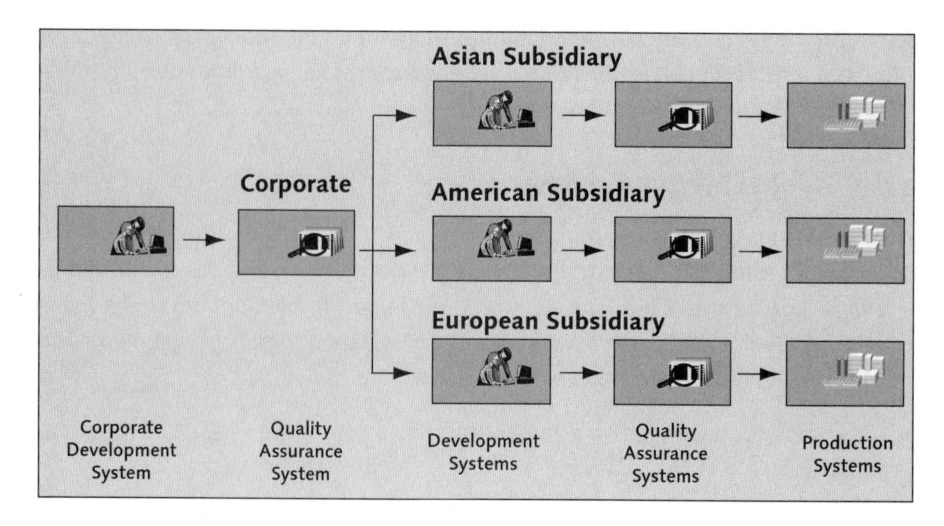


**Figure 3.14** A global system landscape

### Managing a Global Template

The difficulties in managing a global rollout strategy, as depicted in Figure 3.14 (in the previous section), involve the need for a global template. The use of a global template is not a one-time effort. As mySAP ERP expands throughout the organization and more and more business functionality is demanded, new global templates will have to be distributed on a regular basis. This sparks many concerns, particularly within the subsidiaries, and the following questions need to be addressed:

- What is considered global business functionality and what is considered localized? Can Customizing be easily divided into global and local terms?
- What assurance do subsidiaries have that new changes delivered from the corporate development system will not negatively impact local Customizing and developments? With Customizing dependencies and the coupling of SAP ECC function modules causing possible complications, how can global templates be introduced into a subsidiary over time?
- Which dependencies exist between the different products used with mySAP ERP and how can these changes be synchronized across systems?

SAP's first response to these questions is that a strong, centrally managed implementation with representative resources from all subsidiaries is needed. From a technical rather than an organizational perspective, change management in a global system landscapes requires that centrally created Customizing and development objects not be changed locally. Likewise, a global template should not change the Customizing settings or development objects of a subsidiary.

Repository objects have a sense of "ownership." An attribute for every Repository object is the SAP system from which it originated. Therefore, development objects in a global system landscape can easily be managed and protected as follows:

- Every SAP ECC system has a *system change option* (Transaction SE06; **Goto • System Change Option**). Within this option, you can simply disallow modifications to different namespaces. This determines which Repository objects in the SAP system can be changed. If a global implementation requires a lot of central development, one namespace can be created for all global objects. This global namespace can then be protected in all local development systems, disallowing any changes to such objects.
- You can use development classes and naming conventions to prevent the creation of an object with the same name within two different SAP systems.

For more information regarding the use of system change options, namespaces, and development classes for the protection of customer developments, see Chapter 10.

Customizing is more difficult to manage in a global system landscape than in the other landscapes. Unlike for Repository objects, there is no concept of ownership for Customizing settings, nor are there standard methods by which subsets of Customizing can be "locked" or protected against change. To manage a global template from a Customizing perspective, corporate standards must define which Customizing settings are part of the global template and which can be maintained locally. Such a strategy requires detailed definitions, and the procedure must be managed not from within SAP ECC, but as project efforts. This well-defined strategy for protecting both global and local Customizing settings can be realized using one or a combination of the following methods:

- Corporate headquarters determines and documents all global Customizing settings. These global settings are then reentered manually in the local development systems. This ensures successful merging with local settings. However, in addition to the duplication of Customizing efforts, manual reentry of global settings leaves a margin for error. Changes may not be realized in the local development system, or worse, they may be realized incorrectly.
- By assigning specific user authorizations, you can prevent the person performing local Customizing from accessing Customizing activities and tables that are "owned" by the corporate system. This requires added effort to not only single out these activities, but also to develop the proper user profiles to ensure that those performing local Customizing can perform only the appropriate activities.

- *Cross-System Tools*, such as the *Customizing Cross-System Viewer* and the *Transfer Assistant*, allow you to compare clients in different R/3 Systems. Using the Cross-System Viewer (Transaction SCU0), you can find the global template settings that conflict with a subsidiary's local settings before you apply the global template to that subsidiary's local development system. The Transfer Assistant (Transaction SADJ) then uses change request functionality to transfer differences between clients. (See Chapter 11.)
- *Business Configuration Sets* (Transaction SCPR2) allow a local subsidiary to preserve its current Customizing settings and compare local and global settings after applying a global template. This tool provides a mechanism for detecting conflicts between global templates and local Customizing and is therefore the most recommended of the variants introduced here, particularly in its interaction with SAP Solution Manager.

For more information regarding the use of the Customizing Cross-System Viewer, the Transfer Assistant, and Business Configuration Sets as a means to support a global system landscape, see Chapter 11.

Management of a global system landscape is difficult, more from a business application perspective than from a change management perspective. Using a variety of the tools mentioned, you can provide a template of global Customizing and development settings while still maintaining local needs. Global settings can, for example, refer to discounts to be granted while the factory calendars would usually be local due to regional differences. However, you will need to invest a lot of energy in both testing global functionality at each of the local levels as well as regression testing the existing local functionality. Performing valid tests for all local implementations is the ideal method of confirming any functionality—regardless of the advance efforts you make in protecting changes to Customizing and developments.

## 3.7 Questions

1. Which of the following statements is correct in regard to critical client roles as recommended by SAP?

   **A.** Customizing changes can be made in any client.

   **B.** All Customizing and development changes should be made in a single client.

   **C.** Repository objects should be created and changed in the quality assurance client.

   **D.** Unit testing should take place in the Customizing-and-development client.

2. Which of the following activities should not be performed within a system landscape?

   A. Customizing and development changes are promoted to a quality assurance client before being delivered to production.

   B. The SAP ECC system is upgraded to new Releases.

   C. Development changes are made directly in the production client.

   D. Clients are assigned a specific role.

3. Which of the following benefits does the three-system landscape recommended by SAP have?

   A. Customizing and development, testing, and production activities take place in separate database environments and do not affect one another.

   B. Changes are tested in the quality assurance system and imported into the production system only after verification.

   C. Client-independent changes can be made in the development system without immediately affecting the production client.

   D. All of the above.

4. Which of the following statements is correct in regard to multiple SAP clients?

   A. All clients in the same SAP system share the same Repository and client-independent Customizing settings.

   B. No more than one client in the same SAP System should allow changes to client-independent Customizing objects.

   C. If a client allows for changes to client-dependent Customizing, the client should also allow for changes to client-independent Customizing objects.

   D. All of the above.

5. Which of the following statements is correct in regard to the setup of a three-system landscape?

   A. There is only one database for the system landscape.

   B. One client should allow for the automatic recording of client-dependent Customizing and for client-independent changes.

   C. All SAP Systems have the same system ID.

   D. All clients must have unique client numbers.

6. Which of the following statements is correct in regard to the CUST client?

   A. It should allow changes to client-independent Customizing, but not Repository objects.

   B. It should automatically record all changes to Customizing settings.

   C. It should not allow changes to client-dependent and client-independent Customizing settings.

   D. It should allow for all changes, but not require recording of changes to change requests.

7. Which of the following statements is correct in regard to a two-system landscape?

   A. It is not optimal because there is limited opportunity to test the transport of changes from the development system to the production system.

   B. It allows for changes to Customizing in the production system.

   C. It is recommended by SAP because Customizing and development do not impact quality assurance testing.

   D. All of the above.

8. Which of the following statements are correct in regard to a phased implementation?

   A. All Customizing changes made in the production support system must also be made in the development system.

   B. The system landscape requires five SAP systems.

   C. Changes in the production support system do not have to be made in the development environment.

   D. The system landscape needs an environment that supports the production system with any required changes.

9. Which of the following statements is not valid in regard to a global system landscape?

   A. A global template can be used for the rollout of corporate Customizing settings and development efforts.

   B. Management of different Repository objects (those developed by the corporate office versus those developed locally) can be managed using namespaces and name ranges for the Repository objects.

   C. Merging the Customizing settings delivered by the corporate office with local Customizing efforts can easily be done using change requests.

   D. SAP provides different tools to aid in the rollout of a global template.

# 4 Managing Changes and Data in a mySAP ERP System Landscape

Within the mySAP ERP System landscape, you need to be able to transfer both Customizing or development changes and business data from one client or SAP system to another. This chapter explains the tools and strategies for transferring these changes and data. The first half of the chapter concerns managing and distributing changes using the tools in the *Change and Transport System* (CTS). The second half of the chapter concerns the techniques used to transfer business data—master data, transaction data, and user master data—into SAP or from one SAP system or client to another.

mySAP ERP 2004 enables the installation of different ABAP- and Java-based systems. However, change management is not identical in all systems. This is in part due to the fact that there is no Customizing in the sense of SAP ECC for the other products—partly because there is no development workbench, partly because more contents like documents need to be distributed instead of programs, and partially due to other reasons. The following chapters are therefore most applicable for using ABAP-based components like SAP ECC.

## 4.1 Transporting Customizing and Development Changes

The implementation of SAP ECC requires, at the bare minimum, that you customize the SAP ECC system using the IMG. Customizing is performed in a client in the development system; transferred to a client in the quality assurance system for testing; and, finally, made available to a client in the production system. Similarly, changes due to development in the ABAP Workbench require organized techniques of distribution from the development system to the quality assurance system and the production system.

Although it is possible to manually reenter the changes in successive systems, this is not a desirable option due to the quantity and complexity of the changes required. Therefore, enables you to record changes to change requests, which can then be distributed to other clients in the same system or in another system.

**Note** The word "change" is used loosely. It refers to the creation or modification of an Repository object; a change in the attributes associated with Repository objects; or the addition or modification of entries in tables (as often occurs during Customizing).

### 4.1.1 Change Requests and Tasks

In SAP ECC, *change requests* and their constituent *tasks* provide the mechanism with which you can record the objects you have changed. When changes to either Customizing objects or Repository objects are made, the changed objects are recorded to a task. A single user owns each task, which is simply a list of objects changed by that user. Tasks are grouped together into change requests corresponding to specific project objectives.

In addition to listing changed objects, in each task those who customize and develop record their documentation of the change and its purpose. Change requests and tasks provide a complete history of all changes made during SAP ECC implementation.

#### Types of Change Requests

Since the software changes created during SAP ECC implementation are the result of either Customizing or development, there are two types of change requests:

- Customizing change requests
- Workbench change requests

Customizing change requests are used to record only client-specific changes. Since most Customizing activities in the IMG are client-specific changes, they are recorded to Customizing change requests. All client-independent (cross-client) changes are recorded to Workbench change requests. Workbench change requests are used for:

- Client-independent (cross-client) Customizing objects
- All Repository objects created and maintained through the ABAP Workbench

Keep in mind that changes in application and user master data are not recorded to change requests, as depicted in Figure 4.1.

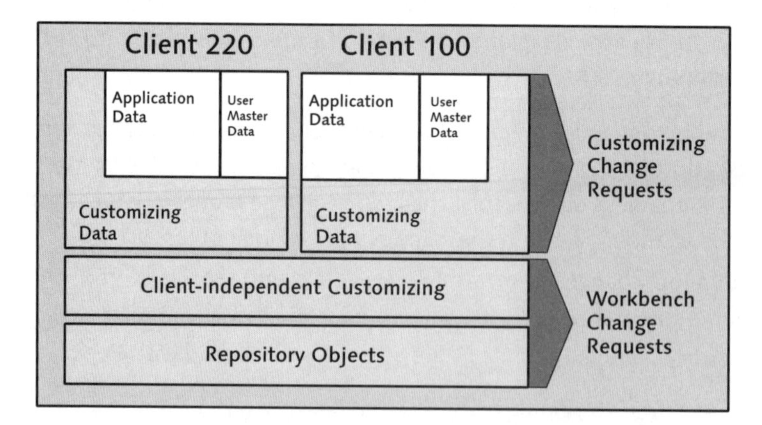


**Figure 4.1** Recording changes to change requests

Customizing activities in the IMG must be performed in a client that permits Customizing changes. To determine whether Customizing changes are permitted in a particular client, and whether these Customizing changes are automatically recorded to a change request, set the client-dependent change option (Transaction SCC4) appropriately. (See Chapter 3.)

**Tip** To ensure that changes are recorded and can be distributed, SAP recommends that you set the client change option for the Customizing-and-development client so that Customizing changes are automatically recorded to change requests.

The IMG guides you through the configuration of business processes, the recording of changes, and the saving of changes to change requests. In the *Customizing Organizer* (Transaction SE10), you can display, create, change, document, and release change requests. The Customizing Organizer enables you to see which Customizing objects have been changed, and whether they have been released. (See Chapter 11.)

The *Workbench Organizer* (Transaction SE09) enables you to display, create, change, document, and release Workbench change requests. When you make a client-independent change, the change is recorded to a Workbench change request for release and transport to the quality assurance system and eventually the production system. As with Customizing change requests, the actual contents of a change request are recorded in a task corresponding to a specific user. Unlike Customizing changes, development changes can be made only in conjunction with a change request. All client-independent changes must be saved to a change request. Therefore, you do not need to specify **Automatic recording of changes** in the client-dependent change option to have development changes automatically recorded to a change request.

You can permit or disallow the creation or modification of Repository objects on two levels:

- To permit or disallow changes from any client in the SAP system, use the system change option (Transaction SE06; **Goto · System Change Option**). (See also Chapter 7.)
- To permit or disallow changes from within a specific client, set the appropriate client-independent change option (Transaction SCC4).

### Technical Representation of Change Requests and Tasks

The ID number for change requests or tasks begins with the three-character system ID—for example, DEV, followed by K9 and a sequential five-digit number. Thus, DEVK900105 is the 105th change request or task to be created on the SAP system DEV. The next task or change request created will be DEVK900106.

A project leader who creates change request DEVK900116 assigns two users to the change request. These users are assigned by creating the tasks DEVK900117 and DEVK900118. If, after other change requests are created, the project leader wishes to add another user as a task to this change request, the corresponding task will receive the next available ID number—for example, DEVK900129. Figure 4.2 depicts these examples as they would appear in the Customizing Organizer.

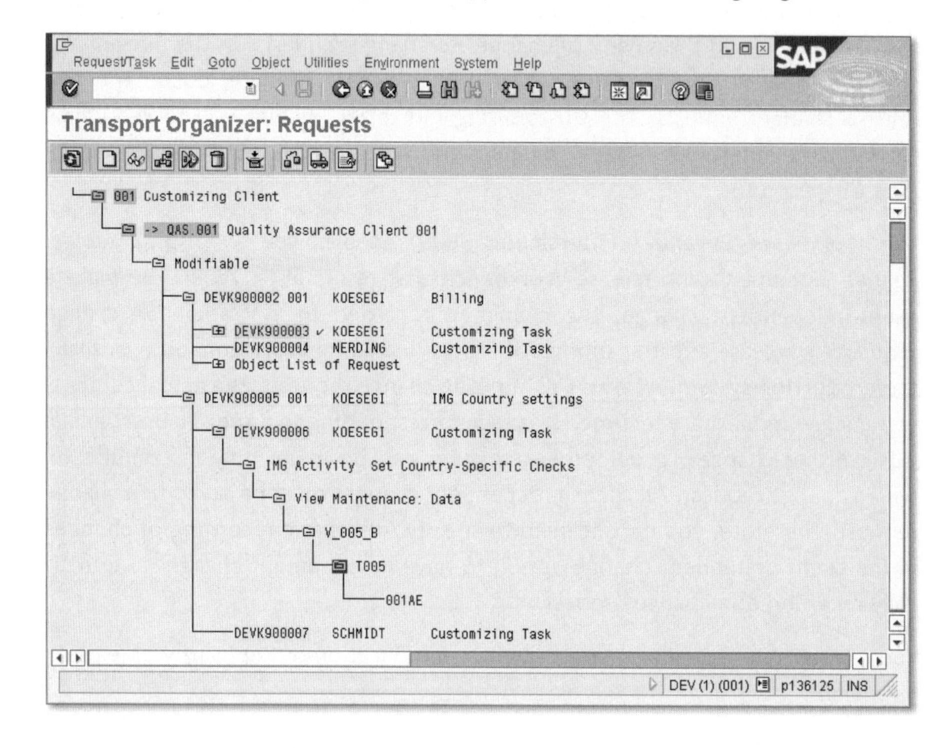


Figure 4.2 The Customizing Organizer displays Customizing change requests and tasks.

The ID numbers of change requests or tasks reveal only the SAP system in which each change request or task was created, and the temporal order of creation. Therefore, it is important to maintain the associated title and documentation for later reference.

### 4.1.2 Promoting Changes

Change requests are simply a collection of tasks that list the different objects in the database that have changed. This information enables you to update any other client within the system landscape with a new copy of the changed objects. To do this, you use the technical procedure for transport, which consists of two steps: promotion and import. Promoting changes involves releasing changes and then exporting them out of their SAP system and onto the operating system level; in a further step, they are imported into another SAP system.

The value of SAP's techniques for promoting and importing changes is the way they enable a system landscape to be kept tidy and orderly. It is only in an orderly landscape that you can know exactly which changes are operative in each system and client, and whether particular clients and SAP systems are functionally identical, or in which functions they differ.

When testing new functionality in the quality assurance system, for example, you need to be sure that the quality assurance system differs from the production system only with regard to the new functionality being tested. This ensures that such testing is meaningful. There is no value in testing new functionality in a system whose Customizing settings and programs differ dramatically or to an indeterminate extent from those in the production system. Functionally identical systems are known as *synchronized* systems.

#### Defining Transport Routes

Before promotion and import can occur, you must define strict *transport routes* between the different SAP systems in the system landscape. To define the routes change requests will follow, use the *Transport Management System* (TMS), which is called with Transaction STMS. The TMS is essentially the "traffic cop" of change requests: it centrally monitors the export process to ensure that changes are delivered in the correct order, and notifies you of errors during import.

During SAP ECC implementation, all clients and systems must be synchronized by defining appropriate and fixed transport routes. Typically, you test and verify changes from the development system in the quality assurance system before importing them to the production system. The appropriate transport routes include a transport route from the development system to the quality assurance system, and a subsequent transport route from the quality assurance system to the production system (see Figure 4.3).

**Figure 4.3** Transport routes defined in the TMS for a standard system landscape

Prior to R/3 Release 4.5, the transport routes defined in the TMS could move change requests only from one R/3 system to another R/3 system as depicted in Figure 4.3. As of R/3 Release 4.5, however, a transport route can also be defined from one client to another client by activating **Extended transport control**. In the example depicted in Figure 4.4, a change request that is released in the Customizing-and-development client is added to the import queue of both the sandbox client and the quality assurance client. After import to the quality assurance client, the change request is automatically added to the import queues of the training client and the production client.

Client-specific transport routes provided by extended transport control from R/3 Release 4.5 onwards allow more control over the delivery of changes, ensuring that changes not only reach all the SAP systems but also all clients.

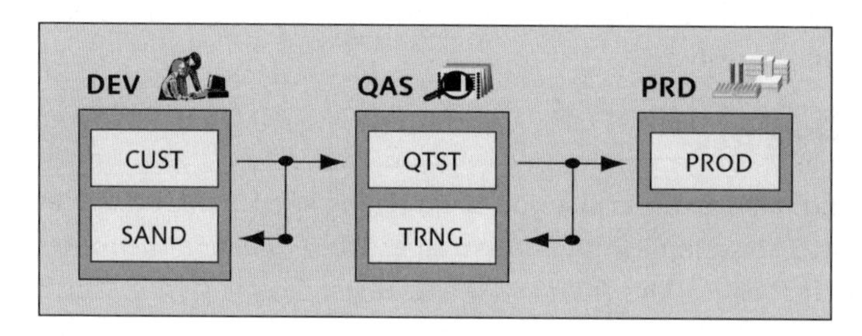


**Figure 4.4** Client-specific transport routes from R/3 Release 4.5 onwards

Regardless of whether you transfer your change requests along transport routes defined in terms of clients or in terms of SAP systems, the important issue is maintaining consistency. The clients and the SAP systems in your system landscape will be synchronized only if all changes are promoted in an orderly way and the import of changes is verified. The TMS provides the necessary tools, but they need to be set up and used properly.

### Releasing Changes

The provision of a collection of changes starts with releasing a change request. If you want to release a change request, either you or the developers assigned to the tasks first need to document and release all these individual tasks contained in the change request. Apart from the background that led to this change and the description of the correction itself, detailed information for carrying out the necessary tests should be part of this documentation.

Before you release the objects recorded in a change request, the objects must be tested for internal coherency and effectiveness. This is known as *unit testing* and can be performed in the current client or another client (see also Chapter 3). To perform *unit testing* in another client, you can use the tool *Client copy according to a transp. request* (Transaction SCC1) to copy the contents of a change request (released or not released) to another client within the same SAP system (see also Chapter 6).

The owner of a task should release the task as soon as it has been completed and unit tested.

### Exporting Changes

Releasing a change request initiates the export process. This process is the physical copying of the recorded objects from the database of the SAP system to files at the operating system level (see Figure 4.5). These files are located in the *transport directory*, which is a file system associated with the SAP system that can be shared by all SAP systems in the system landscape (see also Chapter 7).

A change request is promoted to ensure that its objects reach other clients and systems along the transport route. When the objects in the change request are exported, the change request ID number is automatically added to the *import queue* of the next target client or system, according to the transport route set up in the TMS (see Figure 4.5). The import queue is a list of change requests that have been released and exported and are awaiting import.

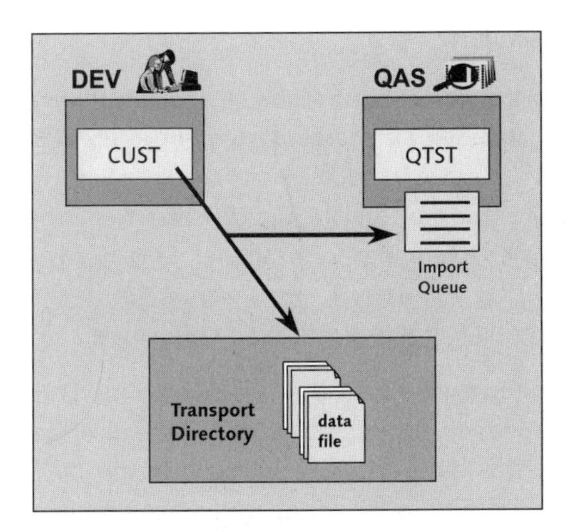


**Figure 4.5** Exporting a change request

### 4.1.3 Importing Changes

Importing is the process by which copies of the changed objects listed in a released change request are brought from the transport directory into the database of the target system and client. The import queue of the target client and system will have been notified during the export process that a request is ready for import. However, no automatic mechanism imports a change request into the target immediately after export. To trigger and monitor imports into SAP systems, use the import queue in the TMS.

**Note** Imports can be started irrespective of the Transport Management System (TMS) using the operating system; however, this procedure should be well considered. The result of the automatic import to QAS after the export from DEV is that DEV and QAS have the same status. If these changes are not immediately imported into the production system—although PRD urgently requires a correction—this correction cannot be accurately tested. An intelligent test environment should have a status that closely resembles that of the production system.

#### The Import Queue

The TMS import queue enables you to determine which change requests have been exported and to ensure that change requests are imported in the same order as they were exported. To access the import queue of a given SAP system, from the TMS initial screen (Transaction STMS), choose **Overview · Imports**. This TMS screen shows all relevant SAP systems. To access the import queue of a particular SAP system, double-click the system name. The import queue is displayed, listing any change requests that are awaiting import.

During an import, files in the transport directory corresponding to each change request are read and copied into the database of the target system. In Figure 4.6, the target system of the development system is the quality assurance system. To examine the various log files generated during the import process, from the import queue screen, choose **Goto · TP system log** (for example). The logs will show whether any errors occurred during the import (see Chapter 13). If the CCMS is set up, it can be used to elegantly monitor errors during transports.

After change requests have been imported successfully, they are deleted from the import queue, and are automatically added to the import queues of the next target clients and systems as defined by the transport route specified in the TMS. Typically, the target SAP system after an import to the quality assurance system is the production system.

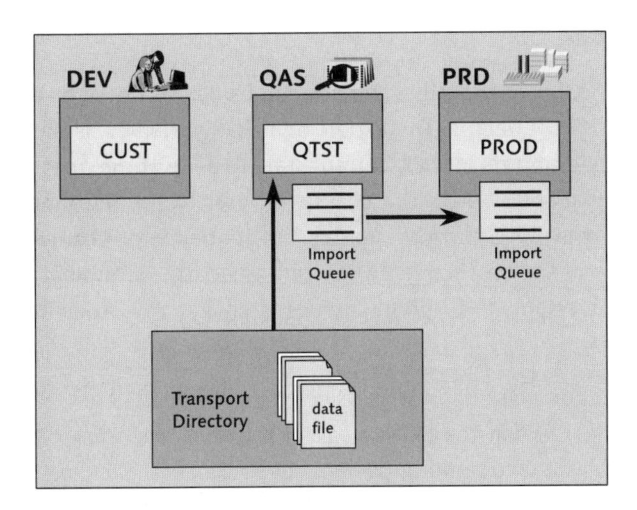


**Figure 4.6** Import to the quality assurance system and delivery to the production system

Subsequent imports into SAP systems such as the production system are similarly monitored and triggered in the TMS. During these imports, the files corresponding to the change requests in the transport directory are again copied to the database of the target system. By using the same files that were originally exported from the development system and tested in the quality assurance system, the TMS ensures that the same changes are delivered to both SAP systems (see Figure 4.7).

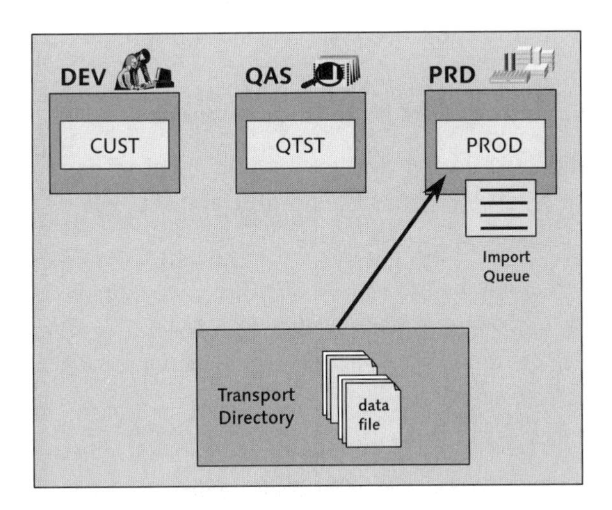


**Figure 4.7** Importing the same files into the production system

### Sequence in Import Queues

Change requests are only lists of changed objects that need to be promoted and imported to other clients and SAP systems. The export of a change request is the process that copies the changed objects in their current state to a file at the operating system level, and simultaneously adds the change request to the relevant import queue as defined by the TMS transport route. The sequence of change requests in the import queue of the respective SAP system is strictly chronological. The order of change requests in the import queues is always the order in which they were exported.

This sequencing is important. For example, if successive change requests are created to change the same object, when they are released, they will each deposit new versions of the object at the operating system level. Since the change requests in the import queue are processed sequentially, the last import of the object will represent the most recent version.

The import process then ensures that defined delivery systems, such as the production system, receive the change requests in the same order in which they were imported into the quality assurance system.

The significance of the import queues is that they control the order in which changes are imported into an SAP system. By ensuring that this order is consistent, import queues enable the various SAP systems to be functionally synchronized. Import queues track the order in which changes are imported and ensure that changes are not imported into the production system in the wrong sequence.

**Example: Sequencing Change Requests in an Import Queue**

Two developers at a multinational company receive the assignment to write data conversion programs in the development system—programs that will be used to convert legacy data.

One developer named Miller creates a program called `ZLEGACY_DATA`. The new Repository object is recorded in change request `DEVK900834`. Miller releases the change request. At the same time, other people are releasing change requests containing Customizing settings.

The second developer, whose name is Schmidt, adds additional functionality to the program `ZLEGACY_DATA` and saves his change to change request `DEVK900876`. Schmidt then releases the change request.

When it is time to import the changes into the quality assurance system, the import queue of the quality assurance system contains the following change requests (in the order in which they were released):

| Change Request | Owner | Description |
|---|---|---|
| DEVK900834 | MILLER | Conversion routine |
| DEVK900912 | HAMM | Customizing for Materials Management |
| DEVK900820 | THOMAS | Organizational data |
| DEVK900876 | SCHMIDT | Conversion routine with validation loop |

Two change requests, DEVK900834 and DEVK900876, recorded changes to the program ZLEGACY_DATA. Therefore, the transport directory contains two different versions of the program. If change request DEVK900876 is imported before change request DEVK900834, the program ZLEGACY_DATA in the quality assurance system will not have the additional functionality programmed by Schmidt, because the version of DEVK900876 which was imported first is simply overwritten with the old version of DEVK900834. The program in the quality assurance system would then differ from that in the development system, and the two systems would be inconsistent.

By having the imports occur in the order indicated in the import queue, the developers ensure that DEVK900834 is imported first, since it was released before DEVK900876. Program ZLEGACY_DATA is imported twice, but the final import, which overwrites its predecessor, is the current version. This helps to ensure consistency between the different SAP systems.

As of SAP R/3 Release 4.6C, another possibility of grouping change requests is available by using *projects*. In projects, transports for specific tasks can be grouped so that a comprehensive import process can be started and the risk of using a wrong transport sequence is reduced. The procedure of a *quality system acceptance* is suitable in this respect as well. In this case, requests are placed in the import buffer of the PRD system only if this is explicitly confirmed after a successful test in the quality assurance system. The related details are described in Chapter 5.2.3.

### Manipulating Import Queues

Within the TMS, users are able to manipulate import queues to add or delete change requests, or to change the order in which they appear in the queue. However, SAP does not recommend such activities, since they may create inconsistencies between the source system and the target system.

Users often wish to delete a change request because it contains incorrect information. However, deleting a change request may delete more than the incorrect data, since change requests typically contain more than one change. In addition, deleting a change request may make the objects in another change request fail, due to a dependency on the objects in the deleted change request. For example, if you delete a change request containing a new data element, all other transported objects containing tables that refer to that data element will fail.

To avoid these inconsistencies, you are strongly advised against manipulating import queues. It is more prudent to make the necessary corrections in the development system and release a new request.

> **Tip** SAP recommends that you do not manipulate an import queue. For example, you should not delete change requests or alter the sequence in the queue.

#### Technical Aspects of the Transport Process

The program `tp` resides on the operating system level and controls both the export and import process. It is responsible for reading the change requests in the import queues and making adjustments to the import queues after completion of successful imports. The TMS import functionality is the user-friendly interface that communicates from within SAP ECC with the transport control program `tp`.

Another relevant program is `R3trans`. To accomplish an export, `tp` triggers another tool on the operating system level called `R3trans`. `R3trans` creates the operating system data file for the export. During import, `R3trans` reuses this data file. `R3trans` is used to communicate with the database to read or insert data.

### 4.1.4 Change and Transport System (CTS)

SAP refers collectively to the tools that support change management as the Change and Transport System (CTS). These tools include:

- **The Change and Transport Organizer (CTO)**
  The CTO consists of the Customizing Organizer, the Workbench Organizer, and the *Transport Organizer*. The most frequently used component is the *Customizing Organizer*. The Customizing Organizer enables the creation, documentation, and release of change requests generated during Customizing. It enables the people implementing SAP ECC to track their changes to change requests, and then view the change requests for which they are responsible and make the changes available to other systems by releasing the change requests. The Workbench Organizer provides similar functionality for developers using the ABAP Workbench. The Transport Organizer then provides support for the

transports that do not fall within the realm of the Customizing Organizer and the Workbench Organizer.

- **The Transport Management System (TMS)**
  You use the TMS (Transaction STMS) to organize, monitor, and perform imports for all SAP ECC systems within a system landscape. For example, you use the TMS to import change requests into the quality assurance system for testing and verification. In addition, you use the TMS to centrally manage the setup of your transport environment by adding SAP ECC systems and defining transport routes.

- **The programs tp and R3trans**
  These are executables on the operating system level used to communicate with the SAP system, the database, and the files in the transport directory necessary for the export and import processes. For example, when you import the objects in a change request into the quality assurance system, `R3trans` copies the data to the database of that system.

The CTS comprises all the tools required to support SAP change and transport management for ABAP-based products (see Figure 4.8). There is a similar tool for Java-based products, the Change Management System (CMS), which is described in more detail in Chapter 18.

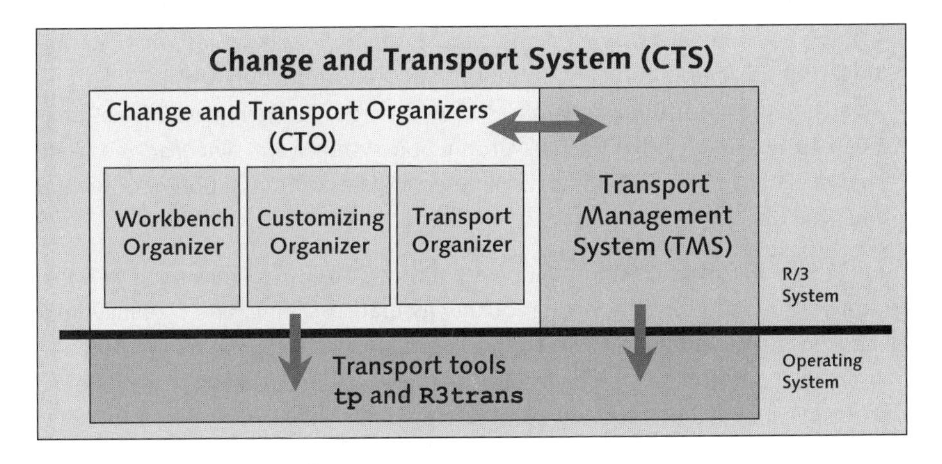


**Figure 4.8** The components of the CTS

## 4.2 Transferring Data

Change requests do not transport application data such as master data, transaction data, and user master data. That you would have to distribute this type of data may surprise you. After all, this data is required for production activities, and there is only one production client in most system landscapes. However, you may need to distribute business data to perform:

- **Functionality testing and end-user training**
  Master data is required for both unit testing in the unit test client in the development system and testing in the quality assurance system. For example, when you test the creation of sales orders, the database needs to contain at least one specified material that a customer can purchase. Ideally, the entire material master list should be available. This is especially the case for quality assurance testing and end-user training.
- **Report testing**
  To test most reports (for example, month-end closing reports) data from multiple business transactions is required—that is, data from various business processing scenarios.
- **Authorization assignment testing**
  Quality assurance testing includes testing authorization assignment for certain users and also for randomly selected users. The test system therefore requires user master data. To avoid having to manually re-create users in the quality assurance system, you may wish to transfer existing user master data from the production system.
- **Production data replication**
  Complex system landscapes, such as those found in companies with international subsidiaries, often contain more than one production SAP ECC system. To ensure the consistency of application data across such a landscape, you may need to ensure that the various production systems are synchronized as to master data records such as customer master data, or transaction data such as financial transaction data.

During the initial and subsequent implementation phases, you may need to transfer application data for unit testing, quality assurance testing, and training. After going live—that is, after work begins in the production system—you may need to transfer application data to synchronize multiple production environments or to share application data with other computer systems.

Transferring business data to different clients is not as straightforward as transferring changes that can be recorded to change requests. The methods used vary according to whether you wish to:

- Transfer application data
- Share application data with other SAP systems or non-SAP computer systems

Whether you need to distribute and the methods for distribution of application data should be determined early in the SAP ECC implementation process.

### 4.2.1 Master Data

Master data is a type of application data that changes infrequently, but is required for the completion of most business transactions. Examples of master data include lists of customers, vendors, and materials, and even the company's chart of accounts. Master data usually exists in an organization prior to the introduction of SAP ECC. Before implementing SAP ECC, you need to determine how to import the data into the SAP system. Ideally, the method used for the initial migration can also be used to subsequently transfer the data between clients.

Since master data changes over time, you must also consider how to provide for data transfer across all your clients to maintain the consistency of master data within the landscape.

#### Importing Master Data into SAP ECC

Master data can be imported into SAP ECC from non-SAP systems using the following techniques:

- Manually entering each data item
- Loading the data from sequential data files outside SAP ECC
- Communicating with other SAP or non-SAP systems through various interface technologies

To save time and ensure consistency, you should import master data either through data loads from external data files or through interface technology. These techniques enable you to supply copies or subsets of the master data to multiple clients. Manual data entry may be more cost-effective for some implementations, since data loading and interface technology can be handled only by someone with programming knowledge or SAP interface experience. However, manual entry is not an efficient way of distributing data to multiple clients.

> **Note** When importing data by loading it from files outside SAP ECC, SAP provides the Data Transfer Workbench and the Legacy System Migration Workbench to help you plan and develop programs to perform your data transfer. For more information on these tools, refer to SAP online documentation.

### Transferring Master Data between SAP Systems

Although master data is relatively static, it will change over time. You need to determine whether changes to master data in the production system will be distributed to all clients in your system landscape. You also need to determine how frequently this synchronization process is required—that is, whether a large delay is acceptable. Master data can be transferred by:

- Manually entering each data item
- Using change requests (only possible for some types of master data)
- Using interface technologies

Manual data entry may be an adequate method for transferring master data to clients other than the R/3 client in the production system. It isn't necessary, for example, to make known a customer's change of address to the quality assurance client, since a change in the details of an address will not affect general business processing. However, if new customers are added to the production system, they can be manually entered into the quality assurance system to ensure their inclusion in testing.

Some master data is transferred using change requests in conjunction with special IMG activities. Examples of this type of master data include the chart of accounts, material groups, and cost accounting areas.

SAP also provides extensive interface technologies that support the transfer of master data. One such technology is *Application Link Enabling* (ALE), which enables you to exchange data between SAP ECC systems or between R/3 systems and R/2 systems or non-SAP programs. ALE is the technology that is most frequently used to support master data in an environment with multiple production clients, or where master data is required to be identical in more than one client. When you use ALE, master data can be either:

- Managed centrally and distributed to other clients when necessary (as is the case in Figure 4.9, where master data is distributed from the SAP system PR1 to clients in system QAS and PR2)
- Managed in different clients and then transferred to a central client and distributed from there to all other clients

To help you implement ALE, SAP provides preconfigured master data templates known as *ALE scenarios*, which you can adapt to meet your specific master data needs. Examples of ALE scenarios for master data include scenarios for materials, vendors, customers, profit centers, chart of accounts, bill of materials, and cost centers. ALE is not limited to master data—it can also be used to distribute transaction data.

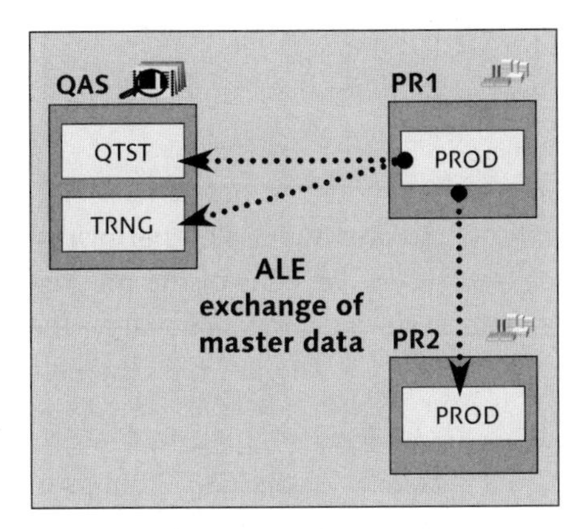


Figure 4.9 An example of ALE data exchange between different SAP systems

In principle, you can use ALE to distribute master data freely between all SAP systems. However, a certain degree of common Customizing is required in the target systems. SAP's *ALE Customizing Distribution* enables you to ensure that the Customizing settings related to ALE scenarios are identical on the different SAP systems in the system landscape.

### 4.2.2 Transaction Data

Transaction data is shared across different computer systems—for example, for testing, training, or multiple production environments. These systems can be other SAP ECC systems or non-SAP systems. Transferring the data requires a communication link using interface technology. Transaction data distribution is complex because of transaction data's high volume, its dependency on the Customizing environment, and its need for master data. These factors mean transaction data cannot simply be transferred from one client to another, nor is there a way to extract a subset of transaction data from one client and distribute it to another.

You must carefully consider how sample transaction data will be made available in different clients for testing and training. Since transaction data is altered during testing and training, you may need to delete and replace all transaction data for each successive test or training course.

#### Creating Sample Transaction Data

Sample transaction data will be required in the quality assurance and training clients in your system landscape. Users can manually create this data during testing or training. However, manual data creation is tedious if testers require many completed transactions—for example, when testing month-end financial reports. SAP recommends that you develop scripts to generate standard sets of transaction data. These scripts can evolve over time to generate data reflecting new functionalities, and can also be used to test existing business processes in *regression testing*. (See Chapter 6.)

A general example of a script is one that creates 20 production orders for a specific plant. If necessary, this script can be copied and altered for all other plants. The data produced by the script is used for testing new versions of the production-planning functionality. During every rollout cycle for this functionality, the script and its data can be altered and used for testing the way in which the new functionality will impact production operations.

The *extended Computer Aided Test Tool* (eCATT, successor of the CATT tool as of Web Application Server 6.20) by SAP provides tools for creating scripts. eCATT allows you to combine and automate business processes as repeatable test procedures and use them to generate sample data. eCATT can also simulate transaction results, analyze the results of database updates, and monitor the impact of changes in Customizing settings.

**Note** Except eCATT, other tools for creating scripts and performing tests make up the SAP Test Workbench. Ideally, these test scripts can be controlled and managed using SAP Solution Manager as a central system, because eCATT can simulate business processes per Remote Function Call (RFC) even across system boundaries.

### Interfaces for Transaction Data

SAP's open interface provides several methods and tools for communication between different types of computer systems (see Figure 4.10). In regard to transaction data, you can create interfaces to:

- Distribute transaction data from one client to another
- Import existing transaction data from a non-R/3 System into the SAP ECC System
- Distribute transaction data to non-SAP systems

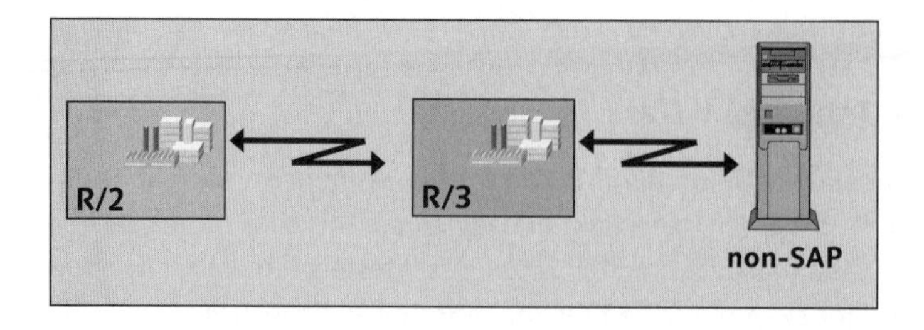


**Figure 4.10** Possible interfaces for sharing application data

As an integral part of mySAP ERP 2004, the SAP Exchange Infrastructure (XI) Release 3.0 provides a particularly flexible way to exchange data, including the conversion between different data types.

**Example: Using ALE with Multiple Production Systems**

Large organizations often require centralization of financial data. Producing millions of sales orders every day conflicts with the management's need for timely reports and with the needs of the finance department. A large computer component supplier decides that while the Customizing and development of the different function modules is possible in a single development system, multiple production systems are required. The production system SAL is used for all sales order entry and processing. A second production system, FIN, is used for financial and accounting data.

To configure SAP ECC for multiple production systems, the company must determine which master data must be shared among the different systems, and how this master data will be shared. The company decides to set up an enterprise reference data "library" to centrally manage all master data. This requires yet another production SAP ECC system, MDR, for the sole purpose of managing master data. ALE is used to transfer master data changes to FIN and SAL.

ALE is also used to share other data between the different production systems. For example, when a sales order is entered in SAL, ALE is used to make the customer's credit information from FIN available to SAL. To ensure that management reports are up to date, ALE enables sales information to be transferred from SAL to FIN, and accounting information to be transferred from FIN to SAL.

All the production environments receive changes originating in the same Customizing and development system, DEV. The company's system landscape and ALE strategy can be represented as follows:

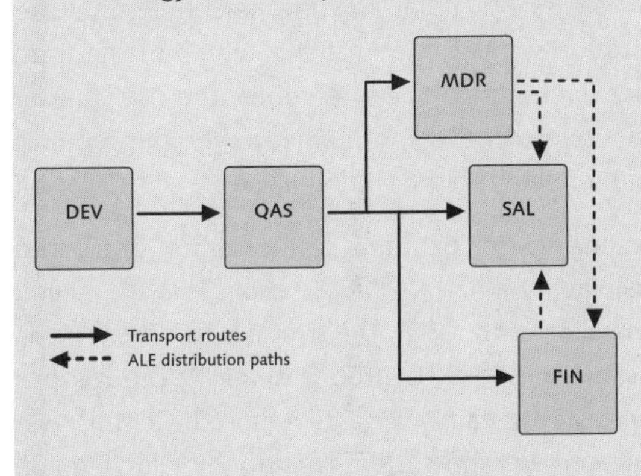


**Figure 4.11** System landscape and ALE strategy

### 4.2.3 User Master Data

User master data includes the data used by the SAP system to validate a user's ID at logon and assign user access rights based on passwords and authorization profiles. User master data also includes the user's name, phone number, and default printers, and the default screen the user will see after completing logon.

User master data is a type of master data—much like material master data and vendor master data. User master data is client-specific data. SAP separates user master data from other types of application data because user master data must be different in different clients, even if master data is the same. For example, in the development client, you must give extensive authorizations to your developers so that they can view tables, change programs, and test reports. However, these developers should not receive such authorizations for the production client. In fact, they may not even need a user account in the production client.

Each *authorization profile* groups together different business objects and transactions that a user may access, and each user may have a number of authorization profiles assigned to their user ID. Authorization profiles are created either manually or, as recommended by SAP, using a tool called the *Profile Generator*. Regardless of how they are created, authorization profiles are technically considered Customizing data and can be recorded to change requests for distribution to other clients.

In SAP ECC Releases prior to R/3 Release 4.5, authorization profiles can be distributed to other clients using change requests, while user master data—including the authorization profiles assigned to the user ID—cannot be transported using change requests. The definition of authorizations is managed in a central location such as the Customizing-and-development client. The user master data is separately maintained in each client to ensure that users have different authorizations in each client and that specific clients are reserved for specific activities.

In SAP ECC Releases prior to R/3 Release 4.5, if you need to have the same user master data and the same authorization profiles in two clients, you must perform a client copy that copies only user data. This procedure copies the user master data and authorization profiles from one client to another. However, this requires that all users be distributed to another client, rather than just some of the users.

As of R/3 Release 4.5, you can manage user data and authorization profiles in your system landscape centrally using *Central User Administration*. This allows you to maintain all SAP users in a single client and assign the user IDs to other clients in the system landscape with the same or different authorizations. Authorizations can be assigned either centrally or locally in each client, as required. Central User Administration simplifies user management and system security by allowing you to globally change a user's data.

**Note** For more information on how to set up and use Central User Administration, refer to the SAP online documentation.

For R/3 releases as of 4.6, the provided *roles* (before: activity groups) are a good alternative with their simplified assignment and grouping of authorizations to end users. In this context, we advise you to use the role maintenance functions and the Profile Generator (Transaction PFCG) to maintain your roles, authorizations, and profiles. Additionally, you can centrally maintain the roles delivered by SAP, or your own newly created roles, and assign any number of users using the functions of Central User Administration (CUA). Furthermore, the Profile Generator provides for integration with HR-Org (Organization management, time dependency).

Using roles, you assign the users the user menu that is displayed to them after their logon to the SAP system. Roles also include the authorizations that users can use to access the transactions, reports, and web-based applications, for example, contained in the menu. Because the SAP standard delivery already provides many roles, you should determine whether you could use these standard roles before you start defining your own.

To obtain an overview of the delivered roles, you can do the following:

- In the SAP Easy Access menu, select **Tools • Administration • User Maintenance • Informationsystem • Roles • Roles by complex selection criteria** and then **Run**.
- Select the input help in the Role field of the role maintenance (**Tools • Administration • User Maintenance • Role Administration • Roles**).

To adapt existing roles, copy the respective standard role and modify this copy. If you don't find any suitable roles, you should define the job descriptions in written form before you start working in role maintenance (see also "First Installation Procedure" or "Organizing Authorization" in the SAP Online Help) (BC-SEC-USR).

## 4.3 Copying SAP ECC Systems and Clients

Repeatedly, the following question is asked: "Why must I record all my changes to change requests—can't I just periodically copy the development system or the Customizing-and-development client?"

The answer to this question is that, technically, you can always copy an SAP system or even a client. However, the result may create extra work or even cause chaos in your system landscape. While copies of SAP systems and clients have their advantages, they should be used only to set up or create a system or client.

A copy of a system or a client does not help you maintain your existing system landscape because it completely overwrites the target system or client, and eliminates all application data.

SAP recommends using change requests to record Customizing and development changes, so that these changes can be distributed to all systems and clients without deleting existing application data.

### 4.3.1 System Copy

A copy of an SAP system is called a *system copy* and is used to create an identical copy of an existing SAP system. A system copy is sometimes referred to as a database copy, because you are copying the database of one system to another system. A system copy copies everything from the source database, including all clients, all Repository objects, and all data such as transaction data.

SAP does not recommend using system copies to set up critical systems, such as the quality assurance system or the production system (see Chapter 5). However, a system copy is useful when you need an exact copy of an SAP system for a limited scope and a limited time frame, or when you need to establish another non-critical SAP system in your system landscape. For example, to set up an system for training purposes, you may wish to use a copy of the quality assurance system. Alternatively, you may wish to make a copy of the production system to use as a temporary system for simulating data archiving routines.

Often, customers make a copy of the production system to set up a quality assurance system with good production data. They believe that a copy of production data is the easiest way to provide for a true quality assurance environment, or even to rebuild a development system. While this may be technically true, remember that since the size of the production system grows dramatically as more and more transaction data is collected, the cost of hardware required to support a copy of the production system may render such a copy unfeasible. For large production systems, consider the alternative methods of transferring business data previously discussed in this chapter.

Avoid using a copy of the production system to create the development system, as you will lose all data stored in the development system. This includes your Enterprise IMG, Project IMGs, and associated project documentation with your change history in the form of change requests and version histories of Repository objects.

**Note** Technical details about making a system copy can be found in the installation guides and in SAP Note 89188.

### 4.3.2 Client Copy

SAP's client copy tools enable you to copy one client to another client in the same or a different SAP system. Whenever you use client copy (except when copying user master data or a single change request), the target client is deleted prior to copying the source client.

Like a system copy, a client copy is useful for creating a client, but generally cannot be used to maintain a client. Because the target client is deleted prior to copying data from the source client, client copy does not provide a way of merging the source client with the target client. Client copy enables you to copy application data that cannot be transferred using change requests (see also Chapters 5 and 9).

## 4.4 Questions

1. Which of the following statements is correct in regard to Customizing and development changes?
   - **A.** All changes are recorded to tasks in Customizing change requests.
   - **B.** The changes should be recorded to tasks in change requests for transport to other clients and systems.
   - **C.** The changes must be manually performed in every SAP system.
   - **D.** The changes can easily be made simultaneously in multiple clients.
2. Which of the following statements in regard to change requests is FALSE?
   - **A.** The Customizing Organizer and the Workbench Organizer are tools used to view, create, and manage change requests.
   - **B.** A change request is a collection of tasks where developers and people performing Customizing record the changes they make.
   - **C.** All changes made as a result of IMG activities are recorded to Customizing change requests.
   - **D.** SAP recommends setting your SAP system so that Customizing changes made in the Customizing-and-development client are automatically recorded to change requests.
3. For which of the following activities is the TMS (Transaction STMS) *not* designed?
   - **A.** Releasing change requests
   - **B.** Viewing import queues
   - **C.** Viewing log files generated by both the export process and the import process
   - **D.** Initiating the import process

4. Which of the following statements is correct after you have successfully imported change requests into the quality assurance system?
   A. The change requests must be released again to be exported to the production system.
   B. The data files containing the changed objects are deleted from the transport directory.
   C. The change requests need to be manually added to the import queue of the production system.
   D. The change requests are automatically added to the import queue of the production system.
5. Which of the following statements is correct in regard to the change requests in an import queue?
   A. They are sequenced according to their change request number.
   B. They are sequenced in the order in which they were exported from the development system.
   C. They are sequenced according to the name of the user who released the requests.
   D. They are not sequenced by default, but arranged in a variety of ways using the TMS.
6. Which of the following techniques can be used to transfer application data between two production systems?
   A. Recording transaction data to change requests
   B. Using ALE to transfer application data
   C. Using the client copy tool
   D. All of the above
7. Which of the following types of data transfer are possible with an appropriate use of interface technologies?
   A. Transferring legacy data to an SAP system
   B. Transferring data between clients
   C. Transferring data to non-SAP systems
   D. Transporting change requests to multiple SAP systems
8. Which of the following statements is correct in regard to user master data?
   A. User master data can be transported in a change request.
   B. User master data is unique to each SAP system, but is shared across clients in the same SAP system.
   C. A specific client copy option enables you to distribute user master data together with authorization profile data.
   D. User master data includes all user logon information, including the definition of authorizations and profiles.

# 5 Setting Up a System Landscape

The strategy you use to set up your system landscape determines how all the SAP ECC systems in your system landscape will be created and will receive Customizing settings and development changes. This chapter outlines the various setup steps—taking you from the initial installation of the development system, through the setup of the quality assurance system, and finally to the production system. The focus will be on how Customizing and development changes are properly transferred throughout the landscape.

Ideally, you should set up your system landscape using change requests. However, since change requests cannot always be used to support the setup of your critical clients, the client copy strategy is a viable alternative. In rare cases, using a system copy may prove an appropriate method for creating your quality assurance system and possibly the production system. The advantages and disadvantages of these different strategies are outlined in this chapter.

## 5.1 Setting Up the Development System

Every SAP ECC implementation begins with the installation of one initial SAP ECC system. Since those individuals in charge of Customizing and development will be anxious to begin configuring SAP ECC to meet your company's different business needs, this first SAP ECC system is typically your development system. This is the system where all changes to the SAP software—both Customizing and development—originate.

Before you make changes to the software, you must ensure that the environment has been properly prepared and is ready for changes to take place. Once you begin making changes to the SAP software, you must record them to change requests to allow for their transport.

### 5.1.1 Post-Installation Processing

After the installation process is complete, you may need to perform any or all of the following activities collectively known as *post-installation processing*:

- **Languages:**
  The SAP system delivered by SAP supports two languages, English and German. If your implementation requires additional languages, you need to install them at this time. A language import inserts language-specific text into the standard client 000. For example, if you import the languages French and Spanish after installation, these languages will be available in client 000. To add

these additional languages to your other clients, use the Language Transport Utility (Transaction SMLT).

- **Industry solutions:**
  To fulfill the unique needs of different industries or business solutions and to help accelerate the Customizing process, SAP ECC's product line includes different industry solutions, such as SAP Discrete Industries, SAP Banking, and SAP Oil & Gas. These types of solutions provide customers with additional R/3 functionality by adding special Repository objects to the SAP system.
- **Support Packages:**
  SAP provides Support Packages, to remedy any possible programming errors. Support Packages are packages of repository corrections of SAP software in which the individual corrections of SAP Notes are delivered in a bundle. Before you start Customizing and development activities, SAP recommends applying all available and relevant Support Packages to your development system.

You should document all of these post-installation activities. You want to use the same setup procedure for the quality assurance and production systems. The documentation will assist you when establishing these critical SAP systems or any other system within the landscape.

### 5.1.2 Setting Up the Transport Management System (TMS)

The Transport Management System, as its name implies, enables you to manage the transport process for all ABAP-based systems within your system landscape. The TMS ensures that all SAP systems share the same transport configuration. This uniformity allows changes to be promoted and delivered to the right clients and systems in the correct order. Without the TMS, you will not be able to save changes to change requests for transport to other SAP systems.

After installing an SAP ECC system, your next task is to set up its TMS (Transaction STMS). This allows you to define the role of the system in your landscape. Since the development system is typically the first SAP system installed, it is also used to define the system landscape and the other SAP systems that will eventually be supported with the same changes and transport process.

Most importantly, you use the TMS to indicate which system is the target for changes promoted from your development system. For example, if you have a three-system landscape, changes from the development system are transferred to the quality assurance system. The TMS helps you create the transport route between the development and quality assurance systems. In a two-system landscape, the transport route leads directly from the development system to the production system.

In many implementations, the quality assurance system is not installed or does not even physically exist until much later in the process. However, you still need to establish a transport route to connect it with the development system. Without this transport route, you cannot create change requests for later release to the quality assurance system. You need a placeholder for the quality assurance system. This *virtual system* is created using the TMS. This procedure requires that you provide a three-character alphanumeric system ID for the virtual system. You should also create a virtual system to represent your production system. For more details on setting up the TMS, including information on creating virtual systems and defining transport routes, see Chapter 8.

Although it is possible to later change the name of the development and quality assurance systems (or the production system), SAP recommends that you maintain the same system IDs throughout your SAP implementation. It is important to keep the relationship between the development and quality assurance systems consistent and the transport route invariant for the following reasons:

- Change requests for Customizing by default cannot export data from the development system without an established target system. The standard transport route defined for the development system determines the target system.
- Customer development objects can be created only for a particular development class. Each development class is associated with a transport layer. The transport layer in turn depends on a transport route to identify the location of the change request after release and export.

Changes are moved from one SAP System to another according to the relationships established by the transport route. Changing an SAP system name and/or transport route will therefore impact existing and future change requests.

### 5.1.3 Creating Clients

Once you have set up the TMS, you can begin creating clients in the development system. After installation, an SAP ECC system contains the SAP-standard clients 000, 001, and 066. SAP reserves clients 000 and 066 for maintenance and support, leaving client 001 for your implementation process. Client 001 can function as your Customizing-and-development client, known as CUST.

However, client 001 may not contain the settings established during post-installation processing, such as applied Support Packages or imported languages. You must integrate all additional settings into this client using tools provided by SAP. Alternatively, you can copy client 000 to create a new client that contains all of the post-installation settings. This copy will ensure consistent settings throughout the system, and allows you to preserve client 001 as it was delivered by SAP. Retaining clients 000 and 001 provides you with a reference for comparing your changes in subsequently created clients with the SAP standard.

**Tip** SAP recommends that you create a new client as a copy of client 000 for Customizing and development efforts.

**Procedure**

To create a client within SAP ECC, follow these steps:

1. Access **client maintenance** (Transaction SCC4).
2. Define the client with a three-digit client number and text description.
3. Select the client's role, restrictions, and client change options. Once this new client has been defined, you can log on to it with the special SAP user SAP*.

Your brand-new client does not contain the data necessary for performing Customizing. This data consists of basic Customizing settings and language data. Neither does the new client have the SAP-standard user authorizations needed to create additional users: SAP-standard authorizations and profiles. After using client maintenance to define the new client, you need a *client copy tool* to copy the contents of client 000 into the new client. A client copy transfers the user data and Customizing data that currently exist in client 000 to the new client.

**Note** For more details on how to use client maintenance and client copy, see Chapter 9.

SAP recommends including a unit test client (TEST) in your system landscape so that you can evaluate new Customizing settings and developments using sample application data. You may also consider creating a sandbox client (SAND) to allow the people performing Customizing to experiment with settings. Use client copies of client 000 to create both the unit test and the sandbox clients (see Figure 5.1).

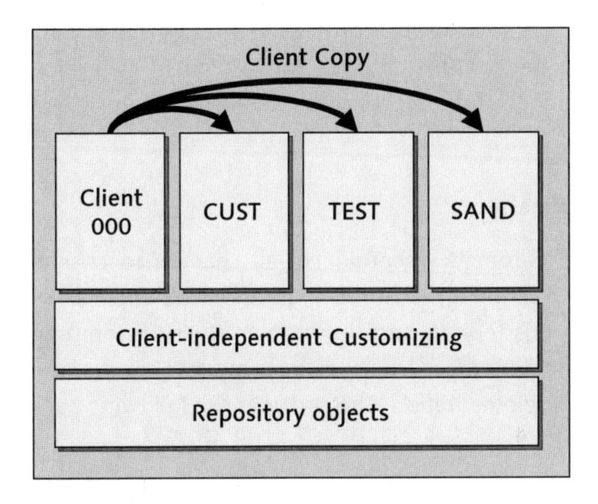


**Figure 5.1** Creating new clients in the development system

### Setting the Client Change Options

Before starting Customizing and development, you must set the client change options for the different clients that you have created. For the development system, SAP recommends setting the client change options in Transaction SCC4 as indicated in Table 5.1.

| Client | Client-Dependent Change Option | Client-Independent Change Option |
|---|---|---|
| Customizing and development (CUST) | Automatic recording of changes | Changes to Repository and client-independent Customizing allowed |
| Unit test (TEST) | No changes allowed | No changes to Repository and client-independent objects allowed |
| Sandbox (SAND) | No transports allowed | No changes to Repository and client-independent objects allowed |

**Table 5.1** Recommended Client Change Settings

Although you may have planned your own unique system landscape, SAP recommends abiding by these development system restrictions set through the client change options for the following reasons:

- All Customizing changes—both client-dependent and client-independent Customizing changes—must originate in a single R/3 client. These changes are then distributed from this client to the rest of the system landscape.

- Client change options provide a solid wall of protection—regardless of user authorizations—by restricting the possible changes within a client (see Table 5.1). You should limit the number of people with the authority to alter client settings.

### Recording Changes Automatically

SAP recommends that you use automatic recording of all changes to change requests for your CUST client. Occasionally, customers question the importance of this procedure, thinking that it is tedious and slows down their Customizing work. Nonetheless, changes should be recorded to change requests consistently from the beginning of your SAP implementation. This provides the following benefits:

- A documented history of the changes to different Customizing settings, including who made them and when they were made.
- A mechanism that copies changes to other clients in the same SAP system prior to the release of the change request. The contents of a change request can be unit tested, modified if necessary, and verified before the actual release of the change request (see Chapter 12).
- A method ensuring that all changes originate in one client and are systematically transported to other clients in the system landscape.
- Project management through the allocation of change requests to teams for the completion of different parts of the Customizing project.

You can track Customizing changes by activating *table logging*. Table logging records the changes made to many tables and Customizing settings (see Chapter 9). Table logging does not, however, provide a method to document and distribute changes. You can also successfully set up clients and systems without automatically saving all changes to change requests. However, you *cannot* maintain clients within a system landscape over time without change requests. There is no other alternative for supplying existing clients with the most recent Customizing changes.

Since all people performing Customizing will eventually need to save changes to change requests to maintain existing clients and systems, you should train them to use change requests early in the implementation process. Changing procedures and providing training in the middle of an implementation is awkward. At such a time, concerns will involve testing and completing business functionality and not learning to work with change requests.

**Tip** To obtain a complete history of all changes made and to simplify your implementation process and future client maintenance, SAP recommends recording all changes to change requests from the very beginning of your SAP implementation.

## 5.2 Setting Up the Quality Assurance and Production Systems

Eventually, you will reach a point when you are ready to test the entire SAP system equipped with your Customizing and development changes. To run this *integration testing*, you will need to set up the quality assurance system. Keep in mind that you also need to start planning for the production system. The quality assurance system acts as your proving ground for production activities. Setting up and testing the quality assurance system ensure that, subsequently, the production system as well as the procedure for setting it up will function properly.

There are different methods for setting up—transferring Customizing and development changes to—the quality assurance and production systems. SAP recommends using change requests to move Customizing and development changes from the development system to the quality assurance system. Another alternative, the client copy strategy, is also available. Each method has certain advantages and disadvantages.

**Tip** SAP recommends that you use the same techniques to set up both your quality assurance and production systems. This is a safeguard for the production system and ensures consistency between the two environments.

### 5.2.1 After Installing the New SAP System

Before using the change request or client copy techniques to distribute Customizing and development changes, you need to install the SAP system that is to become your quality assurance system or production system. Both systems require the same post-installation support that was necessary for the development system. You need to provide the systems with the necessary Support Packages, industry solutions, and languages. After completing the post-installation processing, you can begin setting up the TMS and creating the required clients.

#### Setting Up the TMS

Regardless of how you will subsequently set up the quality assurance system and production systems, after they are installed, you first need to set up the Transport

Management System. The TMS allows you to import change requests into the quality assurance system and ensures that these change requests are also delivered to the production system.

Ideally, your quality assurance and production systems, though not physically present until this point in time, have already been represented in the TMS by placeholders. In other words, virtual systems have been used to define the two systems. Since these virtual systems do not contain any technical details, they need to be deleted before you can continue with the TMS setup on your installed quality assurance or production systems. The TMS includes the new SAP ECC systems and their technical settings in the system landscape (see Chapter 8).

**Tip** Before importing the first change request into the quality assurance system, you must represent the production system in the TMS, either as a virtual system or, if it exists, as the installed system. A transport route from the quality assurance to production system must also be active.

As changes are imported into the quality assurance system, the import queue of the production system also receives notice of the changes. The objective is to ensure that those steps used to create the quality assurance system are recorded and then replicated to create the production system—this includes the import of all change requests in the exact order in which they were applied.

### Creating Required Clients

The quality assurance system requires at least one client, the quality assurance test client (QTST). The production system, in turn, needs the production client (PROD). To import changes or clients from the development system into these clients, you must first create the QTST and PROD clients in their respective systems.

The procedure for creating the QTST and PROD clients is the same as the procedure used for creating the Customizing-and-development client. Using client maintenance, you define the client by providing it with a client number and description as well as selecting its role, restrictions, and client change options. The quality assurance and production clients should both be protected against changes by setting the client change options to **No changes allowed** and **No changes to Repository objects and client-independent Customizing**. For additional protection or to use **Current settings** (see Chapter 11), you can assign the production client the client role **Production**.

Before you can supply the newly created client with the latest Customizing settings and developments using change requests, you must use a client copy tool to copy the contents of an existing client into the new one. To ensure consistency, the QTST and PROD clients are created in the same manner as you created the CUST client—that is, by making a copy of client 000.

### 5.2.2 Change Request Strategy

SAP recommends using change requests to set up your quality assurance system and ultimately your production system. In this way, you can ensure that only those changes promoted or released from the development system are imported into the quality assurance and production systems. Change requests also provide you with a methodical process for adding business functionality to an SAP system after realizing that functionality in a development environment.

#### Requirements

To set up your quality assurance system using change requests, you must have saved all Customizing changes made in the development system to change requests. This is the single requirement for using this setup strategy. If you follow SAP's recommendations regarding the client-dependent change options when setting up your CUST client, your changes are automatically recorded to change requests from the beginning of your implementation. An incomplete recording of Customizing change requests results in only partial functionality in the quality assurance system. There is no easy method for transporting changes that were not recorded; instead, the changes have to be manually assigned to change requests through the respective IMG Customizing activity.

**Tip** If a large number of changes made in your Customizing-and-development client were not recorded to change requests, do not use the change request strategy to set up your quality assurance and production systems. Use a client copy.

#### Procedure

Before and during the installation of your quality assurance system, you record changes to change requests and unit test functionality in the development system. By releasing and exporting the change requests, you cause the changes to be copied to files at the operating system level. There, they are added to the import queue of the quality assurance system. Once you have copied the contents of client 000 into the quality assurance client and selected the appropriate client change options, the changes in the import queue of the quality assurance system can be imported into the system itself.

After the change requests are successfully imported into the quality assurance system, they continue along any other defined transport routes. The next transport route typically leads from the quality assurance system to the production system. After the changes are imported into the quality assurance system, they are also delivered to the import queue of the production system. Eventually, you will import the same changes into the production system, in the same order as they were imported into the quality assurance system.

Figure 5.2 shows the steps involved in setting up a system landscape using the change request strategy. This setup strategy is actually the same method you will use later to maintain the system landscape: Changes are released and exported from the development system, imported into the quality assurance system for verification, and then imported into the production system.

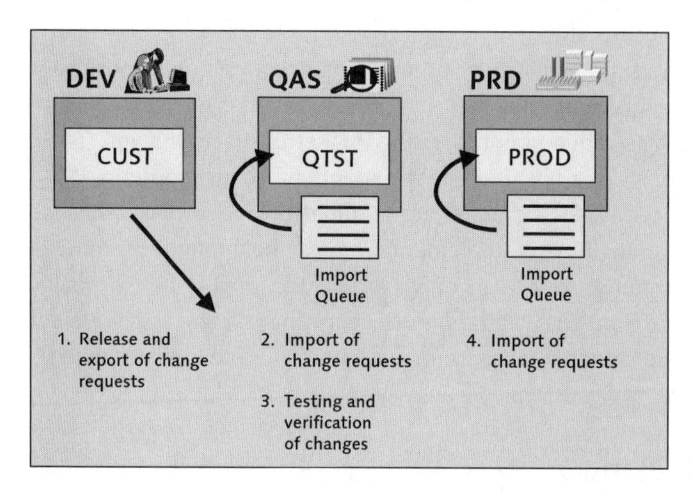


**Figure 5.2** Setting up a system landscape using change requests

At this stage in the implementation procedure, your quality assurance client (and perhaps your production client) contains the latest Customizing settings and developments transported from the development. However, the client contains no application data or user data. Unless you specifically transport user data or manually create users in the client itself, only the default SAP user is defined in this client. Your next step is to verify user accounts and authorizations. Also, since the client has no application data, it also has no master data. Master data will be needed in quality assurance for validation to take place. Ultimately, master data will be needed in the production client prior to the start of production activities.

**Note** For solutions on how to manage master data within a system landscape, see Chapter 4.

### Advantages

The most significant advantage of using change requests to set up your quality assurance and production systems is that this strategy is identical to the maintenance strategy. No additional training or procedures will be required before or after the start of production. The procedures defined during project preparation and system setup are valid for the entire implementation cycle, future upgrades, and the addition of any new business functionality.

The other main advantage of using change requests is that this strategy provides project control and management. It allows the project leader to improve the efficiency of the implementation project by:

- Assigning different tasks or activities to individuals
- Bundling a collection of tasks into one or several change requests
- Ensuring that Customizing and development work has been unit tested before it is released

These steps provide the project leader with an up-to-date overview of the configuration and ensure that only completed Customizing units are transported for quality assurance testing.

## 5.2.3 Quality Assurance Procedure of the TMS

To supplement the change request strategy, SAP provided the *quality assurance procedure* (QA) as an extension to the TMS as of Release R/3 4.6C. This procedure provides a security mechanism to balance the drawback of change requests, that is, that all requests must be imported into the production system, and thereby increase the quality and availability of the production systems.

For this purpose, the QA approval procedure is activated in a system of the transport landscape. As soon as it has been activated, the transports are not forwarded to the downstream recipient systems until all QA approval steps for the respective request and the request as a whole have been approved. If one approval step is not confirmed, the request cannot be approved.

Rejected requests are not imported into the recipient systems of the QA system.

### Prerequisites

If you want to use the quality assurance procedure within the TMS, you must use Basis Release 4.6C or higher, and have set up a system landscape containing at least one QA system. From this QA system, there must also be delivery channels to other systems.

Besides the configured delivery channels, the QA approval procedure has to be set. This includes the information that identifies which system is the QA system and which approval steps must be carried out during the approval procedure.

In a three-system landscape, requests are normally imported from the development system to the QA system. This is where the requests are verified. This verification is carried out using a list of transport requests, which is created in the work list of the QA system. In this work list, a log is generated as well, showing who approved or rejected which transport request at what time. The approved requests are then forwarded or imported to the production system in accordance with given transportation schedules and the sequence of the import queue.

### Procedure

For the QA approval procedure, the same prerequisites and steps apply as for the normal change request strategy. Changes in the system are recorded in change requests. By releasing and exporting from the development system, the changes are copied to files at the operating-system level and are automatically added to the import queue of the quality assurance system.

When importing these changes to the quality assurance system, however, contrary to the normal change request procedure, the imported request is not placed into the import queue of the production system in a way that it can be directly imported, even inadvertently. Instead, this request becomes visible to the transport tools and can be imported only after the corresponding approval steps have been carried out successfully. This ensures that no requests are imported into the production untested.

Additionally, the QA approval procedure can support you in checking transport requests by searching for specific critical objects. Critical objects in this context are any objects like repository objects or objects following a specific naming convention. The objects to be regarded as critical can be specified in a Customizing table of the TMS. Using this information, you can carry out a preliminary check and sort the transport requests from the work list accordingly.

As with the normal change request strategy, you should ensure that no requests—which are referred to by subsequent requests—are refused in the quality assurance procedure as well, because the lack of objects of the refused request would lead to errors in the receiving system. Therefore, in this context, it is safer to correct a change request, which is classified as faulty, by using a subsequent transport.

### 5.2.4 Client Copy Strategy

Although SAP recommends that you use change requests to set up your system landscape, the change request strategy can be used only when most (ideally *all*) changes made in the source client have been saved to change requests. If you are unsure whether this has been done in your implementation, SAP recommends an alternative for the setup of your quality assurance client and eventually your production client—the client copy strategy.

#### Requirements

Before beginning the client copy procedure, you must have installed the quality assurance or production system, completed all post-installation processing, and defined the required quality assurance or production clients. There is no need to copy the contents of client 000 into the new clients. Instead, you will transmit data into the new client using a client copy of the Customizing-and-development client, CUST.

#### Procedure

The setup procedure using the client copy strategy consists of the following steps:

1. Import change requests that have already been released.
2. Begin a *client transport* by exporting data in the source client CUST from the database of the development system to files at the operating system level.
3. Import the files at the operating system level into the target client, providing it with a copy of the data found in the original client.
4. Perform post-import activities with Transaction SCC7. (See Chapter 9.)

Any change requests with new developments must be imported into the new client before commencing with the client transport. A *client transport* (Transaction SCC8) is a special type of client copy used to set up your critical SAP systems. The client transport corresponds to steps 2 through 4 above. It makes use of standard transport functionality; that is, data is exported to files at the operating system level and then imported into the target client.

Several client copy tools are available, including a client transport or a *remote client copy* (Transaction SCC9). A remote client copy employs *Remote Function Calls* (RFCs) to transfer a client from one SAP system to another. A client copy using remote functionality does not provide a method to "freeze" the client; that is, the stream of data that is transferred is not stored at the operating system level (see Chapter 9). Therefore, you do not have a physical copy of the client that can be used later to set up the production system. Since your setup strategy should aim at creating the production system in the same manner as the quality assurance system was created—using the same recorded changes and clients—SAP recommends using a client transport rather than a remote client copy.

**Tip** When you cannot use the change request strategy, SAP recommends using a client transport—not a remote client copy—to set up your quality assurance and production systems.

#### Importing Existing Change Requests

Before and during the installation of your quality assurance system, you may have released change requests with unit-tested changes and functionality from your development system. These change requests appear in the import queue of the quality assurance system. Although they may seem irrelevant for the client copy setup of the quality assurance system, they need special attention.

Some of these change requests contain development changes to Repository objects such as programs. Since the client copy procedure duplicates only client-dependent data and the related client-independent Customizing changes, the client-independent development changes affecting Repository objects will not be transported into the quality assurance system. For this reason, SAP recommends that all change requests promoted before the start of the client transport—that is, those change requests already released and exported—should be imported into the quality assurance client.

**Tip** A client copy does not copy changes to Repository objects made in the ABAP Workbench. Such changes are automatically recorded to change requests and can be imported into a new client from the import queue before performing the client copy.

As the existing change requests are imported into the quality assurance system, they are also placed in the import queue of the production system. When the production system is created, the same change requests are imported into the production system in their correct order.

#### Exporting the Client

When you export a client from an SAP system with Transaction SCC8, you can specify the type of data you wish to copy from the source client. Possible selections include:

- Client-dependent Customizing data
- Client-independent Customizing data
- Application data
- User data

Although you can select different data combinations, SAP recommends that you copy only the two types of Customizing data to create the quality assurance and production clients. Avoid copying application data, since typically the transaction and master data in the CUST client is either nonexistent or simply test data that should not be duplicated.

User data may be included in the copy, but this is potentially problematic. Current users and their authorizations will be distributed from the development system into your production client. For example, your developers will have the same user authorization in the production system that they needed for the development system. This could lead to a possible security problem in the production system.

If you do copy application and/or user data, you will have to "clean up" the new client to remove unnecessary data and users. This clean-up process is complicated and time consuming. It also requires extensive knowledge of the data model to ensure that dependent data is eliminated in the correct sequence. Perhaps the biggest disadvantage is that you will have to repeat the clean-up procedure for the production client.

#### Importing the Client Export

The import of change requests released prior to the client transport ensures that all development changes promoted from the development system exist in the quality assurance system. After you have imported these change requests, you import the exported client into the quality assurance client. This import process (using TMS) has the following steps:

1. The existing quality assurance client, QTST, and any client-dependent data in this client, including Customizing imported in change requests, are deleted.
2. The exported copy of the CUST client is imported into the new QTST client, thereby placing all Customizing data that existed in the development system in the client. This ensures consistency with the CUST client.

**Example: Import Sequence for the Client Copy Strategy**

Assume that your development system has been installed for three months and that you have just recently installed your quality assurance system. Although you recorded all ABAP Workbench changes to change requests, you did not start recording all Customizing changes until the second month of the implementation procedure. Therefore, to set up your quality assurance system, you need to perform a client export of the CUST client from the development system.

After you export the CUST client with all of its Customizing settings, the import queue for the quality assurance system looks like this:

| Order | Change Request | Description |
|---|---|---|
| 1 | DEVK900034 | Conversion routines |
| 2 | DEVK900012 | Customizing for Materials Management |
| 3 | DEVK900020 | Organizational data |
| 4 | DEVK900076 | Sales Reports and New Routines |
| ... | ... | ... |
| 158 | DEVK900410 | Production Reports |
| 159 | DEVK000005 | Client export (client-independent Customizing) |
| 160 | DEVKT00005 | Client export (client-dependent Customizing) |
| 161 | DEVKX00005 | Client export (texts) |

The import queue contains 158 change requests released prior to the client export and three change requests containing the client copy data. Some of the 158 change requests contain reports and programs that you will need but that are not part of the client export. You must first import the 158 change requests into the quality assurance system.

When you import the client export files, both the client-dependent and client-independent Customizing imported from the 158 change requests is overwritten. This is of no consequence since the client export contains all current Customizing settings from your CUST client.

If you discarded the 158 change requests and just imported the client export, your quality assurance system would not contain the new sales reports or conversion routines. If you imported the client export before importing the other 158 change requests, some relevant Customizing settings would have been overwritten by older versions. For example, the change request DEVK900012 is second on the list in the import queue. After that change request was released, you may have modified the Materials Management settings in the CUST client.

If you then imported DEVK900012 after the client export, the settings would revert back to an older and incorrect version. The correct procedure is to import the 158 change requests prior to the client export.

To provide a consistent environment and ensure that the production system is the same as the tested and verified quality assurance system, you must set up the production system in the same way you set up the quality assurance system. The procedure is as follows:

1. All change requests in the import queue of the production system—that is, those change requests released *before* the client export—are imported into the production system.
2. The exported CUST client is imported into the system.
3. Any change requests that appear in the import queue after the client export are imported into the system.

#### Disadvantage

The major disadvantage of the client copy method concerns the type of Customizing settings copied. A client copy copies *all* Customizing settings, even those that provide only partial functionality. There is no way to filter out these incomplete settings. In other words, those Customizing changes that are incomplete or perhaps even unnecessary for the start of production activities will be transferred to the quality assurance client and eventually the production system.

## 5.3 System Copy Strategy

Many customers mistakenly think that a system copy is a viable method for establishing any kind of additional SAP system within a system landscape. A *system copy*, also known as a *database copy*, can be useful for creating optional systems, such as a training system or a copy of the production environment for upgrade tests. However, SAP does not recommend using a system copy to set up a critical system. This means you should not use a system copy of the development system to set up a quality assurance or production system.

SAP has several reasons for advising against the use of a system copy and alternatively recommending either the change request or the client copy strategy:

- A system copy transfers all Customizing settings and developments, even those that are incomplete. The task of removing unwanted Repository objects and Customizing entries to ensure that only complete business transactions exist in the SAP system is a difficult one.

- A system copy transfers application data. While SAP does provide some production start and reset routines to eliminate existing application data, these routines do not exist for all application data.
- A system copy provides you with no true documentation on the creation of the environment. The system copy procedure in conjunction with the manual elimination of data eliminates the audit history and documentation provided by change requests.

### 5.3.1 System Copy of Quality Assurance

SAP strongly advises against using a system copy of the development system to set up your quality assurance system and ultimately your production system. However, on occasion, customers still choose to make a system copy of the quality assurance system to set up their production system. They do this for any of the following reasons:

- They believe that too much time and effort is required to apply the necessary Support Packages, languages, and change requests to the production system.
- They have made manual changes on the quality assurance system that either cannot be transported using change requests or were not performed nor recorded in the development system.
- They have no record of the sequence in which change requests and/or a client copy were applied to the quality assurance system. In other words, the import queue of the production system does not match the list of change requests imported into the quality assurance system.
- They no longer have the data files required by the change requests. The change requests used to build the quality assurance system are no longer in the transport directory, nor can they be located on backup devices.

The three latter reasons are typically the result of poor planning and incorrect procedures. Changes in the quality assurance system should never take place, but if they do, the changes must always be re-created on the development system. Such manual changes should also be performed on the production system. Although it is possible to re-create an import buffer using information currently stored in the quality assurance system, missing data files cannot easily be re-created. By properly planning and structuring your implementation, you can avoid having to make a system copy for any of these reasons.

The time factor, however, may still be compelling. The initial setup of the quality assurance system is straightforward. It requires post-installation processing, possibly a client copy, and some change requests. However, over time, more and more change requests are imported into the quality assurance system. When you begin to install the production system, the list of change requests may number well over a thousand. To complicate matters, during the quality assurance testing, you may have applied additional Support Packages. (See Chapter 15.) Setting up the production system suddenly seems an insurmountable task. A system copy may appear to be the only solution. Keep in mind that this is not a solution recommended by SAP.

**Warning** SAP does not recommend using a system copy to set up your quality assurance or production systems. However, this is a proven technique for creating, for example, a sandbox system for an initial upgrade test (Chapter 15).

### Cleaning Up after a System Copy

If you do use a system copy of the quality assurance system to set up your production system, you will encounter several complications before the start of production. You must ensure that all application data is eliminated and that the new production environment is thoroughly tested.

After performing the database copy and prior to eliminating application data, you must complete the following activities:

- Reinitialize the Change and Transport Organizers (Transaction SE06) to close any open change requests that originated in the source system. (See Chapter 7.)
- Verify that the TMS configuration is correct and active so that change requests can be delivered to the new SAP ECC system.
- Assign the clients in the new system unique logical system names to avoid conflicts with the logical system names of other clients. (See Chapter 9.)
- Use authorization techniques to manage user access to the SAP system.

One of the reasons SAP advises against using a system copy is that production start programs to remove transaction data exist only for certain functional areas. To remove the data not covered by such a program, you could use a combination of archiving, running your own deletion routines, and removing data manually—overall, a very tedious and time-consuming process.

A more practical method of removing the test data copied from the quality assurance system is to use a client copy to generate a client without application data. For example, after the system copy of the quality assurance system, you can make a client copy of what was once the quality assurance client to create the production client. When you make this client copy, you allow only Customizing data to be transferred. This ensures that no application data will be in the production client at the start of production activities. Figure 5.3 illustrates this procedure.

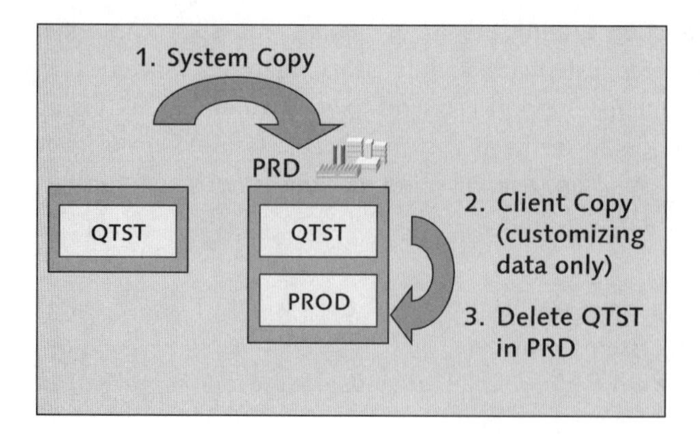


**Figure 5.3** Setting up a production client using a system copy

SAP advises customers setting up a system landscape to always employ the same method when establishing the critical SAP systems. In the system copy procedure, however, the production system—more specifically, the production client—is created in a manner different from that used to create the quality assurance system and client. This means you must verify the new production system before starting production. You should make a system copy of the new production system and use it for testing purposes. These validation tests need to be thorough and comprehensive. Remember that, as in any other step of the implementation procedure, a system copy is only as good as the tests that are performed to verify it.

**Example: Using a System Copy to Set Up a Production System**

An implementation team that lacked the necessary technical expertise early in the project plan hires a woman who is an experienced technical consultant. Her first objective is to determine the best strategy for setting up the production system. Although the quality assurance system has been in place for the past two months, she is unable to determine which change requests have been successfully imported. She discovers that several Hot Packages were applied at various times. Also problematic are the client change settings, which may have allowed additional Customizing changes in the quality assurance client.

The consultant recommends setting up the production system with a system copy. She proceeds as follows:

1. To support a system copy and hopefully provide an opportunity for verifying the production system setup, she creates an additional client in the quality assurance system, client 200. This is a client copy of client 100, the quality assurance test client, and contains only Customizing settings. After creating this client, she makes a system copy of the quality assurance system.

2. The consultant then checks and confirms that no Customizing changes can be made in the quality assurance system. All changes imported into the quality assurance system are added to the import queue of the production system. She also works with the testing teams to migrate all business validation to client 200. While this involves establishing new application data in client 200, it helps ensure that the environment most resembles the soon-to-be production client.
3. When the production system arrives, the consultant installs SAP ECC with the system copy from the quality assurance system. She deletes client 100 from the system and sets up client 200 as the production client with the appropriate settings. Any changes applied to the quality assurance system after the system copy are also applied to the production system.

## 5.4 Release Considerations

When choosing a method to set up your system landscape, you must also consider release levels. Ideally, the release installed within the system landscape should be the same for all systems. However, implementations frequently begin at one release and are upgraded as soon as newer releases become available.

When considering an upgrade within your implementation process, you must keep an important factor in mind: Change requests and the client transport are release-dependent. This means you should not transport changes from one release to another. The change requests used to create a system must originate in a system at the same release level.

**Tip** Change requests and the client copy tools, such as a client transport, are release–dependent.

An upgrade delivered by SAP may contain Repository objects that differ from those in the original release. The table structures that house the Customizing data also vary in the different releases. If the data recorded in a change request originates from a system at a higher level of release, you may not be able to import the data into a system at the lower release level. For the same reason, a client transport can be imported only to an SAP system at the same level of release.

If you need to upgrade your development system prior to the installation of the quality assurance system, first check whether any change requests have been released. If there are no released change requests, you can upgrade the development system and install the quality assurance system at the new release level.

However, if change requests have been released, to ensure that these released changes are distributed to the quality assurance and production systems, you need to employ one of the following methods:

- Install the quality assurance and production systems at the initial release level. After the released changes are imported, upgrade the systems to the latest release.
- Upgrade the development system to the new release. The released change requests are re-recorded to a new change request at the new release level. This *bundling* of several requests *includes* the contents of the old, released change requests in a new change request (see Chapter 10). You install the quality assurance and production systems at the newer release level and then promote this single bundled change request.
- Instead of using change requests for the initial setup of the quality assurance and production systems, upgrade the development system and use the client copy strategy. All change requests released prior to the upgrade are discarded. After the upgrade, you release a change request from the development system for all modified Repository objects. This is accomplished using the Transport Organizer (Transaction SE01) to create a transport of copies (see Chapter 10). This ensures that all Repository changes are transported to the quality assurance and production systems, both of which are installed at the newer release level.

**Example: A Release Upgrade during Implementation**

Based on needs for the latest SAP ECC functionality, a company decides that its development system should be upgraded from R/3 Release 4.6C to release SAP ECC 5.00 in the middle of the implementation process. The company's system administrator, a man named Frank, is concerned that the upgrade will significantly delay his plans for setting up the quality assurance system.

After a little thought, Frank decides to upgrade the development system to release SAP ECC 5.00 and install the quality assurance system at the new release level. Then Frank discovers that change requests were released from the development system. Because the change requests now at the operating system level originated in Release 4.6C, Frank realizes they cannot be imported into an SAP system at the Release SAP ECC 5.00 level.

Frank's alternative plan has the following steps:

1. Install the quality assurance system at the R/3 Release 4.6C level.
2. Apply the R/3 Release 4.6C change requests to the quality assurance system.

3. Upgrade the quality assurance system to the new release.
4. Import any change requests released from the SAP ECC Release 5.00 development system into the quality assurance system.

Frank's manager, Barbara, is not in favor of his plan. She feels it would take too long to install and then later upgrade the quality assurance system. As an alternative, she suggests the following procedure:

1. Upgrade the development system and install the quality assurance system at the SAP ECC 5.00 level.
2. Include all the released 4.6C change requests into a single change request in the upgraded development system; this single bundled change request is then at the SAP ECC Release 5.00 level.
3. Import the bundled change request into the quality assurance system, thereby providing the system with a copy of all Customizing and development changes released earlier.

Frank follows her suggestions. When he installs the production system at the SAP ECC Release 5.00 level, he imports all change requests that were imported into the quality assurance system, including the bundled change request.

## 5.5 Questions

1. Which of the following clients should you copy to create new clients and ensure that all data from post-installation processing is also copied?

   A. Client 001

   B. Client 000

   C. Client 066

2. Which of the following is *not* an SAP-recommended strategy for setting up a system landscape?

   A. Using a client copy from the development system to set up your quality assurance and production systems when the change request strategy is not an option

   B. Creating the production system as a combination of a client copy from the quality assurance system and change requests from the development system

   C. Using the same setup strategy to establish both the quality assurance and production systems

   D. Setting up the quality assurance and production systems by importing change requests promoted from the development system

3. Which of the following are correct in regard to the setup of the TMS?

   A. The TMS should be set up when the development system is installed.

   B. The TMS should include all SAP systems in the system landscape even if the R/3 Systems do not physically exist.

   C. The TMS is critical in establishing the transport route between the development and quality assurance systems.

   D. The TMS should be set up before change requests are created in the Customizing-and-development client.

4. Which of the following is correct in regard to the system copy strategy?

   A. SAP recommends the system copy strategy, because all Customizing and development objects are transferred.

   B. SAP does not recommend the system copy strategy, because there is no easy way to eliminate unwanted application data.

   C. A system copy is the easiest setup strategy recommended by SAP.

   D. A system copy eliminates the need for change requests for your entire SAP implementation.

# 6 Maintaining a System Landscape

In the early phases of your implementation, you require not only a setup strategy, but also a plan for maintaining your system landscape to enable the systematic implementation of changes in SAP systems. This maintenance includes:

- Managing implementation projects through change requests
- Setting up a transport process that ensures that approved changes are distributed to all clients in the system landscape
- Planning and importing SAP Support Packages or SAP Support Package Stacks and performing release changes

The responsibilities, roles, and procedures involved in recording and transporting changes must be clearly defined and documented. In addition, defined procedures are required to support the import of changes outside the standard transport process—for example, when implementing Support Packages.

This chapter focuses on these issues, and outlines the decisions you will have to make. It explains SAP's recommended system landscape maintenance strategy, as well as SAP's recommendations for testing and validating changes, which play an important role in all maintenance strategies. The maintenance strategy mapped out in this chapter is based on the standard three-system landscape recommended by SAP. The processes and procedures presented here can be adapted to cover system landscapes that differ from that standard.

## 6.1 Implementation Plan

A system landscape is in a continuous state of maintenance, and maintenance activities need to be coordinated. The overall maintenance process focuses on successive implementation phases—that is, phases in which new or changed SAP software is to be implemented in the system landscape. To coordinate these implementation phases, you need to map them in an *implementation plan*, as shown in Figure 6.1.

The various implementation phases in the life of an SAP system can be summarized as follows:

- An initial phase to configure the SAP software to meet your business needs and start production
- A series of subsequent phases to introduce new or improved business processes and functionalities

All implementation phases presuppose that changes to be implemented have been created through Customizing and development activities in SAP ECC, and require subsequent *production support*, which is the use of a special SAP ECC system or client to perform the Customizing and development needed to repair any errors associated with the changes already implemented in the production system.

Time and security concerns vary depending on the maintenance activity. Both factors are especially significant for production support. Creating new business processes is not as time-critical as production support, but results in a greater need for end-user training, business process validation, and new test scenarios. Before going live with new or modified business processes, stringent testing is required in the quality assurance system.

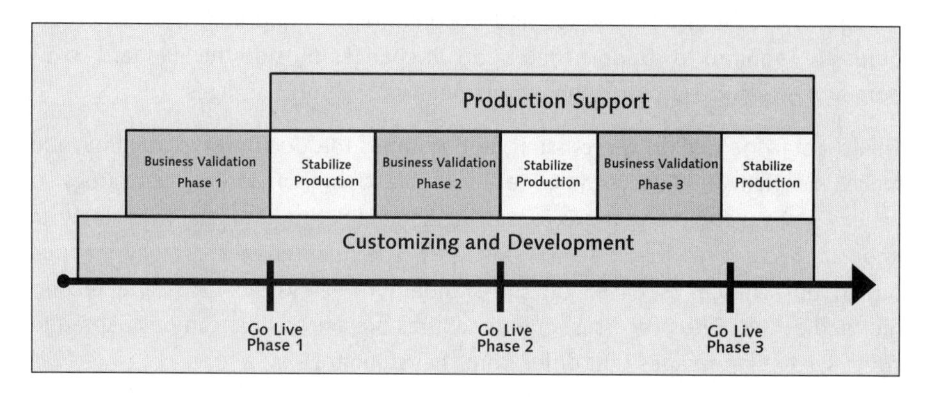


**Figure 6.1** Implementation cycles in the implementation plan

The implementation cycle is indicated as a horizontal bar at the center of the implementation plan in Figure 6.1. It is a repeating pattern consisting of a business validation period followed by a going-live date and a stabilize production period. Prior to the going-live date for each bundle of development or Customizing changes, the *business validation* period consists of:

- ▶ Extensive testing in the quality assurance system of SAP ECC business processes to verify that the changes will work smoothly in the production system
- ▶ Stress tests to validate the technical environment and ensure that the introduction of new changes will not reduce performance in the production system

After going live, the *stabilize production* period is a time that is set aside to allow the production system to stabilize. Any conflicts resulting from the introduction of changes in the production system should be resolved before the beginning of the business validation period of the following implementation phase.

In addition to the business validation and stabilization cycles, Figure 6.1 also shows the related, ongoing activities of production support, and Customizing and development. Customizing and development begins immediately after SAP ECC installation, while production support commences after the start of production.

Your implementation plan will consist of a schedule based on a diagram such as is shown in Figure 6.1, as well as documentation that defines the business processes that you intend to introduce in each implementation phase. The associated Customizing and development tasks are then assigned to particular individuals to prevent conflicts and procedure overlaps. The three main parties involved in an implementation are as follows:

- Project leaders
- Members of the project teams—that is, customizers and developers
- The system administrator responsible for transports

Their roles and responsibilities will be outlined below.

## 6.2 Managing Implementation Projects

To facilitate implementation, you should use the project management capabilities provided by change requests in SAP ECC.

Throughout the implementation procedure, changes made in the Customizing-and-development client must be recorded to change requests. These change requests not only provide a change history and documentation, but also a method of organizing the efforts of the different people who are contributing to the implementation project. Most importantly, change requests provide a method for transporting different implementation projects—first, to the quality assurance system for testing, and then to the production system.

### 6.2.1 Implementation Phases

Most implementation projects introduce new SAP functionality to the production system in successive phases. Initially, one new application component is introduced to the production system, and then, after a few months of production activity, another component is introduced. Although it is possible to Customize and develop for multiple projects and phases in the development system, you want to transport to the quality assurance system and the production system only those changes that are relevant to a specific phase of the implementation project. By using change requests, you can appropriately limit what you release and transport.

If you include all people working on the project as tasks in a single change request, you can then transport the project as a whole by simply releasing the change request. Or, for larger projects, the project needs to be divided into parts using multiple change requests. For transportation to the quality assurance system, you will need to transport together these change requests.

For example, a company may choose to start production activities with the Financials applications, and a few months later, implement the Logistics applications. To save time, Customizing and development for both application areas are done simultaneously. However, change requests related to Logistics will not be released from the development system until it is time to transport them to the quality assurance system, which is after production is stabilized for Financials.

It is not always possible to separate Customizing activities and assign them to specific implementation phases. During quality assurance testing, missing Customizing may be discovered that is due to the dependencies between the different implementation phases. It may then be necessary to release the change requests of a subsequent implementation phase to supply the missing Customizing. Such dependencies between changes in different phases may not become apparent until quality assurance testing.

**Example: Change Requests for Implementing in Phases**

When implementing SAP ECC, a manufacturing firm decides to introduce the software in different phases. The implementation begins in May, when the firm's largest plant goes live with the Production Planning application. In July, the firm's other plants start using SAP ECC. Finally, in October, the Financials applications are added.

To coordinate the procedure, different Project IMGs are created for each different phase of the project. The customizers and developers are careful to save changes to the correct change requests for each different phase. Likewise, project leaders release only those Customizing and development changes that are related to the business processes currently being tested in the quality assurance system. In other words, prior to the start of production in May, only change requests relevant to Production Planning are released.

After the start of production in May, only the changes required for the July implementation phase (implementing SAP ECC at the firm's other plants) are released from the development system for business validation in the quality assurance system. The change requests required for the testing of the Financials applications are released only after the new plants are in production.

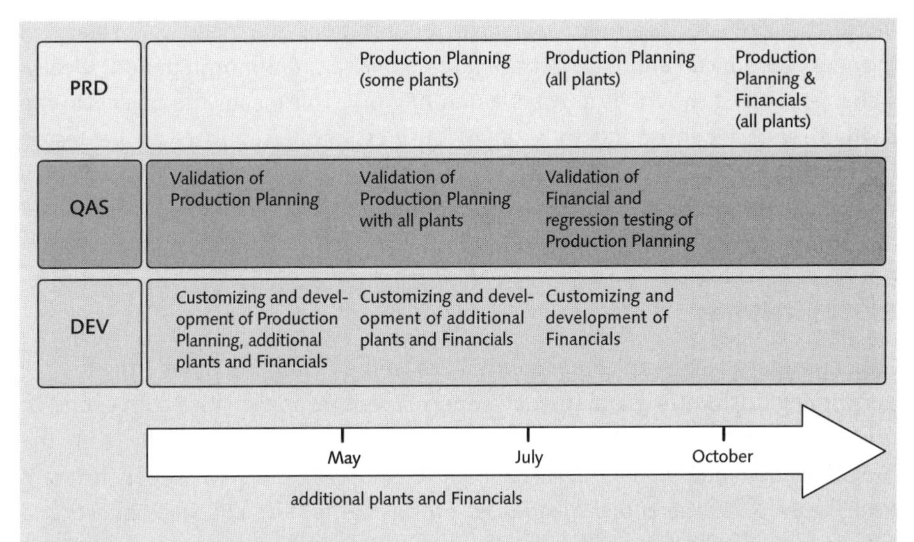


**Figure 6.2** Releasing and exporting change requests in specific phases

Having different change requests for the different implementation phases allows development and unit testing for all phases to occur at the same time in the development system. Only releasing and exporting change requests for a specific phase allow for complete business validation of each successive phase.

### 6.2.2 Managing Change Requests

Ideally, all changes in the implementation process are recorded to change requests. You can do this by using the appropriate client-change settings (see Chapters 3 and 9). A user working in the Customizing-and-development client is then forced to save all changes to a task in a change request. Therefore, to save a change, a user must either be assigned to a task in a change request or have the authorization to create a change request and task. (For more information on authorizations, see Chapter 11.)

**Note** User authorizations and the assignment of users to change requests provide you the ability to manage whether and when an R/3 user can make changes.

Every change made in SAP ECC does not need its own change request. To limit overhead and simplify validation, changes should be grouped in a logical manner by project objectives and collected in a single change request. This is the project leader's responsibility.

In Customizing, for example, a change request does not need to contain all changes made by an entire Customizing team over a three-month period. Ideally, a change request should be a testable unit of work. This means the objects in the change request correspond to a set of business processes that can be tested together, or to an executable program. A testable change request can more easily be unit tested prior to release, and can more easily be verified after being imported into the quality assurance system.

### Responsibilities

Project leaders assign project responsibilities to their team members—the people performing Customizing and the developers. These responsibilities correspond to Customizing activities or development work in SAP ECC. To manage the team, the project leader should create change requests and assign team members to them (see Figure 6.2). The project leader is responsible for the change request, and team members are responsible for their *task* within the change request. Team members, although they cannot create a change request or task, are able to save their changes to the task created by the project leader.

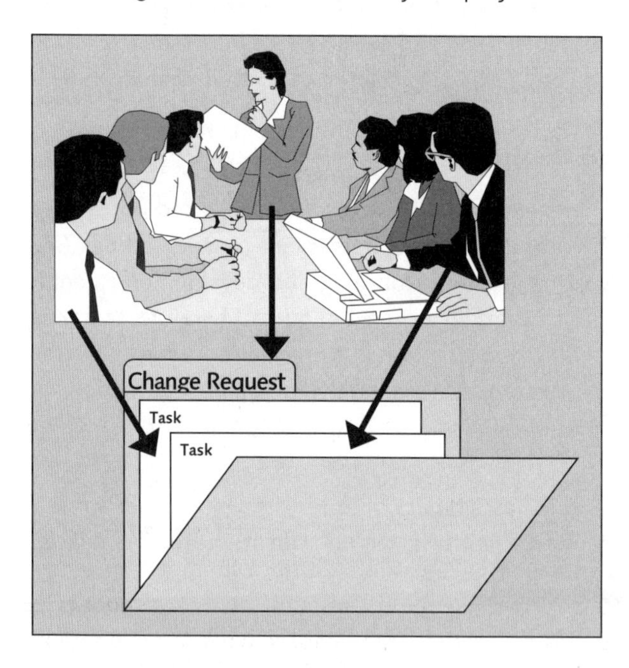


**Figure 6.3** Organizing a project team

The Customizing Organizer (Transaction SE10) and the Workbench Organizer (Transaction SE09) enable project leaders to view, create, and delete change requests. Team members can use these same tools to view any change requests in which they have a task, view the contents of any task in the change request, and record changes to their tasks.

An example of a project objective is to use Customizing to define the process chain for a sales order. After this objective has been agreed on, the project leader, using the Customizing Organizer, creates a change request and assigns each person working on the project to a separate task within the change request.

### Documentation

All customizers and developers working on change requests are required to write documentation associated with a task. The documentation must be completed prior to the release of the task. The documentation should state the aims of the changes, the completion status of the task, and any special features that result from the changes. The objects in the task tell you which objects were changed, the time they were changed, and who made the changes. The documentation provides more details on the status and purpose of the changes.

### Project IMGs

Ideally, you should be able to look at the change requests and determine to which Customizing project they belong. In R/3 Releases before 4.6, the IMG does not automatically set up change requests that recognizably belong to a specific Project IMG; nor can you, from the Customizing Organizer (Transaction SE10), easily determine which Customizing activity was used to modify an object. Therefore, before R/3 Release 4.6, make it your policy to:

- Include the project name in the title of a change request
- Indicate the relationship of the task to the relevant IMG activities in task-level documentation

As of Release 4.6, which contains a technology platform, SAP provides a direct link between change requests and IMG activities. By activating *CTS Project Management*, you can set up change requests specific to a Project IMG. Then, when you perform Customizing activities from within the Project IMG, changes are recorded to change requests of the corresponding project. The project management functionality also organizes the change requests in the import queues in groups according to project. This makes it easier to choose what to import. During import, the project management functionality also detects the sharing of objects between different projects and monitors such dependencies during import activities.

**Note** For more information on the CTS Project Management functionality, see SAP online documentation for SAP ECC Release 5.00.

**Example: Managing Change Requests**

An international travel services group plans to implement SAP's Human Resources applications over a four-month period. During the first month of configuration, a large number of SAP users record changes to change requests, often saving a change to a new change request. At the end of the first month, over 600 change requests have been created.

Fearing that this number will only continue to grow, the system administrator realizes that a strategy for managing change requests is necessary and that the users have to be informed of new procedures. In conjunction with the project leaders, the system administrator defines a change request strategy that includes:

- Changing most user authorizations so that only project leaders can create change requests
- Educating project leaders about the procedure for creating and managing change requests and properly assigning users to change requests

The development projects are made the responsibility of the developers themselves rather than the project leaders. The developers are then directly responsible for their change requests.

At the end of the second month, only 120 change requests have been released and exported and are waiting for import—a much more manageable number than the 600 at the end of the first month.

### 6.2.3 Unit Testing

Before releasing the Customizing and development changes in a change request, you must unit test the changes. Since unit testing requires application data, SAP recommends conducting unit tests in a separate unit test client rather than in the Customizing-and-development client (see Chapter 3). Use the unit test client as follows:

- To copy the latest Customizing changes to the unit test client, use the function **Client copy according to a transp. request** (Transaction SCC1; see Figure 6.4). After performing unit testing, return to the Customizing-and-development client to make any necessary corrections. Again, test the latest changes in the unit test client. This process continues until the task required for the project has been completed and is ready for promotion.

- Since Repository objects are client-independent, a developer does not need to copy development changes from one client to another in the same SAP ECC system. Developers developing in one client can immediately perform unit testing in another client that has sample application data. After developments are completed and unit tested, they can usually be promoted to the quality assurance client for integration testing. If the development consists of SAP-script and report variants, however, which are types of client-dependent data, copying the development to different clients within the same SAP ECC system for testing requires special routines (see Chapter 12).

Performing unit testing in a special unit test client enables you to ensure that the objects in your change request include all the changes that they should contain and that will be required for testing in the quality assurance system.

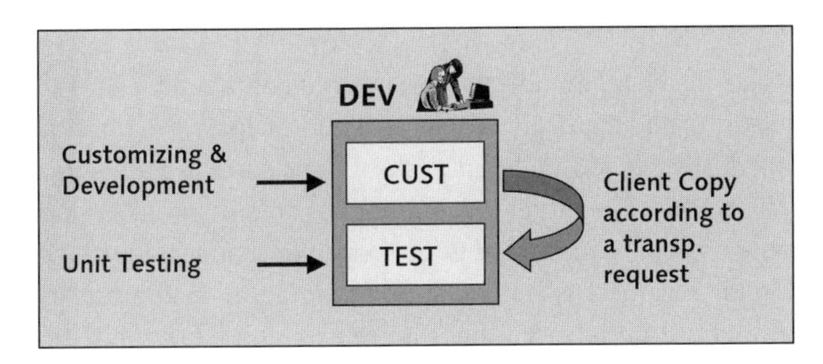


**Figure 6.4** For unit testing, use the function client copy according to a transp. request (in Transaction SCC1).

### Responsibilities

Team members unit test the tasks for which they are responsible. After a team member has completed unit testing at the task level, the task is released.

Releasing a task to a change request indicates to the project leader that the task has been completed. However, it is not as final a step as releasing a change request. If a person performing Customizing or development realizes that additional changes are required after releasing a task, the project leader can create another task for that user.

The project manager performs unit testing of the objects listed in the change request via using the documentation and test instructions included in the transport tasks, before he or she releases the change requests.

### 6.2.4 Releasing and Exporting Change Requests

Before transporting a change request from the development system to the quality assurance system, the project leader must release the change request. In general, releasing a change request automatically initiates the export process. (For details on the release and export processes and examples of change requests that are released but not exported, see Chapter 12.)

Releasing and exporting a change request is a significant step in the overall change management process, and achieves the following:

- It indicates that the changed objects recorded in the change request have been unit tested and are ready to be transported.
- It "freezes" the objects recorded in the change request by copying them in their current state to a file external to SAP ECC.
- It places the change request in the import queue of the target system, which is typically the quality assurance system.

A change request only lists the changed objects—it does not contain the changed objects themselves. Releasing and exporting a change request causes the physical download of the changed objects and table entries—in their current state—to a file at the operating system level. The target system receives an entry in its import queue, indicating that the change request (and its collection of changes) is waiting to be imported. If a change request is not ready for promotion to the quality assurance system, it should not be released, because release and export initiates the transport process for that change request.

> **Tip** Perform release and export only for change requests that are ready to be validated in the quality assurance system.

#### Repository Object Checks

Before you release a change request, you can subject the Repository objects in the request to various checks. Unit testing the change request can reveal errors. In addition, the Workbench Organizer enables you to activate *object checks* for Repository objects contained in a change request (see Chapter 12). Object checks identify and display errors found in customer developments before the change request is released. These errors, such as program syntax errors, must be either corrected or verified by the developer before the change requests are actually released.

> **Tip** SAP recommends that developers activate object checks in the development system.

### Responsibilities

The person who creates a change request—also known as the *owner* of the change request—initiates the release and export process. That person is normally the project leader. Prior to releasing the change request, the owner is responsible for ensuring that the request is ready to be transported. After releasing their change requests or tasks, neither the project leader nor team members play any further role in the transport process. Instead, the system administrator is responsible for importing and managing change requests in the import queue. However, the system administrator does not determine whether a change request is placed in the import queue. The project leader should act as a control point, and release and export only changes that are genuinely ready to be imported into the target system.

> **Tip** SAP recommends that only specific users, such as project leaders, have the authorization to release and export change requests. Chapter 17, which deals with ITIL, presents additional annotations and descriptions of recommended procedures.

## 6.3 Transport Management

The task of transporting change requests is an important responsibility in any SAP implementation. After the start of production, it becomes even more critical because you need to protect the production system from untested changes. Before beginning an SAP implementation, ensure that your system landscape maintenance strategy covers transport management in detail.

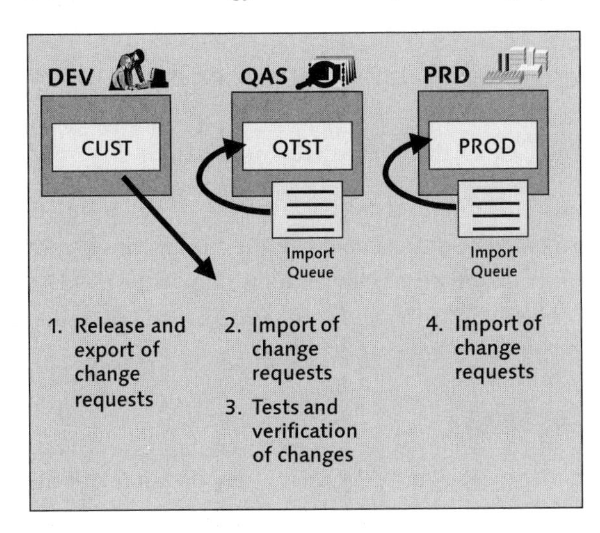


**Figure 6.5** Transporting change requests

Your transport process should be based on change requests as summarized in Figure 6.5 (see also Chapter 4). To establish a transport management plan for your system landscape, focus on the critical steps of the transport process, define how each step is managed, and assign the roles and responsibilities for each.

### 6.3.1 Exporting Change Requests

Releasing a change request in the development system normally automatically triggers the export process and is the first step in transporting the changed objects listed in the change request to the quality assurance system.

During the export process, the changed objects listed in the change request are copied from the database to a data file at the operating system level. The change request is automatically added to the import queue in the target system, the quality assurance system. If data from the source database cannot be exported, or if releasing the change request fails to add the change request to the import queue of the target system, the export will fail.

#### Responsibilities

Only responsible people such as project leaders should release and export change requests in the system landscape. To limit these activities, set the user authorizations appropriately (see Chapter 11).

The person who releases the change request must also verify the success of the export. The owner of a change request can determine the success or failure of an export from the Customizing Organizer and the Workbench Organizer (see Chapter 12). Examples of errors during export include:

- Lack of available disk space in the transport directory for the data and control files
- Inability to connect to the database of the quality assurance system

Sometimes, the failure of an export is due to a technical problem that a project leader cannot solve. Although the owner of the change request is responsible for verifying exports, a technical consultant or system administrator may need to assist in solving any reported problems. For this purpose, a corresponding action and task plan should have been created beforehand.

### 6.3.2 Importing Change Requests

As change requests are released in the development system, they are automatically entered in the import queue of the quality assurance system. Your procedural documentation for performing imports using change requests should include:

- A policy of preventing users from manipulating the order of change requests in the import queue to ensure that target clients receive the released change requests in the correct sequence
- A time schedule for imports and a procedure for managing change requests that fall outside the schedule
- A duty roster assigning responsibility for performing imports and listing who has authorization
- Procedures for verifying imports and handling errors that occur during the import

### Initiating Imports

An import queue displays change requests that are awaiting import. The change requests are listed in the order of their release. The import process, however, is not initiated automatically. To initiate and control imports into SAP ECC systems, use the Transport Management System (Transaction STMS) as described in Chapter 4.

Prior to the introduction of the TMS in R/3 Release 3.1H, the only method for performing imports was to use transport commands at the operating system level. The TMS import functionality consists of a user-friendly interface in R/3 that communicates with the transport control program `tp` using Remote Function Calls (RFCs). Instead of using the TMS to communicate with `tp`, you can still use `tp` directly at the operating system level to perform imports. This requires the appropriate operating system commands. To automate the import process, you can also use tp commands in scripts at the operating system level (see Chapter 14).

> **Tip** For imports, SAP recommends using the TMS or, even better, the Change Request Management, as a part of SAP Solution Manager 3.2 and later versions.

Regardless of whether you use the TMS or the transport control program `tp`, when performing an import, you have the following options:

- Use an **import all** to import all change requests waiting to be imported. This option is accessed in SAP ECC with the menu option **start import**, and is accessed at the operating system level using the command `tp import all`.
- Use a **preliminary import** to import individual change requests. This option is accessed in SAP ECC with the menu option **Request • Import**, and is accessed at the operating system level using the command `tp import <change request ID> u0`. This so-called *U mode* 0 for the `tp` ensures that the request imported

beforehand continues to remain in the import queue and that no error occurs in the order of requests.

Since an **import all** imports all change requests waiting in the import queue, the import sequence plays an important role. By importing change requests in the chronological order in which they were exported—that is, the order in which they are listed in the import queue—you ensure that objects in earlier change requests are replaced by any corrections in later change requests during import.

**Tip** SAP recommends that change requests be imported in the chronological order in which they were exported—that is, the order in which they are listed in the import queue.

To help you import only the change requests you require, you can add an *end mark* to the import queue after the set of change requests you wish to import. When you perform an **import all**, any change requests listed in the queue after the end mark will not be imported.

To add an end mark, in the import queue screen (Transaction STMS; **Overview • Imports**), double-click the system ID and choose **Queue • Close**. The end mark is indicated by the statement **End of import queue** that appears at the end of the import queue.

If required, you can move this statement further up the import queue to include fewer change requests in the next import. For example, you may wish to import only the first 15 change requests in an import queue. To do this, place the cursor on the 16th change request and choose **Edit • Move end mark**. This places the end mark between the 15th and 16th change requests. You can now start the import.

A **preliminary import** allows you to rapidly transfer single requests through the defined transport routes. For example, you may have a production problem that needs immediate correction. The corresponding change request is released from the development system and needs to be tested immediately. Although there are other change requests waiting in the import queue of the quality assurance system, you want to import only the single change request at this time. Therefore, you import the individual change request using a preliminary import. If the contents of the change request successfully correct the problem, you can import the change request to production immediately using another preliminary import.

To minimize the risks associated with preliminary imports, the imported change request remains in the import queue after import and is reimported the next time the entire import queue is imported. This guarantees that export and import sequences are the same and ensures that the target system does not return to the way it was prior to the preliminary import.

To prevent inconsistencies that may result from object dependencies, SAP recommends avoiding preliminary import and using only **import all**. For example, if you import a change request with an ABAP report that refers to a table, and that table is contained in another change request that has not yet been imported, executing the report will only generate short dumps until the table is also imported.

**Example: A Preliminary Import**

A multinational company purchases a new facility and begins making adjustments to its SAP ECC system. After the rollout of the required accounting settings to support the new manufacturing facility, it is discovered during a month-end closing period that the real-estate accounting settings are incorrect, and due to the error, month-end closing cannot be completed. The error is immediately simulated in the quality assurance environment, the problem is pinpointed, and corrections are made in the development system. A change request with the required changes is released from the development system.

The import queue of the quality assurance system looks like this:

| Change Request | Owner | Description |
|---|---|---|
| DEVK901832 | MARY | Plant configuration |
| DEVK901910 | SUE | Real-estate controlling |
| DEVK901830 | ALEX | Rental accounting |
| DEVK901676 | JON | Manufacturing |
| DEVK902015 | BILL | FIX: month-end with new facility |
| DEVK901703 | MARY | Plant maintenance |

The import queue of the quality assurance system already included recently released changes that support manufacturing requirements for the new facility. However, these application settings are neither ready for validation nor required in production immediately.

Change request DEVK902015 contains the changes needed to complete month-end closing. This request needs to be imported immediately. Since the other requests are not ready for validation, an import of the entire import queue is not possible. The individual request itself is imported using a preliminary import.

Importing DEVK902015 to the quality assurance system enters this change request in the import queue of the production system. After the correction contained in this change request has been validated in the quality assurance system, DEVK902015 is imported into the production system with a further preliminary import.

During the next scheduled import into the quality assurance system, DEVK902015 is again imported, this time as part of the listed series of change requests. Because the change request is imported in sequence, changes made to solve the month-end closing problem are not overwritten by earlier requests such as DEVK901910 or DEVK901830, which may contain conflicting changes.

**Import Considerations**

Before importing a change request, consider:

- Importing to all clients in all SAP ECC systems. This ensures consistency of all clients and systems in your system landscape.
- Scheduling imports into the quality assurance system at times that are known to the entire implementation team. This creates transparency for project management and for the business validation team. For a larger number of transport requests, it makes sense to import them as a group to QAS once a week, for example, and to test them altogether before they are imported into PRD.

Typically, a quality assurance system contains more clients than just the quality assurance client. One or two additional clients may be dedicated to end-user training, and another client may be reserved for data conversion tests. Regardless of the number of clients, your import procedure needs to ensure that all clients in the quality assurance system receive the change requests in the same order that they were exported from the Customizing and development system.

To enable you to import to multiple clients, SAP introduced functionality known as **extended transport control** in R/3 Release 4.5, which allows client-specific transport routes. These transport routes allow you to assign imports to multiple clients in a single SAP system at the same time or at different times. Client-specific transport routes use client-specific entries in import queues. (See Figure 4.4 in Chapter 4.)

If you do not use extended transport control, you have to import the change requests several times, once for each client in the system. Ensure that all change requests are imported into all clients in the same sequence so that client-independent functionality is not overwritten by older versions of the functionality delivered in earlier change requests (see Chapter 13).

**Tip** When you have multiple clients in the quality assurance system, SAP recommends that you use a documented strategy to ensure that all change requests are imported to all clients in the quality assurance system.

While development changes automatically impact all clients in the system, Customizing changes are typically specific to the Customizing-and-development client in which they originated. You need to take special steps to ensure that all clients in the development system are also supplied with all client-dependent changes.

Although unit testing copies the changes to the unit test client, importing released change requests into the unit test client provides a way of ensuring that all changes are entered into the unit test client. Similarly, a sandbox client updated with the latest changes ensures that the people working in that client are working in an up-to-date environment.

There are a number of ways to ensure that the clients in the development system contain the latest client-dependent changes:

- Using the client-specific transport routes of the **extended transport control**.
- Performing a **Client copy according to a transp. request** (Transaction SCC1) for all change requests released from the development system.
- Importing released Customizing change requests. To do this, you need to give the development system its own import queue (through transport parameter **testsystems**). Released change requests are then transferred into the development import queue.

**Note** Prior to using the import queue of the development system to import to other clients in the development system, you must eliminate change requests containing development work. This prevents these change requests from overwriting recent changes to client-independent objects in the development system.

- Performing periodic client copies of the Customizing-and-development client to other clients such as the sandbox client. Note that this will eliminate all data including application data in the target client.

Imports into the quality assurance system can be automated to occur at specific, predefined intervals. However, SAP recommends such scheduling only when responsible people such as the project leaders control the release process—whatever is to be released has been checked and is needed in the quality assurance system. If you have established no such control, you must provide some other method by which users can inform a system administrator or technical consultant that released change requests should be imported. This can be a complicated process and may cause misunderstandings.

**Tip** As a prerequisite for scheduling imports to the quality assurance system, import queues should contain only those requests that are ready for import. Therefore, only responsible people such as project leaders should be in charge of the release and export process.

You need to determine when imports should be scheduled. All imports introduce changes and thus invalidate previous test results, even test results for other areas of SAP ECC. Thorough testing is required after all imports. Since thorough testing takes time, the timing of imports is governed by whether the business validation team is ready to perform the testing.

Early in an implementation phase, imports are usually scheduled at regular intervals—for example, once a day; every hour; or at 9:00 A.M., noon, and 4:00 P.M. As you get closer to the going-live date, business validation teams need more time for testing, and you may wish to limit the import process to once a week.

**Tip** Define an import schedule that allows sufficient time for the testing and correction of changes prior to the next import.

As of R/3 Release 4.6, the TMS contains the *Import Scheduler*, which enables you to schedule change requests for immediate import, periodic import, or import at specific times. You can use the Import Scheduler to schedule TMS activities such as **import all**, **preliminary import**, and import to a specific client.

In releases prior to R/3 Release 4.6, you can perform imports at specific intervals either manually or using scheduling programs. To manually schedule imports, the system administrator performs an **import all** in the TMS. Alternatively, at the operating system level, scheduling programs can be used to issue the appropriate tp commands. For example, if Unix is your operating system, you can schedule `tp` commands using the Unix program *cron* (see Chapter 14).

**Tip** Even when your import process is automated, you must still monitor and verify the results of each import.

### Responsibilities

Traditionally, when the import process was more technical and required access to the operating system level, the import process was the responsibility of the system administrator. With the introduction of the TMS, the import process is controlled from within the SAP system. This means any SAP ECC user with the correct user authorization can initiate either an **import all** or a **preliminary import**.

> **Tip** To avoid errors, prevent unauthorized imports by carefully assigning and monitoring all relevant user authorizations.

## 6.3.3 Post-Import Issues

To complete the import procedure, you need to:

- Review the relevant logs
- Resolve any errors that occurred during import
- Notify the people who will perform testing and business validation

### Responsibilities

The post-import issues are the responsibility of both the technical team and the project leaders (or owners of the change requests). Ensure that communication between the people involved is accomplished using a formal notification procedure.

#### Import Logs

Every import activity, such as an **import all** or a **preliminary import**, results in a *return code* in the TMS. These logs can be viewed in the Import Monitor in Transaction STMS as described in Chapter 13. If the return code indicates an error, it is initially the responsibility of the system administrator to evaluate the error. During import, errors can be the result of a particular change request or a problem with the target SAP system.

#### Transport Logs

To determine whether the import of individual change requests was successful, project leaders should check the logs specific to each change request, which are known as transport log files. Using either the Customizing Organizer (Transaction SE09) or the Workbench Organizer (Transaction SE10), you can access an overview of change requests that have been released, exported, and imported. Traffic-light icons on the right-hand side of the initial Organizer screens show the color red to indicate transport errors, yellow for warnings, and green for successful imports.

**Note** The transport logs also contain transport log files that are not assigned to only one transport request (activation or conversion logs for dictionary objects like tables). These transport log files must also be checked for potential errors.

By activating the setting **display transport errors at logon** in the Workbench and Customizing Organizers, a user can obtain information at logon about the status of change requests that have been transported. After this setting is activated, whenever a user logs on and a change request import has failed since the user last logged on, a message box appears informing the user of the failure. The user can access the transport log files and determine which import errors have occurred. You can activate this setting either for an individual user or globally for all users. (See Chapter 12.)

**Tip** SAP recommends having all users automatically informed of transport errors when they log on to both the development and quality assurance system.

#### Problem Resolution

The system administrator should review and evaluate the import log to check for errors after every import. Severe errors can cause the import process to stop, leaving change requests in the import queue and only partially imported into the quality assurance system. Such errors need the system administrator's immediate attention. Even when scheduling routines for import into the quality assurance system are used, a system administrator should always check the import log after each import.

Errors in the import log indicate either problems with the import process or problems with specific change requests. The change request owner, who is normally the project leader, must resolve problems affecting specific change requests. Correcting a problem may simply require releasing additional changes from the development system. In more difficult situations, the project leader may need to consult the system administrator to understand and resolve the problem.

Problems not with specific change requests but with the import process must be resolved by having the system administrator analyze the SAP system and database (see Chapter 14 for troubleshooting tips).

#### Notification of Imports

After the import of change requests into the quality assurance system, the people responsible for the business validation must be notified so that they can begin testing. Notification may occur informally in the early stages of implementation. As the final, more general phase of testing approaches, the business validation team requires more formal notification. The project leaders should provide this notification, since they are responsible for the project at the going-live stage.

### 6.3.4 Importing into the Production System

When planning for import into the production system, your procedural documentation for performing imports using change requests should include:

- Procedures for signing off the change requests that contain approved functionality after testing in the quality assurance system
- A procedure and time schedule for imports of change requests required to support production problems
- Procedures for verifying imports and for the immediate handling of errors that occur during the import
- A duty roster assigning responsibility for performing the import

Imports into the production system are performed using the same tools used to import change requests in the quality assurance system (the TMS and the transport control program `tp`), but the import process itself must be more closely managed. The exact focus of this management differs depending upon whether the import is the going-live step in an implementation phase or is providing production support for current production activities. The support for introducing an implementation phase to production requires more testing and business validation testing. In contrast, imports for production support require more careful management of the import queue.

#### Going Live at the Conclusion of an Implementation Phase

Ideally, all change requests imported into the quality assurance system are also imported into the production system in the same order. This rule applies not only for the initial setup of the production system (as described in Chapter 5), but also for going live at the conclusion of an implementation phase.

Before going live at the conclusion of an implementation phase, a formal business validation of the entire quality assurance client is necessary to ensure that the collection of imported change requests provide the expected business processes. In addition, regression testing is required to ensure that the new business processes do not conflict with existing business functionality. The approved collection of change requests is introduced into the production system by importing the entire import queue.

### Production Support

Even after the introduction of a new implementation phase and a period of time dedicated to stabilizing the production environment, further changes to the production environment may be required—for example, due to the emergence of errors or changed configuration requirements. These changes are the responsibility of production support, which should introduce only urgently required corrections, not new functionality. Every system landscape should include the system resources and transport processes required for production support (see Chapter 3).

Corrections made during production support must be tested in an client that is identical to the production client. This ensures that the testing is a true validation of business functionality and provides a simulation of the impact that the changes will have on the existing production data. Only when a change request has been tested and verified in the quality assurance system should it be imported into the production system.

The change requests required to support production may be the responsibility of different project initiatives, with different priorities. It will not be possible to sign off and import all change requests at the same time. After the start of production activities, the import queue of the production system may contain any of the following:

- Emergency fixes that require one or more change requests to be imported into production immediately (regardless of their position in the import queue sequence)
- Change requests that have been signed off and are ready for import into production
- Change requests that have not been signed off and are not yet ready for import into production

The TMS menu option **start import**, which imports all change requests waiting for import, cannot be used in such a situation. Instead, imports into the production system require you to check whether a change request has been signed off, and to import emergency fixes separately from other signed-off change requests. Thus, the import procedure involves careful manipulation of the import queue to determine the sequence in which change requests are imported into the production system.

#### Indicating Sign-Off after Testing

After business validation testing is completed, the tested change requests are signed off; that is, they are approved for transfer to the production system. When the affected change requests were imported into the quality assurance system, they were also added to the import queue of the production system. However, in releases before R/3 Release 4.6, the import queue of the production system cannot be used to indicate whether change requests have been formally signed off.

The sign-off process is often managed as follows:

- SAP Business Workflow® functionality is used to send a formal sign-off e-mail to the system administrator who will do the import.
- External to SAP, sign-off is recorded using the form shown in Figure 6.6, either on sheets of paper (one for each change request) or in a spreadsheet (as in Figure 6.8 later in this chapter) in a shared file.
- Verbal notification is provided by speaking with the system administrator who will do the import.

| **Change and Transport Request Form** | | | |
|---|---|---|---|
| Requestor | | Date | |
| Source Client | | Target Client(s) | |
| Source R/3 System | | Target R/3 System | |
| Change Request # | | | |
| ☐ Customizing | ☐ Workbench | ☐ Client-dependent | ☐ Client-independent |
| **Description of contents** | | | |
| Tasks/Request | ☐ All tasks released ☐ Change request released ☐ To be released | | |
| Special requirements | | | |
| Approved by (please sign) | | | |
| **It Team USE ONLY** | | | |
| Imported by | | Date | |
| Transport Log Return Codes | ☐ 0 Transport (export and import test) was successful.<br>☐ 4 Warning messages were generated.<br>☐ 8 Error messages were generated<br>☐ ≥ 12 Fatal error has occurred | | |
| Comments | | | |
| Exception handling–Corrected change request # | | Date<br>Reason | |
| **Project Management Approval** | | Date | |

**Figure 6.6** A sample production support change request form

In R/3 Release 4.6, SAP has introduced the *QA Approval Process*, which provides a formal sign-off procedure for change requests waiting for import into an SAP system. The process allows you to define which users are responsible for sign-off. Although a change request may be in the import queue of the production system, it cannot be imported until those people responsible for sign-off have approved the change request. The QA Approval Process is linked with the CTS Project Management functionality in Release 4.6 so that the approval process is linked to change requests as a result of different projects. The approval process can be unique for the change requests of different projects.

### Emergency Production Fixes

Typically, an emergency fix to correct a production problem is performed using a **preliminary import**. This imports the individual change request required to correct a problem, and retains that change request in the import queue of the production system to be reimported in sequence at a later time.

Figure 6.7 shows a sample import queue for a production system, PRD. The seventh and ninth change requests in the import queue have been signed off and are needed in the production system immediately. To achieve this, **preliminary imports** of change requests DEVK901633 and DEVK901638 will be performed.

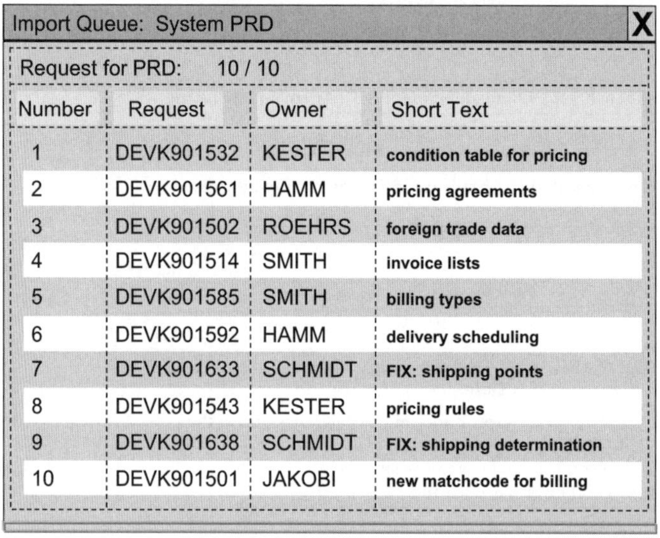

Import Queue: System PRD

Request for PRD: 10 / 10

| Number | Request | Owner | Short Text |
|---|---|---|---|
| 1 | DEVK901532 | KESTER | condition table for pricing |
| 2 | DEVK901561 | HAMM | pricing agreements |
| 3 | DEVK901502 | ROEHRS | foreign trade data |
| 4 | DEVK901514 | SMITH | invoice lists |
| 5 | DEVK901585 | SMITH | billing types |
| 6 | DEVK901592 | HAMM | delivery scheduling |
| 7 | DEVK901633 | SCHMIDT | FIX: shipping points |
| 8 | DEVK901543 | KESTER | pricing rules |
| 9 | DEVK901638 | SCHMIDT | FIX: shipping determination |
| 10 | DEVK901501 | JAKOBI | new matchcode for billing |

**Figure 6.7** A sample import queue for a production system

### Importing Signed-Off Change Requests

Once signed off, change requests that are not part of an emergency fix are normally imported during the next scheduled import. There is a danger of incomplete functionality being imported if change requests that depend on other change requests do not receive sign-off at the same time.

Figure 6.8 gives an example of customer documentation showing an import queue, and also displays the status of the change requests and the dependencies among them. Change requests DEVK901633 and DEVK901638 have already been imported, possibly to provide an emergency fix, but should be imported again with the other change requests in the correct order. As revealed by the indicated dependencies, the change requests numbered 1, 2, 6, and 8 must be imported together to provide the desired functionality. Since they have all been signed off, you can assume that the functionality that will be imported is complete and fully tested. The third change request in the list has been signed off and is ready for import. Both the fourth and fifth change requests have not been signed off. If they are not signed off before the next scheduled import, they cannot be imported.

In such a situation, you should not perform an **import all** of the production import queue. To import the needed changes into the production system, either all change requests must be approved or the needed change requests must be imported individually.

| Number | Request | Status | Dependencies |
|---|---|---|---|
| 1 | DEVK901532 | Approved | DEVK901561, DEVK901592, DEVK901543 |
| 2 | DEVK901561 | Approved | DEVK901532, DEVK901592, DEVK901543 |
| 3 | DEVK901502 | Approved | none |
| 4 | DEVK901514 | | |
| 5 | DEVK901585 | | |
| 6 | DEVK901592 | Approved | DEVK901532, DEVK901561, DEVK901543 |
| 7 | DEVK901633 | Already imported | |
| 8 | DEVK901543 | Approved | DEVK901532, DEVK901561, DEVK901592 |
| 9 | DEVK901638 | Already imported | |
| 10 | DEVK901501 | | |

**Figure 6.8** Sample import queue documentation with sign-off status and dependencies

**Tip** To minimize the need for importing change requests out of sequence, SAP recommends that you ensure all change requests receive business validation and sign-off as soon as possible.

When you need to import change requests and cannot perform an **import all**, you have the following options:

- Set an end mark at a certain point in the import queue and **import all** change requests above the end mark.
- Perform a preliminary import for each individual change request.
- Perform preliminary imports for a group of individual change requests (available as of R/3 Release 4.5).

Either one or a combination of these import options can support the import of change requests into a production environment.

**Note** Support of production activities requires experienced judgement in weighing the advantages of importing change requests in their original sequence against the advantages of performing imports out of sequence to provide emergency corrections to the production system.

To ensure consistency, change requests that are imported out of sequence are always imported again with all other change requests in the sequence dictated by the import queue. For example, after importing the signed-off change requests in Figure 6.8, the import queue would appear as shown in Figure 6.9. (Figure 6.9 no longer shows the first three change requests in Figure 6.8, since these were sequentially imported.) The change requests now numbered 3 through 6 (numbered 6 through 9 in Figure 6.8) will be imported again to ensure they enter the production system in the correct sequence.

| Number | Request | Status | Dependencies |
|---|---|---|---|
| 1 | DEVK901514 | | |
| 2 | DEVK901585 | | |
| 3 | DEVK901592 | Already imported | DEVK901532, DEVK901561, DEVK901543 |
| 4 | DEVK901633 | Already imported | |
| 5 | DEVK901543 | Already imported | DEVK901532, DEVK901561, DEVK901592 |
| 6 | DEVK901638 | Already imported | |
| 7 | DEVK901501 | | |

**Figure 6.9** Import queue after import of approved change requests

### Scheduling Imports into the Production System

Importing change requests brings new Customizing settings and Repository object changes into the production system. These changes affect the runtime environment and have an impact on production activities. Imports into a live production system should be performed at times when online processing activity is low and scheduled background jobs have been completed. This is normally in the evening, when few or no users are in the system. For a global implementation, you can import at a time that represents the close of the business day for one region and the start of a new business day for another. The imports should not take place when the respective developers are not available to make corrections if need be.

**Tip** Before you perform imports, SAP recommends backing up the production system. If the import results in any unexpected problems, you can restore the SAP system with the data preserved in the backup.

When errors occur in the conversion of table structures, or when table structures are wrongly imported with less fields than the target system, you can no longer revert to the original system state using the former object versions, because doing so would lead to a loss of data.

#### Responsibilities

The owner of a change request is responsible for that change request from the time it is created until it has passed through the quality assurance system and has been imported into production.

The business evaluation team takes over responsibility for the change request after it has been imported into the quality assurance system. The business validation team provides sign-off for the change requests (or collection of change requests), which can then be imported into the production system.

The actual import of change requests into the production system is the responsibility of the system administrator. The critical nature of changing a live production environment requires that the person performing the import must understand the current backup strategy, know when the R/3 System is carrying a low system load, and be able to react to any issues or errors that arise due to importing.

## 6.4 Business Validation

A well-managed change and transport process helps to ensure the success of your SAP implementation. However, thorough quality assurance testing is what guarantees the successful addition of new and modified business processes to the production environment. Testing is only as good as the testing plans you devise, so design your testing plans carefully.

Several kinds of testing are required in the quality assurance system:

- **Business validation:**
  The functional verification of your business processes.
- **Technical validation:**
  Performance and stress tests ensure that the new business processes are optimized and supported by the hardware resources.

The technical validation required for production support is not covered in this book.

### 6.4.1 Testing Procedures

Business validation is critical to the success of your SAP implementation. It should always be performed before you import changes into the production system. Testing for production support may not be as time-consuming as the testing at the conclusion of an implementation phase, but it still requires business validation and sign-off. Standard, documented business validation procedures are required throughout the entire implementation process.

Business validation tests and verifies the following:

- New business processes and scenarios
- Existing core business processes (tested using regression testing)
- Customer developments and SAP enhancements

The focus of business validation is on the SAP ECC application processes, but it may also include technical components such as interfaces, input and output methods, and print functions.

#### Designing a Test Plan for Business Validation

Like all other aspects of the SAP implementation, business validation requires a defined procedure with assigned roles and responsibilities. A test plan should determine:

- The business scenarios and processes that require validation—for example, common business activities and core business transactions
- The testing methodology, including the different tools and user groups
- The people responsible for validating test results

SAP ECC's sophistication ensures that there are always several ways of doing a business task. Therefore, it is not easy to define all possible scenarios. Project leaders in collaboration with end-user representatives can define the core business processes and common scenarios that require testing. Project leaders must also define the acceptance criteria that form the objective of the tests.

Your test plans will continuously change over time to deal with the variety of business processes being implemented. For example, your first phase of implementation may require business validation of the Financials components, a large number of data conversion routines, and interfaces to external systems. The subsequent introduction of the Logistics components does not require you to test any data conversion routines, but adds many more business processes and requires the verification of interfaces. In addition, in all testing procedures, you must test existing business processes through regression testing.

Business validation involves the repeated testing of business processes in the quality assurance system until the acceptance criteria have been fulfilled. If the acceptance criteria are fulfilled, the change requests are signed off and are ready for import into the production system. If not, corrections are made in the development system *only*, and then the corresponding change requests are promoted to the quality assurance system for renewed testing.

During this cycle of business validation, it is common to "freeze" the quality assurance system—that is, to prevent the import of any new change requests and thus ensure the testing of a finite group of changes. Before freezing the system, you may wish to create a system backup. Since numerous transactions are run during testing—possibly creating unwanted data—it may be necessary to restore the system from a backup after testing. SAP recommends backing up data so that you can restore the SAP system to its original state at any time.

### Responsibilities

Business validation is process oriented and should be set up and performed in consultation with experts from the business departments who are responsible for the particular process area. For the testing period, the project leaders' responsibilities include:

- Identifying the transactions that need testing (in conjunction with experts from the business departments)
- Defining the testing methodology that best suits the requirements
- Defining the acceptance criteria that form the objective of the tests

After the project leaders have defined the relevant transactions and methodology, the business validation team begins testing and verifying those transactions. The business validation team should represent different business departments and accordingly perform quality assurance tests for their respective SAP ECC settings, reports, and transactions. To enable the business validation team to check the import status for different projects, ensure that team members have display authorization for the Workbench Organizer and Customizing Organizer.

The SAP system administrator should participate in setting up hardware and backups, and provide technical support during the actual testing.

### 6.4.2 SAP Testing Tools

To achieve "perfect" business validation and performance testing, all employees would be required to spend a day or two in an SAP system performing all their normal tasks. Since this procedure is too costly and inconvenient, project leaders generally use either or both of the following:

- Real users, representative of all the different user communities, running actual transactions
- Scripts that simulate SAP transactions and processes

The real-user approach is a simulation using actual, logged-on users. Although this approach allows you to test a realistic transaction mix while operating on actual user data, coordinating such tests may be difficult when many users are involved, especially when users are scattered all over the globe. In addition, such users may not always be available to test business validation when they are needed.

Scripting tools, on the other hand, provide a flexible method for testing a specific set of transactions. These tests are much easier to control, and therefore are easy to replicate. They also provide the option of simulating a different set of transactions and support business validation over time. To facilitate such testing, SAP provides testing tools as part of its core SAP application. These tools make up the *Test Workbench* with its primary tool being the enhanced Computer Aided Test Tool (eCATT).

#### The Test Workbench

Using the Test Workbench (Transaction S001; **Test • Test Workbench**), you can specify the applications to be tested by creating a *test catalog*. Within the test catalog, there are a series of scenarios that need to be tested, also known as *test cases*, which can be performed either manually or through scripting using a tool like eCATT.

After creating different test cases, another tool, the *test organizer*, records which tests are necessary for the current business validation period. As testers perform the different tests in the test organizer, you can use this tool to track the status and results of the tests.

> **Note** For more information on the SAP Test Workbench and on how to organize your business validation testing, refer to the SAP online documentation. We recommend that you use the SAP Test Workbench via SAP Solution Manager as a central test system.

### Enhanced Computer Aided Test Tool (eCATT)

eCATT is an SAP tool of the ABAP Workbench that you can use for automating repeatable transactions in SAP ECC and associated software components, and for recording user activities for systematic tests. eCATT is the successor of Transaction CATT. Contrary to CATT, eCATT can run all SAP ABAP Transactions, even if they were developed using the Control technology. Via RFC, you can also call transactions across system boundaries in another SAP system. You can use eCATT to perform the following tasks:

- Testing transactions
- Checking table values and database updates
- Setting up Customizing tables
- Testing the effect of changes to Customizing settings
- Creating test data

eCATT includes the necessary functions to create, start, maintain, and log test procedures. When a eCATT script is running, eCATT validates user authorizations and produces a detailed result log that can be automatically archived. The eCATT logs contain all information relevant to the test run and are stored centrally in the database of the executing SAP system—either the local system or the SAP Solution Manager.

**Note** For more information on how to build test scenarios with eCATT, see SAP online documentation.

## 6.5 Support for the SAP Standard

To provide an SAP implementation with new and enhanced business functionality and support its customers' growing business needs, SAP periodically delivers new releases. Existing R/3 customers obtain the new functionality in an release upgrade. An upgrade replaces the current SAP standard objects—that is, the repository—with new ones, while preserving customer data and developments.

In addition, SAP provides Support Packages and SAP Notes, which allow the customer to integrate smaller-scale changes and repairs to the SAP standard. As with an release upgrade, Support Packages and SAP Notes ensure that the customer's data and Customizing and development changes will not be changed or lost. Your system landscape must be able to support all three forms of support, and your maintenance strategy should include the relevant procedures.

### 6.5.1 Support for an SAP Release

SAP's Support Packages and SAP Notes are release–specific. Initially, SAP announces a correction for a particular release and provides solutions in an SAP Note. Then, to assist you in maintaining your SAP system, these corrections are bundled into Support Packages. A Support Package contains changes to source code and general improvements. A Support Package can in some ways be compared to an release. For example, both change the SAP standard. Each SAP system not only has an release level, but also a Support Package level that defines the status of the system's SAP standard.

To support your SAP systems at their current release level, you must closely monitor the application of SAP Notes and Support Packages and ensure that:

- You consistently transport changes that are based on SAP Notes
- All SAP systems in your system landscape have the same release level and the same Support Package level
- You do not overwrite modification adjustments that were imported to a system by subsequently applying a Support Package (see Chapter 15)

#### SAP Notes

The solutions provided in SAP Notes typically require you to make programming changes that modify the SAP standard, thereby creating what is known as a *modification*. To simplify applying these changes to your SAP ECC system, the corrections in SAP Notes are bundled into Support Packages, which are available for download from SAPNet and can be automatically incorporated in your SAP system without manual programming or the creation of modifications.

SAP recommends that you apply the corresponding Support Packages instead of making manual changes based on recommendations in an SAP Note. However, you may still be required to make manual modifications for any of the following reasons:

- **Availability:**
  A change documented in an SAP Note has not been bundled into a Support Package.
- **Urgency:**
  A correction documented in an SAP Note is required as soon as possible. Rather than wait for the corresponding Support Package, you make the change in your development system according to the SAP Note. The change request containing the modified SAP object is then transported to the quality assurance system and distributed to production after thorough testing and verification.

- **Verification:**
  Making a single change according to an SAP Note is much easier to verify than multiple changes. A single change requires only limited tests in contrast to the complete business validation of affected objects needed after applying a Support Package.
- **Dependencies:**
  Support Packages must be applied in sequence. Because of this dependency, you cannot apply a Support Package until all of the previous Support Packages have been applied and verified. Additional dependencies may also exist if, for example, you are using industry solutions. However, these dependencies are recognized by the tool importing the Support Packages (SPAM) and any missing Support Packages are requested, if necessary.

Before making modifications based on SAP Notes, verify that the SAP Note applies to your release and that the symptoms documented in the SAP Note correspond to the symptoms apparent in your SAP system. In the case of uncertainty, SAP recommends contacting the SAP Hotline.

You should create all modifications of SAP objects in your development client. The change request containing the modification must then be transported to the quality assurance system for verification. Only after it has been thoroughly tested and signed off should you import the change request containing the modification into the production system.

For more information on the modification procedure, see Chapter 10.

For every customer-changed SAP object, you will be required to perform a modification adjustment during release upgrades and possibly also when applying Support Packages. To help speed up the modification adjustment process, you should document modifications when making them. Your documentation should include the SAP Note number and release dependencies. This information should be recorded in task documentation as well as in the short text of each change request. Then, when you begin a modification adjustment, you can recognize the corresponding change requests in the import queue.

Figure 6.10 shows how properly documented changes made as a result of an SAP Note should appear in the import queue of a target system. Note that the relevant Support Package is also indicated. This enables system administrators to decide whether the change request needs to be imported—it may be preferable to simply apply the corresponding Support Package to the target system.

**Tip** Document all changes to SAP standard objects completely. If the change is based on an SAP Note, include the SAP Note number and relevant Support Package in the change request description.

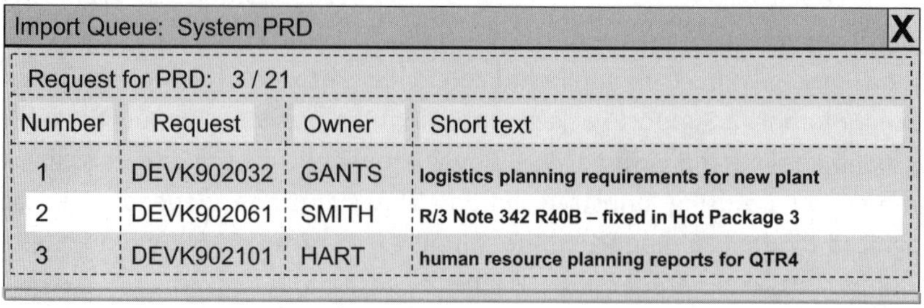

Import Queue: System PRD

Request for PRD: 3 / 21

| Number | Request | Owner | Short text |
|---|---|---|---|
| 1 | DEVK902032 | GANTS | logistics planning requirements for new plant |
| 2 | DEVK902061 | SMITH | R/3 Note 342 R40B – fixed in Hot Package 3 |
| 3 | DEVK902101 | HART | human resource planning reports for QTR4 |

**Figure 6.10** A sample change request resulting from an SAP Note is waiting for import.

## Support Packages

SAP's Support Packages enable SAP to quickly and easily repair software errors in the SAP ECC repository that require urgent attention. By applying Support Packages, you can maintain the latest corrections in your SAP system and avoid making modifications to the SAP standard based on SAP Notes. Support Packages keep your SAP system up to date. However, you cannot apply Support Packages without considering:

- Possible conflicts with any modifications previously made to the SAP standard
- The impact of the corrections on your SAP ECC system, as well as the additional business validation tests required in the quality assurance system

Aside from the Support Packages, SAP delivers so-called *Support Package Stacks* for many products. These stacks provide Support Packages in a specific combination. This is particularly interesting for SAP products like R/3 Enterprise 4.7 or SAP ECC 5.0, for which there are Support Packages for all installed software components. For SAP ECC 5.0, for example, there are up to four SAP main software components and 12 standard SAP add-on components. To avoid problems with cross dependencies between all these Support Packages, using the additionally validated Support Package Stacks provides more security and simplifies the process.

When applying a Support Package, you may be asked to adjust any SAP objects you have modified manually, regardless of whether the modification was made according to an SAP Note or to add customer-specific functionality. Modification adjustment involves choosing whether to retain the changes comprising the modification or delete them to regain the original SAP objects as contained in the Support Package. Ideally, the objective of this adjustment is to return the object to the SAP standard. SAP recommends limiting modifications to the SAP standard to simplify the application of Support Packages.

Support Packages introduce new versions of SAP standard objects into an SAP system. The number of affected objects and application components impacted by the changes varies from Support Package to Support Package. However, since a considerable number of objects are changed, every Support Package (or collection of Support Packages) requires verification before being applied to the production system. Such validation testing is time-consuming and may not be possible within the current implementation plan.

SAP recommends that you apply all available Support Packages at the initial installation of your SAP system or immediately following an upgrade. Subsequent Support Packages for the same release level should be applied at the beginning of a new implementation phase to ensure that they are part of the business validation cycle.

**Example: Applying Support Packages**

An implementation phase has been undergoing business validation for a month. Initial business validation in the quality assurance system has begun to test newly implemented business processes. While large numbers of sales orders are being processed, a performance problem is detected. The system administrator looks for and finds a relevant SAP Note. According to the SAP Note, the solution is to either manually modify three different SAP standard objects or apply the next available Support Package.

Since final validation of the quality assurance system as a whole has not commenced, the customer has a choice—make manual modifications or apply the Support Package. If, however, the performance problem was detected in the middle of final business validation, the implementation schedule would probably cause the customer to decide to make the necessary modifications manually and apply the Support Package in a subsequent implementation phase.

### 6.5.2 Release Upgrades

Although Support Packages provide a select number of new Repository objects, an release upgrade supplies a completely new SAP repository to obtain new SAP functionality. The upgrade procedure requires a wider range of activities than those associated with Support Packages.

Release upgrades require:

- Downtime for each SAP system during the import of the new release
- Modification adjustment
- Customizing

The activities and tools required for an release upgrade are covered in more detail in Chapter 15.

### Release Upgrade Phase

Because of the changes associated with an upgrade, SAP recommends you dedicate an entire implementation phase to the upgrade process. An release upgrade should not be part of an existing implementation phase that is required to introduce changes or creates business processes.

As with the rollout of new business processes, an release upgrade also requires additional upgrade-specific Customizing activities known as *Release Customizing*. The successful implementation of this Release Customizing and the new SAP ECC repository require:

- Technical changes to your SAP ECC environment, such as upgrades to operating system and database software, or to hardware
- Business validation testing
- Stable SAP ECC systems—in particular, a stable production environment

### Responsibilities

Although your system administrator is responsible for production support—for example, applying SAP Notes, Support Packages, and release upgrades—the impetus for applying such changes normally is one of the following:

- A problem arises for which there is a relevant SAP Note or Support Package.
- Business departments want functionality contained in upgrades.

The decision-making process may involve people at many levels within your company.

## 6.6 Questions

1. Which of the following activities is NOT necessary for releasing and exporting a change request?

   A. Documenting every task in the change request

   B. Releasing every task in the change request

   C. Verification of the contents of the change request by the system administrator

   D. Unit testing the change request

2. Which of the following statements is correct in regard to the tasks used in change requests that record Customizing and development changes?

   A. Tasks belong to a change request.

   B. Tasks can be used by several SAP users.

   C. Tasks are the direct responsibility of a project leader.

   D. Tasks record only client-specific changes.

3. Which of the following indicates that a change request has been signed off after quality assurance testing?

   A. The change request is released after unit testing.

   B. The change request is successfully imported into the quality assurance system.

   C. The change request is added to the import queue of all other SAP systems in the system landscape.

   D. The project leader communicates their approval of the change request.

4. Which of the following is NOT an SAP recommendation?

   A. Imports into the quality assurance and production systems should occur in the same sequence.

   B. Even if the import process is automatically scripted, a technical consultant or system administrator should review the results of the import.

   C. Project leaders should manually add change requests to the import queue of the quality assurance system.

   D. Change requests are imported in the same sequence that they were exported from the development system.

5. Which of the following is SAP's recommendation on how to rush an emergency correction into the production system?

   A. Make the change directly in the production system.

   B. Transport the change from the development system to the quality assurance system and production system using a *preliminary import*.

   C. Make the change and use a client copy with a change request to distribute the change to production.

   D. Make the change in the quality assurance system and transport the change using a *preliminary import*.

6. Which of the following transport activities is NOT typically the responsibility of the system administrator?

   A. Importing change requests into all clients within the system landscape

   B. Verifying the success of the import process

   C. Releasing change requests

   D. Assisting in solving either export or import errors

7. Which of the following does SAP provide as customer support?

   A. Release upgrades to provide new functionality

   B. Support Packages to correct identified problems in a specific release

   C. SAP Notes to announce errors and corrections for the reported problems

   D. All of the above

# Part 2
# Technical Tasks

The first six chapters of this book have provided you with an overview of the change and transport concepts and recommendations for the implementation and maintenance of your SAP ECC system landscape. The next part of the book expands on the introduction to the transport mechanism, and outlines the technical tasks required to realize your system landscape. These tasks include:

- Setting up a transport directory at the operating system level
- Setting up the Transport Management System (TMS)
- Creating new clients

This part will be of most interest to those people who are directly responsible for setting up, upgrading, or extending a system landscape. This person is typically the implementation's system administrator.

During the installation of an SAP system, a system ID is assigned to the system and a transport directory is created for it at the operating system level. Chapter 7 focuses on this transport directory, its structure, and the way it is often shared by many different SAP systems. Other post-installation activities covered in Chapter 7 include:

- Configuring a transport profile
- Initializing the Change and Transport Organizer (CTO)
- Setting the system change option

The next step in your implementation is to set up the Transport Management System (TMS). This procedure is explained in detail in Chapter 8. Setting up the TMS is divided into two phases:

- Initializing the TMS
- Configuring the transport flow in the system landscape by defining transport routes

Although you initially install your SAP system with default clients, SAP recommends that you create new clients in the system to perform standard R/3 business processes or to perform Customizing and development. Chapter 9 outlines how to:

- Define a new SAP client
- Define client settings used to restrict the changes that can be made from within the client
- Copy a base set of data to that client
- Log Customizing changes made to a client

# 7 Transport Setup Activities at Installation

To set up the capability for transporting SAP ECC change requests, you must perform certain activities when installing an SAP ECC system. These activities are explained in this chapter and include:

- Specifying the system ID
- Setting up the transport directory
- Configuring the transport profile
- Performing activities within SAP ECC such as:
  - Initializing the Change and Transport Organizer (CTO)
  - Setting the system change option
  - Verifying the background jobs and background work processes required for transports

## 7.1 Specifying the System ID (SID)

When installing SAP ECC, you must determine a name for the new system. The system name is known as the *system ID* (SID). If you perform a standard installation, you must define a name for the system and the database at an early stage in the installation. If the new system is the result of a system copy, you must specify a new SID for the system and the database.

The SID of each system in the system landscape must be unique. When you specify a SID, especially when adding a system to an existing landscape, ensure that the new SID does not conflict with an existing SID.

**Note** Under no circumstances may two systems within a system landscape have the same SID.

Because of the need to set up transport routes early in the implementation of a system landscape, when you set up the development system, a placeholder or virtual system name is assigned—for example, to the production system, despite the fact that the production system has not yet been created. When you install further systems in the system landscape, if a system has already been established within the Transport Management System (TMS) as a virtual system, use the name provided in the TMS and delete the reference to the virtual system. For more information on setting up transport routes and virtual systems, see Chapters 5 and 8.

SIDs that are reserved by SAP and may not be used by customers when naming new SAP systems include ADD, ALL, AND, ANY, ASC, B20, B30, BCO, BIN, COM, DBA, END, EPS, FOR, GID, INT, KEY, LOG, MON, NOT, OFF, OMS, P30, RAW, ROW, SAP, SET, SGA, SHG, SID, UID, and VAR.

**Note** In addition to the names reserved by SAP, you cannot use a number as the first character of the SID.

## 7.2 Setting Up the Transport Directory

After starting the installation, you must specify the path to the system's *transport directory*. The transport directory is a file system located on the operating system level where the objects in change requests that were released and exported from that system are physically copied so that they can subsequently be imported to a target system. The transport directory is an integral part of transporting change requests from one system to another system. The transport directory enables you to perform the following tasks throughout your system landscape:

- Sharing changes, using change requests and client transports
- Applying SAP Support Packages

Because the files in the transport directory corresponding to the objects in the change request must be accessed by different systems within the system landscape, often only one physical transport directory on one system is used, since it can be shared by all other systems. This single shared transport directory is called the common transport directory. Every application server needs to have access to the *common transport directory*.

During installation, at least one physical transport directory has to be created on one system of your system landscape. Quite early in the installation process, you are asked to specify where the transport directory is to be created, or—if a transport directory has already been created—which host system serves as the *transport host*.

**Note** The transport host is the system that physically contains the common transport directory.

All systems that share the same *transport directory* make up a transport group (see Chapter 8). Figure 7.1 shows an example of the common transport directory. The transport host—the system containing the transport directory—is the development system, DEV. The quality assurance system (QAS) and the production system (PRD) share the transport directory of DEV. Together, all three systems—DEV, QAS, and PRD—are part of the same transport group.

**Note** All systems belonging to one transport group share the same physical transport directory, called the common transport directory.

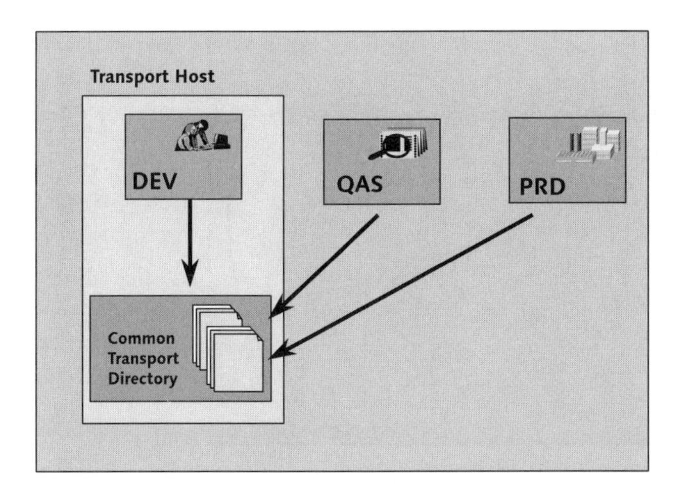


**Figure 7.1** A common transport directory for a three-system landscape

### 7.2.1 One or Many Transport Directories?

Standard practice is to have one common transport directory in a system landscape. However, it may be useful to have more than one transport directory if, for example:

- The network connection to a system is not fast enough.
- There is no permanent network connection between the different systems of the system landscape.
- There are security reasons that prevent direct access to a system.
- There are different hardware platforms that do not allow a common transport directory.

If you require additional transport directories, you should use either further common transport directories (if more than one system share the directory) or a private one (if only one system uses the directory). For example, you can create a transport directory in the production system, and if this transport directory is not shared with other systems, it is called the *private transport directory* (see Figure 7.2).

When you create a new transport directory, a further transport group is added to your system landscape. Customizing and development work can be transported between different transport groups (see Chapter 13). However, transporting between different transport groups requires additional steps, time, and disk space due to the indirect transport through different transport directories.

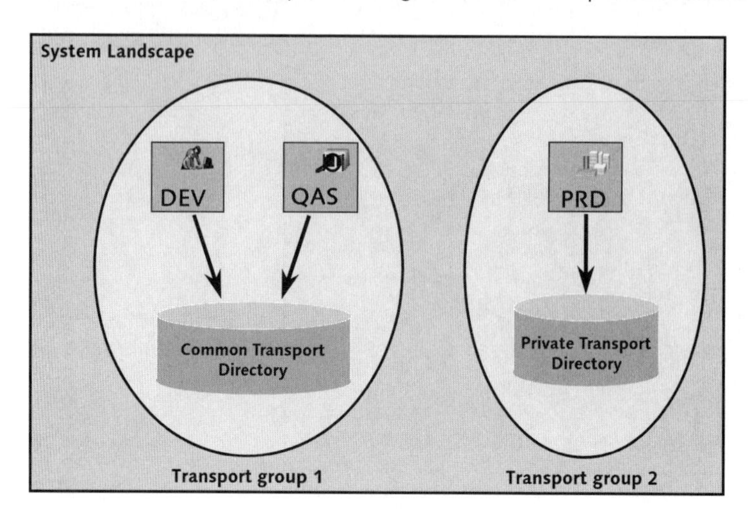


**Figure 7.2** Two transport groups

If you use several transport groups, bear in mind that:

- Log files generated during the export process can be displayed only in systems that are in the same transport group as the source system. The source system is typically the development system.
- Log files generated during the import process can be displayed only in systems that are in the same transport group as the target system. The target system is typically the quality assurance or production system.
- You must maintain the transport profile for each transport group.

**Example of a System Landscape with Two Transport Groups**

To provide a solid, 24-hour maintenance and support solution for a production SAP system, a company outsources its system support for the production system. The internal technology team manages support for the development system and quality assurance system, both of which physically reside at the company headquarters. However, the production system is located in a different facility across town, and for this system, the external support vendor provides support.

While the production system is physically accessible from the company's headquarters through the network and the company's firewall, the production system does not share the same transport directory as the development system and the quality assurance system. The main reason for having separate transport directories is to avoid requiring an NFS (network file system) mount across the network and to protect the production system from nonrelevant transport activities. Consequently, there are two transport groups: one transport group for the development system and the quality assurance system, and another transport group for the production system (see Figure 7.2 earlier in this section).

### 7.2.2 Transport Directory Structure

The subdirectories in the transport directory store all the files needed for transports (see Figure 7.3). No user action is required to create the subdirectories—they are created automatically during the installation of a system.

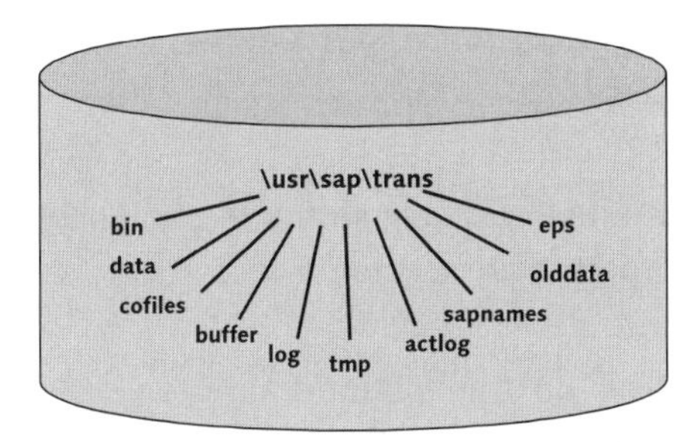


**Figure 7.3** Transport directory structure

The subdirectories in the common transport directory include:

- **bin:**
  This directory contains the transport profile, called `TP_<domain>.PFL` as of R/3 Release 4.5 and `TPPARAM` in earlier R/3 releases.
- **data:**
  This directory stores the actual data files of the related change requests with the Customizing and development changes.
- **cofiles:**
  This directory contains *control files*, or change request information files used by the transport tools on the operating system level. The information in the files includes data on transport types, object classes, required import steps, and post-processing exit codes. These files also contain the current status of the change request in the various systems of the transport group.

- **buffer:**
  This directory contains an import buffer for each R/3 System in a transport group. These buffer files indicate which change requests are to be imported in the respective system. The import queues that have already been mentioned in Chapter 4 are the representation of the import buffer within an SAP system. Buffer files also provide information on the steps that must be performed for import, and the order in which requests are to be imported.
- **log:**
  This directory includes all general log files, as well as all log files generated by the export and import of change requests or client copy activities.
- **tmp:**
  This directory is needed to temporarily store log files and semaphores during transports.
- **actlog:**
  This directory stores the log of user actions in an SAP system for all change requests and tasks. This is the only subdirectory of the transport directory that is not accessed by the operating system `tp`. This directory is accessed only by the Change and Transport Organizer (CTO).
- **sapnames:**
  This directory contains a file for each SAP user working with the CTS. These files log transport activities for each transport request.
- **olddata:**
  This directory is needed when you clean up the transport directory. Old exported data that is to be archived or deleted is stored in this directory.
- **eps:**
  This is the download directory for SAP Support Packages from SAPNet.

For more information on the files contained in these directories, see Chapter 14.

### 7.2.3 Procedure

To set up the common transport directory, you must provide a file system on the system that you have chosen to be the transport host before you run `R3setup` to start the actual installation. Many customers choose the development system as the transport host because it is typically the first system to be installed. When you run `R3setup` from the CDs, the transport directory is automatically created with its subdirectories.

Every computer of the transport group on which an SAP instance is installed should have read access and write access to the transport directory. This is implemented through corresponding authorizations of the operating system user who owns the SAP instance—for example, <sid>adm on Unix platforms. You should ensure that there is sufficient network availability between the systems that belong to the same transport group.

To set up your transport directory:

1. Create the following directory on the transport host:
   - /usr/sap/trans on Unix and AS/400 platforms
   - \sapmnt\trans on Windows NT platforms
2. Mount this directory using operating system tools as part of the installation preparation on the hosts that belong to the same transport group.
3. Ensure that the correct path to the transport directory is stored in the parameter transdir in the transport profile as well as in the parameter DIR_TRANS in the instance profile.

### Technical Requirements

The required free space on the transport directory highly depends on the transport volume. As a rule of thumb for estimating the required amount of disk space for your transport directory, proceed as follows:

- Estimate 100 MB per SAP instance that will be using the transport directory.
- Estimate 20 MB for each user involved in Customizing and development.
  The minimum total amount of disk space for the transport directory deriving from the above two estimates should be 200 MB.
- Add the estimated additional space needed for client exports. This amount of disk space depends on the data to be transported (see also Chapter 9).
- Add the estimated additional space needed for SAP Support Packages (see also Chapter 15). In a system where few development activities are carried out, the memory required for the SAP Support Packages can be the dominating factor. Therefore, at least 100 MB should be reserved for this purpose.

The following sections cover how to set up the transport directory for Unix, Windows NT, AS/400, and a heterogeneous environment.

### Transport Directory on Unix

To set up the transport directory on a Unix platform:

1. Log on to the transport host as user root.
2. Create the file system for the transport directory.

3. Mount this file system as /usr/sap/trans (default value). Ensure that the directory belongs to the group *sapsys* and has the permission 775. After installation, you should restrict the permission to 771.
4. Export the directory using a tool such as NFS (network file system).

**Note** Ensure that group sapsys has the same *group identification number* (GID) on all the computers of the network.

Next, perform the following steps on all other R/3 instances in the transport group:

1. Log on as user root.
2. Create a mount point, /usr/sap/trans.
3. Establish a network connection to the transport directory—for example, using NFS to mount the transport directory from the transport host.

**Note** For details on the command syntax of the specific Unix derivatives, see *Installation on Unix-OS Dependencies*, one of the implementation guides accompanying the SAP installation package.

### Transport Directory on Windows NT

To share a common transport directory, all application and database servers for an SAP system either must be in the same Windows NT domain or, if the domains differ, you must specify an NT *trusted relationship* between them.

For Windows NT, you can choose any computer as the transport host. If you have chosen a computer that contains the SAP ECC central instance to be the transport host, skip the following three steps. Otherwise, if the computer chosen contains an dialog instance or no instance at all, perform the following steps before installation (that is, before running R3setup):

1. Create the directory \usr\sap\trans.
2. Set a global share sapmnt to point to the usr\sap file tree. This allows the transport directory to be accessed through the path \sapmnt\trans.
3. Grant NT access type *Full Control* for *Everyone* on this directory.

**Note** The Windows NT access type *Full Control* is required for the transport directory only during R/3 installation. After the installation, for security reasons, you should restrict this access to write authorizations for operating system users.

You must define the transport host using the alias *SAPTRANSHOST*. Whenever it is necessary to point to the transport host, this alias is used instead of the name of the transport host. Prior to SAP ECC installation, make this alias known to all Windows NT systems within the transport domain by using either of the following techniques:

- On the Domain Name Server (DNS), record the alias SAPTRANSHOST for the transport host. This technique is recommended by SAP and creates what is known as the *central transport host*. Its main advantage is that you do not have to adjust the parameters of every system when moving the transport directory, but only the central record of the transport host on the DNS.
- If no DNS server is available, you can use the hosts file to record the alias SAPTRANSHOST. This file is located in the Windows NT default directory `<drive>:\WINNT\system32\drivers\etc`. Use an editor to add the entry `<IP_address> <hostname> SAPTRANSHOST`. Ensure that this file is identical on all hosts where an SAP instance is installed or will be installed.

**Note** For more information on the configuration of a central transport host, see SAP Note 62739.

Early in the SAP ECC installation process, you are asked to name the host that contains the transport directory. For a common transport directory, enter the alias SAPTRANSHOST. For a private transport directory, enter the host name of the computer that contains the transport directory.

### Transport Directory on AS/400

To enable access to a common transport directory, use the integrated file server QFileSvr.400 on the AS/400 system to provide access to other file systems on remote AS/400 systems.

**Tip** To avoid performance problems, use the QFileSvr.400 file server instead of NFS to connect the SAP systems on AS/400 platforms.

Prior to SAP installation on AS/400:

1. For each host sharing the transport directory, create a subdirectory named with the respective host name in QFileSvr.400. To create such a subdirectory, execute the following command with the respective host name:

   ```
   MKDIR '/QfileSvr.400/<hostname>'
   ```

Create the host directories with the startup program QSTRUP, because these directories no longer exist after the initial program load (IPL) of AS/400, and must be re-created.

2. Create the following operating system users on all AS/400 systems in the transport group:
   - SAP<nn> (as of R/3 Release 4.0; nn denotes the instance number)
   - <SID><nn> (from R/3 Release 4.5 onwards; nn denotes the instance number)
   - <SID>OFR (for the SAP system superuser)
   - <SID>OPR (for the SAP system operator)

**Note** These users must have the same passwords on all computers and need *write* permission on the transport directory.

For each AS/400 SAP system in the transport group, perform the following:

1. When installing the SAP ECC software, in the `R3setup` main menu (**SAP Installation**), select option 3 to change the location of the transport directory `/usr/sap/trans`.
2. Specify the host name of the transport host. As a result, the transport directory can be accessed through `/usr/sap/trans`, which is a symbolic link that points to the directory `/QfileSvr.400/<hostname>/sapmnt/trans`.

For an SAP installation with a private transport directory, perform a default installation for the transport directory. When the SAP installation program asks for the location of the transport directory, agree to the default proposed settings. Accepting the default settings automatically creates the transport directory under `/sapmnt/trans`. The transport directory can be accessed through `/usr/sap/trans`, which is a link to the physical directory `/sapmnt/trans`.

**Note** SAP Note 67213 provides more details on the transport directory for AS/400 platforms.

### Heterogeneous Operating Systems

It is possible to use a common transport directory in heterogeneous operating system environments. The configuration depends on the operating systems. For example, you can set up the physical transport directory on a Unix system and provide network access to AS/400 systems. You can also have the transport directory on an AS/400 server and access it from Unix systems—although this configuration is more complex. In both cases, you must use NFS for the connection between the different platforms.

**Note** For more information on setting up a central transport directory in environments with Unix and AS/400 platforms, see SAP Note 69429.

The implementation of a common transport directory in mixed environments with Windows NT and Unix is more difficult. Some files in the transport directory are written in text mode. On Unix platforms, a *linefeed* is written at each line end. On Windows NT, the line end is indicated by a *carriage return* followed by a linefeed. All SAP systems must be configured so that the transport directory files are written only in binary mode—the line end is indicated by a linefeed on both platforms.

There is no hierarchical file system on Windows NT platforms. It is not possible to create soft links to mount Unix file trees on Windows NT systems, or links that mount Windows NT file trees on Unix systems. To enable this access between the systems, you must install additional software such as SAMBA.

**Note** For more information on setting up a central transport directory in environments with Unix and Windows NT platforms, see SAP Note 28781.

## 7.3 Configuring the Transport Profile

For each transport group, you need to set up and maintain a transport profile. The transport profile contains the settings needed to configure the transport control program `tp` and the transport program `R3trans`. The transport profile is stored in subdirectory `bin` of the transport directory.

In the transport profile, the following parameters must be maintained:

- Database-specific parameters:
  - dbhost
  - dbname
- Path-specific parameters:
  - transdir
  - r3transpath
- Parameters for heterogeneous environments

If you have more than one transport group, the transport profiles should all be identical. The only exception might be parameter `transdir`.

**Warning** In releases prior to R/3 Release 4.5, the parameters in the transport profile are specified in lowercase—for example, `transdir`. As of R/3 Release 4.5, they are specified in uppercase—for example, `TRANSDIR`. For simplicity, the transport profile parameters in this book are written in lowercase.

### 7.3.1 Transport Profile in R/3 Release 4.0

Up to R/3 Release 4.0, the transport profile is stored in the file `TPPARAM`, which is also known as the *global parameter file*. SAP delivers templates as sample profiles, which you have to adapt manually after R/3 installation.

The sample `TPPARAM` file is stored as `TPPARAM.TPL` in the installation directory—for example, in the Unix directory \usr\sap\<SID>\SYS\exe\run\INSTALL. To adapt the default transport profile, copy the default `TPPARAM` file as `TPPARAM` to subdirectory `bin` of the transport directory. To adapt `TPPARAM` to your system landscape, you must use a text editor on the operating system level.

**Example of a Transport Profile TPPARAM for an NT Platform with R/3 Release 4.0**

This example of a transport profile contains only the minimum required parameters:

```
#######################################################
# global Parameters                                   #
#######################################################
transdir = \\$(SAPTRANSHOST)\sapmnt\trans\
dbname = $(system)
#######################################################
# System specific Parameters                          #
#######################################################
#######################################################
# DEV #
DEV/dbhost = twdfmx01
# QAS #
QAS/dbhost = twdfmx02
# PRD #
PRD/dbhost = twdfmx03
```

### 7.3.2 Transport Profile in R/3 Release 4.5

As of R/3 Release 4.5, the file `TP_<domain>.PFL` is used as the transport profile. You no longer need to copy and adapt the profile on the operating system level. It is automatically generated the first time you call the Transport Management System (TMS) and contains the required transport parameter settings. This file is also stored in subdirectory `bin` of the transport directory. It is administered in the TMS.

> **Warning** As of R/3 Release 4.5, you do not modify the transport profile using a text editor on the operating system level.

The transport profile is maintained automatically when certain TMS functions are performed, such as adding a new SAP system. To modify the transport profile, from the SAP initial screen:

1. Call Transaction STMS.
2. Choose **Overview • Systems**.
3. Mark one system and choose **SAP System • Change**.
4. Choose the tab **Transport tool**.

Figure 7.4 shows how the `TP_<domain>.PFL` transport profile is displayed for releases as of 4.5. You may change global, system-specific, and operating system specific parameters. Enter the changes directly in the **Value** column and choose **Save**. This creates a backup file by saving the previous version of the transport profile as `TP_<domain>.BAK` in the transport subdirectory **bin**.

In the **Type** column, the symbols indicate the origin of certain parameters. Via the icon, select **Legend** (see Figure 7.5) to access the legend of these symbols.

In Figure 7.4, the parameter `transdir` is the only parameter that is used explicitly on the operating system level. All database parameters—`dbhost`, `dbname`, and `dbtype`—have been automatically generated by the TMS. The `tp_version` parameter has been added by a user when implementing a current version of `tp`. CTC=1 indicates that the client control of transport routes is activated, and `NBUFFORM=1` allows for an import buffer format with long request names.

To list all the defined parameters and their values, in the screen **Display TMS Configuration: System <SID>**, choose **Goto • TP parameters**.

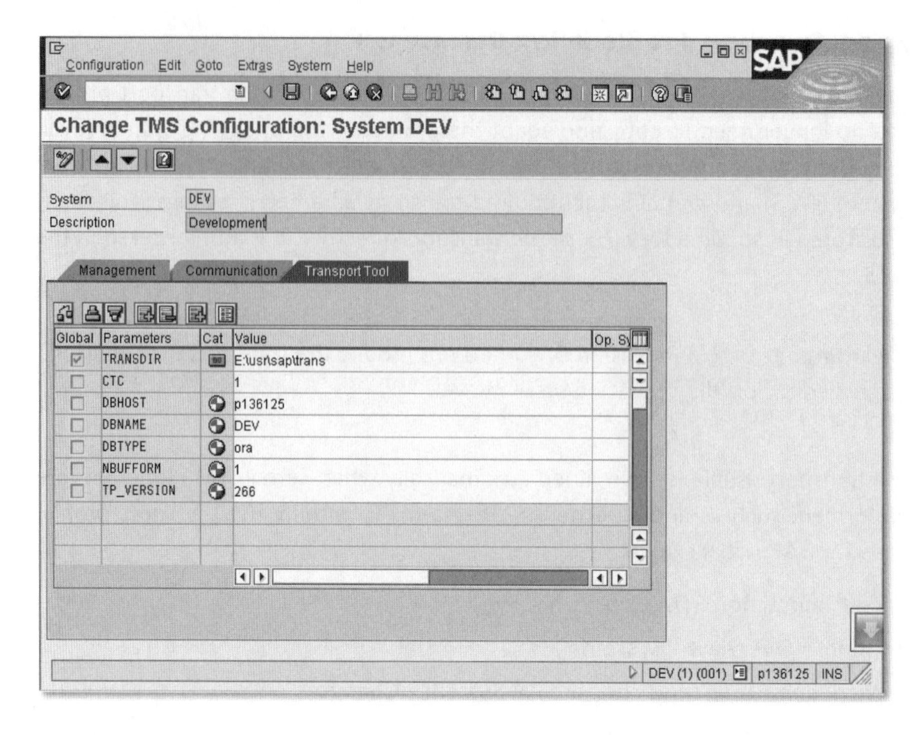


**Figure 7.4** Transport profile parameters

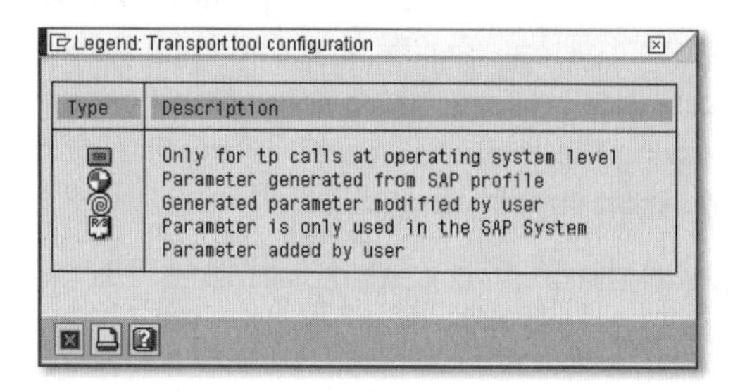


**Figure 7.5** Legend for parameter types

## Upgrading to R/3 Release 4.5 or Higher

After an upgrade to R/3 Release 4.5 or higher your SAP system will contain two transport profiles: `TPPARAM` and `TP_<domain>.PFL`. The transport profile `TP_<domain>.PFL` is always used when calling `tp` from the SAP system. A conflict may arise when you run `tp` on the operating system level if the formerly used transport profile `TPPARAM` still exists in the subdirectory `bin` after the upgrade. To start `tp` from the operating system, you must specify the location of the parameter file with the option `pf=<path of TP_<domain>.PFL>`. Otherwise, `tp` searches for the `TPPARAM` transport profile.

**Warning** If both transport profiles—`TPPARAM` and `TP_<domain>.PFL`–exist, a conflict may arise when you run `tp` on the operating system level. Therefore, when starting `tp` on the operating system level, you must indicate which profile `tp` is to use.

Each SAP system should be described in only one transport profile—as of R/3 Release 4.5, this file is `TP_<domain>.PFL`. To achieve this, copy the settings in `TPPARAM` to `TP_<domain>.PFL` and then delete the entries in `TPPARAM`.

To copy the settings from the former transport profile, `TPPARAM`, to the new transport profile, `TP_<domain>.PFL`, proceed as follows:

1. Call Transaction STMS.
2. Choose **Overview • Systems**.
3. From the screen **System Overview: Domain <domain>**, mark the system that is the source of the parameters to be copied.
4. Choose **SAP System • Change** and then the tab **Transport tool**.
5. Choose **Extras • Copy configuration from TPPARAM**.
6. Choose **Save** and, as described in Chapter 8, distribute these changes to all systems in the transport domain.

### 7.3.3 Profile Syntax

The parameters specified in the transport profile and their syntax are valid for both `TPPARAM` and `TP_<domain>.PFL`. The syntax for `TP__<domain>.PFL` corresponds to how it is represented on the operating system level; within R/3, the parameters are represented as depicted in Figure 7.4 (earlier in the chapter).

**Warning** For R/3 Release 4.0, you must use a text editor on the operating system level to configure the transport profile parameters. As of Release 4.5, these parameters are generated automatically. You do not need to set up the transport profile parameters for a minimum configuration. You can maintain and add transport profile parameters using TMS.

### Parameter Types

Comment lines are preceded by # in the transport profile. All other lines contain parameter definitions, which can be any of the following:

- Global—that is, valid for all SAP systems in the transport domain
- SAP system–specific—that is, valid only for one R/3 System
- Operating system–specific—that is, valid for all systems running a specific operating system
- Database-specific—that is, valid for all systems on a specific database platform

Table 7.1 shows the syntax for the different parameter types in the transport profile.

| Parameter Types | Syntax | Possible Acronyms |
|---|---|---|
| Global | `<parameter>=<value>` | |
| System–specific | `<SID>/<parameter>=<value>` | |
| Operating system–specific | `<CPU>\|<parameter>=<value>` | aix, axp (Open VMS),<br>hp-ux, osf1,<br>sinix, sunos,<br>wnt (Windows NT),<br>as4 (AS/400) |
| Database-specific | `<DB>:<parameter>=<value>` | ora (Oracle),<br>inf (Informix),<br>ada (Max DB),<br>mss (MS SQL Server),<br>db2 (DB2 for OS390),<br>db4 (DB2/400),<br>db6 (DB2 for AIX) |

**Table 7.1** Profile syntax

If a parameter is not specified, the default value is used. SAP recommends grouping global settings at the beginning of the transport profile, because in general, the last setting for a given SAP system, operating system, or database overrides previous settings.

### Predefined Variables

Predefined variables can be used as part of the parameter values of the transport profile. They have the format `$(<variable name>)`. If required, the brackets may be masked with a backslash (\). Table 7.2 lists all possible predefined variables.

| Variable | Description | Possible Values |
|---|---|---|
| $(cpu) | CPU name (important in heterogeneous system landscapes) | alphaosf, hp, rm600, rs6000 sun, wnt, as4 |
| $(cpu2) | Acronym for the operating system | aix, hp-ux, osf1, sinix, sunos, wnt |
| $(dname) | Abbreviation for the day of the week | SUN, MON, ... |
| $(mday) | Day of the current month | 01 to 31 |
| $(mname) | Abbreviation for the name of the month | JAN, FEB, ... |
| $(mon) | Month | 01 to 12 |
| $(system) | System identifier (SID) of the SAP system | For example, PRD |
| $(wday) | Day of the week | 00 to 06 (Sunday = 00) |
| $(yday) | Day of the current year | 001 to 366 |
| $(year) | Year | For example, 1999 |
| $(syear) | Short form of the year | For example, 99 |
| $(yweek) | Calendar week | 00 to 53 |

**Table 7.2** Predefined variables

**Example of Using Predefined Variables**

Transport parameter syslog specifies the file SLOG that is used to monitor the transport activities of a specific SAP system. The file is stored in subdirectory log of the transport directory and contains a general overview of performed imports. The name of this log file can be set in the transport profile using syslog as a global parameter. The default setting for the parameter syslog is SLOG<year><week>.<SID>.

The appropriate configuration is as follows:

- The parameter type is set to global.
- The parameter is set using predefined variables to SLOG$(syear)$(yweek).$(system).

In week 31 of year 2005, this configuration instructs the system to log anything written to the file SLOG in the SAP system QAS to a file called SLOG0531.QAS.

Table 7.3 contains the additional predefined variables that are available on Windows NT platforms.

| Variable | Description |
|---|---|
| `$(SAPGLOBALHOST)` | Points to the host on which the central instance is installed |
| `$(SAPTRANSHOST)` | Points to the transport host |

**Table 7.3** Additional variables for Windows NT

### 7.3.4 Required Parameters

For R/3 Release 4.0, to set up your system landscape for transporting, you must set a minimum number of parameters on the operating system level. These required parameters are automatically set during the setup of TMS as of Release 4.5. The required parameters are described in this section. For information on further uses of these parameters and other transport profile parameters, see Chapter 14 and Appendix B.

#### Database Parameters

Database-specific parameters in the transport profile enable the transport control program `tp` to access the databases. The following parameters are required.

For each SAP system within the transport group, configure the parameter `dbhost` (system-specific). This parameter specifies the host name—that is, the computer on which the database runs or, valid for Oracle and DB2 on AIX, on which the database processes run.

**Tip** On Windows NT platforms ensure that you use the TCP/IP computer host name as the value for parameter `dbhost`.

Parameter `dbname` is used to specify the name of the database instance. Typically, the parameter is realized as a global parameter, and the value is specified using the variable `$(system)`. The transport parameter `dbname` passes over the name of the database, for which `tp` is called.

**Tip** Note that parameter `dbname` is case sensitive on Informix platforms. For SAP DB as well as for DB2, this parameter has to be changed from lowercase to uppercase after the installation.

Exceptions are DB2/400 platforms and SAP standard installations on Oracle platforms. Standard installations use the name of the system for the name of the database instance and for the logical name of the database in the network. On these platforms, you do not need to specify parameter dbname.

Further Database Parameters

Depending on your database platform, you must also set further parameters as listed in Table 7.4.

| Platform | Parameter | Value |
|---|---|---|
| SAP DB | Dbuserkey | Name of the SAP instance |
| DB2/400 (only if opticonnect is used) | Opticonnect | 1 |

**Table 7.4** Additional parameters for database platforms

**Tip** For information on transport profile parameters required for a DB2 database on OS/390, see SAP Note 77589.

### Path-Specific Parameters

The parameters that ensure that the tools involved in the transport process use the correct paths are as follows:

- transdir
- DIR_TRANS
- r3transpath

The transport parameters transdir and r3transpath are specified in the transport profile. DIR_TRANS must be set in the instance profile.

The parameter transdir is located in the transport profile and specifies the name of the transport directory for tp as it has been mounted on all hosts of a transport group.

To set this parameter in a noncomplex landscape that has no special requirements such as special security demands:

1. Set the parameter transdir as a *global* parameter. It cannot be set *system-specific* or *database-specific*, but can be set as *operating system–specific*.
2. Set transdir identically for all SAP systems within a single transport group.
3. Set the default values as listed for the respective platforms in Table 7.5.

**Note** In heterogeneous operating system environments, set the parameter type to operating system–specific. For example, `wnt|transdir = \\trans02\trans\` specifies that for all Windows NT systems, the transport directory can be found on the host trans02 in the directory `trans`.

| Platform | Value for *transdir* |
|---|---|
| Unix | `/usr/sap/trans` |
| AS/400 | `/usr/sap/trans` |
| Windows NT (if you have configured a central transport host with alias SAPTRANSHOST) | `\\(SAPTRANSHOST)\sapmnt\trans` |
| Windows NT (without a central transport host) | `\\<transport host>\sapmnt\trans` |

**Table 7.5** Operating system-specific values for transdir

The parameter `DIR_TRANS` is located in the instance profile. As with `transdir`, it points to the transport directory and is used by several programs, such as the kernel. Whenever the operating system transport tool `tp` is called from the SAP system, the value of `transdir` is overridden with the value of `DIR_TRANS`.

**Note** The transport parameters `transdir` and `DIR_TRANS` should always point to the same directory.

In Windows NT environments, parameter `DIR_TRANS` points by default to directory `\\$(SAPGLOBALHOST)\sapmnt\trans`. If you have configured a transport host—that is, specified the alias SAPTRANSHOST on the domain name server—you must set the value of `DIR_TRANS` to `\\(SAPTRANSHOST)\sapmnt\trans`.

If you have chosen a different path than the one specified by the share `\sapmnt\trans`, you must set parameter `DIR_TRANS` explicitly using the alias $(SAPTRANSHOST). For example:

```
DIR_TRANS = \\$(SAPTRANSHOST)\transport
```

Another way of defining the access path to the transport directory is to set the transport host that is specified in the domain name server to be overridden locally. This is recommended if all systems require a private transport directory.

**Example of the Parameters transdir and DIR_TRANS with Unix**

The following graphic illustrates how the transport directory is accessed using the parameters `transdir` and `DIR_TRANS` on a Unix platform.

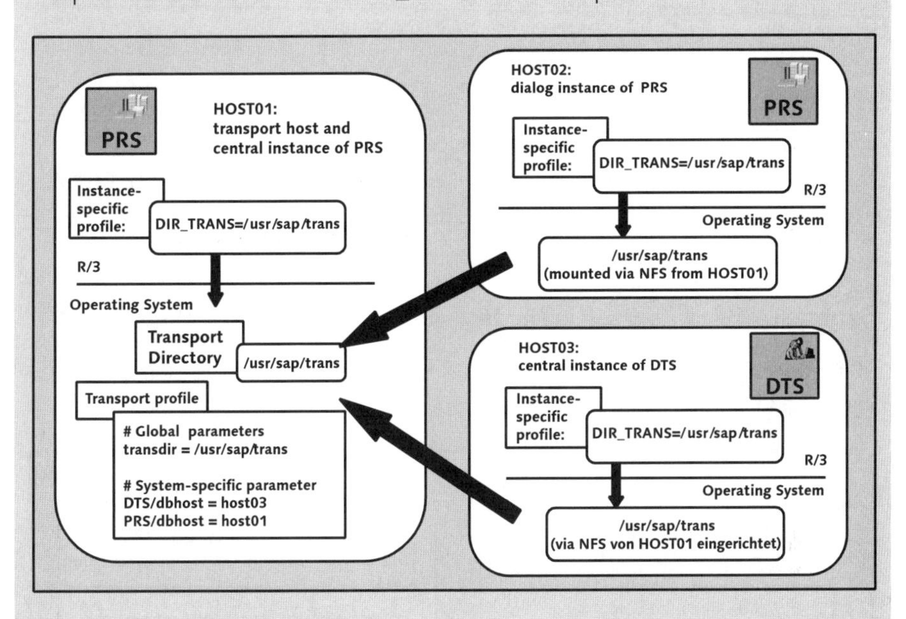


**Figure 7.6** Unix transport directory and 3 host systems

This landscape consists of two SAP systems: the development-and-test system DTS and the production system PRS. DTS consists of a central instance (host03). PRS consists of a central instance (host01) and a dialog instance (host02). DTS and PRS share the same transport directory. Host01 is the physical location of the transport directory `/usr/sap/trans`. In the instance profiles of all instances, the parameter `DIR_TRANS` is set to `/usr/sap/trans`. This directory is mounted on host02 and host03 using NFS from host01.

To cause the transport path stored in the domain name server to be overridden, add the following line to the directory `Winnt\system32\drivers\etc\hosts`:

```
<IP address of private transport host> <TCP/IP name of private trans-
port host> SAPTRANSHOST
```

For example:

```
10.16.162.61      twdfmx05      SAPTRANSHOST
```

The entry in the file `hosts` has to end with a blank line. Keep in mind that the hierarchy governing which parameter value is determinant is as follows:

1. DIR_TRANS in the instance profile
2. Value of SAPTRANSHOST of the local hosts file
3. Value of SAPTRANSHOST of the domain name server

For example, DIR_TRANS will override SAPTRANSHOST.

**Tip** When maintaining DIR_TRANS in the instance profile, you can also maintain parameter DIR_EPS_ROOT. This parameter points to subdirectory eps of the transport directory, which is used to deliver SAP Support Packages (see Chapter 15).

**Example of Parameters transdir and DIR_TRANS with Windows NT**

The following graphic shows an example of how the transport directory is accessed in a three-system landscape on Windows NT.

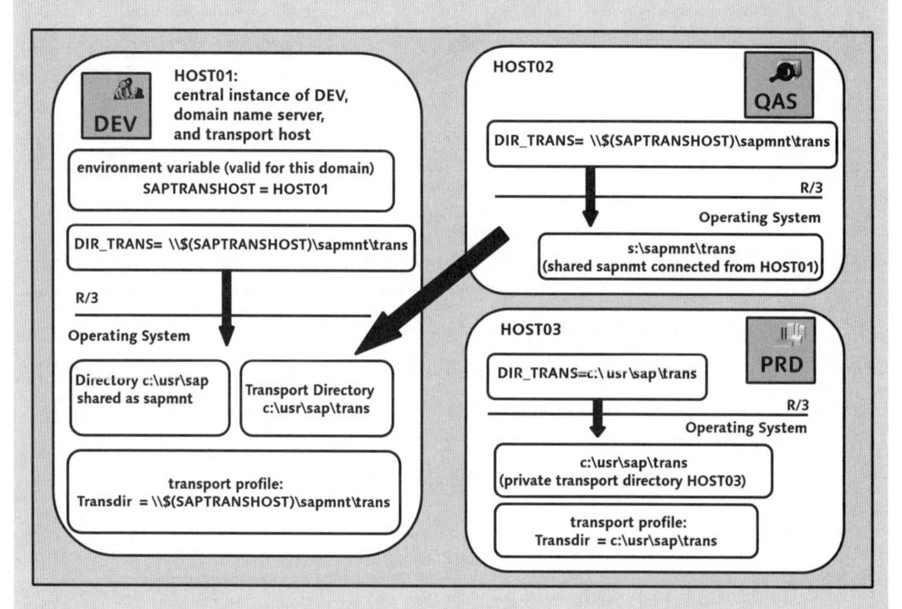


Figure 7.7 NT transport directory and 3 host systems

The landscape consists of the development system DEV on host01, the quality assurance system QAS on host 02, and the production system PRD on host03. DEV and QAS share the same transport directory, whereas PRD has its own private transport directory due to special security demands. Host01 is the physical location of the transport directory (c:\usr\sap\trans) shared by system DEV with system QAS. Directory c:\usr\sap on host01 is shared as sapmnt. DEV is also the domain name server of the Window NT domain, on which alias SAP-TRANSHOST is set to host01. The instance profiles of DEV and QAS contain parameter DIR_TRANS, which is set to \\$(SAPTRANSHOST)\sapmnt\trans. Therefore, for both DEV and QAS, the parameters DIR_TRANS and transdir point to directory c:\usr\sap\trans on host01. Because PRD has its own private transport directory, both DIR_TRANS and transdir point to the private transport directory c:\usr\sap\trans on host03.

Parameter r3transpath specifies which platform-specific version of R3trans is used by tp. The default value—R3trans for Unix and AS/400 platforms and R3trans.exe for NT platforms—normally works. No explicit path is given. The path relies on the correct path definition of the user starting tp. In case of problems or in heterogeneous environments, make sure the specification is correct. Set the value for parameter r3transpath as described in Table 7.6.

| Platform | Parameter Specification | Value |
|---|---|---|
| Unix, AS/400 | r3transpath | R3trans |
| Windows NT | Wnt\|r3transpath | R3trans.exe |

**Table 7.6** Specification of r3transpath

If the system landscape consists of SAP systems running on different database platforms, you must set the parameter to *system-specific* or *operating system-specific* to use different platform-specific versions of R3trans.

**Note** See SAP Note 83327 for more information on transporting in a heterogeneous environment.

### Parameters for a Heterogeneous Environment with Windows NT and Unix

If a transport group includes systems running on Windows NT and systems running on Unix, additional settings are required.

For systems running on Windows NT, perform the following steps:

1. Set binary mode as the default mode for opening a file for tp.exe and R3trans.exe:
   - For R/3 Release 4.0, on the operating system level, choose **Start · Settings · Control Panel · System · Environment · User Variables** to set the environ-

ment variable abap/NTfmode=b in the user environment of the user under whom the kernel was started—that is, either <SID>ADM or SAPService<SID>. Afterward, you have to execute the program NTENV2REG.EXE, which is stored in the R/3 kernel directory. Then, start the SAP Service.

- As of R/3 Release 4.5, set the parameter ababntfmode in the transport profile to b.
- Set the instance profile parameter abap/Ntfmode to b.

2. Make the following entries to the transport profile. Note that all of these entries are platform-specific for Windows NT and, with the exception of parameter transdir, they are also specific to a certain R/3 System:
   - wnt|transdir = <path to the transport directory>
   - wnt|<SID>/r3transpath=\\<NTHOST>\sapmnt\<SID>\sys\exe\run\R3trans.exe
   - wnt|<SID>/sapevtpath=\\<NTHOST>\sapmnt\<SID>\sys\exe\run\sapevt.exe
   - wnt|<SID>/system_pf=\\<NTHOST>\sapmnt\<SID>\sys\profile\default.pfl
3. Maintain parameter DIR_TRANS (and also DIR_EPS_ROOT) correctly in all instance profiles.

**Tip** On Windows NT platforms, the transport profile TPPARAM is edited with SAP's editor SAPPAD, which is stored as sappad.exe in the SAP executable directory \usr\sap\<SID>\SYS\exe\run. SAPPAD lets you save the settings using the Unix formatting option.

## 7.4 Activities within SAP ECC

After installation, the following activities from within SAP ECC are required for the setup of transport capabilities:

- Initializing the Change and Transport Organizer (CTO)
- Setting the system change option
- Verifying the background jobs and background work processes required for transports

Bear in mind that there are different types of "SAP installations," and that how you perform the transport-related tasks described in this section will vary according to which type of SAP installation you are working on. These installation types include:

- **SAP standard installation:**
  An SAP standard installation is installed from the SAP CDs using the program `R3setup`.
- **System upgrade:**
  A system upgrade uses SAP CDs and the program `R3up` to upgrade an existing system release to a higher system release—for example, from R/3 Release 4.6C to SAP ECC 5.0. (See Chapter 15.)
- **System copy:**
  A *system copy* or *database copy* as a method for creating a new system was discussed in Chapter 5. The tools for creating system copies depend on the database and the operating system platform, as well as the demand for migrating the system from one platform to another.

Unlike an SAP standard installation or an release upgrade, a system copy requires you to manage entities carried over from the source system, such as:

- Clients
- Customizing data, application data, and user master data
- Open tasks or change requests
- The system name (SID) for customer-developed Repository objects that remain owned by the source system

### 7.4.1 Initializing the Change and Transport Organizer

After an installation by system copy, you must manually initialize the Change and Transport Organizer (CTO) with Transaction SE06. This causes the SID of the system to be stored in the appropriate database table, and establishes the initial value of the serial ID-number for change requests. This initialization is not required for an SAP standard installation, because when configuring TMS (see Chapter 8), the TMS automatically checks whether the CTO has been initialized, and, if not, initializes it.

To initialize the CTO manually, perform the following steps:

1. Log on to your system.
2. Call Transaction SE06.
3. Select **Database copy or migration** if the R/3 System is the result of a system copy.
4. To initialize the CTO, select **Execute**.

**Note** To use Transaction SE06, you need the administration authorization S_CTS_ADMIN that is found in the authorization profile S_A.SYSTEM.

When initializing the CTO using Transaction SE06 and choosing **Database copy or migration**, Transaction SE06 not only initializes the CTO, it also provides functionality to handle change requests that have been copied into the new system. (Such change requests are not an issue for standard installations, because the SAP-delivered system contains no carryover change requests.) Change requests that have been copied into the new system may cause problems when you upgrade or modify objects. The following activities take place:

- Initializing the control tables for change requests and the release upgrade process.
- Detecting and listing all open tasks and change requests that existed in the originating system—including modifications—that are changes to the SAP standard. You will want to release these open tasks and change requests to delete the locks on the corresponding objects. For documentation purposes, these change requests remain recorded in the new system with the status released.
- Enabling you to decide whether the customer-developed Repository objects belonging to open change requests should be made original objects in the target system. If so, the original system for these objects, which are still "owned" by the source system after a system copy, is changed to the current system (see Chapter 10).

**Note** For information on Repository object locks after system copy, see SAP Note 62519.

### 7.4.2 Setting the Global System Change Option

The global system change option for each SAP system determines whether Repository objects and client-independent (cross-client) Customizing objects can be changed. To set the system change option:

1. Call Transaction SE06 and choose **System change option**.
2. In the screen **System change option**, choose **Global setting**.
3. In the dialog box, choose either **Modifiable** or **Not modifiable**.

The development system should be the only system within your system landscape in which changes to objects are allowed. From the development system, you can transport the changes into the other systems of your landscape.

**Tip** For the quality assurance system and the production system, SAP strongly recommends setting the global system change option to **Not modifiable**.

After setting the system change option to **Modifiable**, from the screen **System change option**, you can determine which specific namespaces and name ranges can be set to **Modifiable**. After selecting or deselecting for specific namespaces or name ranges, select **Modifiable**, **Restricted modifiable**, or **Not modifiable**.

**Tip** If you set the option for a namespace or name range to **Not modifiable**, you cannot change the objects in this namespace or name range, even if the global system change option is set to **Modifiable**.

Figure 7.8 shows the system change settings for a development system DEV. The global system change option is set to **Modifiable**—this is indicated by the message **Global setting: Repository and client-independent Customizing can be changed**. Below this message, the column **Modifiable** indicates the objects in certain namespaces and name ranges that can be changed.

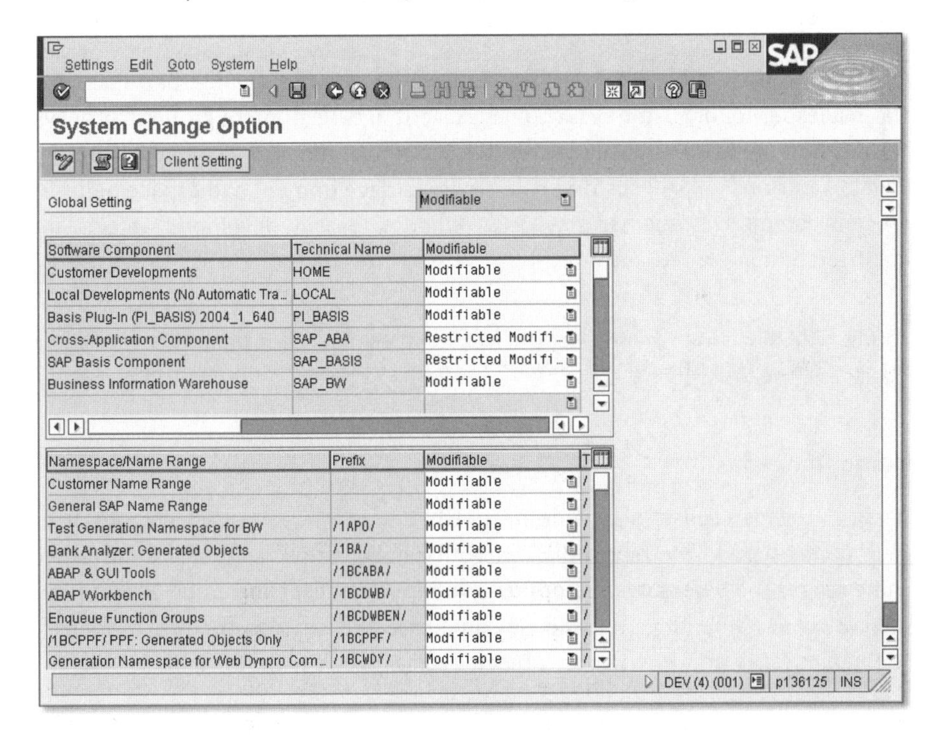


**Figure 7.8** Global System Change Option and Namespace and Name Range Change Option

**Tip** Resetting **Modifiable** for a namespace or a name range prevents changes in a specific namespace or name range, even though changes are globally permitted.

When you save your changes to these settings, the new setting, date, time, and responsible user are logged. To display the log file, from screen **System Change Option**, choose **Log**.

In addition to the global change option and the change option for namespaces and name ranges, you can also set change options on a client basis. (See Chapter 9.)

### Namespaces

A *namespace* is specified by a character set and a permitted name length. All names that match these criteria belong to the corresponding namespace. For example, as of R/3 Release 4.0, the namespace for programs covers all strings with up to 30 alphanumeric characters. Technically, a namespace is implemented by a template—that is, by a field in which all possible names can be entered. This field has a defined length and an integrated validation to check for allowed characters.

As of R/3 Release 4.0, customers can reserve development namespaces at SAP. This makes sense for customers who have a central development group that delivers developments to subsidiaries, as well as for companies that commercially develop add-ons for SAP customers. A reserved development namespace helps to prevent naming clashes that may occur when externally developed objects are imported to a given SAP system.

**Note** For more information on development namespaces for customers and partners, see SAP Note 84282.

### Name Ranges

A name range is a subset of a namespace—that is, an interval within a namespace. Each object type in the repository has both an SAP name range and a customer name range. The SAP name range is reserved for objects delivered by SAP. Within the customer name range, customers can create and develop their own objects. The names reserved for customer objects typically start with "Y" or "Z."

**Note** For more information on the customer name range, see SAP Note 16466.

All customer developments must be made in the customer name range or in a customer namespace. This prevents customer developments from being overwritten during an release upgrade. Objects in the SAP name range should not be changed unless to apply corrections of known errors in accordance with SAP Notes if no corresponding SAP Support Package is yet available (see Chapter 15).

**Example of Namespaces and Name Ranges**

Software object names such as program names are assigned to a namespace when preceded by a prefix placed between slashes: `/<prefix>/<object name>`. This makes it possible to have objects with the same name belonging to different namespaces. Consider, for example, the object name `ZABAP`. The "Z" indicates that it belongs to the customer name range. Within the SAP training organization's namespace, there is another ZABAP program, which is distinguished from the customer report by being called `/SAPTRAIN/ZABAP`.

### 7.4.3 Verifying Required Background Jobs

To control the transport process, the transport control program `tp` requires various operating system programs and SAP programs to run in the background. To run these programs in the background, the *transport dispatcher* `RDDIMPDP` must be scheduled as a periodic background job in each respective client. These jobs are named `RDDIMPDP_CLIENT_<nnn>`, where <nnn> specifies the client. These jobs are automatically scheduled for all delivered standard clients or after a client copy for customer-created clients. The background jobs are scheduled *event-periodic*. They start to run as soon as they receive a certain event.

To help avoid transport problems, check whether the `RDDIMPDP` jobs are running:

1. Use Transaction code SM37. Alternatively, from the R/3 initial screen, choose **Tools • CCMS • Jobs • Maintenance**.
2. In the screen **Select Background Jobs**, enter **RDDIMPDP*** in the field **job name**. Enter * in the field **user** and in the field **or start after event**.
3. To display a list of the jobs that match the search criteria, choose **Enter**. The `RDDIMPDP` jobs should appear in the list.

An alternative way of checking whether the `RDDIMPDP` jobs are running is to call `tp` on the operating system level with the following command:

```
tp checkimpdp <SID of the SAP system>
```

If, for any reason, you must schedule `RDDIMPDP` manually, you can do so by running program `RDDNEWPP`. To run this program, log on to the system using the

DDIC user or another user with the same authorizations, call the ABAP Editor in the respective client using Transaction code SE38, or, in the SAP ECC initial screen, in the SAP Easy Access menu, select **Tools • ABAP Workbench • ABAP Editor**. In the field program, enter "RDDNEWPP" and choose **Execute**.

**Note** For more information on the transport dispatcher RDDIMPDP, see also Chapter 14.

### 7.4.4 Verifying Background Work Processes

All systems from which data will be exported and/or imported require at least two background work processes to support the `RDDIMPDP` jobs. When importing changes into an SAP system, the import dispatcher `RDDIMPDP` is triggered by *tp* and occupies one background work process. Depending on the type of objects to be imported, other background jobs need to run and are scheduled by the dispatcher. To guarantee that `RDDIMPDP` can monitor the status of the specific job runs, at least two free background work processes are needed.

## 7.5 Questions

1. The SAP system ID (SID):

   A. Must be unique for each system sharing the same transport directory

   B. Must be unique for each system in the system landscape

   C. Can start with a number

   D. Can consist of any three-character combination

2. Which of the following statements is correct in regard to the transport directory?

   A. There can be only one transport directory in a system landscape.

   B. All SAP systems within a transport group share a common transport directory.

   C. In system landscapes using heterogeneous platforms, it is not possible to have a common transport directory.

   D. Only the production system can contain the transport directory.

3. The transport control program `tp`:

   A. Is stored in subdirectory **bin** of the transport directory

   B. Uses program `R3trans` to access the databases when transporting changes

   C. Cannot be used directly on the operating system level

   D. Depends on the settings of the transport profile

4. The transport profile:

   A. Is stored in subdirectory **bin** of the transport directory

   B. Contains comments and parameter settings that configure the transport control program `tp`

   C. Is managed from within TMS as of R/3 Release 4.5, but is modified with operating system text editors in earlier releases

   D. Contains only settings that are valid for all SAP systems in the system landscape

5. The initialization procedure of the CTO:

   A. Is especially required after a system copy

   B. Establishes the initial value for change request IDs

   C. Is not mandatory for the purpose of enabling transports

   D. Is performed automatically during SAP installation by program `R3setup`

6. Which of the following statements is correct in regard to the settings governing changes to Repository objects?

   A. Only the customer name range should be modifiable in production systems.

   B. Developments are possible in an SAP system only if you have applied for a development namespace.

   C. If the global change option is set to **Not modifiable**, it is nevertheless possible to make changes in certain name spaces or clients that have their change option set to **Modifiable**.

   D. The global change option should always be set to **Not modifiable** for the quality assurance system and the production system.

# 8 Setting Up the TMS

After installing SAP ECC, to enable change requests to be transported in your system landscape, you need to configure the Transport Management System (TMS). This chapter introduces the setup of the TMS and describes how to configure it in the following steps:

- Creating the transport domain
- Configuring transport routes
- Verifying the system landscape setup

This chapter also explains how to change the TMS configuration when adding more SAP systems, changing the role of an SAP system, or upgrading to a new release. Much of the existing transport functionality has changed—especially in the R/3 Releases 4.0 and 4.6. If you upgrade to R/3 Release 4.0 or higher from an R/3 Release that does not have the TMS functionality, read this chapter to learn how to integrate an existing landscape in the TMS.

This chapter is aimed at people looking for general information on the TMS, as well as system administrators and technical consultants responsible for setting up the system landscape. If you are involved in development and Customizing, you will also want to familiarize yourself with TMS concepts and terminology.

This chapter does not outline the TMS functionality for performing transport activities, such as the importing of change requests. If you are responsible for transporting change requests, you should refer to Part 3 of this book.

## 8.1 TMS Terminology and Concepts

The TMS enables system administrators and technical consultants to centrally manage the transport configuration of multiple SAP systems by using a transport domain and defining transport routes. The TMS offers easy-to-use configuration tools to set up a transport domain and to set up and maintain transport routes.

> **Note** Besides enabling global transport maintenance and configuration, the TMS also provides an R/3 user interface for the transport tools at the operating system level. The TMS allows you to view change requests for ABAP that are waiting for import and to perform and monitor the respective imports from within the SAP system (see also Chapter 13).

SAP introduced the TMS in R/3 Release 3.1H, and its use became obligatory for ABAP-based SAP systems as of R/3 Release 4.0. Note that when you employ the

TMS, you can no longer use Transaction SE06, which was formerly used to set up the Workbench Organizer and to configure transport routes. The tables used by Transaction SE06 are no longer used by the TMS.

### 8.1.1 Transport Domain

All SAP systems that you plan to manage centrally using the TMS form a *transport domain*. Within a transport domain, all SAP systems must have unique system IDs, and transport routes and associated settings are identical for all R/3 Systems.

The system landscape is the set of all SAP systems required to take your implementation from the development stages through production. Typically, your system landscape and your transport domain will contain the same SAP systems. However, you can have several system landscapes in one transport domain—centrally administered using the TMS. Figure 8.1 presents the transport domain of a multinational company that consists of two separate three-system landscapes, one for Asia and one for Europe. Both are administered centrally by system PR1.

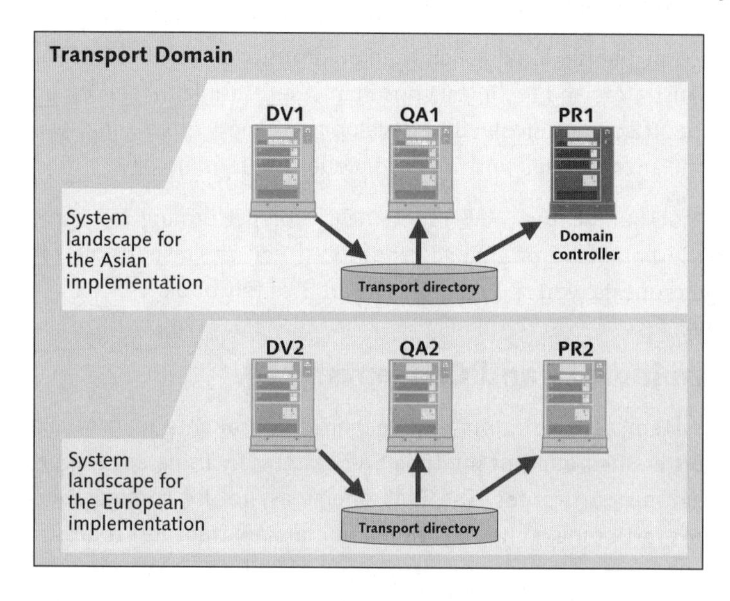


**Figure 8.1** Transport domain including two system landscapes

#### Transport Domain Controller

One of the great benefits of the TMS is the centralized configuration of the entire transport environment. One of the SAP systems in the transport domain holds the reference configuration, and all the other SAP systems hold copies of this reference configuration. The SAP system with the reference configuration is called the *transport domain controller*—for example, system PR1 in Figure 8.1.

From the transport domain controller, you can manage the entire TMS configuration—the configuration of all included SAP systems, their roles, and their interrelationships. The centralized administration of the TMS ensures consistency throughout the transport domain.

Within a transport domain, each SAP system can communicate with all other SAP systems through RFC connections that are generated when the TMS is configured. The transport domain controller, for example, uses RFC connections to distribute configuration changes to all other SAP systems in the transport domain.

### Backup Domain Controller

To manage SAP systems and transport routes, every system landscape requires a transport domain controller. In addition, another SAP system in the transport domain should be designated as the *backup domain controller* (see Figure 8.2). This backup domain controller enables you to perform necessary configuration changes to the transport domain when the transport domain controller is unavailable—for example, when that SAP system is not running. In such cases, the backup domain controller can take over the role of the domain controller, and configuration changes to the transport domain can be made.

However, even if the transport domain controller is unavailable, you can use RFC links to perform transport activities such as viewing import queues and initiating imports from any SAP system in the transport domain. The domain controller is required only for configuration changes to the transport domain.

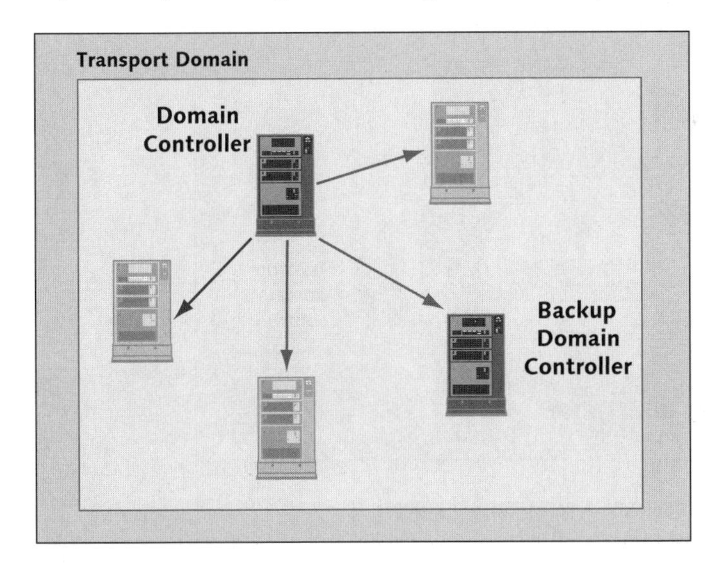


**Figure 8.2** Central administration from the transport domain controller or the backup domain controller

### Transport Groups versus Transport Domains

A transport group is a collection of SAP systems that share the same transport directory (see Chapter 7). A transport group is a technical and physical setup because the involved SAP systems access a common transport directory. Rather than being a physical unit, a transport domain is purely an administrative unit for the TMS.

A transport domain may consist of several transport groups. However, a transport domain typically consists of only one transport group and involves only one common transport directory. Even when multiple transport groups are required (see Chapter 7), all SAP systems in the transport domain are managed centrally, regardless of whether they share the same transport directory.

Figure 8.3 depicts a more complicated transport domain composed of five SAP systems and two different transport groups. The transport domain controller manages the transport configuration of all five SAP systems. The transport routes that determine the flow of change requests are not shown in Figure 8.3. All SAP systems that regularly need to share change requests must be part of the same transport domain (but not necessarily the same transport group). To define transport routes, you first must establish the transport domain and transport groups.

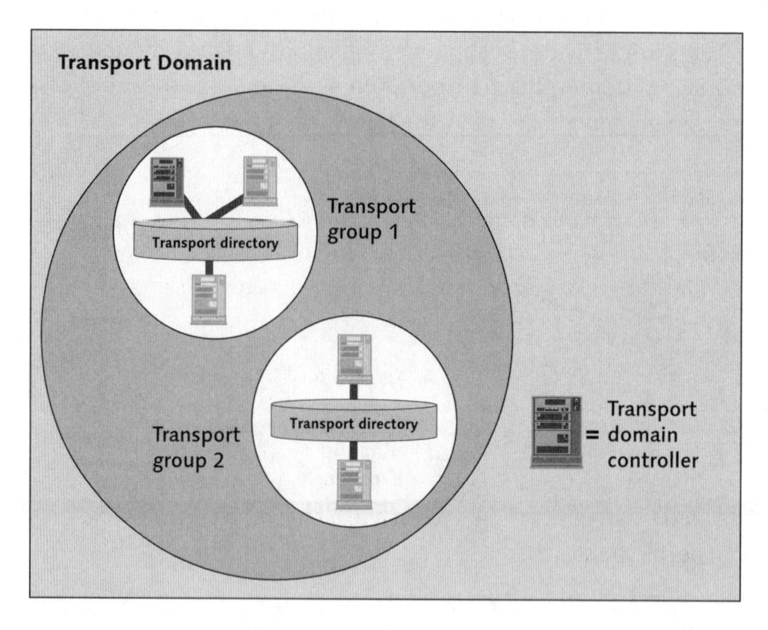


Figure 8.3 A transport domain with two transport groups

### 8.1.2 Transport Routes

The terms *transport domain*, *domain controller*, and *transport group* concern only the physical environment. They do not include the transport relationship between the SAP systems, which is defined by the transport routes. Transport routes are used to indicate the role of each system and the flow of change requests. SAP distinguishes two types of transport routes:

- Consolidation route
- Delivery route

#### Consolidation Route

A consolidation route defines the path (the successive SAP systems or clients) that is followed by change requests immediately after release. The consolidation route is used to accumulate the customer changes that have been integrated with the standard software. Typically, the consolidation route proceeds from the development system to the quality assurance system in a standard three-system landscape, or from the development system to the production system in a two-system landscape.

All SAP systems from which change requests are released and exported require a consolidation route. Such a source system in a consolidation route is known as the *integration system* because it provides the point at which changes are integrated into the SAP system. At the time of export, a change request is added to the import queue of the target SAP system defined by the consolidation route. The target system assumes the role of *consolidation system*.

Consolidation routes are closely associated with *packages* and *transport layers*. Packages are used to group repository objects that are logically related, and act as containers to organize development work. All objects that belong to a package are developed, maintained, and transported together.

A package can be assigned to a transport layer. Each transport layer can be assigned to one consolidation route. The transport layer determines which consolidation route is valid for all objects of a package. Packages and transport layers enable you to specify a consolidation route for each repository object. A consolidation route is defined by an integration system and a consolidation system and is associated with a specific transport layer.

**Note** For information on using packages and transport layers, see Chapter 10.

Because all Customizing changes must follow the same consolidation route, a *standard transport layer* is specified for each integration system. The standard transport layer is used for the transport of changes that have no concept of a transport layer, unlike Repository objects that belong to a package. Assigning a standard transport layer to a consolidation route enables all Customizing changes made in the development system to be transported to the quality assurance system. A standard transport layer is a system attribute of integration systems.

**Note** As of R/3 Release 4.5, transport routes can include not just R/3 Systems but also R/3 clients. Client-dependent changes do not always need to be transported using the standard transport layer, but can be transported using a client-specific transport route (see below, under "Extended Transport Control"), if the respective transport layer has been assigned to the client.

For each integration system, at least two transport layers are defined: the standard transport layer and the SAP transport layer (see below). There may also be several other transport layers. Each transport layer may have several development classes assigned to it. Although an integration system can be the source system for several consolidation routes, each consolidation route has exactly one transport layer assigned to it.

The transport layer *SAP* is the predefined transport layer for the packages of all SAP standard objects. To modify standard objects in the R/3 System and then transport them along the same routes as development and Customizing changes, a consolidation route is assigned to the SAP transport layer. When setting up transport routes using the standard transport route configuration options, the consolidation route is generated automatically (see below, under "Standard Configurations").

### Delivery Route

Delivery routes are used to transport changes from the consolidation system to further SAP systems. Delivery routes are required only in a system landscape that consists of more than two SAP systems. In the standard three-system landscape, for example, a delivery route is specified between the quality assurance system and the production system. This enables changes to be transported to the production system after they have been tested and verified in the quality assurance system.

After change requests have been imported to the quality assurance system, a defined delivery route causes the change requests to be added to the import queue of the next SAP system in the system landscape, the production system.

While consolidation routes dictate which SAP system receives the change request at export, a delivery route determines which SAP system receives the change request after successful import. The definition of a delivery route specifies a source system and a target system.

## 8.2 Setting Up the Transport Domain

To set up a transport domain, first determine which systems should be included in the transport domain. The transport domain should contain all systems in your system landscape and any other SAP systems that will be administered centrally using the TMS. One of these systems must be designated as the transport domain controller. You may later switch the role of domain controller to a different system, but during the implementation process, the first SAP system for which the TMS is initialized is automatically designated as the transport domain controller.

**Tip** To set up the transport domain, you require the authorization profile S_A.SYSTEM.

Figure 8.4 shows the components of a standard configuration. The transport domain includes system DEV as the development system, system QAS as the quality assurance system, and system PRD as the production system. DEV is designated as the transport domain controller. All systems use a common transport directory and thus form a single transport group.

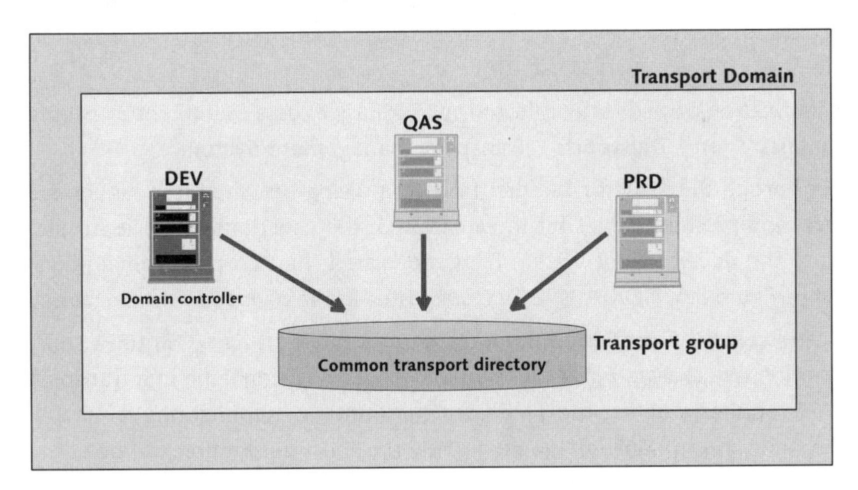


**Figure 8.4** Example of a transport domain

### 8.2.1 Setting Up the Domain Controller

Within a transport domain, the transport domain configuration—that is, the included systems, their roles, and the configured transport routes—is identical for all systems. The transport domain controller stores the reference domain configuration. All other systems in the transport domain have copies of the reference configuration. The advantage of the centralized administration of the transport domain is that it ensures consistency.

The development system is often initially designated as the transport domain controller, because the TMS must be set up to store the released development and Customizing requests in the import queues of the other systems that have not yet been installed.

Because the transport domain controller must provide high levels of system availability, security precautions, and maintenance, it is often subsequently moved to the production system or the quality assurance system. The system load generated by TMS configuration activities on a domain controller is quite low. The system load increases only briefly when the TMS configuration is changed.

#### Initializing the TMS

When using the TMS for the first time after system installation, you are automatically prompted to initialize the TMS. To initialize the TMS for an SAP system, proceed as follows:

1. Log on to the SAP system that you have designated as the transport domain controller in client 000 with a user ID that possesses transport authorization profile S_A.SYSTEM, such as user SAP*.
2. Use Transaction code STMS or, from the SAP Easy Access Menu, choose **Tools • Administration • Transports • Transport Management System**.
3. When starting the TMS for the first time, the dialog box shown in Figure 8.5 appears and prompts values for the creation of the new domain. For example, because the development system DEV is declared the transport domain controller in Figure 8.5, DOMAIN_DEV is suggested as the transport domain name.
4. You can accept the prompted name or enter a different name. Enter a short description and choose **Enter**. Subsequently changing the name of a transport domain requires deleting the TMS configuration and reconfiguring it—for all SAP systems in the transport domain. Only the short description can be easily changed at any time.

**Note** The first system of a transport group from which the TMS is called is automatically designated as the transport domain controller.

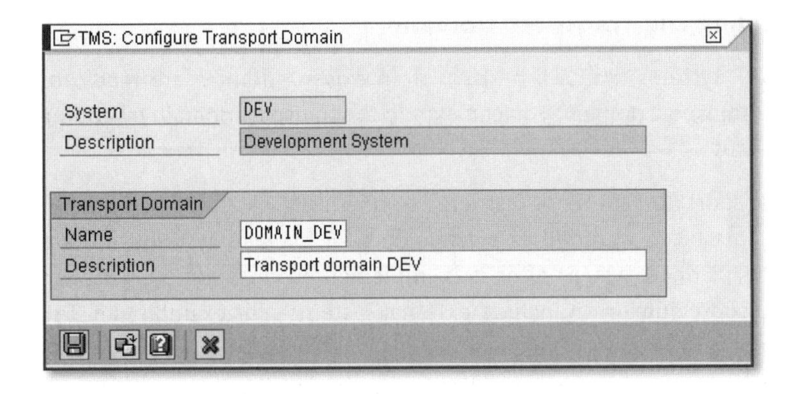


**Figure 8.5** Dialog box that appears when you first use the TMS in a transport domain

Initializing the TMS has several effects on an SAP system (see below, under "Technical Aspects of the Configuration Process"). During initialization, the basic settings of the TMS configuration are stored in file `DOMAIN.CFG` in subdirectory `bin` of the transport directory on the transport domain controller. These settings include the transport domain name, the transport domain description, and the system IDs (SIDs) of all SAP systems in the transport domain. After you install an additional SAP system that shares the same transport directory as the domain controller, the new SAP system reads the already established configuration out of file `DOMAIN.CFG` and automatically recognizes to which domain the new system belongs.

After initializing the TMS, the TMS initial screen indicates which transport domain contains the transport domain controller. Assuming your system landscape consists of only one SAP system at this point, if you now choose **Overview · Systems** from the initial TMS screen, you will see that the transport domain controller is currently the only system belonging to the transport domain.

To obtain detailed information on an SAP system:

1. From the TMS initial screen, choose **Systems**.
2. Select an system and choose **Enter**.
3. The screen **Display the TMS Configuration: System <SID>** appears, providing you with details on the selected system. For example, under the tab **Communication data**, you can see that the system is not only assigned to the transport domain, but also to a transport group with the default name `GROUP.<domain controller SID>`. The screen also shows the generated address information used for communication between the different SAP systems in the transport domain (see below, under "Technical Aspects of the Configuration Process").

### 8.2.2 Extending the Transport Domain

When other SAP systems that will be part of an existing domain are ready for inclusion in the transport domain, you can extend the transport domain by adding these SAP systems.

Extending a transport domain is not restricted to physically installed SAP systems. Virtual systems are often included as placeholders for planned systems and are replaced by the planned system after it is implemented. In addition, you can extend the transport domain to include external systems—for example, an SAP system from another transport domain.

#### New SAP Systems

To add new systems to a transport domain, you must perform configuration activities on both the new SAP system and the transport domain controller. Once you add systems to a transport domain, you should designate one SAP system as the backup domain controller.

To add a new SAP system to a transport domain from within the same transport group, you must perform the TMS initialization process on the new system. Proceed as follows:

1. Log on to the new SAP system in client 000 with a user that has complete transport authorization, such as user SAP*.
2. To access the TMS, use Transaction code STMS or, from the SAP Easy Access Menu, choose **Tools · Administration · Transports · Transport Management System**.
3. If the new system uses the same transport directory as the transport domain controller, the new system will read file `DOMAIN.CFG` in subdirectory `bin` of the transport directory and thus recognize the existence of a transport domain. When you're initializing the TMS on a new SAP system, the dialog box shown in Figure 8.6 appears. The example in Figure 8.6 shows the quality assurance system QAS, which shares a transport directory with system DEV. Choose **Save**.

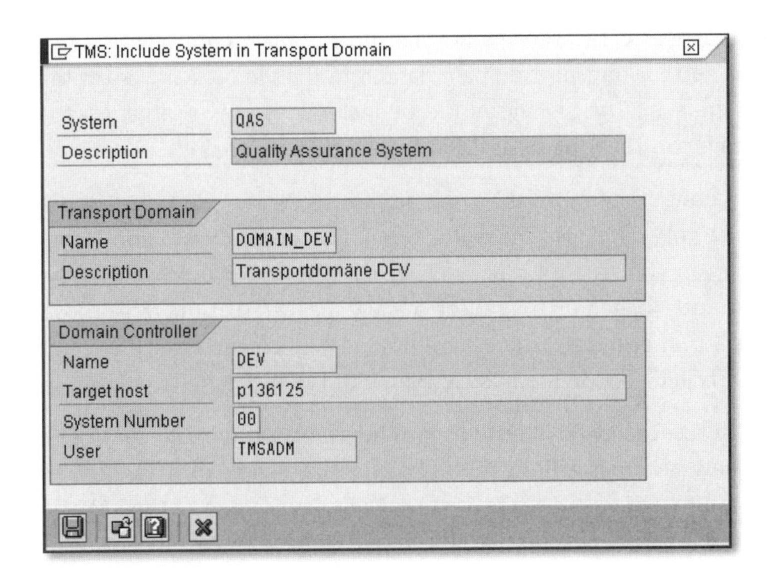


**Figure 8.6** Including an SAP System in an existing transport domain

If the new SAP system is the first system in a new transport group, and therefore does not share a transport directory with another SAP system that is already part of the transport domain, the new SAP system cannot recognize the transport domain in which it should be included. In this case, the TMS automatically tries to configure a new transport domain (see Figure 8.5 earlier in the chapter).

To add an SAP system to an existing domain from a different transport group, you must proceed as follows:

1. Log on to the new SAP system in client 000 using user identification with full transport authority.
2. Access the TMS using transaction code STMS or by selecting **Tools · Administration · Transports · Transport Management System** in the SAP Easy Access menu.
3. Since the new system has not been connected to the TMS yet, a dialog box is displayed for admission to the detected domain. As this is not what we want here, you must open the **TMS configuration** dialog box via the **Other configuration icon** and select **Include system in domain**. If the first dialog box is not displayed automatically, it can also be opened using **System overview**.
4. Specify the transport domain controller of the transport domain in which the system is to be included. Enter the **Target host** and the **System number** of the transport domain controller.

5. Choose **Save**. Using RFC technology, the transport domain controller is automatically contacted for transport domain data from the file DOMAIN.CFG at the operating system level. The SAP system to be included is now waiting for the transport domain controller to accept it in the transport domain.

If the SAP system consists of more than one application server, you can choose one server as the target host. From the dialog box **TMS: Include System in Transport domain**, you can choose to list all possible servers. In R/3 Release 4.0, the server you are currently logged on to is automatically suggested as the target host. As of R/3 Release 4.5, the central instance is automatically suggested as the target host. Ideally, you should choose the host system with the highest availability.

You must explicitly accept new SAP systems into the transport domain controller. Prior to this, the new system is waiting for inclusion into the transport domain. As long as a system waits for inclusion, the **System Overview** screen of the TMS on this SAP system displays only this system and the transport domain.

To accept an SAP system that is waiting for inclusion, proceed as follows:

1. In the SAP system that is the transport domain controller, from the initial TMS screen, choose **Overview · Systems**. The **System Overview** screen appears. Position the cursor on the SAP system that is waiting for inclusion and choose **SAP system · Accept**. The dialog box **Accept system** appears.
2. When asked to include the new system, click on **Yes**. Please note that on accepting this dialog, the TMS configuration is changed. Such a change must always be distributed to all other systems in the transport domain. The **Distribute the TMS configuration** dialog box appears and asks if you want to distribute the new configuration immediately.
   - If you choose **Yes**, the configuration is distributed immediately, and the TMS status of the new SAP system is set to **active**.
   - If you decide to distribute this configuration later, you must distribute it explicitly. As long as the new configuration is not distributed, the TMS status of the new SAP system remains **obsolete**. To distribute the new configuration explicitly and change the TMS status of the new system to **accepted**, from the **System Overview** screen in the domain controller, choose **Extras · Distribute and activate configuration**.

Whenever you change the TMS configuration, the dialog box **Distribute the TMS Configuration** appears by default to ask if you require immediate distribution. To change this default, from the initial TMS screen, choose **Extras · Settings · System overview** (or, from the **System Overview** screen, choose **Extras · Personal**

**Settings**). You can change the default to either automatic distribution after a change or no automatic distribution. These options are shown in Figure 8.7.

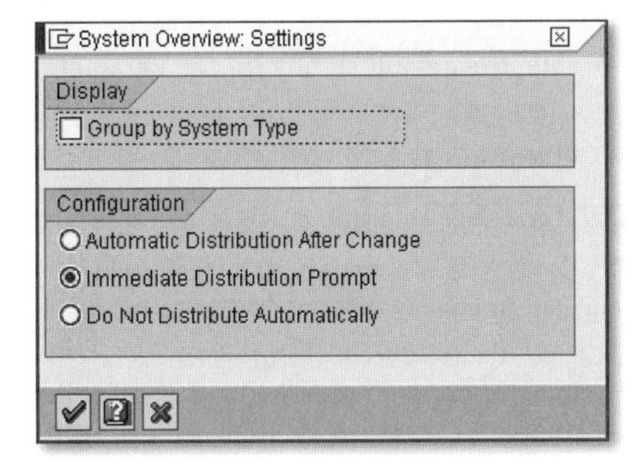


**Figure 8.7** Settings for the distribution process

## Virtual Systems

The TMS allows you to create—that is, enter in the list of SAP systems known to the TMS—SAP systems that are planned but not yet physically installed. These systems are referred to as *virtual systems*.

> **Note** To enable a virtual system to be replaced by an installed SAP system, the virtual SAP system must have the same SID as the subsequently installed SAP system.

By creating virtual systems, you can model the transport routes of the planned system landscape and ensure that the import queues of subsequent systems already exist. In the initial life of an SAP implementation, customers frequently have only the development system physically installed, and store the development and Customizing work in the import queues of the respective planned systems.

To create a virtual system, proceed as follows:

1. Log on to the transport domain controller, with a user ID that has complete transport authorization.
2. From the initial TMS screen, choose **Overview · Systems**. The **System Overview** screen appears. Choose **SAP System · Create · Virtual System**.
3. In the dialog box **TMS: Configure Virtual System**, enter the name of the SAP system and a description text. You also must specify an SAP system as the **Communications system** for the virtual system. The communications system must

be a system that is already part of the transport domain. It cannot be a virtual system or an external system. Choose **Save**.

4. Distribute the configuration change.
5. As of Release 4.5, in the transport profile, the default setting for the parameter `dummy`, which is the correct setting for this system, is `1`. In R/3 Release 4.0, you must add `<sid>/dummy = 1` to the transport profile manually.

Because no RFC address can be created for virtual systems, RFCs are accessed using the transport directory of an already existing SAP system. This system acts as the **communications system**. A virtual system always belongs to the same transport group as the associated communications system. In the dialog box **TMS: Configure Virtual System**, the communications system proposed by default is the transport domain controller.

You can replace a virtual system when the corresponding planned system is realized—that is, it is either physically installed or has been upgraded to an release with TMS functionality. This realized system is what is meant when referring to the *real* SAP system in this context. On the transport domain controller, proceed as follows:

1. Delete the virtual system from the transport domain:
   - From the initial TMS screen, choose **Overview · Systems**. The **System Overview** screen appears. Position the cursor on the virtual system you want to delete.
   - Choose **SAP System · Delete**. Confirm.
   - Distribute the configuration change.

   As soon as the configuration change is distributed, the virtual system is deleted. The import queue for this system in TMS disappears. However, the import buffer at the operating system level remains unchanged.
2. Add the real SAP system to the transport domain:
   - Initialize the TMS on the real SAP system and request the inclusion of that system in the transport domain.
   - On the transport domain controller, accept the system.

   The existing import buffer at the operating system level is assigned to the real system. No change requests will be lost.
3. Distribute the configuration change.

**Tip** After replacing a virtual system with the installed SAP system, ensure the consistency of transport routes between all SAP systems in the transport domain.

### External Systems

You can also add external systems to the transport domain that are not physically part of it. Like virtual systems, they are accessed using a communications system—a real SAP system already included in the transport domain. Unlike virtual systems, external systems have their own transport directory. This transport directory, which must be explicitly defined, resides on a disk partition, is accessed by an SAP system in another transport domain, or resides on an exchangeable data medium such as a CD-ROM. External systems are used for the following reasons:

- To write transport requests to exchangeable data media
- To read transport requests from exchangeable data media
- To provide an intermediate directory to enable you to send transports to other transport domains (see Chapter 13)

To add an external system, proceed as follows:

1. From the TMS initial screen, choose **Systems • Create • External System**. The dialog box **TMS: Configure External System** (shown in Figure 8.8) is displayed.
2. Enter the path to the transport directory of the external system, relative to the communications system (this is the path used by the communications system). The communications system proposed by default is the transport domain controller. In the example in Figure 8.8, the external system is DE2 (the development system of DOMAIN_DE2), and system DEV from DOMAIN_DEV is the communications system enabling transports between the two domains.

As of Release 4.5, the default setting in the transport profile for the parameter `dummy`, which is the correct setting for this system, is `TRUE`. In SAP Release 4.0, you must add `<sid>/dummy = TRUE` to the transport profile manually. Also note that you must create the subdirectories of the external transport directory, which are not created automatically in the specified transport directory.

Unlike virtual systems, external systems do not belong to an existing transport group in the transport domain, but are assigned to a new transport domain whose default name is `EXTGRP_<transport domain controller SID>`.

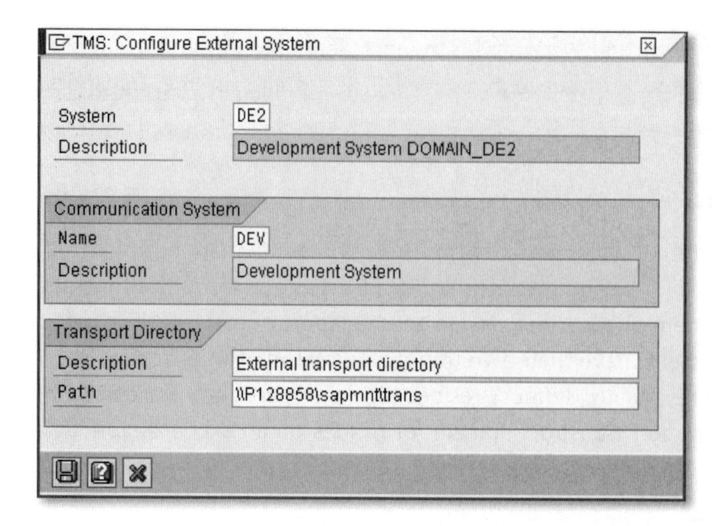


Figure 8.8 Adding an external SAP system to the transport domain

### Changes to the Transport Domain

Changes to the TMS configuration correspond to changes to the transport domain—for example, when you:

- Move an SAP system to another host
- Delete an SAP system from the transport domain
- Cause an SAP system to use another transport directory
- Change the transport profile settings

Such changes to the configuration of the transport domain can be performed only on the transport domain controller and must be immediately or subsequently distributed to the other SAP systems in the transport domain. If you decide to distribute a configuration change later, you must do so explicitly, using the following procedure:

1. From the initial TMS screen, choose **Overview • Systems**. The **System Overview** screen appears. Choose **Extras • Distribute the TMS configuration and activate**.
2. In the resulting dialog box, choose **Yes**.

### 8.2.3 Backup Domain Controller

The transport domain controller is the source system for all configuration data. It is important to designate another SAP system as the backup domain controller, because this gives you a way of performing configuration changes when the transport domain controller is not available. Once an SAP system has been defined as the backup domain controller, you can activate that system as the transport domain controller.

**Note** The system selected as the backup domain controller must be an existing SAP system that is part of the transport domain. It cannot be a virtual or an external SAP system.

#### Defining a Backup Domain Controller

To define an SAP system in the transport domain as the backup domain controller, proceed as follows:

1. Log on to the SAP system that is the transport domain controller. From the initial TMS screen, choose **Overview · Systems**. The **System Overview** screen appears.
2. Position the cursor on a system that is neither a virtual nor an external system and select **SAP System · Change**. The screen **Change TMS Configuration** is displayed.
3. In the field **Backup** (located as of R/3 Release 4.5 in the tab **Communication data**), choose the SID of the SAP system you want to designate as the backup domain controller.
4. Choose **Save**. Distribute the configuration change either immediately or subsequently.

Figure 8.9 shows the screen **Change TMS Configuration** for SAP ECC 5.00. In this screen, the system PRD has been entered as backup domain controller.

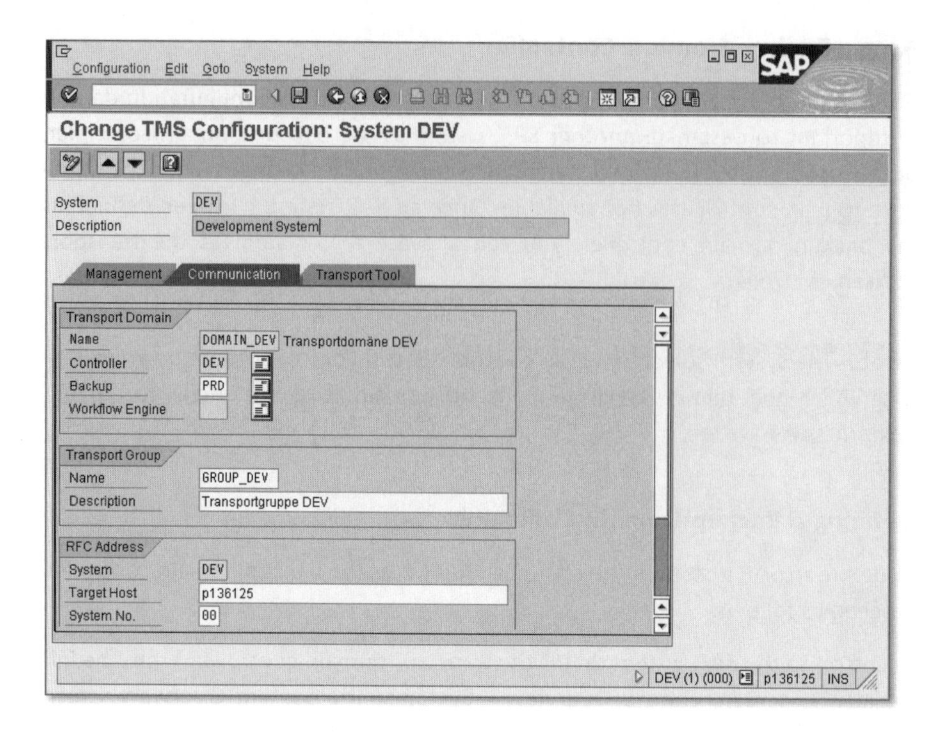


Figure 8.9 Designating a backup domain controller in SAP ECC Release 5.00

### Activating a Backup Domain Controller

To use a backup domain controller to change transport domain configurations, you must activate it as the domain controller. To do this, proceed as follows:

1. Log on to the backup domain controller with a user ID that has complete transport authorizations.
2. From the initial TMS screen, choose **Overview • Systems**. The **System Overview** screen appears.
3. Choose **Extras • Activate backup controller**.

If the SAP system that was previously the domain controller is available, it is automatically designated as the new backup domain controller.

## 8.2.4 Verifying the Transport Domain

You can view a variety of information about the SAP systems in the transport domain on the **System Overview** screen (from the initial TMS screen, choose **Overview • Systems**). For an explanation of the symbols used, choose **Extras • Legend**. The icons beside the SIDs indicate the roles of the respective SAP Systems. These icons and their descriptions are listed in Figure 8.10.

| System | Description |
|---|---|
| | Domain Controller<br>Backup Domain Controller<br>Virtual system<br>External system<br>Other Domain Controller |

Figure 8.10 The key to the icons for system roles in the System Overview screen

### System Status

The icons in the column **Status** of the **System Overview** screen indicate the status of each SAP system (see Figure 8.11).

| Status | Description |
|---|---|
| | System is active<br>System locked<br>System deleted<br>System waiting for inclusion in domain<br>System was not included in domain<br>Communication system is locked<br>Communication system deleted<br>Domain link request made<br>Waiting for domain link |
| | TMS configuration is current<br>TMS configuration must be adjusted<br>RFC destinations were not generated<br>Backup controller not completely activated<br>Status of other system cannot be displayed<br>New configuration from other domain |

Figure 8.11 The key to the icons for system status in the System Overview screen

The various system statuses indicated in the **System Overview** screen can be explained in more detail as follows:

- **System is active**:
  This status means that the TMS has been initialized on this system, and that the system has been successfully included in the transport domain. A system must have this status to be integrated into the transport route configuration and included in the transport flow.
- **System is locked**:
  From the domain controller, you can **lock** an SAP system, thus preventing any TMS activity within the domain from accessing this system. You can do this, for example, to perform hardware maintenance. The TMS transport functionality is deactivated for a system with this status. To lock a system, position the cursor on the SAP system in the **TMS System Overview** screen and choose **SAP Sys-**

**tem · Lock**. To unlock this system, position the cursor on the locked SAP system and choose **SAP System · Unlock**.

- **System was deleted**:
  This status indicates that the system has been deleted from the TMS domain configuration and that no transports via TMS can be performed anymore for this SAP system. Note that the import buffer file of a deleted system is not deleted. Accessing the TMS on a system with this status displays a dialog box requesting the renewed inclusion of the system.
- **System is waiting for inclusion in domain**:
  This status indicates that the TMS has been initialized on the R/3 System, and that this system has not yet been accepted into the domain by the transport domain controller. Therefore, activities in the TMS are possible only after it has been admitted to the domain.
- **System was not included in domain**:
  This status indicates you rejected (rather than accepted) the system in the TMS on the transport domain controller. To reject an SAP system waiting for inclusion (that is, to exclude it from the transport domain), from the **System Overview** screen, choose **SAP System · Delete**. The SAP system disappears from the **TMS System Overview** screen as soon as the deletion has been distributed to all SAP systems in the transport domain.
- **Communications system is locked**:
  This status means the system is a virtual system and that the associated communications system has been manually locked, thus blocking access by the TMS of any other system in the transport domain. But, if you restart Transaction STMS on this SAP system, you can request acceptance into the transport domain again.
- **Communications system deleted**:
  This status means the system is a virtual system and the associated communications system has been deleted in the TMS on the domain controller.
- **Domain Link Request made**:
  This status indicates that you requested the connection of this domain with another domain at the foreign domain controller. For the SAP systems of this domain to communicate with the systems of the other domain, you must confirm the link between the domains with the foreign domain controller.
- **Waiting for Domain Link**:
  This status indicates that a foreign domain controller has requested the connection between this domain and the foreign domain. If you confirm the connection between the domains, all SAP systems in both domains can communicate with each other. You can then, for example, carry out transports between systems from different domains.

### Distribution Status

The icons in the column **Status** on the **System Overview** screen indicates whether the distributed configuration data for the transport domain, as recorded locally on the respective system, is up to date. The options are as follows:

- **TMS Configuration is current**
  This means that the configuration data in the system is up to date, that is, the configuration recorded in the system is identical to the reference configuration on the domain controller.
- **TMS Configuration must be adjusted**
  This means that the configuration data recorded in the TMS of an SAP system is obsolete, that is, it differs from the reference configuration stored on the domain controller. This may be the case if the TMS configuration has been changed on the transport domain controller but has not yet been distributed, or if the specific system was not available when configuration changes were distributed. If the status of a system is obsolete, you must distribute the transport domain configuration from the domain controller.
- **RFC destinations were not generated**
  This means that errors occurred while the RFC destinations were generated during the TMS initialization. If a system shows this status, use the Alert Monitor (see below) to identify and eliminate the error. Then, redistribute the TMS configuration, or from the TMS system overview, select **Extras · Generate RFC Destinations** to recreate the RFC destinations.
- **Backup Controller not completely activated**
  This means that errors occurred when the backup domain controller was being activated as the domain controller. Use the Alert Monitor (see below) to identify and eliminate this error. Then, restart the activation process.
- **Status of other system cannot be displayed**
  You cannot display the status of the TMS configuration for systems of a foreign domain, except for the domain controller.
- **New configuration from other domain**
  This means that the TMS configuration of the foreign domain has been changed. You can now distribute this configuration change to the systems in the local domain. This happens implicitly when you distribute a change of the local configuration. You can also distribute the changes explicitly (see the section on distributing a transport domain configuration).

If the TMS configuration has not yet been distributed to all SAP systems in the transport domain, a warning is displayed on the TMS initial screen in the SAP system that is the transport domain controller.

### 8.2.5 Technical Aspects of the Configuration Process

Whenever you initialize the TMS on an SAP system, several steps are automatically performed on that system:

- In client 000, CPIC user TMSADM is created.
- The RFC destinations required for the TMS connections are generated.

If the system you are initializing is the domain controller, the following additional steps are automatically performed:

- Certain basic settings for the TMS domain configuration are stored in the file `DOMAIN.CFG` in subdirectory `bin` of the transport directory. These settings include, for example, the transport domain's name and description, as well as the transport domain controller's host name, instance number, SID, and transport group.
- As of R/3 Release 4.5, the transport profile for the transport control program *tp* is generated (see Chapter 7).

**Note** In R/3 Release 4.0, you must manually add the required entries for the R/3 system to the transport profile `TPPARAM` using an operating system editor (see Chapter 7).

If the system you are initializing is not the domain controller, the following additional steps are automatically performed:

- The address data of the system is sent to the transport domain controller, as part of the request for membership in the transport domain.
- As of R/3 Release 4.5, the profile parameter for configuring the transport control program `tp` is sent to the transport domain. If there are several transport groups in the transport domain, transport profiles are generated in the transport directory of every group.

**Note** In R/3 Release 4.0, if you have several transport groups in the transport domain, you must adapt the transport profiles TPPARAM so that they are identical in all transport directories. Only the transport profile parameter `transdir` may differ from one transport group to another (see also Chapter 7).

#### RFC Connections

RFC connections are used for communication between the SAP systems in a transport domain. When you're initializing the TMS on an SAP system, RFC destinations are generated to enable access between all involved SAP systems. There are two distinct types of access. One type is for *read* access and any *write* access that is not critical to security—for example, distributing the TMS configuration after a virtual system has been added from the domain controller to all SAP systems in the transport domain. The other type is any *write* access that is critical to security—for example, starting an import. This section explains the underlying techniques of the RFC connections used by the TMS.

### Read Access and Noncritical Write Access

To set up the RFC destinations, user TMSADM of user type CPIC is generated in client 000 during TMS initialization. By default, TMSADM authorizations are limited to *read* and *write* authorization in the common transport directory, RFC authorization in the TMS, and display authorization in the CTS. This user is required for displaying import queues and for distributing the basic TMS configuration settings from the transport domain controller to all systems in the transport domain. For all SAP systems, to enable accesses that are not critical to security, the RFC connection `TMSADM@<SID>.<domainname>` is generated. Figure 8.12 shows the RFC destinations that are generated during TMS initialization.

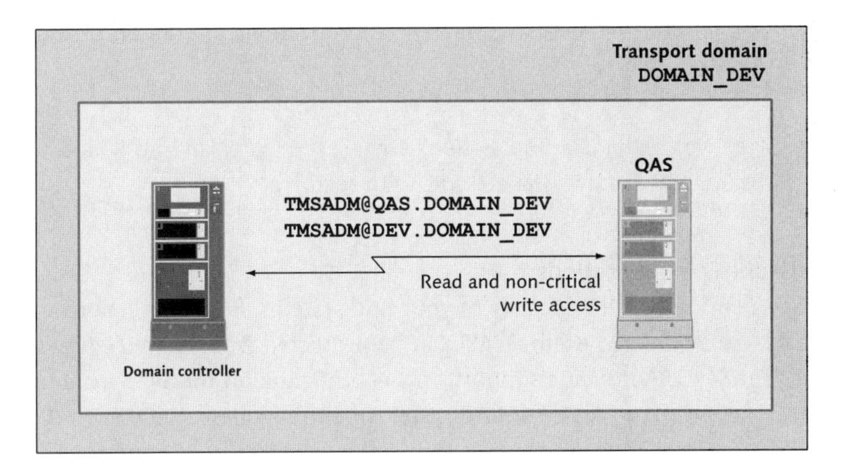


**Figure 8.12** RFC connections required for TMS read access and limited write access

### Critical Write Access

Since *write* accesses can cause changes in the target system—for example, changes to the import queue—the authorizations of user TMSADM are not sufficient to enable write accesses for certain activities. To execute a function that will result in a critical change in the target system—for example, starting an import into an SAP system or changing transport routes—you must log on to this target system and possess sufficient authorization in the target system. The username and password for this RFC link should not be stored in the source system. This security concept has been implemented differently for R/3 Release 4.0 and subsequent releases.

In R/3 Release 4.0, for each target system, a further RFC connection is generated with the address `TMSSUP@<SID>.<domainname>`. No username or password is automatically associated with this destination. Whenever you use this connection, you must log on to the target system. As of R/3 Release 4.5, the destination for critical accesses is calculated at runtime based on the address information stored in the TMS configuration. This concept avoids creating destinations for all targets, which may be very numerous as of R/3 Release 4.5 due to the new functionality for creating client-specific transport routes.

The realization of RFC connections technically differs somewhat between R/3 Release 4.0 and R/3 Release 4.5, but in both releases, the `TMSADM` connection is initially used for all accesses. If the authorizations of `TMSADM` do not suffice, a logon screen is automatically triggered for the target system, and a user with the proper authorizations must log on. If this procedure is too time-consuming—for example, if there is a large number of SAP systems—you may provide user `TMSADM` with the required authorizations through profile `S_A.TMSCFG`. If an SAP system is accessed where the user `TMSADM` has sufficient authorizations, the logon procedure is suppressed.

**Warning** When you extend authorizations for user `TMSADM`, an anonymous user can make system changes that are critical to security.

**Secure Network Communications**

For increased demands on the security of your SAP systems, RFC connections of the Transport Management System (TMS) can be protected with *Secure Network Communication (SNC)*. Automatic support of the configuration for SNC-secured TMS connections is not available for SAP systems before Release 4.6D. For ERP systems, this means that SNC can be used only in this way with R/3 Enterprise 4.7 and ECC 5.00. Additionally, connections producing a logon screen cannot be secured using SNC for technical reasons.

Detailed information about SNC can be found in the SAP Service Marketplace under *http://service.sap.com/SECURITY – Security in Detail – Secure System Management*.

If you're using SNC for RFC connections between SAP systems, you must be aware of the following restrictions:

- The transport workflow cannot trigger any imports to these systems.
- The synchronization of import queues for these systems is possible only via a direct logon.
- For importing transports, you need to log on to these systems directly.

At first, the SAP systems of the transport domain should be set according to the SNC manual so that the systems involved can communicate via SNC-secured RFC connections. You don't need to carry out the reconfiguration of the entire system landscape at once; you can do it step by step.

Note that you should not prevent the insecure RFC access to the systems until all systems of the TMS domain have been reconfigured to SNC. Also consider the aforementioned restrictions in the TMS if you activate the RFC communication over SNC, as obligatory for SAP systems.

As soon as the SNC communication works, adapt the TMS settings as follows:

1. Log on to the SAP system acting as domain controller.
2. Call Transaction STMS.
3. Select **Overview • Systems**. The system overview is displayed.
4. Select **GoTo • Transport Domain**. The **TMS configuration** screen is displayed: **Domain <Domain>**.
5. Select the **Management** tab.
6. Switch to change mode.
7. Under **Security Options**, mark the **SNC Protection** option as **active**.
8. Save your changes and distribute the configuration.

To use SNC, it is necessary for the TMS domain controller to receive SNC-specific information about the systems it maintains. Determine this information via Copy SNC Information, apply it, and distribute it. The RFC connections between the systems of the current transport domain are secured using SNC. If a domain link exists, the communication with foreign systems also occurs via SNC-secured connections.

**TMS Trusted Services**

Apart from using RFC connections for communicating and synchronizing between systems, when working with the Transport Management System (TMS), it is also necessary to log on to all systems that you want to change—for example, by activating transport routes or performing imports—with your user name and your password. This can be inconvenient, particularly in larger system landscapes. With

TMS Trusted Services, you can set your transport domain so that these logon procedures are omitted if you have the corresponding authorization on the target system. TMS Trusted Services are available as of Release R/3 4.6C.

**Note** Note that TMS Trusted Services apply to the systems of only one domain.

Before implementing TMS Trusted Services, you should check whether they comply with your security concept. You should only implement TMS Trusted Services if the same security measures apply to all of your systems, because the most *insecure* system of the transport domain defines the security of all systems in the transport domain.

**Note** Activate TMS Trusted Services only if the user names are unique to all systems and clients of your transport domain.

For later evaluation, however, the TMS records for all actions which user started the action from which system. This information can then be analyzed in the Alert Viewer of the TMS.

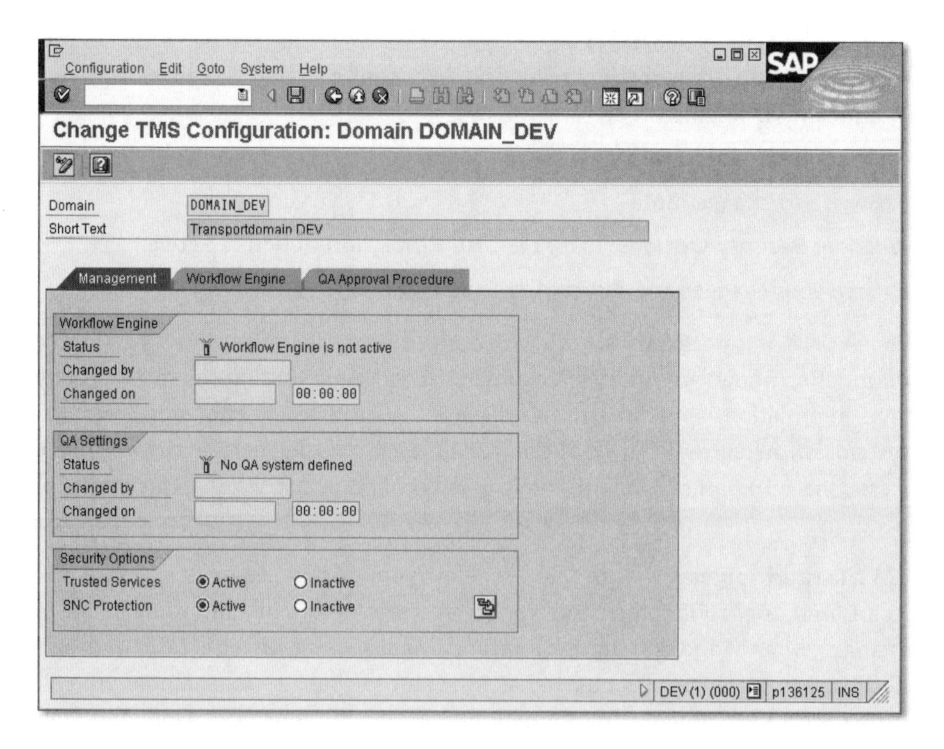


**Figure 8.13** Extending the Security Options in the TMS with Trusted Services and SNC

The TMS Trusted Services are configured as follows:

1. Log on to the SAP system acting as transport domain controller.
2. Call Transaction STMS.
3. Select **Overview • Systems**. The system overview is displayed.
4. Select **GoTo • Transport Domain**. The **TMS configuration** screen is displayed: **Domain <Domain>**.
5. Select the **Management** tab.
6. Switch to change mode.
7. Under **Security Options**, mark the **Trusted Services** option as **Active**.
8. Save your changes and distribute the configuration.

TMS Trusted Services is active for the entire transport domain. From then on, the authorization check on the target system is carried out for the user of the source system. Only if that user does not possess a sufficient authorization on client 000 of the target system, for example, for importing a request, the target system sends a logon screen.

**Example: Usage of TMS Trusted Services**

User MILLER is logged on to client 010 on the SAP system DEV and works with the TMS on that system. He wants to import a transport request into the SAP system PRD. Because he is registered on the PRD system on client 000 as a user with all authorizations in CTS, he can perform the import action without having to enter his username and password on the SAP system PRD.

## 8.3 Configuring Transport Routes

Initializing the TMS and setting up the transport domain define the physical environment only in terms of the transport domain, the domain controller, and the transport group. Next, you must define the transport relationship between each of the SAP systems. Although the TMS has been initialized, you cannot perform transports until the transport routes have been configured and distributed.

Transport routes indicate the role of each system and the flow of change requests. The transport routes are what actually define your system landscape. The prerequisites for configuring transport routes are setting up the transport domain, including all involved systems, and configuring the transport control program *tp*. Configuring a transport route involves:

- Consolidation routes
- Delivery routes
- Target groups (only as of R/3 Release 4.5)

### 8.3.1 Procedure

To ensure consistency, transport routes can be configured only on the transport domain controller. To help define a transport route, the TMS provides a graphical editor and a hierarchical list editor, which can be used interchangeably. After you define a transport route, you must distribute it to all SAP systems in the transport domain and activate it.

SAP recommends creating transport routes as follows:

1. Use one of the standard installation options in the TMS editors. You can choose from a single-system, a two-system, or a three-system landscape. If your system landscape extends beyond a three-system landscape, begin with a three-system landscape and extend the setup using one of the TMS editors.
2. Distribute and activate the transport route configuration to all SAP systems in the system landscape.

**Note** When you are using TMS, Transaction SE06 is no longer used to configure transport routes, and the tables used to store the transport route configuration are no longer TSYST, TASYS, and TWSYS.

#### Standard Configurations

The easiest way to create transport routes and thereby define a system landscape is to use one of the standard configuration options provided by both the hierarchical list editor and the graphical editor:

- **Single system**:
  The option for a single-system landscape
- **Development and production system**:
  The option for a two-system landscape
- **Three system group**:
  The option for a three-system landscape

After you enter the names of the SAP systems that are to form the system landscape, SAP system automatically generates the necessary transport routes and transport layers. To create a more complex environment, initially use a three-system landscape and extend it later. To implement one of the above standard configuration options, proceed as follows:

1. Log on to the transport domain controller with a user ID that has complete transport authorization.
2. To access one of the TMS editors, from the TMS initial screen (Transaction STMS), choose **Overview · Transport routes**.
3. Switch into change mode using **Configuration · Display <-> Change**.
4. Regardless of which editor you are using, choose **Configuration · Standard Configuration** and select one of the three standard configurations.

**Note** By selecting one of the standard configurations, all existing transport routes are deleted. Existing transport layers and packages are retained.

After selecting one of the three standard configurations, proceed as follows.

For a single-system landscape, specify the SID of the SAP system that is to be the single system in the system landscape. You also may specify a transport layer for local developments. For a single-system landscape, you do not need to define transport routes. (Imports can still be performed if necessary.) All object changes that you make in a single SAP system are recorded in change requests of type **local** (see Chapter 10).

For a two-system landscape, enter the SIDs of the development-and-test system and the production system. Choose **Save**. The following steps are performed automatically:

- The transport layer **Z<development-and-test system SID>** becomes the standard transport layer.
- A consolidation route is created from the development-and-test system to the production system through the transport layer **Z<development-and-test system SID>**.
- A consolidation route is created from the development-and-test system to the production system through the transport layer **SAP**.

As a result, all Customizing changes, all developments in packages assigned to the standard transport layer, and all changes to SAP standard objects are recorded in change requests for transport to the production system.

Figure 8.14 shows a standard configuration of a two-system landscape with DTS as the development-and-test system and PRS as the production system. The standard transport layer ZDTS is automatically generated as well as the two consolidation routes, one for customer-developed objects belonging to the transport layer ZDTS and one for SAP standard objects.

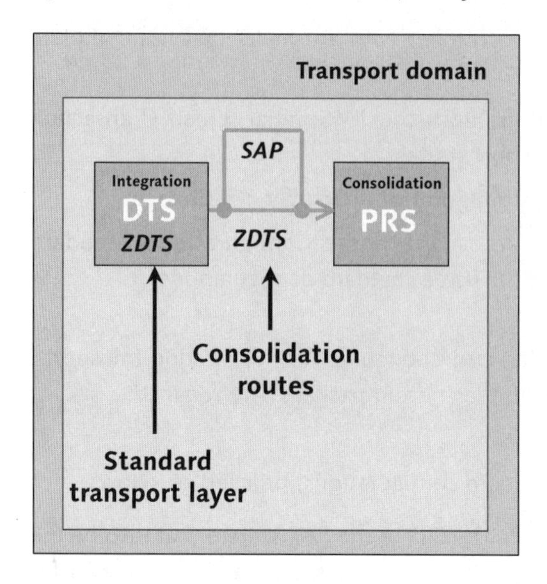


**Figure 8.14** Components of the standard transport route configuration for a two-system landscape

For a three-system landscape, assign SIDs to the development system, the quality assurance system, and the production system. Choose **Save**. The following steps are performed automatically:

- The transport layer **Z<development system SID>** becomes the standard transport layer.
- A consolidation route is created from the development system to the quality assurance system through the transport layer **Z<quality assurance system SID>**.
- To transport SAP standard objects, a consolidation route is created from the development system to the quality assurance system through the transport layer **SAP**.
- A delivery route is created from the quality assurance system to the production system. The production system is the recipient system for the consolidated changes.

As a result, all Customizing changes, all developments in packages that are assigned to the standard transport layer, and all changes to SAP standard objects are recorded in change requests for transport to the quality assurance system for consolidation.

After consolidation, the changes are transported to the production system via the delivery route. Figure 8.15 shows a standard configuration of a three-system landscape with DEV as the development system, QAS as the quality assurance system, and PRD as the production system. ZDEV has been generated as the standard transport layer, and there are two consolidation routes, SAP and ZDEV. Additionally, there is a delivery route between QAS and PRD.

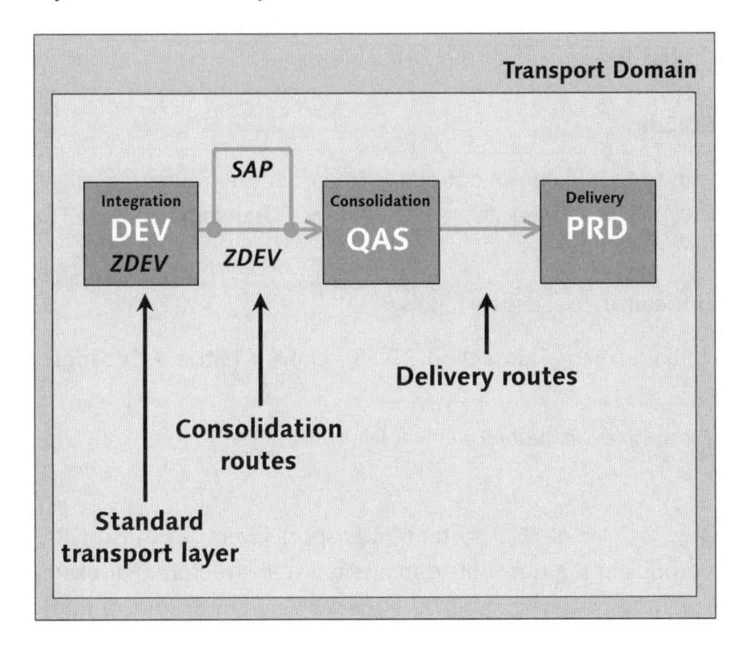


**Figure 8.15** Components of the standard transport route configuration for a three-system landscape

### Distributing and Activating a Standard Configuration

Changes in configuration are not valid until manually distributed and activated. To distribute and activate the changes, from either the hierarchical list editor or the graphical editor, choose **Configuration • Distribute and Activate**.

## 8.3.2 Extending and Changing a Transport Route Configuration

You can extend and change a transport domain's transport route configuration at any time using either of the TMS editors: the graphical editor or the hierarchical editor. The graphical editor is often easier to use for this purpose, because it provides a diagram of the existing environment into which you can "draw" your additions to the landscape.

The transport route configuration can be changed on the transport domain controller only with a user ID that has complete transport authorization. In either editor, to change the transport route configuration—that is, to add, delete, or modify transport routes—you must be in change mode. After making changes, always distribute and activate the changes by choosing **Configuration · Distribute and Activate**. When activating a transport route configuration, you are prompted to log on to all involved SAP systems. To do this, you require a user ID that has complete transport authorization in each of the SAP systems.

### Using the TMS Editors

Either editor can be used to add consolidation routes or delivery routes. To call an editor, from the TMS initial screen, choose **Overview · Transport routes**. The default editor appears.

To change the default editor, proceed as follows:

1. From the TMS initial screen (Transaction STMS), choose **Extras · Settings · Transport routes**.
2. Select either the graphical or the hierarchical list editor.
3. Choose **Enter**.

The *hierarchical list editor* lists all SAP systems, transport layers, and (as of R/3 Release 4.5) target groups in the transport domain in a tree structure. For example, Figure 8.16 shows the tree structure of the hierarchical editor for the transport domain DOMAIN_DEV.

The system landscape diagramed in Figure 8.16 consists of two "real" SAP systems (the development system DEV and the quality assurance system QAS) as listed under the node **Configuration status**. The production system PRD has not yet been installed, but has already been configured as a virtual system to integrate it into the transport route configuration. Node **Single systems** lists the training system TRN, which has not yet been integrated in the transport route configuration. DEV, QAS, and PRD form a standard three-system landscape for which standard transport routes have been configured: two consolidation routes between DEV and QAS, one associated with transport layer SAP for SAP standard objects and one associated with the generated standard transport layer ZDEV for customer objects.

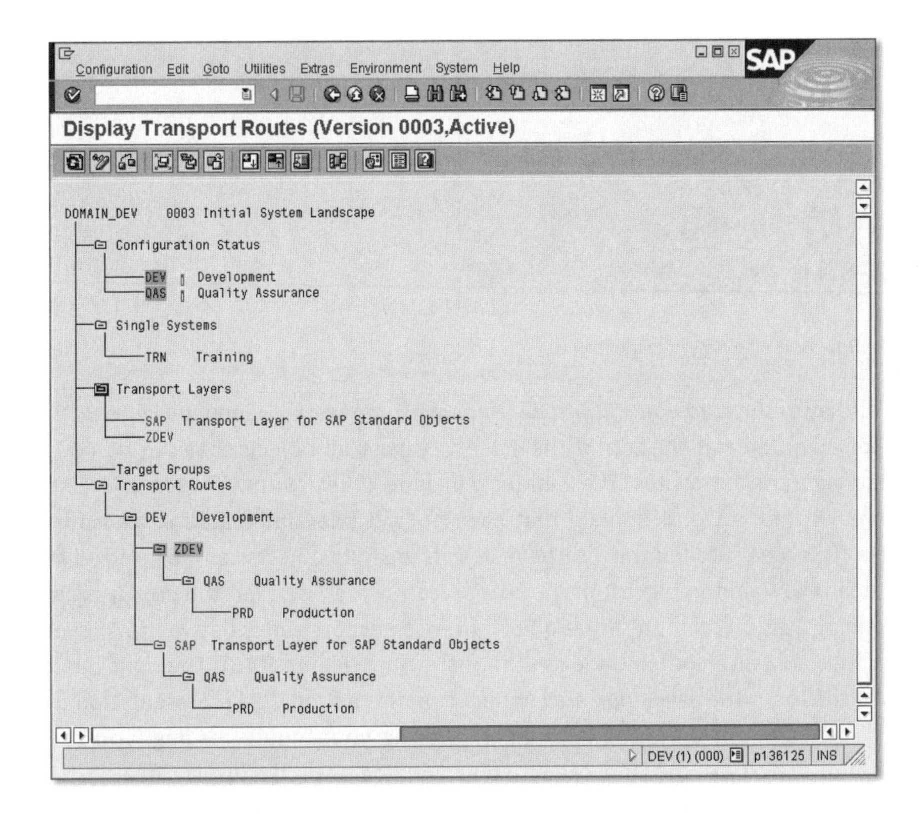


**Figure 8.16** The hierarchical list editor

To add a new transport route using the hierarchical list editor, proceed as follows:

1. Log on to the transport domain controller with a user ID that has complete transport authorization.
2. From the TMS initial screen (Transaction STMS), choose **Overview • Transport routes**.
3. Switch into change mode using **Configuration • Display <-> Change**.
4. Choose **Edit • Transport route • Create**.
5. In the resulting dialog box (shown in Figure 8.17), select the type of transport route you require: either **Consolidation** or **Delivery**.
   - For a consolidation route, you must specify an integration system, a transport layer, and a consolidation system. When a transport layer is assigned to a consolidation route, all objects belonging to the transport layer are assigned to this consolidation route.
   - For a delivery route, you must specify a source system and a recipient system.
6. Choose **Continue** to confirm the settings and save the new transport route.

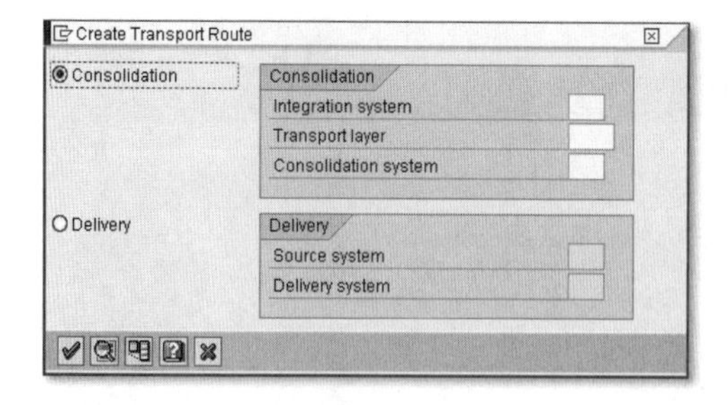


**Figure 8.17** Adding a new transport route

The display of the *graphical editor* is divided into three areas, as seen in Figure 8.18. The left-hand area at the top of the screen displays all objects that can be connected via transport routes. These objects include all real, virtual, or external SAP systems in the transport domain that have not yet been integrated in transport routes. This area is called the *insertable objects area*. Its objects can be inserted in the area below, in the biggest part of the screen, which is called the *display area*, containing a graphical representation of current transport routes between SAP systems. This area also contains a legend (not shown in Figure 8.18). The right-hand area at the top is the *navigation area*, which contains a simplified representation of the display area. In the navigation area, by using your mouse to drag, you can determine the part of the landscape that is shown below in the display area.

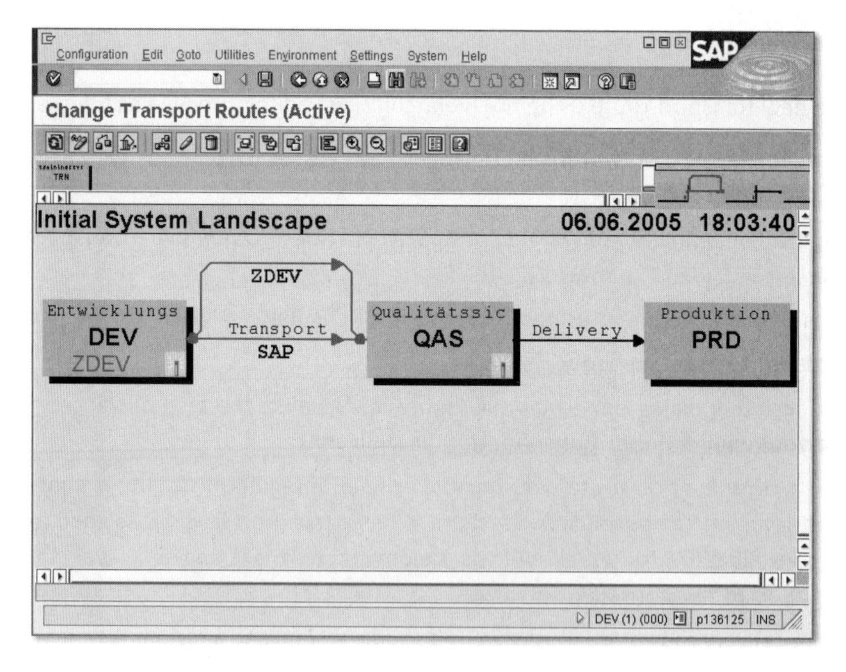


**Figure 8.18** The graphical editor

To add a transport route using the graphical editor, proceed as follows:

1. Log on to the transport domain controller with a user ID that has complete transport authorization.
2. From the TMS initial screen (Transaction STMS), choose **Overview · Transport routes**. If necessary, switch to the graphical editor using the menu option **Goto · Graphical Editor**.
3. Switch into change mode using **Configuration · Display <-> Change**.
4. If a new SAP system (or target group) is to be added to the transport route configuration, use the mouse to drag the SAP system (or target group) out of the insertable objects area and drop it into the display area.
5. Choose **Edit · Transport route · Create**.
6. The mouse now becomes a stylus that you can use to draw a transport route—a line from one SAP system (or target group) to another.
7. After you draw a transport route, a dialog box similar to the one in Figure 8.16 appears. After you select either **Consolidation route** or **delivery route**, the graphical editor—unlike the hierarchical list editor—automatically enters some of the required information.
    - For a consolidation route, you need to specify only a transport layer.
    - For a delivery route, no further entries are required after selecting **Delivery**.
8. Choose **Enter**.

### Additional Consolidation Routes

It is sometimes useful to consolidate specific Repository objects to an SAP system outside the standard transport routes by creating an additional transport layer. Development projects that require this technique are called *multi-layered development projects*.

**An Example of a Multi-Layered Development Project**

A training system TRN is needed. This training system should be identical to the production system, but also requires special programs such as reset routines to return sample data to its original state. These programs only need to be consolidated to TRN, and should never be transported into the production system. To implement this, all training objects are assigned to a package whose transport layer differs from the standard transport layer. This transport layer must be assigned to a consolidation route with TRN as the consolidation system.

### Additional Delivery Routes

One technique for setting up additional delivery routes is known as using *multiple delivery routes*. This technique is frequently used by customers who have more than one delivery system. Multiple delivery routes have the same source system but different target systems. The concept of multiple delivery routes is also called *parallel forwarding*. The import queues of the target systems receive change requests in parallel as soon as the change requests have been imported into the source system of the delivery route.

**Example of Multiple Delivery Routes**

If you have a separate training SAP system, TRN, which is used to train users working in the production system PR1, it makes sense to set up TRN in the same way as PR1 (see Figure 8.19 just below). Both the training and production systems should receive the same changes in parallel after these changes have been verified by quality assurance testing in system QAS. After a standard transport configuration has been created with DEV as the development system, QAS as the quality assurance system, and PRD as the production system, an additional delivery route may be created in the TMS editor with QAS as the source system and TRN as the target system.

Figure 8.19 combines the two examples given above: multi-layered development and multiple delivery systems. In addition, Figure 8.19 shows that a second production system, PR2, is delivered to through the same transport flow as PR1.

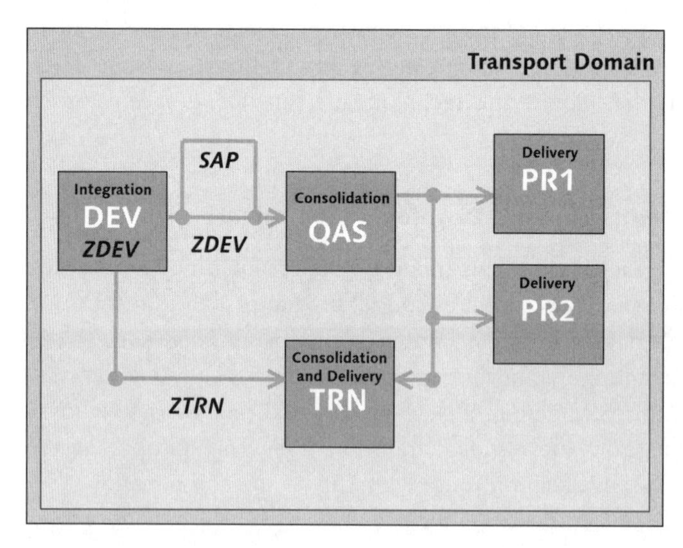


Figure 8.19 Multi-layered development and multiple delivery systems

Another way of configuring more than one delivery system—not shown in the above diagram—is to use *multi-level delivery* or *multi-level forwarding*, which arranges the delivery routes in sequence. This is implemented by defining a recipient system for a recipient system—that is, defining a target system of a delivery route as the source system for an additional delivery route.

An example of multi-level delivery for a complex system landscape of an international company is shown in Figure 8.20. In this example, a standard transport flow exists between the global development system DEG, where global Customizing and development occur, and a global consolidation system QAG. After testing and verification in QAG, changes are delivered in parallel to the development systems of the two regional development systems, DEU for the United States and DEE for Europe.

Because each region requires its own specific Customizing and development, it has its own development system, quality assurance system, and production system. The global changes are delivered to the regional quality assurance systems, and thereafter, to the regional production systems. The concept of multi-level delivery here means that, between the regional development systems and quality assurance systems, there are three transport routes: one consolidation route for regional changes; one consolidation route for SAP objects; and one delivery route for global changes.

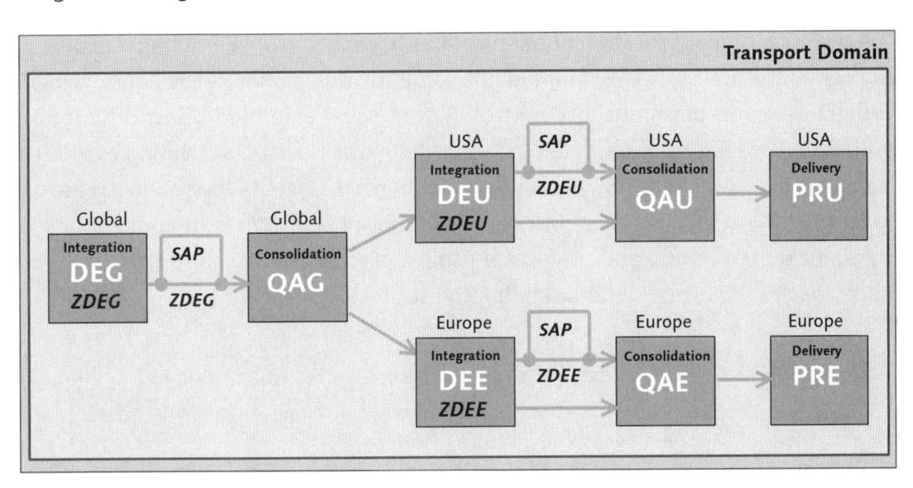


**Figure 8.20** A complex system landscape

## Version Control

The TMS provides a "version control" function for transport route configurations. Each activated configuration is stored with a sequential number and can be reactivated if needed. To reactivate a former configuration version from within the TMS editor, proceed as follows:

1. From the transport routes initial screen, choose **Configuration • Get other configuration**.
2. Select the version from the list of displayed versions. In this case, it is helpful if the short description contains a friendly name, or if you logged the changes you had carried out on a specific date.
3. Choose **Enter**. The selected version is now displayed.
4. If you would like to use the selected old version—as a basis for a change or in its current state—switch to change mode using **Configuration • Change** and adapt the configuration accordingly. Then, save the new configuration with a meaningful short text and activate and distribute it.

### 8.3.3 Extended Transport Control

As of R/3 Release 4.5, there are several additional features for transport route configuration that are summarized as **extended transport control**. Extended transport enables you to assign:

- Clients to transport routes
- Groups of clients (known as *target groups*) to transport routes
- Clients to transport layers

To take advantage of this functionality, in the transport profile, you must explicitly set parameter `CTC` to `TRUE`. The default value for this parameter is `FALSE`, which deactivates extended transport control. Before using extended transport control, you would ideally set parameter `CTC` to `TRUE` globally. After activating extended transport control, you can use either the normal, system-to-system transport routes or client-specific ones, but not a mixture of both types of connections in the same system landscape. If you are using a client-specific transport route, you must specify the clients when defining the source and target.

**Tip** All R/3 Systems that are linked by transport routes must have either client-specific or client-independent source and target specifications, but not a mixture of both.

**Warning** When you switch to extended transport control, if there are change requests in any import queue, those change requests will be highlighted red in the new column **Client** in the import queue, and cannot be transported until you specify a client for them (see Chapter 13).

### Client-Specific Transport Routes

Extended transport control enables you to include R/3 clients in both consolidation and delivery routes (see Figure 8.21 just below). To create a client-specific transport route, proceed as follows:

1. Create an SAP system–specific transport route as described above in the section "Using the TMS editors." In the dialog box **Create Transport Route**, choose **Extended Transport Control**.
2. Select either **Consolidation** or **Delivery**.
   - For a consolidation route, enter the integration system and transport layer. In the field **Target system/client**, enter the SID of either an SAP system and a client, or an existing target group.
   - For a delivery route, enter a delivery source and a delivery system/client. The latter can be either an SID and a client, or an existing target group.
3. Choose **Enter**.
4. Choose **Save**.
5. Distribute and activate the new configuration.

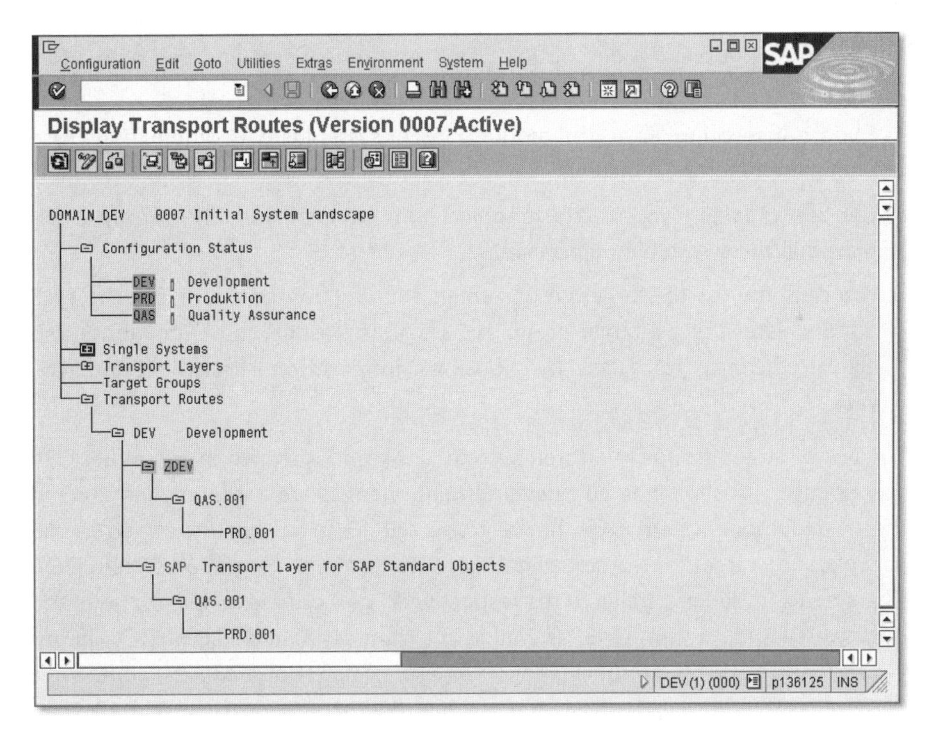


**Figure 8.21** Client-specific transport routes

Figure 8.21 shows a three-system landscape with client-specific transport routes as displayed in the hierarchical list editor. Changes in the development system DEV are transported to client 100 of the quality assurance system QAS. The target of the client-specific consolidation route is `QAS.001`. The delivery route from QAS to the production system PRD must also be client-specific. Client 001 of PRD is the production client, so the target of the client-specific delivery route is `PRD.001`.

### Target Groups

Extended transport control enables you to create *target groups* for consolidations and deliveries. A target group is a group of target clients. Each target client is specified in terms of an SAP system and a client within that system. When you release a change request from the source system of a target group, the change request is automatically added to the import buffers of all targets in the target group. To define a target group, proceed as follows:

1. Access the initial screen of either the graphical or the hierarchical editor in change mode.
2. Choose **Configuration • Target group • Create**.
3. In the dialog box **Create Target Group** (shown in Figure 8.22), enter a name for the target group and a description. The name must begin and end with a forward slash (/).
4. Choose **Insert line**. Enter the required target system client combinations. Use a separate line for each client.
5. Choose **Transfer**. If you use the graphical editor, the created target group is displayed in the insertable objects area.
6. You can now use the target groups when defining transport routes in the TMS editors. After using a target group as part of a transport route, distribute and activate the changes as usual by choosing **Configuration • Distribute and activate**.

The use of target groups in a three-system landscape is shown in Figure 8.23. In this example, Customizing and development changes are made in client 100 in the development system DEV. Target group /GR_QA/ has been specified as the consolidation target for the consolidation route from the integration system DEV. Changes are added in parallel to the respective import buffers for client 100 of the quality assurance system QAS, as well as for clients 300 and 320 of DEV. Target group /GR_PR/ has been specified as the delivery target of a delivery route with `QAS.100` as the delivery source. After change requests are validated in QAS, they are transported into client 100 of the production system PRD as well as into training client 300 of QAS.

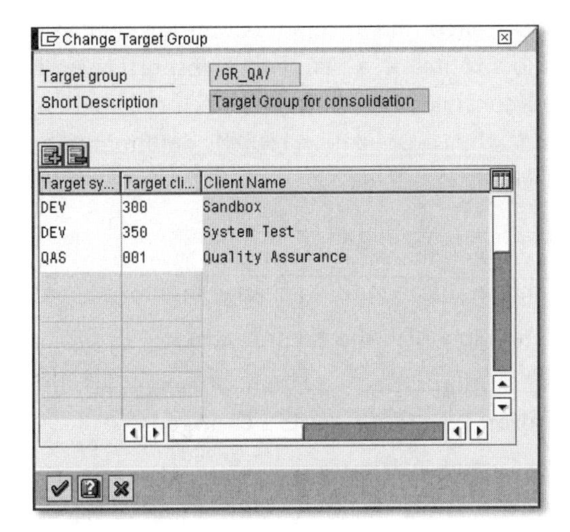
Change Target Group

Target group: /GR_QA/
Short Description: Target Group for consolidation

| Target sy... | Target cli... | Client Name |
|---|---|---|
| DEV | 300 | Sandbox |
| DEV | 350 | System Test |
| QAS | 001 | Quality Assurance |

Figure 8.22 Creating target groups

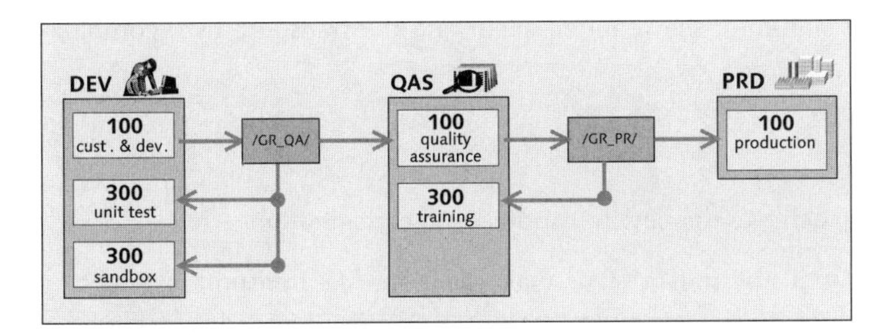


Figure 8.23 Target groups in a three-system landscape

**Tip** After you export change requests from the Customizing-and-development client, SAP recommends using target groups to transport change requests back into the other clients in the development system. This ensures consistency among the clients in the development system.

### Client-Specific Transport Layers

Extended transport control also enables you to give a client its own client-specific standard transport layer for client-dependent changes. Client-specific transport layers do not affect Repository objects. If no client-specific transport layer is created, each client uses the standard transport layer of the SAP system to which it belongs.

With client-specific transport layers, the client in which a Customizing change is released determines the consolidation route. If a standard transport layer is defined for this client, the associated consolidation route is used. If no standard transport layer is defined for this client, the consolidation route is determined by the standard transport layer of the SAP system.

To assign clients to transport layers, proceed as follows:

1. Access either the graphical or the hierarchical editor in change mode.
2. Position the cursor on the SAP system in which the client resides.
3. For the hierarchical editor, choose **Configuration · System · Change**. For the graphical editor, choose **Configuration · System reports · Change**.
4. In the resulting dialog box **Change System Attributes**:
   - To change the standard transport layer for the whole SAP system—that is, for all clients—enter the name of the new standard transport layer.
   - To assign clients to a transport layer, choose **Client assignment**. Choose **Insert line** and enter the required client and the transport layer combinations.
5. Choose **Transfer**.
6. Choose **Save**.
7. Distribute and activate the new transport route configuration.

Figure 8.24 shows a system landscape with client-specific transport layers using the graphical editor. In this example, there is a three-system landscape with a development system (DEV), a quality assurance system (QAS), and a production system (PRD). The SAP ECC application component for Financial Accounting (FI) is configured separately in client 100 in DEV and has its own separate SAP ECC Systems for quality assurance and production (QA2 and PR2). To consolidate all Customizing changes made for FI to QA2, these changes are made in client 200 in DEV (rather than in client 001), for which a client-specific standard transport layer (ZFI) has been defined.

Transport layer ZFI is assigned to a consolidation route with DEV as the integration system and client 100 in system QA2 as the consolidation target. This ensures that all client-dependent Customizing changes made in client 100 of DEV are consolidated to client 100 in QA2. To consolidate Repository objects to QA2, these objects must be created in packages assigned to transport layer ZFI. Finally, all changes that have been imported into QA2 are delivered to PR2, the production system for FI.

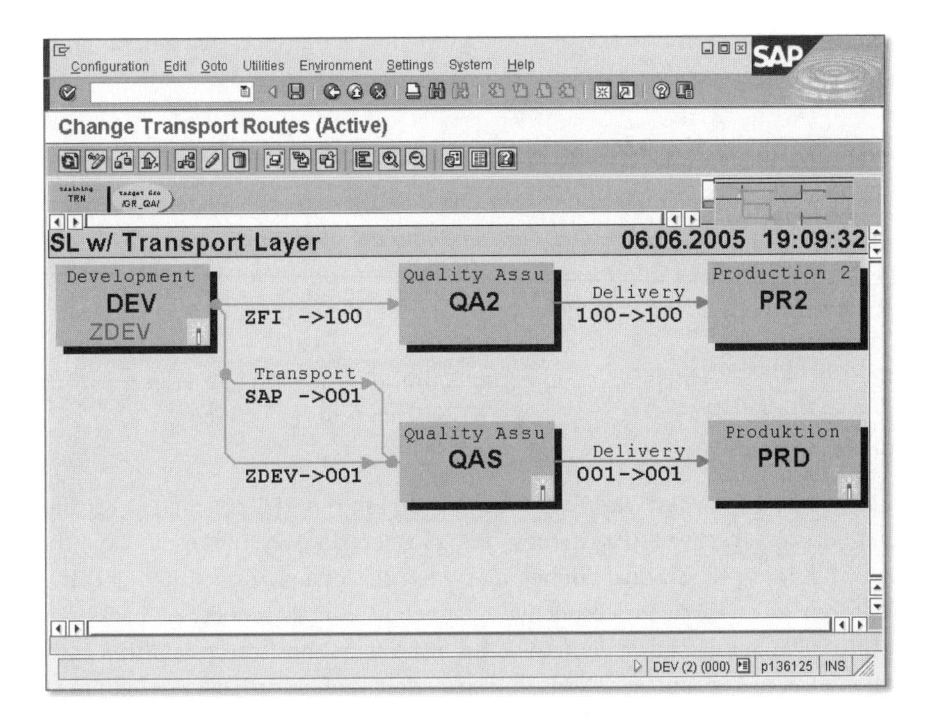


Figure 8.24 Creating client-specific standard transport layers

**Warning** Although client-specific transport layers allow for the consolidation of client-dependent Customizing efforts to different target systems and clients, client-independent Customizing changes will follow only a single transport layer.

## 8.4 Verifying the System Landscape Setup

The TMS provides the following checks and monitor functions to help ensure that your system landscape is set up correctly:

- TMS checks
- Transport route configuration checks
- Alert monitor

You should use these tools to verify your transport configuration and to perform troubleshooting.

**Note** For information on troubleshooting procedures and additional checks for TMS import functionality, see Chapters 13 and 14.

All checks can be performed on any SAP system in the transport domain, not only on the domain controller.

### 8.4.1 Verifying the TMS Setup

To verify whether the TMS has been set up correctly, enter the **System Overview** screen (from the initial TMS screen, choose **Overview · Systems**). Choose **SAP system · Check**. The check is performed on all SAP systems unless you select a particular SAP system by positioning the cursor on it. Choose one of the following checks:

- Connection test
- Transport directory
- Transport tool

During a connection test, the TMS tries to establish the RFC connection for the target hosts of all active SAP systems in the transport domain. The results list indicates whether the individual connections were successfully established and the time taken to establish the respective connection in milliseconds. A "backward check" is also performed to verify whether each target host can establish a connection back to the source system. To display details on a particular RFC connection, click the **status** field for a specific system.

When checking the transport directory, the TMS tries to create, read, and delete test files in all transport directories of the transport domain, including the transport directories of its external systems. The following subdirectories are covered in the check: bin, buffer, cofiles, data, log, sapnames, and tmp. From the results screen of this transport-directory check, you can run another check that tests whether a system is correctly assigned to a transport group. To run this check, choose **Goto · Transport groups**.

The transport tool check gives an overview of the availability of the transport tools. This check may take some time. The check covers the `tp` interface, the transport profile, and the RFC destinations. It tests a `tp` call to every SAP system of the transport domain. This `tp` call includes an RFC call, a database connect, and an offline call.

### 8.4.2 Verifying the Transport Route Configuration

To verify whether you have used TMS correctly to set up your system landscape, access one of the TMS editors. Unless you choose to run the check on a particular SAP system (by positioning the cursor on it), the check is performed on all SAP systems in your system landscape. To start the check, choose **Configuration · Check**. Choose one of the following checks:

- Transport routes
- Request consistency

A *transport routes check* investigates three things. First, it checks whether the transport flow provides deliveries from at least one consolidation system. Second, it checks whether the delivery is multi-level. If so, the check verifies that the parameter `multileveldelivery` is set in the transport profile for any SAP systems in the transport domain with an R/3 Release before 4.0. Third, if extended transport control is activated (that is, if parameter `CTC` is set to `1` in the transport profile and the R/3 Release is 4.5 or higher), the check also verifies that the client-specific transport routes are not mixed with system-to-system transport routes for the same system landscape.

The *request consistency check* can be run either for the local system or for all systems. It checks whether transport routes associated with open tasks and requests are consistent with the current transport route configuration. If inconsistencies are found, it may be necessary to change the **type** of open requests—that is, either from **local** to **transportable** or vice versa, or from **repair** to **correction** or vice versa.

Open requests may also need a new transport destination if the original target system for these change requests does not correspond to the new configuration of the transport routes and does not provide a valid target system. This check also locates inconsistent change requests—change requests that contain invalid object combinations and make release impossible. After running the request consistency check, a list of all inconsistent change requests is displayed. To display details on the type of inconsistency and the required actions, position the cursor on a specific request and choose **Edit • Display long text**.

### 8.4.3 The Alert Monitor

The *TMS alert monitor* enables you to monitor all actions that have been performed with the TMS. Highlighting is used to draw your attention to critical information. To access the alert monitor from the TMS initial screen, choose **Monitor • TMS-Alerts • TMS-Alert Viewer**.

You can display either all messages or just warnings and error messages. The information is SAP system–specific. To display the information corresponding to a different SAP system, choose **TMS log • Other system** in the TMS-Alert Viewer. In the resulting dialog box, enter the appropriate SID in the field **Sys. Name** and choose **Enter**. To display the full text of a message, click the respective line.

The information provided by the alert monitor includes:

- Date and time of the activity
- Name of the user who performed the activity
- Related TMS function
- TMS messages, including error messages and warnings
- SAP system and client where the TMS function was triggered

You should check the alert monitor if there are transport or TMS configuration problems, or to get detailed information to help you solve the problems.

Besides the display options of the TMS alerts in the TMS, you can also transfer information from the TMS to the SAP standard tool for system monitoring, the Computing Center Management System (CCMS). It is built automatically during the TMS configuration. The CCMS alert monitor can be opened by selecting **Monitor · TMS Alerts · CCMS Alert Monitor** in the TMS initial screen.

Basic information about Alert Monitor can be found in the *Computing Center Management System* area of the online help.

The *CCMS Alert Monitor* provides the following functions:

- Display of error alerts that occur in the TMS, or during the export of requests—clearly grouped in a tree structure by subjects
- Analysis method for every alert
- Option to set alerts to the **done** status
- Visibility of alerts as long as they are not completed (completed alerts are visible in the history)

All systems in the current system landscape are added to the CCMS alert monitor. When new systems are added to the system landscape, they also show up in the CCMS alert monitor. Systems deleted from the system landscape disappear from the CCMS alert monitor. Note that open (i.e., not completed) alerts might be deleted as well.

Often, problems are reported that occur locally on a system, that is, problems that the system has with itself or via contact with other systems. At the same time, these alerts are sent to the TMS controller. If you are logged on to the controller, you can view as well as edit all alerts that occurred in the domain.

Note that errors that occurred when writing the CCMS alerts are written to the TMS Alert Viewer. Therefore, you should check the entries in the TMS Alert Viewer on a regular basis.

To open the TMS Alert Viewer or the CCMS alert monitor of the TMS from other places of the Transport Management System, select **GoTo** or **Environment** from the respective menu and then select the corresponding option.

## 8.5 Questions

1. Which of the following statements is correct in regard to the SAP systems belonging to a transport domain?

   A. They all share the same transport directory.

   B. They are managed centrally using TMS.

   C. They belong to the same transport group.

   D. They must run on the same operating system and database platform.

2. Which of the following statements is correct in regard to the domain controller?

   A. It must be the production system.

   B. It occurs once in a transport domain.

   C. It occurs in each transport group.

   D. It can only be the SAP system that was originally designated as the transport domain controller.

   E. It should never be the production system due to the high system load that the domain controller causes.

3. Which of the following statements are correct in regard to the TMS?

   A. It needs to be initialized only on the transport domain controller.

   B. It needs to be initialized only on the transport domain controller and the backup domain controller.

   C. It must be initialized on every SAP system.

   D. It must be set up before you can set up transport routes.

4. Which of the following statements are correct in regard to the RFC destinations for TMS connections?

   A. They are generated automatically when a transport route is created.

   B. They are generated between the domain controller and each SAP system in the transport domain.

   C. They must be established manually before you can use the TMS.

   D. They are generated during the TMS initialization process.

   E. They are only needed for importing change requests.

5. How is the actual system landscape, including SAP system roles and relationships, defined using the TMS?
   A. By including all SAP systems in the transport domain
   B. By configuring transport routes
   C. By assigning a role to each SAP system during the TMS initialization process
   D. By designating real, virtual, and external SAP systems
6. Which of the following statements is correct in regard to a consolidation route?
   A. It is defined by an integration system and a consolidation system, and is associated with a transport layer.
   B. It is created in the TMS by defining only an integration system and a consolidation system.
   C. It is not necessarily required in a two-system landscape.
   D. It can be defined only once in a transport group.
7. Which of the following statements are correct in regard to client-specific transport routes?
   A. They are possible as of R/3 Release 4.0.
   B. They are possible only as of R/3 Release 4.5, and only if extended transport control is activated.
   C. They are only allowed for target groups.
   D. They may not be used in conjunction with client-independent transport routes.

# 9 Client Tools

After SAP ECC installation, you need to set up clients so that users can log on to the system and perform Customizing and other tasks. Setting up the different clients for the SAP systems in your system landscape involves the following tasks:

- Defining the purpose of each client
- Enabling the appropriate users to access the client through user administration and authorization
- Preventing unwanted changes to Customizing settings and Repository objects in a client
- Providing all clients other than the source client CUST with the latest Customizing and developments in an organized and timely manner
- Populating a client with the necessary application data

To perform these tasks or subsequently modify clients to match your changing business needs, SAP provides the tools outlined in this chapter:

- Client maintenance tools (used to define a client and maintain its settings)
- Client copy tools (used to provide a client with the necessary data)
- Client delete tool (used to remove unwanted clients)

This chapter also explains the logging of Customizing changes affecting tables (table logging). Table logging is activated at the client level and needs to be considered when clients are set up.

## 9.1 Creating a Client

To create a client, you make an entry in table T000. Without this entry, you will not be able to log on to the client, import change requests into the client, or copy another client into the client. After creating the client entry, adjust the client settings to define the role of the client within the SAP system landscape.

Please note that not all SAP systems support several clients. The SAP Business Information Warehouse (SAP BW), for example, supports only one client. For these systems, the largest part of the information in this chapter is therefore not applicable.

The newly created client is empty—it contains no client-dependent data. You must provide the client with the necessary user master data, application data, and Customizing data, so that users can log on to the client and perform, for example, Customizing activities or business transactions.

### 9.1.1 Client Entries

You can create, display, and change entries in table T000 using client maintenance (Transaction SCC4).

#### Creating a Client Entry

To create an entry in table T000 and thus create a new R/3 client, proceed as follows:

1. Access client maintenance by calling Transaction SCC4, or, from the SAP Easy Access Menu, choose **Tools • Administration • Administration • Client administration • Client maintenance**.
2. The **Display View "Clients": Overview** screen appears. You are in display mode. Switch to change mode by selecting **Table view • Display • Change**.
3. A message box appears: "The table is client-independent (see Help for further info)". Choose **Continue**—you are now in change mode.
4. Select the button **New entries** or use the menu option **Edit • New entries** to reach the screen **New Entries: Details of Added Entries** (see Figure 9.1).
5. Enter a three-digit client ID in the field **Client**. For example, to create client 145, enter "145" in this field. If this client ID is already in use, the message "An entry already exists with the same key" will appear in the status bar. Provide a new and unique ID number.
6. Save your entry.

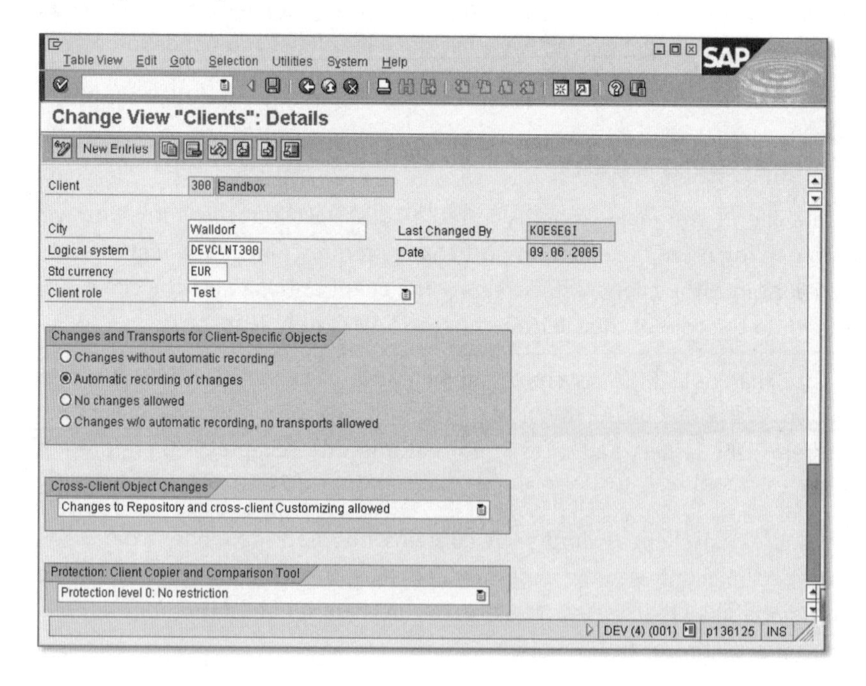


Figure 9.1 The client maintenance screen

### Maintaining a Client Entry

You can use client maintenance (Transaction SCC4) to view and change the settings for a client. From the screen **Display View "Clients": Overview**, you can do any of the following:

- Display the settings for a client by double-clicking the client ID
- Change client settings by choosing **Display · Change** to switch into change mode, then double-clicking the client ID
- Delete a client by selecting the client entry and then choosing **Edit · Delete**

**Warning** You should avoid deleting a client entry from within client maintenance. Instead, use Transaction SCC5.

### Deleting a Client Entry

When you delete a client entry from table T000 with client maintenance (Transaction SCC4), you can no longer log on to the client or update it using change requests. The deletion process, however, does not eliminate the data belonging to that client. This means the client-dependent data remains in your SAP system, possibly without your knowledge, occupying valuable space in the database. To eliminate an client entirely—to delete both the client entry and the client-dependent data—use the client delete functionality (Transaction SCC5), which is explained below in "Deleting an Client."

Deleting a client entry with client maintenance allows you to temporarily lock the client. The deletion procedure preserves the data for that client, but prevents users from logging on to the client or accessing its data. By preventing logon, you can, for example, ensure that no users make changes during a client copy. To restore the client and allow logon, re-create the client entry using client maintenance.

## 9.1.2 Client Settings

When you create a client entry, the only required input is a three-digit client ID. You can also make selections for the client settings or change previously selected settings. These settings are very important, because they further define and restrict the way the client is used. The different client settings include:

- Client name
- Client city
- Logical system name

- Standard currency
- Client role
- Client-dependent change option
- Client-independent change option
- Client protection against a client copy and client compare
- Restrictions

Assigning a name to a client provides you with a description that complements the client ID. The entry in the field **client city** is used to identify the physical location of the hardware for the SAP system or the implementation team that is responsible for the client. Both the client name and city are optional. The other seven client settings provide more critical functions and deserve a more detailed explanation.

### Logical System Name

You define a client within an SAP system by creating an appropriate client ID. You may have other clients with the same client ID in your other SAP systems. For example, you may have a client 145 in both your development and quality assurance systems. To differentiate these two clients, you can provide them with unique 10-character logical system names. Logical system names are crucial for:

- **Application Link Enabling (ALE):**
  ALE is based on a distribution model that defines the message flow (or data exchange) between different logical systems (see Chapter 4).
- **SAP Business Workflow:**
  SAP Business Workflow, often simply referred to as *Workflow*, allows you to automatically control and execute cross-application processes within SAP ECC. To define the steps and events in these processes, you need to know the logical system names of the clients where the events are initiated and performed.

ALE and SAP Business Workflow recognize only logical system names, not client numbers or system IDs. These logical systems can be clients in the same or different SAP systems.

When creating a logical system name, follow these guidelines:

- Use a logical system name only once—each logical system name must be unique within your system landscape.
- Do not change a logical system name once it has been established or used by ALE or the SAP Business Workflow.

**Warning** Avoid changing a logical system name. Such a change could result in the loss of ALE or SAP Business Workflow documents.

### Standard Currency

The standard currency is the default currency used for that client. It is entered as a three-letter code, such as USD for American dollars or EUR for the Euro. For example, if you assign EUR as the client standard currency, whenever you enter a monetary value in that client, SAP ECC will assume that the currency is the Euro unless you specify something different.

To be able to select a default currency for a client, currencies must be defined within the client or copied into the client from an SAP standard client. The SAP standard clients recognize over 100 different currencies. Other currencies can be defined using an IMG client-dependent Customizing activity.

### Client Role

When you create a client, you normally assign a predefined role to it. The role reflects the purpose served by the client and can prevent or limit certain activities. The possible client roles include:

- **Production:**
  A client with this role will not be deleted by a mistakenly initiated client delete or client copy. No client-independent changes can be imported into this client or into its SAP system as part of a client copy. This prevents possible inconsistencies that could affect production. In addition, changing certain Customizing settings in a production client, such as currency exchange rates and posting periods, can be allowed in this client—despite the standard client-dependent change option that is used to prevent Customizing changes in a production client. These *Current Settings* (see Chapter 11) can be maintained in a production client without being recorded to a change request.
- **Test:**
  A client with this role is protected against an release upgrade by the appropriate client restriction (see "Client Restrictions" below).
- **Customizing:**
  The factory calendar can be maintained in and transported from only the client with this role.
- **Demonstration:**
  Setting up a demonstration client allows you to have a separate client for demonstration purposes.

- **Training/Education:**
  Setting up a training client allows you to have a separate client for training purposes.

In future SAP releases, SAP plans to link additional functionality to the client roles to increase the scope of the protection they provide.

### Client Change Options

These settings control the types of changes that can be made in the client and determine whether Customizing changes are recorded to change requests. The default change options for a client are as follows:

- *Automatic recording of changes*
- *Changes to Repository and client-independent Customizing allowed*

Because of the significance of these settings, the client change options were outlined in detail in Chapter 3.

### Client Protection

When you select this client option—**Protection: Client copier and comparison tool**—on the client maintenance screen (see Figure 9.1 earlier in this chapter), the client is protected against being overwritten by a client copy. This option also ensures that sensitive data cannot be viewed from another client during client compares, an activity performed using the Customizing Cross-System Viewer (Transaction SCU0; see Chapter 11). The levels of overwrite-protection you can select are as follows:

- Protection level 0: No Restrictions
- Protection level 1: No overwriting

  This ensures that the client will not be overwritten by the client copy program. It also protects the client from the adjustment activities of the Customizing Cross-System Viewer. Use this setting for your Customizing-and-development client, as well as for clients that contain critical settings or data that should not be overwritten, such as your quality assurance client.

- Protection level 2: No overwriting and no external availability

  This protects a client against being overwritten by a client copy and also against *read* access from another client using the tools of the Cross-System Viewer. Protection-level 2 should be used for clients that contain sensitive data, such as your production client.

### Client Restrictions

The following options enable you to restrict activities in clients:

- **Start of CATT and eCATT processes allowed:**
  Select this option for a client such as the quality assurance test client where you wish to run the Computer Aided Test Tool (CATT) or the enhanced Computer Aided Test Tool (eCATT) to perform scripted validity tests of application functionality. Since CATT scripts generate application data, they should not be run in every client.
- **Currently locked due to client copy:**
  This option is automatically set by the SAP system when you use the client copy tool. You cannot select it manually.
- **Protection against SAP upgrade:**
  You can assign this option only to a client whose role is set to **Test**. This option prevents the introduction of new client-dependent Customizing changes into a client during an release upgrade, thereby preserving the settings that existed prior to the upgrade. After an upgrade, the test client can be used in conjunction with the Cross-System Viewer to compare the client-dependent differences between the two releases.

## 9.2 Providing a Client with Data

After you create a client, it will contain no data: no Customizing data, application data, or user master records. You must copy data into the new client to provide an environment where users can either customize, develop, test, or train, depending on the purpose of the client. A client copy is used to initially populate a client with base data from either the SAP standard client 000 or an existing customer client (see Chapter 5). Change requests are then used to distribute the latest Customizing and developments to the different clients.

The different client copy tools that can be used to initially populate a client with data include:

- Local client copy
- Remote client copy
- Client transport

### 9.2.1 Selecting a Client Copy Tool

To select the most suitable client copy tool in a given situation, you must consider the locations of both the source client and the target client, and the type of data to be copied. To copy a client in an SAP system to another client in the same SAP system, use a local client copy. Either a remote client copy or a client transport can be used to copy a client from one SAP system to another SAP system (see Figure 9.2).

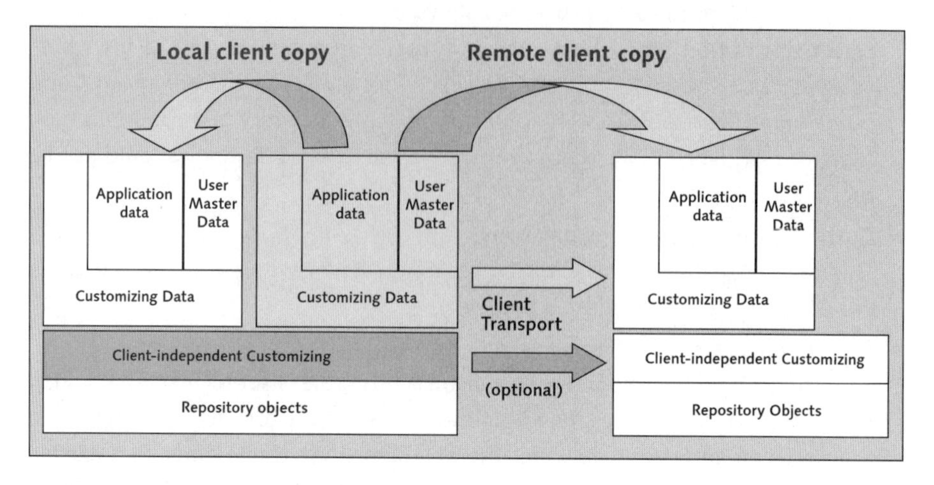


**Figure 9.2** The three client copy tools

## Advantages of a Client Transport

When you copy a client from one SAP system to another SAP system, you can use a client transport to:

- Preserve a copy of the client outside SAP ECC in files at the operating system level. A client transport involves writing a client to the transport directory (similar to the export process for a change request). This provides you with a copy of the client that you can use later, for example, to help create multiple clients based on one client.
- Copy client-independent Customizing. As of R/3 Release 4.6, this can also be done with a remote client copy.
- Schedule the two steps—data export and import—independently.

For these reasons, SAP recommends using a client transport when you cannot use change requests to build a new SAP system (see Chapter 5). A client transport also provides a newly installed target system with the necessary client-independent and client-dependent data.

Note that you should not use a client transport to copy client-independent Customizing to a target system that already contains such Customizing, because the client transport will overwrite the existing client-independent Customizing objects in the target system. This causes inconsistencies when client-dependent data in other clients within the target system depends on the overwritten entries.

**Warning** Importing client-independent Customizing into an SAP system that already contains such Customizing may affect the data and functionality of other clients in the system.

### Advantages of a Remote Client Copy

If you do not need client-independent Customizing in your new client, SAP recommends using a remote client copy to provide the client with data. For example, a remote client copy is ideal if you wish to copy the user data from a unit test client in the development system to the training client in the quality assurance system. A remote client copy transfers data to another SAP system using RFC technology. This client copy tool has the following advantages:

- It can prevent data loss. During a remote client copy, an automatic Repository consistency check is performed. The structure of each table to be copied is checked and compared with tables in the target system. If inconsistencies are detected—for example, tables are missing in the target system or fields are missing in the tables—the client copy is canceled, and an error message is displayed. This kind of check is not performed automatically during a client transport.
- It is faster than a client transport, because it can copy data not only sequentially but also in parallel.
- It does not require the multiple export and import steps required by a client transport.
- It does not generate files at the operating system level and therefore does not take up disk space in the transport directory. In contrast, the client transport of a production client may generate files larger than the available disk space or reach file size limitations set by the operating system.

## 9.2.2 Using Client Copy Profiles to Select Data

Regardless of the client copy tool you select, you must determine the type of data you wish to copy from a source client to a target client. A client copy profile determines the data to be copied. The data that can be copied includes:

- Client-dependent Customizing data
- Client-independent Customizing data
- Application data—both master data and transaction data
- User data, which is a combination of user master data and authorization profiles (see Chapter 4)
- Variants, which are sets of input values saved for programs that you often use

When you begin the client copy procedure, you select a particular client copy profile (see "Local and Remote Client Copy" and "Client Transport" below). The profiles delivered by SAP are displayed in Table 9.1 (here for Release SAP ECC 5.0). Note that you can copy application data only when you also copy Customizing data, because application data depends on the Customizing settings of the client, and is of no value without those settings.

General information about the client copy and about the differences in copy profiles between different releases can also be found in SAP Note 24853.

| Copy Profile | Client-Dependent Customizing Data | Application Data | User Data | Variants | Client-Independent Customizing Data |
|---|---|---|---|---|---|
| SAP_ALL | X | X | X | X | |
| SAP_APPL | X | X | | | |
| SAP_CUST | X | | | | |
| SAP_CUSV | X | | | X | |
| SAP_EXBC* | X | | X | X | X |
| SAP_RMBC** | X | | X | X | X |
| SAP_EXPA* | X | X | X | X | X |
| SAP_RMPA** | X | X | X | X | X |
| SAP_EXPC* | X | | | X | X |
| SAP_RMPC** | X | | | X | X |
| SAP_UCUS | X | | X | | |
| SAP_UCSV | X | | X | X | |
| SAP_USER | | | X | | |

**Table 9.1** Client copy profiles for selecting data

**Warning** Before data is copied from the source client, the contents of the target client are deleted! This is true for all client copy profiles *except* the profile SAP_USER. In addition, if Central User Administration is active, you will not be able to copy user data, regardless of the client copy profile you select.

* These profiles can be selected only for a client transport (SCC8).
** These profiles can be selected for a remote client copy (SCC9) only.

**Example: Using Client Copy Tools to Support Training Needs**

A company whose SAP system has been in production for over a year decides to roll out additional business processes in the production system. This requires training for new users as well as those unfamiliar with the new business functionality.

To provide a training environment, a new client—client 300—is created in the quality assurance system. Client 300 is created as a client copy of the quality assurance client using a local client copy and the client copy profile SAP_ALL. The training staff cleans up client 300 by removing unnecessary data and providing base data for those business transactions the users must learn. Client 300 thus provides a basis that instructors can use to develop training materials.

Prior to the start of training classes, client 400 is created using a local client copy of client 300 with the client copy profile SAP_ALL. To verify profiles and help users feel comfortable in their accounts, user data is copied from the production client into client 400 on the quality assurance system. This is done using a remote client copy with the client copy profile SAP_USER. The training then begins in client 400.

### Displaying Client Copy Profiles

You can display the R/3 client copy profiles from within the different client copy tools. For example, to display the client copy profile SAP_UCUS from within the local client copy tool, proceed as follows:

1. Use Transaction code SCCL or, from the SAP Easy Access Menu, choose **Tools · Administration · Administration · Client administration · Client copy · Local copy**.
2. Use the F4-Help to get a list of the different profiles.
3. Select the profile SAP_UCUS.
4. Display the profile using **Profile · Display Profile**.

Figure 9.3 shows the screen that appears. When you select this profile, Customizing and user data—but not application data—will be copied. This client copy profile also initializes and re-creates the target client—it deletes the target client prior to copying in data. It does not copy variants. This profile is valid for all client copy tools.

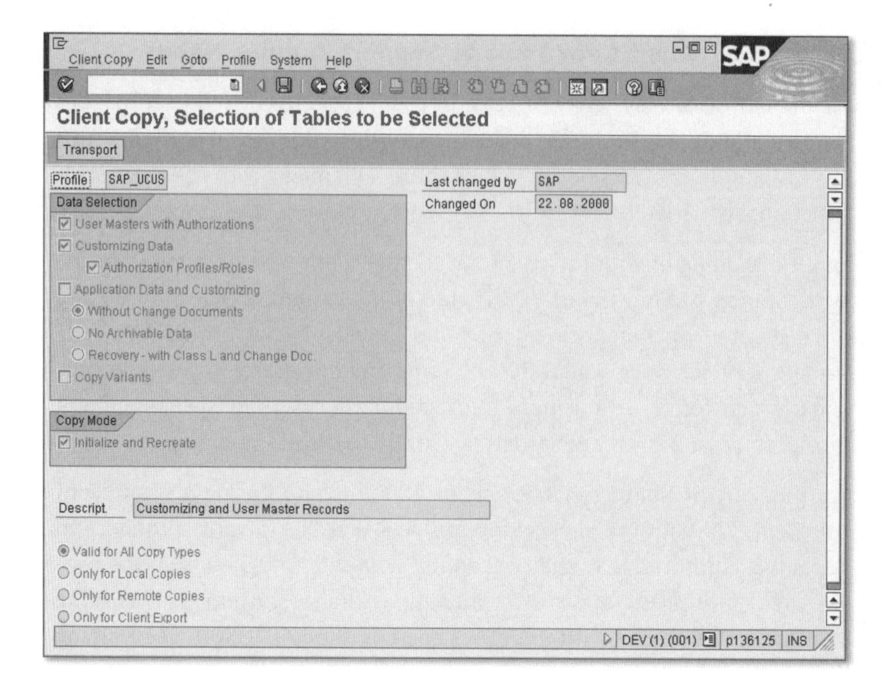


Figure 9.3 Displaying client copy profile SAP_UCUS

### 9.2.3 Local and Remote Client Copy

To perform either a local client copy or a remote client copy, proceed as follows:

1. Use client maintenance (Transaction SCC4) to ensure that the target client is defined in table T000.
2. Log on to the SAP system in the target client.
   - If the target client is new and has no defined users, log on with the user SAP* and the password PASS.
   - If users are defined in the target client, log on with a user that has authorization to perform a client copy, such as the user SAP*.
3. Access the appropriate client copy activity.
   - To copy a client from the same SAP system, access the local client copy tool using Transaction code SCCL or, from the SAP Easy Access Menu, choose **Tools • Administration • Administration • Client administration • Client copy • Local copy**.
   - To copy a client from another SAP system, access the remote client copy tool using Transaction code SCC9 or, from the SAP Easy Access Menu, choose **Tools • Administration • Administration • Client administration • Client copy • Remote copy**.

If a message box appears with the message "The client is locked for data import by client copy", the client protection setting for the target client does not allow overwriting.

4. Select the appropriate client copy profile. To see the available client copy profiles, use the F4-Help for the field **Selected Profile**.
5. Enter the source client information.
   - For a local client copy, provide the client ID of the source client whose Customizing data, application data, and variant information should be copied. In the field **Source client user masters**, you may also enter a client ID for the source client whose user data should be copied. Usually the two source clients are the same, but you may wish to copy user data from a different client.
   - For a remote client copy tool, you must provide an **RFC destination**. An RFC destination (maintained with Transaction SM59) is used to communicate with a client in another R/3 System for the purpose of sharing data. Using the F4-Help for the field **Source destinat.**, select the appropriate RFC destination. The name of the source SAP system and the client ID of the source client are entered automatically. (See Appendix A for information on maintaining RFC destinations.)

   If a message box appears with the message "Source client is protected against data export by client copy", the client protection setting for the source client does not allow external access and cannot be copied.
6. Choose **Execute** or **Execute in background** to start the client copy. Since a client copy is often very time-consuming, SAP recommends performing your client copy as a background job.
7. A **Verification** dialog box appears, which allows you to check and confirm the profile and source information. If everything is correct, choose **Yes** to start the client copy. Select **No** to cancel the procedure.

### 9.2.4 Client Transport

You can think of a client transport as a very large change request that contains the contents of an entire client. The multi-step process requires, first, a client export from the source client to files at the operating system level, and then the import of those data files into the target client. In addition, post-import processing is required to complete the procedure.

### RFC System Check

An SAP system consistency check is automatically performed before data is copied with a remote client copy. With a client transport, such a check is not automatic, but you can opt to perform one. The initial screen of the client transport tool (Transaction SCC8) has an **RFC system check** button that you can use to initiate this check.

The check program first determines what data is to be copied based on the selected client copy profile. RFCs are then used to locate the target system and client, and check whether all ABAP Dictionary definitions exist there in identical form. The check report usually confirms that all structures are consistent. If that is not the case, a list of the ABAP Dictionary table definitions missing in the target system is generated. This will help you to recognize in advance formal problems that may occur during the import of the source data.

> **Tip** To ensure the consistency of the ABAP Dictionary in the source and target SAP systems, SAP recommends performing an RFC system check before starting a client transport.

### Client Export

A client export writes data files at the operating system level. These data files, unlike the data files that result from a standard change request, may be rather large. For this reason alone, SAP does not recommend copying large production clients using the client copy tools. A system copy may be more appropriate. In any case, prior to using a client transport, you should verify that there is enough available disk space in the transport directory using operating system tools.

> **Note** For information on how to copy large production clients, see SAP Note 67205.

To perform a client export, follow these steps:

1. Log on to the SAP system in the source client. Do not log on as user SAP*.

> **Note** Since the user SAP* cannot create a change request, it cannot perform the client export step in a client transport.

2. Access the client export tool using Transaction code SCC8 or, from the SAP Easy Access Menu, choose **Tools • Administration • Administration • Client administration • Client transport • Client export**.
3. Select the appropriate client copy profile. To view the possible client copy profiles, use the F4-Help for the field **Selected Profile**.
4. Enter the system ID of the target system. The exported files will be imported into this SAP system. It must differ from the SAP system in which you are initiating the client export. Only SAP systems defined in your transport domain may be selected. Proceed as follows in these special situations:
   - If the target SAP system is not part of your transport domain, prior to the client export, use the TMS (Transaction STMS) to define the SAP system as either a virtual or an external system.
   - If the TMS is set up with extended transport control, you may provide an SID, a combination of an SID and a client, or a target transport group in the field for the target system.
5. Choose **Execute** or **Execute in background** to start the client export. Since this process can take a long time, SAP recommends performing the client export as a background job.
6. A **Verification** dialog box appears, which allows you to check and confirm the profile and source information. If everything is correct, choose **Yes** to start the client export. Select **No** to cancel the procedure.
7. An **INFO Client Export** message box will appear. This displays any change requests that may be generated as a result of the client export. Choose **Continue** to begin the client export.

### Client Import

A client export generates up to three change requests for import into the target SAP system. Table 9.2 displays the change requests for a sample client export. These change requests and files will be found in the transport directory for the 15th client export from the development system DEV. Since this sample client export uses the client copy profile SAP_EXPA, which includes all client-dependent and client-independent data from the source client, three change requests were generated. If the client copy profile SAP_USER, which selects only user data for export, had been selected for the sample client export, the `DEVKO00015` change request would not have been created.

| Change Request | Data Contents | Data File | Command File |
|---|---|---|---|
| DEVKO00015 | Client-independent data | R000015.DEV | K000015.DEV |
| DEVKT00015 | Client-dependent data | RT00015.DEV | KT00015.DEV |
| DEVKX00015 (None prior to R/3 Release 4.5) | Client-dependent text, such as SAPscripts | RX00015.DEV (SX0015.DEV prior to R/3 Release 4.5) | KX00015.DEV (None prior to R/3 Release 4.5) |

**Table 9.2** Sample Change Requests from a Client Export

Note that the client export files have a naming convention distinct from Customizing and Workbench change requests. Like those change requests, the ID number for client export files begins with the system ID of the source system (here, DEV), and ends with a sequential five-digit number. In the middle, however, there is a combination of the letters K and O (for client-independent data), T (for client-dependent data), or X (for client-dependent texts). These letters allow you to quickly distinguish a client export change request from standard change requests when viewing an import queue.

As a result of the client export, the change requests are added to the import queue of the target system. To view the import queue of a system, call Transaction STMS and choose **Overview · Imports**; then, double-click the system ID.

Figure 9.4 shows a sample import queue. A total of six change requests are waiting for import, three of which resulted from a client export initiated by user KOESEGI. Since client export change requests are special requests that, in most cases, delete and re-create a client as well as provide a client with new data, they cannot be imported using standard import commands (in Transaction STMS: **Start import** or **Preliminary import**). They must be imported as individual change requests. Such change requests are highlighted in a different color to indicate that they will not be imported. To determine the meaning of the different icons and colors, use the **Legend** button on the import queue screen.

All change requests, including those released as a result of a client export, should be imported in their correct order—the order in which they appear in the import queue (see Chapter 5). Before you import change requests as part of your client export process, import those change requests higher up in the import queue. For example, in Figure 9.4, the first two change requests should be imported before the client export.

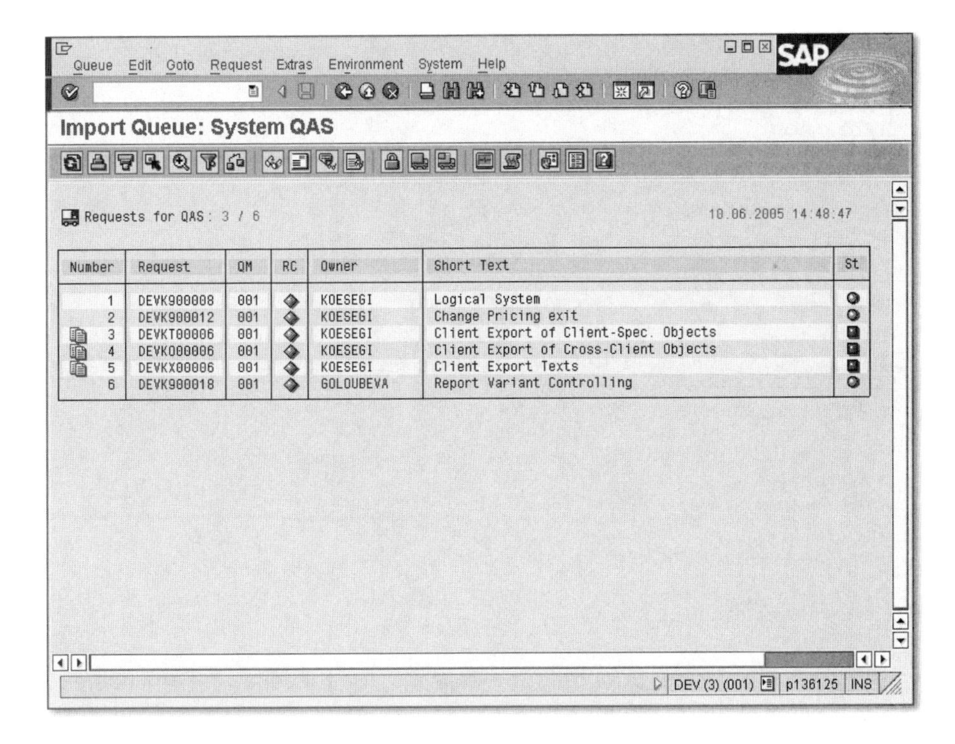


**Figure 9.4** A sample import queue with client export change requests

If your R/3 System is at R/3 Release 4.5 or higher, follow these steps to import the client data that has been exported and is waiting in the import queue:

1. Call Transaction STMS and then choose **Overview · Import**. Double-click the target SAP system of the client export to display its import queue.
2. Select the first client export change request waiting for import and choose **Request · Import**. By selecting this change request, you initiate the import for all the client export change requests.
3. The screen **Client Import**, as shown in Figure 9.5, will appear. It lists the names of the change requests to be imported. Enter the client ID of the target client.
4. Execute the import by selecting the **Import** button. The import of the change requests occurs as a background job.

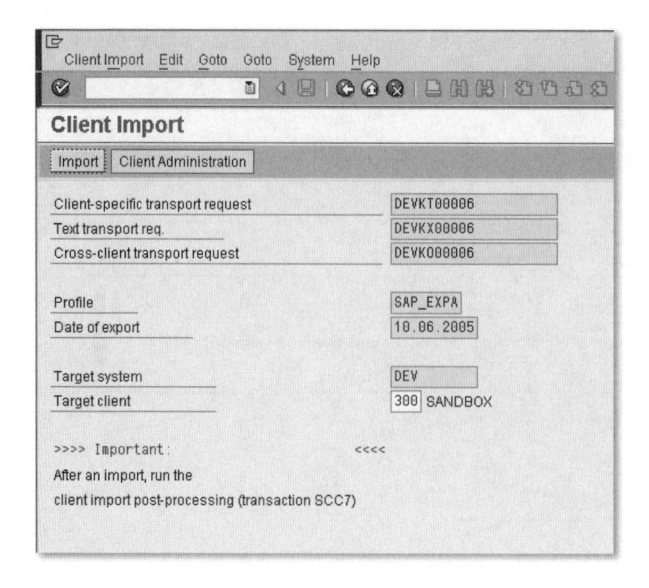


**Figure 9.5** The client import screen

For systems with releases prior to R/3 Release 4.5, use the following procedure to import change requests resulting from a client export:

1. Call Transaction STMS and then choose **Overview · Import**. Double-click the target R/3 System of the client export to display its import queue.
2. If the client export has created a client-independent change request—for example, in Figure 9.5, `DEVK000015`—import this change request first.
   - Select the change request and choose **Request · Import**.
   - Enter the client ID of the desired target client.
   - Because the import may be time-consuming, schedule the import to occur in the background by selecting the button **Expert mode** and choosing **Start import in background**.
   - To start the import of the change request, choose **Start import**.
3. Import the client-dependent change request—for example, `DEVKT00015`.
   - Select the change request and choose **Request · Import**.
   - Provide the client ID of the desired target client.
   - Because the import may be time-consuming, schedule the import to run as a background job by selecting the button **Expert mode** and choosing **Start import in background**.
   - To start the import of the change request, choose **Start import**.

Since a change request does not exist for text files in releases prior to R/3 Release 4.5, they will not be involved in the import process. Instead, they are included in post-import processing.

#### Post-Import Considerations

For all SAP releases, after successful import, the client export change requests remain in the import queue of the target system. You should delete these change requests by individually selecting each change request in the import queue and choosing **Request · Delete**.

Client export change requests do not continue along the standard transport routes. In other words, if you import a client into the quality assurance system, the change requests will not be added to the import queue of the production system. If the client export is to be imported into other SAP systems or clients, you must add the change requests to the import queues accordingly.

#### Post-Import Processing

No one should work in the client until the necessary post-import activities have been performed successfully. The only exception to this is when you perform a client import that contains only user data. Post-import processing includes:

- Deleting data from certain imported tables, including tables with delivery class "L" (explained in more detail below in "Table Delivery Classes")
- Importing texts (prior to R/3 Release 4.5)
- Generating reports, screens, and other Repository objects
- Adjusting number ranges

To perform post-import processing:

1. Log on to the target SAP system in the target client.
2. Use Transaction code SCC7 or, from the SAP Easy Access Menu, choose **Tools · Administration · Administration · Client administration · Client transport · Post-process import**.
3. The screen **Client import - postprocessing** appears (see Figure 9.6). It shows the name of the client-dependent change request from the client import process. The name of the profile used during the client export is also displayed. To begin post-import processing, choose either **Execute** or **Execute in background**.
4. If client-independent Customizing objects were copied, you will be prompted to process the cross-client Customizing changes. If the SAP system contains none of its own unique client-independent Customizing, choose **Yes**.

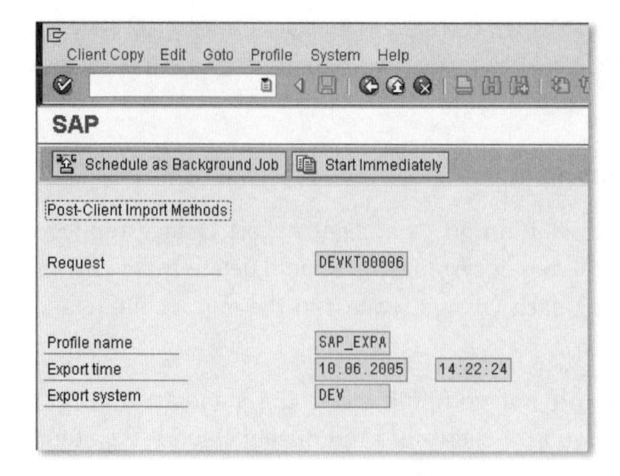


**Figure 9.6** Client import post-processing screen

Post-import processing needs to be performed only once. If you try to restart post-import processing, one of the following messages will appear in the status bar:

- "A physical client transport with tp has not taken place". This message appears when post-import processing has been completed.
- "Client has not yet been generated by a data import". This message appears when a client import has not occurred or the import of the client data was not successfully completed.

### 9.2.5 Monitoring and Verifying a Client Copy

While a client copy is running, throughout the rather long procedure, you can view the status in the **Client Copy Log**. After the procedure is complete, you can also use the log to verify whether the client copy was a success or failure before you begin working in the target client.

To access the Client Copy Log, use Transaction code SCC3 or, from the SAP Easy Access Menu, choose **Tools • Administration • Administration • Client administration • Copy logs**. The screen displays the current status of all local and remote client copies, listed by the target client number. Figure 9.7 shows a sample screen indicating client export logs for three different target clients. The column **Number Runs** indicates how many client copy log files exist for the target client. The most important column, **Status text**, displays the status of the last client copy. Possible status texts include:

- Initializing ...
- Processing ...

- Successfully completed/exported
- Completed with errors
- Canceled
- R3trans export (see SE01)

These texts are also valid for a client transport. In fact, the last text is client transport–specific and is explained below in "Special Transaction for Client Transports."

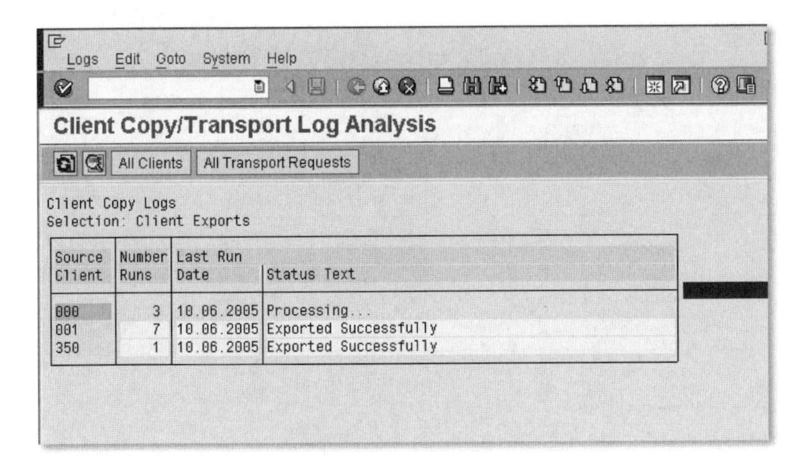


| Source Client | Number Runs | Last Run Date | Status Text |
|---|---|---|---|
| 000 | 3 | 10.06.2005 | Processing... |
| 001 | 7 | 10.06.2005 | Exported Successfully |
| 350 | 1 | 10.06.2005 | Exported Successfully |

**Figure 9.7** Client Copy Log Analysis screen

With Transaction SCC3, you can also monitor the client export and import activities that make up a client transport. In R/3 Releases prior to Release 4.5, the client export log files are displayed on the initial screen of Transaction SCC3 with "EXP" in the column **Target Client**. With these Releases, import logs can only be found using the Transport Organizer (Transaction SE01). To view import logs as of Release 4.5, from the initial screen of Transaction SCC3, you can choose either **Client exports** or **Client imports**.

To access the logs for a particular target client, double-click that client ID. A list of all available log files for that client will be displayed. A sample screen is shown in Figure 9.8. The table on this screen contains a variety of information, including the client copy profile (column **Profile**) and the client copy type (column **Mode**). In the column **Test**, the entry "R" indicates that a resource check was run, and "X" refers to a simulation (explained below in "System Resources"). By double-clicking a particular log file, you can obtain the following information:

- For client copy logs resulting from a test run (an entry in the column **Test**), you have detailed access to the tables impacted by the copy as well as an estimated resource analysis.

- For client copies that have the status **Processing**, you can see the table whose data is currently being processed and the number of tables still to be copied.
- For client copies with the status **Successfully completed**, you can verify the tables that were copied and the number of table inserts and deletes.
- For client copies with the status **Canceled** or **Completed with errors**, to determine the cause of the error, you can view the log files.

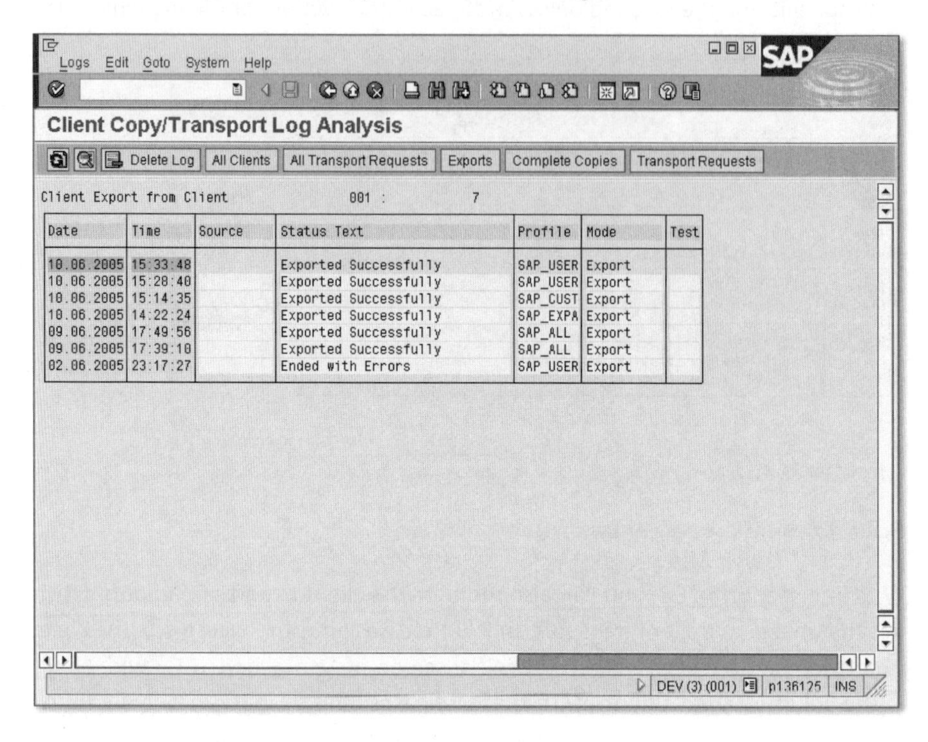


**Figure 9.8** Client copy runs for a single client

### Special Transaction for Client Transports

When data is being extracted for a client export, the status for the client copy log in this transaction will read "R3trans export (see SE01)". Because client transports use `R3trans`, a database tool external to R/3 (see Chapter 7), you can view only limited log files within Transaction SCC3.

To see all the export and import log files generated during a client transport process, access the Transport Organizer by calling Transaction SE01. From the initial screen, select **Client transports** as the request type, and click **Choose**. This displays client transport change requests in the same hierarchical manner used for standard change requests in the Customizing Organizer or Workbench Organizer.

## Restarting a Canceled Client Copy

Table 9.3 lists the most common reasons why a client copy is terminated, and presents possible solutions.

| Cause of Termination | Solution |
|---|---|
| A user stops the program. | Restart the client copy. |
| A user shuts down the R/3 System, or the system fails. | Restart the client copy. |
| The program terminates due to inadequate storage space in the database. | To monitor the database fill level and size of objects such as tablespaces or tables, use Transaction DB02. Using database tools such as SAPDBA, increase available space and restart the client copy. |
| You receive an ABAP dump with the error cause **timeout**. | Either increase the maximum online runtime (profile parameter `rdisp/max_wprun_time`) and restart the client copy, or perform the client copy in the background (covered below in "Background Scheduling of a Client Copy"). |
| The program terminates due to an error in an EXIT module. You receive an ABAP dump. | Review the copy logs to determine which program failed. Using SAP's Internet site, SAPNet, search for SAP Notes related to the failed program to find a correction. Correct the problem or contact the SAP Hotline for further support. |
| An inconsistency occurs between the database and the SAP system. You receive an ABAP error message noting a database inconsistency. | Data cannot be copied properly because table structures in the source and target systems differ. Correct the inconsistencies and restart the client copy. (Refer back to "RFC System Check.") |

**Table 9.3** Common Causes and Fixes for a Failed Client Copy

After correcting the problem, restart the client copy by again calling the appropriate client copy transaction (Transaction SCCL, SCC9, or SCC8). Since the initial client copy failed, the **Restart** option will be proposed by default. For example, if a local client copy failed because of inadequate tablespace, you would remedy the problem and then call Transaction SCCL. The parameters you initially used for the canceled client copy would still be present, and the field **Restart mode active** would be selected. To run the client copy from the point of failure—that is, to begin copying the table where the failure occurred—choose either **Execute** or **Execute in background**. To perform a completely new client copy, choose **Restart · New start**.

**Tip** If a terminated client copy was a recent run, which will be indicated in the status line, SAP recommends restarting the client copy from the time of the termination. This will save the time required for recopying data that has already been successfully copied.

### Additional Tools

In addition to reviewing the client copy logs, you can also monitor and verify a client copy with the following tools:

- Analyze a client copy error by calling Transaction SM21 (**System Log**) and checking the system log. This indicates whether database problems are responsible for the client copy error. Correct any database problems and then restart the client copy.
- Check the status of a client copy started as a background job by calling Transaction SM37 (**Background Job Overview**). This indicates whether a background client copy job has started, is active, or has been completed.
- Monitor the progress of a particular client copy by using Transaction SM30 (**View Maintenance**) to access view V_CCCFLOW. This view contains, for example, the runtime and processing status of a local client copy, the number of already copied tables, and the name of the table currently being copied.
- View the log files physically stored in the transport directory at the operating system level. Log files are named `CC<number>.<SID>`, where `<number>` is the six-digit serial client copy number, and `<SID>` is the source system ID. For example, the 21st client copy on the development system will generate the log file `CC000021.DEV`.

## 9.2.6 Considerations for a Client Copy

The client copy process impacts not only the performance, memory, and database resources of the involved SAP system (or systems), but also the availability of the source and target clients. Before starting a client copy, you must evaluate the system resources and client availability in your system landscape. In addition to technical issues, you must also consider the impact a client copy has on certain data, including number ranges and address data.

### Client Impact

Unless you are copying only user data, a client copy or client import reinitializes the target client by deleting it. The key entries of the tables corresponding to the target client are deleted.

To ensure data consistency in the target client during the client copy or client import, the target client's restriction **Currently locked due to client copy** is activated automatically, and only the users DDIC and SAP* can log on to the target client.

No user should work in the source client during the copy procedure. This prevents possible inconsistencies, particularly in the number ranges, resulting from changes in tables that are being copied. You should schedule a client copy for a time when the source system's usage is minimal—for example, in the evening.

**Tip** Users should not make changes in a source client while it is being copied.

### Background Scheduling of a Client Copy

The client copy program has a long runtime. Therefore, it should always be started in the background. This has the following advantages:

- The client copy will not use or block work processes required for online processing.
- The client copy will not be terminated if it exceeds the allowed execution time. This is important when very large tables are involved in the copy. Although the maximum execution time for online work processes (profile parameter `rdisp/max_wprun_time`) is usually too short to allow a complete client to be copied, this runtime restriction does not apply to background processing.
- Changes to tables during online processing are not blocked. (While the client copy is in progress, to prevent possible inconsistencies, no changes can be made to tables in the source client.)

To perform a client copy as a background job, choose **Execute in background** when initiating the client copy. Next, schedule the job as immediate or specify a start time, preferably a time when the system is not being used. Provide the print parameters for the spool output. Once you save these parameters, the client copy is scheduled for background processing.

### System Resources

As pointed out in Chapter 3, every client requires both hardware and administrative resources. To copy a client, you must ensure that adequate space is available in the target SAP system. In other words, the target SAP system database must have enough free storage space available in existing tables for the client copy to succeed. In addition, you need enough system memory to process the copying of data. Without the required system resources, a client copy will fail.

#### Tablespace Requirements

For an SAP system whose database management system (DBMS) is Oracle, Informix, MaxDB (formerly known as SAP DB), or DB2/CS you can determine whether the database space for each table suffices by performing a test run of the proposed client copy. After a test run, you receive a list of all database areas (tablespaces) that will be extended during the copy. In addition, since these test runs are logged, you can use the log to check how much space the entries require.

To perform a client copy as a test run, simply execute the client copy with the option **Test run** selected. A test run can be executed either online or, more appropriately, as a background job. To start the test run, choose either **Resource Check** or **Simulation**. These two types of test runs differ as follows:

- A resource check estimates the required database space by counting the records to be copied. It is faster than a simulation.
- A simulation estimates the required database space by reading all records to be copied without updating them in the database.

There is no way to exactly determine the range of free storage space available in existing tables. For every table copied, the number of required inserts is calculated. However, since database deletions are not possible in some databases until after reorganization, these deletions are not taken into account. This means the forecasted database requirements may be considerably larger than the actual requirements. If a resource check or a simulation indicates that you have enough tablespace to perform a client copy, you can be certain the client copy will not fail because of a lack of tablespace.

Note that the space requirements can only be estimated, because space that is reserved but not yet occupied is not taken into account. A client without application data requires a storage space of roughly 500MB in the database. Additionally, you must consider that in most databases, the space that is freed by deleting data only becomes available after a reorganization. For pool tables, the estimate is very imprecise, because their extent sizes is very substantial. Nevertheless, you have to assume that a new extent is required for every pool table, which increases the estimated value. For more information, refer to SAP Note 118823.

#### Memory Requirements

A client copy requires a great deal of system memory. If your system memory is limited, you should not perform any other activities in the system during the copy procedure. In this case, SAP recommends running the client copy as a background job at a time when the normal activity of the system is greatly reduced.

### Table Delivery Classes

By selecting a particular client copy profile, you determine which data is copied in a client copy. In turn, the SAP system uses table delivery classes to determine which data corresponds to the client copy profile.

A table delivery class indicates the type of data housed in a table—application data, Customizing data, or some type of system data. Every table in the ABAP Dictionary is assigned a table delivery class. Release upgrades and the client copy tools use this information to determine which table data to copy to target clients.

Table 9.4 displays the different table delivery classes and indicates when the different classes are copied. For example, if you select the client copy profile for client-dependent Customizing data only, the client copy will select the client-dependent data from those tables with the delivery class "C." In addition, the client copy selects the client-dependent data from system tables with the delivery classes "G," "E," and "S."

| Table Delivery Class | Type of Table | Copied* When? |
|---|---|---|
| A | Application data | When selected |
| C | Customizing data | When selected |
| L | Temporary table | Never |
| G | Customizing table protected during an upgrade | Always |
| E | Control table | Always |
| S | System table that you cannot maintain | Always |
| W | System table | Never |

**Table 9.4** The role of table delivery classes in a client copy

You do not need to select particular delivery classes, because they are tied to the client copy profile. However, when you are debugging, the table delivery class may help you discover why a certain data type was not included in a client copy. For example, if data is stored in a table with the table delivery class "W," you know the data will not be part of any client copy. However, if you selected a profile that included application data, and the data from a table with delivery class "A" was not included in the copy procedure, one of the following has occurred:

- The data was entered into the source table after the client copy.
- The data was deleted from the target client after the client copy was completed.
- The table containing the data is assigned to the temporary development class $tmp. Data in tables that are assigned to a temporary development class is not copied during a client copy.

* It is assumed that the copy mode is set to Initialize and recreate.

- There is a programming problem. In this case, check SAP's Internet site, SAP-Net, for a specific SAP Note, or report the problem to the SAP Hotline.

To view the delivery class of a table, use Transaction code SE11 or, from the SAP Easy Access Menu, use **Tools • ABAP Workbench • Development • Dictionary**. Enter the name of the table and select **Display**.

#### Number Ranges

When performing Customizing activities within the IMG, you often adjust *number ranges*. A number range is the set of consecutive numbers that can be assigned to business objects—or their sub-objects—of the same type. Examples of such objects include addresses, business partners, general ledger accounts, orders, posting documents, and materials. Number ranges are assigned to application data—master data in the case of business partners or transaction data for orders. When working with multiple clients and using client copies to create new clients, you should evaluate the status of your number ranges. For example, you may wish, for the purpose of testing, to use different number ranges in different clients, or perhaps the same number ranges for certain master data but not necessarily for transaction data.

If you copy only Customizing data, the target client will contain no application data after the completion of the client copy. In this case, the number ranges will be automatically reset to default values during the copy procedure. In all other cases, the number range status remains unchanged or is copied from the source client.

**Tip** After a client copy, SAP recommends that you evaluate number ranges in the target client and reset them when necessary.

**Note** Address number ranges can be problematic when information is shared between clients. For more details on avoiding possible address inconsistencies in your system landscape, see SAP Note 25182.

## 9.3 Deleting a Client

When you delete an client from your system landscape, you have to remove:

- All of its associated client-dependent data
- Its entry in table T000

Deleting a client is a permanent step. The client can be reinstated only by restoring the entire database of the SAP system from a backup.

**Warning** Once you have deleted an client, you cannot simply undo the procedure. A restore of the SAP system database is the only way to bring back a client.

To delete a client's data and its entry in table T000:

1. Log on to the SAP client you wish to delete.
2. To access the client delete tool, use Transaction code SCC5 or, from the SAP Easy Access Menu, choose **Tools · Administration · Administration · Client administration · Special functions · Delete client**.
3. Select a client delete option. Choose from either:
   - **Test run**: To simulate the deletion process and see what table entries will be deleted
   - **Delete entry from T000**: To delete the client ID from client maintenance
4. Select the button **Delete online** or **Background** to start the procedure.

## 9.4 Table Logging for a Client

Table logging is different from recording changes to change requests. Logging table changes made in a client provides an audit trail that allows you to verify who made exactly what change to the data and when. For example, if a user changes the company name associated with a company code:

- A change request would record that the key value—in this case, the company code—has been changed by a particular user.
- Table logging would indicate the actual field that changed in a table and would store the original company name. It would record who made the change and when.

When you log table changes made as a result of Customizing activities, you can pinpoint the actual change. For example, you can determine whether data in a particular field was changed or whether a new record was added to a table. In releases prior to R/3 Release 4.5, all table logging is displayed at the table level. Beginning with R/3 Release 4.5, you can also display table logs at the Customizing-activity level. To activate table logging, see below.

### 9.4.1 Resource Constraints

Table logging saves a "before image" by documenting the complete set of table entries before a change is made. Each time a Customizing change is made, a new before image is created. Therefore, table logging will constrain your system resources in the following way:

- Each before image requires storage space in the database of your SAP system. Table logging is not suitable for recording or managing large quantities of data.
- Activating table logging causes twice as many database updates as before, resulting in a higher database memory load and reduced system performance. However, as long as table logging is restricted to Customizing tables (not application data tables), performance should not be greatly reduced.

This tool has the potential to produce large amounts of data, more than you may be able to actually review and evaluate. For all of these reasons, SAP recommends using table logging only in those clients where Customizing changes must be closely monitored. Most Customizing changes occur in the Customizing-and-development client. However, it should suffice to rely on the information provided by change requests in this client. Table logging is more appropriate in the production client, providing you with a complete audit of any immediate changes to Customizing settings or changes that usually occur in the production client, such as adjustments to currency exchange rates.

### 9.4.2 Activating Table Logging

To activate the logging of table changes for Customizing, the SAP system profile parameter must be set to `rec/client = <client ID>`. To change the SAP system profile, use Transaction code RZ10 (**Maintenance of profile parameters**) or, from the SAP Easy Access Menu, choose **Tools • CCMS • Configuration • Profile maintenance**.

For example, to activate the recording of table changes in the production client 400, the profile for the production system requires the entry `rec/client = 400`. Possible variations of the profile parameter include the following:

- `rec/client = 300, 400` activates logging in two clients, 300 and 400.
- `rec/client = OFF` deactivates logging for all clients.
- `rec/client = ALL` activates logging in all clients within the SAP system.

**Tip** For changes in the SAP system profile to take effect, an SAP system must be restarted.

### Activating Logging during Imports

When you activate table logging using the `rec/client` profile parameter, you ensure that table changes made within the client or clients will be logged. However, since Customizing changes may also be imported into the client, you can record them by setting the transport parameter `recclient = <client ID>` in the transport profile (see Chapter 7).

The transport parameter should have the same setting as the SAP system profile `rec/client`. In other words, if you have activated table logging for client 300 and client 400 by setting the profile parameter (`rec/client = 300,400`), the transport profile should be identical (`recclient = 300,400`).

Logging imported change requests as well as table logging in the SAP system provide a comprehensive, collective audit of all Customizing changes. If you do not have logging turned on during import, you can always use change requests in conjunction with table logging to get a similar audit history. In fact, this may be a more viable alternative, since logging imported changes can negatively impact system resources and unnecessarily inflate the amount of data collected.

SAP has predetermined the tables that are logged. These tables contain Customizing settings and were chosen because of their significance to the flow of business processes within SAP ECC. When you activate table logging for a client, a history of changes will be collected for those tables in the ABAP Dictionary selected by SAP. Technically, these are the tables for which SAP has activated the **Log data changes** option in the ABAP Dictionary. To check if a specific table will be logged when you activate table logging, display that table in the ABAP Dictionary Maintenance (Transaction SE11); then, choose **Technical Settings** to see if **Log data changes** is indicated for that table.

Starting with R/3 Release 4.5, logging has advanced beyond the table level to the Customizing-activity level. Technically, logging still occurs at the table level using the **Log data changes** option in the ABAP Dictionary. However, from within each IMG Customizing activity, you can view the tables associated with each Customizing activity and learn which have table logging activated.

Using Table Maintenance (Transaction SE13), you can change the technical settings for a specific table, including changing the **Log data changes** option for a table. However, SAP does not recommend altering this setting. If you deactivate logging for an object, an analysis of changes will result in inconsistencies. Activating table logging for a table may also negatively affect system performance. This applies particularly to application tables, due to the frequent changes to application data.

### 9.4.3 Viewing Table Logs

After you have activated table logging in a client, changes to tables are saved to **change documents**, often referred to as **change logs**. Using the tools provided by SAP, you can view these change documents in detail and compare older change documents with present table entries to obtain a before and after picture of your Customizing settings.

The table log analysis has slightly changed between the different releases. In the releases prior to 4.5B, you could only analyze tables. As of Release 4.5B, this was also possible for views and Customizing entries. Then, the display changed again with the SAP Web Application Server (SAP Web AS).

#### Table Log Analysis

To view the audit history for tables, use Transaction code SE38 (*ABAP Editor*) and execute the ABAP program `RSTBHIST`. Alternatively, from the R/3 initial screen, choose **Tools · Business Engineer · Customizing · Tools · Table History**. From the resulting screen, you can do any of the following:

- List all logged Customizing changes that occurred on the current day (only before R/3 Release 4.5)
- List all logged changes that occurred during a given time period (for example, over the last 15 days), or only those in a specific table
- List all tables for which table logging is active
- Compare the present contents of a table (for which logging is active) with its contents at a previous date and time

For example, to compare the current exchange rates (table TCURR) in an R/3 System with the values on June 13, 1999, you would:

1. Log on to the client whose data you wish to analyze.
2. Access the table history tool by using Transaction code SE38 and executing program RSTBHIST. Alternatively, from the R/3 initial screen, choose **Tools · Business Engineer · Customizing · Tools · Table History**.
3. To compare the current values of the table with its contents in the past:
   - In releases prior to R/3 Release 4.5, choose **Comparison**.
   - As of R/3 Release 4.5, select **Comparison: History <-> Current**, and choose **Function · Analyze change documents**.
4. Provide the name of the table whose values you want to compare—in our example, table TCURR. Enter the date (June 13, 1999) and, if you wish, a time.
5. Choose **Compare** to begin the comparison.

In the displayed screen, the first column, **Status**, is particularly interesting. This column permits the following entries:

- **Status "M":**
  The current value and the past value are different.
- **Status "C":**
  A current table entry did not exist in the table at the past date.
- **Status "S":**
  A table entry at the past date no longer exists in the current table.
- **No status:**
  The values for the table entries are identical.

### Customizing Activity Logging

Starting with R/3 Release 4.5, you can also analyze table logs from within a Customizing activity. This allows you to see the changes to tables that are part of a Customizing activity without knowing the specific names of the tables involved. Using Customizing activity logs from within an IMG activity, you can:

- Examine the tables involved in the current Customizing activity and determine which of the involved tables have table logging activated
- View the current changes that have been logged for the Customizing activity

If you want to see, for example, which tables are affected by the Customizing activity for **Currencies Exchange rates** and which tables are logged, proceed as follows (this example refers to SAP ECC Release 5.0):

1. Access the IMG (Transaction SPRO) and select **Implementation projects • Display SAP Reference IMG**. In the tree structure, select **SAP NetWeaver • General settings • Currencies • Enter exchange rates**.
2. Select **GoTo • Change log** to display information about table logging with regard to the activity.
3. Select the button **Logging: Display status** to display the logging status of the current client and the tables that are being logged in the current Customizing activity.

The results of this analysis are shown in Figure 9.9. The table involved in this activity is TCURR.

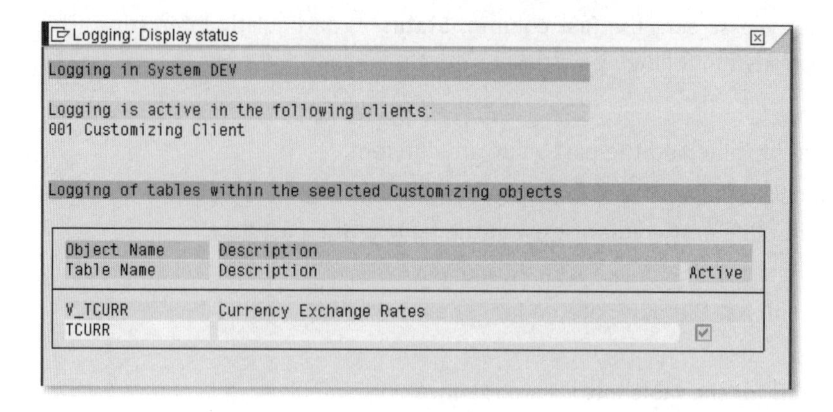


**Figure 9.9** Customizing activity logging status

You can also view the actual changes that have been recorded for a particular IMG Customizing activity. To do this, begin the Customizing activity and then choose **Utilities • Change logs**. For example, to view the changes that have taken place in a production system for the Customizing activity to change currency exchange rates, proceed as follows:

1. Access the IMG (Transaction SPRO) and select **Implementation projects • Display SAP Reference IMG**. In the tree structure, select **SAP NetWeaver • General settings • Currencies • Enter exchange rates**.
2. Select **GoTo • Change logs** to display information about table logging with regard to the activity.
3. Enter the time frame you wish to view.
4. Select the button **Execute** to display the logged information for the current Customizing activity during the specified time frame.

Figure 9.10 displays the results of this analysis. The column **Key Fields** shows the table entries that were adjusted. The actual changes are shown in the second column, **Function Fields, Changed**. Here, you can see whether the entry was changed, deleted, or newly created.

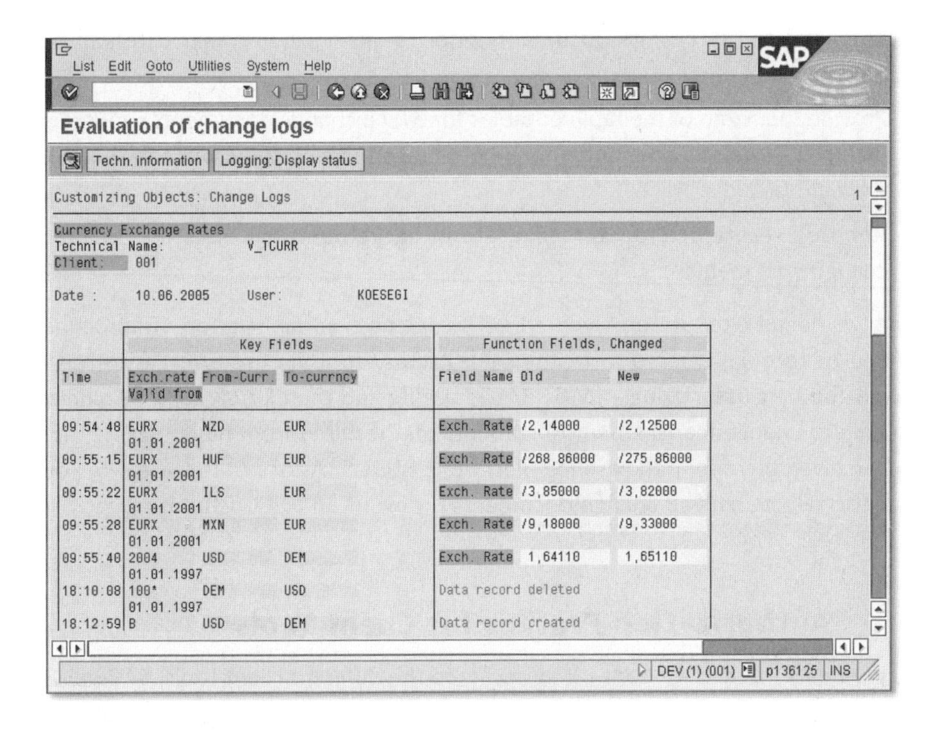


Figure 9.10 Change documents for a Customizing activity

### 9.4.4 Removing Change Documents

As more and more Customizing changes impact different tables, the number of change documents increases over time and occupies valuable space in the database. Therefore, it is important for you to manage the growth of change documents. SAP ECC provides you with two alternatives: You can either delete change documents that contain table logging data or archive the documents for retrieval and analysis at a later date in time. Archiving is the ideal method for preserving a complete audit history.

To delete unnecessary change documents, proceed as follows:

1. Log on to the client where you wish to delete change documents.
2. Access the table history tool by using Transaction code SE38 and executing program RSTBHIST; or, from the SAP Easy Access Menu, choose **Tools • Customizing • IMG • IMG Logging**.
3. To delete change documents:
   - In releases prior to R/3 Release 4.5, choose **Administration • Delete documents**.
   - As of R/3 Release 4.5, choose **Edit • Change docs • Delete**.

4. Enter a date. All change documents prior to and including that date will be deleted.
5. Provide the name of the table or tables for which change documents should be deleted. To delete all change documents regardless of the table name, leave this field blank.
6. Choose **Execute** or **Program • Execute in background** to delete the selected change documents.

Change documents are archived using the archive administration (Transaction SARA) or through a jump from the table history tool via the SAP Easy Access menu **Tools • Customizing • IMG • IMG logging** and then **Edit • Logs • Archive**. To archive change management documents that resulted from table logging, use the archive object for database log files, BC_DBLOGS. As of R/3 Release 4.5, you can also select archived change documents for inclusion in a Customizing activity log analysis.

## 9.5 Authorization Profiles for Client Tools

To provide a method for controlling access to the different client tools, SAP delivers its software with standard authorization objects. In addition to these authorization objects, you can rely on the client protection setting defined for each client to protect its data from being overwritten or accessed externally. Once a client has this setting, no matter how many authorizations a user has, that person cannot overwrite the data in the protected client by performing a local client copy.

Table 9.5 provides a list of the authorizations delivered by SAP that are relevant for the client copy tools. It also indicates whether that authorization is required for the user account in the target client and/or the source client. For example, in a remote client copy, the source client's user is defined by the RFC destination used during the client copy. To perform a remote client copy, the user referenced in the RFC destination must at least have the authorization S_ TABU_RFC.

| Authorization Object | Description of Permitted Activities | Local Client Copy | Remote Client Copy | Client Transport |
|---|---|---|---|---|
| S_TABU_CLI | Maintenance of client-independent tables | Target | Target | Source and target |
| S_TABU_DIS | Maintenance of the client copy control table CCCFLOW | Target | Target | Source and target |

**Table 9.5** Authorization objects needed in source/target clients when using the client copy tools

| Authorization Object | Description of Permitted Activities | Local Client Copy | Remote Client Copy | Client Transport |
|---|---|---|---|---|
| S_DATASET | Writing log files to the operating system level | Target | Target | Source and target |
| S_CLNT_IMP | Importing data into a client | Target | Target | Source and target |
| S_CTS_ADMI with TTYPE 'CLCP' ACTVT '01' | Creating object lists for client transport and copying them to another client | | | Source and target client |
| S_TRNSPRT | Exporting data | | | Source |
| S_USER_PRO | Copying user profiles | Target | Source and target | Source |
| S_USER_AGR | Copying roles | Target client | Source and target client | Source client |

**Table 9.5** Authorization objects needed in source/target clients when using the client copy tools

A client entry and its settings are stored in table T000. Since this is a client-independent table, a user needs the authorization object S_TABU_CLI to maintain client entries using Transaction SCC4. To delete a client, you must have three authorization objects: S_TABU_CLI, S_TABU_DIS, and S_DATASET. Analyzing table logs and Customizing activities requires two authorization objects: S_TABU_CLI and S_TABU_DIS.

**Tip** User SAP* has complete authorization to use all client tools. However, because SAP* cannot create a change request, SAP* cannot perform the client export step in a client transport.

## 9.6 Questions

1. After you create a new client entry in table T000, which of the following activities enables you to provide the client with data?
   A. A remote client copy to populate the client with data from a client in another SAP system
   B. A client transport to import data from a client in another SAP system
   C. A local client copy to import data from a client within the same SAP system
   D. All of the above
2. Which of the following *cannot* be used to restrict a client from certain activities?
   A. The client role
   B. The client-dependent change option
   C. The client ID-number
   D. A client restriction
   E. The client-independent change option
3. Which of the following tasks can be performed using the client copy tools?
   A. Merging application data from one client into another client
   B. Copying only application data from one client to another client
   C. Copying only Customizing data from one client to another client
   D. All of the above
4. Which of the following tasks can be performed using the client copy profiles?
   A. Scheduling a client copy to occur at a time when system use is low
   B. Selecting the subset of application data that will be copied when a client copy is executed
   C. Providing required user authorization for the use of client tools
   D. Determining the data that will be copied when a client copy is executed
5. Which of the following statements is correct in regard to table logging?
   A. Table logging should be used instead of change requests whenever possible.
   B. Table logging provides an audit history of who made what changes and when.
   C. Table logging does not negatively impact system resources.
   D. All of the above.

# Part 3
# Tools

Part 1 of this book provided an overview of the change and transport concepts and recommendations for your R/3 System landscape. Part 2 covered the technical requirements and setup of these tools. Part 3 will explain in detail how to use the following change and transport tools:

- Workbench Organizer (Chapter 10)
- Customizing Organizer (Chapter 11)
- Transport Management System (TMS) (Chapters 12 and 13)
- Transport control program `tp` (Chapter 14)
- SAP Patch Manager (SPAM) (Chapter 15)
- R/3 Transactions for modifications and adjustments (SPDD and SPAU) (Chapter 15)

The first four chapters of Part 3, Chapters 10–13, will be of most interest for those people who are directly involved in making changes to the R/3 System—the customizers and developers—as well as for those responsible for importing change requests.

Chapter 14 contains detailed information on the import process, which is particularly helpful when it comes to troubleshooting. In most cases, these tasks are handled by system administrators and technical consultants.

Chapters 15 and 16 deal with maintaining and upgrading the SAP system landscape. These chapters are of interest for system administrators who are responsible for these tasks. Project leaders, however, are also invited to get an overview over necessary activities and efficient approaches in maintaining and upgrade projects.

Chapter 17 describes new functionalities of SAP Solution Manager in the area of Software Change Management. It focuses on Customizing Synchronization in a system landscape and on managing change requests.

Chapter 18 finally provides an outlook on transport tools in the Java environment.

# 10 Managing Development Changes

Technically, development changes in an mySAP ERP system are changes to Repository objects using the tools of the ABAP Workbench. These changes are recorded to Workbench change requests, which are then managed using the Workbench Organizer. Development changes include creating and changing customer-developed or SAP-delivered objects.

Proper management of development changes, which ultimately ensures that all changes can be validated and distributed to all mySAP ERP systems in the system landscape, can be divided into the following areas:

- Development prerequisites
- Change requests and tasks
- Repairs and modifications
- The Object Directory

## 10.1 Development Prerequisites

As prerequisites to performing development, ensure that:

- The client-independent change option and the system change option allow changes to Repository objects
- Each developer has the appropriate authorizations and obtains an SAP Software Change Registration (SSCR) key
- Development classes and object names are used that enable the transport of new Repository objects

A user with developer authorizations can perform development work only if the current SAP client allows for client-independent changes—changes to Repository objects. In addition, the system change option must allow the relevant types of objects to be changed—for example, local objects, customer-developed objects, or SAP-developed objects.

> **Note** See Chapter 11 for more information on developer authorizations, Chapter 9 for information on client-independent changes, and Chapter 7 for information on the system change option.

### 10.1.1 SSCR Registration of Developers

Any user who wishes to use the ABAP Workbench to create, change, or delete Repository objects (including customer-developed objects) in the SAP system must be registered using the *SAP Software Change Registration* (SSCR) key. Such users are often referred to as *development users* or *developers*.

The first time that development users attempt to create or change an object, the system displays the **Add developer** dialog box, which asks for their access key (see Figure 10.1). To obtain this access key, enter the developer's user ID and the system's installation number in the SCCR area in SAPNet. Copy the resulting 20-digit key into the appropriate field in the **Add developer** dialog box.

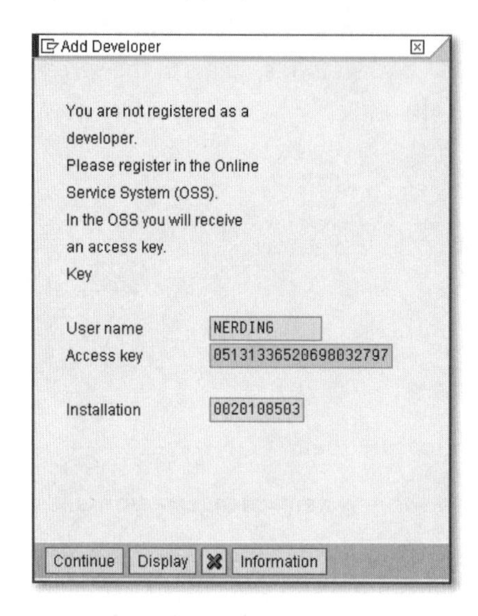


**Figure 10.1** SSCR key for a developer

After a developer has been registered through SSCR, the system will not request an SSCR key for that developer's subsequent attempts to create or change Repository objects.

**Note** For more information on SSCR, see SAP Note 86161 in SAPNet.

### 10.1.2 Packages

Today, SAP ECC consists of more than 300,000 development objects (programs, tables, dynpros, BAPIs, function modules, types, etc.). These objects are grouped in more than 1,700 development classes at the same level.

In general, every developer can use every development object. Therefore, a developer can hardly configure a protection against the use of his or her own development objects. Similarly, it is almost impossible to identify those development objects that should be made available to others. Additionally, the possibilities of a tentative technical modularization, for example, via module pools, function groups or classes, are very limited. Thus, appropriate mechanisms for a technical modularization are missing both on a large and on a small scale.

This is where packages come in. They are an enhancement of today's development classes with new additional semantics and serve to split, encapsulate and decouple mySAP ERP on a large and small scale.

### Package Concept

The previous development classes, being simple containers for development objects, are provided with a transport layer specifying the transport route. As an extension of development classes, the packages are characterized by the basic properties nesting, interfaces, and visibility, as well as use access.

- *Nesting* is the ability of packages to embed other packages.
- *Visibility* denotes a property of package elements. An element can be visible outside of its pakkage. It is always visible within its package, but never within embedded packages. If an element is visible from the outside, it is placed in at least one *package interface*.
- A *use access* is associated with a one-sided right of a package to use the visible elements of an interface of another package.

The following figure illustrates the basic properties of packages in a graphical way.

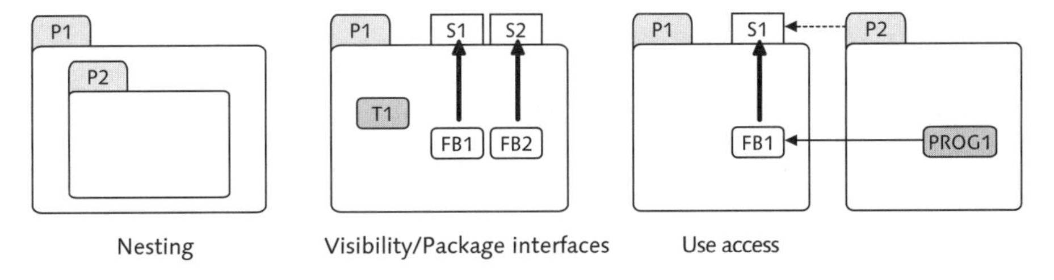


**Figure 10.2** Package concept

Using interfaces and visibility, a package can identify its range of services. All visible elements can potentially be used by other packages. Elements that are not visible cannot be used by other packages. Therefore, a package can protect its elements from arbitrary foreign use and encapsulate its contents.

Use access limits the use of visible elements of foreign interfaces. Not all visible elements can be used as well. Only if a use access for an interface of a foreign package exists, can a package use the visible elements of this package.

Nesting allows for a hierarchical organization of larger units of mySAP ERP. Through the combination of interfaces and use access, the package elements can be hidden easily and thus be protected from unauthorized use.

The highest level of the package hierarchy is formed by structure packages, which usually comprise several main packages. Starting with the respective main package, they create the corresponding partial packages.

This package concept enables you to split and encapsulate R/3 into technical units in the form of packages, to reduce the high dependencies, and to therefore decouple the system on a large and on a small scale.

### Creating a Customer Package

By default, package validation is deactivated on the customer system. In this case, the packages have the same properties as the previous development classes. They are simply a container for SAP objects that logically belong together.

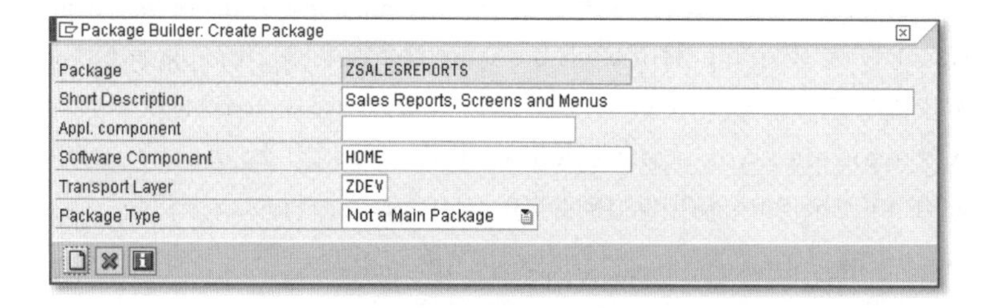


**Figure 10.3** Creating a customer package

If you want to create new programs, screens, or tables for transport to other SAP systems, you need at least one customer package. A customer package for your development environment is created as follows:

1. Access the Repository Browser using Transaction code SE80, or, in the initial screen select **Tools · ABAP Workbench · Overview · Object Navigator**.
2. In the screen **Object Navigator: Initial screen**, select Package.
3. Enter a name for the new package. The name can be up to 30 characters long and must be within the customer namespace or name range. For example, use a name like Y<Name> or Z<Name>, where <Name> should be a short description of the package.
4. Choose **Display**. The system checks whether the package exists. If it doesn't, the **Create Object** dialog box is displayed where you can specify whether or not the package should be created. Select **Yes**.

5. The **Create Package** dialog box is displayed (see Figure 10.3). Enter the following information:
   - A short description of the new package.
   - Starting with Release 4.5, you can also assign an application component to the package if all objects to be secured in the package are intended for the same application component.
   - A software component of the new package—normally, the HOME software component—must be assigned
   - A transport layer—normally you should use the standard transport layer suggested by default.
   - A package type—if you don't use package validation, you can keep the suggested standard package type.
6. Select **Save**. The SAP system prompts you for a change request identification. You have the following two options:
   - Enter the change request identification of an existing change request.
   - Select **Create Request** to create a new change request. The system displays the **Create Request** screen (see Figure 10.8). Enter a descriptive name for the change request.
7. Select **Save**. The screen **Repository Browser: Package <Package>** is displayed showing your new package at the top of the package list. Since the package is new, it has not yet been assigned any repository objects.

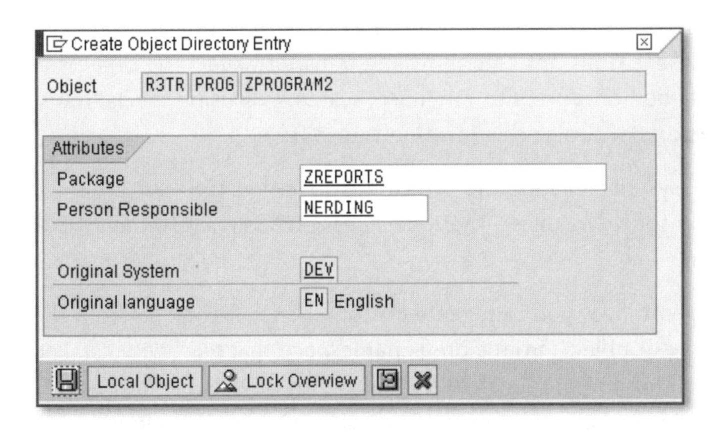


**Figure 10.4** The creation of a new repository object requires the assignment of a development class

### Naming Conventions for Packages

The packages starting with the letters [A–S] or [U–X] are reserved for the objects of the SAP standard version from the SAP name range. Customer-specific objects or objects from prefix namespaces cannot be created in these packages.

Note that a package name can consist of a maximum of 30 characters. Furthermore, the package semantics should be reflected in the name. For *neighboring* packages, we advise you to use similar names.

Changes to objects of these packages are recorded by the Transport Organizer and can therefore be transported. These packages belong to the SAP transport layer and are assigned to an SAP software component (e.g., SAP_BASIS, SAP_APPL).

In packages starting with Y or Z, you can create customer-specific objects from the customer name range. Changes to objects of these packages are recorded by the Transport Organizer and can be transported if the SAP system has been configured accordingly.

These packages are assigned to the HOME software component.

In a package starting with a T, you can create customer-specific objects from the customer name range or objects from a prefix namespace that has been installed to your SAP system using the producer role.

When creating such a package, you can specify whether the package should be connected to the Transport Organizer. If this is what you want, objects being edited are recorded by the Transport Organizer in local requests that are not transported. The package does not belong to any transport layer. The objects of this package can only be transported to other SAP systems via using special transport requests (transports of copies or relocation transports).

Newly installed SAP systems include the private test package TEST, which is not connected to the Transport Organizer. These packages are assigned to the LOCAL software component.

In a package starting with a $, you can create customer-specific objects from the customer name range, or objects from a prefix namespace that has been installed to your SAP system using the producer role. Changes to objects of this package are not recorded by the Transport Organizer. The package does not belong to any transport layer. The objects cannot be transported.

Newly installed SAP systems contain the local $TMP package.

Like other repository objects, packages can belong to a prefix namespace if the corresponding namespace is installed in the SAP system. The package name starts with a namespace prefix enclosed by slashes (/).

The prefix namespace has the following effects: In such a package, you can only create objects belonging to the same prefix namespace. Changes to objects of these packages are recorded by the Transport Organizer and can be transported if the SAP system has been configured accordingly.

### Package Architecture in R/3 Enterprise

The design of the package architecture in R/3 Enterprise is based on the following objectives:

- Structure the software in a better way
- Encapsulate the functionality in a stronger way
- Provide well-defined interfaces throughout the environment
- Provide a better transparency of responsibilities

Especially for R/3 Enterprise, the application of the package concept is to ensure that the R/3 Enterprise Core and the extensions are developed individually with the goal of installing and maintaining them separately. The package concept can thus be used both within the R/3 Enterprise Core and in between the individual extensions for structuring and encapsulating.

Because the previous software components combine packages that are always delivered together, they form the basis of the new package architecture of R/3 Enterprise. Every software component is directly identified with one structure package each.

Therefore, the structure packages BASIS, ABA, HR and APPL emanate from the software components SAP_BASIS, SAP_ABA, SAP_HR and SAP_APPL.

| Software component | Description |
|---|---|
| SAP_BASIS | SAP Web Application Server (before: SAP Basis) |
| SAP_ABA | Cross-application component |
| SAP_HR | Human Resources Management |

**Table 10.1** Software components in R/3 Enterprise

| Software component | Description |
|---|---|
| SAP_APPL | Logistics and accounting |
| HOME | This software component contains packages with non-local objects that are not delivered to customers. |
| LOCAL | Comprises packages with local objects only. |

**Table 10.1** Software components in R/3 Enterprise (cont.)

Several extensions are grouped in an Enterprise add-on and delivered together. The individual extensions are not dependent on each other. They represent decoupled software units and are implemented using one structure package each. The R/3 Enterprise add-on is used as a container for the extensions and also corresponds to a software component.

Examples of extensions are EA_HR, EA_FIN, EA_TRAVEL, or EA_RETAIL.

The upgrade or the installation of R/3 Enterprise always includes the R/3 Enterprise Core, the R/3 plug-in, and some extensions that are grouped together in an R/3 Enterprise add-on.

To be able to use the extensions, they must be activated first.

The software components delivered with R/3 Enterprise are hierarchically structured. Using the hierarchy (see Figure 10.5), you can see which dependencies are caused by using a software component. For example, SAP_HR uses objects from the SAP_ABA component which, in turn, is dependent on SAP_BASIS.

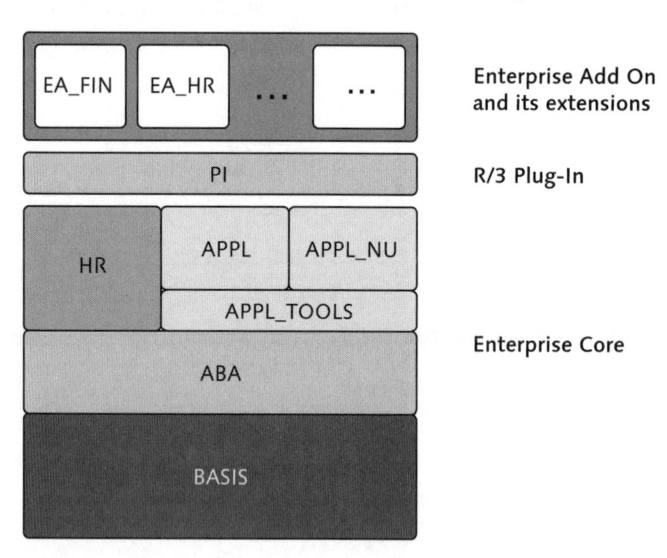


**Figure 10.5** Structure packages in R/3 Enterprise

### Creating Packages in Customer Scenarios

In certain customer scenarios, it is beneficial to activate package validation. For this purpose, the global package validation switch needs to be activated. The corresponding procedure is described in SAP Note 648898.

**Scenario 1:** Being an SAP customer, you install R/3 Enterprise but also want to start with your own development and to deliver your own tools, not only to R/3 Enterprise but also to other products like SAP Advanced Planner and Optimizer (SAP APO) or SAP Customer Relationship Management (SAP CRM). You make your applications dependent only on the structure packages BASIS and ABA. How can you proceed in this case to effectively implement the package concept?

1. Create a structure package that is to comprise all customer-specific developments.
2. Create main packages within the new structure package.
   The main packages are used for further structuring within the customer structure package and represent disjointed technical areas.
3. Define the usage relationships for the new structure package.
   Considering that your own structure package is dependent on only the two Enterprise components BASIS and ABA, the usage relationship of the new structure package needs to be defined accordingly:
   - Define the usage relationship at structure package level.
     This requires you to create the use access of the new structure package to the virtual pakkage interface of BASIS and of ABA. Additionally, the use access needs to be created to the respective filter package interface of BASIS and ABA.
   - Create the use access for all inner packages of the customer structure pakkage that are affected by the usage to the virtual package interface of BASIS and ABA.
4. You switch on the package check using the global package check switch.
5. To continue modularizing your customer developments, you make the package check stricter, step-by-step. In particular, you can set the **Package Check as Client** and **Package Check as Server** flags for the new structure package.
6. You import a copy of your customer development into the APO system in order to make it available there.

**Scenario 2:** Being an SAP customer, you already have many customer-specific developments and perform an upgrade to R/3 Enterprise. How can you proceed to structure your own developments?

Prerequisites

- Determine all development classes for the customer-specific development.
- Determine the packages on which the customer-specific developments should depend.
- Merge all of your own developments in a structure package.

Procedure

1. Create a structure package for all customer-specific developments.
2. Create main packages within the new structure package.
3. Assign all of the customer-specific packages to the new structure package. You have the option to assign packages to the structure package in a single step by using the report `RS_ASSIGN_TO_STRUCTURE_PACKAGE`.
4. Determine the dependencies of these packages on Enterprise structure packages BASIS, ABA, HR, APPL, APPL_TOOLS.
5. Create use access in the customer structure package to the interfaces of Enterprise structure pakkages (use access at structure package level).
6. Create the corresponding use access for all packages contained in the customer structure package.
7. Activate package validation using the global package check switch.

**Scenario 3:** Being an SAP customer, you have merged your own developments in a structure package and then want to further promote the decoupling in certain areas.

1. Another modularization can be effected by creating additional structure packages. In this case, however, the dependencies of the structure packages among each other need to be considered. If such dependencies exist, you need to create the corresponding package interfaces (for providers) or the use access (for users).
2. The decoupling can be further promoted by preassigning a specific error gravity to a use access. Thus, the degree of the access permission is specified and existing uses can be gradually reduced by increasing the error gravity.

### Restricting Customer Object Names

To ensure that your objects are not overwritten by SAP-delivered objects during the import of Support Packages or an upgrade, SAP has reserved name ranges for customer-developed objects and SAP-delivered objects. When creating a new Repository object, SAP developers must use the SAP name range, and you must use the customer name range.

**Note** For more information on customer name ranges, naming conventions, and examples of names, refer to online documentation.

**Warning** SAP delivers a few system objects with names that fall within the customer name range. To avoid using these names, consult the list in table TDKZ.

Most mySAP ERP implementations feature a single development system in which all customer developments are created. Performing all development work in a single SAP ECC system ensures that each object name can be used only once for a program, table, or other object type.

Performing development efforts in multiple systems may cause difficulties if there are objects created with the same name in various systems. This may happen, for example, when development changes are made centrally at a company's headquarters and then delivered to its subsidiaries. An attempt to import an object into a development system that already contains an object with the same name will fail, because, by default, objects in their original systems cannot be overwritten. If the target system is not a development system, the imported object will overwrite an object that has the same name in the target system. This may cause inconsistencies if the objects were originally developed in different systems.

You may not notice that there is a naming conflict until you transport your development work. At this late stage, resolving the conflict requires renaming the objects and all references to them. To avoid this type of conflict:

- Define naming conventions in the view V_TRESN (as described below) in all systems. The ABAP Workbench will prevent you from creating objects with the same names in different systems.
- Register a namespace with SAP through SAPNet. Large corporate implementations or development partners may require a unique namespace to use for developing objects. This ensures that, when centrally developed objects are delivered to other systems, they will not conflict with locally developed objects.

The first characters in the name of an object correspond to a naming convention in the ABAP Workbench. You can define a naming convention for a development class. The Workbench Organizer refuses to create an object if the developer tries to assign it to a development class other than the one dictated by the naming convention. This ensures, for example, that all Repository objects beginning with the naming convention ZSALES are assigned to the development class ZSALESREPORTS. Naming conventions are stored in the view V_TRESN.

To define a naming convention for a development class:

1. Use the Call View Maintenance screen (Transaction SM30). Enter the view name "V_TRESN". Choose **Maintain**. The **Change View "Naming Conventions in the ABAP Workbench": Overview** screen appears.
2. Choose **New entries**. The **New Entries: Details of Added Entries** screen appears.
3. Enter data in the respective fields as follows:

| Field | User Entry |
|---|---|
| **Program ID** | R3TR or R3OB. |
| **Object type** | To select the object type for which the naming convention applies, position the cursor in the field and use the possible entries arrow. |
| **Name range (generic)** | Enter the naming convention to be used—that is, specify the first characters of all object names that are to correspond to the development class. |
| **Devel. Class** | Enter the development class that is to correspond to the naming convention. |
| **Reservation type** | Retain the default value D, which indicates a standard name range reservation. |
| **Person responsible** | Enter the name of the person responsible for reserving the name range. |
| **Short description** | Enter a short text to describe why the naming convention was assigned to a particular development class. |

4. Choose **Save**.

For consistent naming protection, the view V_TRESN must be the same in all systems in the system landscape. New entries to V_TRESN should be recorded to a change request and distributed to all systems in the system landscape.

**Example: Naming Conventions for Development Classes**

In a system landscape connecting company subsidiaries in various countries, the corporate headquarters creates a standardized package of Customizing settings and development objects such as reports in the development system COR.

The two regional headquarters that receive the package, Asia and Europe, each have their own development systems. The Asian development system is ADV, and the European development system is EDV.

To avoid having Repository objects with the same name on the various development systems (COR, ADV, and EDV), the following entries are added to the view V_TRESN on the development system COR and transported to all other Systems in the system landscape:

| PgId | Obj | Name Range | Type | Dev. Class | Descriptions |
|---|---|---|---|---|---|
| R3TR | PROG | Y | D | ZCORPORATE | Programs |
| R3TR | TABL | Y | D | ZCORPORATE | Tables |
| R3TR | DOMA | Y | D | ZCORPORATE | Domains |
| R3TR | PROG | ZA | D | ZASIA | |
| R3TR | PROG | ZE | D | ZEURO | |

These entries ensure that centrally developed programs, tables, and data domains beginning with a Y belong to the development class ZCORPORATE. Programs for the Asian region will begin with ZA and receive the development class ZASIA; programs for the European region will begin with ZE and receive the development class ZEURO.

## 10.2 Workbench Change Requests

When you create or change a nonlocal Repository object, the object is recorded to a *Workbench change request*. To manage Workbench change requests, use the Workbench Organizer (Transaction SE09).

Unlike Customizing change requests, Workbench change requests are divided into the following types:

- Transportable
- Local
- Unclassified

Unless specified, a change request is created as an unclassified change request. When an Repository object has been recorded to a task in a change request, the change request becomes either a transportable change request or a local change request. The development classes of objects recorded to tasks in the change request determine the type of change request. For example, any object whose development class indicates that it is local is not recorded to a change request, or any object whose development class uses a transport layer that does not have an associated transport route in TMS is recorded to a local change request.

### 10.2.1 Transportable Change Request

Since most changes are created with the aim of transporting them to other systems, the transportable change request is the most commonly used type of Workbench change request.

A transportable change request is a change request that can be released and exported for transport to other systems. It contains Repository objects that can be transported—that is, Repository objects with a development class that is assigned to a valid transport layer. A transport layer is considered valid by the TMS if the system in which the object is created or changed is the source system of a designated consolidation route. For example, in Figure 8.18 (see Chapter 8), the training transport layer ZTRN is the consolidation route from the development system to the training box TRN. If the TMS is set up according to Figure 8.18, all Repository objects with a development class whose transport layer is ZDEV, SAP, or ZTRN can be recorded to transportable change requests.

**Note** Repository objects that are to be consolidated to different systems must be recorded to different change requests. For example, an object with the transport layer ZTRN cannot be recorded to the same change request as an object with the transport layer ZDEV. The export cannot occur because the target systems differ; the same change request cannot be simultaneously consolidated to the training system and the quality assurance system (see also Chapter 8).

### 10.2.2 Local Change Request

Changes to Repository objects whose transport layer is invalid are automatically recorded to local change requests. A transport layer is invalid if it is not assigned to a consolidation route that includes the current system as the source system. For example, the TMS typically does not list a consolidation system for the quality assurance system and the production system. Therefore, there is no valid transport layer for these systems. A change to an Repository object in a quality assurance system or production system is not transportable and will be recorded to a local change request.

A local change request can be released, but not transported. To transport the objects in a local change request, release the change request and then either:

- Create an appropriate transport layer for the object's development class. For example, to transport a change made to an SAP-delivered object in the quality assurance system to the production system, use the TMS to add the consolidation route from the quality assurance system to the production system for the transport layer **SAP**.

- Using Transaction SE80 (see below, under "Displaying an Object Directory Entry"), assign the object to another development class or change the development class for the object and assign it to a valid transport layer for the current system.

### 10.2.3 Tasks

As long as no changes have been recorded to a task, its status in the Workbench Organizer (see below) is **Not assigned**. This status is sometimes also referred to as *unclassified*. When an Repository object is first recorded to a task in a change request, the task is classified as either:

- Development/correction
- Repair

Most changes are recorded to *development/correction* tasks, which contain changes to objects that originated in the current system.

A *repair* is a change to an Repository object that originated on an system other than the current system. The object can be an SAP-delivered object or a customer-developed object. For example, since all SAP-delivered objects are defined as belonging to the original system SAP, if you change such an object, the change is regarded as a repair. As another example, consider a customer-developed program, `ZPROGRAM`, created in the development system DEV. If you try to change this program in the training system TRN, you are automatically required to save the change to a task of type **repair** since the object does not originate in TRN.

**Tip** Changing an object on a system other than the system in which it was originally created will be recorded in a task of type **repair**.

To complete your development activities, you may need to include both types of tasks—*development/correction* tasks and *repair* tasks—in a change request. For example, after creating a new Repository object and saving it to a task in a change request, if you try to add a repair to the same change request, a **Create Task** dialog box automatically appears to indicate that a new task must be created in the change request.

### 10.2.4 Viewing Workbench Change Requests

To view Workbench change requests and the associated tasks, access the Workbench Organizer by using Transaction code SE09 or, from the initial screen, by choosing **Tools • ABAP Workbench • Overview • Transport Organizer**. Figure 10.6 shows the initial screen of the Transport Organizer. Enter your selection criteria to determine which change requests will be displayed. These selection criteria include the user who created the change request and its type. The default selections are as follows: transportable change requests and local change requests that are modifiable (that is, not released). Under **Last changed**, you can enter dates to limit the displayed change requests to those that were last changed in a certain period.

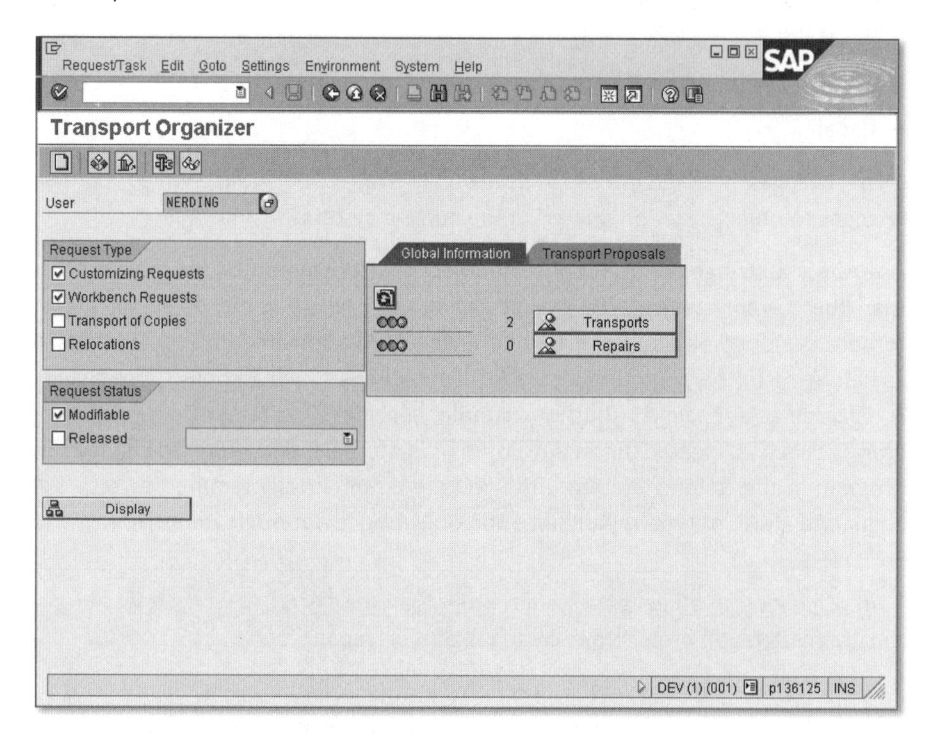


**Figure 10.6** Initial screen of the Transport Organizer

To accept the selection criteria and display the corresponding change requests, choose **Display**. The screen **Transport Organizer: Requests** appears, showing a tree structure containing change requests and tasks (see Figure 10.7). The change requests listed include both change requests that were created by the user whose name you entered on the initial screen and the change requests in which that user is assigned to a task. To see the tasks associated with a particular change request, expand the list using the + sign beside the ID number of the change request.

The example shown in Figure 10.7 represents the display of all change requests from the user NERDING. The list specifies that both DEVK900027 and DEVK900002 are transportable change requests. In change request DEVK900027, the user NERDING has the task DEVK900028 that records two changed repository objects, the development class ZREPORTS, and the program ZPROGRAM. The user KOESEGI is the owner of the change request DEVK900002. The user NERDING also possesses a task in this change request, but has not yet recorded any changes in it.

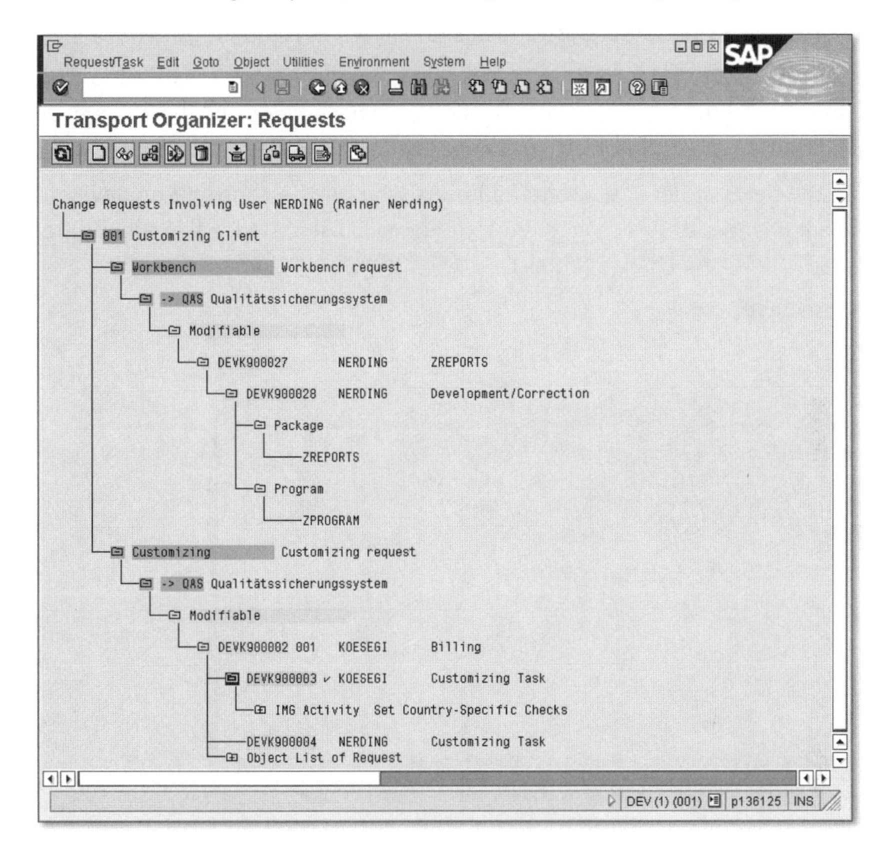


Figure 10.7 Hierarchical display in the Transport Organizer

### 10.2.5 Creating a Workbench Change Request

A Workbench change request can be created either prior to or during development work. To simplify project management, SAP recommends creating change requests before starting development work. This makes it easier for developers from the same development project to record their changes to a single change request that can be released and exported as a testable unit. A project team leader or development manager should be responsible for creating the change request and assigning the various developers to it. To create a change request, you require the authorization profile S_A.CUSTOMIZ (see also Chapter 11).

To create a transportable Workbench change request in the Transport Organizer (Transaction SE09), proceed as follows:

1. In the screen **Transport Organizer: Requests**, choose **Request/Task • Create**.
2. In the resulting dialog box, select **Workbench request**. Choose **Enter**.
3. The dialog box **Create Request** appears (as shown in Figure 10.8):
   - In the field **Short description**, enter a short text to identify the development project, describe the functionality, indicate the urgency of the change, or indicate whether the change is a modification.
   - In the fields under **Tasks**, enter all users who will be contributing development changes to this change request. For each user listed, a task will be created in the new change request.
4. Choose **Save**.

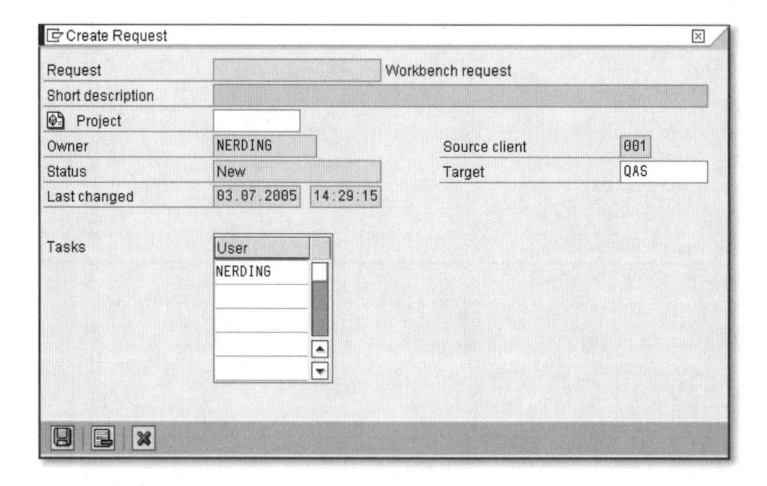


**Figure 10.8** Creating a change request and assigning initial tasks

When creating a Workbench change request, there are some default settings you cannot change. These include:

- Name of the user who created the change request
- Status
- Date and time stamp
- Category
- Source client in which the change request was created

The change request category is always SYST, indicating that this change request is a Workbench change request.

The source client is always the client in which the change request was created. It is only from within this client that you can perform the following activities:

- Recording changes to the change request
- Changing the owner of the change request or of its tasks
- Adding additional tasks to the change request
- Releasing the change request

### Adding Further Users to a Workbench Change Request

To add further users to a Workbench change request you previously created, proceed as follows:

1. In the screen **Transport Organizer: Requests**, position the cursor on the appropriate change request ID.
2. In the menu, select **Request/Task • Request • Add User**. The **Add user** dialog box appears. Enter the name of the user for whom you wish to create a task. To find a user, you can use the possible entries arrow (or place the cursor in the username field and choose F4).
3. Choose **Enter**.

**Note** You can add users only to a change request that has not been released. A change request or task cannot be changed after it has been released.

### Changing Ownership of Change Requests and Tasks

Every change request and task is owned by an user. When a user creates a change request, that user automatically receives ownership of the change request and a task in the change request. The owners of all other tasks in the change request are those people assigned to a task by the owner of the change request. Only the owner of a change request can perform the following activities for either change requests or tasks:

- Deleting tasks in the change request
- Changing the object list
- Releasing (exception: a user with the authorization profile SAP_ALL)
- Changing attributes, such as the short description
- Changing the owner

The owner of a change request can specify another person as the owner of the change request or the tasks it contains. To do this, proceed as follows:

1. In the **Workbench Organizer: Request** screen, position the cursor on the ID of the change request or task whose ownership you want to change. Choose **Request/Task • Change owner**.
2. In the **Change owner** dialog box, enter the username of the new owner, or use the possible entries arrow to select a user.
3. Choose **Enter**.

### Protecting a Workbench Change Request

You can protect a Workbench change request to ensure that only the creator of the change request can add users to the change request. This even prevents users with the authorization profile S_A.CUSTOMIZ from adding users to the change request (see also Chapter 11).

To protect a change request you have created, in the **Workbench Organizer: Request** screen, position the cursor on the ID number of the change request that you want to protect, and choose **Request/Task • Request • Protect**.

To remove this protection from the change request, choose **Request/Task • Request • Remove protection**.

## 10.2.6 Recording Repository Objects to Change Requests

When creating or changing an Repository object, you will be required to specify the Workbench change request to which the object can be recorded unless:

- The object is already recorded in a change request that has not yet been released.
- The object is assigned to a local development class, such as $TMP, whose objects are not recorded in a change request.

Figure 10.9 shows the dialog box that appears for recording a new or changed object to a change request. There are three ways to specify the change request ID:

- Manually enter your change request ID.
- Choose **Own requests**. From this list, double-click the change request to which you wish to record the object. This list will display only change requests to which this object can be saved.
- Choose **Create request**. (You require the appropriate authorization.) In the **Create Request** screen, enter the required data (see Figure 10.8 earlier in the chapter).

After specifying a change request, choose **Continue**. The object is recorded to this change request.

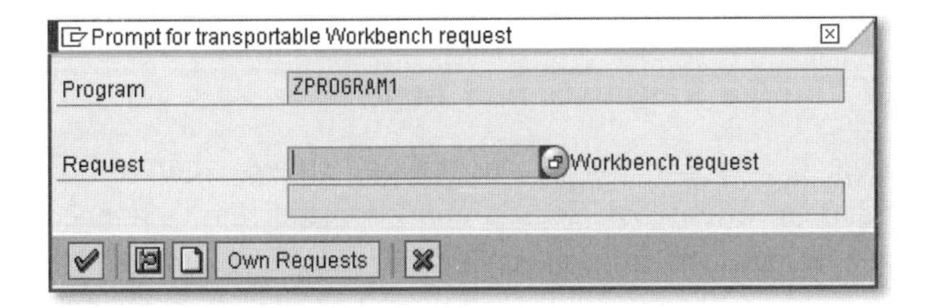


**Figure 10.9** Recording an Repository object to a change request

When recording the development change to a Workbench change request, you must select a change request:

- In which you have a task or the authorization to create a task
- With the correct type, either transportable or local

You must save the change to a transportable change request if the object's development class is associated with a defined transport route. Otherwise, you should record the change to a local change request. The correct type of change request for development work matches the Repository object's defined transport layer and the associated transport routes for the current system as defined in the TMS.

### Object Locking

When you record a new or changed Repository object to a task, the Workbench Organizer locks the object so that only those users who have tasks in the change request can modify the object. Another kind of locking—through an R/3 enqueue—ensures that only one user can change an object at one time.

When the Workbench Organizer locks an object, this prevents users outside the development team from changing any of the objects in the change request. For example, if a user does not own a task in change request `DEVK900586`, but tries to edit the program `ZABAP` using the ABAP Editor, that person receives the error message "Object ZABAP locked by request/task DEVK900586". This user can do only one of three things:

- Display the object, but not make changes to it
- Have a new task created for the user in change request `DEVK900586` by someone with authorization to create tasks
- Change ownership of the task containing the locked object to the user wanting to change it

If you try to change an object that is already being held by an enqueue lock, you receive the error message "User ARCHER is currently editing ZABAP". This ensures that only one user at a time can modify an object in the system.

### 10.2.7 Object List of Change Requests and Tasks

An object list records objects that have been changed and shows what will be transported when the change request is released and exported. Each changed object has an entry in the object list. The object list of a change request is filled after the tasks in the change request have been released (see also Chapter 12). The entries in the object list correspond to the entries in the *Object Directory* described later in this chapter.

The ABAP Workbench tools that record your changes to tasks automatically include the corresponding objects in the object list. Workbench Organizer tools also enable you to manually include or delete objects in the object list. In certain situations, you may wish to manipulate an object list by, for example, removing the only listed object that is not ready to be released. When you remove an object, it is no longer in a change request. It is not locked by the Workbench Organizer and will not be transported. In addition, the Workbench Organizer no longer indicates that this object has been changed. Therefore, manual changes to the object list should only be made with caution.

**Warning** Use caution when making manual changes to the object list.

To display the object list, in the **Transport Organizer: Request screen**, double-click the change request or task ID. In the sample object list in Figure 10.10, each object that has been recorded in the task is represented by a combination of entries in the columns **PgmID** (program identification), **Obj** (object type), and **Object name**. The object represented in the row `R3TR DEVC ZREPORTS` is the package `ZREPORTS`. The ABAP program `ZPROGRAM` is represented in the row `R3TR PROG ZPROGRAM`.

In the object list shown in Figure 10.10, the entry in the **ObjStatus** column for every object is LOCKED. These are Workbench Organizer locks. In other words, the program `ZPROGRAM` and the development class `ZREPORTS` can be changed only by the users who are specified in the change request `DEVK900027`. The Workbench Organizer locks the objects in the request until the entire change request has been released.

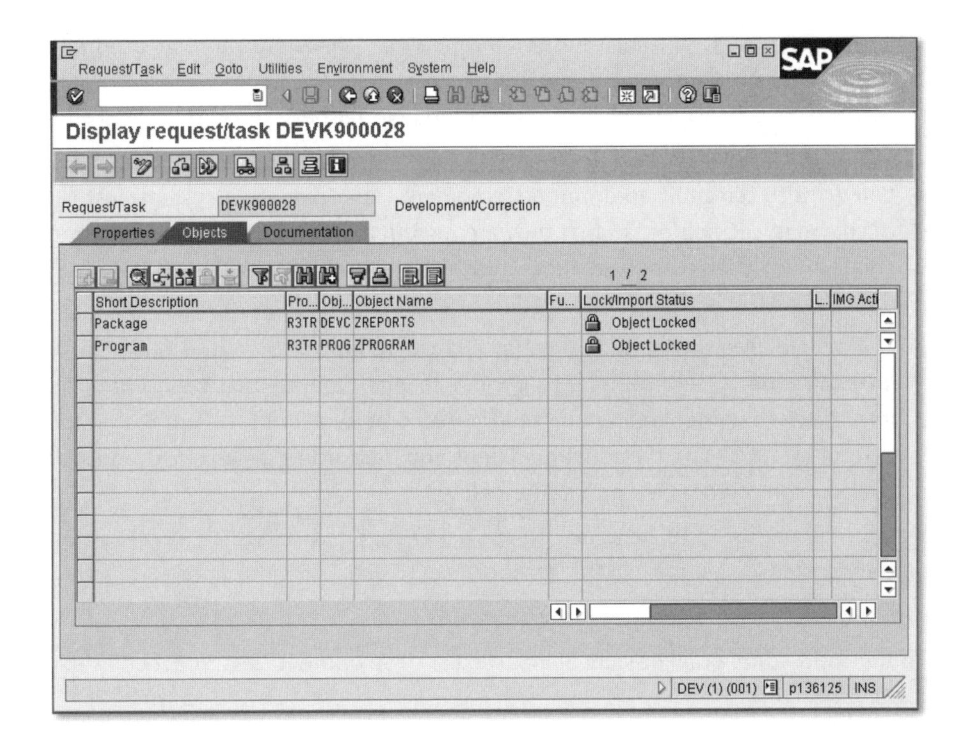


Figure 10.10 An object list

The change request or task does *not* contain the actual table entries or the object content that has changed. A change request or task does *not* even record whether the change was an addition, modification, or deletion. A change request or task only *lists* the changed objects. Each row in the object list is a pointer to the actual objects—programs, tables, data domains, views, and so on—that are physically located in the Repository. As an example, task `DEVK900028` is a result of creating, modifying, or deleting the program `ZPROGRAM` and the development class `ZREPORTS`.

**Note** A change request or task only *lists*—it does not actually contain objects. The objects exist outside the change request in the Repository.

### Manual Additions to the Object List

There are times when the standard, automatic procedure for recording new or modified Repository objects or Customizing changes to a change request is too cumbersome and time-consuming. Situations in which you may instead need to manually add objects to a new or existing object list include the following:

- A change request did not transport properly and needs to be rereleased and reexported. After a change request is released, it cannot be rereleased. Instead, you can include its object list in a new change request and then release the new change request.
- You want to transport an entire development class to another system. Instead of changing each object so that they are recorded to a change request, you can create a new change request and enter the objects in its object list. (See procedure below.)
- You would like to combine several change requests to form a single new change request—for example, to bundle change requests that were imported into the development system or need to be copied to another client within the current system using the function **Client copy according to a transp. request** (Transaction SCC1). (See procedure below.)
- Objects may need to be added to special change requests such as **relocation transports** (see below, under "Transporting Objects Using the Transport Organizer").

To transport some or all objects of a particular development class, proceed as follows:

1. Create a transportable change request. To do this, from the **Transport Organizer: Request screen** (in Transaction SE09), choose **Request/Task · Create**. In the resulting dialog box, choose **Workbench request** and then choose **Enter**. A second dialog box appears—enter a short description and choose **Enter**.
2. Position the cursor on the newly created change request and choose **Request/Task · Object List · Include objects**. Select **Freely selected objects**. Choose **Enter**.
3. The **Add Objects to Request <change request ID>** screen is displayed. Enter the name of the development class for which you would like to display the object list. Choose **Execute**.
4. A tree structure is displayed containing all objects that belong to the development class. Position the cursor on individual objects or collections of objects and choose **Select/deselect**.
5. When all the required objects have been selected, choose **Save in request**. All selected objects will be added to the object list of the new change request.

**Note** You can include objects in the object list of a change request, but not a task, using the **Include objects** functionality.

To merge a copy of an existing object list from one or several change requests into a new change request, proceed as follows:

1. Create a transportable change request. To do this, from the **Transport Organizer: Request screen** (in Transaction SE09), choose **Request/Task • Create**. In the resulting dialog box, choose **Workbench request** and then choose **Enter**. A second dialog box appears. Provide a short description and choose **Enter**.
2. Position the cursor on the newly created change request and choose **Request/Task • Object List • Include objects**. Select **Object list from multiple requests**. Choose **Enter**.
3. The **Merge Object lists in request <change request ID>** screen appears. Enter selection criteria for the change requests and tasks whose object lists are to be included in the new change request. Examples of selection criteria include:

| Field | User Entry |
|---|---|
| Owner | Name of a particular user or users. |
| Date | Begin dates and end dates. This entry selects all change requests that were last modified during a specified time period or periods. |
| Request type | Use the possible entries arrow to specify the type of change requests and tasks to be included—for example, *transportable change request*. |

**Table 10.2** Selection criteria

4. In the same screen, select the status of the change requests and tasks to be included from the following options:
   - Modifiable
   - Open (faulty status)
   - Released
5. Choose **Execute**.
6. A list of all change requests matching the selection criteria is displayed. Select the individual requests or collections of change requests that you require by choosing **Select/deselect** (or F7).
7. Once you have selected the required objects, choose **Merge object lists**. A dialog box appears asking "How should action be performed?" Proceed as follows:
   - To combine a small number of change requests, choose **Online**.
   - To combine a large number of change requests, choose **In background**. You are automatically asked to schedule the merger as a background job.
8. Choose **Enter**. All selected objects are added to the object list of the new change request.

You can manually change the object lists of change requests or tasks by adding or deleting objects. A user should not need this function often, since almost all changes to objects are automatically recorded to change requests. Occasionally, expert users with a detailed knowledge of the respective objects may need to add or remove them manually.

If you want to change an existing object list, in the screen **Transport Organizer: Requests** (in Transaction SE09) set the cursor to the task or the change request to be modified and select **Request/Task · Display**. The object list is displayed. Switch to change mode. You have the following options:

- To add entries to the object list, choose **Insert line**. Enter the program name, object name, and object type. To make manual additions to the **Change object list** option, you must be familiar with certain technical data for an object, including the program ID, object type, and other objects that may be affected. You may prefer the procedure described above under "Including All Objects of a Development Class" to add individual objects to the object list.
- To delete objects in the object list, choose **Delete line**. Before deleting entries from the object list, use your knowledge of the objects to ensure that the deletion does not jeopardize dependent objects.

**Warning** SAP does not recommend deleting objects from an object list, because it may jeopardize consistency between your systems.

### Locking and Unlocking Objects in Object Lists

Adding an object manually to the object list does not automatically lock the object. Any other user can record this object to a change request and perform changes on it. To prevent this, after adding objects to an object list, you are advised to manually set a lock on the objects as follows:

1. In the **Transport Organizer: Requests** screen (in Transaction SE09), position the cursor on the change request you want to lock.
2. Choose **Request/task · Object list · Lock objects**.

You may receive an error message indicating that one or more objects are already locked in another change request or task. If the objects are locked, you may need to release the change request containing the locked objects.

To manually unlock an object in a change request, you require the authorization S_CTS_ADMIN, which is provided in the authorization profile S_A.SYSTEM. When you have this authorization, you can unlock an object in a change request using the Organizer Tool (Transaction SE03). In the tree structure under **Objects**

**in Requests**, access the function **Unlock objects**. Enter the request or task you wish to unlock and choose **Execute**.

## 10.3 Repairs and Modifications

Every Repository object has an *original system*, which is the SAP ECC system in which the object was created and should be edited. If you change an object in a system that is not the original system, you are changing a *copy* of the object and not the original itself; this is called a *repair*. In the production system, for example, if you change a copy of a program that originated in the development system, the changed object is considered a repair.

The original system for all SAP-delivered objects is defined as SAP. A change to an SAP-delivered object is a special type of repair known as a *modification*.

Certain risks are associated with repairs and modifications. For example:

- If you did not create the original object, you may not be able to guarantee application functionality after changing the object.
- The repair can be overwritten by imports if it has been confirmed (and therefore the repair flag is no longer set).
- Performing an upgrade is more complex if there are modifications in the pre-upgrade system.

Making a repair requires two steps that are not required when changing an object in the original system:

- Setting a repair flag for the object
- Monitoring and controlling the changes made to the Repository object with the *Modification Assistant*

### 10.3.1 Setting a Repair Flag

When you change an Repository object in a system that is not its original system, regardless of whether it is an SAP-delivered object or a customer-developed object, the **Set Repair Flag** dialog box will appear. To continue, you must choose **Object for repair**. This sets the repair flag for this object.

The repair flag protects an Repository object from being overwritten if it is subsequently reimported from the source system. When the repair flag is set, an error message appears during import indicating that the object has not been imported because it was repaired in the target system.By default, the repair flag is deleted when the transport request is exported.

In Transaction SE03, Transport Organizer Tools, you can display the list of all repaired objects and remove the repair flag manually, if necessary.

### 10.3.2 Modification Assistant

As of Release 4.5, the ABAP Editor offers the Modification Assistant to guide you during repairs to objects that are not in their original system. Although the name *Modification Assistant* may imply that it is used only to make modifications, this tool is designed to help manage the repair of any object, whether it is SAP-delivered or customer-developed.

The Modification Assistant ensures that repairs to an object outside its original system are made using only the options **Insert**, **Replace**, and **Delete**. This preserves a record of the original form of objects, and indicates the change request that is used to make the change. For example, using the Modification Assistant, you can no longer simply change an existing line of code in a program. You must use the **Replace** option. This option inserts an asterisk to preserve the original line of code as a commentary (as in line 444, in Figure 10.11). The option **Modification undo** simplifies undoing all changes made during the repair.

> **Note** The Modification Assistant preserves a copy of that part of an object that was changed in a repair or modification.

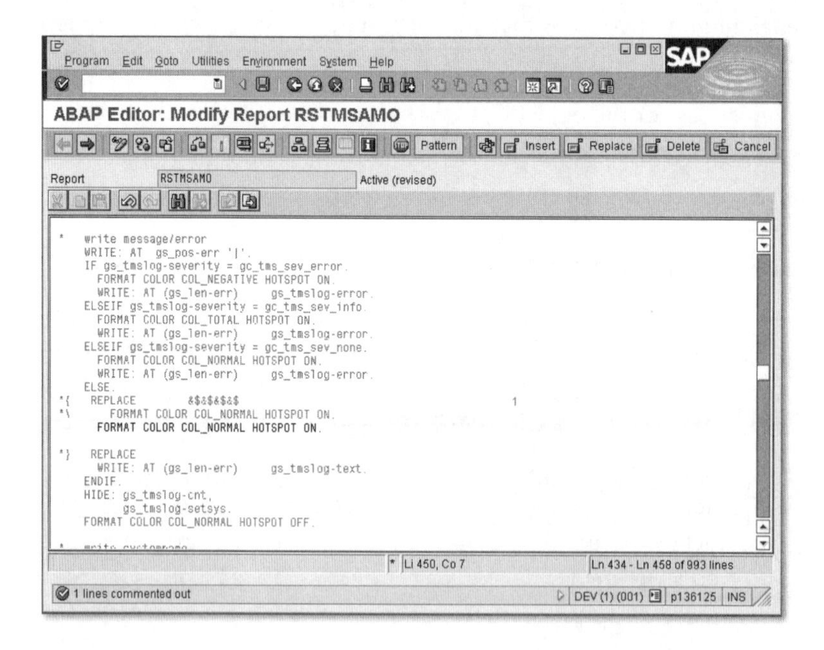


```
*   write message/error
    WRITE: AT  gs_pos-err '|'.
    IF gs_tmslog-severity = gc_tms_sev_error.
      FORMAT COLOR COL_NEGATIVE HOTSPOT ON.
      WRITE: AT (gs_len-err)      gs_tmslog-error.
    ELSEIF gs_tmslog-severity = gc_tms_sev_info.
      FORMAT COLOR COL_TOTAL HOTSPOT ON.
      WRITE: AT (gs_len-err)      gs_tmslog-error.
    ELSEIF gs_tmslog-severity = gc_tms_sev_none.
      FORMAT COLOR COL_NORMAL HOTSPOT ON.
      WRITE: AT (gs_len-err)      gs_tmslog-error.
    ELSE.
*{   REPLACE        &$&$&$&$                                    1
*\      FORMAT COLOR COL_NORMAL HOTSPOT ON.
      FORMAT COLOR COL_NORMAL HOTSPOT ON.

*}   REPLACE
      WRITE: AT (gs_len-err)      gs_tmslog-text.
    ENDIF.
    HIDE: gs_tmslog-cnt,
          gs_tmslog-setsys.
    FORMAT COLOR COL_NORMAL HOTSPOT OFF.
```

**Figure 10.11** The ABAP Editor when used with the Modification Assistant

This detailed documentation provided by the Modification Assistant in the ABAP Editor helps to dramatically reduce the amount of effort needed to apply Support Packages and upgrade your SAP ECC system.

Occasionally, you will have to disable the Modification Assistant—for example, to upload a program into the ABAP Editor. To disable the Modification Assistant, before making changes, from within the ABAP Editor choose **Edit · Modifications · Disable assistant**. Repairs and modifications made when the Modification Assistant is deactivated will still be registered as repairs in the Workbench Organizer. However, you lose the pre-change documentation provided by the Modification Assistant. When performing modification adjustments during an upgrade or when applying a Support Package, to gain insight into changes that were made without the Modification Assistant, you will have to use the version management functionality of the ABAP Workbench (see Chapter 12).

**Warning** To simplify future upgrades, SAP recommends having the Modification Assistant activated at all times.

### 10.3.3 Modification Browser

To display a tree structure listing all repairs and modifications in the Modification Browser, use Transaction code SE95 or, from the initial R/3 screen, choose **Tools · ABAP Workbench · Overview · Modification Browser**. The selection screen of the Modification Browser appears, which enables you to specify the criteria for the repairs and modifications to be displayed. For example, you can select:

- All repairs, or only the repairs for a specific development class and/or time period
- Repairs made with and/or without the Modification Assistant
- Modifications to SAP objects that may subsequently need to be adjusted during an upgrade or Support Package application (see Chapter 15)

In the Modification Browser, to access the ABAP Workbench tool relevant to a particular object type (such as the ABAP Editor for a program), position the cursor on a specific object and choose **Display** or **Change**.

To undo repairs made with the help of the Modification Assistant, in the Modification Browser, place your cursor on a specific object and choose **Reset to original**. Using this function returns the object to its original state and causes the object to be deleted from the Modification Browser.

### 10.3.4 Modifications

*Modifications* are a specific type of repair—they are changes to the SAP standard. Modifications may be made in the following ways:

- By applying the corrective coding provided to customers in an SAP Note
- By adapting the SAP ECC system to your specific business needs

**Warning** A modification is a change that is more serious than a repair. Making a modification changes the functionality delivered by SAP and may negatively impact the performance and functionality of the SAP ECC system.

Prior to making modifications based on SAP Notes, ensure that the SAP Note is applicable to your mySAP ERP release and that the symptoms in the SAP Note are the symptoms apparent in your SAP ECC system. In the case of uncertainty, contact the SAP Hotline.

Before making modifications with the goal of adapting SAP ECC to your specific business needs, you should be well acquainted with the existing construction and flow logic of the application component. This knowledge will help you evaluate modification possibilities and enable you to decide on a sensible modification design. This knowledge will also help you determine when SAP enhancement technology provides a better alternative to performing a modification.

When you make a modification, you need to set a repair flag. In addition you need:

- An SSCR key so that the SAP-delivered object can be modified
- Documentation in change requests and attached to the affected objects to assist the modification adjustment process during the application of future Support Packages or mySAP ERP release upgrades
- Correct timing for transporting the modification in relation to the time when Support Packages are applied (see Chapter 15)

**Tip** SAP recommends that you perform all modifications to SAP-delivered objects in the Customizing-and-development client.

#### SSCR Key for Modifications

The first time an SAP-delivered Repository object is changed, the ABAP Workbench prompts the developer for an object-specific SAP Software Change Registration (SSCR) key through the dialog box shown in Figure 10.12. You can obtain the key from the SAP Service Marketplace (using the procedure described above under "SSCR for Developers").

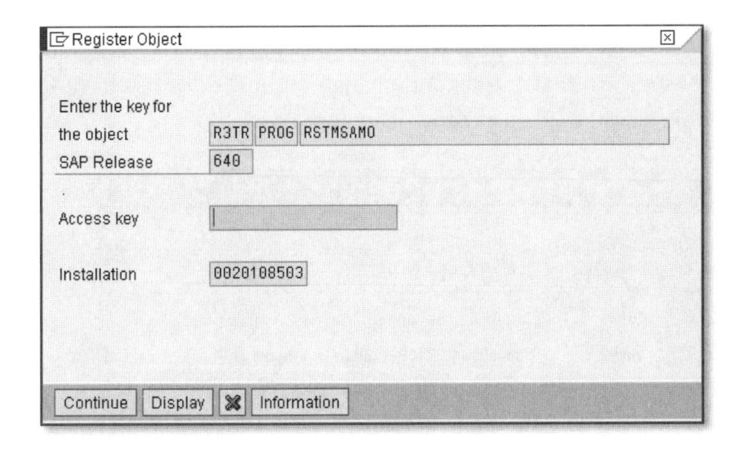


**Figure 10.12** The ABAP Workbench requests an SSCR key when you try to modify SAP objects.

After you enter the key in the dialog box shown in Figure 10.12, the key is automatically added to the table ADIRACCESS in the current system. The SSCR key is specific to the program ID and object type of the Repository object, as well as to the installation number and mySAP ERP release of the SAP ECC system. Therefore, you have to register the Repository object that you want to modify only once per system and mySAP ERP release level.

**Note** Repository objects that do not require SSCR registration include matchcodes, database indexes, buffer settings, customer objects, and objects generated through IMG Customizing activities.

### Documentation Requirements

Creating modifications makes mySAP ERP release upgrades or the application of Support Packages more complex due to the need for a modification review and possible adjustments during upgrade. To simplify decision making during this review process, when creating modifications, you should document all changes thoroughly in both the change request and the documentation attached to the object.

Include the SAP Note number and mySAP ERP release dependencies in the field **Short description** when you create the relevant change request and in the task-specific documentation (under **Goto • Documentation** in the Workbench Organizer). The change request description, for example, will then inform the person performing the upgrade that the modification was made as a result of an SAP Note and can be safely overwritten by the new mySAP ERP release. The short description of the change request will also be recognizable in the import queue. This is shown in Figure 10.13, where the SAP Note number and the relevant Support Package number indicate that the second change request does not have to be imported if Support Package 3 has already been applied.

Import Queue: System PRD

Request for PRD: 3 / 21

| Number | Request | Owner | Short text |
|---|---|---|---|
| 1 | DEVK902032 | GANTS | Logistics planning requirements for new plant |
| 2 | DEVK902061 | SMITH | R/3 Note 342 R40B-fixed in Hot Package 3 |
| 3 | DEVK902101 | HART | human resource planning reports for QTR4 |

**Figure 10.13** A sample import queue with a change request that is the result of an SAP Note

**Tip** All changes to SAP standard objects should be well documented in the relevant change requests and tasks. If the change is a result of an SAP Note, be sure to include the SAP Note number as part of the change request description.

## 10.4 The Object Directory

When you create an object, a corresponding Object Directory entry is also created. The key data for this entry is visible in the object list for each change request or task. Although this information is created automatically, there may be situations in which it is useful to display and possibly change the Object Directory entry for a particular object.

The Object Directory in the table TADIR is a catalog of all Repository objects in the SAP ECC system, including the SAP standard objects that are delivered with systems and all objects you create using ABAP Workbench tools. These objects include ABAP programs, module pools, function groups, and ABAP Dictionary objects (domains, data elements, and tables).

The primary key of the table TADIR comprises the following fields:

- Program identification (PgmID)
- Object type (Obj.)
- Object name

For the majority of Repository objects, the PgmID is R3TR. The object type classifies the object—for example, PROG denotes an ABAP program, and TABL denotes a dictionary table structure. Examples of common object entries are listed in Table 10.3.

| PgmID | Object Type | Description |
|---|---|---|
| R3TR | PROG | ABAP programs |
| R3TR | DEVC | Development class |
| R3TR | VIEW | Table view |
| R3TR | FORM | ABAP form |
| R3TR | CMOD | Customer enhancement |
| R3TR | TABL | Table structure |
| R3TR | DTEL | Data element |
| R3TR | DOMA | Domain |
| R3TR | TRAN | Transaction |
| R3TR | FUGR | Function group |

**Table 10.3** Sample object entries

When reviewing the object list of a task or change request, you may see the entry LIMU in the column **PgmID**. LIMU indicates that the object is a sub-object of either an R3TR or an R3OB object. These sub-objects do not have their own Object Directory entry, but, instead, they are included in the entry for the respective object. Sub-objects can be transported separately so that the entire Repository object does not have to be transported every time a change is made.

When, for example, the ABAP program ZPROGRAM is created, the corresponding Object Directory entry R3TR PROG ZPROGRAM is automatically created. This entry is then used in the object list of the task and, when the task is released, in the object list of the change request. After an object is initially created, all of its components are transported. Subsequent changes to the object transport only the changed sub-objects. Sample sub-objects for an ABAP program are listed in Table 10.4.

| PgmID | Object Type | Description |
|---|---|---|
| LIMU | REPS | Program source |
| LIMU | DOCU | Documentation |

**Table 10.4** Typical sub-objects for ABAP programs

| PgmID | Object Type | Description |
|---|---|---|
| LIMU | REPT | Text elements of the report |
| LIMU | VARI | Program variants |
| LIMU | ADIR | Object directory entry |

**Table 10.4** Typical sub-objects for ABAP programs (cont.)

### 10.4.1 Object Attributes

The Object Directory also contains the *object attributes* of each Repository object. You can display these attributes as described in the next section. They include:

- Development class
- Original system
- Person responsible for object
- Original language
- Generation flag
- Repair flag

You can change the attribute **original system**—the system in which the object was created—by making a *relocation transport* in Transaction SE01 (described below). In general, if there are problems with a particular object, consult the person indicated in the attribute **person responsible for object**.

The **original language** attribute is an attribute for the language-specific components of each object, such as text elements, and is equivalent to the logon language in which the object was created. If you are developing in more than one language, the system asks you whether you want to change the original language when you log on in another language and proceed to edit the object.

If an object is flagged as **generated**, it was automatically created as an indirect result of other user activities, such as particular Customizing transactions (see "Client-Independent Customizing Activities" in Chapter 11).

### 10.4.2 Displaying or Changing an Object Directory Entry

There are several ways of displaying Object Directory entries. The most common way is to use the Repository Browser, which lets you display and change the Object Directory entries for Repository objects in the current SAP ECC system. To display objects in the Repository Browser, proceed as follows:

1. Use Transaction code SE80 or, from the R/3 initial screen, choose **Tools • ABAP Workbench • Overview • Objekt Navigator**.
2. In the resulting selection screen, the upper and lower screen areas enable you to perform the selection in two different ways:
   - In the top half of the screen, you can generate an object list and then select the particular object you wish to display. To do this, mark one of the radio buttons offered and, in the adjacent field, enter the corresponding development class, program, function group, or user. Choose **Display**. Expand the object list if necessary, and position the cursor on a particular Repository object.
   - The lower half of the screen enables you to display an individual object. Select the type of object and choose **Edit**. A new selection screen appears. Enter the object name and choose **Execute**.
3. To display the object's directory entry, select **Edit • Object directory entry**. The dialog box **Change Object Directory Entry** appears (see Figure 10.14), enabling you to view the Object Directory entry, or to change the development class or person responsible.

For example, when you want to transport an object with development class $TMP, you would use this dialog box to change the development class to a customer development class. You can also change the owner of an object—for example, if a developer has left the project and all of his or her objects need to be assigned to another developer.

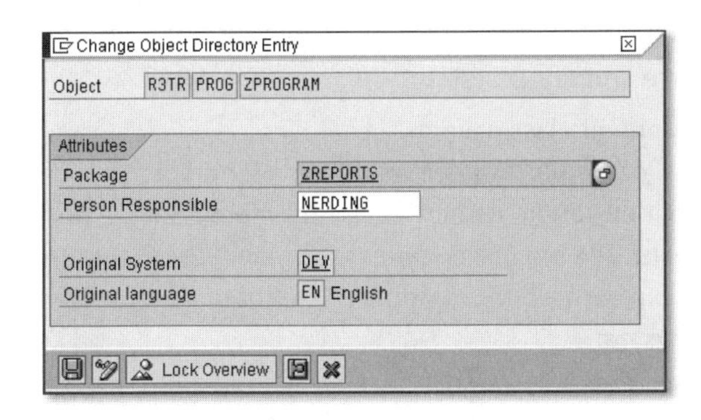


**Figure 10.14** Displaying or changing the Object Directory entry

Some attributes cannot be changed from this dialog box in the Repository Browser. For example, if you need to assign the current SAP ECC system as the original system of an object, use Transaction SE03. A tree structure is displayed listing various tools. Choose **Object directory**, and double-click an entry to perform the respective Object Directory task.

No matter which method you use to change Object Directory entries, keep the following points in mind:

- With authorization profile S_A.SYSTEM and using Transaction SE03, you can modify all attributes except **original language**.
- After changing the development class, responsible person, generation flag, or repair flag for an object, you must save your changes to a change request. Exceptions include objects local to the current system such as those assigned to the development classes $TMP.
- When changing the development class of an object that has already been released and exported, the new development class ideally has the same transport layer as the previous one. This helps to ensure that the affected objects continue to be transported along the same transport route.

### 10.4.3 Transporting Objects Using the Transport Organizer (Extended View)

The *Transport Organizer* (Extended View, Transaction SE01), is used for all non-standard transports—that is, for transports that are not performed using the Workbench Organizer and the Customizing Organizer. In particular, the Transport Organizer enables you to create change requests to perform the following kinds of transports:

- **Transports of copies:**
  Used to transport a collection of Repository objects and Customizing objects to a specified system. The Object Directory entry of the objects remains unchanged in both the source and target system.
- **Relocations without development class change:**
  Used to change collections of objects in another system on a temporary basis—for example, to make special developments that do not interfere with the normal development environment. The original system of the objects becomes the target system. The same type of relocation transport is later used to return the objects back to the source system.
- **Relocations with development class change:**
  Used to change the development system of individual objects on a permanent basis. The original system of the objects becomes the target system. Assign a development class that ensures the objects will be associated with the right transport route after import into the target system. Once the objects have been imported into the target system, you can record them to a transportable change request without making any further changes to their Object Directory entry.

- **Relocations of complete development classes:**
  Used to permanently change the transport layer of a development class and the original system of the objects. The object list of the change request for this transport is set up automatically and contains all objects in the development class.

To perform any of these four types of Transport Organizer transports, proceed as follows:

1. Enter Transaction code SE01 or, from the initial R/3 screen, choose **Tools · Administration · Transports · Transport Organizer**.
2. Select **Transport of Copies**, **Relocation** and then press **Choose**.
3. Choose **Create**. In the resulting dialog box, select one of the following:
   - Transport of copies
   - Relocation of objects w/o dev. class change
   - Relocation of objects with dev. class change
   - Relocation of a complete development class
4. Choose **Enter**. The dialog box **Create request** appears, enabling you to create an appropriate change request as follows:

| Field | User Entry |
|---|---|
| Short description: | Enter a short text describing the change request. |
| Target: | Enter the name of the target system (or, if extended transport management is active, the target system and client). The target system must be one that is defined in the TMS. |
| Target dev. Class: | This field appears if you selected Relocation with dev. class change. Enter the name of the target development class for the Repository objects. The development class must be defined in the current R/3 System and assigned to a transport layer specific to the target R/3 System. |
| Development class and Target transp. layer: | These fields appear if you selected Relocations of a complete development class. Enter the name of the development class for the objects to be copied, and the target transport layer for the development class. |

**Table 10.5** Creating a change request

5. After completing the required entries, choose **Save**.
6. The **Display request** screen appears, showing the newly created change request. To modify the details you entered in the previous dialog boxes, position the cursor on the change request and choose **Request/task · Display/change**.

Unless the change request is a relocation for an entire development class, the newly created change request does not contain any Repository objects. To add objects to the change request, in the **Display request** screen, select the change request and choose **Request/Task · Object List · Include objects**. Then, proceed as described above, under "Object List of Change Requests and Tasks." After adding objects to the change request, you can release and export the change request.

**Example of Using Relocation of a complete development class**

A large pharmaceutical company implementing R/3 initially wants a standard three-system landscape (DEV, QAS, and PRD). Due to the development and testing requirements of Internet interoperability, however, the company decides to create a second development system, NET, to be used solely for the development needs of SAP's Internet Transaction Server. DEV will still be used for traditional forms of development work such as the creation of special reports and legacy conversion routines.

The system NET is created as a system copy of the current development system. The TMS and transport routes for NET are configured as shown in the following diagram:

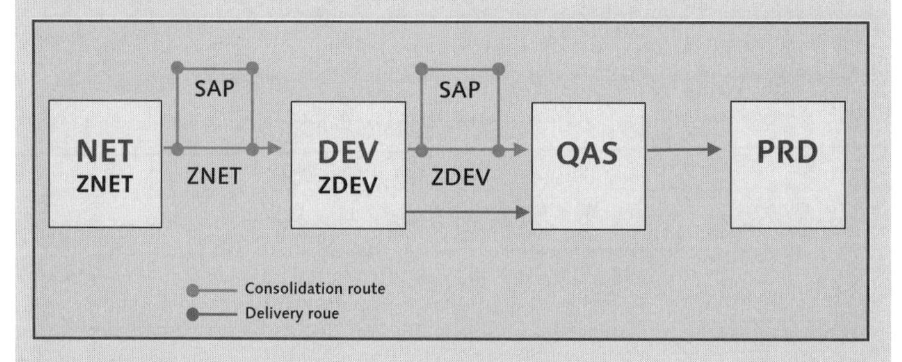


**Figure 10.15** Configuration of TMS and transport routes for system NET

New Repository objects that support Internet activities are created in NET and assigned to the development class `ZINTERNET`, whose transport layer is ZNET. These objects are recorded to change requests and transported to DEV. The delivery route between DEV and QAS ensures that changes from NET are subsequently delivered to the quality assurance system and ultimately to the production system.

To ensure that objects created in NET and DEV have unique names, naming convention entries are added to the view V_TRESN. Only an object whose name begins with "ZNET" should receive the development class ZINTERNET. New objects on DEV cannot be named using "ZNET."

The system NET helps to bring Internet transactions to the production environment. Over time, the need for NET disappears, and all Internet development is to be concentrated in DEV. To support the switch from NET to DEV, all Repository objects created on NET (those objects with the development class ZINTERNET) are copied from NET to DEV by relocating the entire development class. The development class is assigned the new transport layer ZDEV. DEV then solely supports all development efforts, including those required for Internet functionality.

## 10.5 Questions

1. Which of the following statements is *false* in regard to development classes?
   A. Development classes facilitate project management by grouping similar Repository objects.
   B. All Repository objects are assigned to a development class.
   C. A development class determines the transport route that a changed Repository object will follow.
   D. A local object does not need a development class.
2. Which of the following kinds of changes are transported using Workbench change requests?
   A. Client-independent changes
   B. Modifications to SAP-delivered objects
   C. Changes made using the ABAP Editor and ABAP Dictionary
   D. Repairs to Repository objects that originated in another SAP ECC system
   E. All of the above
3. Which of the following data is *not* contained in the object list of a task?
   A. The actual change made to the objects listed in the task
   B. The list of changed objects recorded to the task
   C. Whether the objects recorded to the task are locked
   D. The complete Object Directory entry for the object

4. Which of the following statements are correct regarding repairs and modifications?

   A. Repairs are changes to SAP-delivered objects; modifications are changes to any object that originated on an SAP ECC system other than the current SAP ECC system.

   B. A repair flag protects an Repository object against being overwritten by an import.

   C. All repairs are saved to Workbench change requests.

   D. A modification is a change to an SAP-delivered object.

   E. All of the above.

# 11 Managing Customizing Changes

This chapter explains the tools that enable you to perform Customizing and manage the change requests containing Customizing changes. Proper management of Customizing changes can be divided into the following areas:

- Customizing prerequisites
- Customizing change requests
- Nonstandard Customizing activities
- Support tools for Customizing

## 11.1 Customizing Prerequisites

To enable Customizing activities in SAP systems:

- Ensure that Customizing changes occur only in a single SAP client in your system landscape.
- Ensure that Customizing changes are recorded to change requests.
- Assign user authorizations to the Customizing team.
- Set up the necessary Project IMGs.

To ensure that Customizing changes occur only in a specific SAP client, use the client and system change settings to allow or disallow Customizing in each SAP system and client. As described in Chapter 3, to enable Customizing changes in a specific client, the client settings for that client in Transaction SCC4 should be as follows:

- The client-dependent change option allows changes and is preferably set to **Automatic recording of changes**.
- The client-independent change option allows changes to client-independent Customizing objects.
- The client's role is not **production**.

In addition to providing the client settings, to enable Customizing, you must set the system change option for the SAP system to **Modifiable** to support client-independent Customizing (see Chapter 7).

To limit who can create and release change requests and tasks, assign user authorizations based on the following authorization profiles:

- S_A.CUSTOMIZ:
  This profile is for project leaders and enables them to create and release change requests, and to assign tasks to team members.

- **S_A.DEVELOP:**
  This profile is for team members and enables them to perform Customizing and development activities, and to work with the Customizing and Workbench Organizers. Team members can release their tasks after unit testing, but they cannot release the change request.

You can use SAP-delivered authorization profiles as templates for creating your own authorizations.

**Note** For information on the authorization objects and authorizations related to the profiles S_A.CUSTOMIZ and S_A.DEVELOP, see R/3 online documentation.

### 11.1.1 Setting Up Project IMGs

Customizing management during implementation is ideally realized using Project IMGs (introduced in Chapter 2). Project IMGs subdivide the functionality of your application components, enabling you to focus your Customizing on particular areas. Project IMGs also provide project management capabilities that enable project leaders to monitor the status of their project and review relevant documentation. After you have generated Project IMGs, the Customizing team can begin its work.

To create Project IMGs, you must first generate the Enterprise IMG by selecting the desired application components and compiling the list of required Customizing for the selected components. To generate the Enterprise IMG, proceed as follows:

1. Use Transaction code SPRO or, from the R/3 initial screen, choose **Tools • Business Engineer • Customizing**.
2. Choose **Basic Functions • Enterprise IMG • Generate**. Enter a distinctive title for the Enterprise IMG and choose **Continue**.
3. Choose **all countries** or, to focus on country-specific activities, only the countries relevant for your company. Choose **Confirm**.
4. A tree structure is displayed showing SAP's entire application components list (the SAP Reference IMG). Select the components that your company requires. Choose **Generate**.

After generating the Enterprise IMG, you are ready to create the various Project IMGs by dividing the Enterprise IMG into several parts, as well as filter the Project IMGs to create various **views** based on task priority. To create a Project IMG and the associated views, proceed as follows:

1. Use Transaction code SPRO_ADMIN or, from the R/3 initial screen, choose **Tools • Customizing IMG**. Choose **Project Management**. The **Project Management** screen appears.
2. Choose **Project • Create**. Enter a unique number for the new project and choose **Continue**. The **Change Project** screen appears (see Figure 11.1).
3. Enter a descriptive name, a default project language, a project owner, a start date, and an end date. Select the desired project management and documentation options. Choose **Generate Project IMG**. The dialog box **Generate Project IMG** appears.
4. Choose **Select countries and application components** and select **Continue**.

**Note** Avoid selecting the option **Use whole Enterprise IMG**, since this does not reduce the Project IMG to a subset of the Enterprise IMG.

5. In the resulting dialog box, choose all countries or only the countries relevant for your project. Choose **Continue**. The **Select business application components** screen appears, showing the list of application components in the Enterprise IMG.
6. Select the application components you want to include in the Project IMG. Choose **Generate**. The dialog box **Generate views of the Project** is displayed.
7. Select the project views to be created and choose **Generate**.

Project IMGs provide project management capabilities that are not contained in the Enterprise IMG. These include time scheduling, status maintenance, documentation, and Customizing task priority. The project leader should create Project IMGs for the respective implementation phases (see Figure 11.1).

You can subsequently extend the Enterprise IMG and regenerate it without losing the originally selected components. This is necessary, for example, after release upgrades, because new releases include new application components and new Customizing activities. To re-create the Enterprise IMG, repeat the above procedure for creating the Enterprise IMG. After generating the Enterprise IMG, regenerate each Project IMG as follows:

1. Use Transaction code SPRO or, from the R/3 initial screen, choose **Tools • Customizing IMG**. Choose **Project Management**. The **Project Management** screen appears.
2. To regenerate a single Project IMG, select the Project ID and choose **Project • Change**. Choose **Generate Project IMG**.

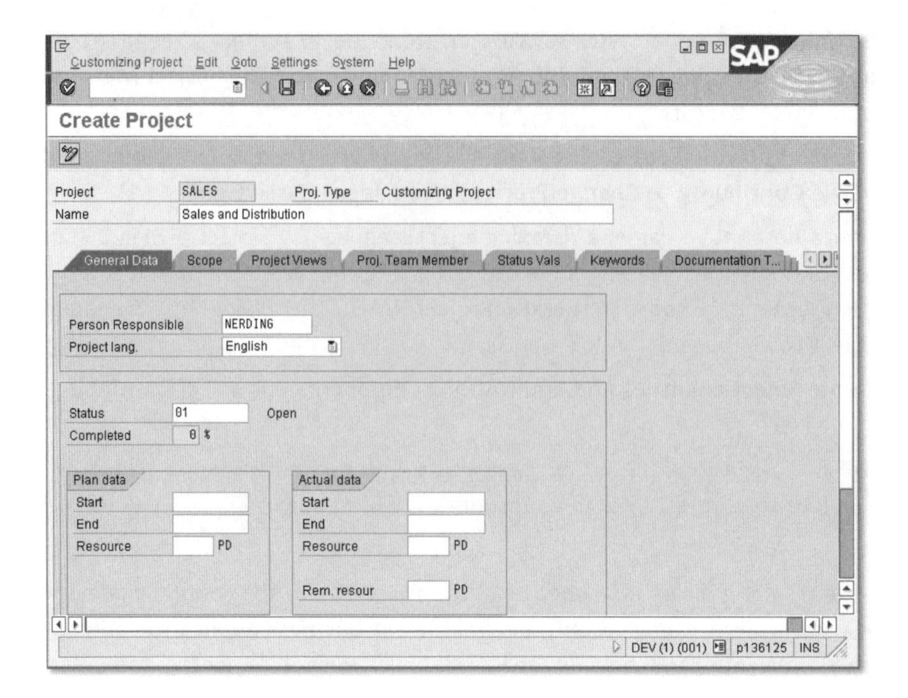


Figure 11.1 Creating a Project IMG

## 11.2 Customizing Change Requests

Customizing is performed in the activities specified in a Project IMG. After an activity has been completed, the changes should be recorded to change requests so they can be transported to other systems and clients. Most Customizing activities of the IMG are client-dependent and affect only the current client. These changes are recorded in a Customizing change request. Client-independent Customizing changes require Workbench change requests.

Project leaders are responsible for creating Customizing change requests and assigning tasks within those change requests to Customizing team members (see Chapter 6).

### 11.2.1 Viewing Customizing Change Requests

To view the Customizing change requests that a user owns, as well as the Customizing change requests in which that user owns a task, proceed as follows:

1. Access the Transport Organizer using Transaction code SE10 or, from the R/3 initial screen, by choosing **Tools · Customizing · IMG · Transport Organizer (Extended View)**. The initial selection screen of the Customizing Organizer appears (see Figure 11.2).

2. Select the user ID of the change request or task owner, as well as the types of change requests you would like to view, and choose **Display**. Select the **request type** and the **request status** and then select **Display**.
3. The screen **Transport Organizer: Requests** is displayed, showing a tree structure listing all change requests that match the selection criteria. To expand the tree structure, click a folder icon. If the folder icon you click is beside a change request ID number, a list of the associated tasks is displayed. If the folder icon you click is beside a task, a list of the objects recorded in the task is displayed.

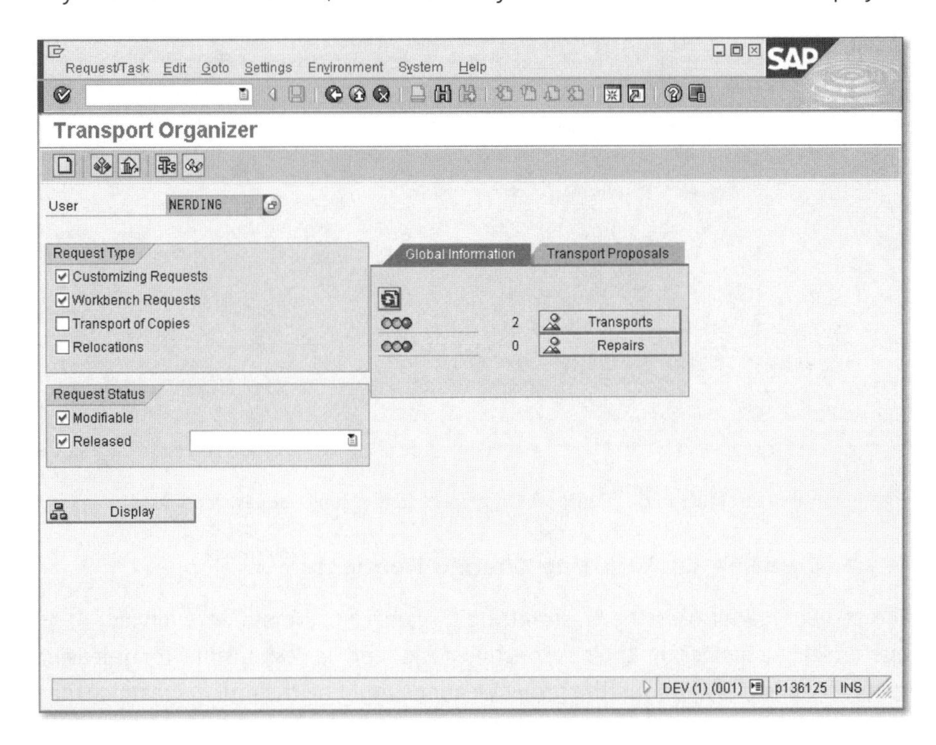


**Figure 11.2** The initial selection screen of the Transport Organizer

Figure 11.3 shows an example of the tree structure with all modifiable Customizing requests where the user KOESEGI is involved. KOESEGI is the owner of the requests `DEVK900002` and `DEVK900005`, in which the users NERDING, KOESEGI, and SCHMIDT own tasks. The task `DEVK900006` of KOESEGI contains changes to the view V_005_B that consists of the table T005.

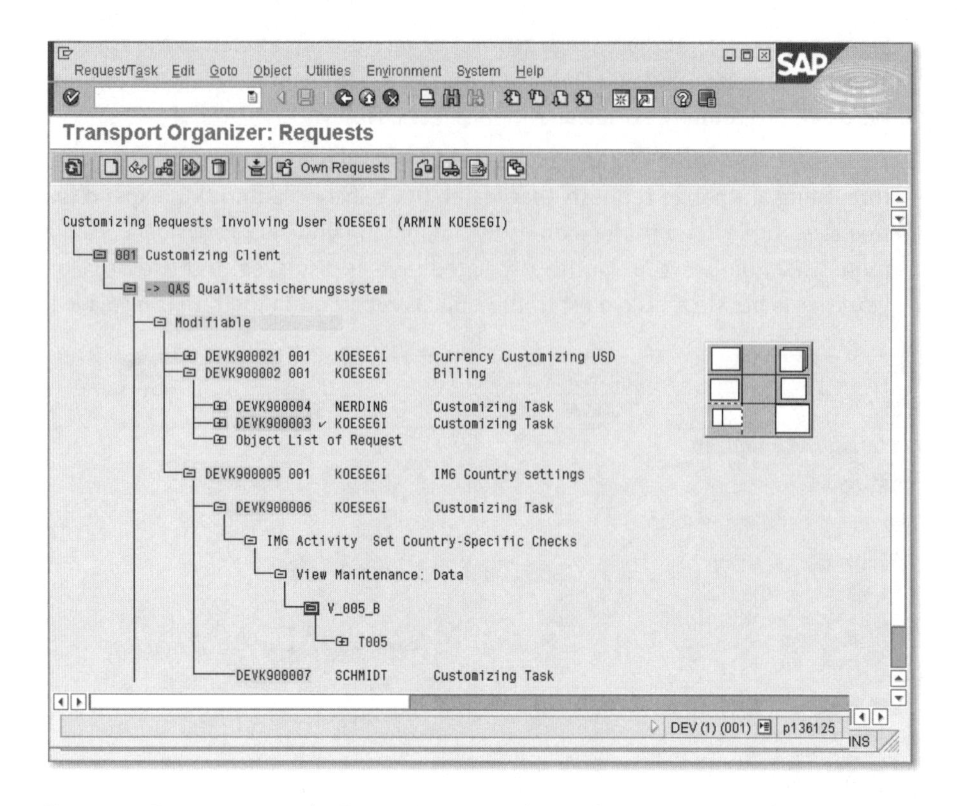


Figure 11.3 Tree structure in the Transport Organizer listing change requests and tasks

### 11.2.2 Creating Customizing Change Requests

The project leader uses the Customizing Organizer to obtain an overview of all Customizing changes in their respective tasks and is responsible for releasing change requests. Therefore, the project leader should be the one to create change requests and assign project team members to them. Ideally, this should be completed well before project team members begin performing Customizing activities. SAP recommends recording all Customizing activities for a particular project objective to a single change request, thereby enabling their subsequent release and export as a testable unit.

To create a Customizing change request and assign project team members to tasks, proceed as follows:

1. From Transaction SE10, display the screen **Transport Organizer: Requests**.
2. To create a new change request, choose **Request/Task • Create**. The **Create Request** window is displayed (see Figure 11.4).

3. Provide a short description for the change request including, for example, project information, a description of the changed functionality, or the urgency of the change.
4. Enter the names of the users who will be contributing Customizing changes to the change request. Each user automatically receives a task in the new change request.
5. Choose **Save**.

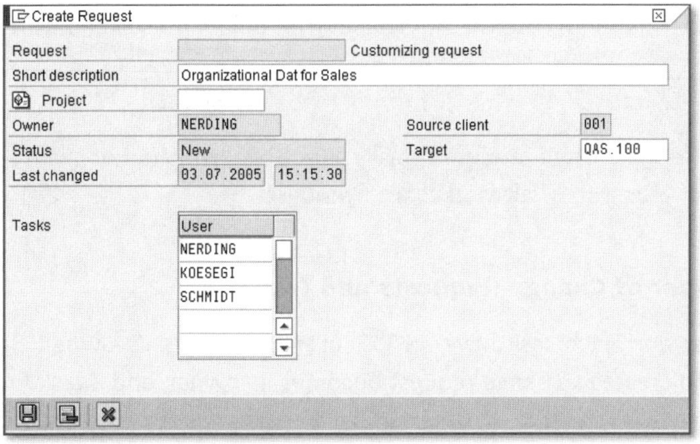

**Figure 11.4** Creating a customizing change request

When creating a Customizing change request, you cannot change the following default settings:

- Name of the R/3 user who created the change request
- Status
- Date and time stamp
- Source client in which the change request was created
- Change request category

The source client is always the client in which the change request was created. Only from within this client can you perform the following activities:

- Recording changes to the change request
- Changing the owner of the change request or of its tasks
- Adding additional tasks to the change request
- Releasing the change request

The change request category is always CUST, indicating that this change request is a Customizing change request and can record only client-dependent changes.

### Adding Additional Users to a Change Request

You can add users to a change request at any time in the interval between creating and releasing a change request. To add users to an existing Customizing change request, thereby creating a task for these users, proceed as follows:

1. From Transaction SE10, display the screen **Transport Organizer: Requests**.
2. Position the cursor on the change request ID to which you wish to add a user. Choose **Request/Task · Create**. The **Add user** dialog box is displayed.
3. Enter the name of the user, or use the possible entries button to select a user.
4. Choose **Copy**.

**Tip** After it is released, a change request or task cannot be changed. For example, you cannot add a user to a released change request.

### Changing the Owner of Change Requests and Tasks

Each change request and each task have an R/3 user defined as its owner. By default, the user who creates a change request becomes its owner, and a task for that user is automatically created. If other users are assigned to the change request, tasks are automatically created for those users.

You may wish to change the owner of a change request or task—for example, to reassign it to another user or to become its owner so that you can change its attributes or delete an empty task. To change the owner of a change request or task, proceed as follows:

1. In Transaction SE10, access the screen **Transport Organizer: Requests**.
2. Position the cursor on the ID of the appropriate change request or task. Choose **Request/Task · Change owner**.
3. Enter the name of the user, or use the possible entries button to select a user.
4. Select **Confirm**. The new user now owns the change request or task.

## 11.2.3 Customizing in Project IMGs

To perform Customizing as a member of the project team, proceed as follows:

1. Use Transaction code SPRO, or in the R/3 initial screen, select **Tools · Customizing · IMG · Execute Project**. The screen **Customizing: Execute Project** is displayed listing the created project IMGs.

2. Choose the project you need to customize by double-clicking the Project ID. The Project IMG tree structure is displayed.
3. To display Customizing activities for the Project IMG, expand the tree structure (see Figure 11.5).

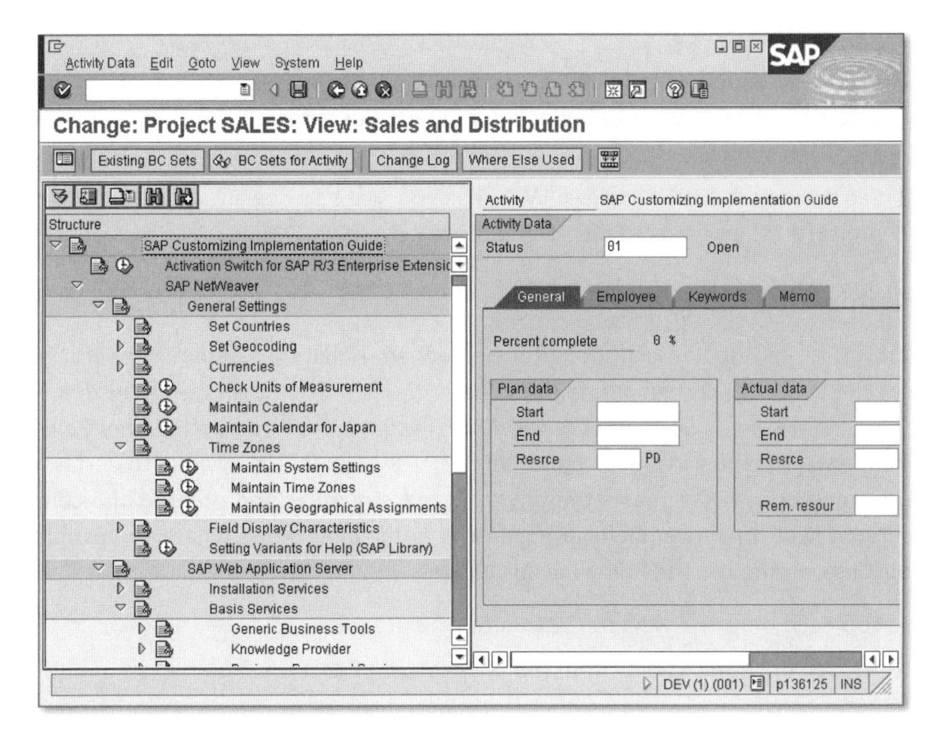


Figure 11.5 Project IMG tree structure

Double-clicking the appropriate icon to the left of the description of each Customizing activity takes you to various related tasks.

- ▶ The large check mark takes you to the documentation of the relevant Customizing activity.
- ▶ The pencil-and-paper icon takes you to the relevant Customizing transaction.

**Note** Customizing activities are performed in the Project IMG tree structure. These activities include maintaining project status information, project documentation, and Customizing settings.

### Setting a Default Project IMG

Customizers usually work in a single Project IMG over a period of time. To eliminate the need for selecting the Project ID to access the relevant tree structure, you can set a default Project IMG that appears every time you access Transaction SPRO. To set a default Project IMG, proceed as follows:

1. Use the Transaction code SPRO, or in the R/3 initial screen, select **Tools · Customizing · IMG · Execute Project**. The screen **Customizing: Execute Project** is displayed showing the created project IMGs.
2. Set the cursor to the project IMG that you want to specify as the standard project IMG and select **Edit · Default project/view · Define**.

### Customizing Using Views

Most Customizing transactions in R/3 are defined so that the Customizing settings for you to change correspond to the settings in views rather than the tables themselves. Views are logical tables in the ABAP Dictionary that group together fields from physical tables to create a uniform business context. Using views to perform Customizing activities masks the physical table structures and presents the constituent fields in a meaningful arrangement. Using table views wherever possible for Customizing has the following advantages:

- You need only one view to Customize several tables.
- You see only those fields from the physical tables that are relevant to the business object.
- The presentation and your processing of Customizing data are standardized.

Some business objects, such as material types and document types, cannot be represented in a view. Rather than having standardized maintenance transactions, these objects are maintained using special transactions, which can differ from object to object and, instead of views, use object-specific screen sequences.

**Tip** Customizing objects, whether simple or complex, are defined by SAP and can be viewed using Transaction SOBJ.

## 11.2.4 Recording Customizing Changes

Customizing changes performed in the respective Customizing transactions can be either automatically or manually saved to a change request for transport to other clients and systems.

SAP recommends that the client in which you make Customizing changes has its client-dependent change option set to **Automatic recording of changes**. In Figure 11.3 (earlier in this chapter), for example, when you create a new controlling area and save the change, you will be automatically required to save it to a change request.

If the client in which you are performing Customizing changes is not set to **Automatic recording of changes**, you can manually record the change to a change request, either after saving the change or at a later time.

**Note** Certain Customizing activities, referred to in this chapter as *manual transport* Customizing activities, are not automatically recorded to a change request, even if the client is set to automatic recording. These Customizing activities are transported using a method that varies according to the activity.

### Automatically Recording Changes to Change Requests

If the setting for client-dependent changes in your Customizing-and-development client is set to **Automatic recording of changes**, when you save a Customizing change, you must indicate a change request to which the change can be recorded. The dialog box **Enter Change Request** is displayed (see Figure 11.6). In this dialog box, you can do one of the following:

- Enter the change request ID of a change request in which you have a task.
- Choose **Own requests** and select a change request from the change requests offered (see Figure 11.7).
- Choose **Create request** and (assuming you have the appropriate authorization) create a new Customizing change request in which you automatically also have a task.
- Choose **Cancel** and thereby not save your Customizing changes.

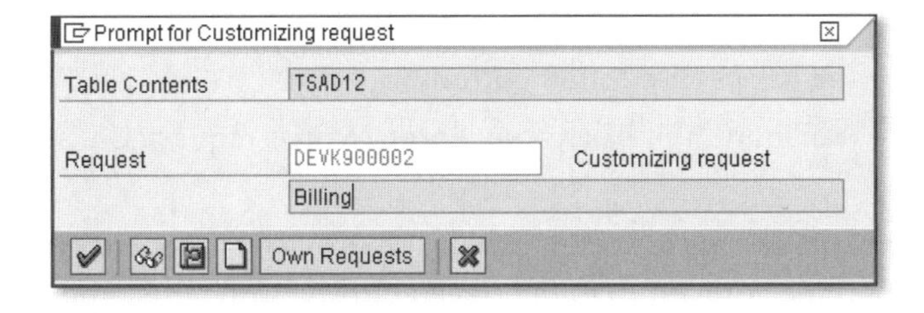


**Figure 11.6** Recording a change to a change request

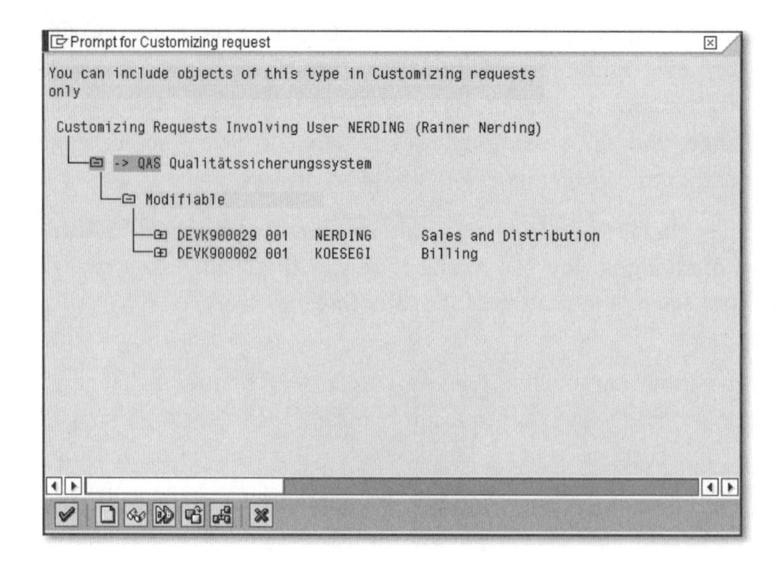


**Figure 11.7** Selecting from a list of available change requests

### Manually Recording Changes to Change Requests

If a client is not set to automatically record Customizing changes to a change request, you can save Customizing changes without recording them to a change request. Subsequently, you can manually record the existing Customizing changes to a change request. Manual recording of Customizing settings can also be used to record existing entries that, while they already may be in a change request, should be transported together in a single change request. To manually record existing Customizing entries, proceed as follows:

1. Use the IMG (Transaction SPRO) to access the Customizing activity. Click the large check mark to display the existing Customizing data you wish to manually record to a change request.
2. Select the Customizing entries to be recorded to the change request. To do this, select all entries using **Edit · Selections · Select all**, and then deselect individual entries by clicking the adjacent selection buttons.
3. Choose **Table view · Transport**. The dialog box **Enter change request** is displayed.
4. Enter the ID number of the change request to which the selected entries will be recorded. Choose **Continue**. You return to the screen displaying the Customizing data.
5. Choose **Include in request**. This records all the Customizing entries you selected to the defined change request. Choose **Save**.

Not all Customizing activities allow changes to be manually recorded to a change request. When you display such Customizing settings, the menu option **Table view • Transport** is not available. To transport such Customizing, you may need to activate automatic recording of changes and edit the existing entries to force them to be recorded to a change request.

### Setting Your Default Change Request

When using automatic recording of change requests, you can set a default Customizing change request to eliminate the need for specifying the change request. As a result, whenever you save a client-dependent Customizing change, it is recorded to your default change request. To set a default change request, proceed as follows:

1. In Transaction SE10, access the screen **Transport Organizer: Requests**.
2. Position the cursor on the change request you want as your default change request and choose **Utilities • Standard request • Set**. The change request appears in the **Transport Organizer: Requests** screen in a different color.

When you have a default change request and try to save your Customizing changes, no dialog box appears to ask you to indicate a change request. Your default change request is valid for one week unless you change the validity period. To change the validity period, choose **Utilities • Standard request • Set validity period**.

If you no longer want a particular change request to be the default change request, from the **Transport Organizer: Requests** screen, position the cursor on the default change request and choose **Utilities • Standard request • Reset**.

## 11.2.5 Object Lists for Customizing Change Requests

The object list records objects that have been changed and shows what will be transported when the change request is released and exported. Each changed object has an entry in the object list. The object list of a change request is filled only after the tasks in the change request have been released (see also Chapter 12).

By expanding the hierarchical structure of a Customizing change request, you can display the list of objects recorded in a change request. For example, Figure 11.8 shows the Customizing objects (values in tables) that were changed in task `DEVK900022`. The owner of this task is the user KOESEGI. The figure shows that changes to the views V_TCURF and V_TCURR have been carried out. The views have been expanded so that you can see the tables (TCURF and TCURR) on which these views are based, as well as the primary keys of the table entries changed during Customizing. For the table TCURF, for example, this change request recorded the primary key `001B USD DEM 80029898`.

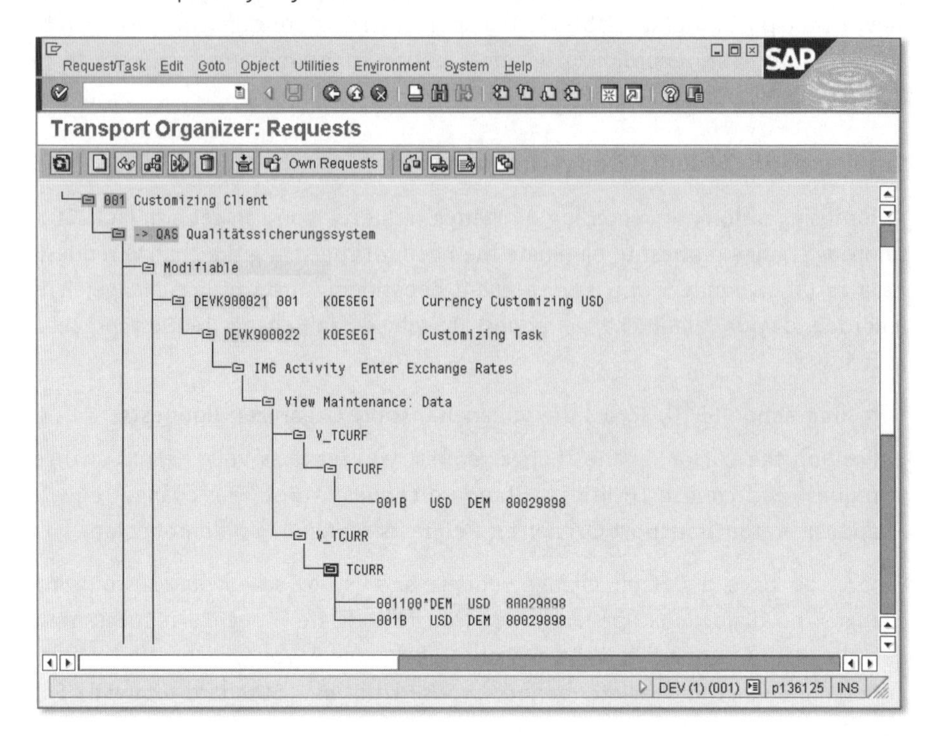


**Figure 11.8** Objects in the tree structure for Customizing change requests

You can view more information on these objects if you display the object list by double-clicking the request identification. The object list of task DEVK900022 is presented in Figure 11.9. The program identification PgmID and the object description Obj specify the type of objects that have been changed. R3TR VDAT specifies view data. Note that a key symbol is shown in the Funct. column for the entries V_TCURF and V_TCURR. This symbol shows that a primary key has been recorded for these specific objects. If a primary key is recorded, not all of the rows of the specified table or view need to be transported. Instead, only the individual rows that match the key definition are transported.

For a better understanding of the primary key that has been recorded for the changed Customizing entry, double-click on the key symbol in the object list and then double-click on the primary key value. A screen like the one shown in Figure 11.10 appears, displaying the key data of the table TCURR. Figure 11.10 shows that the primary key consists of the client, the exchange rate type, the source currency, the target currency, and a validity date. When this change request is released and exported, the current table entries are extracted to this primary key.

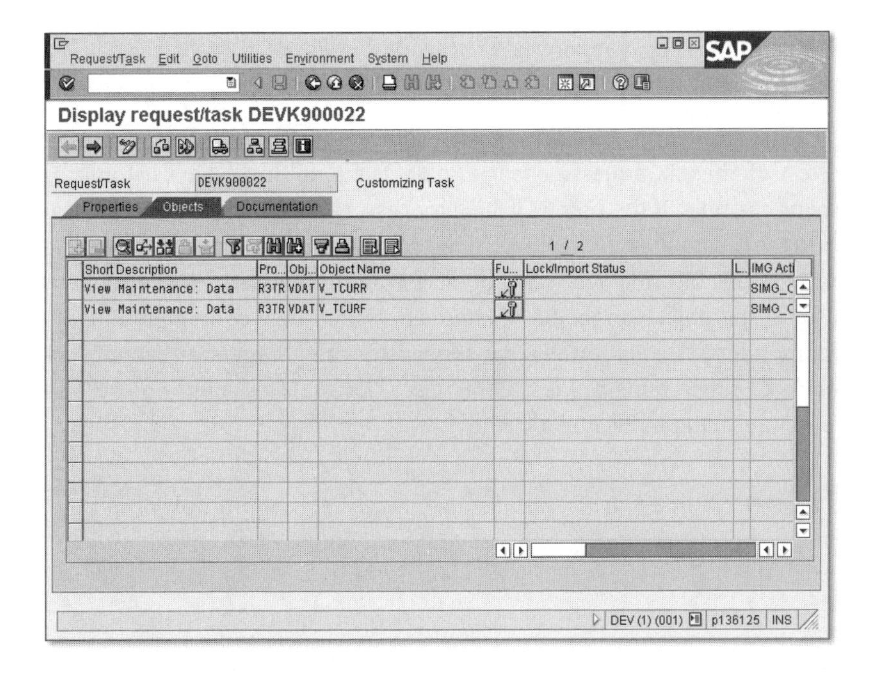


Figure 11.9 Object list for a Customizing task

Display Key for Table TCURR

| Med.field label | Field Name | Ty... | Lngth | Key Value |
|---|---|---|---|---|
| Client | MANDT | C | 3 | 001 |
| Exch.rate type | KURST | C | 4 | 100* |
| From currency | FCURR | C | 5 | DEM |
| To-currency | TCURR | C | 5 | USD |
| Valid from | GDATU | C | 8 | 80029898 |

Figure 11.10 Details of a primary key for a recorded Customizing change

Customizing change requests contain only client-dependent Customizing objects. For changes recorded in a Customizing change request, the client ID number is included in the primary key value. At the time of release and export, the primary key is used in an SQL `SELECT` statement to access the changed table entry.

A change request does *not* contain the actual table entries or the object that has changed. A change request does not even record whether the change was an addition, modification, or deletion. All that is recorded in a change request is the list of the objects (views, tables, and/or key values) that have changed. The objects in task `DEVK900022` shown in Figure 11.9 can be the result of creating, deleting, or changing entries in the currency table, for example.

**Note** A Customizing change request records, but does *not* contain, the actual table entries that have changed.

Contrary to Workbench requests, changed objects are not locked in Customizing requests. For example, if the user KOESEGI makes a change to the sales organization PRNT, the Customizing Organizer does not prevent other users from also modifying this Customizing setting while it is in an unreleased change request. Since Customizing objects in the SAP system are shared between different application components, it is important that the Customizing Organizer cannot lock entire tables or single table entries. Otherwise, Customizing could not be performed by more than one user in a client.

**Note** Changes recorded to a Customizing change request are not locked by the change request and can be changed and recorded to other change requests.

### 11.2.6 Identifying Change Requests with the Same Object

Unlike Workbench change requests, Customizing change requests do not lock objects. It is possible for more than one person to change the same Customizing settings. If this shared access to Customizing objects creates a misunderstanding among project team members, it may be necessary to see which users are changing the same Customizing object.

To view all tasks or change requests that include the same Customizing object, proceed as follows:

1. Access the Transport Organizer Tools by using Transaction SE10 and choosing **Goto · Transport Organizer · Tools**.
2. The **Transport Organizer: Tools** screen will appear, listing the available tools in a tree structure. Expand the node **Objects in requests**.
3. Double-click the option **Search for objects in requests/tasks**. The screen **Search for Objects in Requests/Tasks** appears (see Figure 11.11). This is a selection screen where you can define the object for which you are searching.
4. Select the appropriate object type and then, in the adjacent field, enter the name of the object. For example, if the object is in a view, enter the object type VDAT and then enter the name of the view.
5. Other selection criteria include the type of change requests, whether the change requests have been released, the owners of the change requests, and a time period in which the objects were last modified. If you are searching for

Repository objects, the option **Also search for sub-objects** will display tasks and change requests containing LIMU entries (see Chapter 10).

6. After making your selections, choose **Execute**. A list of change requests and tasks containing the object is displayed.

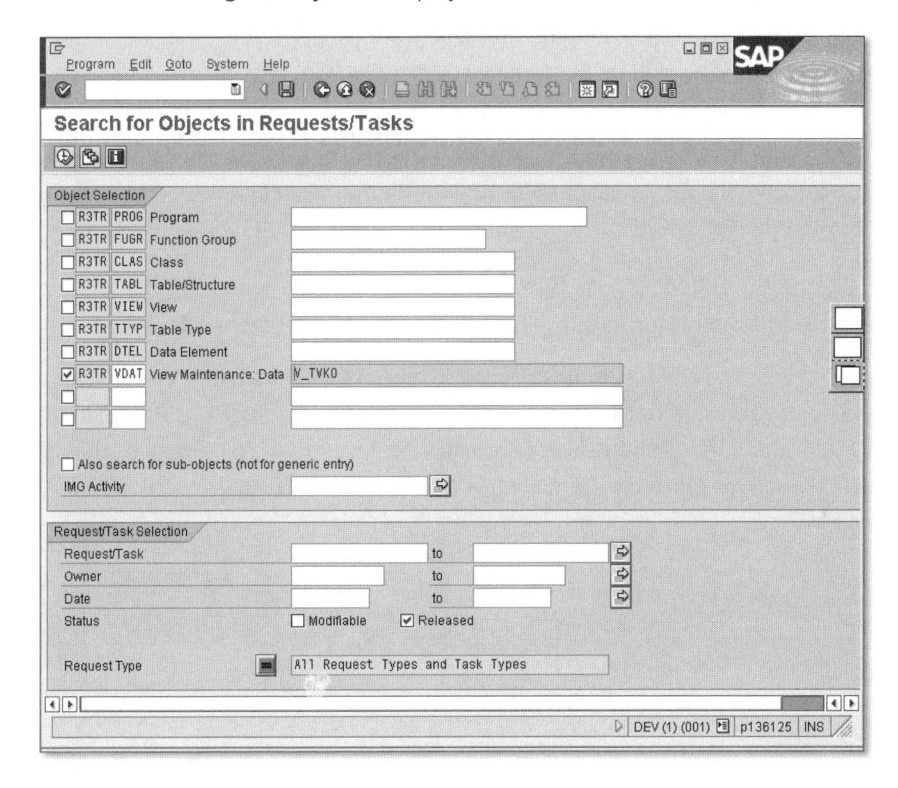


Figure 11.11 Searching for change requests or tasks with common objects

## 11.3 Nonstandard Customizing Activities

Customizing activities are typically client-dependent changes to views and tables that are made by a user through IMG activities. However, an implementation phase usually includes other Customizing activities that are considered nonstandard because they have one or more of the following characteristics:

- They are client-independent and, therefore, affect not only the current SAP client but all clients within the SAP system.
- They require a manual method for transport instead of being automatically recorded to a change request.
- They can be performed both in the IMG and by alternative means (since they commonly need to be performed in the production client).

### 11.3.1 Client-Independent Customizing Activities

Although most Customizing objects of type CUST are client-dependent and are recorded in Customizing change requests, client-independent Customizing objects are of type SYST and are recorded in Workbench Organizer change requests. Changes to client-independent Customizing settings can also create ABAP Workbench objects (known as *generated objects*).

#### Determining whether a Customizing Activity Is Client-Independent

To determine which Customizing activities are client-independent (or *cross-client*), proceed as follows:

1. Display either the Enterprise IMG or a Project IMG tree structure.
2. Select **Additional Information · Technical Data · Client Dependency**.

Figure 11.12 shows the resulting screen. Cross-client IMG activities are indicated on the right-hand side of the screen. In the example in Figure 11.12, the maintenance of calendars is **client-independent** and requires a Workbench change request to be transported. The activity **Check Units of Measurement** is client-dependent.

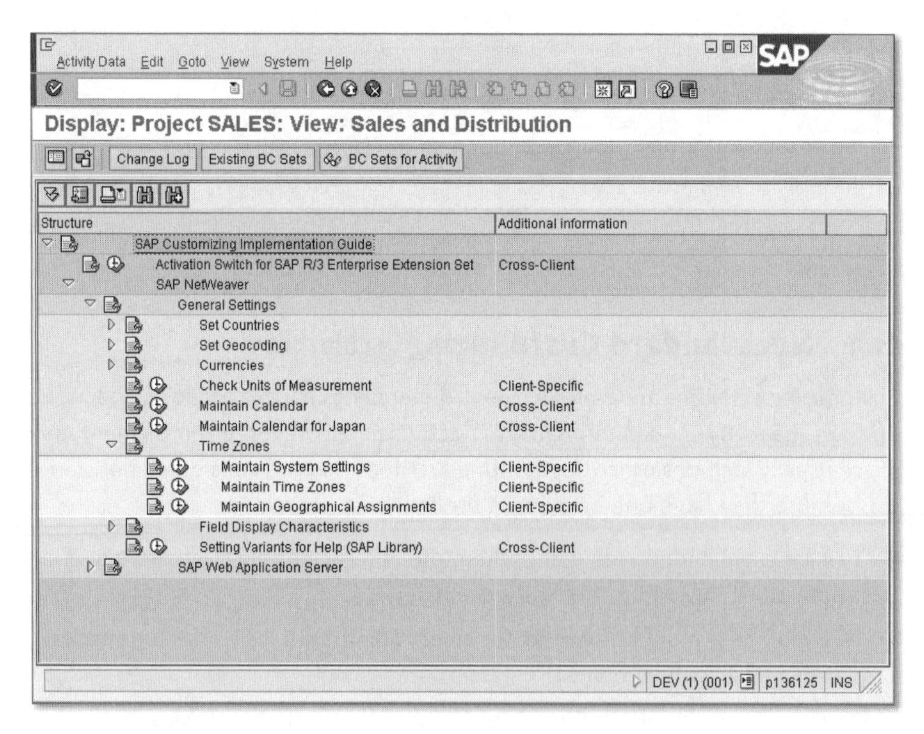


**Figure 11.12** Displaying cross-client Customizing activities in the IMG

### Recording Client-Independent Customizing Changes

When you save changed Customizing settings that are client-independent, a dialog box always appears requesting you to record your change to a Workbench change request, regardless of the client settings. You can either select a Workbench change request from a list after choosing **Own requests** or create a new Workbench change request with **Create request**.

### Assigning Generated Customizing Objects to a Development Class

Cross-client Customizing activities sometimes result in the automatic generation of new R/3 Repository objects. Before these are generated, in the relevant Customizing transaction, you are required to provide a name for the new object. Next, a dialog box appears requesting a development class. Finally, a dialog box appears requesting a change request of type Workbench. The development class determines whether the objects can be transported. Most likely, you will want to transport all Customizing changes that trigger the creation of new R/3 Repository objects, and will therefore need to assign a customer development class with a valid transport layer (see Chapter 10).

**Example: Objects Generated Automatically during Customizing**

An example of a client-independent Customizing activity that results in the creation of new Repository objects is defining pricing condition tables. To access this Customizing activity in the IMG, choose **Sales and Distribution · Basic Functions · Pricing · Pricing control · Define condition tables**. Performing this Customizing activity automatically generates a pricing table, which stores various pricing criteria. After specifying the object name (such as 601, which automatically generates the object name A601) and defining pricing criteria in the relevant dialog boxes, you must assign a development class and save the object to a Workbench change request. After saving the generated object to a Workbench change request, if you access the object list corresponding to the change request, the list will show the objects recorded to the change request as the result of creating the pricing condition table A601:

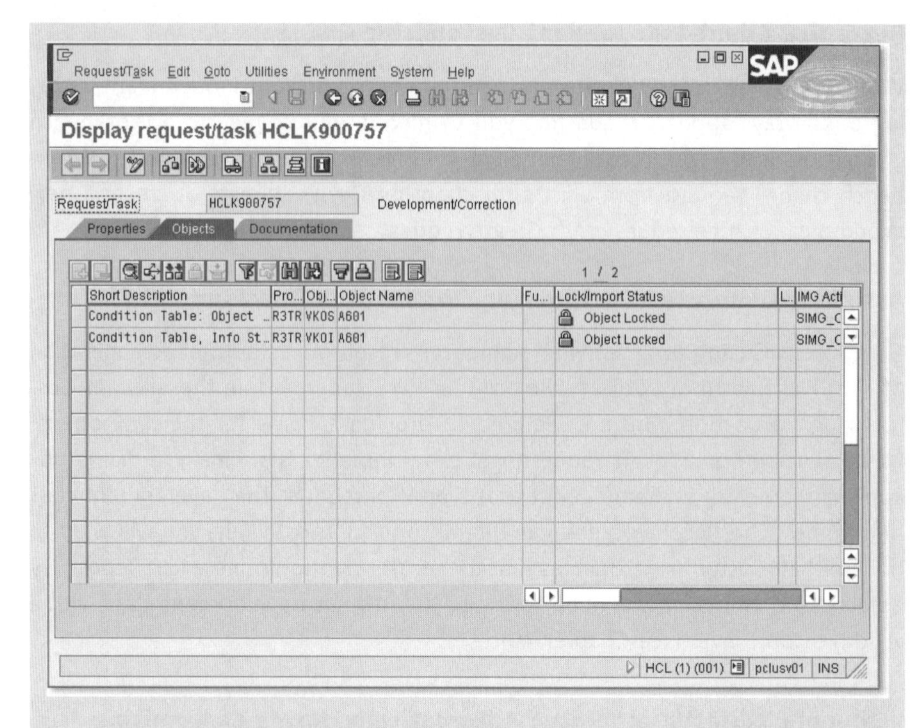


Figure 11.13 Object list corresponding to change request

The two objects in the object list are not the pricing condition table A601, but rather the information required to generate that table. The definition of the object to be generated and not the object itself is recorded in the change request and subsequently transported. After export and during import into the quality assurance and production systems, the definition information is used to generate the required object.

To check whether the object has been generated, use Transaction SE11, enter "A601" beside **Database table**, and choose **Edit · Object directory entry**. The screen displayed is the one shown below. This screen shows A601 flagged as a generated object whose original system is SAP. Since its development class does not begin with a Y or a Z, it is an SAP-delivered development class. The field **Generation flag** contains an X; therefore, the object was generated by SAP.

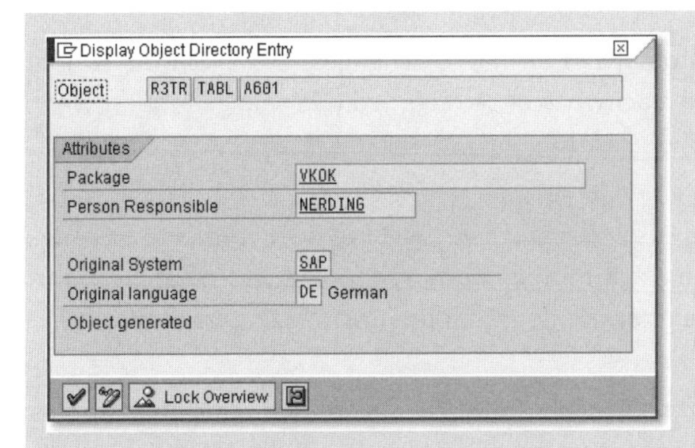


**Figure 11.14** Object catalog entry

The objects defining the generated pricing condition table that are recorded in the change request are assigned to a customer development class. They do not appear as generated objects, and their original system is the customer's development system. To verify this, use Transaction SE11 to display the above screen for the objects in the change request.

Generated Customizing objects often are not transported. The definitions and instructions for the creation of the required Customizing object are transported.

### 11.3.2 Manual Transports and Other Transport Types

For most IMG Customizing changes, if the client setting specifies automatic recording of changes, the changes are automatically saved to a change request. However, there are some Customizing activities for which automatic recording to a change request is not possible. Such Customizing activities are considered *manual transport* Customizing activities.

Automatic recording to a change request is generally not possible when the entries for a Customizing object cannot be transported individually—the entire object (all of its entries) must be transported as a unit. Changes to such critical Customizing settings require a manual method of transport when the project leader recognizes that the entire object is ready for transport.

In the tree structure of the enterprise IMG or of a project IMG, select **Additional Information · Technical Data · Transport Type** to determine which Customizing activities require manual transport. A screen like that shown in Figure 11.13 is displayed. The right-hand side of the screen indicates the transport method for each Customizing activity. The transport methods may include:

- **Automatic transport:**
  If the client is set to automatic recording of changes, the client-dependent changes to the Customizing activity will be recorded to a change request when saved.
- **Manual transport:**
  Individual changes to the Customizing activity will not be recorded to a change request. To transport the Customizing settings, the changes must be transported using a special menu option found in the Customizing transaction.
- **No transport:**
  Changes to the Customizing activity cannot be transported. This often applies to SAP system–specific changes that are of a technical nature and not related to Customizing. It also applies when the IMG activity is a check routine that enables you to verify settings and data in the current SAP client. These IMG activities are not changes to Customizing settings and therefore do not require transport.

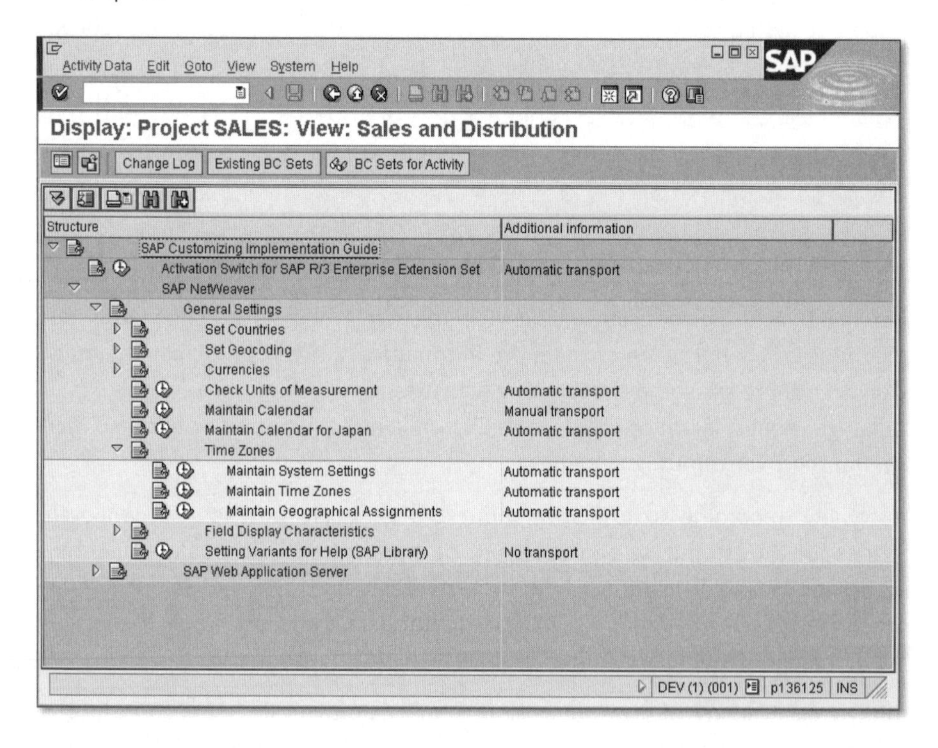


**Figure 11.15** Displaying transportability in the IMG

In Figure 11.15, the transport method **Automatic transport** is assigned to the Customizing tasks for checking the units of measurement and maintaining the calendar for Japan. The Customizing activity **Maintain Calendar** requires a manual transport. To transport changes to the calendar, use the **Transport** button in the Customizing transaction, which will transport not just the most recent change but the entire calendar.

### 11.3.3 Customizing in a Production Client

For your production client, SAP recommends setting the client-dependent change option to **No changes allowed**, thereby ensuring that all Customizing and development occur in the development system. However, some Customizing activities in the IMG concern minor changes that a customer may need to make on a regular basis. Examples of these changes include interest rates, health insurance premiums, pension schemes, tax schemes, and currency exchange rates. These types of changes are known as *data-only* Customizing changes.

Making such changes in the development system and transporting them regularly to the production system is tedious and increases the amount of work necessary for maintaining import queues and monitoring import logs. To avoid having to use change requests for these changes, SAP has introduced the **Current Settings** function. This function enables Customizing in a production client for client-dependent changes that do not impact the business flow.

#### Activating Current Settings

As a prerequisite for using the **Current Settings** function, the following settings must be made in Transaction SCC4 for the production client:

- The client role is **Production**.
- The client-dependent change option is **No transports allowed**.

> **Note** For more information on using **Current Settings** in a production client, see SAP Note 77430.

#### Customizing Activities in Current Settings

The Customizing activities that can be performed in a production client using the **Current Settings** function are listed in the database table CUSAMEN.

You can add Customizing activities to table CUSAMEN, allowing you to perform them in the production client with the **Current Settings** function. SAP recommends that you add Customizing activities to CUSAMEN only if it is necessary and only if the changes resulting from these activities are data changes that:

- Are required on a regular basis
- Do not require a formal quality assurance sign-off
- Are not required in the other clients within the system landscape to maintain consistent Customizing environments

Adding an entry to table CUSAMEN results in a modification (see Chapter 10).

**Tip** For more information on adding Customizing activities to the table CUSAMEN so that they can be performed using the **Current Settings** function, see SAP Note 135028.

An alternative to adding Customizing activities to the table CUSAMEN is using ALE to distribute Customizing data. ALE enables you to distribute a change to all SAP clients without the need for a change request. This requires ALE development, because SAP does not provide ALE scenarios for Customizing activities (see also Chapter 4, under "Transferring Master Data between SAP Systems").

## 11.4 Support Tools for Customizing

To enable you to compare Customizing settings in different clients, SAP provides the following tools:

- Customizing Cross-System Viewer
- View/Table Comparison
- Business Configuration Sets
- Customizing Transfer Assistant

To use any of these tools, you must:

- Have a user authorization that includes authorization S_CUS_CMP in both the logon client and the comparison client. To compare client-independent objects, you also need the authorization S_TABU_CLI.
- Create an RFC connection between the logon client (RFC target client) and the comparison client (RFC source client). To find out how to create an RFC connection, see Appendix A. When you create the RFC connection, the user you are required to define should be a user whose authorization in the target client does not exceed the authorization required to use these tools. For example, you can define a CPIC user who has only the authorization S_CUS_CMP.
- Set client protection in the comparison client to either **Protection level 0** or **Protection level 1**. (See "Client Protection" in Chapter 9.)
- To transfer Customizing settings from a comparison client, set the client protection in the logon client to **Protection level 0**.

### 11.4.1 Comparing Customizing in Two Clients

To compare the Customizing settings of two clients, in releases prior to Release 4.5, use the function **client compare**. As of Release 4.5, use the Customizing Cross-System Viewer, which is an improved version of the client compare function.

Using either of these tools enables you to compare Customizing objects and tables in one SAP client (comparison client) against the settings in the current client (logon client). The result is an overview screen, showing differences between the two clients. In this screen, you can drill down the listed items to display the corresponding Customizing entries. To change these entries, you can use direct links to the corresponding IMG activity or a function that allows you to adjust the differences between the entries.

During implementation, you often need to compare the contents of tables or views located in the same SAP system or in different SAP systems. Comparing clients can help you to:

- Identify the differences between the Customizing settings of two R/3 clients, or verify that both clients have consistent Customizing settings
- Compare current Customizing settings to those of a reference client such as client 000
- Compare Customizing settings delivered from a central corporate development system with the local Customizing settings

When you access the Customizing Cross-System Viewer using Transaction SCU0, a selection screen like the one shown in Figure 11.16 appears. This selection screen shows the kinds of objects you can compare. It contains the following selection options:

- **IMG activities:**
  This option selects Customizing objects related to an entire Project IMG or Enterprise IMG.
- **Application components:**
  This option selects Customizing objects related to one or more branches of a business application component.
- **Customizing object list/transport:**
  This option selects all Customizing objects recorded in an object list or a change request. This option is available as of Release 4.0.
- **Business configuration set:**
  This option is available only in the Cross-System Viewer. It selects all objects recorded in the Customizing snapshot known as a Business Configuration Set.

- **ALE Distribution Group:**
  This options selects all objects belonging to an ALE distribution group
- **Manual selection:**
  This option selects the Customizing objects and ABAP Dictionary tables that you specify.

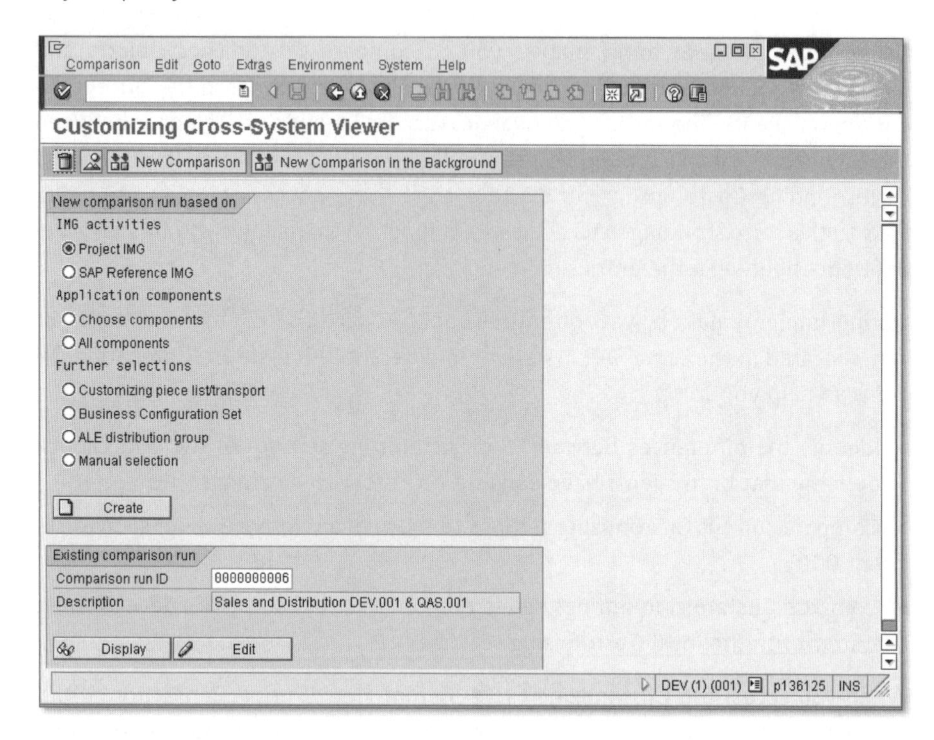


**Figure 11.16** Selection screen of the Cross-System Viewer (containing options similar to those on the selection screen for client compare)

### The Customizing Cross-System Viewer

To perform a client comparison, proceed as follows:

1. Access the Customizing Cross-System Viewer. To do this, use Transaction code SCU0 or, from the R/3 initial screen, choose **Tools · Customizing · IMG · Customizing · Cross-System Viewer**.
2. The selection screen for the Cross-System Viewer is displayed. Select the criteria for comparison and choose **Create**. You may need to indicate, for example, the Project IMG, the different application components, or a change request ID.
3. After you choose **Create**, a **comparison run ID** (a sequential value also referred to as the *worklist ID*) is automatically generated. A **Selection by:** screen appears:

- Enter a description for the comparison. The description should enable you to remember what selection criteria you are using. Note that, to subsequently display the results of the comparison, you will need the comparison run ID.
- To include client-dependent Customizing objects, select **Client-specific**.
- To include client-independent Customizing objects, select **Cross-client**.
- Provide an RFC connection to the comparison client.

4. To schedule the comparison as a background job, choose **New comparison in background**. To begin the comparison immediately (if the comparison involves only a few objects), choose **New comparison**. Alternatively, to get a list of Customizing objects that can be compared so that you can limit the comparison, choose **Object overview**.

### Displaying the Results of a Client Comparison

The results of the comparison are the starting point for the display and subsequent adjustment of the differences between the logon client and the comparison client.

To display the results of a client comparison, proceed as follows:

- Use Transaction SCU0.
- In the field **Existing comparison run**, enter the worklist ID (the comparison run ID) for the client comparison you wish to display.
- Choose **Display**.

The results screen shows the differences for each compared object, a description of the object, and the **comparison status** in the column **Comp**. The comparison status indicates the equivalence or nonequivalence of the object in the respective clients.

The comparison results of the Cross-System Viewer are known as a *worklist*. You can use the worklist to review completed comparisons and maintain status information. The worklist also uses traffic-light icons to indicate processing status information—whether you are still analyzing or have already corrected found differences.

Figure 11.17 displays sample differences between the logon client, client 001 of system DEV, and the comparison client, client 001 of system QAS. The Customizing in the views V_T005K, V_T005_BAS, V_TCURF, and V_TCURR differs in the two clients. The Customizing in view T_005S is the same. The right-hand side of the screen compares the number of entries of this object in the two clients.

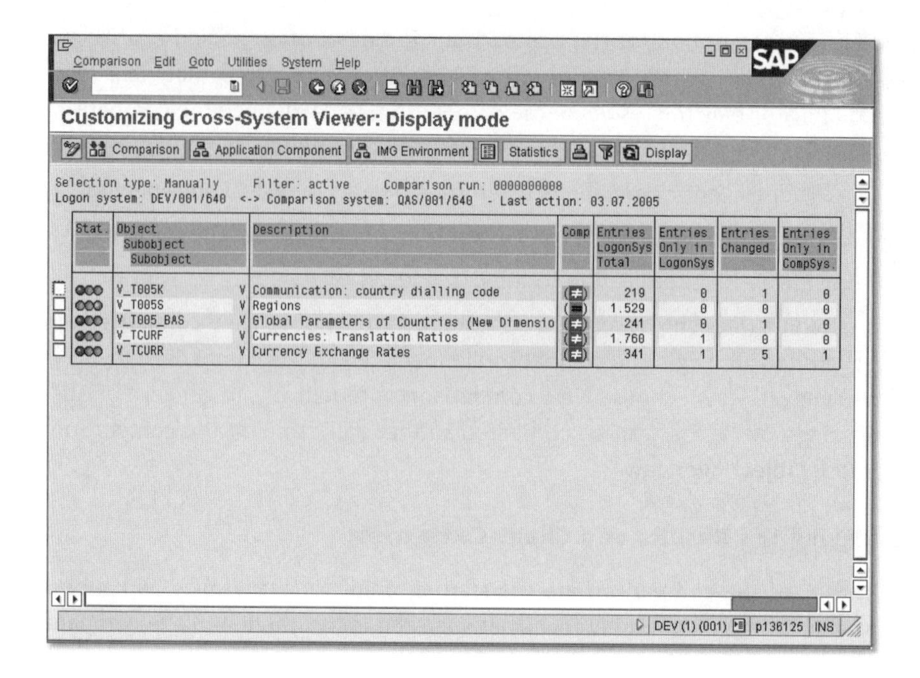


**Figure 11.17** The result of comparing two SAP clients

The column showing the comparison status, **Comp**, may indicate the following:

- Contents are identical.
- Contents are not identical.
- Contents are identical, but the ABAP Dictionary structure of the object differs.
- Contents are not identical, and the ABAP Dictionary structure of the object differs.
- Contents could not be compared.

There are several reasons why a comparison may not be possible. For example:

- The table or view does not exist in a local or a remote client.
- The sum of the length of all fields in the table or view exceeds the byte limitations of the standard compare tool (this is very rare).
- The structure of the table or view is not consistent between the two clients. For example, the primary key differs, or a field in one client is defined as a character field, while being defined as numeric in the other client. This can occur when the clients have different Release levels.
- The table is a system table and is therefore excluded from comparison.

The processing status indicated as a traffic light enables you to distinguish those objects that have already been processed from those that still need to be processed. Red indicates **not processed**, yellow indicates **in process**, and green indicates **completed**. Initially, the process status is set as a result of the comparison so that all red traffic lights indicate a difference in the two clients or the inability to compare the object. A green traffic light indicates that the comparison found no differences.

The processing status can be set manually—for example, from red to yellow to green. To do this, choose **Comparison run • Display • Change** and then click the traffic light until the desired color indicator is displayed. Remember to save the changes. By manually setting the processing status, you can track your progress as you analyze and possibly adjust the differences for each object.

For example, in Figure 11.17, during the review of table V_T005K, the status for this object can be changed to yellow to indicate to other members of the Customizing project that the difference is currently being analyzed. During your analysis, you may discover that the difference is simply due to the fact that a change request has not yet been transported from client 001 of DEV into the quality assurance system. In this case, the difference will be resolved when that change request is imported, and no adjustment is required in the comparison results screen. You can change the processing status from red to green.

To analyze the differences between two clients, you can:

- Filter the comparison results screen according to various criteria for processing status, comparison status, and object type
- Display a statistical overview showing differences and object types
- Display the relevant IMG activity for particular objects
- Display the application component for a particular object in the application component hierarchy
- Perform a single comparison, as described below

#### Performing a Single Comparison

To view the corresponding records of the table or view, display the comparison results list, position the cursor on an object, and choose **Single comparison**. The screen **Overview comparison** is displayed. To make the differences easy to identify, the entries of the respective views of each object are shown consecutively. The results of the comparison are color-coded. For an explanation of the colors, choose **Legend**. The different comparison statuses are shown in Table 11.1.

| Status | Description |
|---|---|
| <blank> | The listed entry is identical in both clients. |
| ML | The entries are not identical; the listed entry is the logon client entry. |
| MR | The entries are not identical; the listed entry is the comparison client entry. |
| L | Entry exists only in logon client. |
| R | Entry exists only in comparison client. |
| (M) or (E) | Differences only in fields that you have hidden from the comparison (for example, you may wish to exclude a noncritical field such as **LastChangedAt** from comparison). |

**Table 11.1** Single comparison status indicators

An example of the results of a single comparison of object V_T005K is shown in Figure 11.18. The view includes telephone area codes to call from or to a country. The entry for the country AZ is different. On the logon client, the **Tel. from** field contains "00". On the comparison client, this field is empty.

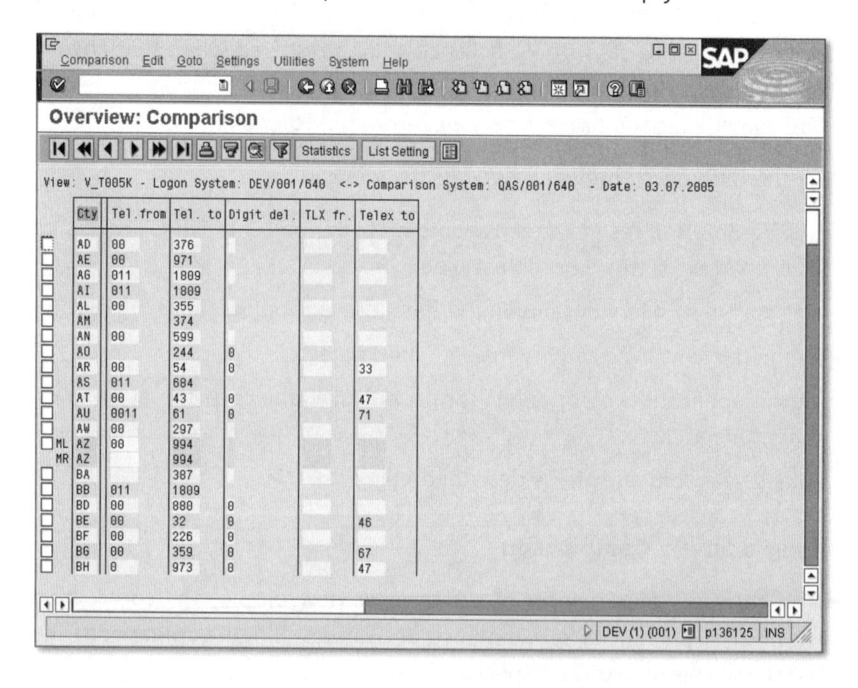


**Figure 11.18** A single comparison for a view

When you analyze a particular Customizing object by performing a single comparison, the window **Restrict selection set** appears, asking whether you would like to compare all values or restrict the comparison. To optimize performance, you may wish to restrict the comparison. If the object to be detailed does not contain a lot of table entries—for example, fewer than 500—you do not need to restrict the comparison.

### Adjusting the Customizing Differences between Clients

To adjust the Customizing differences between clients, you need to transfer view and table entries or the contents of individual fields from a comparison client to the logon client as described below. Keep the following points in mind:

- Table and view entries can be changed only in the logon client, not in the comparison client.
- The adjustment can be performed for only one object at a time.
- The adjustment can be performed for only the tables and views that can be maintained using Table Maintenance (Transaction SM30). Other objects can be compared, but not adjusted.
- The data transferred to the logon client is subjected to the standard validation checks, which may prevent you from saving the transferred data. This may occur, for example, if you transfer a row, and part of the data comprising the primary key is missing in the logon client.
- Customizing objects cannot be adjusted for Business Configuration Sets.

**Warning** All differences as the result of a comparison cannot be adjusted for technical reasons.

You can transfer the following kinds of data from the comparison client to the logon client:

- An entire row in a view or table. If the entry is present only in the comparison client, it is added to the logon client. If the row is present, but different in the two clients, it is copied into the logon client.
- A specific field in a row. Only the contents of the field you select are copied. The contents of all other fields are not affected.
- All entries of a table or view in the comparison client.
- An entire column of data. In this way, values are only added, not replaced.

In addition, you can delete entries in the logon client to resolve a difference.

You can access the tools for performing adjustments in the Cross-System Viewer. To perform an adjustment, from within the client you wish to adjust, proceed as follows:

1. In Transaction SCU0, access the worklist for which you wish to initiate a transfer by providing the worklist ID and choosing **Display**.
2. The screen **Customizing Objects: Difference list** (see Figure 11.17 earlier in the chapter) appears. In this screen, to switch to change mode, choose **Display <-> Change**.
3. Position the cursor on the Customizing object to be adjusted and choose **Edit • Interact. Copy**.
4. The screen **Overview: Comparison** appears. Position the cursor on the entry you wish to adjust and choose **Adjust**.
5. The screen **Detail View: Adjust** appears. Choose the type of adjustment to be made. For example, to copy an entry from the comparison client to the current client, choose **Entry**.
6. At this stage, the data has been transferred but not saved (entered into the database). Choose **Back** to leave the adjustment tool. You will be prompted to save your changes. To save them, choose **Yes**. Choosing **No** returns the table or view to its original state.
7. If automatic recording of changes is active, you are prompted for a change request.

### 11.4.2 Single Comparison with Transaction SCMP

The Customizing Cross-System Viewer and the **client compare** tool are useful for comparing many objects at once—for example, when comparing objects from a project or application perspective. However, you may wish to simply compare a single Customizing object or table. Since the Customizing Cross-System Viewer and the **client compare** tool are specifically designed for Customizing objects, you cannot use them to compare tables that are not considered Customizing objects. Such non-Customizing objects include, for example, tables that contain application data.

> **Warning** Single comparisons read the view or table contents into memory before performing a comparison. Therefore, views or tables with a lot of entries, such as an application table, will negatively impact system performance.

To compare a single R/3 object or a non-Customizing object, the simplest option is to use Transaction SCMP. To do this, proceed as follows:

1. Use Transaction code SCMP.
2. The screen **View/Table Comparison** appears (see Figure 11.19). Enter the name of the view or table to be compared and the name of the RFC destination (R/3 connection).
   - To limit the comparison to specific key values, select **Enter selection requirements**.
   - To see only entries that differ between the two clients, select **Display differences only**.
   - To schedule the comparison as a background job, select **Background execution**—the results will be available as spool output only.
   - To limit the CPU required for the comparison, select **Restrict fields to be compared**.

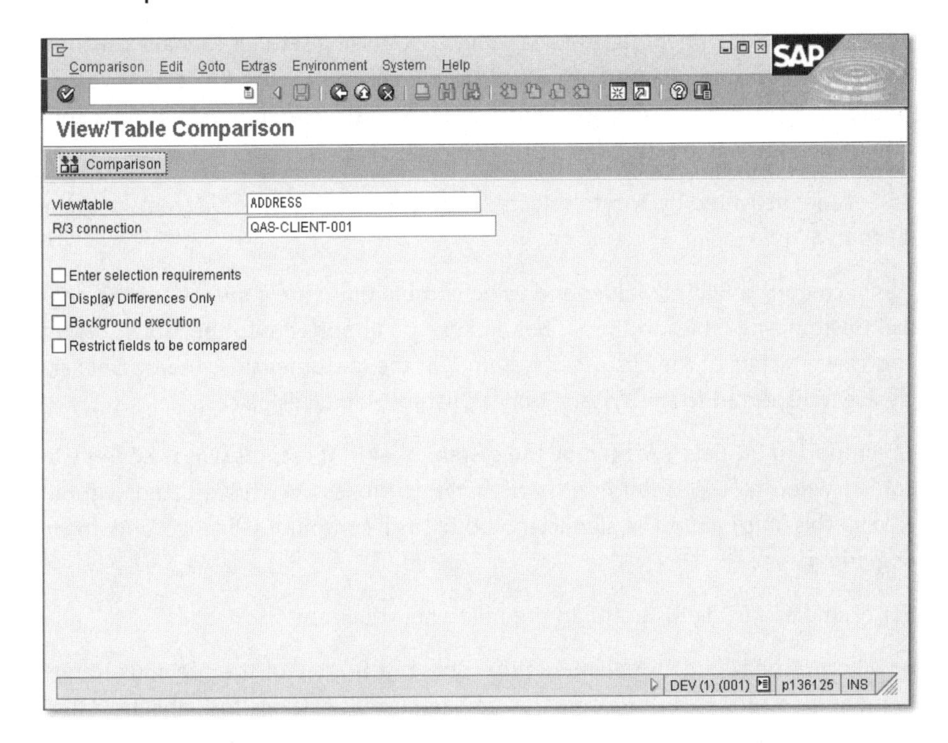


**Figure 11.19** Single comparison with Transaction SCMP

3. To run the comparison, choose **Single comparison** (or **View/table** in releases prior to Release 4.5). Depending on what you selected in the previous step, you may be prompted for information regarding selection requirements or the restriction of the number of fields that will be compared.

4. The comparison list is displayed. The results are identical to those of a single comparison from within the Cross-System Viewer. For example, the status **L** indicates that the entry exists only in the current logon client and not in the comparison client.

**Warning** In single comparisons using Transaction SCMP, restrict the number of fields to be compared if more than 500 entries are involved.

### 11.4.3 Business Configuration Sets

Business Configuration Sets (BC Sets) are containers in which you can store Customizing settings. They are transportable and versionable. Thus, previous settings can be compared to current settings.

BC Sets are for documenting and analyzing Customizing settings to make Customizing more transparent. Additionally, BC Sets can be used for a global rollout where the Customizing settings are forwarded as a structured bundle from a consolidation parent to its subsidiaries.

BC Sets are delivered by SAP to selected industries and can also be created by the customer.

When creating a BC Set, values and value combinations are copied from the original Customizing tables to the BC Set and can be imported into the tables, views, and view clusters of the customer system. On the customer side, the BC Sets are always transported to the system where Customizing takes place.

The import of BC Sets is logged by the system, that is, it records which BC Set was copied when to the system and whether this process was completed without errors. This information is significant both to a continuous change and to an upgrade.

For example, a BC Set is useful in the following situations:

- When testing a new implementation phase, a BC Set of the previous implementation phase can be compared to the current settings to highlight differences and to identify the Customizing settings that could affect existing processes in the production operation.
- Customizing standards that were specified in an enterprise development system are often delivered to subsidiaries using change requests. Since Customizing can neither be locked nor protected, a subsidiary can change the delivered enterprise standards. Furthermore, by using a BC Set delivered by the enterprise system, subsidiaries can regularly compare their current Customizing set-

tings to the enterprise standards recorded in the BC Set. All deviations discovered must be solved both locally in the subsidiary and in the development system of the enterprise.

- After a system upgrade, the BC Set settings can be compared to the system data using the Customizing Cross-System Viewer so as to ensure data consistency.
- Industry systems are easier to create and to maintain.
- To a great extent, Customizing can be carried out on a business level.

Change Management can be handled faster and more securely.

Use Transaction SCPR3 to edit BC Sets in the system. Using Transaction SCPR20, you can activate BC Sets in the system and view activation logs using Transaction SCPR20PR.

More information on BC Sets can be found in the online documentation and in Note 669542.

### 11.4.4 Customizing Transfer Assistant

A new R/3 tool as of Release 4.5, the Customizing Transfer Assistant (Transaction SADJ) lets you compare the client-dependent changes that have been imported by a change request with the settings of the current client. The Customizing Transfer Assistant imports changes into a temporary, "holding" client and allows you to avoid importing individual changes that you may not want in the current client. This is useful in the following situations:

- An international implementation often involves the delivery of changes from a central development system to each of the subsidiaries. Because there is no protection against the overwriting of Customizing settings during import, a subsidiary may choose to import the changes from the central development system to a holding client and check the new settings against the client-dependent settings in the subsidiary's Customizing-and-development client. If the changes do not conflict with the local settings, they are transferred to the local Customizing-and-development client.
- Customizing efforts for a new implementation phase have been made in another SAP system, such as a predevelopment system. To eliminate the need to redo these changes in the Customizing-and-development client in the development system, the Customizing changes from the predevelopment system are imported into a holding client, and the Customizing Transfer Assistant is used to adjust the settings in the Customizing-and-development client.

- During production support, emergency changes are made in the production system. These changes need to be made in the development system to ensure consistency. To avoid overwriting the changes currently being created in the development system for the next implementation phase, the production system changes can be imported into a holding client and checked with the Customizing Transfer Assistant.

**Warning** When importing changes to the holding client, ensure that you do not overwrite client-independent changes that apply to the entire SAP system.

Before using the Customizing Transfer Assistant, set up an appropriate holding client. The Customizing Transfer Assistant creates a *worklist* to enable you to compare the Customizing objects in a change request of type **Customizing** that has been successfully imported into the holding client and therefore has the status of **released**.

After importing the change request to the holding client, to create the worklist, proceed as follows:

1. Log on to the client into which you will transfer Customizing changes.
2. Start the Customizing Transfer Assistant using Transaction code SADJ.
3. Provide the change request ID that will be used to create the worklist. This change request ID must be a change request that has already been imported into the SAP system in the comparison/holding client.
4. Choose **Create** to create the worklist.
5. The screen **Create New Worklist for Request to be Imported** appears, indicating the worklist ID (which you need, for example, to obtain the comparison results when the worklist is generated as a background job).
   - Provide a description for the worklist.
   - Provide the RFC connection to the comparison client.
6. To display the differences between the changes imported into the holding client and the corresponding Customizing entries in the logon client, choose **Determine status**. If the change request contains a large number of Customizing objects and will therefore require a lot of processing time, choose **Determine status in background**. Alternatively, to display a list of objects that will be compared so that you can selectively initiate the comparison for particular objects, choose **Object list**.

### Displaying and Transferring Differences

If not scheduled as a background job, the worklist is displayed immediately following the execution of the comparison. If the comparison has been scheduled in the background, to subsequently display the worklist, enter the worklist number in the Customizing Transfer Assistant (Transaction SADJ) and choose **Display**.

As when using the Customizing Cross-System Viewer, you can display more details by choosing **Single comparison**; you can display statistics; and you can filter the list. The first column of the resulting worklist, **Stat.**, indicates the *copy status* for each Customizing object. The copy status shows whether the object can be automatically transferred or, if the transfer is complete, whether it was successful. For an explanation of copy statuses, choose **Legend**.

By switching into change mode using **Display • Change**, you can copy entries from the comparison client to the current client. Copy options available from the menu using **Edit • Copy** include:

- **Interactive:**
  You perform the adjustment of single entries manually as described above, under "Adjusting the Customizing Differences between Clients."
- **Automatic direct:**
  All differences are automatically transferred.
- **Autom. Background:**
  Automatic adjustment is performed as a background job.

## 11.5 Questions

1. Which of the following requirements must be met before you can change both client-dependent and client-independent Customizing settings in a client?

   A. The client settings must allow for changes to client-independent Customizing objects.

   B. The client role must be **Production**.

   C. The system change option must be set to **Modifiable**.

   D. The client settings must allow for changes to client-dependent Customizing.

2. Which of the following statements are correct when project leaders and project team members receive only the recommended authorizations?

   A. Only developers can create change requests.

   B. Only project leaders can create change requests and are therefore responsible for assigning project team members to change requests.

C. Project team members can create and release change requests.

D. Project leaders can release change requests.

3. Which of the following statements are correct with regard to Project IMGs?

   A. The Project IMG provides access to the Customizing activities defined for a particular project.

   B. Customizing is performed in the Project IMG tree structure.

   C. The Project IMG enables you to display project status information and document Customizing activities.

   D. All of the above.

4. Which of the following activities are performed using the Customizing Organizer?

   A. Viewing all Customizing change requests related to a particular user

   B. Viewing all Workbench change requests related to a particular user

   C. Viewing all change requests related to a particular user

   D. Managing change requests you own or reviewing change requests in which you have assigned tasks

5. Which of the following statements is correct in regard to Customizing?

   A. All Customizing activities in the IMG are client-dependent.

   B. All changes resulting from IMG activities can be transported.

   C. All Customizing changes are automatically recorded to a change request if the client change option is set to **Automatic recording of changes**.

   D. A Customizing activity may involve the creation of client-independent objects and therefore requires a Workbench change request.

6. Which of the following activities are performed using client comparison tools?

   A. Comparing the Customizing settings of two SAP clients in the same SAP system or in a different SAP system

   B. Adjusting the Customizing differences between two different SAP clients

   C. Transporting Customizing settings into the production client

   D. Comparing the objects listed in the object list of a change request with an SAP client

# 12 Promoting Change Requests

When you *promote* a change request, you release and export it. Often, the words *export* and *release* are used interchangeably. Technically, however, they are two different processes:

- The *release* process acts as a sign-off for the development or Customizing work in the task or change request. This process verifies ownership and user authorization for the respective changes—first at the task level, and then at the change request level. It also causes the respective Repository objects to be released by the Workbench Organizer and copies a version history of them to the version database. You can release a change request only if all tasks belonging to the change request have been documented and released. Before releasing the change request, ensure that the changes it records have been unit tested and verified.
- The *export* process physically copies the objects and tables referred to in the change request from the R/3 database of the development system to a file in the transport directory at the operating system level. In addition, this process adds the change request to the import buffer of the target system defined by the relevant transport route.

This chapter covers the release process and export process, as well as documentation, unit testing, and version management. The topics are covered in the chronological order in which the activities are performed.

## 12.1 Documenting Change Requests and Tasks

SAP recommends that you write thorough documentation for all tasks in a change request while performing Customizing and development. This makes it easier to reconstruct the configuration process if necessary. The documentation is transported with the changes, thus becoming available in the quality assurance system, and is also a requirement for releasing the change request in the development system. In your documentation for change requests and tasks, you should include the following information:

- The purpose of the development or Customizing project
- The current status of the project (IMG status information is maintained within the Project IMG, not within change request documentation)
- Areas of responsibility and the people responsible, as well as contact people
- Sources of other documentation or instructions
- The expected impact of the changes on the implementation
- Interdependencies between this and other projects

The object lists of change requests and tasks indicate the objects that have changed. Action logs recorded by the SAP system give you information on various activities, such as who created, released, or changed the ownership of a change request or task. The object list and documentation together with the action logs provide a detailed audit history of all changes made.

### 12.1.1 Creating and Changing Documentation

To create or change documentation for a task or change request, proceed as follows:

1. In the Transport Organizer (Transaction codes SE09 or SE10), choose **Display**. The screen **Transport Organizer: Requests** is displayed, listing the change requests and tasks related to your user ID.
2. Double-click on the task or the change request for which you want to write documentation. Change to the **Documentation** tab and switch to change mode.
3. Enter the detailed documentation and choose **Save**.
4. Choose **Back** to return to the change request hierarchy.

You can release a task only if it has been documented. Before a task or change request has been released, you can add documentation to it at any time. Once the task or change request is released, documentation cannot be changed.

When the task is released, the associated documentation is copied to the documentation of the change request containing the task. The documentation of the change request then contains its own documentation and the documentation of any of its released tasks. For example, suppose that there are two tasks in a change request, and both have been documented and released. Until the change request is released, the documentation for both tasks can be viewed and changed within the documentation of the change request.

### 12.1.2 Action Logs for Change Requests

In the **action log** of each change request, the R/3 System automatically logs the occurrence time and user responsible for the following actions in regard to that change request or any of its tasks:

- Creation
- Ownership change
- Deletion
- Release

To see the action log for a particular change request, position the cursor on the change request in the screen **Transport Organizer: Requests** and choose **Goto • Action log**.

The action log of each change request is physically located as a separate log file in the transport directory *actlog*. The name of this log file is *<SID>Z<change request ID number>.<SID>*, where SID is the system ID of the system on which the change request was created. The change request ID number is a six-digit number beginning with 9. For example, the log file for the change request DEVK900747 is *DEVZ900747.DEV*. This log file is located at the operating system level and can be accessed from any SAP system within the same transport group.

## 12.2 Unit Testing

Before releasing a change request or task, it should be unit tested as described in Chapter 6. For a change request, this means unit testing the combined contents of all tasks as a unit.

If unit testing is to occur in a unit test client, before performing testing, you must copy the client-dependent changes to the unit test client. Client-independent changes automatically impact all clients within the SAP system and therefore can be verified by simply logging on to the unit test client and performing verification. As explained below, client-dependent changes may be of the following types:

- Client-dependent Customizing
- SAPscript styles and forms
- Variants

### 12.2.1 Client-Dependent Customizing

To unit test client-dependent Customizing changes in a client other than the one in which the changes were originally recorded to change requests, copy the changes into the applicable client using the client **copy transaction client copy according to a transp. request** (Transaction SCC1). This transaction enables you to verify the contents of your tasks before release. The owner of a change request can also use this transaction to verify the contents of the change request and all of its tasks before release.

You can only use Transaction SCC1 to copy the changed objects recorded in a change request or task from one client to another client in the same SAP system.

Although Transaction SCC1 can be used to copy objects recorded in tasks and change requests that have been released, you should not release the respective change requests and tasks before using the transaction to perform unit testing. If unit testing reveals missing or incorrect Customizing settings, you can still record additional changes to the unreleased task or change request.

### Copying Changes with Transaction SCC1

To use Transaction SCC1 to copy changes, you require the necessary authorizations in the unit test client for testing the relevant business processes, as well as the user authorization S_CLNT_IMP. Once you have the proper authorizations, log on to the unit test client—the client into which you wish to copy the recorded changes of a particular change request or task—and proceed as follows:

1. Use Transaction code SCC1 or, from the initial screen, choose **Tools • Administration • Administration • Client Administration • Special Functions • Copy transport request**. The screen **Copy as per Transport Request** is displayed (see Figure 12.1).
2. Enter the source client ID number, as well as the ID of the change request or task to be copied.
3. If copying a change request, select the option **Incl. tasks for request** to ensure that changes recorded in unreleased tasks are also copied.
4. To start copying the change request, choose either **Execute** or **Execute in background**.
5. If you choose **Execute**, a dialog box appears indicating the number of objects to be copied. If this number is zero, no changes will be copied. In that case, choose **Cancel** and retry this procedure using a different change request or task ID.

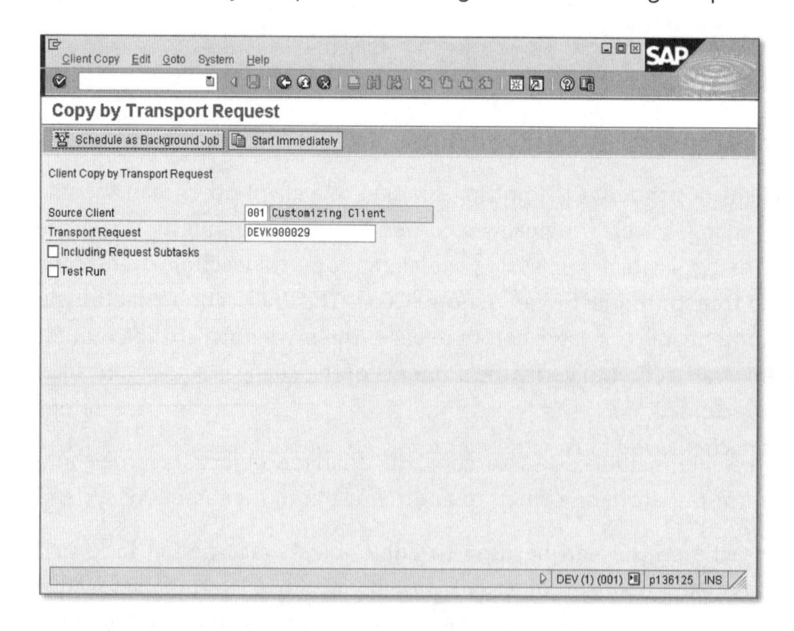


**Figure 12.1** Client copy according to a transport request (Transaction SCC1)

### Reviewing the Log Files for Transaction SCC1

To review the log files generated by Transaction SCC1, proceed as follows:

1. Access the Client Copy Log using Transaction code SCC3 or, from the R/3 initial screen, by choosing **Tools · Administration · Administration · Client administration · Copy logs**.
2. Choose **Transport requests**. The screen displays the current status of all client copies based on a transport request (that is, a change request). These client copies are listed by the ID number of the target client.
3. Double-click the ID number of the client into which you copied changes using Transaction SCC1. The various log files for the copied change requests are displayed. The column **Transport** indicates the change request or task IDs.
4. To see more information on a client copy based on a change request, double-click the related change request or task ID.

## 12.2.2 SAPscript Styles and Forms

SAPscript is the word-processing functionality of SAP systems. At its core, there are *forms* (often referred to as *layout sets*) and *styles*. Forms are used to control page layouts. Styles are format definitions for paragraphs and characters that can be used to format the text itself. Although SAPscript styles and forms are client-dependent, when they are created or changed, they are recorded to a Workbench change request. To unit test styles and forms as of R/3 Release 4.0, you should use Transaction SCC1 to copy the styles and forms in the Workbench change request.

**Note** In releases prior to Release 4.0 Transaction SCC1 cannot be used for copying SAPscript styles and forms from one SAP client to another.

However, for copying SAPscript styles and forms from one client to another client of the same SAP system, you can also use SAPscript functionality **Copy from client**. In releases prior to 4.5, choose **Tools · SAPscript · Form · Utilities · Template from client**. As of release 4.5, choose **Tools · SAPscript · Form · Utilities · Copy from client**.

**Copy from client** works only if the objects to be copied are not locked in a change request. By default, all Repository objects in a change request are locked. Before using **Copy from client**, you must either unlock the recorded objects or release the change request containing the objects. However, unlocking the recorded objects is time-consuming, and releasing the relevant change request prevents you from being able to add corrections to the change requests. For these reasons, as of Release 4.0, SAP recommends that you use Transaction SCC1 to copy SAPscript styles and forms from the client in which they are created to the unit test client.

### 12.2.3 Report Variants

Although R/3 programs (often referred to as **reports**) are client-independent, **report variants** are client-dependent. Report variants are used to record data that is supplied to an ABAP program so that you do not need to enter the same selections repeatedly. When report variants are created or changed, by default, they are not recorded to a change request. Since report variants are usually localized to the current environment and have little value for other clients, they are not usually transported. If needed, variants can be copied to other clients. In some cases, the variants must then be added to a change request for transport.

To copy variants to a unit test client, use one of the following techniques:

- From the unit test client, execute the program RSDBVCOP. This program copies variants from another client within the same SAP system.
- In the client in which the variant was created, manually add the variant to a change request by creating the object-list entry *LIMU VARX <program name><variant name>*. Then, use Transaction SCC1 to copy the recorded variants in the change request to the unit test client.

**Note** For more information on how to transport variants, see SAP Note 128908.

## 12.3 Releasing a Task

Promoting changes recorded in a change request begins with releasing the relevant tasks. Releasing a task indicates that the owner of the task has completed his or her Customizing or development work, that unit testing was successful, and that the appropriate documentation is complete. The technical requirements for releasing a task are as follows:

- The task contains a recorded object.
- The task has been documented.
- You own the task (or you have authorization S_A.SYSTEM).

To release a task, proceed as follows:

1. To list the change requests that you are working on, in either the Workbench Organizer (Transaction code SE09) or the Customizing Organizer (Transaction code SE10), choose **Display**. The request overview is displayed.
2. To view all the tasks assigned to a particular change request, expand the tree structure. Position the cursor on the task you wish to release and choose **Release**.

3. If you have not yet entered documentation for the task, the documentation maintenance screen appears. Document your changes, save the documentation, and choose **Back**. (For more information on providing documentation, see "Creating and Changing Documentation" above.) If the task is successfully released, in the status bar, you will receive the message "Task <task ID> has been released to request <change request ID>."
4. Released tasks are highlighted with a particular color in the request overview. To see the color key, choose **Utilities · Key**.

### 12.3.1 Release Errors

If the task cannot be released, an error message appears in the status bar to indicate, for example, that:

- The task can be released only by the owner of the task (or a user with the authorization profile SAP_ALL).
- The task cannot be released because it contains no recorded objects and has been classified as **Not Assigned** (as opposed to **Development/correction** or **Repair**).

If there is a more serious error, no message will appear in the status bar. Instead, the screen **List of entries cannot be locked** is displayed. Such errors may occur with development work in tasks belonging to Workbench change requests. Examples of these errors include:

- **Object locked in another request/task:**
  Prior to release, all Repository objects in a task or change request require a Workbench Organizer lock. This message indicates that the Workbench Organizer cannot lock (and therefore release) objects in the task because the objects are already locked in another task or change request.
- **Transport object to target system <SID> only:**
  The development class and its transport layer for objects in the task do not consolidate to the target system defined when the change request was created. For example, an object has a development class that consolidates to the quality assurance system, but the target for the change request is the training system. This means that, after the object was recorded to a task, someone manually changed the target system for the change request, or changed the transport routes for the development system using the TMS.

Correcting these errors may require you to:

- Modify the object list of a change request to acquire proper Workbench Organizer locks

- Change the target system for the change request
- Change the transport routes defined within the TMS

To remedy the problem, the owner of the task may need the assistance of the system administrator.

### 12.3.2 Impact on the Change Request

When you release a task, the task object list and the relevant locks and documentation are automatically copied to the object list of the change request that contains the task. Before a task is released, the object list of a change request is empty (unless objects have been added manually).

Figure 12.2 demonstrates these processes. The task DEVK900003 in the Customizing change request DEVK900002 has been released. Prior to its release, no objects were listed at the change request level. After the release of the task, a *Comment* is added to the request overview, which, when the relevant node is expanded, indicates when the task was released.

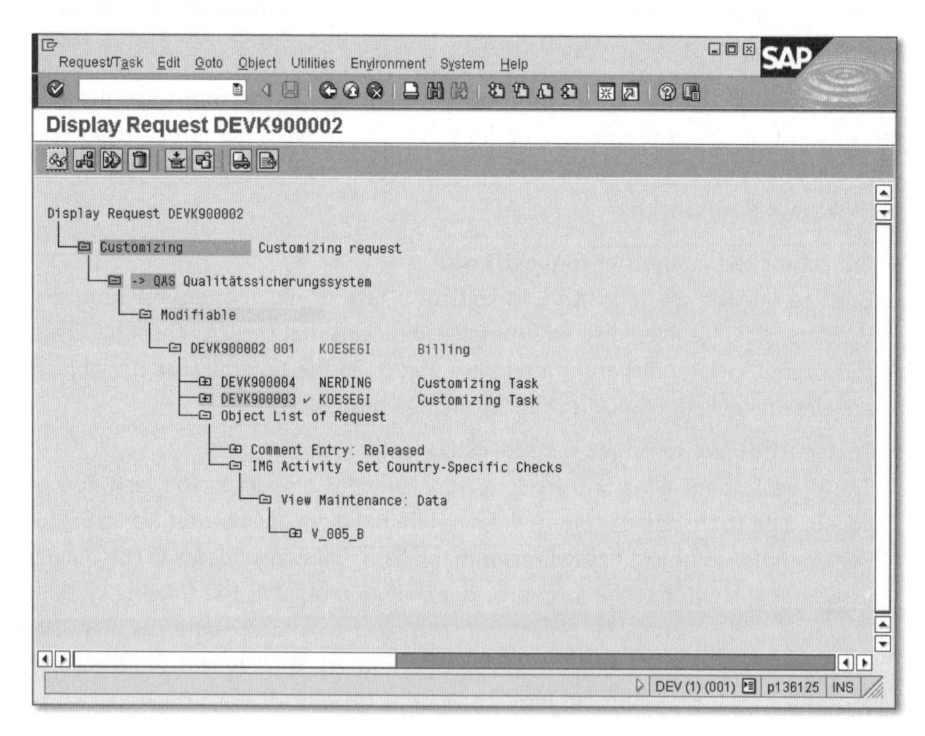


**Figure 12.2** Upon release, the object list of a task is copied to the object list of its change request.

This information can also be displayed in the object list of the change request. In Figure 12.3, for example, the object list entry *CORR RELE DEVK900003*

*20050608 215306* indicates that the task was released on June 8, 2005. The other entry, the contents of view V_005_B, is the contents of this task. This object was transferred from the task to the request.

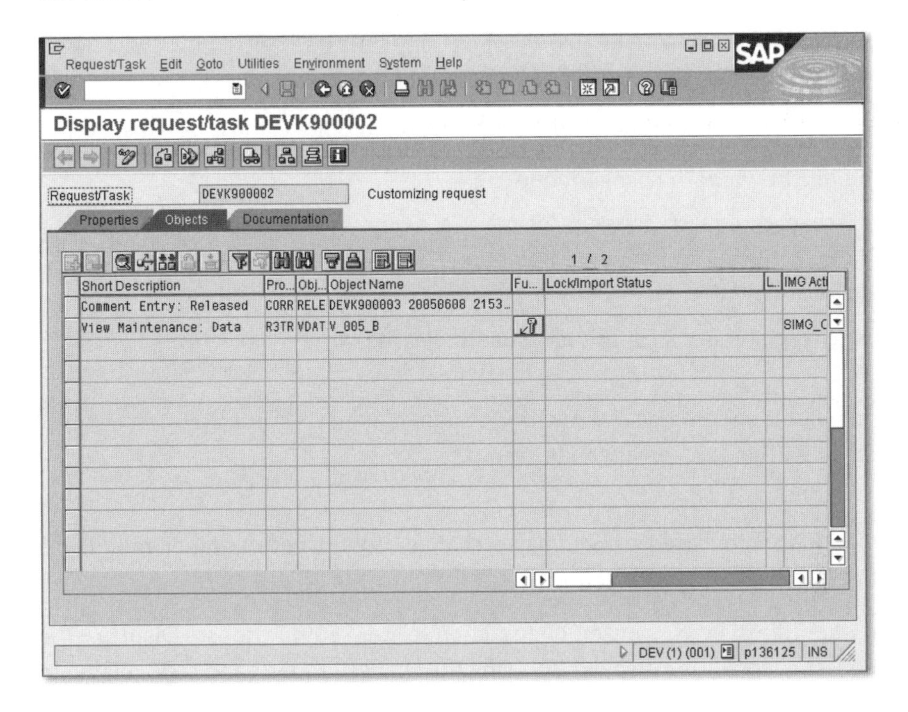


**Figure 12.3** Object list of a change request showing the released task and locked Repository objects

## 12.4 Releasing a Change Request

By releasing a change request, you indicate that it has sufficient documentation, the changes recorded in it have been unit tested, and the changes are ready to be transported using the TMS transport routes. During the export process triggered by the release, the objects recorded in the change request are copied from the R/3 database to a file external to R/3. This copy "freezes" the objects in their present state. In addition, a record of the change request is automatically added to the import queue of the defined consolidation system.

Releasing and exporting a single change request generates export logs and import logs. Testing in the quality assurance system and sign-off are necessary before import into the production system. To support the validation process and limit the technical and administrative overhead, SAP recommends merging change requests of a project prior to export.

### 12.4.1 Merging Change Requests

Combining multiple change requests into a single change request to create a testable unit is useful only if the change requests for a particular project are ready to be transported at the same time. This is usually the case when the change requests are related and need to be tested together.

To merge two change requests, the following requirements must be satisfied:

- You must own both change requests.
- The change requests must be of the same type—for example, a Customizing change request can be merged with only another change request of type *Customizing*.
- The change requests cannot have been released.

**Note** You cannot merge a task with a change request. A change request can be merged with only another change request.

To merge an unreleased or *modifiable* change request with another modifiable change request, proceed as follows:

1. In the Transport Organizer (Transaction code SE09), choose **Display**. The request overview is displayed, showing the change requests and tasks related to your user ID.
2. Position the cursor on the change request you wish to include in another change request. Select **Utilities · Reorganize · Merge Requests**. The Merge Request/Task screen is displayed (see Figure 12.4).
3. Enter the change request ID of a second change request in the second field. This change request will contain both merged change requests at the end of the merging process. Choose **Continue**.

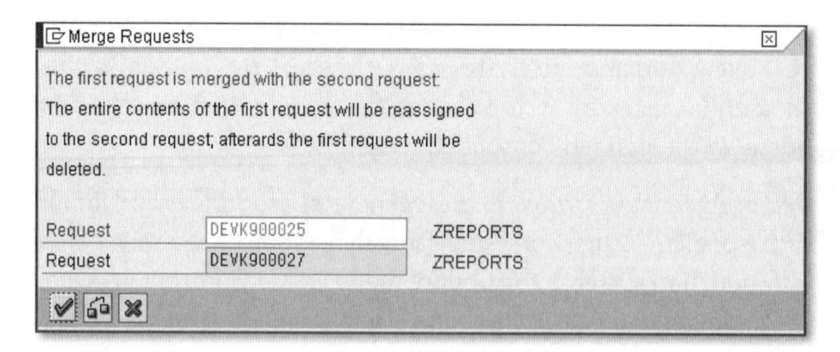


**Figure 12.4** Merging two change requests

Only change requests of the same type can be merged using the above procedure. However, you can also combine a Customizing change request with a change request of type **transportable** (see Figure 12.6 in the next subsection).

## 12.4.2 Procedure for Releasing a Change Request

To release a change request you own, proceed as follows:

1. In the Transport Organizer (Transaction code SE09), choose **Display**. The request overview is displayed, showing the change requests and tasks related to your user ID.
2. Position the cursor on the change request you wish to release and choose **Release**. Depending on the type of change request, this results in the following:
   - For a transportable change request, if the release is successful, this automatically starts the export process.
   - For a local change request, if the release is successful, this automatically results in the following message in the status bar: "Local request released (objects no longer locked)."
3. When the export process starts, the screen **Overview of Transport Logs** appears, showing the transport logs specific to the change request. The export process has the status **In process**. You can wait for the export to complete or choose **Back** to return to either the Customizing Organizer or the Workbench Organizer. (Reviewing the transport logs to verify the success of an export process is explained below under "Transport Logs").

### Release Errors

If a change request cannot be released, an error message will appear in the status bar indicating, for example, one of the following situations:

- There are tasks in the change request that have not been released. Before the change request can be released, all tasks in the change request must be released.
- The change request can be released only by the owner of the change request (or a user with the authorization profile SAP_ALL).
- Not all Repository objects in the request could be locked. The Workbench Organizer cannot lock an object that is already locked in another task or change request. Before the change request can be released, all R/3 Repository objects in the change request must have a Workbench Organizer lock.
- The transport routes defined from within TMS have changed since the change request was created. The target system for the change request is not defined in the TMS as a consolidation system; therefore, the change request cannot be

released. To change the target system for the change request, in the request overview, position the cursor on the change request and choose **Request/task • Display/change**.

- The development class and its transport layer for an object listed in a transportable change request no longer consolidate to the target system defined when the change request was created. To solve this problem, change the development class of the object, change the target system defined for the change request, or delete the object in the object list of the change request.
- A system administrator has disallowed release from the SAP system. If you create the file `T_OFF.ALL` or `T_OFF.<SID>` in the transport directory *bin*, the release of change requests for either all SAP systems in the transport group or a specific SAP system can be prevented. This option is useful when the target SAP system is being upgraded or problems at the operating system level have been reported. If the export of change requests has been disallowed, the change request will not be released and exported, and will require the owner to release and export the change request later.

### Object Checks

When you release either a transportable or a local Workbench change request, you can activate object checks that identify and display errors such as program syntax errors. This reduces the risk of importing "bad" Repository objects that will not be able to be activated or generated in the target systems.

If activated, these checks automatically run when you release a Workbench change request. They include a program check with Transaction SLIN, as well as an ABAP Dictionary check to verify that all ABAP Dictionary objects in the request have the status **Active**.

Activating Object Checks
As a user with the CTS administration authorization (S_CTS_ADMIN), you can either:

- Activate or deactivate the object checks for all users
- Leave it up to the user to decide whether to activate or deactivate the checks

To activate or deactivate the object checks, proceed as follows:

1. Use the Transaction code.
2. Expand the **Administration** hierarchy and double-click **Global Customizing Transport Organizer**. The screen **Global Customizing Transport Organizer** is displayed (see Figure 12.5).

3. Under **Object checks at request release**, select one of the following:
    - **Globally activated**: This activates automatic checking of all objects before release.
    - **Globally deactivated**: This deactivates automatic checking of all objects before release. A user cannot set the automatic checking of objects before release as an individual default.
    - **Can be set for specific user**: This enables a user to use Transaction SE09 to set automatic object checking as their user default.
4. To save your settings, choose **Continue**.

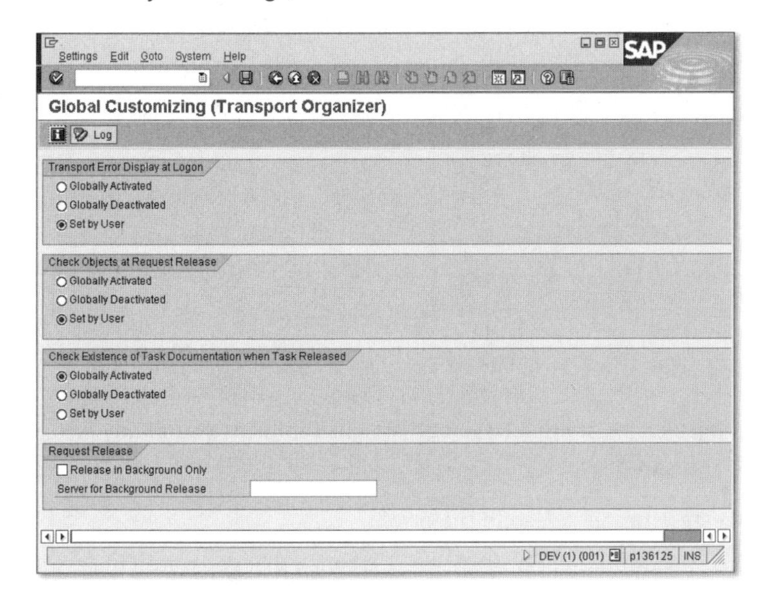


**Figure 12.5** Global activation of transport error display and object checks in Transaction SE03

If the global option **Can be set for specific user** is set, individual users can activate or deactivate the checks themselves. From the initial screen of either the Transport Organizer (Transaction SE09 or SE10), the user chooses **Utilities • Settings • Transport Organizer** and selects **Check objects on request release**.

> **Tip** Regardless of whether object checks are activated globally, you can check the objects in a change request at any time. To do this, from the request overview of the Workbench Organizer, position the cursor on the appropriate change request or task and choose **Request/task • Overall checks • Objects (syntax check)**.

If you have activated object checks, the objects in a Workbench change request are automatically checked at change request release. When you release the change request, if no previous object check for this change request has been run, the **Object checks** window appears (see Figure 12.6). You have the following options:

- Run the object check in the background. If the objects contain no errors, the release process is started automatically in the background. When the background processing is completed, a dialog box tells you that errors were found or that the change request was released.
- Run the object check in the foreground, which automatically displays the results of the checks. After this, you must complete the release of the change request manually.
- Cancel the object check and do not release the change request.

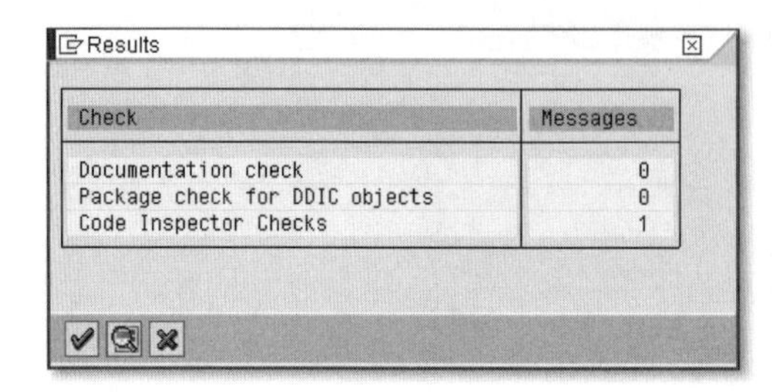


**Figure 12.6** Automatic object check prompt when releasing a Workbench change request

When the object check is finished, a **Results** dialog box informs you of any errors that were found. You can then:

- Continue the release process despite the errors
- Display the errors by double-clicking the specific check that generated the error
- Cancel the release process

### The Sort and Compress Function

When a change request is released, its object list is automatically sorted and compressed to remove duplicate entries. This process does not delete objects that were changed, but simply deletes redundant listings. Often, different users of a change request record the same objects in their object lists because they are pursuing overlapping objectives within the same Customizing or development project. Suppose, for example, that two tasks of a change request contain the object entry *R3TR TABL ZNEWTABLE*. When the tasks are released, the object list of the change request shows the entry twice. After the change request is released, thanks to the **sort and compress** function, the object occurs in the object list only once.

You can also manually initiate a **sort and compress** at any time. If you do this prior to releasing the change request, it may speed up the release process or prevent release failure due to a long runtime. To manually initiate a **sort and compress**, from the request overview in either the Customizing Organizer or the Workbench Organizer, choose **Request/Task · Object list · Sort and compress**.

### 12.4.3 The Export Process

Releasing either a Customizing change request or a transportable change request automatically initiates the export process. Understanding what happens during export highlights its significance and aids in troubleshooting. During export, the following processes occur:

1. The changes recorded in the change request are copied from the database to a data file in the transport directory at the operating system level. In addition, a control file and an export log file are created and written to the transport directory (see Table 12.1).
2. The change request is added to the import queue of the target system, which is typically the quality assurance system.
3. By default, a "test import" is performed in the target system. The test import verifies the connection to the target system's database and checks the objects to be imported.
4. The Workbench Organizer lock is removed for the objects in the object list of the exported change request, thus enabling them to be included in other change requests.

Table 12.1 provides details on the three files created in the transport directory: the data file, the control file, and the export log file.

| Naming Convention[1, 2] | Transport Sub-Directory | Contents | Example: Files Created for Request DEVK900747 |
|---|---|---|---|
| `R<request #>.<SID>` | data | Data file containing exported data | R900747.DEV |
| `K<request #>.<SID>` | cofiles | Control file with instructions for import and import history for the change request | K900747.DEV |
| `<SID>E<request #>.<SID>` | log | Log file with details about the success of the export process | DEVE900747.DEV |

**Table 12.1** Transport Directory Files Created during the Export of a Change Request

1 The *request #* is the six-digit request number from the change request ID. By default, it begins with the number 9.

2 The SID is the system ID for the source R/3 System from which the change request is released.

The programs tp and R3trans are used during the export process. The program tp manages the export of a change request and issues calls to R3trans. R3trans physically extracts the recorded changes from the database of the source SAP system and writes the data file and the control file. Because the data files written to the transport directory are in R3trans format and not a database-specific format, the data file can be imported into any other SAP system regardless of its database platform.

After writing the data file and the control file for a change request to the transport directory, the transport control program tp adds the change request to the end of the import buffer—to the file <SID> in the transport subdirectory buffer, where SID is the system ID of the target system. The target system is the consolidation system defined for the change request (typically, the quality assurance system).

### Exported Data

Change requests record only what has changed and do not contain actual changed objects. The export of the change request physically copies the changed objects in their current state to a file in the transport directory at the operating system level. The data can be either an Repository object or table entries associated with Customizing.

To return to the example in Figure 11.8 (see Chapter 11), one of the Customizing changes recorded in the change request was a change to the sales organization PRNT. Exactly which table entries are copied by the export is determined by the primary key values recorded in the change request. The primary key of table TVKO consists of the client and the sales organization. The primary key values recorded in this change request are 001PRNT (where 001 is the client and PRNT is the sales organization). These values identify the table row that will be extracted during export.

Customizing change requests record table entries rather than entire tables. Since table entries are not locked, two users may change the same table entry. Regardless of whether the change was a creation or an edit, the primary key and the object list in each of the change requests will be identical. When the change requests are released and exported, the table row corresponding to the primary key will be extracted from the database. The data from this row as it appears at the time of export is saved to the transport directory and eventually imported into the downstream system. This is illustrated in the following example.

**Example: Exporting Customizing Changes with the Same Primary Key**

The user THOMAS creates a new plant called PHL1 with the description **Philadelphia**. Later, the user JANE decides to change the description of the plant PHL1 to **Philadelphia West**. Both users have saved their changes to different change requests.

What happens when user THOMAS releases and exports his change request depends on whether he releases and exports his change request before JANE makes her change.

- If the change request of THOMAS is released and exported before JANE makes her change, the data file in the transport directory will contain the description **Philadelphia** for plant PHL1.
- If THOMAS releases and exports after JANE has made her changes, the data file in the transport directory will contain the description **Philadelphia West** for the plant PHL1.

### Test Imports

In addition to entering the exported change request in the import buffer of the target system, by default, the transport program `tp` initiates a test import in the target system. The test import is not an attempted import so much as a screening of the objects to be imported. The test import process connects to the database of the target R/3 System and reviews the objects listed in the object directory. An error is indicated in the transport log file for the change request if (for any Repository object):

- The target system is the original system
- A repair flag is set in the target system
- The table into which data will be imported does not exist in the target system

If the error occurs because the target system is the original system, you may need to perform a nonstandard import or choose not to import the object to prevent overwriting the corresponding object. If a repair flag is the source of the error, this can be corrected by confirming the repair prior to importing the change request. A missing table in the target system is a serious problem and will require the transport of the table from the development system before the import of the change request that contains data for that table.

To perform a test import, the transport program `tp` must be able to connect to the target system's database. This is not possible if, for example, the target system has not been installed and is simply a virtual system, or if the target system is in a different network for security purposes. In such situations, you may wish to deactivate the test import functionality.

To deactivate the test import as the default setting, set the transport profile parameter **testimport** to FALSE. This parameter can be set either globally—for all SAP systems in the transport domain—or for a specific SAP system. When setting the parameter for a specific system, set it in the source SAP system and not in the target SAP system. For example, to deactivate test imports into the quality assurance system, proceed as follows:

- In releases before Release 4.5, add the entry `DEV/testimport=FALSE` to the TPPARAM file.
- As of Release 4.5, use the TMS to set **testimport** in the transport parameter to FALSE for the development system (Transaction STMS; choose **Overview · Systems**).

### 12.4.4 Authorizations

The release and export process is critical because it initiates the transport process for changed objects. Therefore, SAP recommends that only specific users be authorized to release change requests. As explained in Chapter 11, the relevant user authorization profiles are S_A.CUSTOMIZ (for the project team leader) and S_A.DEVELOP (for project team members). These authorizations enable a project leader to create and release change requests, and a team member to change and release only their own tasks.

**Example: Using Authorizations to Control the Release and Export Process**

A company initially allows all users in the development system to create and release change requests. The users inform the system administrator when a released change request is ready for import. The sequence in which change requests were imported is not taken into account.

During an important testing period, the quality assurance validation team reports several consistency problems with regard to the organization and functionality of basic business processes. After analyzing several problems, they discover that—since change requests are being imported on demand, out of sequence, and partly not imported—the quality assurance system has older versions of settings and is missing Customizing. Everyone agrees that the change requests require better management.

The idea of restricting the creation and release of change requests to the project leader is regarded as unrealistic. For this R/3 implementation, project leaders are focused on planning and are unavailable to handle the day-to-day activities of creating change requests. It is decided that all users should be able to create change requests. However, only specific users receive the authorization to release change requests or change the ownership of a change request and then release it. To release a change request, other users contact a power user, define the purpose of the change, and ask the power user to release the change request.

As a result of this new procedure, change requests are imported into the quality assurance system in the same order in which they are released—not simply whenever someone asks for a change request to be imported. This prevents older versions of settings from replacing the latest versions.

## 12.5 Transport Logs

The release and export of a change request is the beginning of its transport process, which is when the first transport log file—the export log file—is automatically generated. Transport log files reside in the transport directory and can be displayed within the SAP system as follows:

- A system administrator can view all transport log files for a change request in an import queue. To do this, display the import queue of a particular SAP system (Transaction STMS; **Overview · Imports · Import Queue · Display**). Position the cursor on the change request and choose **Request · Display · Logs**.
- Any user can view all transport log files relating to a specific user. To do this, access the Transport Organizer (Transaction SE09 or SE10). Enter the relevant user ID and, under **Global information**, choose **Transports**.
- Any user can view all transport logs for a particular change request. To do this, call the Organizer Tools (Transaction SE03), drill down under **Request/task**, and choose **Display transport logs**. Enter a change request ID and choose **Enter**.

After you use any of these methods, the screen **Overview of all Transport Logs** is displayed (see Figure 12.7). This screen shows a tree structure of released change requests and the respective export and import processing steps, grouped according to target systems. The success of individual steps is indicated by the highlighting color, comment, and return code. (For more information on return codes for exports and imports, see Chapter 14.) If the change request was imported, the import log files for the various R/3 Systems are displayed.

Figure 12.7 shows the export steps for change request DEVK900032. The operating system check finished without errors (return code 0), as did the export of changes. In the quality assurance system, however, the test import was cancelled by the transport control program tp (return code 8) and therefore was not successful.

To see more information about the failure of a processing step, you can drill down to the associated error message or warning.

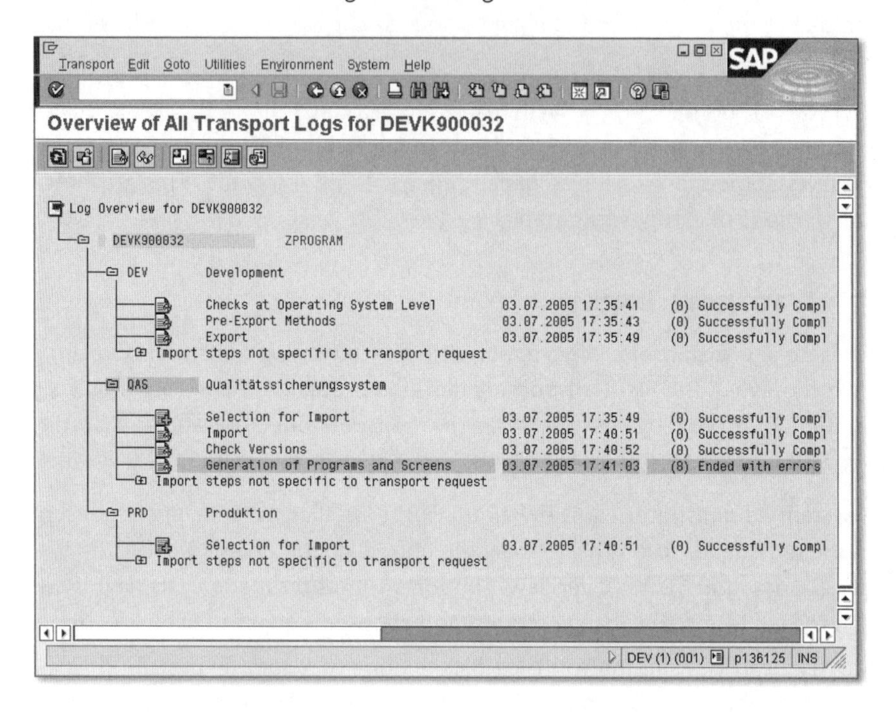


**Figure 12.7** Transport logs displayed in the SAP system

### 12.5.1 Managing Transport Logs

Managing the transport logs involves reviewing errors and possibly marking them as corrected, and deleting unnecessary transport logs

If an error occurs in relation to either export or import, the corresponding change request receives the transport log status **Incorrect**. Incorrect change requests can easily be identified when you look at the overview of your transport logs—the incorrect change requests are flagged in red and appear at the top of the hierarchical list.

Over time, the number of transport logs associated with the various change request owners will increase. The only transport logs of interest are the most recent logs, not the logs either of the last implementation phase or that have received quality assurance sign-off. To facilitate your transport log analysis, you can delete old change requests from a user's list of transport logs.

### 12.5.2 Displaying Transport Errors at Logon

By changing a default setting, you can cause transport errors to be automatically displayed when you log on to an SAP system within the transport domain.

The release and export process is the responsibility of the person who released the change request. Therefore, it is the responsibility of the owner of the change request to monitor and correct transport errors, even if this requires the help of a system administrator. SAP recommends that you use the default setting that automatically informs users of failed exports and imports at the time of logon.

The dialog box that appears at logon to indicate the transport errors is shown in Figure 12.8. In this dialog box, you can select:

- **Continue** or **Cancel** to bypass viewing the errors and access the R/3 initial screen instead
- **Display** to see a list of transport logs for the affected change requests
- **Transport Organizer** to go directly to the Transport Organizer (Transaction SE09)
- **Never display again** to prevent the respective tasks from being displayed in this list.

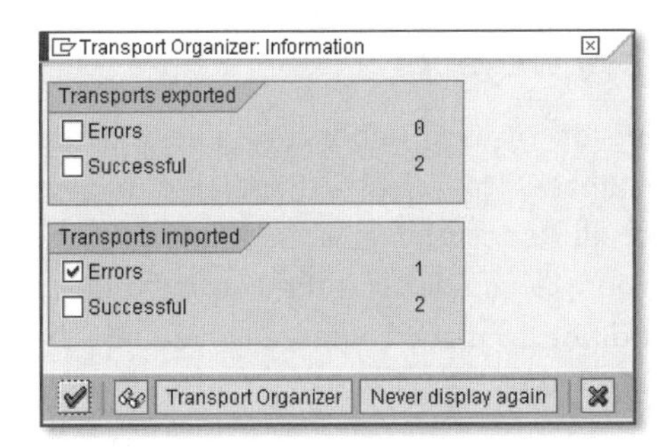


**Figure 12.8** Transport error notification at logon

#### Activating the Automatic Display of Transport Logs at Logon

By default, errors during export or import are not displayed when a user logs on to an SAP system. You can globally activate or deactivate the automatic display of transport errors at logon for all users, or you can allow users to make the automatic display one of their individual default settings.

If you are the system administrator (a user with the CTS administration authorization S_CTS_ADMIN) and you want to globally activate or deactivate the transport logs at logon, proceed as follows:

1. Use Transaction code SE03.
2. Drill down in the tree structure at **Administration** and double-click **Global Customizing Transport Organizer**.
3. The screen **Global Customizing Transport Organizer** appears (see Figure 12.5 earlier in this chapter). Choose one of the following options under **Transport error display at logon**:
   - **Globally activated**: Transport errors will be automatically displayed at logon for all users.
   - **Globally deactivated**: The automatic display of transport errors is deactivated. A user cannot set the automatic display of transport logs as an individual default.
   - **Can be set for specific user**: Users can select the automatic display of transport errors as one of their individual default settings.
4. To save your settings, choose **Continue**.

If the option **Can be set for specific user** is set, to make the automatic display of transport errors one of your individual default settings, from the initial screen of the Transport Organizer (Transaction SE09 or SE10), choose **Settings · Change & Transport Organizer**. Select **Display transport errors at logon** and choose **Enter**.

## 12.6 Versioning for Repository Objects

When a change request is released, a version of each Repository object in the change request is added to the version database. This enables the release process to provide a complete change history for all Repository objects. Another automatically created version is the *active* version, which displays the current state of all active objects in the SAP system. In addition to the automatically created versions, you can also create versions at any time, which are known as *temporary* versions.

The different types of versions are stored in two different sets of tables (two different databases) in the SAP system database:

- The *version database*, which stores versions saved as a result of a released change request and temporary versions
- The *development database*, which stores the active version of an object (its current state in the SAP system)

Both the development database and the version database are maintained in the development system, since this system is where Repository objects are created, changed, and released. If you discontinue a development system, you will lose all version history for all customer developments and modifications to SAP objects made in that system.

### 12.6.1 Version Management

You can access version management for a particular Repository object using any of the following:

- Repository Browser (Transaction SE80)
- Transport Organizer (Transaction SE09)
- Display and maintenance transactions for Repository objects, such as the ABAP Editor for ABAP programs and the ABAP Dictionary for tables, domains, and data elements

For example, to view the versions maintained for the ABAP program `ZPROGRAM`, proceed as follows:

1. Access the ABAP Editor using Transaction code SE38 or, from the R/3 initial screen, by choosing **Tools • Development • ABAP Workbench • ABAP Editor**.
2. Enter the name of the ABAP program whose versions you wish to view.
3. Choose **Utilities • Version management**. The versions stored for the ABAP program are displayed (see Figure 12.9).

The display of versions for a Repository object includes both the version in the development database and the versions in the version database. If, as in Figure 12.9, a change request ID is indicated for the active version, the object is currently locked by the change request and was changed by the indicated user. If no change request ID appears for the active version, the object is currently not recorded to a change request and not locked by the Workbench Organizer.

Versions in the version database are numbered starting with 0001. The first version for a customer object will always be of type **S**, indicating that it is the original creation of the object. Because most versions in the version database are the result of a released change request, the change request number and owner of the change request are also indicated.

Temporary versions are indicated as type **U**. These versions are created if, when maintaining an object, you use the option **Generate version**. In the ABAP Editor, for example, you would choose **Program • Generate version**. Temporary versions are deleted when a change request is released, since releasing a change request writes a permanent version to the version database.

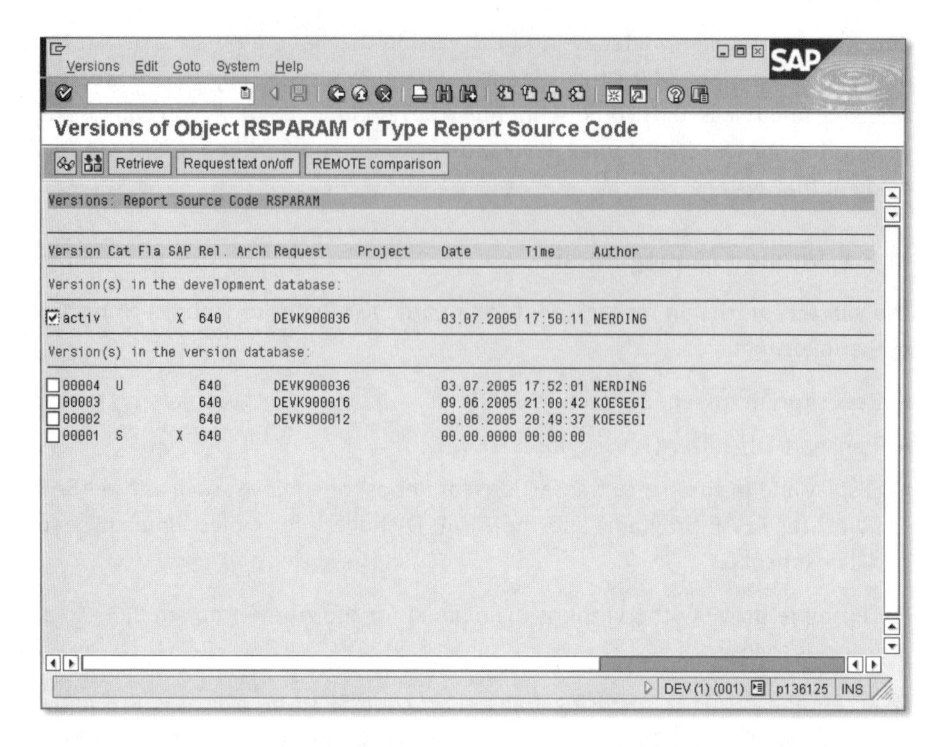


**Figure 12.9** Versions of an ABAP program

From the display of versions for an Repository object, you can:

- Display a particular version by selecting the version and choosing **Display**.
- Compare two different versions by selecting the two versions and choosing **Compare**. A split screen will show the differences between the two versions.
- Restore a version by selecting the version and choosing **Retrieve**. This causes the currently active version to be overwritten by the older version you select. If the object is not already recorded to a change request, you must record the change to a change request. To use **Retrieve**, the Repository object's maintenance screen must be in change mode.

### 12.6.2 Versions in Nondevelopment Systems

By default, Repository objects are not versioned upon import. This restricts version histories to the development system. The quality assurance and production systems have only the currently active version for each Repository object. This version indicates the change request that caused the import of the object, but cannot be used to display or compare older versions.

Versions cannot be transported between SAP systems. Because versions reside only in the development system, if the development system is removed from the system landscape, all versions in the version database are lost.

As of Release 4.5, you can create versions at import, enabling you to preserve your version history for all Repository objects if the development system is removed from the system landscape or overwritten with a database copy. If versioning upon import is activated, when you import change requests into an system, versions of the imported objects are added to the version database of that system.

Versioning at import can be achieved by setting the transport parameter **vers_at_imp** to either C_ONLY or ALWAYS. The value C_ONLY causes only relocation transports (see Chapter 10) to create versions in the target system. The value ALWAYS makes all imports create versions. This transport parameter can be set specifically to an SAP system or globally for all systems.

**Note** Activating versioning at import increases the number of import processing steps during the import of a change request. To minimize the amount of time required for import into the production system, you may wish to avoid activating versioning at import for that system.

## 12.7 Questions

1. Which of the following is a prerequisite for copying client-dependent changes to a unit test client using a **client copy according to a transp. request** (Transaction SCC1)?

   A. The change request has been released.

   B. The tasks have been released, but the change request has not.

   C. The tasks have been released after successful unit testing by the owner of the task.

   D. The change request has not been released.

2. Which of the following are the result of releasing a task?

   A. A data file is created in the transport directory and contains the objects recorded in the change request.

   B. The object list and documentation for the task are copied to the change request.

   C. All objects recorded in the task are locked.

   D. You can no longer save changes to that task.

3. Which of the following are the result of releasing and exporting a change request?
   A. A data file is created in the transport directory to contain copies of the objects recorded in the change request.
   B. Versions are created in the version database for all Repository objects in the object list of the change request.
   C. All repairs recorded in the change request are confirmed.
   D. You can no longer save changes to that change request.
4. When you release a Customizing change request, you have the option to do which of the following?
   A. Release the change request to another Customizing change request.
   B. Schedule the release of the change request for a later time.
   C. Release the change request to a transportable change request.
   D. Initiate immediate release and export.
5. Which of the following is a prerequisite for releasing a transportable change request?
   A. There are no syntax errors in the ABAP programs recorded to the change request.
   B. You must own the tasks in the change request.
   C. All Repository objects in the change request are locked by the change request.
   D. The change request has documentation.
6. The export process initiates which of the following activities?
   A. The creation of files in the transport directory
   B. The automatic import of change requests into the target system—for example, the quality assurance system
   C. The addition of the exported change request to the import buffer of the target system.
   D. The deletion of the change request within the SAP system.
7. Which of the following activities result in a version history for all Repository objects?
   A. A Repository object is recorded to a change request.
   B. Change requests are imported into an SAP system, and the transport parameter **vers_at_imp** is activated.
   C. A task containing a Repository object is released.
   D. A change request containing a Repository object is released.

# 13 Importing Change Requests

The Transport Management System (TMS) provides customers with a tool for importing change requests from within the SAP system. While the use of operating system tools could not always be avoided up until Release 4.0, it is eliminated almost entirely in Release 4.5.

The information in this chapter prepares you to:

- Understand import queues
- Perform imports
- Manage import queues
- Schedule imports
- Monitor imports
- Transport between transport groups and transport domains

**Note** Before reading this chapter, you may wish to reread the sections related to imports in Chapters 6 and 8.

## 13.1 Understanding Import Queues

The most important tools for performing imports using the TMS are the *import queues*, which reflect the same information in the SAP system as the system-specific *import buffers* at the operating system level. (For more information on import buffers, see Chapter 14.) The import queue displays the change requests that are to be imported, in the order of their export.

In the TMS (Transaction STMS), you will find two screens that are relevant to the import queues: **Import Overview** and **Import Queue**.

### 13.1.1 Import Overview

The **Import Overview** screen shows the import queues of all SAP systems in the transport domain (see Figure 13.1). To access the import overview, from the TMS initial screen (Transaction STMS), choose **Overview · Imports**.

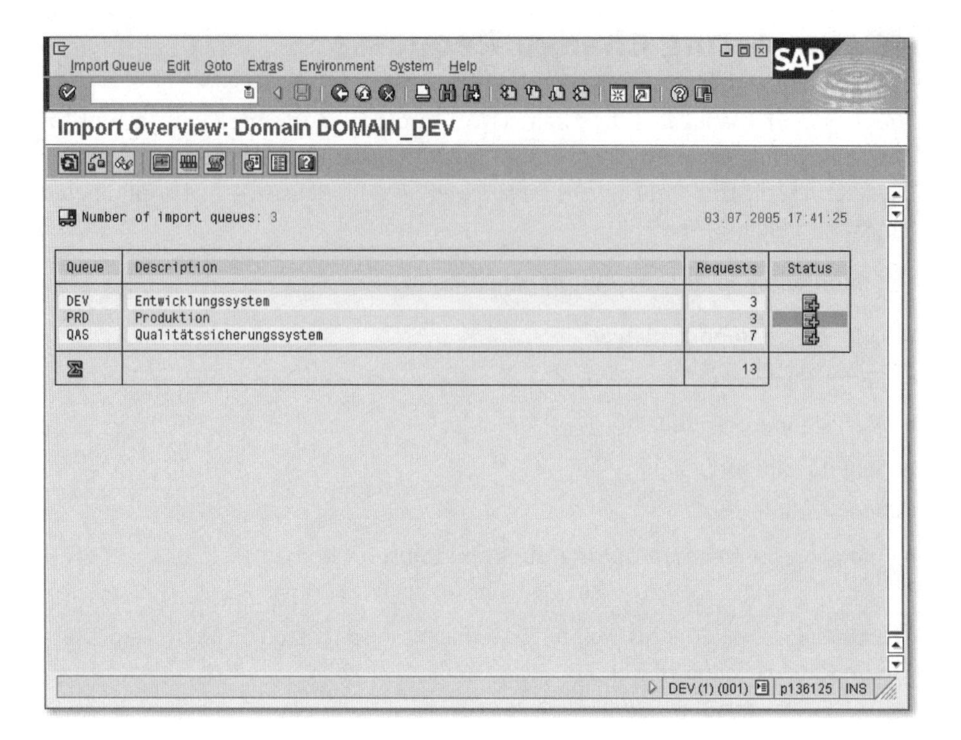


Figure 13.1 The import overview

In the import overview, the column **Requests** contains the number of change requests ready to be imported. This number may differ from the total number of requests listed in the import queue for the following reasons:

- The change requests occur after an end mark in the import queue. The system administrator can set the end mark to separate the change requests that will be transported in the next import from those change requests that will not be included in the next import.
- The change requests are excluded from being imported due to certain parameter settings in the transport profile; for example, the transport profile parameter **sourcesystems** in the transport profile for the target system does not include the source system for some of the change requests in the import queue. (See Appendix B for more information on the transport parameter **sourcesystems**.)
- The change requests have already been imported—for example, change requests that belong to a client copy—and have not yet been deleted from the import queue.

The column **Status** in the **Import Overview** screen indicates the current status of each import queue in the transport domain. For an explanation of the colors and symbols indicating the status, from the **Import Overview** screen, choose **Extras • Legend**. Each combination of colors and symbols is also explained in Table 13.1.

| Symbol | Color | Status | Explanation |
|---|---|---|---|
| | Green | Import queue is open. | New change requests can be added and will be imported during the next import if they are located before the end mark. |
| | Green | Import queue is closed. | The import queue is closed, and the system has set an end mark. All change requests before the end mark will be imported during the next import. |
| | Green | Import is running. | All change requests before the end mark are currently being imported. |
| | Yellow | Errors occurred during import. | Errors occurred during import, but the import did not terminate. |
| | Red | Import was terminated. | Serious errors occurred during import, and the import terminated. |
| | Red | Import queue could not be read. | To determine why an import queue could not be read, click the symbol. One reason may be that certain files could not be accessed at the operating system level. |

**Table 13.1** Status Information of Import Queues

### 13.1.2 Import Queue

To display the import queue of an SAP system, in the **Import Overview** screen, position the cursor on the SAP system and choose **Import Queue • Display**. The import queue lists the change requests in the order in which they will be imported; as a rule, this is the order in which they have been exported. The owner and the related short text are also indicated for each change request (see Figure 13.2).

The colors and symbols used in the **Import Queue** screen indicate the status and type of change request. For an explanation of these colors and symbols, choose **Extras • Legend** (see Table 13.2).

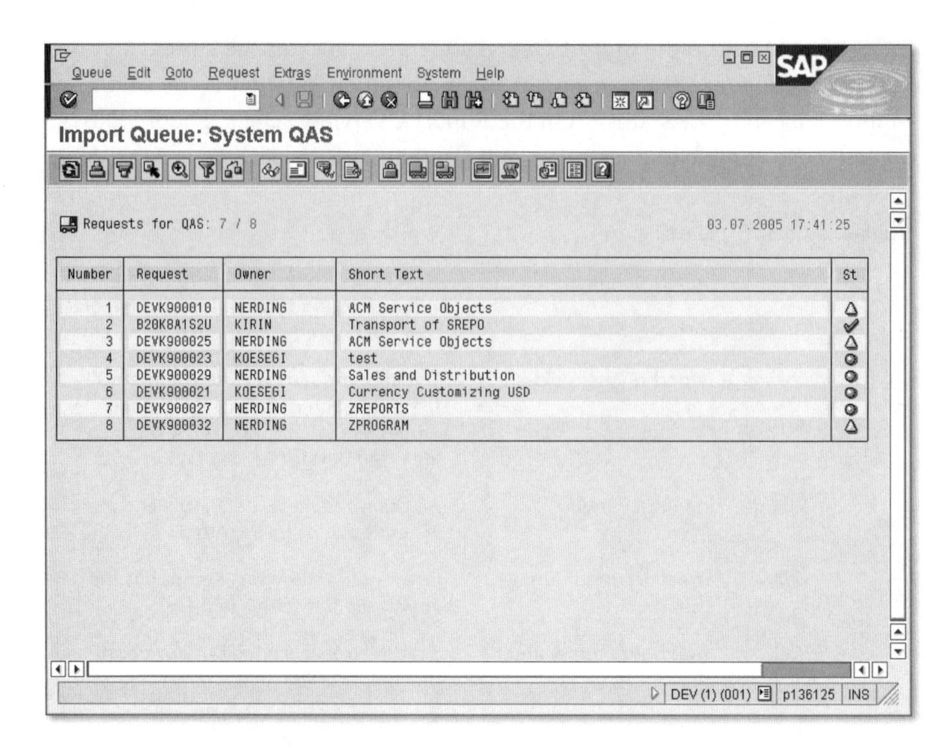


**Figure 13.2** Import queue for a particular SAP system

| Status | Explanation |
|---|---|
| Request waiting to be imported | The change request will be imported during the next import. |
| Request was already imported | The change request is displayed in the import queue, but will not be imported with the next import—for example, because it was already imported with a client transport or as an individual import with the preliminary import option deselected (see below, under "Preliminary Imports"). |
| Request was already transported | The change request was already transported as a preliminary import. To ensure consistency, it will be imported again during the next import of the entire queue. |
| Request will not be imported | The settings for specific transport profile parameters prevent import of the change request. For example, if the transport profile parameter **k_import** is set to FALSE, all Workbench change requests are excluded from the import, but will still be displayed in the import queue. Another example is a change request whose source system is not defined in the transport profile parameter **sourcesystems** as described earlier in this chapter. Note that these excluded change requests are not common and are only a result of special transport profile parameters that have been added to the transport profile for the target R/3 System. |

**Table 13.2** Status possibilities for change requests in an import queue

| Status | Explanation |
|---|---|
| Request after end mark | The change request is after the end mark. Therefore, the change request will not be imported during the next import. |
| Client transport | The change request results from a client transport and must be imported individually (see Chapter 9). |

**Table 13.2** Status possibilities for change requests in an import queue (cont.)

### Additional Display Options

For further information about the import settings for change requests, in the **Import Queue** screen, choose **Edit • Display more**. The screen displays two additional columns (see Figure 13.3 later in this section):

- Column **T**, which specifies the transport request type
- Column **QM**, which specifies the source client
- Column **RC**, which specifies the maximum return code of the import
- Column **I**, which specifies the `tp` import indicator of this change request
- Column **UMO**, which specifies the import options of this change request
- **Project** column, which specifies the CTS project to which the transport belongs

The column **T** shows the transport request type. The most common values are "K" for a Workbench request, "W" for a Customizing request, "T" for a transport of copies, and "M" for a client transport.

In column **I**, the value of the `tp` import flag (also known as the `tp import indicator`) is specified. It reflects the type of change request and under what conditions a change request is or is not imported. To display a short description of the various import flags, position the cursor in column **I** and choose F4. The most common import flags are a "w" indicating a Customizing change request and a "k" representing a Workbench change request. If either of these letters is capitalized, it indicates that the change request is excluded from transport.

To prevent the import of Workbench change requests into an SAP system—for example, to supply client-dependent changes back to a client in the development system without impacting client-independent efforts—you would set the transport profile parameter `k_import` to FALSE. All Workbench change requests added to the import queue for the development system would have the import flag **W**. (See Appendix B for more information on the transport profile parameter `k_import`.)

On the operating system level and in R/3's TMS, you can assign **import options** to your imports to override specific rules of the Change and Transport System (CTS).

These import options are also known as **unconditional modes**. You can access these import options in the TMS through the **expert mode** (see below). In Figure 13.3 (later in this section), the single character in the column **U modes** denotes the import option assigned to a change request. For details on import options on the operating system level, see Chapter 14.

Transport requests can be combined in projects. This enables you to filter and import all transport requests belonging to the same project. This functionality was introduced in Release 4.6 and meets the common practice of carrying out imports to the production by project.

The result of an import for a change request is indicated by the *maximum return code* as depicted in column **RC** in the **Import Queue** screen (see Figure 13.3). Every import activity results in a return code in the TMS. The return code may warn you about problems with the target R/3 System or about an error that has occurred during import. The system collects all the return codes and displays the *maximum* return code—the code with the highest numerical value. For example, the return code 0004 represents a warning, whereas 0000 indicates that the import was successful. If you import the entire queue and these two return codes are collected, the 0004 will be displayed to alert you of the warning (see Chapter 14).

To display the source client in column **N** of a change request, from the **Import Queue screen**, choose **Extras • Settings • Display source client**.

If the transport domain is running with extended transport control in Release 4.5, the **Import Queue** screen also shows the target client in the column **Clt**.

In addition, if you position the cursor on a change request and choose **Request • Display** in the **Import Queue** screen, you can display further details about the import queue, such as:

- Object list
- Owner
- Documentation
- Logs (export and import log files)

Bear in mind that not all log files can be displayed when you are dealing with different transport groups (see Chapter 7). See also the section "Transporting between Transport Groups" later in this chapter.

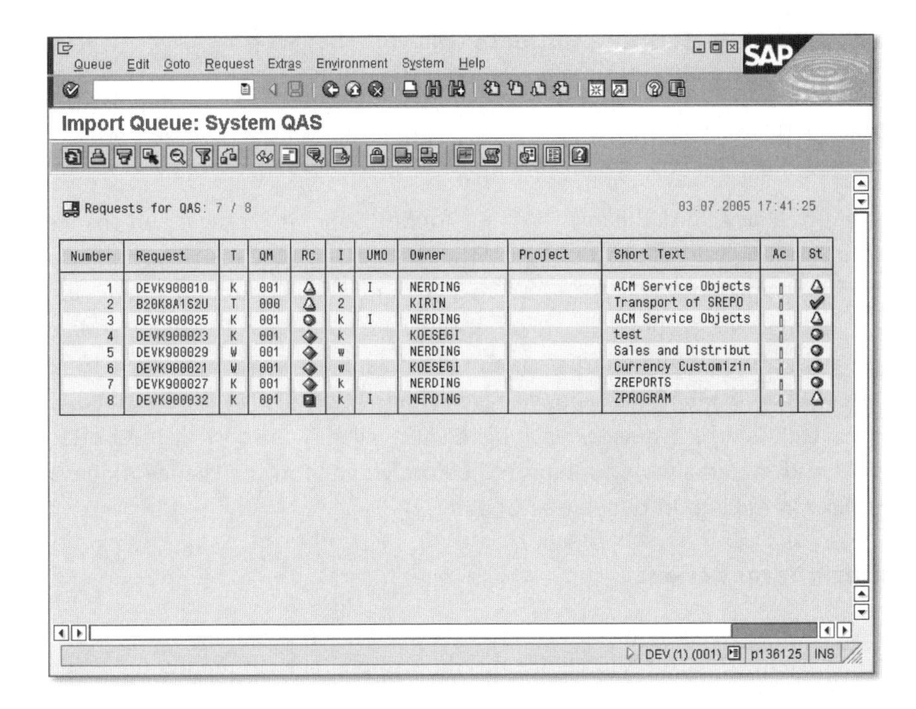


Figure 13.3 Additional display options in the import queue

### Refreshing the Import Queue

To improve performance, data is read from the transport directory only the first time you access the TMS. After that, the data in the import overview and import queue is buffered in the database of the SAP system. The time stamp in the screen indicates how recent the data is. The internal buffers of the TMS become invalid each day at 0:00.

To refresh the data in the display, from either screen, choose **Edit • Refresh**. It may be more convenient to have the data refreshed periodically in the background. To do this, schedule the report `RSTMSCOL` to run at regular intervals in the SAP systems in which you frequently use the TMS. SAP recommends scheduling `RSTMSCOL` to run hourly.

## 13.2 Performing Imports

Importing is when you bring exported changes into another SAP system. Because there is no automatic mechanism for importing a change request into a target system, you have to use the tools provided in the TMS or at the operating system level. The procedure for using the TMS is covered in this chapter. For information on performing imports at the operating system level, see Chapter 14.

### 13.2.1 Before Performing Imports

Before starting an import, you should ensure that the transport environment is set up to properly fulfill your particular import needs. By taking certain precautions, you can facilitate the import procedures and avoid unnecessary work.

You should always check the import queue for SAP Support Packages and change requests resulting from client transports. The changes included in a Support Package and a client transport depend on their sequence in the import queue and should be imported accordingly. However, they are not imported using standard **import all** or **preliminary import** steps. For example, Support Packages have to be imported using the SAP Package Manager (Transaction SPAM) as described in Chapter 15. Change requests resulting from a client transport are imported together and should always be imported before you import the change requests that follow in the import queue (see Chapter 9).

#### Setting a Target Client

During import, change requests are by default imported into the client that has the same client ID as the source client. For example, change requests released from client 110 in the development system are by default imported into client 110 in the quality assurance system. If this does not satisfy your import needs, you must specify the required target client number during the initial steps of an import. At that time, a dialog box appears—either **Import Transport Request** for individual requests or **Start Import** for imports of entire queues—allowing you to enter a target client number.

**Note** If you have not set the target client, the change requests will be imported into the client that has the same number as the source client.

#### Target Clients with Extended Transport Control

When extended transport control is activated, there is no need to specify the target client's number in the dialog boxes **Import Transport Request** and **Start Import**. Extended transport control from Release 4.5 onwards requires that transport routes specify client and system combinations; therefore, every change request in the import queue will have associated with it the client number into which it needs to be imported. You do not have to provide a target client. Figure 13.3 (earlier in the chapter) displays an import queue for the system QAS.

When extended transport control is activated, there is the possibility that change requests in an import queue do not have a target client specified. For example, if you activate the extended transport control while there are still change requests in any of the import queues, the requests will not have a target client specified. The column **Clt** will be highlighted in red. You cannot perform any operations on the import queue until you specify a target client for these old requests.

To set a target client for a change request:

1. From the **Import Queue** screen, mark the respective change request.
2. Choose **Request · Target client · Set**.
3. Enter the target client number and choose **Enter**.

To change a specified target client before starting an import, proceed as follows:

1. From the **Import Queue** screen, mark the respective change request.
2. Choose **Request · Target client · Change**.
3. Enter the target client number and choose **Enter**.

The advantage of extended transport control is that you can ensure change requests are delivered to all clients in your system landscape in their correct sequence. Because change requests now have an additional indicator in the import queue—the target client—you can choose to specifically import only the change requests destined for a particular target client by setting a *target client filter*.

To set a target client filter, follow these steps:

1. From the **Import Queue** screen, choose **Edit · Target client filter**.
2. Enter the target client number and choose **Enter**.

### Closing the Import Queue by Setting an End Mark

You close an import queue and set an end mark at the end of the import queue: All change requests that are released after the import queue is closed are added to the end of the import queue in their correct sequence—but after the end mark. This will prevent these recently released change requests from being imported during the next import activity. When an import of all waiting requests is started, all the change requests before the end mark will be imported. SAP recommends freezing certain states of development and Customizing using this closing technique.

To close the import queue, from the **Import Queue** screen, choose **Queue · Close**. Similarly, to open an import queue, choose **Queue · Open**. This removes the end mark.

If you do not close the import queue manually, the initial step in the import procedure is to close the import queue. The transport control program will automatically close the import queue and set the end mark. After the import, the queue is opened again automatically, and the end mark is removed. Setting an end mark at the end of the import queue is necessary to protect the import process from additional change requests while in the middle of performing different import steps.

### 13.2.2 Import All

Once you have verified the target client settings and have closed the import queue, you are ready to start your import. To initiate an import, use the TMS option **Start import** (explained below), which is also referred to as **import all** because it imports all change requests waiting to be imported. Importing a collection of change requests waiting to be imported ensures that the objects are imported in their correct sequence—the sequence in which they were released and exported from the development system. (See the section "Sequence in Import Queues" in Chapter 4 and "Importing Change Requests" in Chapter 6.)

Imports can be started from any SAP system in the transport domain. If you start the import from an SAP system other than the target system, you will be required to log on to the target system. Following logon, the TMS starts the transport control program `tp` in the target system. For the duration of the import, `tp` continues to run in the background so that the user session is not blocked. After the import, the queue is opened again automatically, and the end mark is removed.

To import all change requests waiting to be imported in the import queue of an SAP system, perform the following steps:

1. From the TMS initial screen (Transaction STMS), choose **Overview · Imports**.
2. Mark the system into which you want to import, and choose **Import queue · Display**.
3. From the **Import Queue** screen, choose **Queue · Start import**.
4. The dialog box **Start Import** appears. If necessary, enter the target client number.
5. If special import options are required, choose the **Expert mode** icon (see below).
6. Choose **Continue** to initiate the import procedure.

Once change requests have been imported successfully into a system defined as the source system of a delivery route, the change requests are automatically added to the import queues of the respective target SAP systems. The transport route configuration specifies which change requests are automatically delivered to which target systems.

### Expert Mode

The **expert mode** for an import allows you to handle special import requirements, such as reimporting change requests and overwriting objects. To use the expert mode, select one of the following required import options in the **Start Import** dialog box (mentioned above) and then choose **Continue**:

- **Select all requests for new import:**
  When you select this option, all imported change requests are kept in the import queue after the import instead of being deleted immediately. In this way, they can be imported into further clients in the SAP system (see the section "Importing into Multiple Clients"). This import option is similar to the preliminary import option when importing single change requests (see below).
- **Overwrite originals:**
  If a change request contains objects that originate in the target system, the import overwrites the existing original in the target system.
- **Overwrite objects in unconfirmed repairs:**
  If a change request contains objects that are currently being repaired in the target system and not yet confirmed, the import ignores the repair and overwrites the object in the target system.

**Warning** SAP recommends using export mode options only when necessary. Export mode selections should not be used during every import of an import queue.

## 13.2.3 Preliminary Imports

As an alternative to importing entire import queues, you can also import single change requests. This is called a preliminary import because it enables you to send one change request as a preliminary through the defined transport route. To minimize the risks associated with *preliminary imports*, the request remains in the import queue and is reimported the next time the entire import queue is imported. This helps to ensure that export and import sequences are always the same.

**Warning** To ensure object dependencies and consistency, SAP strongly recommends importing all or a collection of sequenced change requests. You should limit your use of preliminary imports to exceptional situations.

As of Release 4.5, the default setting for importing individual change requests is to perform preliminary imports—although you also have the option of deselecting this function in expert mode (see below).

To import a single change request, perform the following steps:

1. In the **Import Queue** screen, mark the change request to be imported.
2. Choose **Request • Import**.
3. The dialog box **Import Transport Request** appears. If necessary, enter the target client number.
4. If you wish to select special options, choose the **Expert mode** icon (see below).
5. Choose **Continue**.

### Multiple Change Requests

You can select multiple change requests to be imported using a preliminary import. Choose the change requests you wish to import by positioning your cursor on the change request and either choosing **Edit • Select • Select Request** or pressing F9. Once the change requests have been selected, perform a preliminary import as described above. Each highlighted change request is imported one after the other—they are not imported as a collection of change requests as with an **import all** (see the section "tp Processing Sequence" in Chapter 14).

### Expert Mode

If you have special import requirements for your preliminary import, use the expert mode. The expert mode for preliminary imports allows you to specify:

- Import options
- Execution type

> **Warning** Setting import options during the import of change requests should be done in exceptional situations only.

In expert mode, you can select the following **Import options**:

- **Preliminary Import of transport request:**
  When performing a preliminary import, the default setting is that the change request remains in the import queue and is reimported when you import the entire queue. This import option is selected by default. As of Release 4.5, you are able to deselect this option. The change request remains in the import queue, but is not imported again with the next import of all waiting requests.

To remove such a change request, you must manually delete the change request from the import queue.

**Warning** To ensure consistency and object dependencies, SAP strongly recommends that you do not deselect the preliminary import option.

- **Ignore that the transport request was already imported:**
  If a change request has already been imported into the target system, this option allows you to import it again without error.
- **Overwrite originals:**
  If a change request contains objects that originate in the target system, the import overwrites the existing original in the target system.
- **Overwrite objects in unconfirmed repairs:**
  The import ignores any repairs and overwrites the unconfirmed object in the target system (see above, under "Import All").
- **Ignore invalid transport type:**
  This option overrides the transport profile parameters that exclude a transport type. For example, if the transport profile parameter `k_import` is set to FALSE, Workbench change requests (type **k**) are excluded from being imported. If this option is selected, transport profile parameters restricting the type of imports will be ignored, and, in this case, imports of Workbench change requests will be possible.

In the expert mode for preliminary imports from within TMS, there are two selections for the execution of the import:

- Start import in foreground
- Start import in background

By default, individual imports are set to start in the foreground. It is unlikely that performing an import in the foreground will exceed the dialog work process runtime (300 seconds), because work process time is consumed only for receiving and displaying `tp` status messages, not for the time `tp` is actually running. Therefore, starting the import in the background makes sense only if you do not want to have the user session locked.

## 13.3 Managing Import Queues

To help manage single and multiple change requests, additional functionality is provided from within the **Import Queue** screen. To use the selection option, choose **Edit · Select**. You can use the following functionalities:

- Forwarding a change request
- Deleting a change request from an import queue
- Adding a change request to an import queue
- Moving the end mark in an import queue
- Performing checks on the import queue

> **Tip** As of Release 4.5, you are able to select multiple change requests in an import queue prior to performing different functions on those change requests. In earlier releases, only a single change request can be selected.

### 13.3.1 Forwarding a Change Request

The TMS enables you to manually forward a change request. When you *forward* a change request, you add it to the import queue of a selected SAP system. The target of a forwarded change request can be an SAP system or—with extended transport control in Release 4.5—a specific client within an SAP system. Forwarding of a change request is used to add a change request to an import queue outside the predefined transport routes and therefore should be used only in exceptional cases.

To forward a change request to a target system outside the predefined transport routes, proceed as follows:

1. From the **Import Queue** screen, mark the respective change request.
2. Choose **Request · Forward · System**. Provide the name of the SAP system to which the change request should be forwarded. If extended transport control is active, you will be required to forward the change request to a client and system combination.

With extended transport control, you can forward a request into a specific client of the same system. To do this, from the **Import Queue** screen, choose **Request · Forward · Client**.

If the source and the target systems belong to different transport groups, you must adjust the import queue of the target system. For more details on adjusting import queues, see the section "Transporting between Transport Groups" later in this chapter.

**Example: Forwarding a Change Request**

A company has a four-system landscape that consists of the systems development, quality assurance, production, and training. The development system consolidates to the quality assurance system. A delivery route is specified between the quality assurance system and the production system, and then between the production system and the training system.

A program included in a change request is imported into the quality assurance system. It is urgently needed in the training system, but an import into the production system is not possible at this time. A manual forward of the change request that contains the respective program is performed to rush it to the training system before it has been imported into the production system.

### 13.3.2 Deleting a Change Request from an Import Queue

To delete a change request from an import queue, mark the change request in the **Import Queue** screen and choose **Request · Delete**.

Object dependencies may cause inconsistencies in the target system after the next import. For example, if you delete a request containing a new data element, all other requests containing tables that depend on that data element will fail.

**Warning** To avoid inconsistencies, you are strongly advised not to delete individual change requests. Make your corrections in the development system and release a new request instead.

There are situations in which deleting change requests from an import queue is necessary. These situations include:

- Change requests from a client transport. After successful import of a client transport, the change requests for that client transport still remain in the import queue and will need to be deleted (see Chapter 9).
- In Release 4.5, if you have deselected the preliminary import option when importing a single change request, the change request will remain in the import queue and will need to be manually deleted after import. To do so, from the **Import Queue** screen, select the change request that has the status **Request was already imported** and choose **Extras · Delete imported requests**.

### 13.3.3 Adding a Change Request to an Import Queue

If you have manually copied a change request to the transport directory or if you wish to reimport a change request that no longer is in the import queue, you must manually add the change request to the respective import queue. To do this, choose **Extras • Other requests • Add**. Provide the change request ID for the change request to be added and choose **Enter**. Note that if extended transport control is active, you will also have to enter a value for the target client.

### 13.3.4 Moving an End Mark

When an import queue is closed, an end mark is added at the very end of the import queue. To move the end mark to another position within the import queue, position the cursor on a change request and choose **Edit • Move end mark**. The end mark will then be positioned above the selected change request. For example, Figure 13.4 shows the result of selecting change request `DEVK900021` and then performing a **Move end mark**.

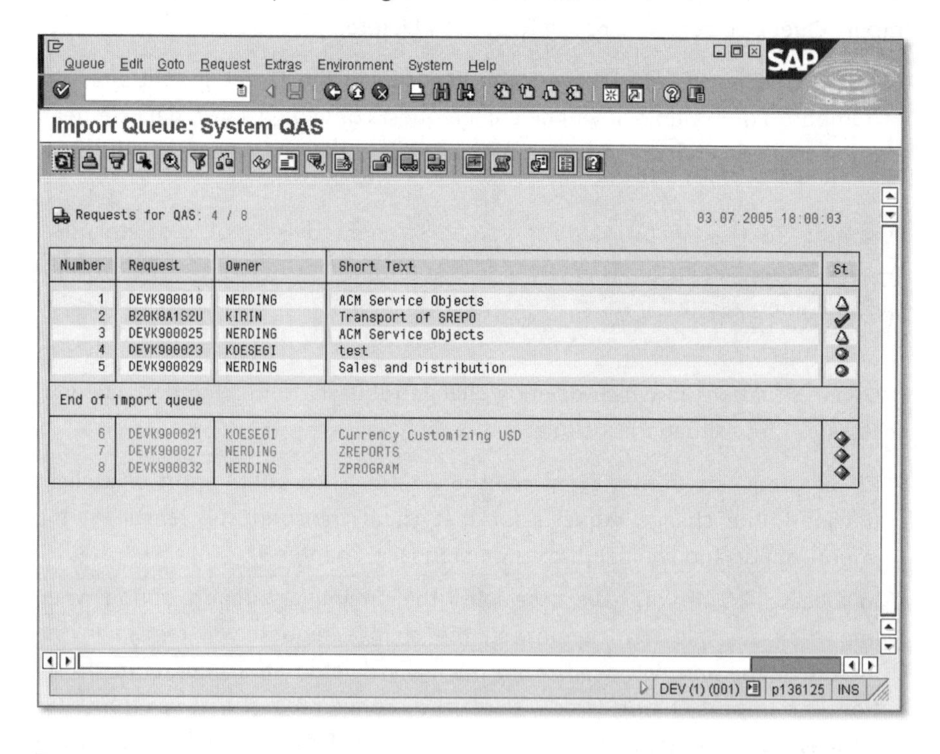


**Figure 13.4** Moving an end mark

### 13.3.5 Performing Checks

To ensure that your import runs smoothly, you should run checks on the import queue before performing the import. To start these checks, from the **Import Queue** screen, choose **Queue • Check**. Then, choose one of the following checks:

- Consistency
- Transport tool
- Critical objects

#### Consistency Check for the Import Queue

This check function verifies that all data files and control files that belong to a change request exist in the transport directory and can be read.

To run this check, from the **Import Overview** screen, choose **Import Queue • Check • Consistency**. The **Check Import Queue** dialog box appears.

- By default, this dialog box is set to **No**. If you choose **No**, the system displays whether the corresponding files are available in the transport directory and whether they are readable. Consistent files are indicated by a check mark on the right side of the screen **TMS: Import Queue Check** that appears. If the corresponding files are not available or are not readable, the system marks the files or the directory with an **x**. If an error occurred, you can access more information by clicking the **x**.
- If you choose **Yes** in the **Check Import Queue** dialog box, the size of the files and directories is displayed in addition to information concerning the consistency of the directories.

#### Transport Tool Check

Before starting an import, it is also helpful to check the transport tools to ensure that they can function and have the appropriate settings for performing imports. You can check the transport tools for one or all SAP systems within a transport domain (except for virtual systems and external systems). The check examines the following:

- **tp interface:**
  The status of the transport control program
- **Transport profile:**
  The readability of the transport profile at the operating system level
- **RFC destination:**
  The status and success of required RFC calls to the transport control program

- **tp call:**
  The status of the communication link between the transport control program and the database of the SAP system

To perform a transport tool check, from the **Import Queue** screen for an SAP system, choose **Queue • Check • Transport tool**. The screen **TMS: Check Transport Tool** appears and will indicate whether the transport tools have the appropriate settings for performing imports. To display more information about the individual tools and potential errors, expand the tree structure. A green check mark indicates a successful test. If a particular check is marked with an **x**, its check was not successful, indicating either an error at the operating system level or a problem with the current transport profile parameters.

### Critical Objects

As of Release 4.5, the TMS can search for objects that you have defined as critical. A *critical object* is an object that you expect to cause problems during import or an object that is critical for security. By defining critical objects, you can help to protect against the import of objects into certain SAP systems that may cause serious errors or damage settings in the SAP system.

An example of a critical object is authorization profiles created in the development system that you do not want to transport into the production system for security reasons. You can define authorization profiles as critical objects in the production system. (The critical object list is specific to each SAP system in the system landscape—you have to define the critical objects for each target system within your landscape.) Once the authorization profiles are defined in the critical object list, to ensure that change requests including authorization profiles are not accidentally imported, you need to perform a check for critical objects prior to each import.

To define critical objects, proceed as follows:

1. From the **Import Overview** screen, choose **Extras • Critical transport objects**.
2. Choose **Enter**.
3. To add an object to the table, switch to change mode by choosing **Table view • Display • Change**.
4. Choose **Edit • New Entries**.
5. Specify the critical objects. You can define an object as critical only if its Object Directory entry has a program ID of *R3TR* (see Chapter 10).
6. Save your entries.

**Note** If you have defined critical objects for a system, you should always run the critical objects check on the import queue of that system before importing.

To start the check for critical objects in the import queue, from the **Import Queue** screen, choose **Queue · Check · Critical objects**. The system then searches the object list of the import queue for critical objects in the table of critical objects (see Figure 13.5). The results of the search are displayed in the screen **TMS: Critical Objects in Requests**.

Bear in mind that this check offers only a display function. Neither the check nor the definition of critical objects automatically prevents you from importing change requests that include critical objects. It is the responsibility of the system administrator to ensure that the respective change requests are not imported. He or she must also reexport any noncritical objects that are contained in the list of change requests into another change request from the source system. This must be done in a way that preserves the original sequence of the change requests.

**Warning** The critical objects check is only a display function. It is the responsibility of the person performing imports to manage critical objects located during a critical object check.

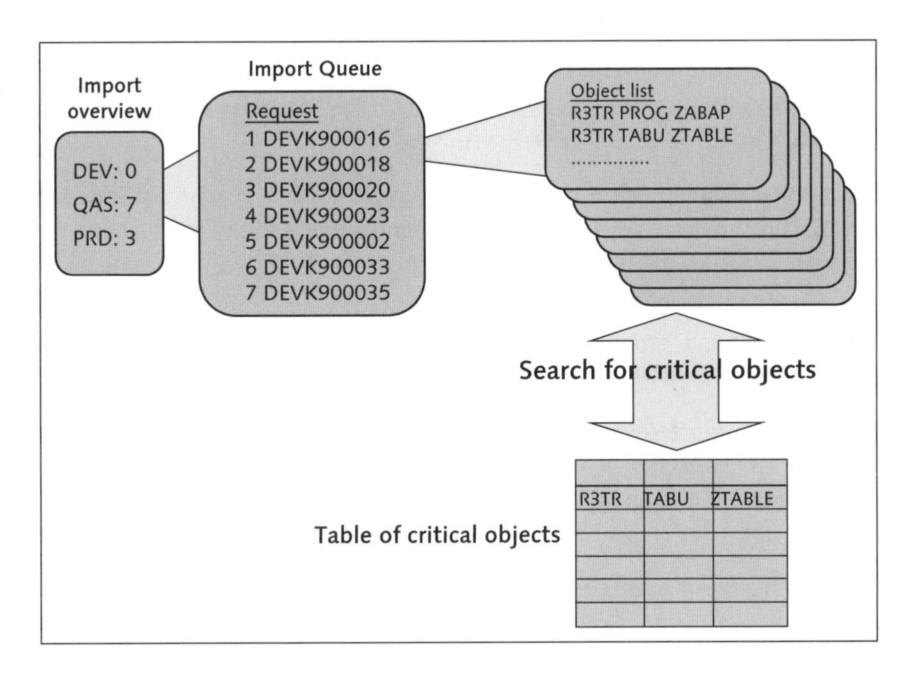


**Figure 13.5** Scanning for critical objects

## 13.4 Scheduling Imports

After export, a change request is not automatically imported. To import the change requests, you have two options: You can perform an import either manually, or schedule it as a job on the target system.

> **Note** Even when scheduling a background job, you need to check the import results for problems.

When planning imports, ensure that you include enough time to accommodate post-import tasks such as quality assurance testing. SAP recommends performing imports of entire import queues (*import all*) at regular intervals—for example, monthly, weekly, or daily. A more frequent import rate is not advisable. The import rate depends on how soon the changes are required in the production system.

Because imports into a production system affect the runtime environment, you should schedule them for times when they are least likely to affect running transactions and programs (see Chapter 14). This is especially important when you import data into a production system, because an import can invalidate some SAP buffer contents, forcing them to be reloaded and consequently reducing performance. Furthermore, inconsistencies may affect running programs and their environment. You should schedule imports into production systems to run at night in the background, or perform a detailed check on the jobs that would be running at the same time and monitor the effects carefully. Before importing into a production system, perform a complete SAP system backup.

Ideally, no users should be working in an SAP system when change requests are imported. This is particularly important when importing into the production system. For this reason, you should make sure that you choose appropriate times and send a system message telling users to log off.

### 13.4.1 Importing into Multiple Clients

Often, a customer wishes to import change requests into multiple clients throughout the system landscape—a procedure that poses certain problems. These problems and their possible solutions are outlined in more detail in this section.

Figure 13.6 shows an example of transport route requirements for imports into multiple clients. After the release of change requests from the CUST client, the changes are to be imported into not only the TEST client and the SAND client in the development system, but also into the QTST client and a DATA client in the quality assurance system. Once the change requests are imported into the QTST client, the change requests will be transported to the TRNG client and the PROD client in the production system.

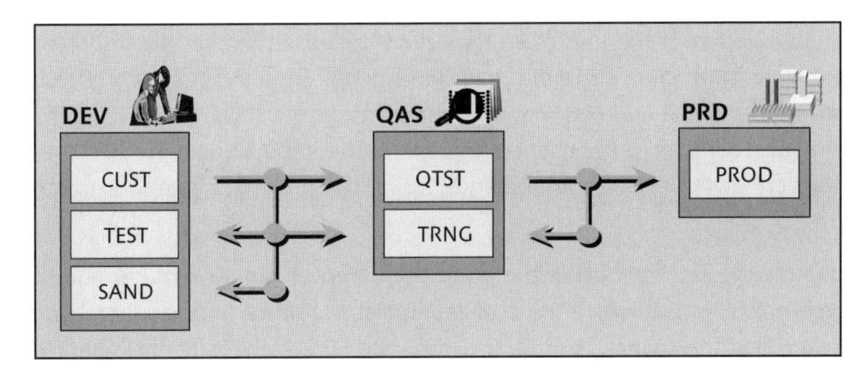


**Figure 13.6** Transporting into multiple clients

As of Release 4.5, you can rely on extended transport control to ensure that all clients in the system landscape contain the latest changes that originate in client CUST. The change requests are automatically placed in the import queues of specified SAP systems and clients. Extended transport control also ensures that client-independent objects in a change request are imported into an SAP system only once, protecting newer versions of objects from being overwritten. For example, if a change request that contains an ABAP program is released from the CUST client, the program itself is imported into the quality assurance system only once, while the change request may be in the import queue for multiple clients. On the other hand, client-specific changes are imported into each client.

**Note** As of Release 4.5, you can use extended transport control to set up client-specific transport routes, which allows you to import into multiple clients in a single R/3 System at the same or different times (see Chapter 8).

### Importing into Multiple Clients without Extended Transport Control

If extended transport control is not available or if extended transport control is not activated, you cannot take advantage of client-specific transport routes. Instead, you must manually import the change requests that originate in client CUST to all the clients in the system landscape. Although it is possible to import change requests into the quality assurance client and then wait to import them into the other clients in the same system at a later time, this requires complex management of change requests and import queues.

**Note** Without client-specific transport routes defined using extended transport control, you have to manually import the change requests several times, once for each client in the system.

The standard is that at the end of an import of the entire queue, the imported change requests are removed from the import queue of the target system. If you wish to import change requests into another client, you will want to import the change requests and keep the change requests in the import queue in their prescribed order. This can be accomplished by using the preliminary import option during import.

Importing change requests using the preliminary import option requires you to decide the next client to which the change request should be imported, and you must ensure that the change requests are imported into all the different clients in the system. Managing imports into multiple clients at different times requires you to track change requests outside of the SAP system and its transport tools.

SAP recommends that you import change requests into multiple clients in a sequential process. This ensures consistency in the import queues and ensures that all clients have received the latest change requests. If this is not possible, use client copy tools to assist in maintaining the consistency of different clients in the target system. For example, a data conversion test client could be re-created periodically as a copy of the quality assurance test client. Or, the training client could receive the latest Customizing changes on a weekly basis through **client copy according to transp. request**.

The easiest way to support imports into multiple clients is to schedule them for a time when a group of change requests are sequentially imported into all clients within the quality assurance system, starting with the quality assurance client. In this way, the change requests are imported first into the quality assurance client, and the other clients wait until their scheduled times to receive the import.

To manually perform the import of a collection of change requests into multiple R/3 clients, first close the import queue of the target system. Then, to keep the change requests in the import queue in their correct order for imports into other clients, import the import queue into all the target clients except the last target client using a special import option. When you perform the import into the last target client, perform an import with no import option.

To perform a preliminary import into multiple clients, proceed as follows:

1. From the **Import Queue** screen, choose **Queue · Start import**.
2. In the **Start Import** dialog box, enter the respective target client.
3. To perform preliminary imports of the entire queue, choose **Expert mode** and:
   - For R/3 Release 4.0, select the import option **Flag all requests for further import**.
   - For R/3 Release 4.5, select the import option **Select all requests for new import**.
4. Choose **Continue**.

For the last client to receive changes, you should perform the import without selecting the expert mode option for a preliminary import. This final import will then remove the change requests from the import queue of the target system.

For all the target clients except the last target client, to transport a single change request originating in client CUST to all other clients within the system landscape, follow these steps:

1. From the **Import Queue** screen, select the change request to be imported.
2. Choose **Request · Import**.
3. In the **Import Transport Request** dialog box that appears, enter the respective target client number.
4. Choose **Continue** to initiate the import.

Remember that by default single imports are set to **Prelim. Import of transport req** in the expert mode. Therefore, you do not need to specify the expert mode. For the last client to receive changes, you will have to change the expert mode. To change the expert mode for the last target client and thus remove the change request from the import queue of the quality assurance system:

1. From the **Import Queue** screen, select the change request to be imported.
2. Choose **Request · Import**.
3. In the **Import Transport Request** dialog box that appears, enter the respective target client number.
4. Choose the **Expert mode**. Deselect the import option **Prelim. Import of transport req**.
5. Choose **Continue** to initiate the import.

## 13.5 Monitoring Imports

The TMS provides several tools for monitoring the transport activities in your transport domain. Bear in mind that to open these tools, you must branch into them successively from the previous tool.

Additional information on TMS activities is provided by the Alert Monitor, which was discussed in Chapter 8. For details on monitoring and troubleshooting, see Chapter 14.

### 13.5.1 Import Monitor

To display status information about currently running and completed imports, start the **Import Monitor**. To access the import monitor for a specific SAP system, from the Import Overview screen, position the cursor on the system and choose **Goto · Import monitor**. The import monitor displays the information for each `tp` import command, regardless of whether it imported a single change request or the entire queue. The information includes:

- `tp` command
- Start mode (online or offline)
- Start time (date and time)
- `tp` process ID
- Last change (date and time )
- `tp` status (current status of the *tp* command)
- Maximum return code
- `tp` message

In the **TMS Import Monitor** screen, to update the display of a currently running import in the import monitor, choose **Edit · Refresh**. If you notice that the last change date of an import has not changed in a long time and the status of the `tp` command is **still running**, it may be due to one of the following reasons:

- The data volume of the change request(s) is large.
- An error has occurred that is shown in the TP System Log.
- `tp` has been terminated with operating system tools.

The `tp` message indicates the step currently being processed and then either the successful completion of the import or the error that last occurred.

### 13.5.2 TP System Log

The TP System Log displays an overview of the transport activities for the current SAP system—for example, all `tp` calls and errors, as well as the return codes, which indicate the success of each import. To branch to the TP System Log, from the **TMS Import Monitor** screen, choose **Goto • TP system log**. The **TP System Log** screen appears. The file is stored on the operating system level in the subdirectory `log` of the transport directory. This file is also known as the *SLOG*.

### 13.5.3 Action Log File

The *action log* contains the transport activities and the return codes for all transport activities. Each transport group has its own action log file. To branch to the action log, from the **TP System Log** screen, choose **Goto • Transport steps**. The **Transport Step Monitor** screen appears. This file is stored on the operating system level in the subdirectory `log` of the transport directory. This file is also known as the "ALOG".

### 13.5.4 Single Step Log Files

For each transport activity, the system writes a log file, called the *single step log file*. If an error is indicated in the Import Monitor, you can branch to the TP System Log and the action log. From the **Transport Step Monitor** screen, you can open the single log file to analyze the error. To open the single log files, on the action log file screen, position the cursor on a change request and choose **Request • Logs**.

## 13.6 Transporting between Transport Groups

Usually, all SAP systems in a transport domain share a common transport directory. In certain situations, multiple transport directories may be required (see Chapters 7 and 8), and the transport domain will consist of multiple transport groups, one for each transport directory that is used. The TMS supports transports between transport groups. Each transport group reflects the configuration of the transport domain; that is, each transport group includes import queues for all SAP systems belonging to the transport domain. Nevertheless, change requests can be imported into a target system only if they exist in the import queue of the transport group to which the target system belongs.

**Note** If more than one transport group exists, each transport group contains a local import queue for each SAP system belonging to the transport domain.

After a change request has been released, it is stored in the transport directory of the source system and recorded in the local import queue of the target system, where *local* means that this import queue belongs to the transport group of the source system.

If the source and the target system belong to different transport groups, the import queue of the target transport group has to be adjusted. Figure 13.7 depicts a simplified example of this process, based on the sample systems DEV and QAS.

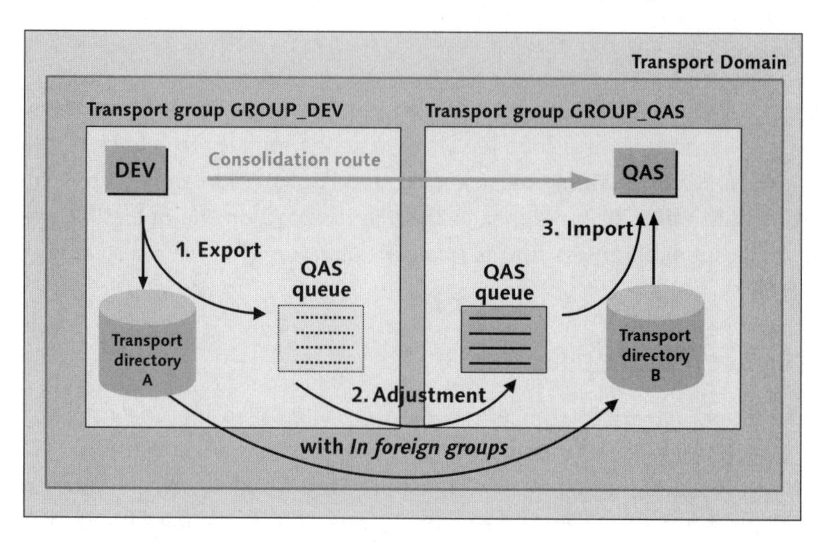


**Figure 13.7** Transporting between transport groups

Figure 13.7 shows a system landscape with two transport groups: GROUP_DEV and GROUP_QAS. Customizing and development changes are performed in the development system DEV. A consolidation route is defined between DEV and the quality assurance system QAS. When a change request is released and exported from DEV, the data file and control file are created on the transport directory local to DEV—the transport directory for GROUP_DEV. Also, the change request is added to the import queue of QAS—the import queue that is local to the development system. For an import of the change request to take place, the data file and control file as well as the import queue entry need to be local to the quality assurance system. In other words, the files need be adjusted from the transport group GROUP_DEV to GROUP_QAS. The process for moving the required files and entries from one transport group to another is known as *adjusting*.

### 13.6.1 Adjusting Transports

Before change requests can be imported into a system whose transport group is different from its delivering system, the different transport groups need to be adjusted. The TMS adjusts the import queue in the target system's transport group to search for change requests waiting for import into the target SAP system, which are stored in transport directories belonging to other transport groups, and to add these change requests to the transport directory of the target system's transport group.

There are three steps to perform when transporting between SAP systems that belong to different transport groups (as depicted in Figure 13.7 above):

1. The user releases and exports a change request.
2. The person responsible for imports must adjust the import queue.
3. The user imports the change request into the target system.

To perform such an adjustment, from the **Import Queue** screen of the target system, choose **Extras · Other requests · In foreign groups**. Similarly, to adjust an import queue with requests originating in an external group, choose **Extras · Other requests · In external groups**. When you confirm the transfer of these change requests, the TMS will transfer the requests to the import queue of the target system (QAS). Accordingly, the corresponding data files and control files are transferred. If an error occurs, you can still restart the adjustment despite the message that will appear stating that the import queue is locked. In this situation, you can ignore the message.

## 13.7 Transporting between Transport Domains

A transport domain is an administrative unit. Generally, all SAP systems that are connected by transport routes and that have a regular transport flow belong to the same transport domain. Even if you are forced to use more than one transport directory, by taking advantage of the concept of transport groups, all SAP systems can be kept in one domain and administered centrally by the domain controller.

Occasionally, there may be reasons to have more than one transport domain. For example, global companies or groups may configure one domain for the headquarters and one domain for each subsidiary. Possible reasons for multiple transport domains are as follows:

- Organizational or political reasons require that you have separate administrative units.
- The number of SAP systems (50 to 100) is too high to be administered within one transport domain.
- There are network limitations or considerations that technically make it advantageous to have separately administered transport domains.

Before configuring several transport domains, determine whether this is really necessary. Transports between SAP systems in different transport domains are possible, but increase the administrative workload.

Figure 13.8 shows the simplified representation of two SAP systems—GDV and DDV—that belong to different transport domains: DOMAIN_HDQ and DOMAIN_ESP. GDV is the SAP system for the headquarters of a multinational organization, and DDV is the SAP system of a subsidiary in Spain belonging to the organization. Only the involved systems are shown in this example. The system administrator wants to transport from the SAP system GDV into DDV.

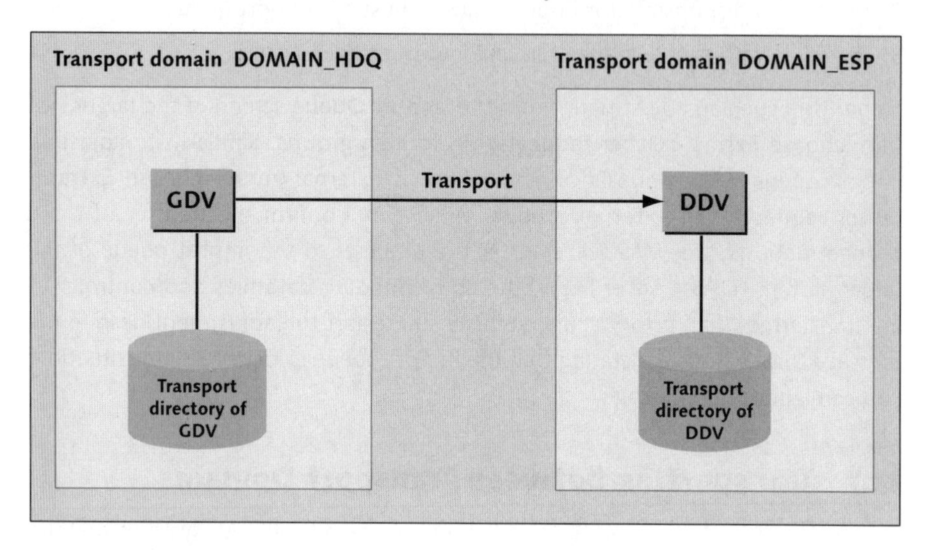


**Figure 13.8** Logical transport flow between two transport domains

### 13.7.1 Configuration

To implement the transport route depicted in Figure 13.8, the system administrator has to create an external system DDV in DOMAIN_HDQ and an external system GDV in DOMAIN_ESP. The external systems are placeholders for the real systems. For both external systems, a transport directory, called the *external transport directory*, must be defined, which is accessible from both transport domains. Within each domain, one available SAP system has to be defined as the *communications system* for the respective external system and must have access to the external transport directory. Figure 13.9 shows that GDV serves as the communications system for the external system DDV in DOMAIN_HDQ, and DDV serves as the communications system for the external system GDV in DOMAIN_ESP.

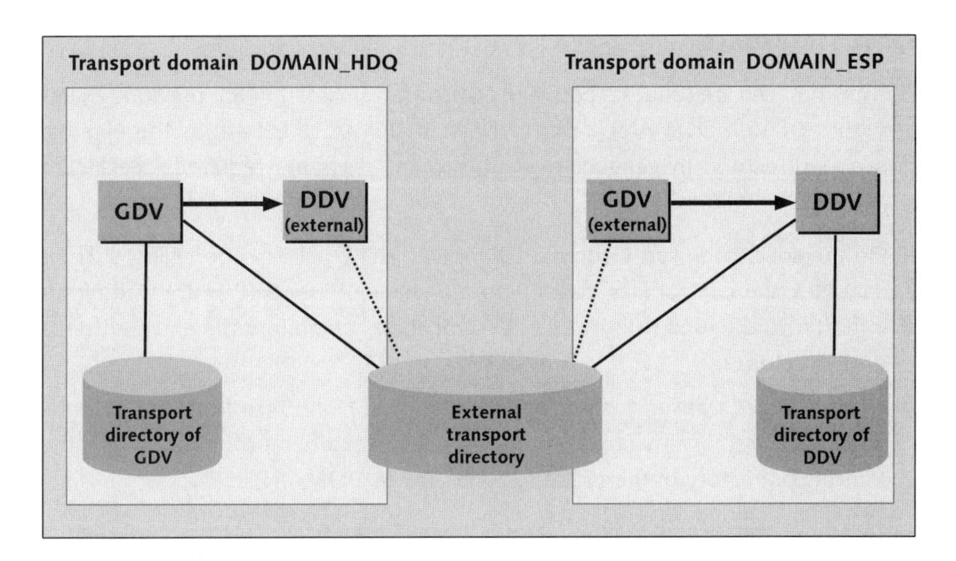


**Figure 13.9** Configuration of the transport domains

To configure the transports between two domains, follow these steps:

1. Manually create the external transport directory (see Chapters 7 and 8). Ensure that all transport subdirectories exist.
2. To ensure access to the external transport directory, check whether the communications systems in both transport domains have read and write authorizations on all subdirectories. In the example in Figure 13.9, all files that are written by user GDVADM from DOMAIN_HDQ into the external transport directory have to be readable and replaceable by user DDVADM (the reverse also must be possible).
3. Create an external system in both transport domains (see Chapter 8). Ensure that the SID of the external system in one transport domain is identical with the SID of the SAP system in the other domain, and vice versa.
4. To check the access authorizations in both transport domains, from the initial **Systems Overview** screen, choose **SAP System • Check • Transport directory** (see Chapter 8). The **Check Transport Directory** screen appears.
5. To check whether there are discrepancies between the transport group configuration of the TMS and the configuration of the transport directories on the operating system level in both transport domains, from the **Check Transport Directory** screen in step 4, choose **Goto • Transport groups**.
6. Configure a transport route from the available SAP system GDV to the external system DDV in DOMAIN_HDQ. The transport route can be a consolidation route or a delivery route.

### 13.7.2 Transport

Transporting change requests between transport domains—in the previous example, from GDV in DOMAIN_HDQ to DDV in DOMAIN_ESP—uses the external transport directory. In general, two adjustment steps are required (see Figure 13.10):

- On the source transport domain (DOMAIN_HDQ), all transport files, such as data files and control files, that belong to change requests that are waiting for import into the external system (DDV) must be copied into the external transport directory.
- On the target transport domain (DOMAIN_ESP), the files from the external transport directory must be copied into the target transport directory, the transport directory of the target system DDV in DOMAIN_ESP.

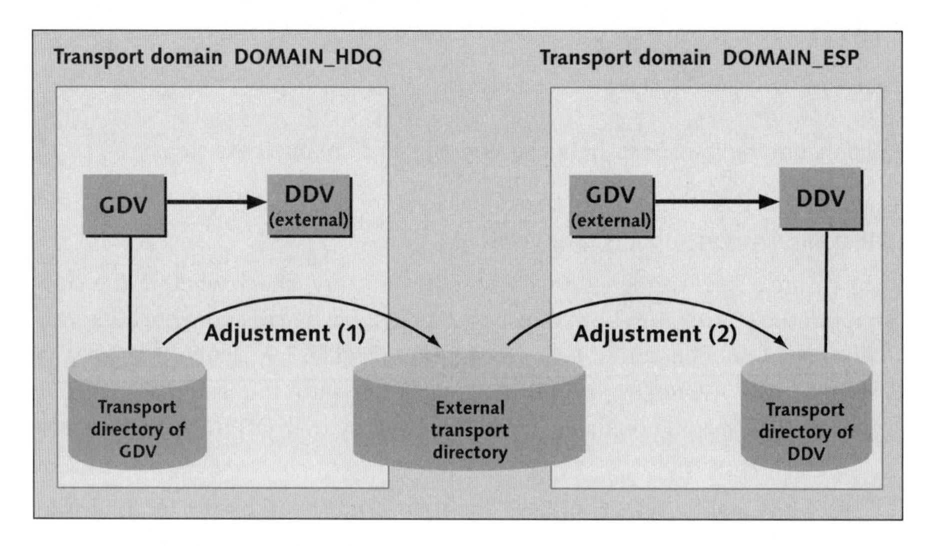


**Figure 13.10** Adjusting import queues

To transport a change request as in the example in Figure 13.10—that is, from GDV in DOMAIN_HDQ to DDV in DOMAIN_ESP—proceed as follows.

In the transport domain for the headquarters:

1. Release the change request in the "real" system GDV. As a result, the corresponding files are written to the transport directory of GDV. Because of the configured consolidation route in this example, DDV is specified as the target system of the change request. If the configured transport route is a delivery route, the change request would have to be imported into GDV instead of being released.

2. For the first adjustment step, use the TMS to search for the change request. To do this, from the **Import Queue** screen of the external system DDV, choose **Extras · Other requests · In foreign groups**.

In the transport domain for Spain:

1. For the second adjustment step, use the TMS to search for the change request. To do this, from the **Import Queue** screen of the "real" system DDV, choose **Extras · Other requests · In external groups**.
2. Choose **Enter**. As a result, the change request is copied to the transport directory of the "real" system DDV.
3. The change request is now part of the import queue of DDV in the Spanish domain and can be imported as usual.

### Requesting a Link Between Two Domains

To request a link between two domains, you must proceed as follows:

1. Logon to one of the two domain controllers.
2. Call Transaction STMS.
3. Select **Overview · Systems**. You are now in the system overview.
4. Select **SAP System · Create · Domain Link**. The **Request Domain Link** dialog opens.
5. Enter the system name, host name, and system number of the domain controller for which you want to request the domain link, and confirm your entries.

Your SAP system automatically performs the following actions:

- The required RFC destinations are generated.
- The address data of the controller is sent to the external domain controller.
- The system overview now shows that the domain link to the external domain has been requested.

### Confirming a Link Between Two Domains

For reasons of security you must confirm the link between the two domains with the external domain controller. Proceed as follows:

1. Logon to the external domain controller.
2. Call Transaction STMS.
3. Select **Overview · Systems**. You are now in the system overview.

4. Place the cursor on the domain controller that has requested the domain link, and select **SAP System • Accept**.
5. Confirm the security prompt and distribute the configuration.

The two domain controllers now exchange all the required system information for the two domains. This information is distributed to all systems of the domain you are currently logged-on to, and a transport profile is generated that contains all systems of both domains.

The information on the systems of the external domain is not automatically distributed to the systems of the domain in which you requested the domain link. For this reason, you must distribute the new configuration to those systems.

#### Result

A domain link has been established between the two transport domains. The system overview and import overview now display all systems from both domains. You can now carry out transports between systems from different domains. Note that only systems from Release 4.6C onwards can be displayed.

### 13.7.3 Linking Domains Using Domain Links

If you set up several transport domains and want to carry out transports between systems from different domains, you can link two domains simultaneously via domain links. For this purpose, there must be a permanent network connection between the systems, like the connection between the systems within a domain. The domain controllers of both domains must use SAP Release 4.6C or higher.

To link two domains via a domain link, the connection between the domains must be requested and confirmed.

## 13.8 TMS Authorization

The TMS uses RFCs for the connections between the SAP systems in a transport domain (see Chapter 8). Performing imports is not restricted to the domain controller. With proper authorizations, you can initiate imports into any SAP system from each SAP system within the domain. When using the TMS, a user's authorization is checked twice during the import process:

1. To initiate an import in the TMS, the system validates the user's authorization in the current client.
2. The TMS makes a remote function call to the target system. The user must log on to the target system with a username and password. After the user's authorization is validated in the target system, the import process begins in this target system.

To perform imports using the TMS, a user requires authorization in the client from which the import command will be issued as well as in the target system. This authorization concept allows you to assign from which client and into which target SAP systems a user may perform imports.

SAP provides the authorization S_CTS_ADMIN for importing change requests using the TMS. This authorization is required to confirm that imports into the target system are allowed.

There is no SAP profile simply allowing import functionality. You can assign the authorization profile S_A.SYSTEM to users who need to perform CTS administrative activities, including the initialization of the Change and Transport Organizer, as well as all TMS functions—for example, setting up the TMS to perform imports. Alternatively, you may wish to assign a user the ability to perform imports without the ability to initialize or set up any parts of the CTS. Rather than assigning the profile S_A.SYSTEM, you can restrict this user to performing imports by creating a new authorization profile for the authorization object S_CTS_ADMI and assigning the user the new profile. This authorization profile then prevents the user from accessing administrative functions.

## 13.9 Questions

1. Which of the following statements are correct in regard to import queues?
   A. Import queues are the TMS representation of the import buffer on the operating system level.
   B. You have to manipulate import queues to transport change requests.
   C. Import queues should be closed before starting an import using TMS.
   D. You can import only an entire import queue.
2. Which of the following statements are correct in regard to preliminary imports?
   A. SAP recommends using preliminary imports rather than imports of entire queues.
   B. Preliminary imports should be performed only in exceptional cases.
   C. Change requests imported as preliminary imports remain in the import queue.
   D. Change requests are deleted from the import queue after preliminary imports. This prevents them from being imported again with the next import of the entire import queue.

3. Which of the following statements is correct in regard to imports into an SAP system?
   A. Imports can be performed only by using the **start import** functionality in the TMS.
   B. Imports can be performed only by using `tp` commands on the operating system level to prepare the import queue and then using the **start import** functionality in the TMS.
   C. Imports can be performed only by using `tp` commands at the operating system level.
   D. Imports can be performed by using either a `tp` command on the operating system level or the TMS import functionality.
4. Which of the following statements is correct in regard to transports between different transport groups?
   A. They are not possible.
   B. They can be performed only by using `tp` on the operating system level with special options.
   C. They can be performed using the TMS with special options provided by the expert mode.
   D. They require you to adjust the corresponding import queues.
5. Which of the following statements are correct in regard to transports between different transport domains?
   A. They are not possible.
   B. They require you to create a virtual system and a virtual transport directory.
   C. They require you to configure identical transport groups within the different transport domains.
   D. They require you to create an external system and an external transport directory.
   E. They require you to adjust the corresponding import queues.

# 14 Technical Insight—the Import Process

The previous chapter described how imports are performed using the Transport Management System (TMS). When you use the TMS interface, you are not aware of the activities that take place on the operating system level during imports, such as calls for the transport control program `tp`. This chapter provides an insight into the technical side of the import process on the operating system level. You will learn:

- How to perform imports on the operating system level using `tp`
- About the `tp` processing sequence and the import steps
- How to use log files and return codes for troubleshooting
- How buffer synchronization affects transports
- How to identify file naming conventions in the transport directory
- About the different transport tools, their activities, and the way they communicate

By covering these issues, the chapter provides the system administrator with the background knowledge needed to use `tp` on the operating system level and to perform successful troubleshooting. This chapter is also of interest to a project leader, because learning details on what happens beyond the TMS—for example, the `tp` processing sequence and the R/3 buffer synchronization—allows a better understanding of the concepts and strategies that were introduced in Part 1 of this book.

## 14.1 The Transport Control Program tp

The transport control program `tp` is a tool on the operating system level that uses special programs (such as C programs), operating system commands, and ABAP programs in SAP systems to control transports between SAP systems. Accordingly, `tp` stands for "transports and programs."

`tp` controls the exports and imports of objects between SAP systems by ensuring that the steps for exporting and importing are performed in the correct order and that the change requests are exported and imported in the same order.

As a rule, it is not necessary to call `tp` directly because you can perform most transport activities using the TMS. Nevertheless, you may occasionally need to use `tp` commands on the operating system level instead of the TMS or in conjunction with the TMS. With each new release, SAP offers more advanced transport functionality through the TMS. Although the TMS provides a wide range of functions, to perform certain tasks, such as cleaning up the transport directory, you must still call tp directly.

### 14.1.1 Prerequisites

To use tp, the following prerequisites must be fulfilled (for details, see Chapter 7):

- All SAP systems in the transport domain must have a unique system name (SID).
- Each SAP system involved must have access to a correctly installed transport directory.
- The transport profile must be maintained correctly. The transport profile configures the transport control program tp.
- Each source system and each target system must have at least two background work processes.
- The transport dispatcher RDDIMPDP must be scheduled as an event-periodic background job in each SAP system that acts as a source system for exports or a target system for imports.

#### Authorizations for Using tp

Because tp is an operating system level command, you require operating system level authorization to access it. To call tp, you have to log on to the operating system of the computer that houses the transport directory of the target system as one of the following users:

- <sid>adm on Unix and Windows NT
- <SID>OPR on AS/400 platforms

Typically, only technical consultants and system administrators have access to the operating system level and therefore are responsible for issuing tp commands. If necessary, you can write scripts to enable users to perform imports without logging on as user <sid>adm or <SID>OPR.

### 14.1.2 Command Syntax

To call tp directly on the operating system level, follow these steps:

1. Log on to the operating system.
2. Change to subdirectory bin in the transport directory.
3. Execute a tp command with the following syntax:

```
tp <command> [argument(s)] [option(s)]
```

Table 14.1 contains a list of tp commands that may be helpful for troubleshooting or everyday operations.

| tp Command | Function |
|---|---|
| tp help | Provides general information about tp functionality—for example, about syntax and available tp commands. |
| tp <command> | Describes the syntax and function of the specified command. |
| tp go <SID> | Checks the database destination by displaying the environmental variables required for accessing the database of a specific SAP system. To do this, tp checks the values in the transport profile. Note that this command does not actually establish a database connection. |
| tp connect <SID> | Checks whether a connection to the database of the specified system can be established. |
| tp showinfo <change request> | Displays information about a specific change request, including the owner and the type of change request. |
| tp count <SID> | Displays the number of change requests waiting to be imported into the specified SAP system. |
| tp checkimpdp <SID> | Displays how the transport dispatcher RDDIMPDP is scheduled for the specified SAP system. |
| tp showparams <SID> | Displays all current transport profile parameter settings for the specified SAP system. |

**Table 14.1** Helpful tp Commands

### 14.1.3 Import Queues and Import Buffers

In the previous chapter, you learned how to use the import queue in TMS to manage and import change requests. On the operating system level, the same change requests are contained in the import buffer. The subdirectory buffer of the transport directory contains an import buffer for each system in the transport group. The buffer file is named after the corresponding system ID and contains transport control information such as the following:

- Which change requests are to be imported
- The order to follow when importing the change request
- The possible import options (explained below in the section "Import Options")
- The import steps (explained below in the section "tp Import Steps")

Import queues are the TMS representation in the SAP system of the buffer files located on the operating system level. Import queues show all change requests that are listed in the corresponding import buffer.

When an end mark is set in the TMS, the change requests that will not be included in the next import are grayed out in the import queue. By definition, these change requests no longer belong to the import queue. Consequently, more change requests may belong to the import buffer than to the import queue. For example, in Figure 14.1, the import queue displays the four change requests before the end mark as included in the next import, whereas the three change requests after the end mark would be grayed out—that is, they are not included in the next import.

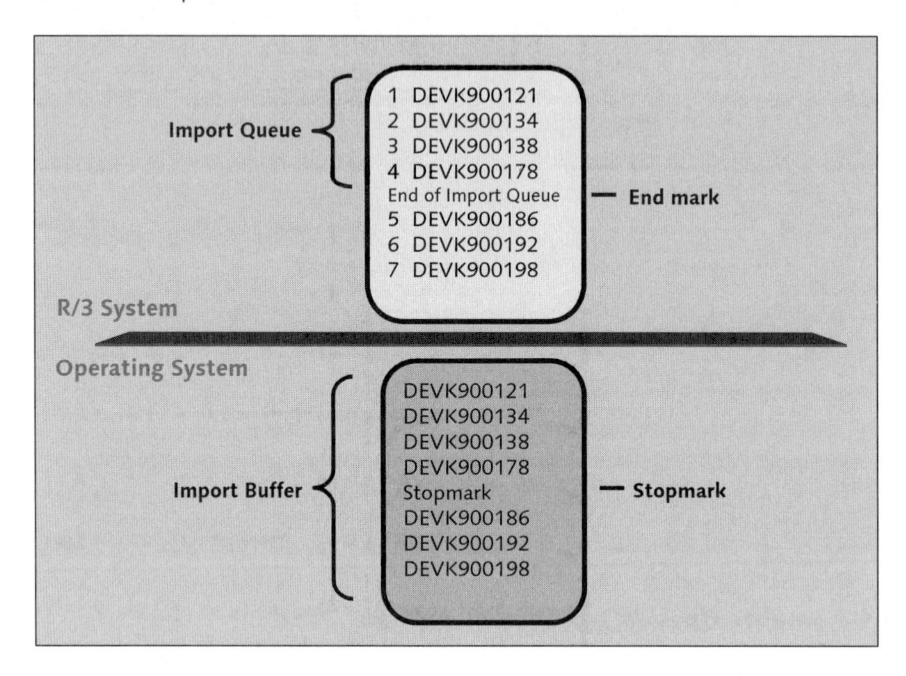


**Figure 14.1** Import queue and import buffer

An end mark is indicated in an import queue by the statement **End of import queue**, whereas on the operating system level, the import buffer shows the term **stopmark** (see Figure 14.1). Regardless of where the marker is created, it is always set in both the import buffer and the import queue. There can be only one end marker or stopmark in each import queue or buffer.

To set an end mark, and therefore simultaneously set the stopmark, close the **import queue** by choosing **Queue • Close** from the TMS import queue screen. The operating system level equivalent is the command `tp setstopmark <SID>`. If you have not set the end mark/stopmark before starting an import, `tp` will automatically execute this command and place a stopmark at the end of the existing import queue right after the import command has been issued.

To manually remove an end mark/stopmark, open the import queue from the TMS import screen by choosing **Queue • Open**. The operating system equivalent is the command `tp delstopmark <SID>`. This command is normally not needed because `tp` will automatically remove the marker after an import process has been successfully completed.

### tp Commands for Import Buffers

In addition to the `tp` commands already mentioned, you can use the `tp` commands listed in Table 14.2 to access and maintain the import buffers.

**Warning** When you access import buffers, it mostly results in mixing up the correct order of the change requests and thus may cause serious inconsistencies. These `tp` commands should be used only in exceptional cases.

| Command | Description |
| --- | --- |
| `tp showbuffer <SID>` | Displays the buffer entries of the specified SAP system. |
| `tp addtobuffer <change request> <SID>` | Adds the specified change request as the last request to be imported, and therefore places it at the end of the import buffer of the specified SAP system. If the change request has already been added to this buffer, it will be removed from its current position and placed at the end of the buffer. |
| `tp delfrombuffer <change request> <SID>` | Deletes the specified change request from the import buffer of the specified SAP system. |
| `tp cleanbuffer <SID>` | Removes successfully imported change requests from the import buffer of the specified SAP system. If you perform an import of an entire queue (that is, an *import all*), `tp` automatically executes this command at the end of the import. |

**Table 14.2** tp commands affecting import buffers

All commands listed in Table 14.2 affect both the import buffer and the related import queue. If you execute any of these `tp` commands on the operating system level, you must refresh the import queue display in the TMS to see the results.

**Note** The import buffer is the basis of all operations, regardless of whether `tp` is called through the TMS or on the operating system level.

### 14.1.4 Performing Imports Using tp

Although SAP recommends that you use the TMS to perform imports, you may need to use `tp` commands for the following reasons:

- To script the import process so that it can be automated and scheduled
- If you use third-party tools

The `tp` commands allow you to perform imports of all change requests (*import all*) as well as imports of single change requests (*preliminary imports*).

#### Importing All Change Requests

To import all the change requests in the import buffer, execute the `tp` command `tp import all <target SID> [client=<target client number>`.

If you are using the TMS to import an entire queue, the TMS will automatically trigger the above `tp` command on the operating system level. This command imports all change requests before the end mark/stopmark in their export sequence into the target system and specified target client number. If no target client number is provided, the change requests are imported into a target client with the same client ID as the source client.

As already mentioned in Chapter 6, if change requests near the start of the import and change requests near the end of the import affect the same object, the version of the object at the end of the import will overwrite the earlier versions with the latest changes. This ensures that incorrect object versions that have been corrected will not affect your production environment (see also the section "tp Processing Sequence" later in this chapter).

**Note** The command `tp import` is reentrant. If an error occurs during import, after you have eliminated the cause of the error and restarted `tp`, `tp` will automatically restart the import at the point where it was interrupted.

#### Importing Individual Change Requests

To import a single change request, execute the `tp` command `tp import <change request> <target SID> client=<target client number> u0`. This `tp` command is the operating system equivalent of the TMS function **preliminary import**.

**Note** To ensure object dependencies and consistency, SAP strongly recommends using the **import all** function.

To ensure that the objects that were imported individually are not overwritten by an older version, always use the preliminary import option u0 (see the section "Import Options") to import individual change requests. If you use this import option, the change request will remain in the import queue. When the entire import queue is later imported, the request will automatically be imported again in the correct export sequence.

SAP recommends avoiding the import of individual requests without this import option, because the export sequence will not be maintained. Consequently, newer versions of objects may be overwritten by older versions when the entire import queue is imported.

### Import Options

When performing imports in the TMS, you can select import options using the expert mode (see Chapter 13). Import options are also referred to as unconditional modes. On the operating system level, *unconditional modes* are options that you can assign to tp commands to override specific rules of the Change and Transport System (CTS).

Each unconditional mode is represented by a digit. To use an unconditional mode, add a leading u followed by a concatenated list of single digits representing the different unconditional modes that should affect the tp command. For example, if you want to import a change request that should be kept in the import queue after the import, add u0. If you additionally want to ignore that originals in the target system are overwritten by imported objects, you can simply specify u02 as follows: tp import <change request> <SID> u02.

**Note** Use unconditional modes carefully. SAP recommends transporting according to the rules of the Change and Transport System (CTS).

Table 14.3 lists the unconditional modes that you can use in conjunction with tp commands for performing imports.

| Unconditional Mode | Description |
|---|---|
| 0 | This option is used to preliminarily import a change request. After import, the change request remains in the import buffer and is marked to be imported again. This import option is also called *overtaker*. |
| 1 | Despite the fact that the change request has already been imported, tp will import it again when the entire import queue is imported. |

**Table 14.3** Unconditional Modes

| Unconditional Mode | Description |
|---|---|
| 2 | Objects in change requests will overwrite the original objects in the target system. |
| 6 | Objects in change requests will overwrite objects that are currently being repaired in the target system and that have not yet been confirmed. |
| 8 | This option will ignore transport restrictions for table delivery classes. |
| 9 | This option will override certain transport profile settings that otherwise would have prevented the change request from being imported. For example, despite the fact that the transport profile parameter `t_import` has been set to FALSE, change requests resulting from a transport of copies (type **T**) will be imported. |

**Table 14.3** Unconditional Modes (cont.)

In the import buffer in column **Umode** and also in the import queue in column **U modes** in the TMS, you may find a character that indicates certain conditions for the next `import all` caused by a previous import with the overtaker option (`u0`). Table 14.4 lists the possible letters and the corresponding conditions for the next import of all change requests waiting for import.

| Indicator | Description |
|---|---|
| I | The import of the change request will be repeated from the beginning. |
| J | The import of the change request into the respective client is repeated from the beginning, but client-independent objects are not imported again. |
| F | The buffer entry is in the wrong position. `tp` will resolve this problem by implicitly executing the command `tp addtobuffer`. |

**Table 14.4** Indicator in the Import Buffer

### Importing into Multiple Clients

As of Release 4.5, to perform imports into multiple clients, you can use the TMS and its import options and the extended transport control (see Chapter 13). If you don't use the extended transport control, you must carry out imports at operating-system level using `tp` with specific information.

To import change requests into the client with the same number as the source client, execute a regular `tp` command without any import options: `tp import all <target SID>`. This can be bypassed by specifying the client name as follows: `tp import all <target SID> client=<target client number>`.

These commands will ensure that a single client receives all client-dependent changes recorded in the change requests and that the SAP system will receive all client-independent changes. However, if there are several target clients, you encounter problems because:

- Only one target client can be specified.
- The change request will be deleted from the import buffer after a successful import and therefore cannot be imported into other R/3 clients.

This will result in problems if other clients are waiting to receive the changes. One solution is to specify the preliminary import option u0. This import option will keep the change request in the buffer so that it can be imported again when the entire import queue is imported.

**Example: Importing into Multiple Clients**

A company's quality assurance system has three clients:

- Client 100 for business integration validation
- Client 200 for testing data migration routines
- Client 300 for user training

Because the company is using Release 4.0B, they do not have the option of using the extended transport control with its client-specific transport routes. Therefore, the import queue of the quality assurance system contains a list of change requests that need to be imported into all three clients. To import into the three clients, the system administrator will execute the following *tp* commands:

```
tp import all QAS client=100 u0
tp import all QAS client=200 u0
tp import all QAS client=300
```

The last command is the import command for the last remaining client. At this point, all clients have been delivered with the changes—the change requests are no longer needed in the import queue. To delete the change requests from the import buffer after the import, the system administrator can leave out the import option u0.

### Setting a Stopmark

A stopmark prevents all change requests that are positioned after the stopmark in the queue from being imported. This also applies to change requests that are released during a running import, because they are placed after the stopmark in the import queue.

`tp` automatically sets a stopmark at the beginning of an import and removes it at the end of the import. This removal is a problem when importing into multiple clients, because subsequent imports will include change requests that were after the stopmark in the previous imports.

As a solution, `tp` does not remove the stopmark after import when the overtaker option (`u0`) is used.

If you have an earlier `tp` version, there is still a way to perform imports into multiple clients. In this case, you have to add one stopmark explicitly for each client into which you will import before starting the first import to ensure that all clients receive the same change requests. These additional stopmarks prevent change requests from being added to the import buffer between the import processes. Although this option will technically work, SAP recommends that you have the latest version of `tp` for your release as listed above.

### 14.1.5 tp Processing Sequence

The contents of the import buffer are organized as a table. Each column represents an import phase, except the last one, which specifies the import option (UMODE). The numbers in the columns indicate whether the import step is necessary or the number of objects in the request that require the step. Figure 14.2 shows an example of an import buffer. The transport control program `tp` does not process all import steps for one request before proceeding to the next change request. Instead, `tp` collectively processes each import step for all change requests in an import queue before proceeding with the next import step.

During an import, a change request passes through nine *import phases*. These phases are shown in Figure 14.2. The import phases are the technical names for the *import steps* in the `tp` processing sequence. Only the import phase ACTIV contains more than one import step (see Table 14.5 in the next subsection).

During an `import all`, `tp` first processes any changes requests containing changes to the ABAP Dictionary—that is, `tp` first imports these objects. This occurs during the **ABAP Dictionary import** phase (DDIC). In Figure 14.2, the change requests `DEVK900069` and `DEVK900092` contain such changes and are therefore processed by `tp` in the first phase. In the second phase (ACTIV), `tp` activates any objects that have been imported in phase DDIC. In Figure 14.2, this again affects change requests `DEVK900069` and `DEVK900092`. In the third phase, `tp` returns to the first request in the list, and performs the main import (MAIN I) for that change request and then all subsequent change requests in the buffer. This continues until each phase has been completed for all requests in the import queue. The required steps for each change request are listed in the import buffer.

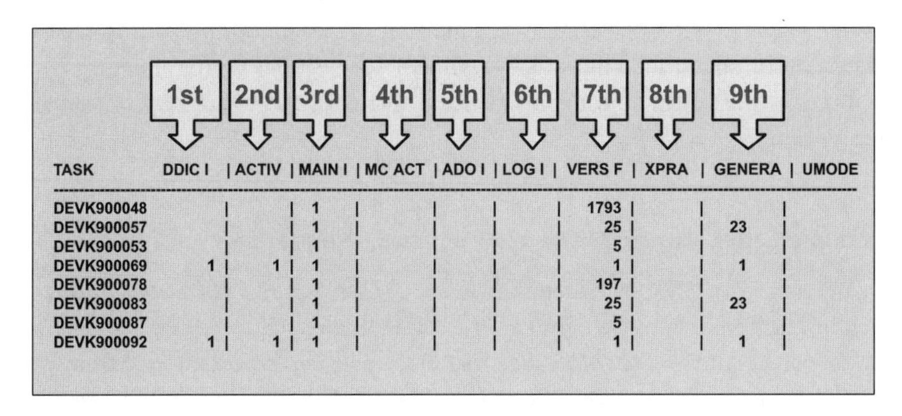


| TASK | DDIC I | ACTIV | MAIN I | MC ACT | ADO I | LOG I | VERS F | XPRA | GENERA | UMODE |
|---|---|---|---|---|---|---|---|---|---|---|
| DEVK900048 | | | 1 | | | | 1793 | | | |
| DEVK900057 | | | 1 | | | | 25 | | 23 | |
| DEVK900053 | | | 1 | | | | 5 | | | |
| DEVK900069 | 1 | 1 | 1 | | | | 1 | | 1 | |
| DEVK900078 | | | 1 | | | | 197 | | | |
| DEVK900083 | | | 1 | | | | 25 | | 23 | |
| DEVK900087 | | | 1 | | | | 5 | | | |
| DEVK900092 | 1 | 1 | 1 | | | | 1 | | 1 | |

**Figure 14.2** tp processing sequence for imports

Processing the import buffer in a particular sequence of phases technically and logically allows the import of multiple change requests for the following reasons:

- Dictionary structures (such as table structures) are imported and activated prior to the main import phase. The current structures are thereby able to "receive" new data (such as table entries) that may be imported in the same or another change request during the main import phase.
- The Repository objects with the fewest dependencies (the ABAP Dictionary objects) are imported and checked for consistency before ABAP programs and screen definitions are imported. This is important because these objects tend to highly depend on proper ABAP Dictionary settings.
- Since ABAP program generation takes place after the main import process, only the last imported version of the programs and screens is activated. Consider this situation: A "bad" version of a program is released and exported, and then corrected in a change request released later. Even though the bad version was imported, it is quickly overwritten during the main import phase with the "good" version of the program that is contained in the latest change. When the generation phase eventually takes place, only the correct version of the program is generated.
- The amount of import time required for importing multiple change requests is lower than that needed for individual requests imported one at a time. Time is saved because standard activities and generic import steps (such as post-activation conversions) take place collectively for all change requests in the queue and not for each individual change request.

**Note** The processing sequence ensures that if you detect an error in a change request that has already been released, you can correct the object in a new change request. After releasing and exporting the change request, the next *import all* command then imports the whole import buffer in the sequence of export, and the faulty object is overwritten and does not affect your production system.

**Example: Advantages of the tp Processing Sequence**

Change requests DEVK900069 and DEVK900092 (see Figure 14.2 earlier in this section) both contain changes to the same table structure. By mistake, DEVK900069 contains a "bad" change that deletes a very important field from a table containing critical data. Through testing in the quality assurance system, the error is detected before DEVK90069 is imported into the production system. Change request DEVK900092 is released from the development system to correct the problem by redefining the field in its original state. Because the change requests are imported in the proper sequence, as is the case with tp processing, the bad change does not affect the production system, and the data in the important field is not deleted. While the bad table structure is imported in the first phase during ABAP Dictionary import, the corrected version of the table structure is then imported and overwrites what is faulty. The table structure activated during import is the table structure imported in change request DEVK900092. The table structure in change request DEVK900069 is never activated in the production system.

### Import Steps

The import process includes several import steps (see Table 14.5) that are performed by different transport tools. All of these steps are coordinated by tp. Phase ACTIV is the only phase that contains more than one import step. In addition to the activation of ABAP Dictionary objects, this phase includes the generic import steps: distribution, structure conversion, and the moving of nametabs. Generic steps are not related to certain change requests, but are performed for all change requests in one step. Another generic step is the enqueue conversion, which is performed in the phase MC CONV. Note that you cannot display the log files related to generic steps using the TMS. However, you can view them on the operating system level.

For each import step, Table 14.5 lists the character (a letter or number) that is used to represent the step in the different log files and a description that includes the transport tool involved.

| Import Phase | Import Step | Char. | Description | Supporting Transport Tool |
|---|---|---|---|---|
| DDIC I | Import of ABAP Dictionary objects | H | To enable imports into production systems, the transport program `R3trans` imports the ABAP Dictionary structures inactively. | `R3trans` |
| ACTIV | Activation of ABAP Dictionary objects | A | Runtime descriptions (nametabs) are written inactively, but during this phase, the steps required for activation are initiated. | `RDDMASGL` |
| ACTIV | Distribution of ABAP Dictionary objects | S | Logical checks decide what additional actions are required to bring the new ABAP Dictionary objects into the running system. | `RDDGENBB (job name: RDDDISOL)` |
| ACTIV | Structure conversion | N | ABAP Dictionary structural changes are made. | `RDDGENBB (job name: RDDGENOL)` |
| ACTIV | Move nametabs | 6 | The new ABAP runtime objects are put into the active runtime environment. | `pgmvntabs` |
| MAIN I | Main import | I | Import of all data including table entries. | `R3trans` |
| MC ACT | Activation and conversion of enqueue objects | M | Enqueue objects such as matchcodes that were not previously activated are now activated. These objects are used immediately in the running system. | `RDDGENBB` |
| ADO I | Import of application defined objects (ADOs) | D | Import of additional objects including SAPscript forms and styles, and printer definitions. | `RDDDIC1L` |
| LOG I | Logical import | U | This phase is currently not active and is ignored during the import process. | |
| VERS F | Versioning | V | Versions of Repository objects are created on the R/3 System from which the objects were exported. The import process modifies the object's *Version counter*, which is incremented during this step for all Repository objects imported. | `RDDVERSL` |

**Table 14.5** Import steps

| Import Phase | Import Step | Char. | Description | Supporting Transport Tool |
|---|---|---|---|---|
| XPRA | Execution of post-import methods | R | Post-import methods are required activities (such as the execution of an ABAP program) that rely on transported data. | RDDEXECL |
| GENERA | Generation of ABAP programs and screens | G | The generation of imported objects. | RDDDIC03L |

**Table 14.5** Import steps (cont.)

From the beginning of the step that moves nametabs until the end of the main import, inconsistencies may occur in the SAP system. After the main import phase, these inconsistencies will be removed because the SAP system returns to a consistent state. However, it is not until after the generation of ABAP programs and screens at the end of the import process that you can be assured business activities in the SAP system will be unaffected (see "R/3 Buffer Synchronization" below for more details).

## 14.2 Using Log Files for Troubleshooting

Occasionally, you will encounter problems during import. The information provided in the following areas will help you to solve these problems:

- Log files stored in the transport subdirectory `log`
  - Generic log files
  - Single step log files
- Return codes

In addition to this information, certain troubleshooting techniques will prove beneficial in remedying errors to ensure a successful import.

### 14.2.1 Generic Log Files

The transport control program `tp` creates and writes three *generic log files*: the SLOG file (more commonly known as the `TP` System Log), the ALOG file (referred to as the Transport Step Monitor), and the ULOG file.

The `TP` System Log that reports the contents of the SLOG file is accessed from within TMS (Transaction STMS) using the menu option **Overview · Imports · Goto · TP System Log** (see Chapter 13). The `TP` System Log contains a general overview of performed imports, including the respective return code, and thus indicates the success of each import. You can use the `TP` System Log to monitor the transport activities of a specific SAP system. To set the name of the SLOG file in the transport profile, use the global transport parameter syslog. The default naming convention is SLOG($syear)($yweek).($system), where ($syear) represents the calendar year, ($yweek) is the week of the year, and ($system) is the system ID for the SAP system.

The Transport Step Monitor that reports the contents of the ALOG file is accessed from within TMS (Transaction STMS) using the menu option **Overview • Imports • Goto • TP System Log • Goto • Transport step** (see Chapter 13). The Transport Step Monitor records the return codes for all transport steps handled in the common transport directory. To set the name of the ALOG file in the transport profile, use the global transport parameter alllog. The default value is ALOG($syear)($yweek), where ($syear) represents the calendar year and ($yweek) is the week of the year. Each entry in the ALOG file represents a single step log file from within the Transport Step Monitor.

The ULOG file records all tp commands that have been executed and are free of syntax errors. This log uses the naming convention ULOG($syear)_<one digit>, where ($syear) represents the current calendar year and the single digit represents the quarter of the year. For example, ULOG05_4 specifies the log for the fourth quarter—October, November, and December—of the year 2005. The file contents are organized as a table consisting of a row for each tp command and three columns containing the following information:

- The operating system user who issued the tp command
- The time stamp
- The complete tp command executed on the operating system level containing all options and paths

**Tip** The ULOG file is not available from within TMS, but can be viewed on the operating system level in the transport directory log.

### 14.2.2 Single Step Log Files

For each import step, the respective transport tool, either R3trans or one of the ABAP programs involved (whose names all begin with "RDD"), writes a log file to the transport directory. The log files are written to the subdirectory tmp. At the end of an import, tp moves all log files contained in subdirectory tmp to subdirectory log (see Figure 14.3).

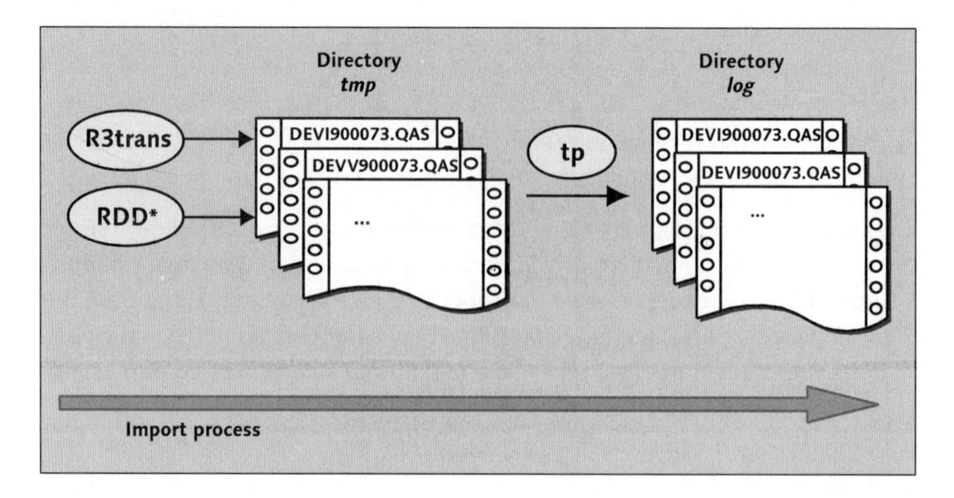


**Figure 14.3** Single step log files

Each log file contains a list of message texts containing either information, warnings, or errors, which reflect the results of the respective import step. At the end of the log file, the exit or return code of the transport tool is specified. This code indicates the overall success of the import step.

Table 14.6 lists log files for the sample change request `DEVK900021` after all import steps have been performed. The naming convention for single step log files is `<source SID><import step><6 digits>.<target SID>`. The import step is represented by a single character (see Table 14.5 earlier in this chapter). The six digits following the import step denote the corresponding change request.

The generic import steps—distribution, structure conversion, move nametabs, and enqueue conversion—are not related to certain change requests like the other steps. These log files cannot be displayed in the TMS. The naming convention for these log files is `<import step><year><month><day>.<target SID>`.

| Log File | Import Step | Import Phase |
|---|---|---|
| `DEVH900021.QAS` | Dictionary import | DDIC I |
| `DEVA900021.QAS` | Dictionary activation | ACTIV |
| `DS991005.QAS` | Distribution | ACTIV |
| `N991005.QAS` | Structure conversion | ACTIV |
| `P991005.QAS` | Move nametabs | ACTIV |
| `DEVI900021.QAS` | Main import | MAIN I |

**Table 14.6** Possible import log files generated for sample change request DEVK900021

| Log File | Import Step | Import Phase |
|---|---|---|
| DEVMS900021.QAS | Activation of the enqueue definitions | MC ACT |
| N991005.QAS | Enqueue conversion | MC CONV |
| DEVD900021.QAS | Import of ADOs | ADO I |
| DEVV900021.QAS | Versioning | VERS F |
| DEVR900021.QAS | Execution of XPRAs | XPRA |
| DEVG900021.QAS | Generation of ABAP programs and screens | GENERA |

**Table 14.6** Possible import log files generated for sample change request DEVK900021 (cont.)

### 14.2.3 Return Codes

Each transport tool involved in the import process exits with a *return code* to tp that is also recorded in the respective log file. In addition, tp may receive signals and messages from the operating system or the database. tp interprets the return codes and calculates its own return code, which indicates the result of the whole import process (see Figure 14.4).

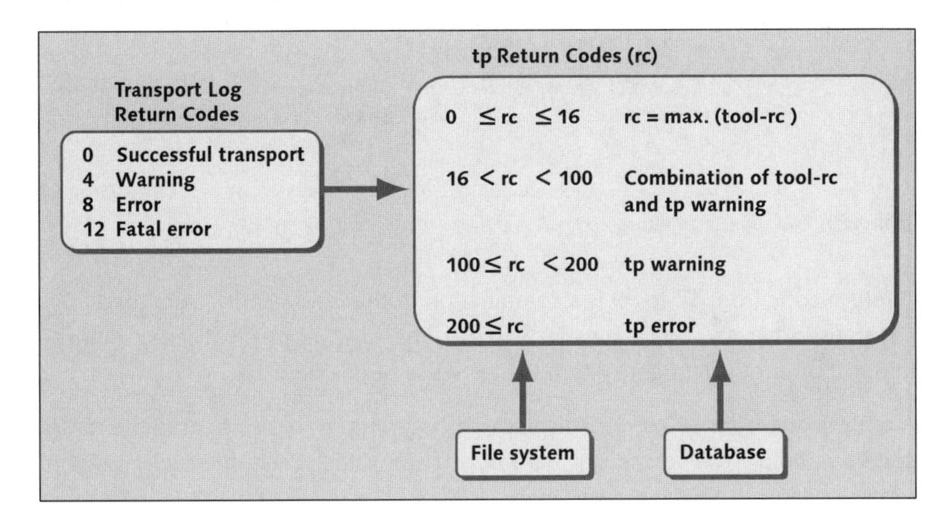


**Figure 14.4** Return codes

Typically, tp receives return codes only from the transport tools that have a value between zero and 16 (see Table 14.7). The overall success of the import then depends on the highest return code that has occurred in an import step. If no other problems occurred, tp will display the return code with the highest value received from a transport tool. This is called the *maximum return code*.

By default, if tp receives a return code larger than eight during an import phase, tp will abort the import process. The transport profile parameter stoponerror defines which return code value will cause tp to abort.

| Return Code | Description | Example |
|---|---|---|
| 0 | The transport activities were successful. | |
| 4 | Warnings occurred during the transport. All objects were transported successfully, but irregularities occurred. | A change request contains an object deletion. |
| 8 | The transport was carried out with errors; however, there is at least one object that could not be transported successfully. | An ABAP program had a syntax error and, while imported, was not able to be generated due to the error. |
| 12 | The transport was terminated. A serious error occurred, but was not caused by the contents of a change request. | During the import process, the database of the SAP system was unavailable for import—for example, because of a lack of tablespace. |
| 13 | The transport tool was terminated by a signal from the operating system. | R3trans contains a serious error. |
| 16 | The transport tool terminated due to an internal error. | There is a possible development error in tp or R3trans for which you will need to contact SAP's Hotline for assistance. |

**Table 14.7** Examples of tp return codes

A return code from 17 to 99 is a combination of the return codes from the different transport tools. This results in a tp warning, such as one indicating that the import buffer of the target system has no write permission.

A return code from 100 to 199 displays a tp warning. tp has calculated the return code by adding 100 to the original return code value. There are two groups of return codes resulting in tp warnings:

- Return codes from 100 to 149 indicate "normal" tp warnings—that is, tp could not perform all tasks. For example, RDDIMPDP could not be triggered by the program sapevt. To evaluate this kind of return code, refer to its last two digits.
- Return codes from 150 to 199 are rare and indicate incorrect user operation. For example, if tp tries to import a change request that is not included in the import buffer, the return code 152 will be displayed. To evaluate the return code, refer to its last two digits.

A return code of 200 or more indicates a `tp error`. For example, if `tp` could not access a file as required by the import process, the return code 212 will be displayed.

**Tip** To display the text of a specific `tp` return code, use the `tp` command `tp explainrc <value of return code>`.

### 14.2.4 Troubleshooting Techniques

At the beginning of the implementation phase of an SAP system landscape or after TMS configuration changes, SAP recommends using the Alert Monitor, which records all TMS transport activities, to eliminate the obvious TMS setup issues. To call the Alert Monitor, use Transaction STMS and choose **Monitor • Alert monitor**. The following information is displayed for each TMS function:

- Date and time
- Username
- TMS status message
- Target R/3 System

To display the full text of an error message, double-click the error message. The Alert Monitor reveals mainly TMS configuration errors and TMS connection errors. Once your TMS configuration is stable, you can detect the cause of errors and problems in the related log files.

Once your TMS configuration is stable, always use the import monitor in the TMS to ensure that imports run smoothly. If the import monitor indicates problems and errors, SAP recommends performing the following steps:

1. Use TP System Log in TMS (or the SLOG file on the operating system level) to monitor the transport activities of an SAP system and determine the results of an import.
2. If import failures are recorded in the TP System Log, drill down to the Transport Step Monitor in TMS (or the ALOG file at the operating system level) and locate the import step that sent the return code listed in the TP System Log.
3. From the Transport Step Monitor, locate the log file for the specific change request that produced the error and evaluate the cause of the problem. Note that although all transport log files for a specific change request can be viewed from within TMS (see Chapter 12 and Chapter 13), single log files of generic import steps cannot be displayed using the TMS.

These steps can be performed either in SAP ECC or on the operating system level. The procedure for using the TMS in SAP ECC is described in the following example.

**Example: Troubleshooting an Import Problem**

As shown in the following graphic, there are four change requests in the import queue of system PRD.

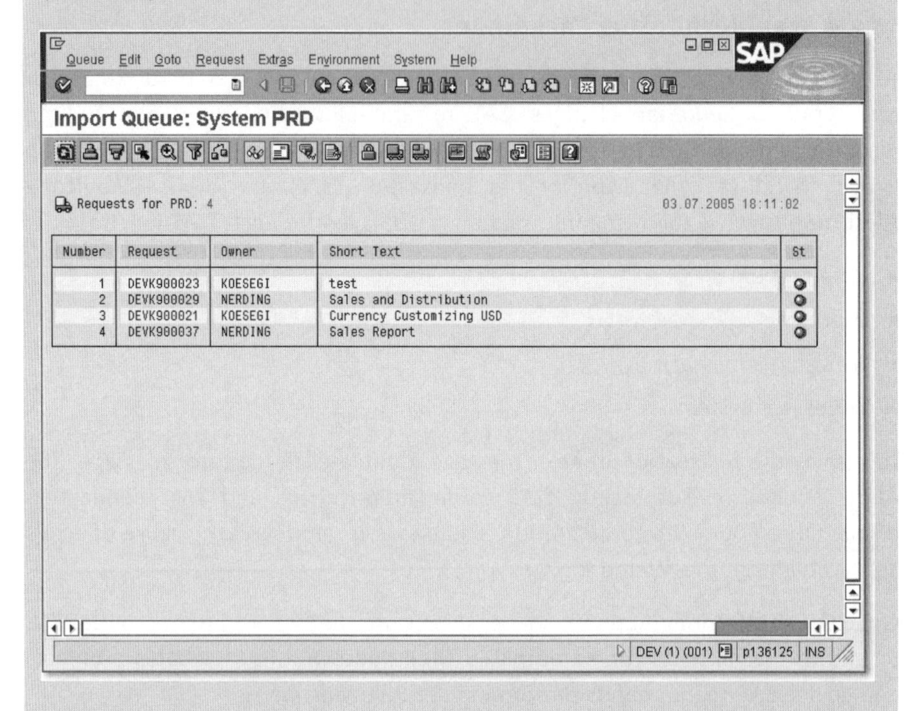


Figure 14.5 Change requests in the import queue of system PRD

From the import queue screen of PRD, the import is started using **Queue • Start import**.

The import process is monitored by choosing **Goto • Import monitor**. The display is refreshed using **Refresh**. The following graphic shows the import monitor as the import is finished (status **tp finished**). It shows that the import process resulted in a maximum return code of 0008. The return code indicates that errors occurred during the import process by `tp`, but no other details are provided, so you must check where and why the error occurred.

To check whether this error originates from setup errors, from the TMS menu, choose **Monitor • Alert monitor**. In this example, the Alert Monitor has not recorded any errors for the time frame of this import (screen not depicted).

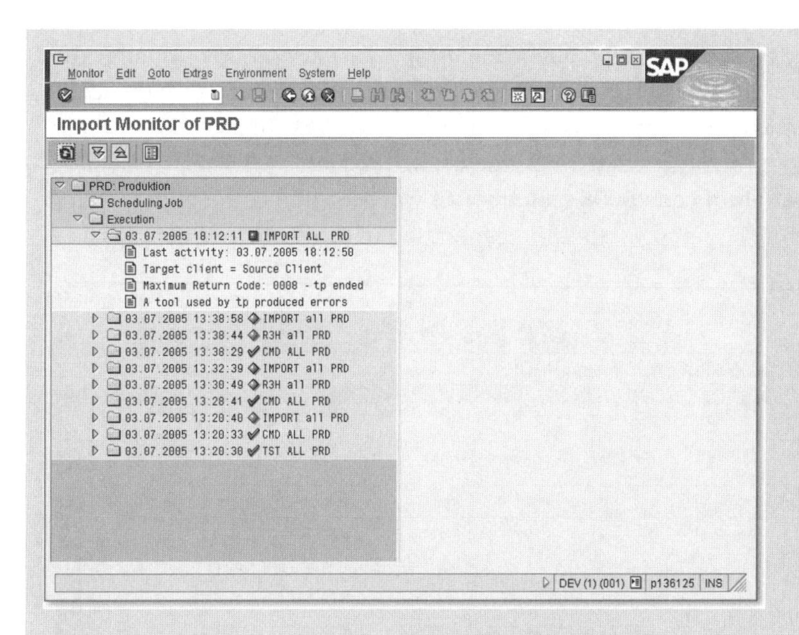


Figure 14.6 Import monitor screen after completed import

In the next step, the TP System Log is checked using **Goto · TP system log** from the import monitor screen. As shown in the following graphic, the TP System Log indicates that the import has been completed and that it ended with a return code of eight (0008 in the fifth row from the bottom).

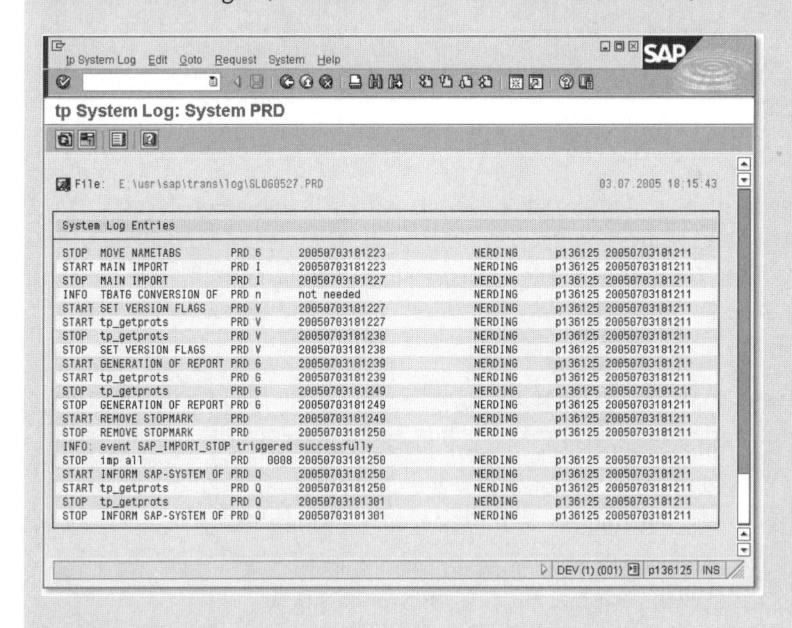


Figure 14.7 TP System Log

To display more information about the error, the Transport Step Monitor (the log file ALOG) in the TMS is opened using **Goto • Transport steps** from the screen **TP System Log: System QAS**. As shown in the following graphic, the Transport Step Monitor indicates that when the change request DEVK900037 was processed, the return code 0008 (column **RC**) was sent during the import step G (column **S**). This import step is the **generation of programs and dynpros**.

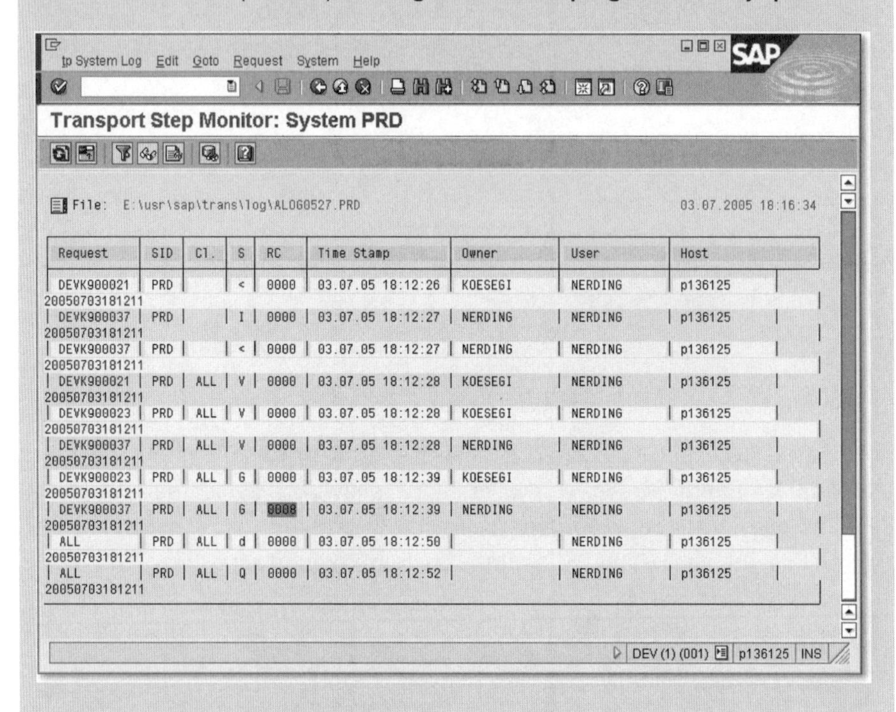


**Figure 14.8** Transport step monitor

Now that the change request that caused the error has been located, the respective single log file is accessed. To do this, the cursor is positioned on change request DEVK900037. Then, **Request • Logs** is chosen from screen **Transport Step Monitor: System PRD**. As shown in the following graphic, an overview of all transport logs is given.

In the screen **Overview of transport logs**, the log file for the import step **Generation of programs and dynpros** is highlighted and listed with a return code of eight.

To display the log file for this import step, the highlighted line is double-clicked.

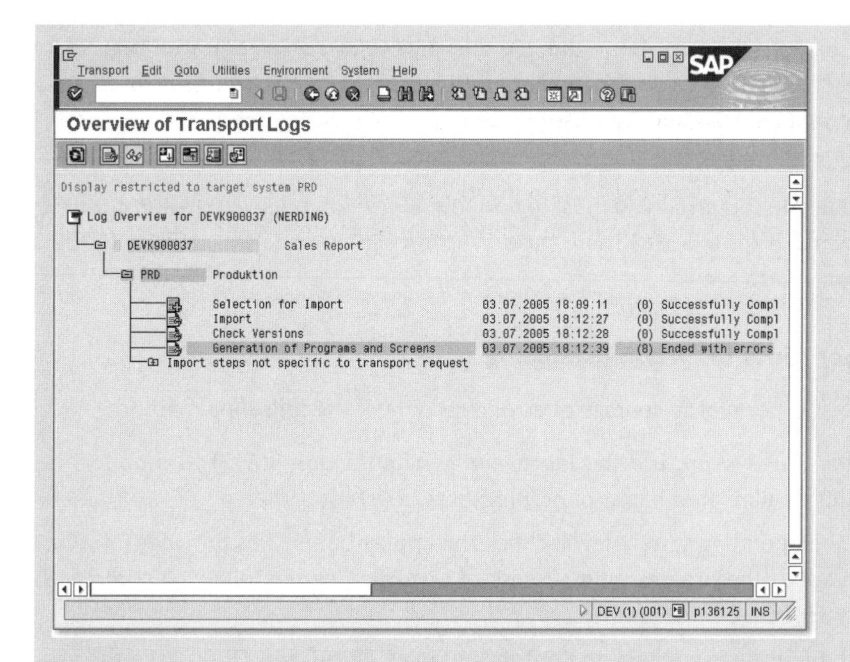


Figure 14.9 Overview of transport logs

As shown in the following graphic, the single step log file for the import step **Generation of programs and dynpros** is displayed.

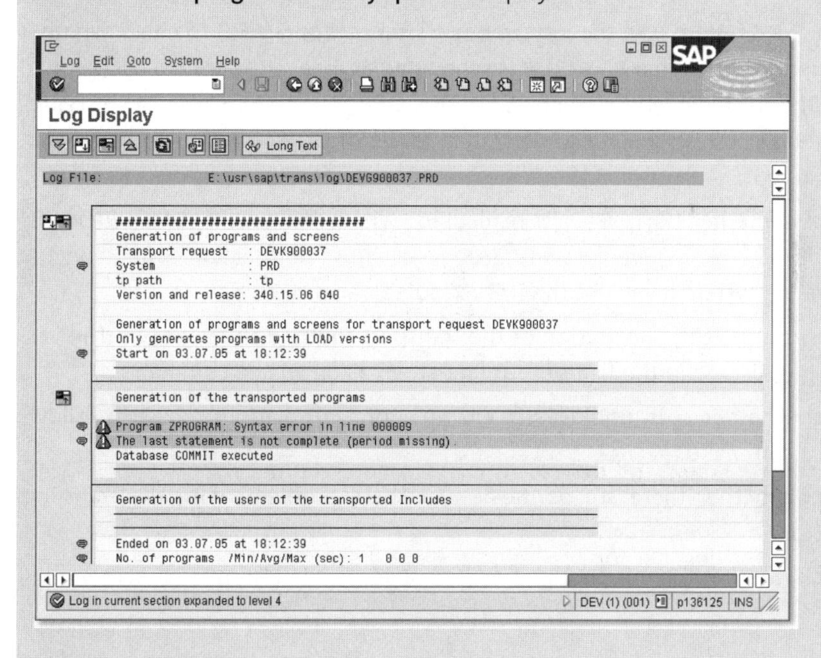


Figure 14.10 Single step log file

The previous section from the log file DEVG900037.PRD indicates that the change request DEVK900037 includes the program ZPROGRAM. The program could not be activated because line 9 contains a syntax error. Although the report was implemented, it could not be generated.

To eliminate this error, you must log on to the development system and correct the syntax error in SE38. Then, the correction can be imported along with the faulty request.

### Further Hints for Troubleshooting

To detect other typical sources of errors, use any of the following methods:

- In the SAP system, use the job overview (Transaction SM37) to monitor the results of all related background processes (RDD*-jobs).
- On the operating system level, check the import buffer. This provides information about the progress and success of imports. Use the following command: `tp showbuffer <target SID>`.
- In the SAP system, check the entries in tables TRBAT and TRJOB (see the section "Communication between `tp` and ABAP Programs"). You should also compare them with the log file and import buffer entries on the operating system level.
- In the SAP system, use the job overview (Transaction SM37) to check whether the import dispatcher RDDIMPDP is scheduled as an event-periodic background job. The related event has to be SAP_TRIGGER_RDDIMPDP. You can also perform this check on the operating system level using the following `tp` command: `tp checkimp <target SID>`.
- Check whether RDDIMPDP is executed when the event SAP_TRIGGER_RDDIMPDP is triggered. In the SAP system, use Transaction SM64; on the operating system level, use the R/3 executable `sapevt`.
- If necessary, verify the version of the transport tools `tp` and `R3trans`. The version is indicated in the first output line after calling any `tp` command.
- Check whether `tp` is running—for example, on Unix platforms, use the following `tp` command: `ps -ef | grep tp`.
- Check whether there are permission or share problems with the transport directory.
- Check whether there is enough free disk space in the transport directory.

## 14.3 R/3 Buffer Synchronization

To reduce database accesses and network load, as well as improve system performance, frequently used data in an SAP system is stored in R/3 buffers. These buffers are located in the shared memory of an application server. Every work process in an instance accesses these buffers. Data stored in the R/3 buffers includes ABAP program, screens, ABAP Dictionary data, and company-specific data, which normally remains unchanged during system operation.

If an SAP system consists of several instances on multiple application servers, changes to data stored in the local buffers of the application servers must be updated at regular intervals. This prevents inconsistencies between the local buffers on each instance. The synchronization process is asynchronous to minimize network load. Imports into an SAP system may also affect R/3 buffers, because imported objects can be objects that are stored in one of the R/3 buffers. Therefore, central systems with only one instance should also be synchronized.

Due to the required amount of network and database accesses, updating buffers places a high load on the system. In large systems, it may take two to three hours for performance to stabilize again after a complete buffer reset. You must take this into consideration when importing change requests.

**Warning** Importing data into a production system can significantly impact performance.

Data inconsistencies can occur if an application server reads data from its buffer between two synchronization procedures. If, at the time of access, the data is being processed by another server or is in the process of being imported, it will not be up to date. The following examples illustrate the risk of temporary and permanent inconsistencies when importing changes into production systems.

**Example: Temporary Inconsistencies**

A change to the structure of a table—that is, a Dictionary change—has been entered by an import into an SAP system. Before the buffers are synchronized, a dependent program is loaded. The program is generated with the old structure and saved with a time stamp indicating a time after the new structure was imported and activated. After the subsequent buffer synchronization, the program retains the incorrect structure. This is an inconsistency that cannot be easily detected. When this dependent program runs, the work area of the table will no longer match the structure used when the work area was generated. When the program is executed, it will terminate with the runtime error GETWA_CANT_CLEAR. To correct the inconsistency, you must manually regenerate all the related programs that are listed in the short dump.

**Example: Permanent Inconsistencies**

Program A is being generated in the production system, so the database sets a lock on the program data. While program A is being generated, `tp` imports an include program, on which both programs A and B depend. During buffer synchronization, the system tries to set a new change time stamp for programs A and B. Although the time stamp is specified, it cannot be set because program A is still being generated and is thus locked by the database.

After program A has been generated, the system sets a generation time stamp for program A, and the database lock is removed. The program then tries to set the change time stamp for programs A and B. Program B is regenerated because its last generation time stamp was set before the change time stamp. Program A, however, will not be regenerated because its most recent generation time stamp was set after the change time stamp was determined. The program retains the old structure. Consequently, this inconsistency will remain in the SAP system until program A is changed.

Temporary inconsistencies are less critical than permanent ones because temporary inconsistencies exist only until the transaction is restarted. Restarting the transaction causes the buffers to be synchronized, which restores the consistency between the object and the buffers.

**Warning** Transporting programs and ABAP Dictionary data can cause both temporary and permanent inconsistencies if they affect running programs and their environment. SAP recommends scheduling imports into production systems to run at night in the background when there is low system load. Alternatively, you could perform a detailed check on the jobs that are running and monitor the effects carefully.

## 14.4 Naming Conventions in the Transport Directory

Chapter 7 introduced the transport directory and its subdirectories. Because the transport control program `tp` runs on many different operating systems, the files of the transport directory use restrictive naming conventions. The naming conventions are applied to the files automatically and can help you with troubleshooting. Once you have identified a change request that caused errors, you can use the naming conventions to access the related log files and find out how to resolve the errors.

Figure 14.11 illustrates the file naming conventions for the subdirectory files that are related to a specific change request. The sample change request `DEVK900073` serves as the basis for the subdirectory files. The user SMITH created the change request in the development system, DEV. There is a consolidation route between DEV and the quality assurance system, QAS. QAS is the first system into which the change request will be imported. Therefore, DEV is the source SID of this change request; QAS is the target SID.

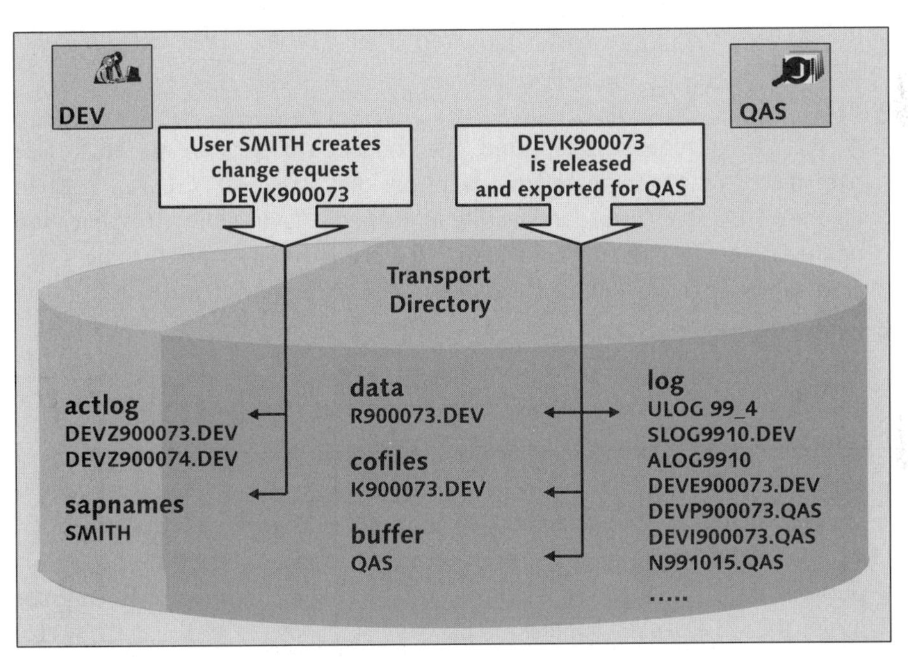


**Figure 14.11** Transport directory naming convention

As mentioned in Chapter 4, change requests are named following this convention: `<source SID>K9<5 digits>`. `K9` indicates that this is a customer change request. The subsequent five digits are a serial number. The naming convention for the subdirectories in the transport directory follows these rules:

- **actlog:**
  For each change request and also for each task, one file named <source SID>Z9<5 digits>.<source SID> is written. The file records each user action on the request or task—for example, creation, release, or change of ownership. In Figure 14.11, the files DEVZ900073.DEV for the change request and DEVZ900074.DEV for the only related task have been stored. If, for example, the owner of the task is changed, a new entry containing this action will be added to DEVZ900074.DEV.

- **sapnames:**
  A file is automatically created for each R/3 user who performs transport activities on a change request. This file is updated when the user releases a request. The naming convention is the user's logon name. In Figure 14.11, this file is named SMITH.

- **buffer:**
  When the change request is released, an entry is added to the import buffer for the target system, QAS. The naming convention for the import buffer is the SID of the target system. In Figure 14.11, the change request is added to the import buffer QAS.

- **data:**
  As the change request is exported, the contained objects are stored to files named according to this naming convention: R9<5 digits >.<source SID>. In Figure 14.11, the corresponding file is named R900073.DEV. If application defined objects (ADOs) are contained in the change request, another file is created, which begins with D9 instead of R9.

- **cofiles:**
  When exporting, a control file named K9<5 digits>.<source SID> is stored. This control file contains, for example, the import steps that have to be performed. The control file in Figure 14.11 is named K900073.DEV.

- **log:**
  Various log files are contained in this subdirectory. The generic log files ULOG, ALOG, and SLOG either get new entries or are created if they did not previously exist. The change request in Figure 14.11 was transported in October 1999. Thus, the generic log files are ULOG 99_4, SLOG9910.DEV, and ALOG9910. (For information on the naming convention of these files, see the section "Generic Log Files.") For each executed transport step, a single step log file is stored. Some sample log files related to the change request include DEVE900073.DEV, DEVP900073.DEV, DEVI900073.QAS, and N991015.QAS. (For information on the naming convention of these files, see the section "Single Step Log Files.")

### 14.4.1 Removing Files from the Transport Directory

In the course of time, many large files may accumulate in your transport directories. These files will become obsolete over time. Depending on your transport activities and your amount of free disk space, you should occasionally clean up the transport directory. This activity can be performed only on the operating system level using the appropriate `tp` commands. To clean up the transport directory, proceed as follows (see also Figure 14.12):

1. Execute the following command:

   `tp check all`

   This command reads all import buffers and searches in subdirectories `data`, `cofiles`, and `log` of the transport directory for files that are no longer needed. Such files refer to change requests that are no longer contained in any import buffer. The names of these files are listed in the file `ALL_OLD.LIS` in the transport subdirectory `tmp`.

2. Execute the following command:

   `tp clearold all`

   `tp` checks each file listed in `ALL_OLD.LIS` to determine whether it has exceeded a maximum age. The maximum age is specified in days by the transport profile parameters `datalifetime` (default 200), `olddatalifetime` (default 365), `cofilelifetime` (default 365), and `loglifetime` (default 200). `tp` then processes the files in the following way:

   - Data files in the transport subdirectory `data` that are older than the value specified in the parameter `datalifetime` are moved by `tp` to the transport subdirectory `olddata`.
   - Files in the subdirectories `log` and `cofiles` are immediately deleted by tp if they are older than the value specified by the parameter `loglifetime` or `cofilelifetime`.
   - Files in `olddata` are deleted if they are older than the value specified in the parameter `olddatalifetime`.

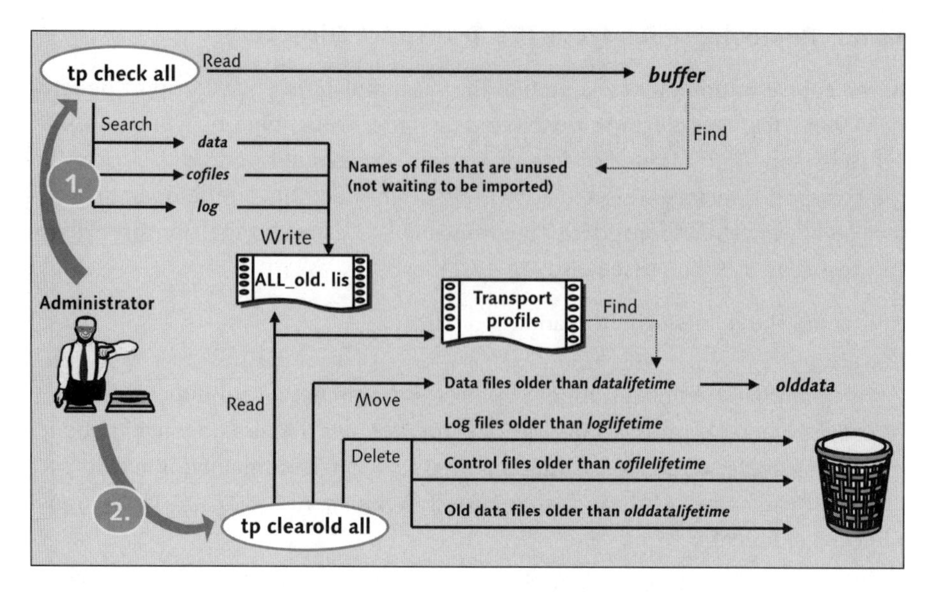


Figure 14.12 Cleaning up the transport directory

## 14.5 Understanding Transport Tools

The Change and Transport System (CTS) uses several transport tools to transport data to and from an SAP system. On the operating system level, these tools include the transport control program `tp` (`tp.exe` on Windows NT platforms), the transport program `R3trans` (`R3trans.exe` on Windows NT platforms), and the program `sapevt` (`sapevt.exe` on Windows NT platforms).

These tools are automatically installed as executables on the operating system level during the installation process of an SAP system. Note that they are not stored in the subdirectory `bin` of the transport directory, but in the following directory, which houses most R/3 executables:

- `/usr/sap/<SID>/SYS/exe/run` on Unix and AS/400 platforms
- `\usr\sap\<SID>\SYS\exe\run` on Windows NT platforms

**Tip** After an release upgrade, check the transport directory `bin`. If you find variants of the programs `tp` and `R3trans` that have been stored by a former release, delete the programs to ensure that the correct transport programs are used from the executable directory.

Several R/3 components are involved in performing transports. These include the transport dispatcher RDDIMPDP and several ABAP programs that carry out various steps required in the transport process—for example, generating imported reports. (See Table 14.8 later in this chapter in the column **ABAP Programs**.)

### 14.5.1 The Transport Program R3trans

`R3trans` is the transport tool on the operating system level that actually transports data between SAP systems. `R3trans` exports objects from the source database and stores them in data files on the operating system level. During import, `R3trans` reuses the data files and imports the objects into the target database.

The format of the data files written by `R3trans` is also known as `R3trans` format and is independent of the platform. Thus, you can transport data between different databases or operating systems. Additionally, upward compatibility is guaranteed; that is, you can export data with an old `R3trans` version and import the data with a newer version.

> **Note** Although exports and imports are independent of the `R3trans` version, the database platform, or the operating system, due to logical dependencies, SAP does not support using `tp` or `R3trans` for transports between different releases.

`R3trans` is called by other programs, such as `tp` and the upgrade control program `R3up`. Because `R3trans` is not the only tool needed to perform a complete and correct import of change requests, SAP does not recommend directly calling `R3trans`. Always use `tp` to ensure that all export and import steps, including `R3trans` activities, are completed successfully.

#### Transport Tool Interaction on the Operating System Level

On the operating system level, `tp` interacts with `R3trans`. In the import process, `tp` tracks the extracted objects, ensuring that they are added to the database of the target system. The interaction between `tp` and `R3trans` is depicted in Figure 14.13.

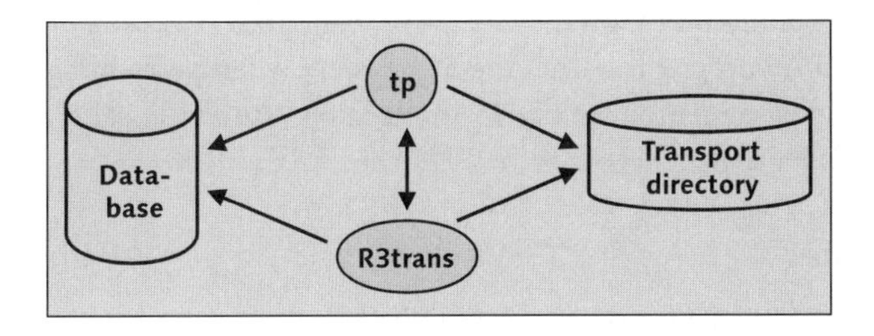


**Figure 14.13** Transport tool interaction on the operating system level

`tp` always reads the transport profile in the transport directory that determines how `tp` should behave. This transport file also specifies the host, database, and path information through certain parameter settings.

When starting an import, `tp` sets a stopmark at the end of the import buffer of the target system and reads the import buffer to determine which change requests have to be imported and which import steps have to be performed for which change request. In addition, `tp` reads the corresponding control file in the subdirectory `cofiles` for details on the steps to be performed.

`tp` passes a control file to the transport subdirectory `tmp` for use by `R3trans`. `tp` then calls `R3trans` by initiating a new process using the following operating system commands:

- `fork()` on Unix platforms
- `CreateProcess()` on Windows NT platforms
- `spawn()` on AS/400 platforms

`R3trans` reads the control file in the subdirectory `tmp`. This control file determines what activities `R3trans` should perform. `R3trans` reuses the data files that it stored to the subdirectory `data` during exports and connects to the database of the target system to import the objects. When importing objects to the target database, `R3trans` updates, inserts, and deletes data in the database.

`R3trans` is responsible for the import steps **ABAP dictionary import** for the import of ABAP Dictionary definitions and **main import** for the import of table contents (see the section "Import Steps").

`R3trans` always passes a return code to `tp` when exiting. For each transport action, `R3trans` writes a log file in the transport subdirectory `tmp`. After `R3trans` completes its work, `tp` interprets the return code from `R3trans` and moves its log file to the transport subdirectory `log`.

After the import process, `tp` cleans up the import buffer and removes the stopmark.

`R3trans` does not interact with the other transport tools. In contrast, `tp` communicates extensively with ABAP programs within the SAP system when performing certain steps in the target system (see below in the section "Communication between tp and ABAP Programs").

### 14.5.2 ABAP Programs

Importing change requests involves different ABAP programs within the SAP system, depending on the import steps that have to be performed—for example, activating the ABAP Dictionary, converting structures, or generating reports and screens. The ABAP programs are executed as background jobs.

**Note** Because the ABAP programs are executed as background jobs, there must be at least two background work processes running in the target R/3 System.

To execute the necessary transport steps, `tp` uses the control tables TRBAT and TRJOB to communicate with the various ABAP programs. TRBAT and TRJOB are control tables that contain temporary data. After reading the control file (subdirectory `cofiles`) for the import of a change request, `tp` writes entries to the control table TRBAT, specifying the steps to be performed for the respective request. Table 14.8 lists the ABAP programs, the related job name, a description of the function, and the function code specifying the function to be performed in table TRBAT.

| Function Code | Job Name | ABAP Program | Description |
|---|---|---|---|
| X | RDDDICOL | RDDDICOL | ADO export |
| J | RDDMASGL | RDDMASGL | Mass activator (new) |
| B | RDDTACOL | RDDTACOL | TACOB activator |
| S | RDDDISOL | RDDGENBB | Distributor |
| N | RDDGENOL | RDDGENBB | Import converter |
| M | RDDMASGL | RDDMASGL | Mass activator (Enqueue) |
| Y(n) | RDDGENOL | RDDGENBB | Matchcode converter |
| O | RDDGENOL | RDDGENBB | Batch converter (not in Upgrade) |
| D | RDDDIC1L | RDDDIC1L | ADO import |
| V | RDDVERSL | RDDVERSL | Create version |
| R | RDDEXECL | RDDEXECL | XPRA execution |
| G | RDDDIC3L | RDDDIC3L | Generation |

**Table 14.8** Functions of ABAP Programs during Change Request Import

The interaction between `tp` and the ABAP programs is depicted in Figure 14.14. After making the required entries to table TRBAT, `tp` triggers the import dispatcher `RDDIMPDP`.

As a prerequisite, RDDIMPDP must be scheduled as an event-periodic background job in client 000 of the target system. Additionally, a similar background job must be scheduled in every target client. This background job is called RDDIMPDP_CLIENT_<nnn>, where <nnn> represents the client ID. These jobs are normally scheduled automatically after a client copy. You can also schedule them manually by running the program RDDNEWPP in the respective client (see Chapter 7).

RDDIMPDP reads the information on import steps that tp writes to the control table TRBAT and then starts the corresponding programs as background jobs. The names of these programs and jobs all start with "RDD"—for example, RDDMASGL is for mass activation, RDDGENDB is for conversion, and RDDVERSL is for versioning. Each RDD*-job (as they are commonly referred to) collectively receives a job number, which is recorded in table TRJOB. The jobs report their status and final return code back to table TRBAT and delete the corresponding TRJOB entry just before they finish.

They also write log files into the transport directory in the subdirectory tmp. At the end of an import, these log files are moved to the subdirectory log by tp.

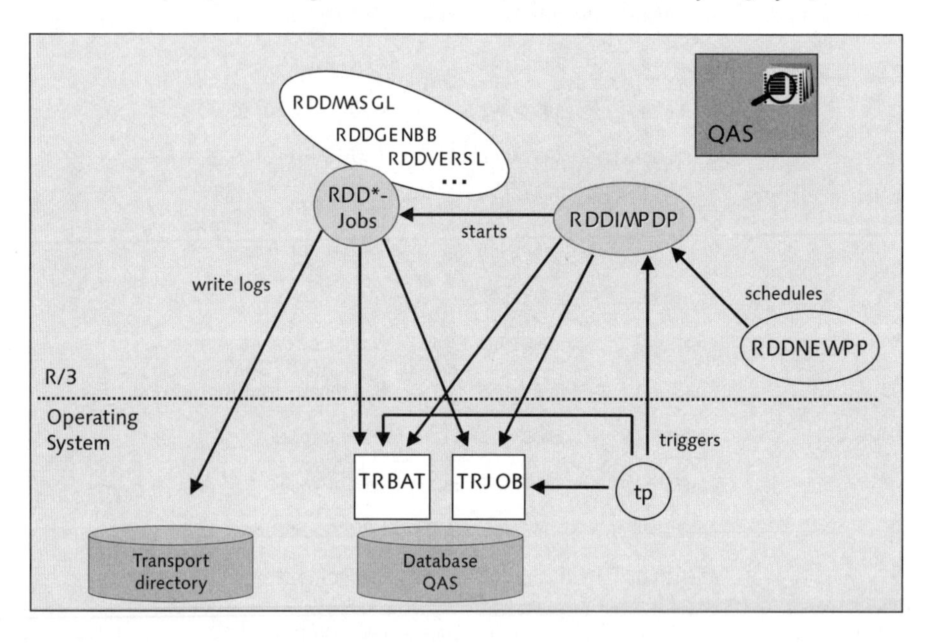


**Figure 14.14** Interaction between ABAP programs and tp

### Communication between tp and ABAP Programs

The following section focuses on how `tp` communicates with the ABAP programs that are involved in the import process. The main components for performing an import are depicted in Figure 14.15. The figure is divided into three parts: the operating system (OS) level, the database, and the ABAP programs within the SAP system.

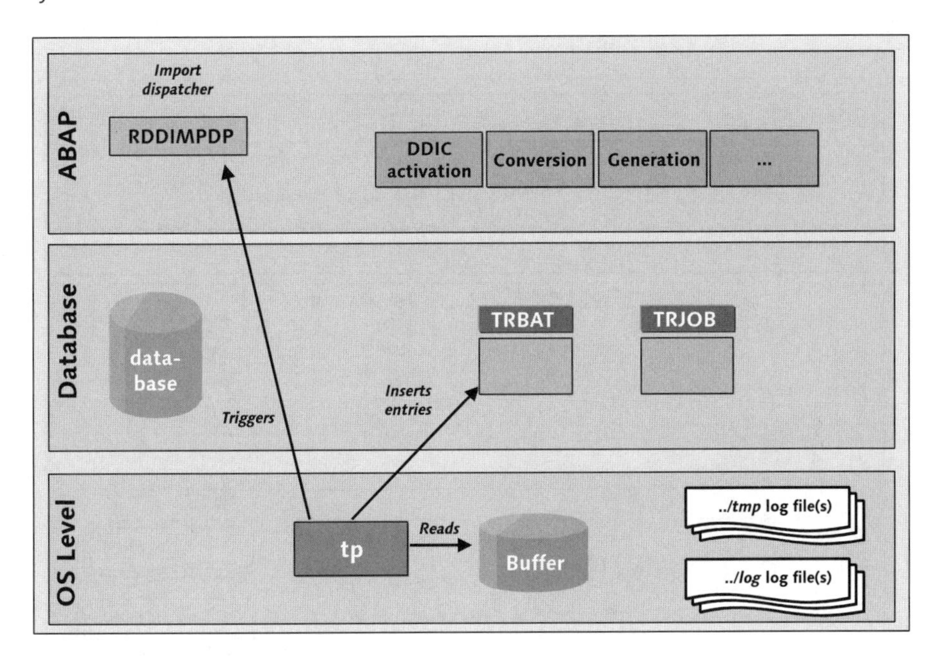


**Figure 14.15** tp starts the import process

When you perform an import, `tp` reads the import buffer and then writes an entry to the control table TRBAT for every change request in the import buffer. `tp` groups the change requests according to the import step to be performed. The entry in table TRBAT contains the name of the change request, the function performed during the import step, the return code, and the time stamp. The import function is represented by a character. For example, **J** indicates that the *mass activator* is performing the import step **ABAP Dictionary activation**. For a list of TRBAT function codes, refer back to Table 14.8. As a signal to `RDDIMPDP` to start processing, `tp` writes a **header entry** after every group of change requests that have the same function code.

**Note** For generic import steps that are independent of certain change requests, such as distribution and structure conversion, `tp` only writes a header entry in table TRBAT.

To trigger the import dispatcher RDDIMPDP, tp calls the operating system tool sapevt, which sends the event SAP_TRIGGER_RDDIMPDP to the SAP system.

When RDDIMPDP starts processing, it checks table TRBAT to find out whether there is an import step to be performed, such as mass activation, distribution, or table conversion. It sets the return code of the header entry to R (for "run"), starts the appropriate RDD* program as a background job, enters the job number of the new job into table TRJOB, reschedules itself, and then exits (see Figure 14.16).

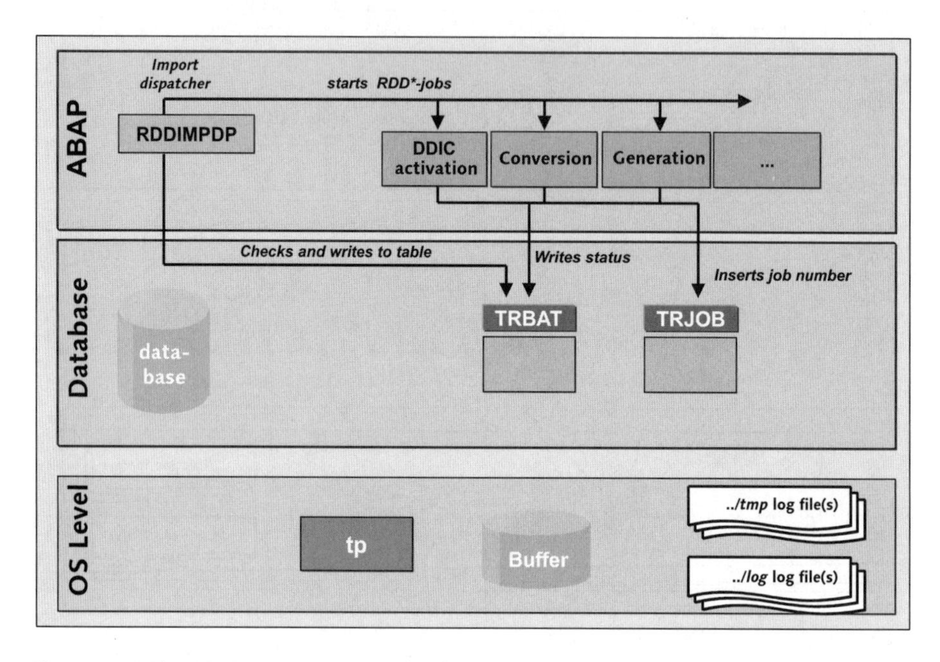


**Figure 14.16** The ABAP programs access the database tables

Each RDD* background job receives a job number generated by R/3 background processing. The job number and the function code are recorded in table TRJOB. The respective RDD*-jobs indicate their status in table TRBAT by logging their current return code.

When the background jobs exit, they write their final status as return codes in table TRBAT and delete the corresponding job number in table TRJOB. Return codes other than 9999 and 8888 indicate that the import step is complete. In table TRBAT, the column **Timestamp** contains the time of completion. When all the necessary actions have been performed for all change requests, the respective RDD* job sets the header entry to F (for "finished") (see Figure 14.17).

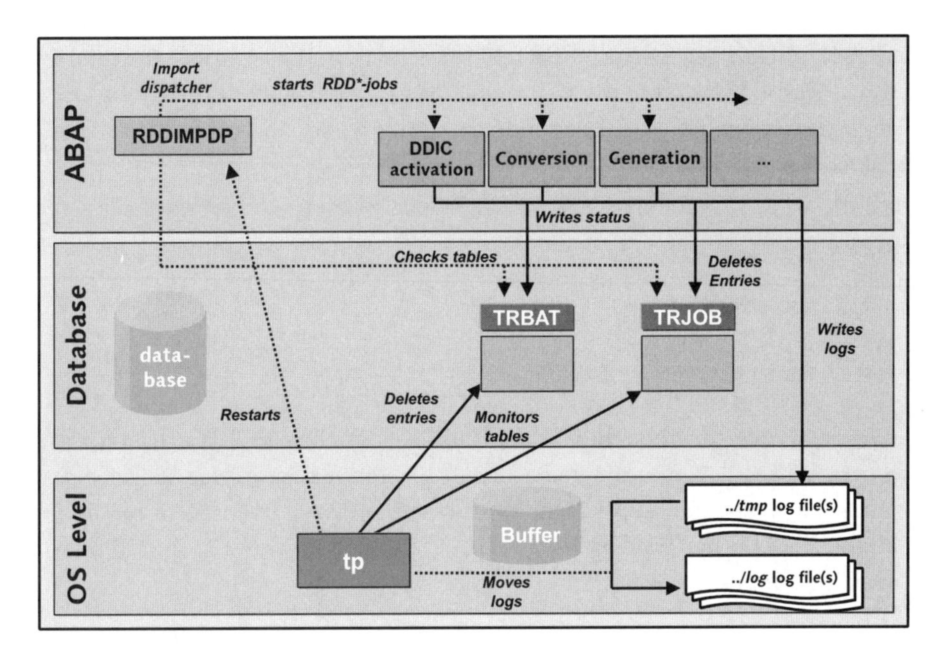


**Figure 14.17** RDD* job exits

All background jobs log the steps they perform either in the database or in the transport subdirectory `tmp`. `tp` monitors the entries in the tables TRBAT and TRJOB. When an entry that is not a header entry has a return code other than 8888 or 9999, the job is considered finished. Then, `tp` copies the log file from the subdirectory `tmp` to the subdirectory `log` and deletes the corresponding TRBAT entry. When the header entry in TRBAT is set to F and TRJOB is empty, the ABAP programs have completed their role in the import steps.

If `tp` detects problems when monitoring the tables TRBAT and TRJOB, `tp` retriggers `RDDIMPDP` using `sapevt`. `RDDIMPDP` automatically recognizes whether an import step is still active or has been aborted by checking tables TRJOB and TRBAT. If a step was aborted, `RDDIMPDP` will restart this step.

**Example: TRBAT Entries during an Import**

When `tp` reads the import buffer of the target system, it notices that three of the change requests require the import step **ABAP Dictionary activation**. Therefore, `tp` writes the three change requests to table TRBAT, and it assigns the function code J to the change requests. This indicates that **ABAP Dictionary activation** has to be performed.

`tp` then writes a header entry to tell RDDIMPDP to start processing. The return code 9999 indicates that the step is waiting to be performed. For the header entry, `tp` inserts a `B` (for "begin") as the return code. The contents of table TRBAT are as follows:

| Request | Function Code | Return Code | Time Stamp |
|---|---|---|---|
| DEVK904711 | J | 9999 | 00000001 |
| DEVK904712 | J | 9999 | 00000002 |
| DEVK904713 | J | 9999 | 00000003 |
| HEADER | J | B | 19983103143701 |

After `RDDIMPDP` sets the return code of the header entry to R, it activates the program `RDDMASGL`. The program `RDDMASGL` is the *mass activator*, which performs the import step **ABAP Dictionary activation**. While `RDDMASGL` is running, the status of the first entry in table TRBAT is changed to "active," which is indicated by the return code 8888.

| Request | Function Code | Return Code | Time Stamp |
|---|---|---|---|
| DEVK904711 | J | 8888 | 00000001 |
| DEVK904712 | J | 9999 | 00000002 |
| DEVK904713 | J | 9999 | 00000003 |
| HEADER | J | R | 19983103143903 |

When the program `RDDMASGL` (the *mass activator*) has completed the import step **ABAP Dictionary activation**, it enters the return codes for each change request in table TRBAT and changes the status of the header entry to F. In this way, `RDDIMPDP` will recognize that the import step **ABAP Dictionary activation** has been completed.

| Request | Function Code | Return Code | Time Stamp |
|---|---|---|---|
| DEVK904711 | J | 4 | 19983103144202 |
| DEVK904712 | J | 0 | 19983103144357 |
| DEVK904713 | J | 0 | 19983103144512 |
| HEADER | J | F | 19983103144512 |

## 14.6 Questions

1. Which of the following statements are correct in regard to the transport control program `tp`?

   A. To perform imports, `tp` must always be used directly on the operating system level.

   B. SAP recommends that you use the TMS instead of `tp` to perform imports.

   C. `tp` is responsible for exporting and importing objects from and to SAP systems.

   D. `tp` does not observe the sequence of change requests in the import queue when performing imports.

2. Which of the following statements are correct in regard to import queues and import buffers?

   A. Import queues are the TMS representation in SAP system of the import buffer files on the operating system level.

   B. Import queues and import buffers are completely independent of each other.

   C. Import buffers have to be manipulated before imports can be performed on the operating system level.

   D. Manipulating import buffers may cause serious inconsistencies and should be performed only in exceptional cases.

3. Which of the following statements are correct in regard to the import options formerly known as *unconditional modes*?

   A. Import options cannot be used when imports are performed on the operating system level using `tp`.

   B. Import options are used to cause specific rules of the Change and Transport System (CTS) to be ignored.

   C. Import options must be used when importing into multiple clients using `tp`.

   D. Import options can be selected in the TMS using the expert mode.

4. Which of the following statements are correct in regard to the sequence of processing steps `tp` follows when performing imports?

   A. `tp` collectively processes each import step for all change requests in an import queue before proceeding with the next import step.

   B. `tp` processes all import steps for a single request before proceeding to the next change request.

C. The processing sequence followed by tp ensures that when a change request with a faulty object is followed in the import queue by a change request with the corrected object, the faulty object will not affect the runtime environment of the target system.

D. tp imports and activates ABAP Dictionary structures prior to the main import phase to ensure that the current structures are able to receive new data during the main import phase.

5. Which of the following statements are correct in regard to troubleshooting imports?

A. In R/3, you cannot display log files that do not depend on a specific request. For example, you cannot display log files related to generic import steps, such as structure conversion.

B. SAP recommends that you check the SLOG file and the ALOG file before checking the single step log files.

C. By default, all return codes greater than eight cause tp to abort a running import.

D. tp is the only transport tool that uses return codes.

6. Which of the following statements are correct in regard to buffer synchronization?

A. Transport activities do not affect buffer synchronization.

B. Imports affect buffer synchronization even in central SAP systems.

C. R3trans can invalidate buffer content.

D. Importing data into a production system can significantly impact performance, because some buffer content may be invalidated and reloaded. This causes high system load.

E. Importing programs and ABAP Dictionary data cannot cause inconsistencies in the target system, even if the programs or data affect running programs and their environment.

7. Which of the following statements are correct in regard to the interaction between transport tools?

A. During exports, tp calls R3trans to access the database of the source system and extract the objects to be transported.

B. tp triggers the transport daemon RDDIMPDP in the SAP system using the operating system tool sapevt.

C. Using the tables TRBAT and TRJOB, tp communicates with ABAP programs involved in the transport process.

D. tp communicates with only RDDIMPD.

# 15 Maintaining SAP Software

In this chapter, you will learn about the software maintenance strategies and tools that SAP provides, and in particular, about Support Packages and SAP Notes. Support Packages correct all the errors in a system that have been identified within a specific time period, while SAP Notes correct individual errors as they occur. This chapter also explains the modification adjustment steps you need to take when importing Support Packages.

The tools dealt with in this chapter are as follows.

- The Note Assistant (Transaction SNOTE) is used to import Notes with code corrections.
- The SAP Patch Manager (Transaction SPAM) is used to import Support Packages.
- The Note Assistant (Transaction SNOTE) is used to import Notes with code corrections.

This chapter is primarily intended for system administrators and technical consultants who are responsible for maintaining and updating an SAP system landscape. Nonetheless, project leaders and strategic consultants will also benefit from this information, because it's helpful for planning package upgrades and for estimating the time and staff costs involved. Experience shows us that the main factors that cause difficulties in Support Package implementation projects are the necessary downtime, the time and effort required for testing, and the indispensable code freeze. Section 15.3 addresses these aspects, and also describes the benefits gained from importing Support Packages.

## 15.1 Making Manual Corrections on the Basis of SAP Notes

If a specific problem occurs with the mySAP Enterprise Resource Planning (ERP) software and this problem is corrected, details of the correction are published in an SAP Note. The correction is also included in the next Support Package.

But, if the problem is particularly urgent, you may not be able to wait for the Support Package. In that case, you will have to manually make the correction with the help of a SAP Note.

SAP provides the SAP Note Assistant to enable customers to import SAP Notes containing corrections in ABAP. This tool considerably reduces the amount of manual work required to implement the Note and to make modification adjustments later on.

Particularly important Notes—like those about faults with serious consequences such as system breakdown or data inconsistencies—are classified as HotNews and are published on the SAP Service Marketplace.

### 15.1.1 SAP HotNews

SAP HotNews items are SAP customer Notes with Priority 1 (very high). These Notes contain the solutions to problems that could cause a system breakdown or data loss in the SAP system. Therefore, if one of these Notes applies to your system, it is very important that you take it seriously.

The new SAP HotNews process enables you, the user, to display only HotNews items that are relevant to your area(s). The shared personalization interface for SAP HotNews and SAP TopNotes (see below) allows you to create multiple filters for the applications that you use (such as SAP R/3 or SAP CRM). Using the filter maintenance functions, you can select the products (such as SAP R/3), product versions (such as SAP R/3 4.6C), software components (such as SAP Basis 4.6C), and Support Packages that are relevant to you, and the system returns only the HotNews items that are relevant to your criteria.

SAP HotNews items are located in the SAP Service Marketplace under the */notes* Quick Link: *http://service.sap.com/notes*. (You need a Service Marketplace user to be able to view this content.)

You can also have the SAP HotNews you are interested in emailed to you in the SAP Service Marketplace newsletter. To subscribe to the topic area **News for Administrators (incl. SAP HotNews)** of the SAP Service Marketplace newsletter, make the required settings in the SAP Service Marketplace under **My Profile**. Once you have done this, you will be informed automatically as soon as there is a new SAP HotNews item that is relevant to your settings.

If you receive a SAP HotNews item that contains information that is extremely important for the operation of your SAP system, you should confirm receipt of this item in the SAP Service Marketplace. When you confirm receipt of this item, this Note is no longer displayed to you. SAP is notified that you have read the Note and that you have taken the recommended measures.

As an SAP system administrator, you should regularly review all SAP HotNews items or ensure that this is done, and if necessary, proactively implement them in your system.

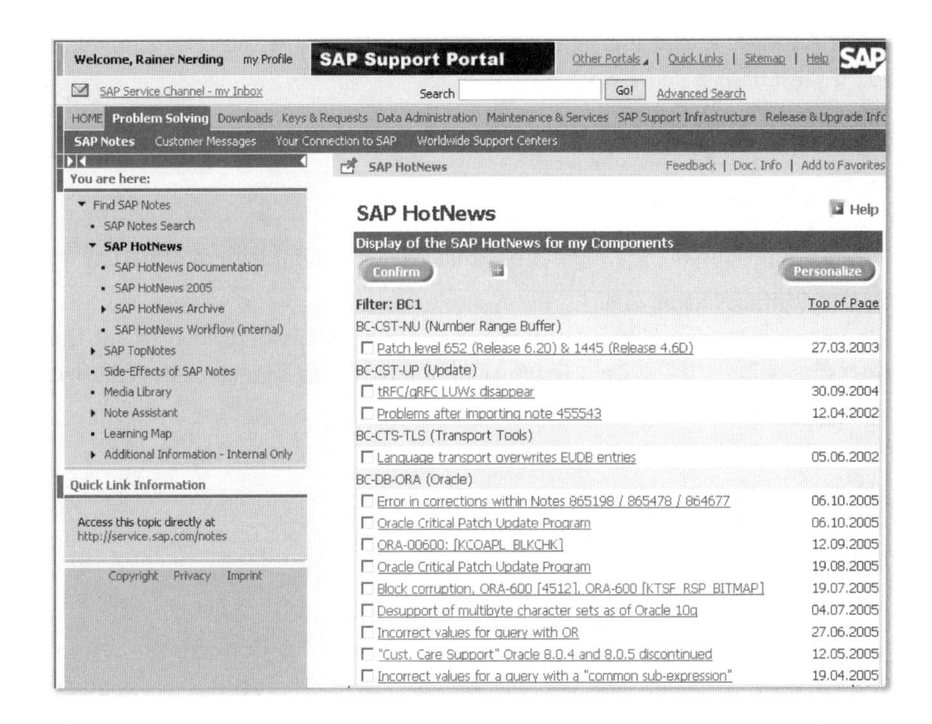


**Figure 15.1** SAP HotNews browser in the SAP Service Marketplace

### 15.1.2 SAP TopNotes

SAP TopNotes are the most important Notes in a component or sub-component (such as FI). These are the Notes that are most frequently appended to customer problem messages. Every month, the system identifies the 10 most common messages for the component in question. Then, the TopNotes are checked manually, and other important SAP Notes can be added to them or replace them. This concept is described in detail in Note 557703.

SAP TopNotes are also located in the SAP Service Marketplace under the */notes* Quick Link (*http://service.sap.com/notes*). As with SAP HotNews, you can also be notified of new SAP TopNotes by email.

## 15.2 Implementing Notes with the SAP Note Assistant

The SAP Note Assistant can automatically implement Notes that contain corrections to source code. Other changes, such as Customizing changes or changes to a table, cannot be automatically implemented. Always make sure to read the Note carefully before implementing it using the Note Assistant, since it may contain information about prerequisites, interdependencies, and references to clean-up steps that you'll need to consider in the implementation process.

The Note Assistant is available as an add-on from Release 4.5B, and is included as standard from Basis Release 6.10.

The functions of the Note Assistant are as follows:

- **Reporting**
  Provides an overview of the Notes existing in a system, their processing status and of all the source-code corrections that have been implemented to date.
- **Project administration**
  Allows you to assign Notes to processors. These processors can then set the processing status. The system notifies you if a Note has an inconsistent status.
- **Retraceability**
  The system automatically logs the processing steps.
- **Error correction**
  You can automatically implement source-code corrections (correction instructions) that are described in Notes.
- **Integration**
  When Support Packages are imported or upgrades are performed, the system automatically identifies the Notes that the Support Package or upgrade resolves and which correction instructions have to be re-implemented.

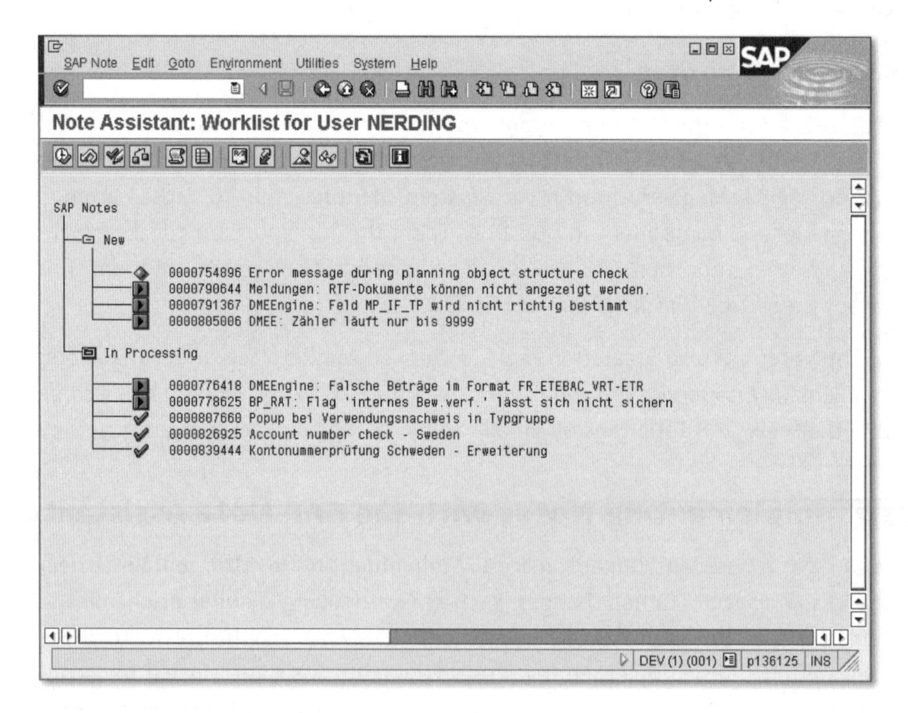


Figure 15.2 SAP Note Assistant

### 15.2.1 Registering Manually-Implemented Notes

If you implemented corrections from Notes into your SAP system before installing the Note Assistant, you can retroactively 'tell' this to the Note Assistant. Because the Note Assistant cannot automatically determine whether a Note correction was implemented in your system manually (that is, without the use of the Note Assistant), this is important to do. Proceed as follows:

1. In the ABAP Editor (Transaction SE38), call the program `SCWN_REGISTER_NOTES`.
2. In the program's input screen, enter the numbers of the Notes you want to register and that have been fully implemented.
3. This can cause the following situations to occur:
   - If you created a Remote Function Call (RFC) connection to the SAPNet-R/3 frontend, the program automatically loads the Notes to be registered into your system's database.
   - If you did not create an RFC connection, first load the Notes to be registered from the SAP Service Marketplace. Then, upload the Notes in the Note Assistant.
4. The program checks whether the Notes are valid for your release and Support Package level. It also verifies whether the Notes are already registered as having been implemented in the Note Assistant. The system then outputs the results of these checks to a list.
5. To register the Note, select **Execute**.

**Note** To be able to register the Note as implemented, the system has to enter the details of the Note and the objects that it corrected in a change request. When you transport this request, you are registering the Note as implemented, even in your follow-on systems. If it is not possible to include the Note and its objects in one request—because, for example, some objects have already been locked in other requests—the system will reject the registration.

### 15.2.2 Processing Notes

To correct an error in a program using the Note Assistant, proceed as follows:

1. Load the Note into your system. In the loading process, the Note Assistant checks whether the characteristics of the Note (software component, release level, and Support Package level) match those of your system. It then states whether the corrections can be implemented.
   Only Notes with source-code corrections (correction instructions) can be automatically implemented.

2. Read the Note description carefully.

**Note** The Note description may contain information about prerequisites and interdependencies, and references to post-processing steps (for example, changes that need to be made to a table), which the Note Assistant does *not* automatically recognize. If you do not read and, if required, act upon this information, serious problems can result. It is therefore absolutely imperative that you read the Note before you start the implementation.

3. Determine whether the Note is relevant to you. Classify the Note in accordance with the processing status.
4. Implement the correction.
5. Carry out any post-processing steps that may be specified in the Note.
6. Test whether the error has been successfully corrected.
7. Set the processing status to **Completed**.
8. Release the transport request and import the corrections into the follow-on systems in your system landscape.

### Search for Note

The Note Browser enables you to search through all the SAP Notes in your system. It also displays Notes that are assigned to another processor and Notes that have already been implemented.

1. Select a search criterion for the Note:
    - Note number
    - Application component
    - Processing status
    - Implementation status
    - Processor
2. Select which option you require:
    - Restrict the selection process to certain software components and their releases.
    - Sort the Notes according to their number or the application component to which they belong.
3. Confirm your selection.

The Note Browser then displays a list of the Notes that match your criteria, and their Note number, short text, component, processing status, implementation status, and user. You can also implement Notes directly from the Note Browser.

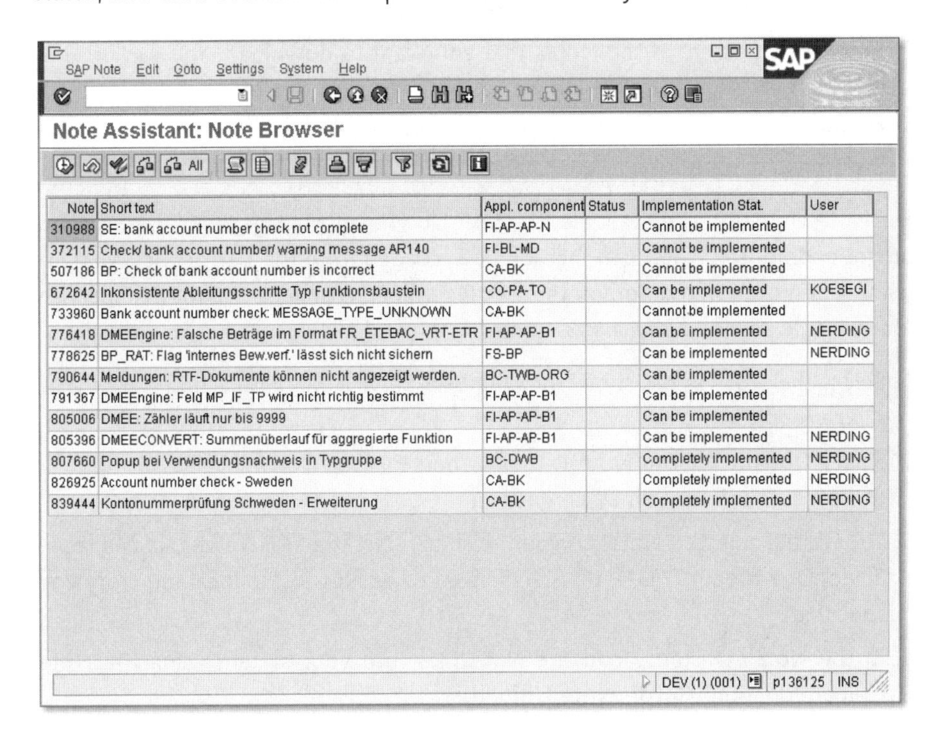


| Note | Short text | Appl. component | Status | Implementation Stat. | User |
|---|---|---|---|---|---|
| 310988 | SE: bank account number check not complete | FI-AP-AP-N | | Cannot be implemented | |
| 372115 | Check/ bank account number/ warning message AR140 | FI-BL-MD | | Cannot be implemented | |
| 507186 | BP: Check of bank account number is incorrect | CA-BK | | Cannot be implemented | |
| 672642 | Inkonsistente Ableitungsschritte Typ Funktionsbaustein | CO-PA-TO | | Can be implemented | KOESEGI |
| 733960 | Bank account number check: MESSAGE_TYPE_UNKNOWN | CA-BK | | Cannot be implemented | |
| 776418 | DMEEngine: Falsche Beträge im Format FR_ETEBAC_VRT-ETR | FI-AP-AP-B1 | | Can be implemented | NERDING |
| 778625 | BP_RAT: Flag 'internes Bew.verf.' lässt sich nicht sichern | FS-BP | | Can be implemented | NERDING |
| 790644 | Meldungen: RTF-Dokumente können nicht angezeigt werden. | BC-TWB-ORG | | Can be implemented | |
| 791367 | DMEEngine: Feld MP_IF_TP wird nicht richtig bestimmt | FI-AP-AP-B1 | | Can be implemented | |
| 805006 | DMEE: Zähler läuft nur bis 9999 | FI-AP-AP-B1 | | Can be implemented | |
| 805396 | DMEECONVERT: Summenüberlauf für aggregierte Funktion | FI-AP-AP-B1 | | Can be implemented | NERDING |
| 807660 | Popup bei Verwendungsnachweis in Typgruppe | BC-DWB | | Completely implemented | NERDING |
| 826925 | Account number check - Sweden | CA-BK | | Completely implemented | NERDING |
| 839444 | Kontonummerprüfung Schweden - Erweiterung | CA-BK | | Completely implemented | NERDING |

**Figure 15.3** The note browser displays all notes that have been implemented using the SAP note assistant

## Load Note

You can load SAP Notes into your system from the SAP Service Marketplace or the SAPNet-R/3 frontend, using either a direct RFC connection (Note download) or by file transfer (Note upload). Note download has the following benefits:

1. You can transfer the Note in the Note Assistant from the SAPNet-R/3 frontend directly to your system.
2. If the Note in question specifies other Notes as prerequisites, the Note Assistant automatically downloads these in the implementation process.
3. You can download updated versions of the Notes at the touch of a button.

To download a Note, you have to create an RFC connection to the SAPNet-R/3 frontend. To upload a Note, on the other hand, a permanent RFC connection to the SAPNet-R/3 frontend is not necessary. Instead, first load the required Note from the SAP Service Marketplace and save it locally on your PC. Then, upload the Note from inside the Note Assistant.

1. Select **Note Download** in the Note Assistant.
2. Enter the numbers of the Notes that you want to download. You can use the selection function to select individual Notes or a list of Notes.
3. Confirm your selection. The system then loads the matching Notes from the SAPNet-R/3 frontend into your database.

For Note Upload to be available, the SAP Download Manager must be installed on your computer. Notes can then be downloaded from the SAP Service Marketplace. For more information on the SAP Download Manager, see the SAP Service Marketplace at *service.sap.com/swcenter*.

1. Select the Note in question from the SAP Service Marketplace under *service.sap.com/notes*.
2. Select **Download**. The Note is then added to your Download Basket. Repeat this process as many times as required.
3. To save the selected Notes to your local PC, start the SAP Download Manager. Select **Download**. The Notes are then saved as files to the local directory you specified.
4. In the Note Assistant, load the Note files into your system using the Note Upload function (**Goto · Note Upload**).

After you have successfully downloaded or uploaded a Note that was not previously in your system, it is listed with the processing status **New**.

### Classify Note

This function allows you to specify the relevance or processing status of a Note. Read the Note carefully and decide whether its content is relevant to the situation in your system. Then proceed as follows:

1. If the Note is relevant to your system, set its status to **In Processing**. This informs other users that you are already processing this Note.
2. Closely follow the recommendations given in the Note. If the Note contains a correction instruction, implement this in your system.
3. If you want to assign the Note to another processor, enter the user name of the processor.

All your actions are recorded in the log file for the Note. You can also enter additional comments in the log file, such as information you may want to pass on to another user.

If the Note is not relevant to you, set the processing status to **Not Relevant**. This signals to you and to all other users that this Note can be disregarded.

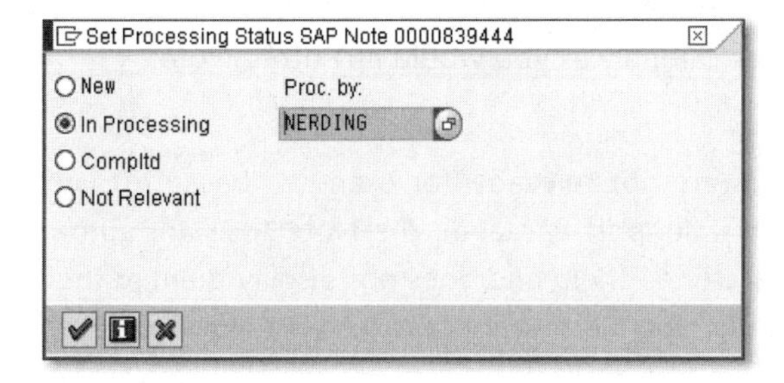


**Figure 15.4** Processing statuses for implementing notes

### Implement Correction Instruction

There is a function that implements the correction instruction contained in a Note. If you have previously modified the object that is the subject of a correction instruction, you can also adapt the correction to your modifications.

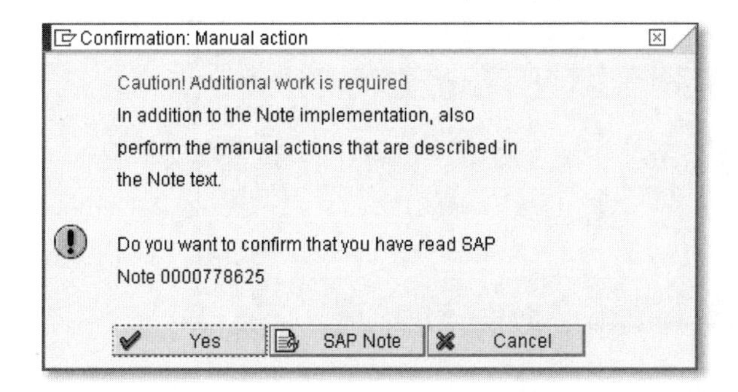


**Figure 15.5** Additional manual action required in note implementation

1. To implement the correction instruction of a Note in your system, place your cursor on the title of the Note in the initial screen of the Note Assistant and select **Implement Note**. First, the system checks which correction instruction from the Note is appropriate for your release level and Support Package level. It then checks whether any corrections from other Notes are a prerequisite to the implementation of this correction. If there are prerequisite Notes, the system displays these in a dialog field.
   - If you have an RFC connection to the SAPNet-R/3 frontend, you can automatically download these Notes by confirming the dialog field.
   - Otherwise, load them from the SAP Service Marketplace and then upload them using the Note Assistant.

If the prerequisite Notes are relevant to your system, they are then displayed in the order in which they are to be implemented. If possible, the system implements all prerequisite Notes in one step.

Read the prerequisite Notes as carefully as you would any other Notes.

**Note** If any prerequisite Notes are not relevant (for example, because they have already been imported in a Support Package), the Note Assistant automatically assigns the relevant status to them and does not display them in the list. To view these Notes, call the Notes Browser and select the **Not Relevant** processing status.

Before the system corrects the objects, it opens a dialog window in which you can select the change request.

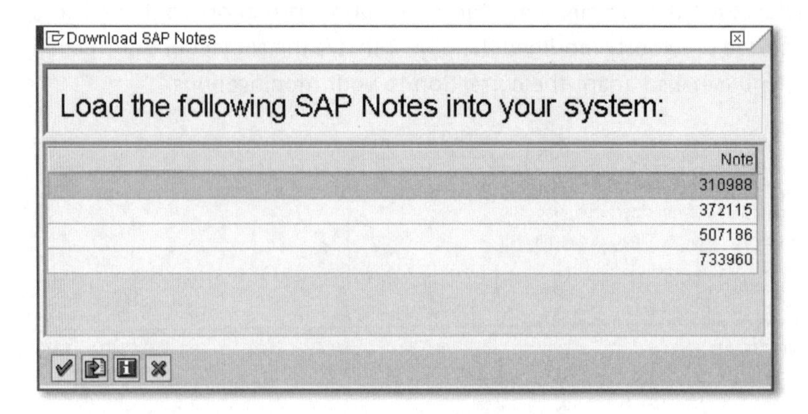


**Figure 15.6** Prerequisite notes

2. Either select a suitable change request, or create a new one.

   The Note (R3TR NOTE), including all correction instructions (R3TR CINS) and all changed objects, is entered into the request. The transport request then transports all corrections to the follow-on systems.

   Note that all objects to be corrected, plus details of the Note, must be entered in a request. This is the only way to ensure that the corrections are transported in their entirety to the follow-on systems.

**Note** No SSCR key is required for automatically implementing Note corrections.

3. A dialog window opens that lists all the objects to be changed. A traffic light icon shows whether the system can automatically implement the correction.

   Click on the object name to open an editor. The editor shows you the changes in detail.

   If you previously modified the objects to be corrected, the Note will have an amber light. You can then adapt the corrections to suit your modifications (also see: Split-Screen Editor).

   If you make manual changes when implementing Notes, the system cannot judge whether the corrections have been implemented properly. Therefore, you must confirm in a separate dialog window that the corrections can be classified in the system as fully implemented.

**Note** If the system cannot automatically implement a correction, even though the objects in question were *not* previously modified, you should first attempt to import the Note using the split-screen editor. In many cases, minor differences in the source code cause the automatic implementation to fail. If the implementation still does not work, it is probably because the Note contains an error of some sort. If this happens, contact SAP Support by creating a problem message under the component of the Note (for example, FI-AR-CR).

4. Check that the corrected objects do not contain any syntax errors. This is particularly important if the corrected objects also contain customer-specific modifications. Note that currently the system can automatically implement only source-text changes. If any other changes are required (changes to Dictionary objects, for example), they are described in the Note text and must be manually implemented in your system.
5. After implementing the corrections, test the function in question to ensure that it has been fully corrected by the Note.

   You can display all objects that were corrected by the Note; simply select **Corrected objects** to call the modification browser.
6. Set the processing status to **Completed**.

**Note** In exceptional cases, you can remove correction instructions that you have implemented. This undoes all implemented changes. The Note in question remains in your system and is reset to the status it had prior to it being implemented. To remove certain correction instructions, select **Reset SAP Note Implementation**.

7. Once you have solved your problem via the Note, release the change request that was created when you implemented the correction instruction. This transports the corrections and the Note data to the follow-on systems in your system landscape.

If a particular Note has prerequisite Notes, the Note Assistant identifies the prerequisite Notes when the Note is being implemented and instructs you to load the prerequisite Notes into your system. As soon as the prerequisite Notes are available, the Note Assistant displays the Note you selected plus all additional Notes in a dialog field called the Note queue. The Notes have to be implemented in the order shown in the Note queue. Before you start the implementation process, read the prerequisite Notes as carefully as you would any other Notes.

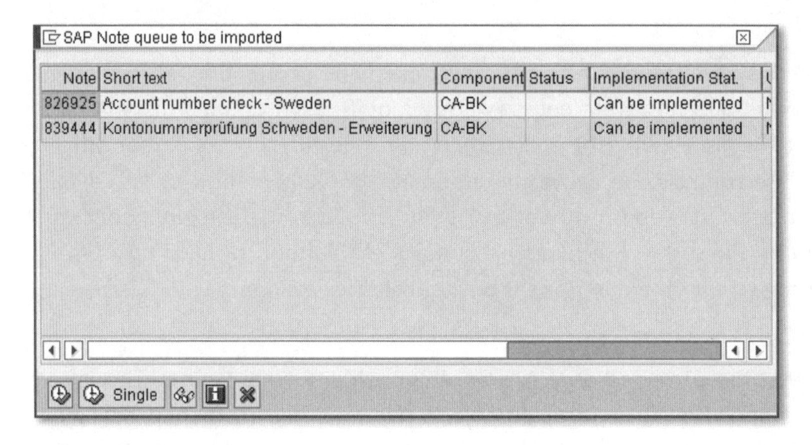


**Figure 15.7** Implementing a note queue

You have the following options:

- **Implement multiple Notes in one step**
  If you select this option, the system implements as many of the specified Notes as possible, in one step and in sequence. The Notes that can be implemented at the same time are highlighted in color.

  The system can implement multiple Notes in one step only if all corrections can be transferred in unmodified form from the Notes. If you have made your own modifications to the includes in question, the system may be unable to insert individual changes. The system always implements such Notes individually, so that you can adapt your modifications.

- **Implement all Notes individually**
  The system implements the specified Notes individually. This option allows you to review in detail what source-code changes belong to which of the specified Notes, and to modify the changed source code, if necessary.

▶ **Cancel SAP Note implementation**
The system does not make any changes to the source code.

The **Confirm Changes** dialog field shows you which objects will be changed by the implementation of the Note, and whether the Note Assistant can copy in the changes. If you confirm this dialog field, the system implements the corrections into the specified objects. If you select **Cancel** here, the system does not make any corrections.

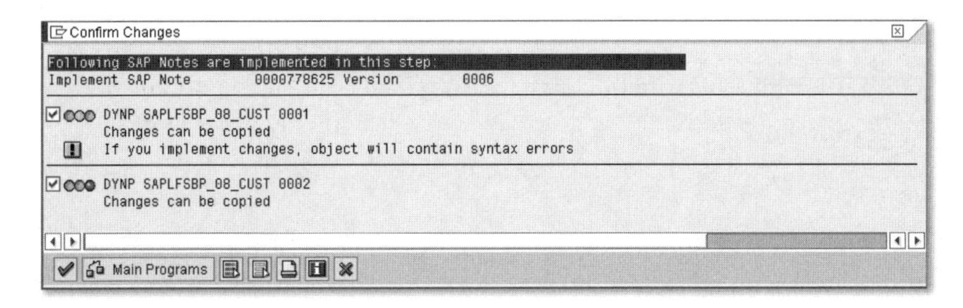


**Figure 15.8** Display of objects to be changed

The traffic light icons show you whether the corrections in a Note can be implemented. The different colors have the following meanings:

- ▶ **Green light:** The corrections can be implemented without any changes.
- ▶ **Amber light:** Some of the corrections can be implemented.

  Before you confirm the implementation, you should adapt the corrections in such a way that the object changes can be imported correctly. To do this, click on the object name or on the traffic light icon. The split-screen editor opens, enabling you to edit the source code here.
- ▶ **Red light:** The object changes cannot be implemented.

  This can occur for a variety of causes; for example, the object has to be created from scratch, or is locked by another change request.

  There is a corresponding message text for every object (for example, "Corrections have not been included completely"). If you click on the text, the system displays the appropriate long text with detailed information.

To implement the corrections, select all the objects for which you want to implement corrections, and select **Continue**.

**Tip** Note that only those objects that you selected will be changed.

This editor provides a detailed display of all corrections in an object. You can use this editor to adapt the corrections to your own modifications, if necessary.

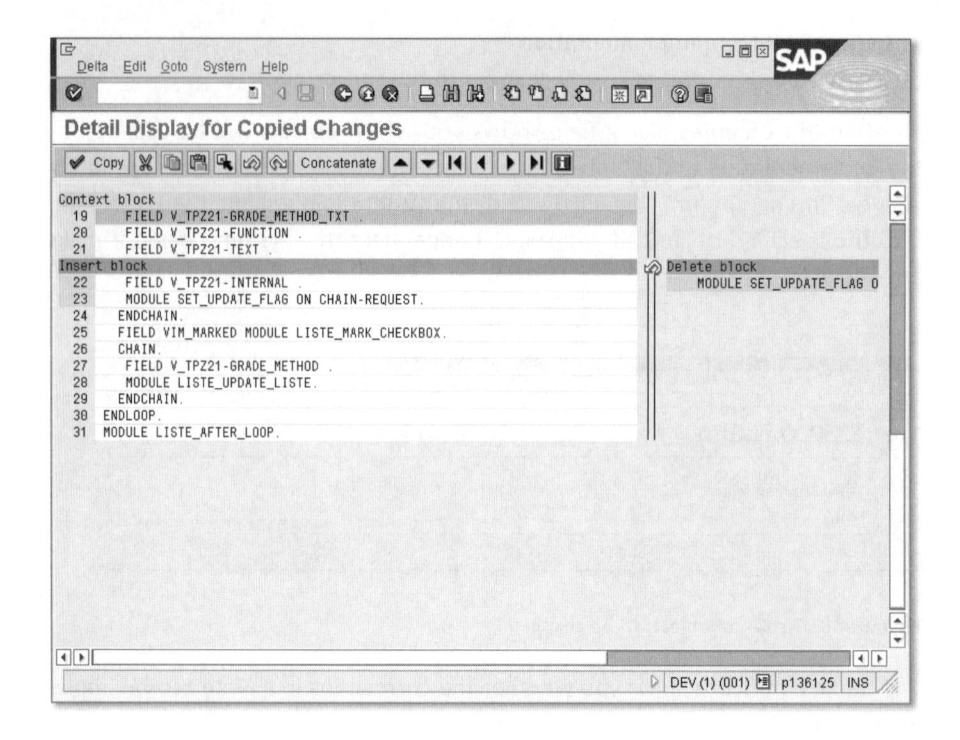


**Figure 15.9** Split-screen editor

The split-screen editor is divided into two areas:

- On the left-hand side of the screen, you see the source code as it looks after the changes have been implemented. The changes are highlighted in color. You can edit the source code in this part of the screen.
- On the right-hand side of the screen, you see the parts of the program that have been deleted, and corrections that the Note Assistant cannot implement automatically. These deletions and corrections are displayed in the form of context blocks, delete blocks, and insert blocks.

You can do the following on the left-hand side of the screen:

- Manually edit the program
- Select, cut, copy and paste blocks

**Note** To select a block that is highlighted in color, simply place your cursor on the header line and choose **Select**. You can also select multiple lines. To do this, place your cursor on the first line of the block that you want to select and choose **Select**. Then place your cursor on the last line and choose **Select** again.

- Select **Undo** to undo all changes, step by step, that you made in the split-screen editor.
- Select **Redo** to restore all changes that you undid.
- Use the arrow buttons to go to the next or last change.
- Select **Concatenate** to attach two lines to each other.

If a block has been inserted or deleted, the **Undo/Redo** button appears between the left-hand and the right-hand side of the editor. You can use it to undo or redo individual changes. The technical function of the undo and redo buttons is to exchange individual delete and insert blocks.

### Technical Details of Correction Instructions

Technical details of correction instructions contains information on the following topics:

- Format of correction instructions
- Validity of correction instructions
- Prerequisites of correction instructions

Correction instructions describe how the source code of ABAP programs has to be changed in order to resolve an error. These correction instructions are located at the end of each SAP Note. You use correction instructions to automatically correct the source code of ABAP programs, ABAP includes, function modules, method implementations, Dynpro flow logic, and type groups.

Every change contains information about the object (for example, the include or the function module) and the modularization unit (such as FORM routine) in which it is to be made. The location of the change is identified by the unique number of the unchanged lines that directly precede the lines to be changed (context block). The lines to be deleted are then listed (delete block), followed by the lines to be inserted (insert block). A correction instruction can consist of multiple contexts, delete blocks, and insert blocks.

When automatically implementing a correction instruction, the system finds the context blocks in the include or function module to be corrected, checks whether the context blocks follow the lines to be deleted, and replaces these lines with the lines to be inserted.

If the include or function module to be corrected contains customer modifications, sometimes the system can't find the context blocks specified in the correction instruction, or in the lines to be deleted. In other words, the system cannot fully implement the correction. In this case, you can use the split-screen editor to adapt the corrections in the Note to your modifications.

Since 1998, correction instructions have been formalized to such a degree that they can be implemented automatically. However, older Notes may still be in a non-standardized format, and the Note Assistant will be unable to automatically implement these Notes completely. However, as before, you can manually edit the source code, using the split-screen editor. We recommend that you do this to ensure that the Note Assistant can register the Note in your system.

Every correction instruction specifies the release levels and Support Package levels in which you can implement the correction instruction. These release and Support Package levels are known as the *area of validity* of the correction instruction.

For example: if an error is detected in Release 4.6C, and Support Package 5 corrects this error, the validity period of the correction instruction in question will be specified as "4.6C Support Packages 1–4."

A Note can also specify that a correction instruction may not be implemented if the system contains a specific software component (such as an add-on). This may be the case if, for example, a correction makes changes to a part of a program that is required in its unmodified form by another software component.

If such a condition exists, it is displayed in the header area of the correction instruction under *Not valid for <software component, release, Support Package level>*.

The Note Assistant automatically checks the validity and implements a correction instruction only if the status of the system is included in the specified validity area.

In certain cases, correction instructions can be implemented only if other correction instructions have already been implemented. This is due to interdependent changes made to the same points in the source code, or to semantic dependencies.

These dependencies are described in the header area of the correction instructions. If there are dependencies, you will have to implement not just one Note, but also a series of Notes.

### Log File

A log file is created when you download a Note. A log file contains information about the main processing steps and the date, time, system and user in question. It therefore allows you to trace the steps that have already been taken.

You can also save your own notes or remarks in the log file, provided that you are entered as a processor for this Note.

The information in the log file cannot be deleted.

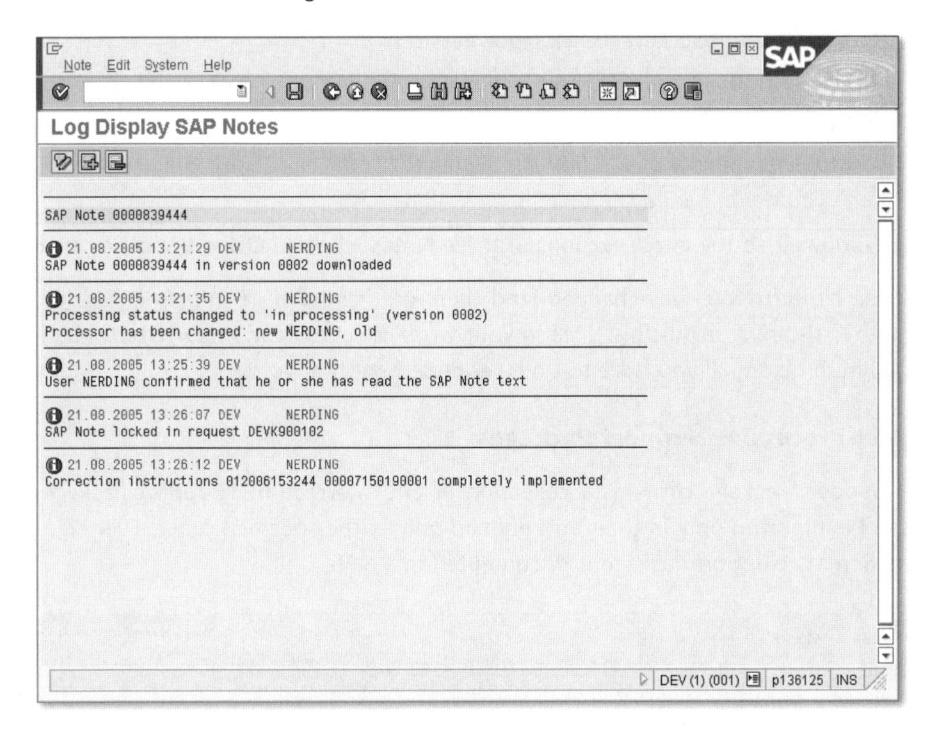


**Figure 15.10** Log file

## Update Note

This function enables you to compare the version of a Note in your system with the current version in the SAPNet-R/3 frontend. You can thus check at any time whether the Notes in your system are up to date. If necessary, the system downloads the latest version.

You have the following options:

- Compare an individual Note from within the Notes display
- Compare all the Notes listed in your work list
- Compare all the Notes listed in the Notes browser

**Note** Notes can be automatically updated only if you have set up an RFC connection to the SAPNet-R/3 frontend.

To update a Note, proceed as follows:

1. Choose **Download Latest SAP Note Version**.

   The system checks whether your system contains the latest versions of the Notes listed on the screen.

   It also displays in a dialog box the Notes that SAP has changed since the last time you downloaded them.

2. To download the latest versions of these Notes, click on **OK** in the dialog box.

If the current Note was changed, and therefore has to be re-implemented, the Note Assistant displays this Note in your work list under the **Inconsistent** heading. In this case, all you have to do is re-implement the Note.

### Post-processing Support Packages

A Support Package contains a collection of error corrections. Support Packages can be imported only in their entirety and only in the specified order. Every correction in a Support Package is documented in a Note.

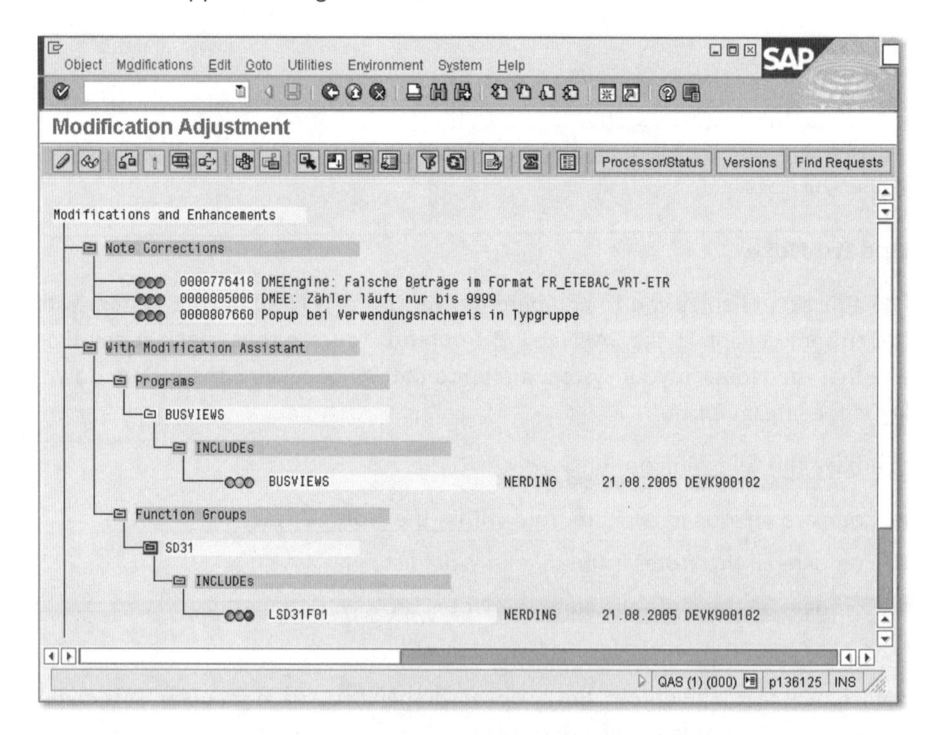


**Figure 15.11** Post-processing support packages in transaction SPAU

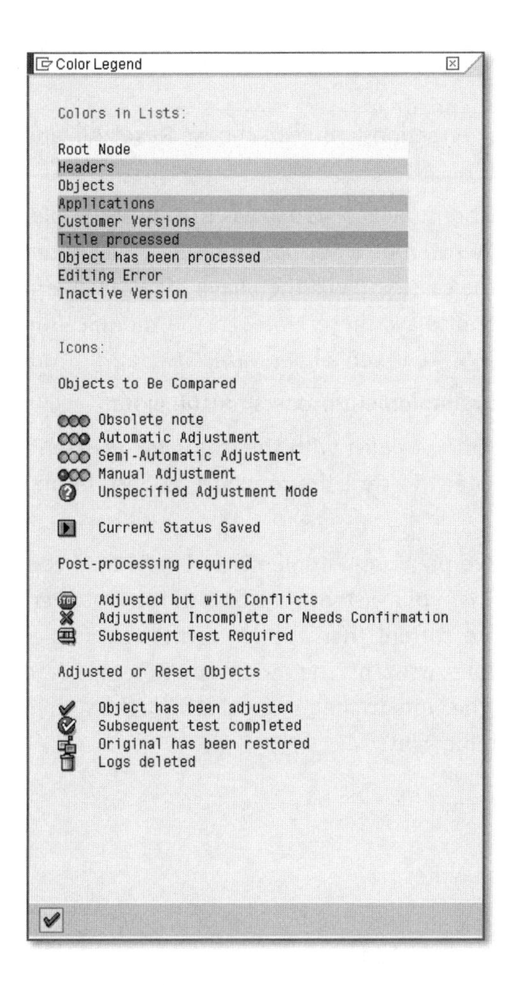


**Figure 15.12** Color legend in transaction SPAU

After you import a Support Package, you should execute the modification adjustment using Transaction SPAU. The cases that can arise are as follows.

1. When a Support Package is imported, the system automatically checks whether you have previously implemented individual corrections from this Support Package in the form of Notes. In the modification adjustment function (Transaction SPAU), these Notes are displayed with a *traffic light icon with no colors* and are therefore marked as obsolete.

   You must reset the objects they contain to their original SAP status. You can do this in one of the following ways:

   - Click on the traffic-light icon.
   - Position the cursor on the Note number. Choose **Reset to Original**.

A dialog box opens. In this box, confirm that you want to reset the Note correction to the original status.

If you have selected multiple Notes corrections, you can choose **Reset All**, and the dialog box does not open.

2. The system checks whether corrections, which you have previously implemented via a Note, have been overwritten by a Support Package that did not contain these corrections. If this is the case, you will then have to reimplement these Note corrections. The system displays these Notes in the modification comparison function (Transaction SPAU) with an *amber traffic light*.

   Click on the traffic light to start the reimplement process for the Note.

   These Notes are also displayed in your work list with the status **Inconsistent**, that is, they have to be reimplemented. To start the reimport, choose **Implement SAP Note**.

3. The system checks whether you have previously implemented individual corrections from the Support Package into your system via Notes. If the Note version in the Support Package is more current than the Note that was implemented in your system using the Note Assistant, the modification comparison function cannot reset the objects in the Note to their original status. The system displays this Note with an amber traffic light.

   In this case, proceed as follows:

   - Open the Note Assistant.
   - Download the latest version of all Notes.
   - Recalculate the adjustment modes in the modification adjustment. Then choose **Goto · Determine Adjustment Modes**.

   If SAP has not changed the Note, its traffic light icon has no colors. You can reset it to its original status as described in Step 1.

   If SAP has changed the Note, its traffic light icon is amber. In this case, proceed as described in Step 2.

4. An example of this case would be a Note that contains several correction instructions, each of which has a different validity period. This can have the following effect: When a Support Package is imported; one correction instruction may become obsolete, while another may still be valid. In such cases (which are, admittedly, rare), the Note has a *green traffic light* icon.

   If you click on the icon, correction instructions that are no longer relevant are reset to their original status.

5. The adjustment modes for Notes corrections are calculated in a background process after a Support Package is imported. However, if this process is not started for some reason, or if errors occur, a *green question mark* is displayed in

front of the object in the hierarchy display. Click on the question mark to restart the process. This process can take a few minutes.

**Note** If an object contains your own modifications and Note corrections, first you must process the Note corrections in the modification adjustment function (SPAU), and then adjust your own modifications.

The system does not support modification adjustments in the **With Modification Assistant** subtree if the object is contained in Note corrections that have not yet been adjusted, or that have not yet been reset to their original status.

In all cases, in a modification adjustment or when correction instructions are reset to their original status, the objects contained in the Note are placed into transport requests. This ensures that they are transported to the follow-on systems.

### 15.2.3 Implementation Status and Processing Status of Notes

The Note display in the Note Assistant contains two statuses: **implementation status** and **processing status**. The implementation status of a Note is determined by the system, based on existing information. The processing status, on the other hand, is specified by the user.

You should note that the system checks whether the processing status you specify is consistent with the implementation status of the correction instructions.

For example, you may set the processing status to **Completed** only if all the relevant corrections have been implemented (implementation status **Completely implemented** or **Cannot be implemented**).

If the implementation status changes afterwards and if it is no longer consistent with the processing status (for example, after a Support Package is imported), the system marks this Note as "inconsistent" in the Note overview.

#### Implementation Status

If a Note contains correction instructions, the implementation status indicates whether all relevant correction instructions of the Note have been implemented in the system.

The system automatically sets the implementation status. The possible values are as follows.

- **Incompletely implemented**
  Not all relevant correction instructions have been implemented, or a particular correction instruction has not been completely implemented. The objects in

question are therefore considered to be in an inconsistent state, and you should re-implement the relevant Note.

- **Obsolete version implemented**
  SAP has corrected a Note that contained errors. Re-implement the Note into your system.
- **Can be implemented**
  The Note contains correction instructions that you can implement in your system, if necessary.
- **Undefined Implementation State**
  The implementation state is undefined.
- **Completely implemented**
  The corrections in the Note have been fully implemented in your system. In this case, you don't have to take any action.
- **Cannot be implemented**
  The Note does not contain any correction instructions that you can implement in your system. In this case, you don't have to take any action.
- **Obsolete**
  After you implemented the corrections in the Note, you then imported a Support Package that also contains these corrections. The error has therefore been completely resolved.

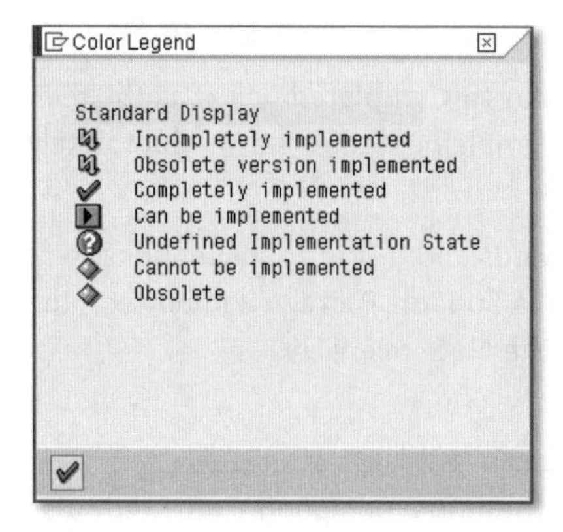


**Figure 15.13** Possible implementation statuses of a note

### Processing Status

The processor of a Note sets its processing status. This status tells other users and the system whether this Note has already been processed and if so, to what extent. This status is set in the Note Assistant and can be one of the following:

- **New**
  The Note has been loaded into your system but has not yet been processed.
- **In processing**
  The Note is being processed.
- **Completed**
  The instructions in the Note have been executed; any corrections have been implemented in the system. Consequently, processing is completed.
- **Not relevant**
  The Note has been read and classified as not relevant. A possible reason for this is that it pertains to a function that you don't use.

## 15.3 SAP Support Packages

SAP regularly publishes Support Packages for different types of program correction and updates, both for ABAP and Java.

Support Packages can be downloaded from the SAP Service Marketplace under the Quick Link */swdc* (*http://service.sap.com/swdc*). SAP also provides collections of Support Packages on CD-ROM. You can order these Support Packages from the SAP Software Shop at *http://service.sap.com/softwarecat*.

SAP provides a range of tools that make it easy and convenient for you to obtain Support Packages and to import them automatically.

The new reporting tool called *Side Effects of SAP Notes* helps you to avoid any undesirable side effects of Support Packages after you import them. This tool discovers whether the SAP Notes in a Support Package could have side effects on other areas of your SAP system, and outputs a list of additional SAP Notes that you can implement to prevent these side effects from occurring.

Support Packages provide the following benefits:

1. **Proactive solution of known problems**
   Support Packages solve known problems that have occurred in other SAP customers' systems, and thus proactively remove potential problems. This in turn leads to better system stability.
2. **Prerequisite to problem-solving**
   In rare cases, a problem can be solved only if a certain Support Package has been imported. In such cases, it is not possible to solve the problem with a series of Notes. If the problem in question occurs, the required Support Package will be have to be imported at short notice.

3. **Improved repair and maintenance**
   If a problem occurs, it is easier to find a solution if the latest Support Package has been imported. This is because you can exclude from the possible solutions all Notes that are contained in the Support Packages that have already been imported.
4. **Reduced repair and maintenance**
   If you import the Support Packages for your system, there is no need to import all the individual Notes. If the kind of error occurs that necessitates the implementation of a Note, this Note may have several prerequisite Notes that also have to be implemented. If you don't have the latest Support Packages, the list of prerequisite Notes may be very long, thus increasing the amount of time and effort required for error correction.
5. **Prerequisite for implementation projects**
   An up-to-date Support Package is often a prerequisite for the implementation of new functionality in a system. In such cases, if the Support Package level is not current, the implementation process will have to be put on hold until the appropriate Support Package is imported.
6. **Prerequisite for interfaces to other SAP systems**
   In some cases, it is necessary to import the latest Support Packages so that other SAP systems with newer Support Packages can use interfaces to your system.
7. **Statutory changes**
   Support Packages comply with the latest statutory requirements. This is especially relevant to the HR area, but also to statutory changes in the FI/CO area.

Support Packages contain quality improvements to the SAP system and make any adjustments that may be necessary (due to statutory changes, for example). They do this by replacing the affected objects in your system.

Every Support Package is valid for one specific release level (but for all databases and operating systems) and has a prerequisite number of predecessors. An upgrade of the next release level or correction level contains all Support Packages for the preceding levels that were available when the upgrade was delivered.

The Support Package Manager ensures that Support Packages are imported only in the correct order.

To prevent problems from occurring, import Support Packages at regular intervals. This is the best way to keep your system landscape up to date.

The following types of Support Packages are available:

- **SPAM/SAINT update**
  A SPAM/SAINT update (PAT) contains updates and improvements to the Support Package Manager and the SAP Add-On Installation Tool.
- **Component Support Packages**
  A Component Support Package (COP) applies to a particular software component (such as SAP_BASIS, SAP_HR, and SAP_APPL) and contains quality improvements to Repository and Dictionary objects in this specific component.

  Support Packages for the SAP_HR component also contain changes made in response to statutory changes, as well as the usual improvements.
- **Add-on Support Package**
  An add-on Support Package (AOP) always applies to an add-on with a specific release. It contains quality improvements to this add-on.
- **Conflict Resolution Transport**
  A Conflict Resolution Transport (CRT) is used exclusively for add-ons, such as IS-IS or IS-OIL. Its purpose is to adapt a Support Package to an add-on.

**Tip** Note that a CRT that applies to a specific add-on release also contains all changes made for earlier releases of this add-on. A CRT may also contain other quality improvements for the relevant add-on. Thus, a CRT can also be a special add-on Support Package.

The naming convention for Support Packages is as follows:

| Software component | Name |
| --- | --- |
| SAP_APPL | SAP ERP Support Package |
| SAP_BASIS | Basis Support Package |
| SAP_ABA | Application Interface Support Package |
| SAP_HR | SAP HR Support Package |
| SAP_APO | APO Support Package |
| SAP_BW | BW Support Package |
| BBPCRM | BBP/EBP and CRM Support Package |

Java Support Packages contain corrections and updates to Java components. They are delivered in the form of software component archives (SCAs). Unlike ABAP Support Packages, Java Support Packages always contain the full version of the development component in question. It is therefore sufficient to import only the latest one. If there are dependencies between the current Java Support Package and other Java Support Packages, these dependencies are described in an SAP Note.

Java Support Packages have been delivered since SAP Web Application Server (SAP Web AS) 6.20 and are imported using the Software Delivery Manager (SDM). The SDM is delivered with the SAP Web AS from Version 6.20. SAP Note 544244 contains more detailed information on this topic.

### 15.3.1 Importing SAP Support Packages

#### Support Package Manager

The Support Package Manager (Transaction SPAM) enables you to import SAP Support Packages into your system simply and efficiently.

You can open the SPM in one of the following ways:

- Choose **SAP Menu · Tools · ABAP Workbench · Utilities · Maintenance · Support Package Manager**.
- Enter the transaction code SPAM.

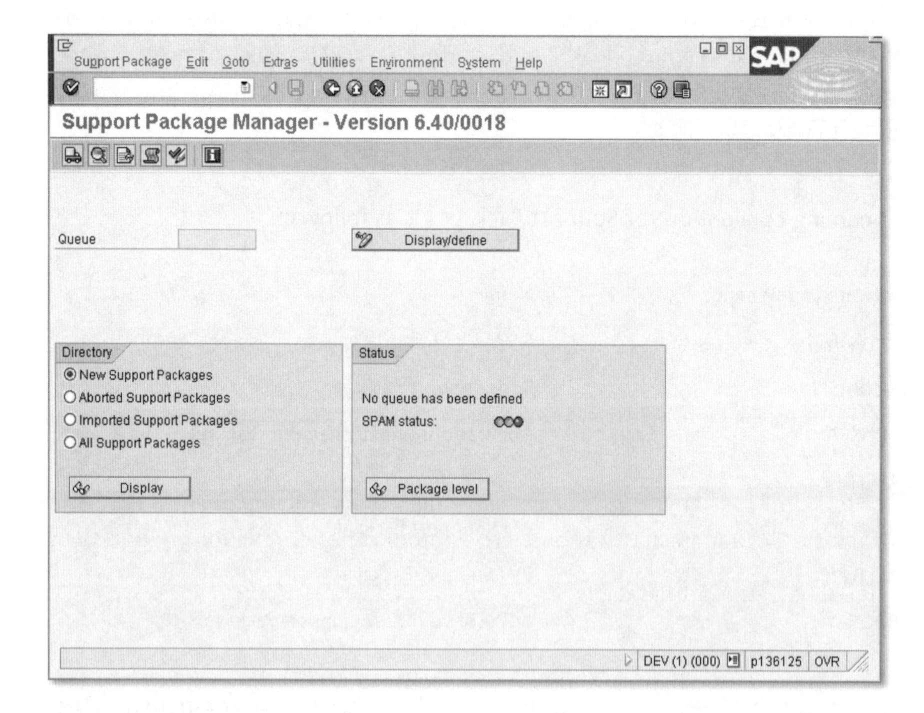


**Figure 15.14** Initial screen of transaction SPAM

The Support Package Manager has the following features:

- **Support Package loading**
  You can load Support Packages into your system from the SAP Service Marketplace, the SAPNet-R/3 frontend, or from collection CDs.
- **Restartability**
  When the Support Package Manager imports a Support Package into your system, it adheres to a fixed order of steps.

  If the import process has to be canceled for any reason, you can then resume processing at a later stage from the point that had been reached.
- **Display import status**
  You can use the Support Package Manager to find out the current import status of your system at any time.
- **Special import procedure**
  A special import procedure minimizes downtime.
- **Start time control**
  The individual phases of the Support Package Manager are grouped into modules. This allows you to set the start time of the modules to any time you like.
- **Background processing**
  You can also schedule the modules to run in background processing, with predefined start times.

You need the following authorizations to be able to use all the functions of the Support Package Manager:

- S_TRANSPRT
- S_CTS_ADMIN

Both authorizations are contained in the S_A.SYSTEM authorization profile.

If you log on to client 000 and your user master contains the relevant authorization profile, you can use all the functions of the Support Package Manager. If you log on to another client, or if you don't have the required user profile, you can use only the display functions.

You should only assign this authorization profile to the system administrator. Also, only the system administrator should have authorization for the following actions:

- Download Support Packages
- Import Support Packages
- Confirm successfully imported Support Packages
- Reset the status of a Support Package

Choose **Extras • Settings** to open a dialog box in which you can make general settings for the Support Package Manager. These settings affect the behavior of the system when loading and importing all types of Support Packages. One exception is SPAM/SAINT updates, which have special predefined settings.

You only have to make the settings once, since they're saved and used every time the Support Package Manager is called. Note that these settings also apply to the SAP Add-On Installation Tool.

An exception to this is the settings for the *Downtime-minimized* import mode: This does not automatically apply to the SAP Add-On Installation Tool.

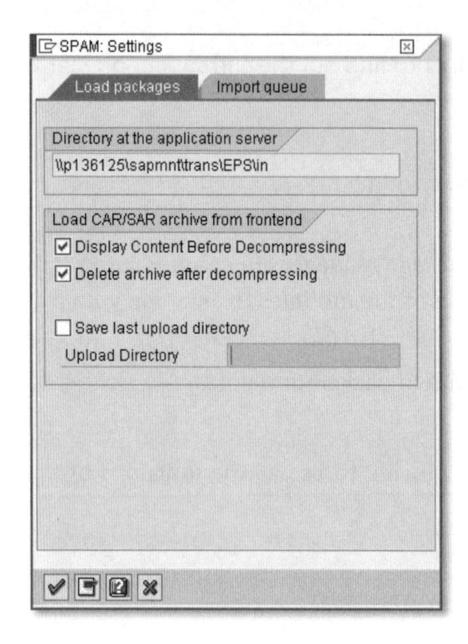


**Figure 15.15** Load packages tab page

You can change or check the following properties:

- **Load CAR/SAR archive from frontend**
  - **Transmission Monitor**
    The Transmission Monitor is a graphical monitor that enables you to monitor the loading of Support Packages from the SAPNet-R/3 frontend. Otherwise, the progress of the load process is indicated in the status bar.
  - **RFC destination**
    Displays the name of the RFC destination, which is used for the connection to the SAPNet-R/3 frontend. You do not usually need to change the standard setting **SAPOSS**. Transaction OSS1 is used to set up the SAPOSS destination.

- **Directory at the application server**
  Shows you the application server directory in which the Support Packages are stored.
- **Load CAR/SAR archives from the frontend**
  - **Display content before decompressing**
    Allows you to specify whether you want to view a dialog box containing the archive content before the CAR/SAR archive is decompressed. This is checked by default.
  - **Delete archive after decompressing**
    Allows you to specify whether the CAR/SAR archive that was transferred to the application server should be deleted after it is successfully decompressed. This is checked by default.
  - **Save last upload directory**
    Allows you to specify whether the most recently used upload directory on your front-end computer should be saved. If you select this option, this directory is then automatically displayed as the start directory in the archive selection dialog box the next time you use this transaction. This is checked by default.
    You can also enter an upload directory of your choice in the **Upload Directory** field. This upload directory is then displayed as the start directory in the archive selection dialog box.

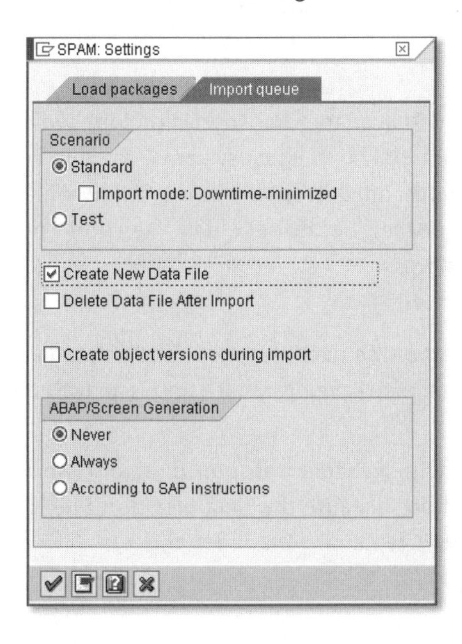


**Figure 15.16** Import queue tab page

- **Scenario**

  By selecting a scenario, you are specifying which actions will be carried out during the import of the Support Package.

  - **Standard**
    Select the standard scenario if you want to fully import Support Packages and to execute all the steps involved.
  - **Import mode: downtime-minimized**
    If you select the standard scenario, you can also select *downtime-minimized* import mode to reduce the length of the downtime. This is not selected by default, which means that if you don't select this option, the packages are imported by the conventional method. For more information on this import mode, see the relevant section below.
  - **Test**
    The test scenario allows you to determine whether you need to carry out a modification adjustment, or whether there are conflicts that need to be removed before the import, that is, before the Support Package itself is imported. No data or objects are imported into your system in the test scenario. There is no test scenario for SPAM/SAINT updates. Therefore, if you select this option when importing a SPAM/SAINT update, it is simply ignored.

- **Create new data file**

  This option allows you to specify whether the data files in the EPS packages should be decompressed with every attempted import. This is checked by default.

  If you have a multisystem landscape with a shared transport directory, we recommend that you switch on this option only in the first system into which you import Support Packages, and to switch off this option in the follow-on systems. This saves time in the import process, because the data files don't need to be re-created in the follow-on systems.

- **Delete data file after import**

  This option allows you to specify whether the data files should be deleted after a Support Package is imported. This helps to save disk space and is activated by default.

  If you have a multisystem landscape with a shared transport directory, we recommend that you switch on this option, because the data files don't need to be recreated in the other system (see "Create new data file" above).

- **Create object versions during import**

  This option does not apply to SPAM/SAINT updates.

It allows you to specify whether versions should be created of the objects of the Support Packages in the import process. This option is deactivated by default. This is because versioning makes sense only if it is activated for all imports, and also because it increases the run time and takes up additional space in the database.

**Note** If you activate the versioning option, note that when configuring the transport tools in the Transport Management System (Transaction STMS), you must set the `VERS_AT_IMP` parameter to `ALWAYS`.

- **ABAP/screen generation**

  These options allow you to specify whether the programs and screens that come with the Support Package should be generated during the import.

  They have no effect with SPAM/SAINT updates.

  - **Never**
    If you select this option, the programs and screens are generated only when they are first called.
  - **Always**
    If you select this option, the programs and screens are always generated. Note that the generation process can take a very long time and may cause errors to occur.
  - **According to SAP instructions**
    If you select this option, the programs and screens are always generated if the generation option is activated during the import process for these Support Packages.

The Support Package Manager has the following basic settings:

| Option | SPAM basic setting |
|---|---|
| Transmission Monitor | Off |
| RFC destination | SAPOSS |
| Display content before decompressing | On |
| Delete archive after decompressing | On |
| Save last upload directory | On |
| Scenario | Standard |
| Downtime-minimized import mode | Off |

| Option | SPAM basic setting |
|---|---|
| Recreate data file | On |
| Delete data file after import | On |
| Create object versions during import | Off |
| ABAP/screen generation | Never |

All actions that the import tools perform run in *phases*. These phases, in turn, are grouped into modules. The modules have the following properties:

- You can run them individually.
- You can start them in a background process.
- You can set the start time of the modules to any time you like.

The import process is subdivided into the following modules:

- **Preparation module**
  This module carries out all the preparation and testing steps (such as a test import and add-on conflict checking). It can run during live operation.
  After you have run the Preparation module, you can reset the queue if, for example, you find that you have to import a different number of Support Packages. If you proceed to the Import 1 module, the data is changed in the database and you won't be able to reset or delete the queue from this point on.
- **Import 1 module**
  This module imports and activates Dictionary objects (and carries out a modification comparison of Dictionary objects, if necessary). Any changes that are made in the process of importing and activating the Dictionary are still in an inactive state in the system. This means that the runtime system cannot yet "see" these changes. If you are sure that there are no manual changes to be made and that no transports will be imported into the system, this module can also run during live operation. This is usually the standard in production systems.
- **Import 2 module**
  This module carries out the remaining import steps, including the activation of inactive Dictionary name tabs. To avoid inconsistencies, this module cannot run simultaneously with live operations, since it imports changes to various development objects.
- **Clean-Up module**
  This module handles all post-import ("clean-up") steps, especially modification comparison for the Repository objects. Live operations can resume once all modifications have been compared.

Because the package import process can be stopped after every module, it is possible to run the Preparation and Import 1 modules during live operations, if no modifications have been made to Dictionary objects. Once the system is transferred to non-live operations, the Import 2 module and, if necessary, the modification comparison can then be carried out, after which live operations can resume.

**Tip** Note that no company-specific transports, apart from modification comparison transports, can occur during the time between the Preparation and Import 2 modules (or during the time up to the modification comparison), and that no manual changes can be made to Repository objects (ABAP programs and Dictionary objects) in the same period. The time between Import 1 and Import 2 should be as short as possible.

The Support Package Manager uses the status bar to indicate which phase is currently being executed. If you want to know which phases are executed for which scenario (test or standard scenario), run program `RSSPAM10`.

The following list provides an overview of all the modules and phases in the order in which they are executed by the Support Package Manager:

- **Preparation module**
  - PROLOGUE
    This phase checks whether you're authorized to import Support Packages.
  - CHECK_REQUIREMENTS
    This phase checks various import prerequisites, such as whether the transport control program `tp` can log on to your system.
  - DISASSEMBLE
    This phase extracts the data files from the relevant EPS packages and stores them in the transport directory.
  - ADD_TO_BUFFER
    This phase adds the queue to the transport buffer of your system.
  - MODIFY_BUFFER
    This phase modifies the transport buffer so that it can process the next import phases correctly.
  - TEST_IMPORT
    This phase carries out a test import using the transport control program `tp` for the current queue. In doing so, it checks whether any objects are currently in repair and will be overwritten during the import, and whether there are any other factors that will prevent an object from being imported.

- IMPORT_OBJECT_LIST
  This phase imports into the system the object lists for the Support Packages in the queue.
- OBJECTS_LOCKED_?
  This phase checks whether there are any objects that will be overwritten in the import and that are contained in requests that have not yet been released.
- ADDON_CONFLICTS_?
  This phase checks whether there are any conflicts between objects in the queue and installed add-ons.
- SCHEDULE_RDDIMPDP
  This phase schedules the transport demon (program RDDIMPDP).

- **Import 1 module**
  - CREATE_VERS_BEFORE
    If this option is selected, this phase creates versions of the objects of the Support Packages in the queue.
  - SPDD_SPAU_CHECK
    This phase checks whether a modification comparison (transactions SPDD/SPAU) is required.
  - DDIC_IMPORT
    This phase imports all ABAP Dictionary objects in the queue.
  - AUTO_MOD_SPDD
    This phase checks whether modifications to ABAP Dictionary objects can be automatically compared.
  - RUN_SPDD_?
    This phase instructs you to compare your ABAP Dictionary object modifications by calling Transaction SPDD.
  - LOCK_EU (only in *Downtime-minimized* import mode)
    This phase locks the development environment.
  - DDIC_ACTIVATION
    This phase activates the imported ABAP Dictionary objects.
  - INACTIVE_IMPORT (only in *Downtime-minimized* import mode)
    This phase imports program code and texts in an inactive state.
- **Import 2 module**
  - IMPORT_PROPER
    This phase imports all Repository objects and table entries that were not imported in the INACTIVE_IMPORT phase. Actions such as table conversions and name-tab activation are carried out beforehand.

- PREPARE_XPRA
  This phase prepares the execution of the XPRAs and after-import methods.
- UNLOCK_EU (only in *Downtime-minimized* import mode)
  This phase unlocks the development environment.
- AUTO_MOD_SPAU
  This phase checks whether modifications can be automatically compared.
- XPRA_EXECUTION
  This phase executes the XPRAs and after-import methods.

- **Preparation module**
  - ABAP_GENERATION
    This phase generates the runtime objects for imported Repository objects (ABAP source code, screens).
  - RUN_SPAU_?
    This phase instructs you to compare your Repository object modifications by calling Transaction SPAU.
  - CLEAR_OLD_REPORTS (only in *Downtime-minimized* import mode)
    This phase deletes obsolete versions of program code and program texts from the database.
  - EPILOGUE
    This phase closes the import. The system also checks whether the queue has been fully processed.

### Import SPAM/SAINT Update

SPAM/SAINT updates (known as SPAM updates for short) provide you with updates and improvements to the Support Package Manager and the SAP Add-On Installation tool. Every release comes with a SPAM update, which is then updated as necessary over time. It is stored in the following locations in the system:

- In the short description; for example, *SPAM/SAINT update version <REL>/0001*
- In the package name; for example, *SAPKD<REL>01*

A SPAM update is always first in the list of Support Packages in the SAPNet-R/3 frontend. You can also find the latest SPAM update in the SAP Services Marketplace under *http://service.sap.com/patches*.

**Note** We recommend that you always import the latest version of a SPAM update before importing Support Packages or Installation Packages.

A SPAM update can be successfully imported only if the system does not contain any canceled packages. If the system does contain such packages, a dialog box informs you of this, in which case, you can do one of two things:

- First, you can fully import the queue and then import the SPAM update.
- Delete the queue, import the SPAM update, and then import the queue.

You can delete the queue only if the Import 1 module has not yet been started (up to phase SCHEDULE_RDDIMPDP).

To import a SPAM update, proceed as follows:

1. Open the Support Package Manager (Transaction SPAM).
2. Check that the SPAM update in question is more up-to-date than the version that is currently in your system. (The latest version is displayed in the title bar of the Support Package Manager.)
3. Once you're satisfied that the update you will be importing is the latest one, choose **Support Package · Import SPAM update**. SPAM updates are automatically confirmed after they have been successfully imported.

### Loading Support Packages

Before you can import a Support Package, you first have to load it. SAP makes its Support Packages available via the following channels:

- The SAPNet-R/3 frontend
- The SAP Service Marketplace
- Collection CDs

Proceed as follows to load Support Packages from the SAPNet-R/3 frontend so that you can import the Support Packages in question with the Support Package Manager:

1. Request the Support Packages you require in the SAPNet-R/3 frontend. To do this, see Note 97621.
2. Load the Support Packages from the SAPNet-R/3 frontend to your SAP system by choosing **Support Package · Load Packages · From SAPNet-R/3 Front End**.

   The system displays a list of Support Packages. You can select the Support Packages you require before loading them.

   The size of the uncompressed Support Packages is shown in bytes. This figure gives you a rough idea of the time needed for the Support Package to load.
3. The status bar indicates whether the load process was successful.
4. Choose **Goto · Back** to return to the Support Package Manager.
5. Define the queue.

**Note** Before loading a Support Package from the SAPNet-R/3 frontend, make sure that the network parameters for logging on to the SAPNet-R/3 frontend are correct. You do this by using Transaction OSS1.

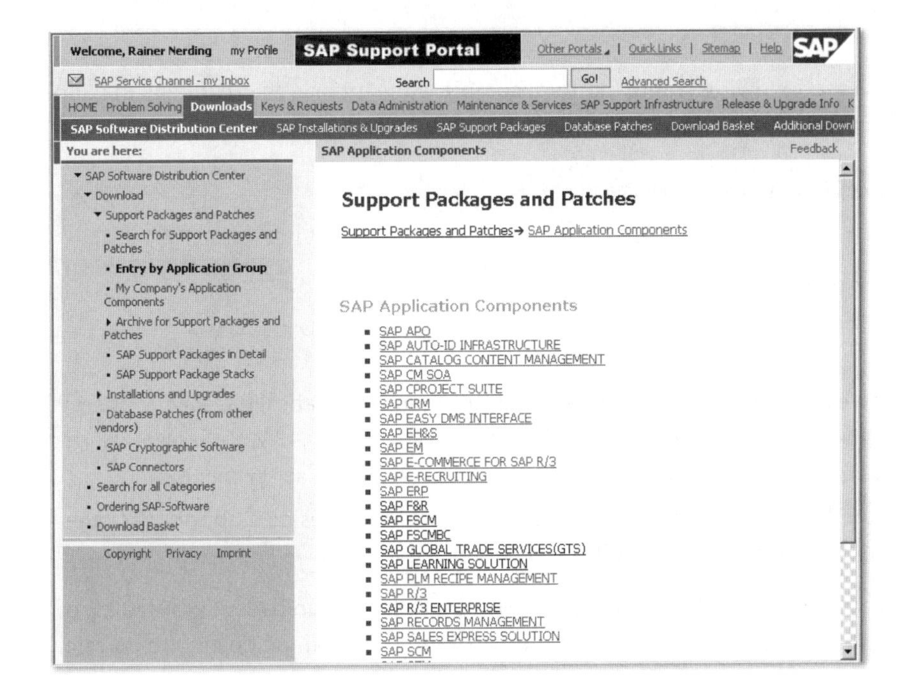


**Figure 15.17** Loading support packages from the SAP Service Marketplace

Support Packages in the SAP Service Marketplace and on Collection CDs come in a compressed format. You therefore have to *decompress* them before using them.

If the archives are located on your front-end computer, you can transfer these directly to the application server from within the Support Package Manager and decompress them there. However, if the archives are *larger than 10 MB*, proceed as follows:

1. Load the Support Packages from the SAP Service Marketplace or mount the relevant CD.
2. Log on with the following user:

| Operating system | User |
|---|---|
| Unix | <sid>adm |
| IBM eServer iSeries | <SID>OFR |
| Windows | <SID>adm |

3. Switch to the following subdirectory in your system:

| Operating system | Subdirectory |
|---|---|
| Unix and IBM eServer iSeries | trans |
| Windows | TRANS |

4. Use the following command to decompress the archive that contains the Support Packages:

| Operating system | Command |
|---|---|
| Unix | SAPCAR -xvf /<CD_DIR>/<PATH>/<ARCHIVE>.CAR |
| IBM eServer iSeries | SAPCAR '-xvf /QOPT/<VOLID>/<PATH>/<ARCHIVE>.CAR' |
| Windows | SAPCAR -xvf <CD_DRIVE>:\<PATH>\<ARCHIVE>.CAR |

   The decompressed Support Packages are then automatically placed in the EPS Inbox of your transport directory (Unix and IBM eServer iSeries: /usr/sap/trans/EPS/in; Windows: <DRIVE>:\usr\sap\trans\EPS\in).

5. Now load the Support Packages into your system using **Support Package • Load Package • From Application Server**.

A list is displayed of the Support Packages that you just uploaded, which are now known to the SAP system with all their attributes and can be dealt with correctly by the Support Package Manager.

1. Choose **Back** to return to the initial screen of the Support Package Manager.
2. Define the queue.

If you want to load the archives (*.CAR/*.SAR) from the frontend to the application server, and if the archives are *smaller than 10 MB*, proceed as described below. If the archives are *greater than 10 MB*, the procedure described below will not be efficient. Therefore, in this case, first transfer the Support Packages to the application server by FTP, for example, and then load them from there.

1. Open the Support Package Manager (Transaction SPAM).
2. Choose **Support Package • Load Packages • From Front End**. The dialog box for archive selection opens.
3. Select the relevant archive. This archive is transferred to the application server. The archive's table of contents is then read and displayed in a dialog box.
4. Select **Decompress** to transfer the archive to the application server and decompress it. If you select the **New Support Packages** option and choose **Display**

under **Directory** in the initial screen, the corresponding package is displayed in the Support Package Manager after the archive has been decompressed.

5. Choose **Goto • Back** to return to the Support Package Manager.
6. Define the queue.

### Define Queue

The queue determines which Support Packages are imported into your system by the Support Package Manager, and in what order. If the queue has not yet been fully defined, you now have to define the queue, making your selection from the available Support Packages. If the queue has been fully defined, it is simply displayed, and you cannot change it. However, you can delete the queue entirely, if required, by choosing **Delete Queue**.

**Note** You can delete the queue only if the Import 1 module has not yet been started (up to phase SCHEDULE_RDDIMPDP).

The Support Package Manager ensures that only Support Packages that are suitable for your system are displayed in the queue. Support Packages that are intended for another release, or for an add-on that you have not installed, don't appear in the queue, even if you loaded them into your SAP system.

You can define the queue on the basis of either the software components in your system or a target Support Package.

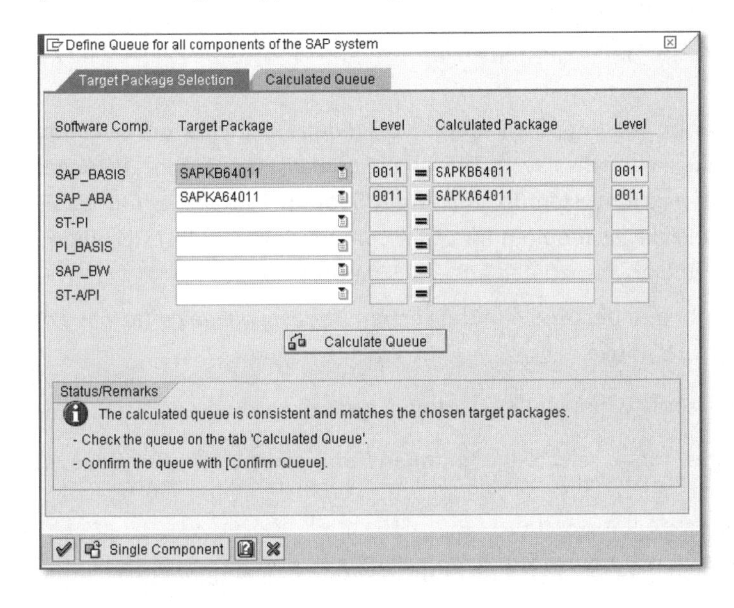


**Figure 15.18** Defining the import queue

1. To define a queue on the basis of software components, click on **Display/Define** in the initial screen of the Support Package Manager.

   The **Component Selection** dialog box opens, and the list of installed software components is displayed (such as SAP_BASIS, SAP_HR, SAP_BW).
2. Select the component you want. Alternatively, you can calculate a common source for all software components in the system by selecting **All Components**.
3. The available queue is then displayed. The queue contains the Support Packages that are available for the selected component(s) in your system, and possibly also any Support Packages required for other components, Conflict Resolution Transports (CRT), and any associated add-on Support Packages.

   If you want to define the queue for another software component, select **New Component**.
4. You now have the following options:
   - If you're happy with the queue as displayed, choose **Confirm Queue** to confirm and close the dialog box.
   - You also have the option to reduce the queue selection. To do this, select the Support Package that you want to be the last in the queue. The queue is then recalculated. You can also explicitly re-calculate the queue by selecting **Recalculate Queue**.

To define the queue on the basis of a target Support Package, proceed as follows:

1. In the initial screen of the Support Package Manager, choose the **New Support Packages** option under **Directory**.
2. Click on **Display**. The system displays a list of the Support Packages in the system.
3. Place your cursor on the Support Package you require and click on **Calculate Queue**. The queue is then displayed. This queue contains the Support Packages that are available in your system for the target Support Package, and possibly also any Support Packages required for other components, Conflict Resolution Transport (CRT), and any associated add-on Support Packages.
4. Proceed as described under Step 4 in the section *Defining queue on the basis of software components* above.

The following rules apply when you're creating a queue:

- Support Packages for a selected component are placed in the queue in sequence.
- If Support Packages in the queue are linked to Support Packages of another component (such as another predecessor relationship or a required CRT), other

Support Packages are added to the queue until all predecessor relationships are accounted for.

**Note** The Support Package Manager takes into account the configuration of your SAP system and places in the queue only those Support Packages that your system can accept.

**Import queue**

The Support Package Manager provides the following two scenarios for importing Support Packages or the queue:

The test scenario is used to identify any conflicts or problems (for example, repairs that have not been released) before the actual import process. The test import creates the list of objects to be compared in transactions SPDD and SPAU, and should therefore be run in the project preparation phase. If you want to run the test scenario, you have to specify so explicitly.

This scenario allows you to estimate—and, if necessary, to minimize—the time and effort required to import Support Packages. No data is imported into the system in this scenario, and if errors occur, you can continue the import without having to correct them.

**Note** After the test scenario has run, the queue is then empty again and you will have to redefine it. You then also have to explicitly select the standard scenario.

In the standard scenario, the Support Packages contained in the queue are fully imported. If errors occur, you can continue and complete the import only once you have removed or resolved the errors.

Once you have selected the standard scenario, you can choose between conventional import mode and *Downtime-minimized* import mode. The latter reduces the length of the downtime.

Proceed as follows to import the queue in the standard scenario:

1. To set the standard scenario, select **Extras · Settings**.
2. On the **Import Queue** tab page, select **Standard** and make the other import settings.
3. Select the import mode that you require.

4. Select **Support Package · Import Queue**. You can also use this function to resume a previous import procedure that was canceled.
5. The dialog box for selecting the start options opens. Specify the required start options and confirm the dialog box.

The Support Package Manager then completes the import, in accordance with the import mode and start options you selected.

If you accept the standard start options without changing them, the Support Package Manager handles the whole import process in the dialog box. The status bar provides you with information about the progress of the import and the current phases of the Support Package Manager. Note that your system should no longer be live at this point.

If you selected a start time or **Continue Manually** for the Import 2 module, you can keep the system in live mode until the Import 2 module starts.

If you accepted the standard start options without changing them, you can keep the system in live mode for the time being, as the Support Package Manager will explicitly request you to stop live operations when the time comes.

As usual, the Support Package Manager carries out all the preparatory and checking steps (Preparation module). It then imports the inactive objects (Import 1 module), during which process the system can stay live.

The development environment is locked when the Import 1 module starts, so that objects are not unintentionally modified and therefore the consistency of the system is not jeopardized when objects are accessed by this module.

The Support Package Manager then notifies you in a dialog box that you have to stop live operations for the next import module (Import 2).

- Click on **Cancel** to do this in an orderly manner.

  Close any background jobs that are running. Request all users to close any transactions that they are running and to log themselves off from the SAP system.

- Click on **Continue** to continue the import.

  The Import 2 module activates the objects that were previously imported in an inactive state and imports the remaining objects from the Support Packages in the queue.

  Once this module has finished, the Support Package Manager informs you that you can resume live operations in the system, provided that no changes, or at most only small changes, were made to SAP objects.

- If you made changes to SAP objects, the Support Package Manager instructs you to finish the modification comparison process.

  If you have to compare Dictionary objects (Transaction SPDD), you must do this immediately, whereas with Repository objects (Transaction SPAU), you can either compare these objects immediately or at a later point, or in parallel with the clean-up steps after importing a Support Package. To do this, proceed as described in Section 16.3.

- To complete the import process, select **Import Queue** again.

  The clean-up steps are carried out on the next import module (Clean Up), and the import process is completed and closed.

You can define the start options for the individual modules in accordance with the requirements of your system. If you confirm the dialog box without making any specific settings of your own, the import tool uses the standard settings of the selected import mode. You can store any settings you make as a template for future import procedures.

The tab pages in the **Start options for the queue** dialog box allow you to select the options you require for every module:

- **Start in dialog immediately**
  Select this option if you want this module to start running immediately in the dialog box. If you select this option for multiple modules, they are executed immediately one after the other. The mode remains blocked for the duration of the import.
- **Start in background immediately**
  Select this option if you want this module to start running immediately in the background. If you select this option for multiple modules, they are executed immediately one after the other.
- **Start in background later**
  Select this option if you want this module to start running in the background at a later time. Specify the start date and start time you require in the input fields. The **No start after** option allows you to specify that this module is to run only in the period between the **Planned start** time and the current time. If no background process is available in this time period, this module is not started.
- **Manual Start/Continue Manually**
  Select this option if you want to manually start processing of this module. The import tool stops the processing process once the previous module has finished.

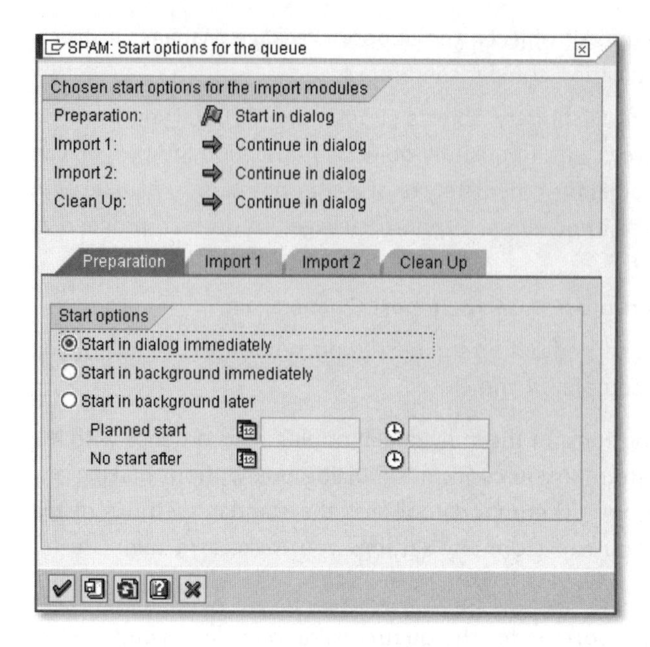


Figure 15.19 Defining the start options

If you selected the conventional import procedure (*Downtime-minimized* is not activated), the following standard settings apply:

| Module | Option |
|---|---|
| Preparation | Start in dialog immediately |
| Import 1 | Continue in dialog immediately |
| Import 2 | Continue in dialog |
| Clean Up | Continue in dialog |

If you have selected *Downtime-minimized* import mode, the following standard settings apply:

| Module | Option |
|---|---|
| Preparation | Start in dialog immediately |
| Import 1 | Continue in dialog immediately |
| Import 2 | Continue manually |
| Clean Up | Continue manually |

### Downtime-Minimized Import Mode

As a rule, the process of importing the latest OCS packages (Support Packages, Add-on Installation Packages, add-on upgrades) requires a relatively long system downtime due to the size and scope of these packages. Although the system is not restarted in the import process, it should still not be used for live operations during this process. This restriction is a distinct disadvantage in many live systems.

Thus, *Downtime-minimized* import mode was developed to reduce the downtime required for package imports. This mode enables you to import the majority of import objects while keeping the system live. The objects in question are program code and program texts. Therefore, downtime can be reduced greatly if a package contains a high proportion of program code and texts. (This figure is approximately 70–80 % for SAP Basis and SAP_APPL Support Packages.)

In *Downtime-minimized* import mode, the objects are imported into the database in an inactive state and are mostly "invisible" to the system. The system can continue to stay live.

This procedure contains new actions (activation of inactive objects) and more organizational steps than the previous mode, which means that the whole import process takes longer in this case. The efficiency and time-savings in the non-live phase of this mode, as compared to conventional mode, depend on two things: the proportion of inactively imported objects of the overall volume of imported data, and the amount of time consumed by additional actions that have to be carried out during the downtime (such as the handling of after-import methods and XPRAs).

**Note** Import the packages in queues that are as large as possible. Ideally, put all packages in one queue to benefit most from this method. You should note, however, that in some cases Support Packages cannot be imported in one queue using the Support Package Manager. Consult the relevant SAP Note in your release for more information.

Because the inactively imported objects are stored in the database at the same time as the active versions, more space is temporarily required in the database.

The objects are activated later by a defined process that is provided by the import tool (Support Package Manager/SAP Add-On Installation Tool). Nevertheless, inactive objects are not fully isolated from the system, which means that parallel changes can cause unwanted activations and therefore system inconsistencies.

During the import, you should ensure the following:

- There is enough free storage space in the database
- There are no simultaneous imports of transport requests
- The development environment is not in live use

Use *Downtime-minimized* import mode in the following situations:

- In live systems
- In test systems, if you want to test the expected downtime in the live system

During the import process, you should treat the systems like live systems (no manual changes to program objects, no parallel imports of other transport requests).

Do not use *Downtime-minimized* import mode in the following situations:

- In development systems or in systems into which a lot of regular imports are made (such as QA or test systems)

  System consistency cannot be guaranteed during the import if manual changes are made to program objects, or if other transport requests are imported at the same time.
- To import Support Packages to BBP/CRM systems

  The additional preparation and clean-up steps required by the special Support Package Manager for BBP/CRM mean that the whole import process effectively takes place during downtime.
- To import Preconfigured Systems (SAP Best Practices) using the Add-On Installation Tool

### Importing Support Packages into a System Landscape

Support Packages can be imported in groups or individually. If you have multiple SAP systems in a system landscape like DEV, QAS and PRD, you must import Support Packages into each of these systems.

You can use the aforementioned procedure to import Support Packages into your landscape's development system, but the procedure is different for the other SAP systems in your landscape, especially if you have to carry out a modification adjustment. Figure 15.20 shows an example of how Support Packages can be distributed in a three-system landscape.

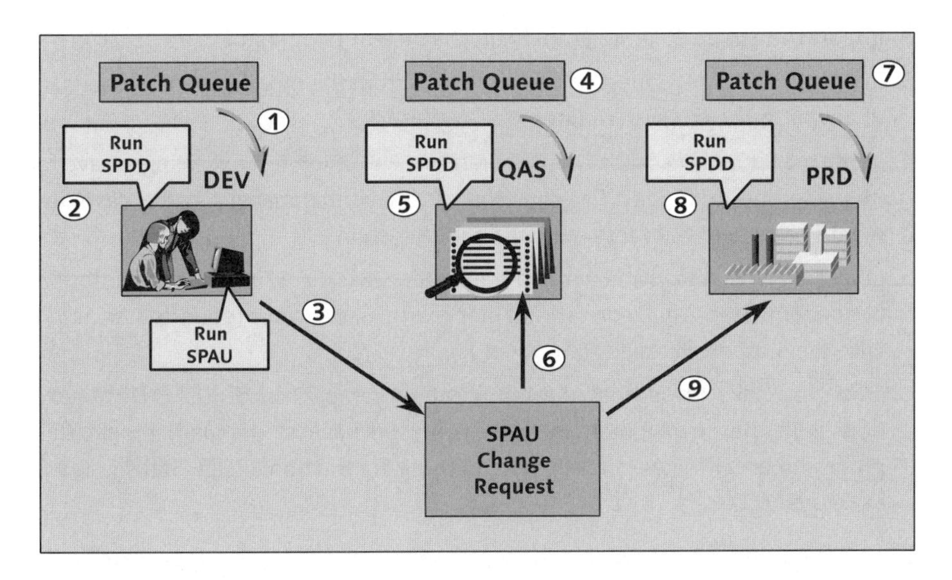


**Figure 15.20** Distribution of support packages in a three-system landscape

Ideally, all SAP systems have the same release level, which is the case after they are installed, after an SAP release upgrade, or after the rollout in the implementation phase. If all SAP systems have the same release level, you can import one or more Support Packages in the same way as you import change requests:

1. Import the Support Packages into the development system (Step 1 in Figure 15.20). The system compares all objects that were imported with the Support Package and that have been modified by the customer:
   - You may need to carry out a modification comparison for the Dictionary objects using Transaction SPDD in the development system (Step 2 in Figure 15.20). The changes that result from the comparison can then be included in a change request. However, unlike with release upgrades, this request cannot be used for an automatic modification comparison of ABAP Dictionary objects in follow-on R/3 systems (see below). Instead, the comparison procedure must be repeated manually in every SAP system (Steps 5 and 8).
   - You may need to carry out a modification comparison for the SAP Repository objects using Transaction SPAU in the development system (Step 3 in Figure 15.20). The changes that result from the comparison can then be included in a change request. This change request can be used to transport the modification comparison of the SAP Repository objects to other systems. If extensions were used to make changes to the SAP system (see Chapter 2), there is no need for a comparison, since extensions don't introduce modifications.

2. Import the Support Packages into the QA system (Step 4 in Figure 15.20).
3. Import the change request with the changes from the modification comparison (if any) into the QA system (Step 6 in Figure 15.20).
4. Verify the Support Package using operational validation tests. If changes have to be made due to Support Package imports, make the changes in the development system and then test them in the QA system.
5. Once you have tested and verified the Support Packages, import them into the live system (Step 7 in Figure 15.20) along with all transport requests associated with the Support Packages (Step 9 in Figure 15.20).
6. Once you have carried out the modification comparison of ABAP Dictionary objects in the development system, you then have to manually repeat this process in every follow-on SAP system, using Transaction SPDD (Steps 5 and 8 in Figure 15.20).

It is a prerequisite of this process that no change requests for the import are waiting to be processed in the QA or in the live system. To put it another way, the SAP systems—especially the QA and the live systems—must all have the same release level. The validation process in the QA system ensures that the Support Package and all the change requests that result from the modification comparison can be imported into the live system.

### Support Packages and Development Projects

It is more difficult to schedule Support Package imports if large development projects are ongoing in your system landscape. This is because you're not supposed to make transports between systems with different Support Package levels. Therefore, development projects cannot be imported into the live system until the Support Packages have been imported into all systems in the landscape.

Despite efforts to keep this "code freeze" period as short as possible, experience shows that one to two weeks have to be allotted for the SPAU comparison in the development system, and then approximately two to four weeks must be scheduled for the integration test in the QA system. Of course, these time periods are average values and are subject to change in different systems.

The time and effort required for the SPAU comparison increases along with the number of modified and customer-specific objects. In addition to the objects listed in SPAU, any customer-specific objects that access SAP standard code also have to be checked. The SAP Code Inspector (Transaction SCI) is an automated tool for performing this task, and enables you to carry out an extended syntax check for all customer-specific objects.

The time and effort required for this check depends on the number of business processes in use. The SAP system administrator has to decide whether to test only the most important business processes, or whether more minor processes should also be included in the test. Therefore, it is necessary to categorize the business processes according to their importance (ABC analysis) in advance. A well-organized test management process and the ready availability of automated test cases (eCATT tool) reduce the time and effort required for the test and thereby shorten the duration of the code freeze period.

Before Support Packages are imported into the development system, any open change requests should be released and imported to the follow-on systems. Once the Support Packages have been imported into the development system and the SPAU comparison is complete, you may be able to resume development work in the development system. But, the danger still exists that errors detected in the Support Package tests may be difficult to solve in the development system, because the development system may have a more up-to-date software release. The safer option would therefore be to resume work in the development system only once the Support Packages have been tested and found to be error-free. In every case, all transports in the QA system must be suspended for the duration of the integration test.

Because of these effects on development work, the timing of Support Package imports must be carefully planned and coordinated with the development project teams.

Some SAP customers first test Support Package imports and the SPAU comparison in a sandbox environment in order to minimize the code freeze period. Initial functional tests can also be carried out in the sandbox system.

You can also use the latest Support Package level for the relevant development projects, and then transport the changes along with the Support Packages through the maintenance landscape. The advantage of employing this method is that only one test is required for Support Packages and development projects. Note that this approach requires a phase-based system landscape, as described in Section 3.6.2.

### 15.3.2 Modification Comparison

The modification comparison must be run for Support Packages imports, just as it does for a release upgrade. However, with Support Package imports, unlike with release upgrades, the SPDD comparison must be run separately in every system. A transport request can be imported from the development system to the follow-on systems for the SPAU comparison only.

Because Section 16.3 deals with the topic of modification comparison in greater detail, we won't discuss it further here.

## 15.4 Support Package Stacks

In 2003, SAP added 'Support Package stacks' (SP stacks) to its Support Package strategy for some product versions. This new strategy supports the import procedure of most customers and Support Packages, improves quality and service, and thus reduces ongoing operating costs.

The increasing range and complexity of components within individual product versions makes it necessary to improve the transparency of Support Packages and patches, and to clearly specify the recommended or permitted combinations. Therefore, a new SP stack is compiled for every product version that is updated via the new strategy, usually on a quarterly basis. This stack contains the optimal combination of Support Package and patch levels for the individual components at the time of the stack release.

The SP stacks are therefore combinations defined by SAP for each product version. SAP recommends that you import these SP stacks on a regular basis instead of choosing different Support Package levels per different Software Component. While the underlying technology of the individual Support Packages and patches does not change with this stack approach, an SP stack is intended to be regarded as a whole. In other words, while you should take into account any minimum requirements of or dependencies between the individual components, the Support Packages and patches contained in the stack must be imported together to utilize the benefits shown in the following chapter.

By reducing the range of theoretically possible combinations to practical, real-world combinations, there are several benefits for the customer that result:

- The quality of the individual Support Packages is improved, as other associated components are maintained to a known minimum level, so that corrections are less complex and of a higher quality.
- Quality and compatibility within the set combinations are improved, as SAP's own tests can focus more on these combinations.
- Download pages that are specially tailored to SP stacks make it easier to download required Support Packages and patches.
- Import instructions can also be tailored for the combination to be imported, thereby reducing the time and effort required for the import process.
- The general level of knowledge about any restrictions, and transparency about side effects and their solutions, are better overall for SP stacks than for individ-

ual combinations. Potential problems can be prevented and, when they occur, solved more effectively, which, in turn, reduces operating costs.

SP stacks support the requirements of customers with live applications for regular Support Package and patch recommendations, plus their need for the minimum total cost of ownership (TCO). For customers with upgrade or implementation projects, the minimum requirements may involve other (higher) recommendations than the most recent SP stacks.

Implementing SP stacks leads to a reduction in complexity, increased quality, improved transparency, and simplified repairs and maintenance. SP stacks further reduce the risks to live operations and help to expedite the resolution of any problems. They are just another step toward reducing the total cost of ownership (TCO).

Once an SP stack is released, details of the relevant information and download site are available from the SAP Service Marketplace via the Quick Link */sp-stacks* • *SP Stack Information & Download* or under the */patches* alias (head of the navigation hierarchy) • *(Product)* • *<Product version>*.

Additional information on specific SP stacks is available from the pertinent Release and Information Note (RIN), which is available via a link on the aforementioned page.

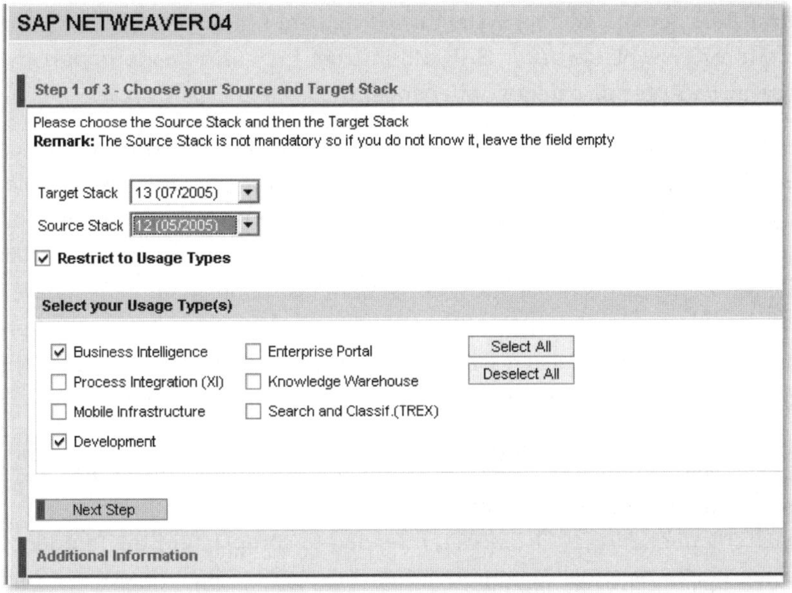

**Figure 15.21** Downloading support package stacks from the SAP Service Marketplace

### 15.4.1 SP Stack Strategy with the Usual Import Procedure

It has been shown that most customers carry out planned maintenance for each live application between one and four times a year, and that this maintenance process usually covers all the components of each application.

In practice, the frequency of planned maintenance operations depends on many factors. These include the following:

- The customer's own specific situation (projects, live status, etc.)
- The product in question (technical factors, statutory changes, etc.)
- The benefits of having the latest release when support is required
- The customer's own assessment of the risk of encountering known errors (and thus of incurring unnecessary costs and having to react at short notice)
- The expected costs of a planned maintenance operation

There is therefore no standard rule for calculating the optimal time and frequency of planned maintenance operations. Customers decide on the optimal conditions for themselves, with regards to their own individual circumstances. However, SAP recommends that customers run a planned maintenance operation at least once a year, and preferably two to four times a year, whether or not problems have arisen, so that the risks outlined above don't become too great. SAP assumes that the latest SP stack will be imported as part of a planned maintenance operation, and that the SP stacks in use in a system landscape are not retained beyond one year. As before, if problems occur, SAP can instruct the customer to import the latest Support Packages or patches, independently of the SP stack cycle.

Unexpected problems can occur at any time, regardless of planned maintenance operations. They have to be fixed as quickly and as straightforwardly as possible. A range of different mechanisms is available for this purpose, and the decision regarding which device to use depends on the affected component and the actual problem. These mechanisms include correction instructions for ABAP-based tracks (which can solve problems relatively locally and in a targeted way) and kernel patches (which, for technical reasons, usually contain other problem solutions and whose effects are therefore less restricted to the local environment).

The SP stack strategy runs with this conventional combination of planned maintenance and interim local corrections.

- The quarterly frequency of SP stacks is intended to complement the frequency of planned maintenance operations. This does not mean, however, that planned maintenance must be carried out every quarter. Based on your assessment of the aforementioned factors, you can temporarily postpone the import of an SP stack, provided that your system does not contain any errors that necessitate the import of up-to-date Support Packages or patches. You can catch up with any Support Packages that you postpone when you import the next SP stack.

- SP stacks contain Support Package combinations that you should change only in exceptional cases; for example, if a problem has occurred that can be solved only by a change. In such cases, you should keep the modification as small and as local as possible. Of course, you can also import new Support Packages or patches as a preventative measure, if circumstances in the system are such that the error in question is likely to occur. But, in many cases, you will be able to make a local correction via the correction instruction in a Note, for example.
- Components of an SP stack that are not in use, or not in live use, in a system landscape don't have to be patched when an SP stack is imported, provided that they have no technical or logical dependencies with any components that are in active use. But you should note that the Support Package or patch levels of components that are in use cannot be lower than the levels of the combination set in the SP stack.

If unexpected problems are identified after the release of an SP stack, these problems will be resolved by additional single notes, which will be added to the side effect notes reporting.

A Release and Information Note (RIN) is used to inform all customers of the general release of an SP stack and possibly also about potential problems. As before, notice of critical errors is communicated via HotNews Notes. A special reporting tool in the SAP Service Marketplace can be used to find out about known side effects of all kinds of Support Packages (Quick Link */side-effects*).

An SP stack thus remains valid until the next SP stack is released. Unexpected problems are communicated to customers according to the problem's level of severity. The focus in SP stacks on specific combinations means that potential problems can be identified and solutions can be found earlier on in the process.

Any differences between Support Package levels or patch levels and the relevant SP stack should be documented in Notes. This approach is used only for problems or other special cases (such as statutory changes or for customers' project or implementation phases). This also applies to Support Packages or patches that have been created since the last SP stack and that will be part of subsequent SP stacks.

It is also possible that there may be Support Packages or patches that are more up-to-date than those contained in the last SP stack. Nevertheless, as long as your system is not experiencing any particular problems, the general recommendation is that you use the combination contained in the latest SP stack. Any Support Packages or patches that are created in the interim are reserved for the special cases mentioned above.

### 15.4.2 Details of the Components in SAP Support Package Stacks

Based on one 'leading' application component, SP stacks represent one combination of preset or recommended Support Package levels and patch levels of the other components of a product version. Dependencies are defined step-by-step in a "top-down" fashion (see the example below).

Stacks specify one level for each possible release for some components, such as the SAP GUI. Other components may be optional; that is, the relevant Support Package or patch level must be fulfilled only if the component in question will be in use in a production system (for example, an R/3 Enterprise Extension).

The basic rule here is that the other components must have at least the specified level for it to be possible to import a Support Package for the leading component. Also, a higher level is recommended for most components only for those problems where there is no local correction (such as a correction instruction) or a workaround.

An SP stack can consist of the following:

- A Support Package level of a leading application component (such as SAP_APPL 4.6C), which serves as the name of the SP stack
- A Support Package level of the application basis (such as SAP ABA 4.6C) that is a prerequisite for the aforementioned application Support Package and that would not usually be overwritten until the next SP stack
- A Support Package level of the basis layer (such as SAP Basis 4.6C) that is a prerequisite for the aforementioned ABAP Support Package and that would not usually be overwritten until the next SP stack
- A recommended kernel patch level (such as SAP KERNEL 4.6D) that would not usually be overwritten until the next SP stack, provided that there are no problems
  This kernel patch level is intended for use on the operational level and can be higher than the level of an upgrade for the release in question (in this case, follow the instructions in the upgrade documentation or the relevant Notes).
- A minimum patch level for every possible SAP GUI release (such as 4.6D/6.20 for Windows, 6.20/6.30 for Java)
  Note that the releases in this case should initially be regarded as alternatives and that each patch level is a minimum requirement that can be overwritten at any time. This minimum requirement within an SP stack will be increased in

exceptional cases only. But, because the SAP GUI is a component of almost all SAP products, the requirements of the SP stacks of various products that are used in parallel must be coordinated with each other. In this case, the maximum required SAP GUI releasehis case, the maxoimuumthe maxoimumoducts can be pocase, follow if problems for which thration is still that you use th with the maximum required patch level is what is relevant. Other conditions may arise in the context of product-specific GUI add-ons.

- Possibly, a minimum patch level for every possible SAP ITS release (such as 4.6D, 6.10, 6.20) could occur. The various releases should be regarded as alternatives, similarly to the SAP GUI.
- Another condition that might arise could be that other optional components require the specified level only when the component in question is in production use.

### 15.4.3 SP Stack Calendar

Either the product versions listed in the SP stack calendar are already supported by SP stacks, or SP stacks will be introduced for them in the near future. Every SP stack is "led" by a particular component or Support Package track, and the relevant Support Package is a central component of this. Once the first SP stack is released, this signals the start of the new strategy for that product version.

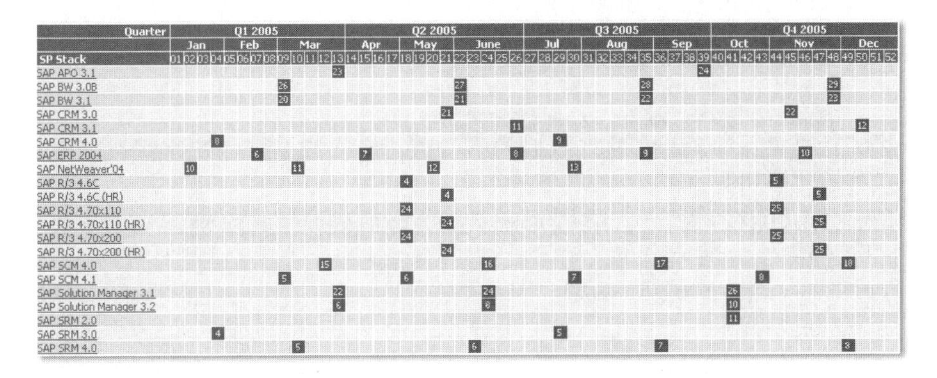

| Quarter | Q1 2005 | | | | | | | | | | | | |
|---|---|---|---|---|---|---|---|---|---|---|---|---|---|
| | Jan | | | | Feb | | | | Mar | | | | |
| SP Stack | 01 | 02 | 03 | 04 | 05 | 06 | 07 | 08 | 09 | 10 | 11 | 12 | 13 |
| SAP APO 3.1 | | | | | | | | | | | | | 23 |
| SAP BW 3.0B | | | | | | | | | 26 | | | | |
| SAP BW 3.1 | | | | | | | | | 20 | | | | |
| SAP CRM 3.0 | | | | | | | | | | | | | |
| SAP CRM 3.1 | | | | | | | | | | | | | |
| SAP CRM 4.0 | | | | 8 | | | | | | | | | |
| SAP ERP 2004 | | | | | | | 6 | | | | | | |
| SAP NetWeaver'04 | | 10 | | | | | | | | 11 | | | |
| SAP R/3 4.6C | | | | | | | | | | | | | |
| SAP R/3 4.6C (HR) | | | | | | | | | | | | | |
| SAP R/3 4.70x110 | | | | | | | | | | | | | |
| SAP R/3 4.70x110 (HR) | | | | | | | | | | | | | |
| SAP R/3 4.70x200 | | | | | | | | | | | | | |
| SAP R/3 4.70x200 (HR) | | | | | | | | | | | | | |
| SAP SCM 4.0 | | | | | | | | | | | | 15 | |
| SAP SCM 4.1 | | | | | | | | | 5 | | | | |
| SAP Solution Manager 3.1 | | | | | | | | | | | | | 22 |
| SAP Solution Manager 3.2 | | | | | | | | | | | | | 6 |
| SAP SRM 2.0 | | | | | | | | | | | | | |
| SAP SRM 3.0 | | | | 4 | | | | | | | | | |
| SAP SRM 4.0 | | | | | | | | | | 5 | | | |

| Quarter | Q2 2005 | | | | | | | | | | | | |
|---|---|---|---|---|---|---|---|---|---|---|---|---|---|
| | Apr | | | | May | | | | June | | | | |
| SP Stack | 14 | 15 | 16 | 17 | 18 | 19 | 20 | 21 | 22 | 23 | 24 | 25 | 26 |
| SAP APO 3.1 | | | | | | | | | | | | | |
| SAP BW 3.0B | | | | | | | | | 27 | | | | |
| SAP BW 3.1 | | | | | | | | | 21 | | | | |
| SAP CRM 3.0 | | | | | | | | 21 | | | | | |
| SAP CRM 3.1 | | | | | | | | | | | | | 11 |
| SAP CRM 4.0 | | | | | | | | | | | | | |
| SAP ERP 2004 | | 7 | | | | | | | | | | | 8 |
| SAP NetWeaver'04 | | | | | | | 12 | | | | | | |
| SAP R/3 4.6C | | | | | 4 | | | | | | | | |
| SAP R/3 4.6C (HR) | | | | | | | | 4 | | | | | |
| SAP R/3 4.70x110 | | | | | 24 | | | | | | | | |
| SAP R/3 4.70x110 (HR) | | | | | | | | 24 | | | | | |
| SAP R/3 4.70x200 | | | | | 24 | | | | | | | | |
| SAP R/3 4.70x200 (HR) | | | | | | | | 24 | | | | | |
| SAP SCM 4.0 | | | | | | | | | | | 16 | | |
| SAP SCM 4.1 | | | | | 6 | | | | | | | | |
| SAP Solution Manager 3.1 | | | | | | | | | | | 24 | | |
| SAP Solution Manager 3.2 | | | | | | | | | | | 8 | | |
| SAP SRM 2.0 | | | | | | | | | | | | | |
| SAP SRM 3.0 | | | | | | | | | | | | | |
| SAP SRM 4.0 | | | | | | | | | | 6 | | | |

| Quarter | Q3 2005 | | | | | | | | | | | | |
|---|---|---|---|---|---|---|---|---|---|---|---|---|---|
| | Jul | | | | Aug | | | | | Sep | | | |
| SP Stack | 27 | 28 | 29 | 30 | 31 | 32 | 33 | 34 | 35 | 36 | 37 | 38 | 39 |
| SAP APO 3.1 | | | | | | | | | | | | | 24 |
| SAP BW 3.0B | | | | | | | | | 28 | | | | |
| SAP BW 3.1 | | | | | | | | | 22 | | | | |
| SAP CRM 3.0 | | | | | | | | | | | | | |
| SAP CRM 3.1 | | | | | | | | | | | | | |
| SAP CRM 4.0 | | | 9 | | | | | | | | | | |
| SAP ERP 2004 | | | | | | | | | 9 | | | | |
| SAP NetWeaver'04 | | | | 13 | | | | | | | | | |
| SAP R/3 4.6C | | | | | | | | | | | | | |
| SAP R/3 4.6C (HR) | | | | | | | | | | | | | |
| SAP R/3 4.70x110 | | | | | | | | | | | | | |
| SAP R/3 4.70x110 (HR) | | | | | | | | | | | | | |
| SAP R/3 4.70x200 | | | | | | | | | | | | | |
| SAP R/3 4.70x200 (HR) | | | | | | | | | | | | | |
| SAP SCM 4.0 | | | | | | | | | | 17 | | | |
| SAP SCM 4.1 | | | | 7 | | | | | | | | | |
| SAP Solution Manager 3.1 | | | | | | | | | | | | | |
| SAP Solution Manager 3.2 | | | | | | | | | | | | | |
| SAP SRM 2.0 | | | | | | | | | | | | | |
| SAP SRM 3.0 | | | 5 | | | | | | | | | | |
| SAP SRM 4.0 | | | | | | | | | | 7 | | | |

| Quarter | Q4 2005 | | | | | | | | | | | | |
|---|---|---|---|---|---|---|---|---|---|---|---|---|---|
| | Oct | | | | Nov | | | | | Dec | | | |
| SP Stack | 40 | 41 | 42 | 43 | 44 | 45 | 46 | 47 | 48 | 49 | 50 | 51 | 52 |
| SAP APO 3.1 | | | | | | | | | | | | | |
| SAP BW 3.0B | | | | | | | | | 29 | | | | |
| SAP BW 3.1 | | | | | | | | | 23 | | | | |
| SAP CRM 3.0 | | | | | | 22 | | | | | | | |
| SAP CRM 3.1 | | | | | | | | | | | 12 | | |
| SAP CRM 4.0 | | | | | | | | | | | | | |
| SAP ERP 2004 | | | | | | | 10 | | | | | | |
| SAP NetWeaver'04 | | | | | | | | | | | | | |
| SAP R/3 4.6C | | | | | 5 | | | | | | | | |
| SAP R/3 4.6C (HR) | | | | | | | | 5 | | | | | |
| SAP R/3 4.70x110 | | | | | 25 | | | | | | | | |
| SAP R/3 4.70x110 (HR) | | | | | | | | 25 | | | | | |
| SAP R/3 4.70x200 | | | | | 25 | | | | | | | | |
| SAP R/3 4.70x200 (HR) | | | | | | | | 25 | | | | | |
| SAP SCM 4.0 | | | | | | | | | | 18 | | | |
| SAP SCM 4.1 | | | | 8 | | | | | | | | | |
| SAP Solution Manager 3.1 | | 26 | | | | | | | | | | | |
| SAP Solution Manager 3.2 | | 10 | | | | | | | | | | | |
| SAP SRM 2.0 | | 11 | | | | | | | | | | | |
| SAP SRM 3.0 | | | | | | | | | | | | | |
| SAP SRM 4.0 | | | | | | | | | | 3 | | | |

**Figure 15.22** Support package stack calendar

## 15.5 Side Effects

The SAP Service Marketplace contains a new reporting tool that helps you to avoid unwanted side effects. Side effects can occur in rare cases after a Support Package or a SAP Note is imported. The aforementioned tool enables SAP customers to reduce their internal support costs and to increase the stability of their SAP solution.

SAP Support Packages consist of several SAP Notes, each of which contains software corrections. Importing Support Packages and Notes increases system stability and protects the system from known problems. Nonetheless, it can still happen that a Note that is intended to solve one problem can actually cause another problem. To solve this new problem, a new Note is then created that is linked to the first Note.

The new tool is intended to make these dependencies easier to handle. If you're importing a Support Package or a SAP Note, you can search for any known side effects and correct these, if necessary. This tool enables you to proactively prevent problems that could occur after an import.

Information about side effects is defined in the Note attributes. The reporting tool identifies all the side effects that will be caused by the Notes contained in the Support Package. Therefore, to protect your system from unwanted side effects, import these Notes after you import the Support Package.

The Quick Link *http://service.sap.com/notes* in the SAP Service Marketplace contains information about known side effects of individual SAP Notes.

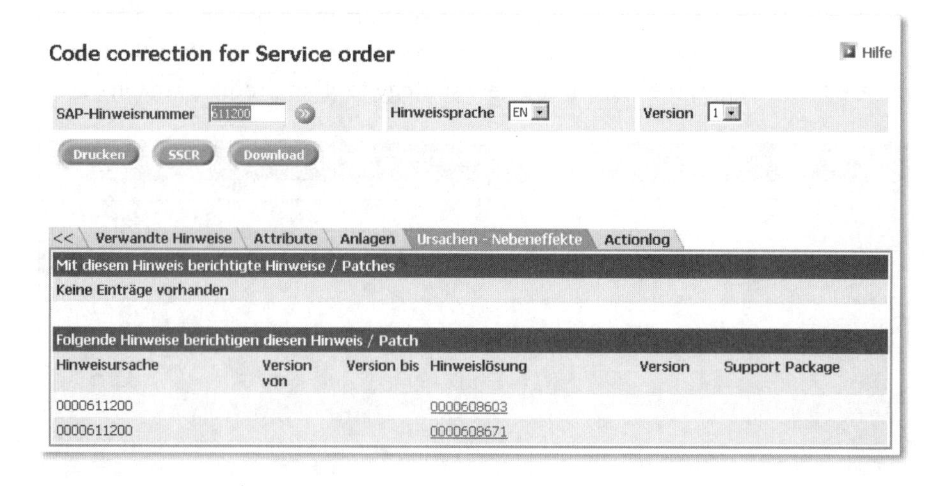


**Figure 15.23** Side effects of an individual note

To obtain a list of all the side effects of a Support Package or an SP stack, use the reporting tool in the SAP Service Marketplace (Quick Link: *http://service.sap.com/patches • Support Packages in Detail • Side Effects of SAP Notes*.)

Use this tool just before you import the Support Package in question to see the most up-to-date list of side effects.

Side effects that have already been eliminated by other Support Packages in the same queue are automatically removed from the results list. The results list is specially tailored to your Support Package queue. It is sorted by application component, so that you can easily skip Notes that belong to applications that you don't use.

Note that it can take several hours to create the results list. Therefore, the system sends you an email when the list is complete.

SAP began its side-effect reporting activities in July 2003. There is no complete information available on the side effects of earlier Notes.

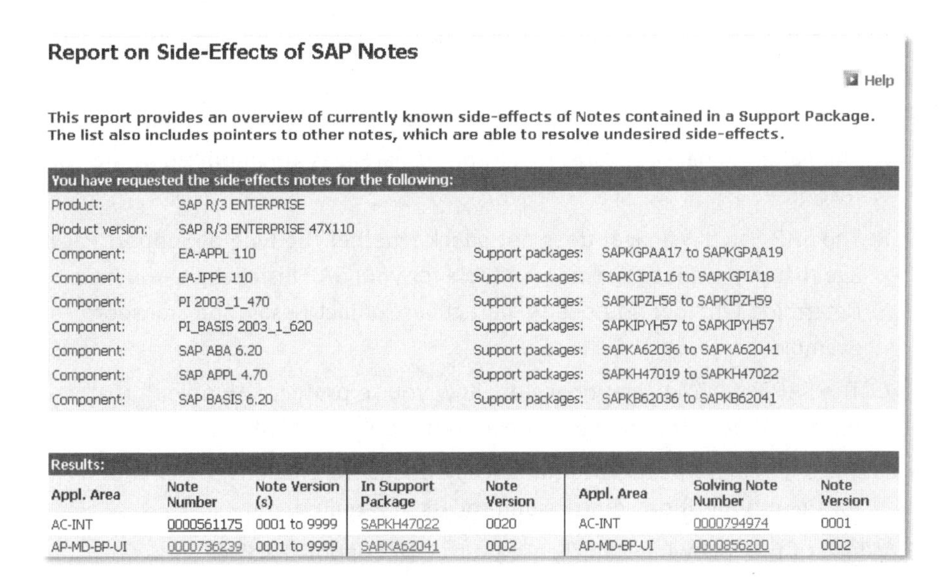

**Report on Side-Effects of SAP Notes**

Help

This report provides an overview of currently known side-effects of Notes contained in a Support Package. The list also includes pointers to other notes, which are able to resolve undesired side-effects.

You have requested the side-effects notes for the following:

| | | | |
|---|---|---|---|
| Product: | SAP R/3 ENTERPRISE | | |
| Product version: | SAP R/3 ENTERPRISE 47X110 | | |
| Component: | EA-APPL 110 | Support packages: | SAPKGPAA17 to SAPKGPAA19 |
| Component: | EA-IPPE 110 | Support packages: | SAPKGPIA16 to SAPKGPIA18 |
| Component: | PI 2003_1_470 | Support packages: | SAPKIPZH58 to SAPKIPZH59 |
| Component: | PI_BASIS 2003_1_620 | Support packages: | SAPKIPYH57 to SAPKIPYH57 |
| Component: | SAP ABA 6.20 | Support packages: | SAPKA62036 to SAPKA62041 |
| Component: | SAP APPL 4.70 | Support packages: | SAPKH47019 to SAPKH47022 |
| Component: | SAP BASIS 6.20 | Support packages: | SAPKB62036 to SAPKB62041 |

Results:

| Appl. Area | Note Number | Note Version (s) | In Support Package | Note Version | Appl. Area | Solving Note Number | Note Version |
|---|---|---|---|---|---|---|---|
| AC-INT | 0000561175 | 0001 to 9999 | SAPKH47022 | 0020 | AC-INT | 0000794974 | 0001 |
| AP-MD-BP-UI | 0000736239 | 0001 to 9999 | SAPKA62041 | 0002 | AP-MD-BP-UI | 0000856200 | 0002 |

**Figure 15.24** Side effects of support package queues

## 15.6 Questions

1. What are the benefits of importing **SAP Support Packages?**

   **A.** Proactive solution of known problems

   **B.** Functional extensions to SAP software

   **C.** Improved ease of maintenance and reduced time and effort for repairs and maintenance

2. Which of the following statements are true of the SAP Note Assistant?

   **A.** It simplifies the maintenance of programs in the customer namespace.

   **B.** It enables you to import Notes that contain code corrections.

   **C.** It simplifies the process of making changes to Data Dictionary objects.

D. It identifies dependencies between SAP Notes.

E. It can replace the process of importing Support Packages.

3. Which of the following statements are true of Support Packages?

   A. They change the SAP standard of your SAP system before the next release upgrade.

   B. You can import all types of Support Packages into all SAP systems, regardless of the components installed in the target system.

   C. Support Packages are available only to customers who are taking part in the ramp-up.

   D. Different types of Support Packages may be required for SAP systems with different components.

4. Which of the following statements are true of the SAP Patch Manager?

   A. The Patch Manager ensures that Support Packages are imported in the correct order.

   B. The SAP Patch Manager does not check whether the type of Support Package that you want to import is suitable for your SAP installation. You have to determine whether you need a particular Conflict Resolution Transport, for example.

   C. The SAP Patch Manager does not allow you to protect SAP objects that you have modified. These objects are automatically overwritten.

   D. The SAP Patch Manager automatically opens transactions SPDD and SPAU for the modification comparison process, if required.

5. Which of the following statements are true of Support Package stacks?

   A. Support Package stacks are combinations of Support Packages that are recommended by SAP.

   B. Support Package stacks should be imported only if an urgent problem is preventing an import from being carried out.

   C. Support Package stacks are Support Package combinations that have been particularly well tested by SAP.

   D. The SAPGUI version also must be upgraded to the latest level with every Support Package stack upgrade.

# 16 Change of SAP Release

This chapter describes the general guidelines to be observed when changing to another SAP release. They should be regarded as a supplement to the corresponding upgrade guidelines, which show the individual steps and necessary actions in detail. Because this chapter does not explain these administrative actions down to the lowest level, it should prove useful to system administrators and technical consultants who ultimately conduct the upgrade, as well as project managers who are instrumental in the planning of the upgrade project. In particular, this chapter addresses the general recommendations and services, which are discussed in more detail, in addition to the description of the technical upgrade procedure.

## 16.1 Life Cycle of a Productive SAP System

Over time, your productive SAP system undergoes a development process that enables you to respond better to changing business requirements. Apart from the corrections mentioned in the previous chapters using SAP notes or support packages, you will, for example, have carried out customizing changes for currency adjustments, created new clients or company codes for additional company sites or subsidiaries, or deployed more modules into operation. Additionally, you will often want to implement a new functionality with the system. SAP delivers these new functions to their customers in a new release.

### 16.1.1 SAP Release and Maintenance Strategy

For the efficient planning and support of the life cycle of your production environment, you should know SAP's *release and maintenance strategy*.

Within the scope of maintenance, apart from the corrections in notes that have been mentioned on several occasions, SAP develops new functions and adaptations to meet the requirements of the current technology. It is therefore possible to use improved hardware or newer versions of databases or operating systems, for example. Often, this is even feasible without changing the release by simply importing a newer version of the SAP kernel.

For your planning, it is also important to know the timeframe for this SAP maintenance. The so-called *standard maintenance* lasts five years for SAP products that use SAP NetWeaver '04 as a technology platform. This means that within this period all note or support package corrections, as well as the legal adjustments, for example, for tax rates in payroll accounting, are covered in the maintenance fees. For an extended period of one respectively two more years, the delivery of the aforementioned corrections is still possible for an increased maintenance fee. However, after this period, that is eight years after implementing a release, corrections are only created individually within the scope of customer-specific maintenance and are charged by the required effort.

For most SAP customers, this timeframe is more than adequate, because this so-called *5-1-2 maintenance strategy* provides eight years of planning reliability. However, sometimes the demand for using a new functionality arises earlier. Extensions or creations of completely new application functions are usually implemented in a new release, which is why the question whether to change to a customer-specific maintenance usually does not come up. Because SAP ensures that the change of release is supported by corresponding tools and methods in a way that the applications already implemented can still be used with only very small adjustments and since the effort is much smaller than what is required with a new installation, this decision is less difficult to make.

According to the former release strategy, the latest extended business processes and functions were first delivered in a "functional release" to a limited number of customers. Additionally, the SAP recommendation was not to use these functional releases productively, because there was only limited support for corrections via support packages. These functions were created mainly for the "correction release", which contained customizations and necessary improvements based on the functional release. This correction release was then available to all customers. The maintenance timeframes between the functional release and the correction release varied, which is why users of a functional release had to either import a *Final Delta Patch* or carry out an upgrade for the correction release.

In contrast to these formerly used installation procedures or types of releases, respectively, SAP has introduced new releases using a *ramp-up procedure* (see Figure 16.1).

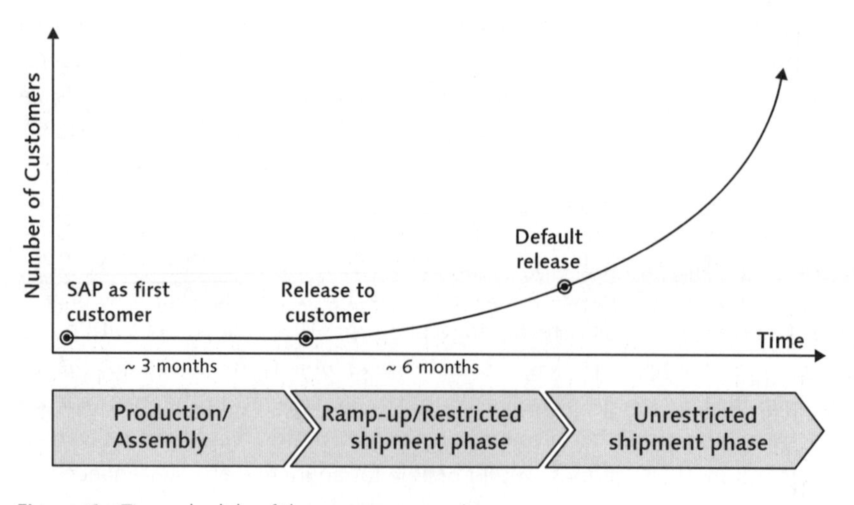


**Figure 16.1** Time schedule of the ramp-up procedure

After the development of new functions has been completed, an SAP-internal department will implement these functions for a longer period and then check them thoroughly using a detailed validation process. This process covers everything from documentation via installation or upgrade procedures up to customizing and using specific functions. This ensures that the reduced number of ramp-up customers receive a software that can already be used productively. A smart selection of ramp-up customers from the most diverse usage areas will then make sure that an extensive bandwidth of the application will be further verified. For this purpose, SAP provides enhanced support to solve any problems in the most expedient way. As soon as the stability criteria for the ramp-up has been achieved, the ramp-up is completed and the new release is made available to all clients.

### 16.1.2 Upgrade Motivation

Which reasons motivate SAP customers to change the release? To answer this question, a large-scale survey was conducted in 2004, where more than 700 SAP customers were interviewed about upgrades. Among other things, this survey investigated the motives for a change of release.

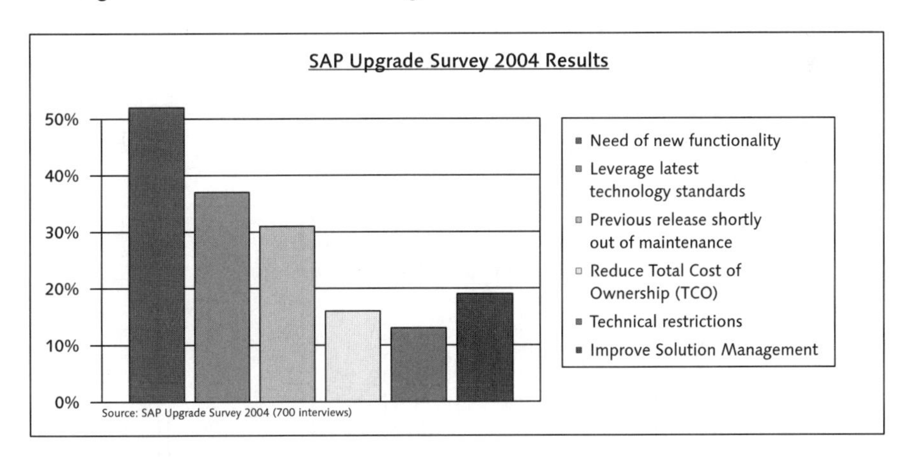


**Figure 16.2** Motivation for a change of release

As you can see from the evaluation in Figure 16.2, the main incentive for a change of release is the demand for new application functions, or the use of current technology standards followed by the intention to remain within the standard maintenance. Furthermore, the aspects of cost reduction and improved operation optimizations are becoming increasingly important, especially with regard to the current release, mySAP Enterprise Resource Planning (mySAP ERP) 2004. Additional results of this survey, as well as recommendations based on it, are listed in Section 16.5.

Therefore, a good planning of an upgrade project requires you to synchronize your IT strategy with the SAP maintenance strategy. Due to the availability of the 5-1-2 maintenance strategy, you can now synchronize these strategies with more flexibility. Therefore, before the end of the standard maintenance time of five years, you should determine whether it is reasonable to carry out a change of release in parallel with other running projects, for example, or if it would be preferable to use a maintenance extension.

## 16.2 Change of Release Process

### 16.2.1 Overview

In contrast to support packages that contain only a small number of new repository objects, a change of release delivers a large number of elementary changes and new objects because of the new functionality. Since new applications require a corresponding Customizing to enable the mapping of business processes according to specific demands, it is apparent that these activities require more efforts than the import of a support package. This section introduces you to the technical upgrade procedure and helps you to plan and carry out such a change of release.

Figure 16.3 presents an overview of the main phases of the technical upgrade procedure.

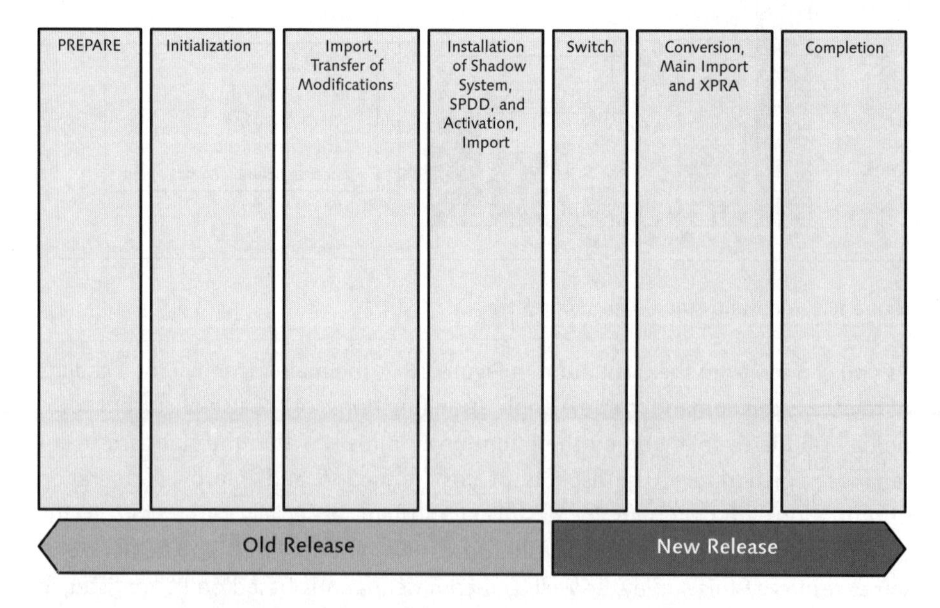


**Figure 16.3** Overview of the technical upgrade procedure

During the preparation phase of an SAP change of release, the PREPARE script is run at operating-system level. This script performs preliminary checks that save time for the actual upgrade procedure. Among the things that are checked are, for example, the available disk space or the existence of corrections in change requests that have not been released yet. According to the results of this check, you can adapt your SAP system, if necessary. For example, it might be necessary to increase the size of the table spaces and to make additional disk space available. The following phases are then executed by the program R3up or, from the SAP releases based on SAP NetWeaver 2004s, SAPup.

During the initialization phase, some of the PREPARE checks are repeated. As soon as you have resolved all problems that were reported during the execution of PREPARE, the initialization phase should run smoothly. The reason why some of the checks are repeated is that it is advisable to run PREPARE not only immediately before the upgrade, but even several weeks ahead; PREPARE can be repeated several times. This ensures that the most important checks can be performed without starting the actual upgrade program, but still have the ability to evaluate all areas that are significant to the upgrade process. If changes have occurred to the initial upgrade situation after PREPARE was executed successfully, the upgrade process must be able to verify the situation again, which takes place during the initialization phase.

During the "import and transfer of modifications" phase, the repository objects for the new release are transferred from the delivery CDs or DVDs to the system. After this transfer, these objects are compared to the objects that already exist in the customer repository in order to identify changes.

During the next phase, the shadow instance is created. This is an SAP Web Application Server (Web AS) ABAP of the target release, which is necessary in order to carry out the activation of data dictionary objects even before downtime. For this purpose, all objects to be included in the target repository are merged. In the event of data dictionary object conflicts, you must first adjust the two versions using Transaction SPDD. This adjustment must be carried with great care, because there is the risk of data loss if it is not done properly. As soon as the adjustment is completed, the activation is started. Contrary to what one might expect from, for example, Transaction SE11, this activation does not create a corresponding version of these objects in the database. Instead, it creates a new version of the *runtime object* that is needed for the structure changes, which are calculated in a subsequent step.

The downtime of the upgrade process starts with the switch between the old and the new versions of the repository objects at the latest. At this stage, the change to the new versions of the kernel and the repository takes place.

Finally, in the "conversion, main import, and XPRA" phase, the changes caused by the new repository are written to the database. During these steps, the system is not available—this is called the "downtime" of the system. Depending on various factors, this downtime can last for several hours. After some table imports, as well as logical customizations have been carried out, the system is available with the new functions.

During the "completion" phase, further actions are taken regarding the last adjustments of objects, and the call for synchronizing the remaining repository objects in Transaction SPAU is started.

### 16.2.2 System Switch Upgrade Procedure

The system switch upgrade procedure was introduced with the upgrades to systems with SAP Web AS ABAP 6.10 and higher. It replaces the repository switch procedure, which was used previously.

Earlier upgrade procedures of an R/3 system were carried out by importing the new repository objects into the system, using a well-defined sequence of transports. With an increasing number of objects, and therefore more and larger transports, this led to an increased period of time during which the system was in a fuzzy state between the start release and the target release and therefore could no longer be used. Therefore, following the generally held belief that the number of SAP repository objects exceeds the number of customer repository objects by far, and that the size of the repository tables makes only a small part of the size of the application tables, the so-called *repository switch upgrade* was developed. What this inherently means is that the new repository is positioned adjacently to the repository still in use in order to exchange it with the old one in operation. After this process, to complete the upgrade, you only need to take care that the application data matches the new repository objects. An analysis of many upgrade duration evaluations results from the downtime statistics for repository switch upgrades shown in Figure 16.4.

As you can see, the activation time (ACT phase) increases with the number of support packages included in the upgrade. Thus, the decision had to be made whether to import as many support packages as possible during the upgrade project to reach a current software state, or whether to stay at a comparably old correction level without support packages so as to have a shorter downtime.

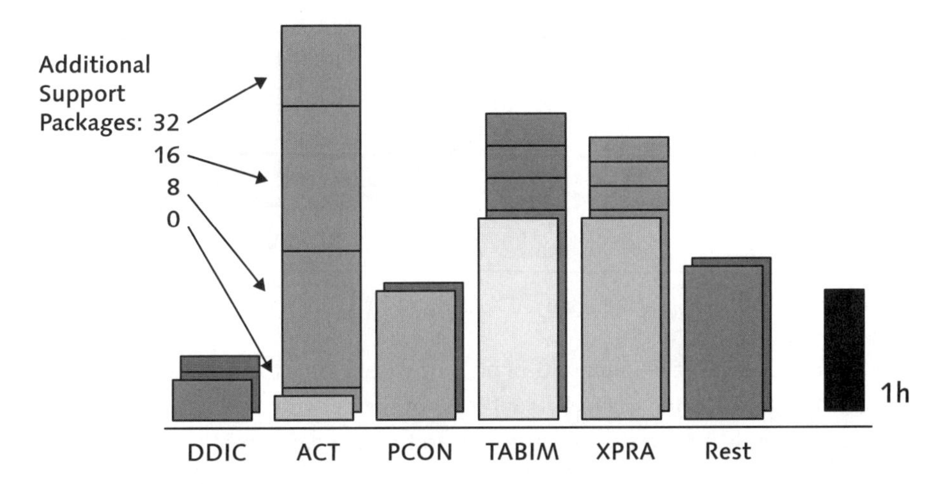


**Figure 16.4** Changes of downtime depending on the number of implemented support packages for the repository switch upgrade

The reason for this result is that a runtime version of the SAP Data Dictionary must exist for all data dictionary objects to be able to adapt the objects in the database. To save time, SAP delivers this version along with the CDs or DVDs for the new release. Objects that are taken over from the set of support packages into the new repository, however, do not have this information and must therefore be activated. Those objects that are taken over into the new release due to customer developments must perform this step as well. Since the activation alone can take several hours, especially for upgrades to releases with a lot of support packages, it was necessary to find a way to save this time as well, in favor of a reduced downtime. The result of this optimization is the system switch upgrade.

### 16.2.3 System Switch Upgrade in Detail

This chapter discusses the phases of the currently used technical upgrade procedure outlined above in detail using the example of an upgrade from R/3 4.5B to mySAP ERP 2004 ECC 5.00. This is important for understanding certain recommendations like modification adjustment. The following figures present a schematic outline of the SAP system with its share of the repository (bottom), as well as the associated data (top). The data area contains all application data like documents and materials, and the repository includes the executable programs and information about the table structure.

During the `PREPARE` phase, the actual system is not changed by the upgrade yet (Figure 16.5). Therefore, live operations are not affected at this stage.

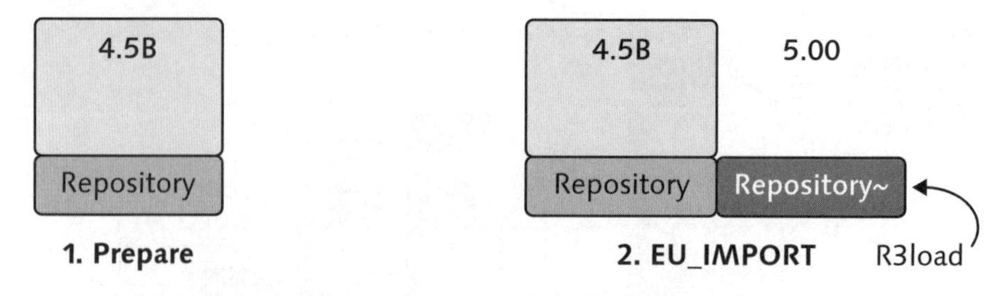


Figure 16.5 PREPARE phase and EU_IMPORT phase

As mentioned above, the initialization phase basically runs the checks of the PREPARE phase again. During the individual steps of the data transfer, the R3load program loads the data from the upgrade CDs to the database (phase EU_IMPORT). In doing so, a trick is used which is important for the fast accomplishment of the switch: The data is stored in a second repository next to the existing one. Because this area of the database was created with a changed name (all relevant names were extended by "~xx", where "xx" represents a specific release), the normal operation is not affected. These areas are not visible to standard SAP programs like, for example, the kernel. After this repository information has been created, the tables that are delivered with the new release—and which do not yet exist in the database—are generated .

To ensure that no customer developments are lost during the upgrade, the last part of the data transfer makes certain that these objects are saved. These objects are either directly taken over into the new repository following certain rules, or a copy of the current version is stored in the version database (see Figure 16.6).

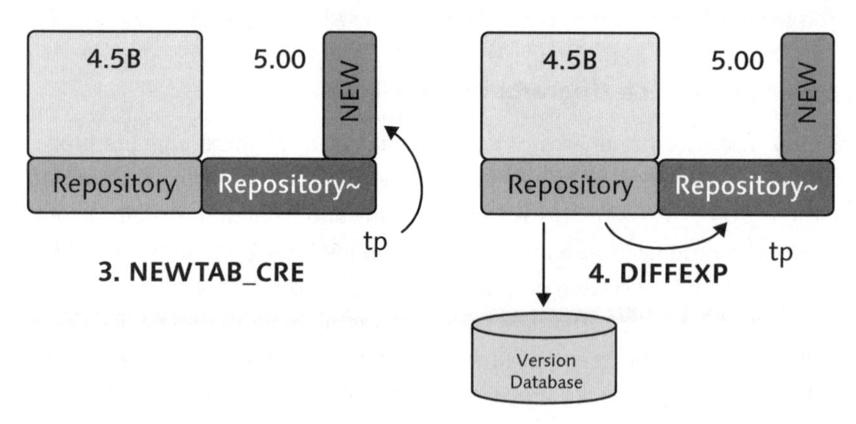


Figure 16.6 Creation of new tables and salvage of modifications and customer developments

Now that all objects exist in the new repository, the shadow system will be built next (see Figure 16.7). For mySAP ERP 2004 ECC 5.00, this is SAP Web AS ABAP with Release 6.40. Initially, the modification adjustment for data dictionary objects like tables or data element definitions must be done if these objects have been changed. This is carried out via Transaction SPDD. More details about the modification adjustment can be found in the "Modification Adjustment" section.

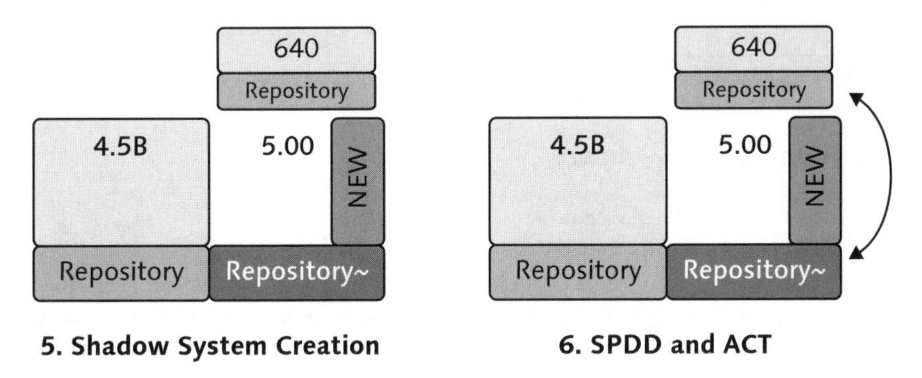


**Figure 16.7** Creation of the shadow system and execution of SPDD and activation

Due to the chronology, it's apparent that you need to determine what a table in the new release should look like prior to creating the runtime information in the "activation" step. The second instance is required because the old release doesn't often know the rules, according to which the runtime objects are created in the new release. Therefore, both the SPDD adjustment and the activation were a time-critical step during the downtime in the old upgrade procedure of the repository switch. By reorganizing the individual phases and building up another "system," the system switch procedure allows for the performing of these activities while the system is still being used productively. But even the system switch upgrade uses the switching mechanism as will be apparent to you in the next step. As soon as the activation is completed and the collected data has been copied to the database area that will still be available later, the shadow system will be uninstalled.

Eventually, in the ICNV phase, potentially pending table conversions can be started concurrently with live operations in order to save some downtime (see Figure 16.8). Another means of reducing downtime is that specific data is copied in advance during the "shadow_import." Database mechanisms ensure that data, which was changed after the copy action during live operations, is copied another time. Although this copying of data will be carried out during downtime, it is vital to ensure data consistency.

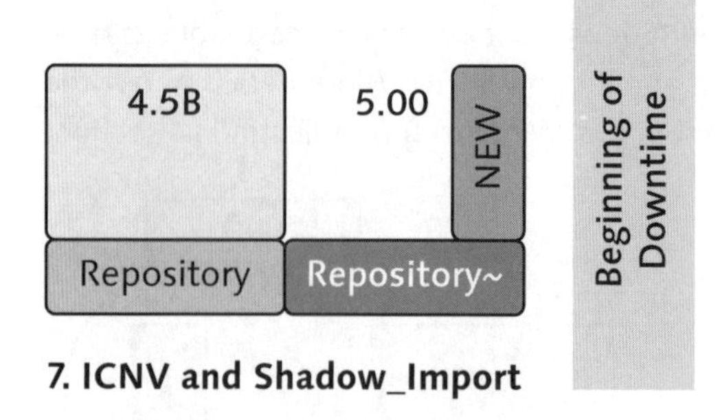


**Figure 16.8** Final activities before downtime

The upgrade then stops before the step that starts the system downtime. Thus, the productive system can be stopped at a specific time; for example, on a Friday evening after completing your work day activities. As soon as the downtime starts, the old repository is deleted. Since it was created according to a specific naming convention, this action can be performed very quickly. After that, the switch is effected. The names of the repository that was previously created in parallel are changed to new names by using a quick database operation. At this stage, the new programs and transactions are already available in theory.

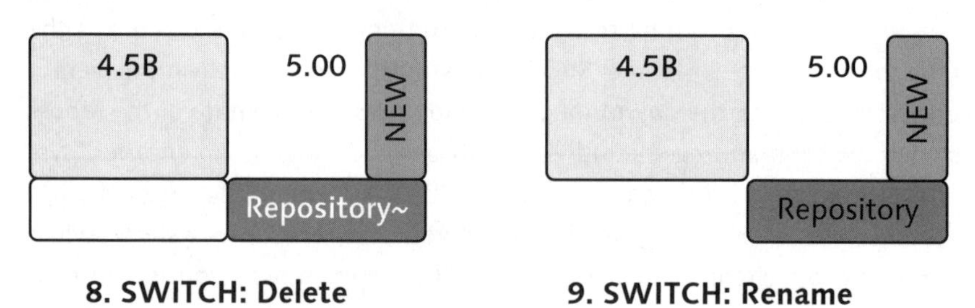


**Figure 16.9** Actions during switching

As you can see in Figure 16.9, however, the area with the application data is not above the new repository. This shows that tables were extended or changed in some way during the upgrade process. The adjustment of data to these new structures is carried out in the next phase, the conversion (see Figure 16.10). Using the data determined during the activation, these changes are calculated and, depending on the result of these calculations, the table is then adapted with the application data in the database. This can be reflected in the creation of new indexes and the extension or deletion of the table structure by several fields.

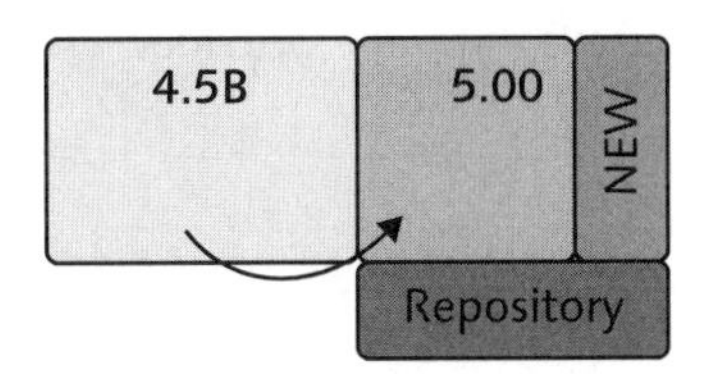


**Figure 16.10** Adjustment of the table structures between database and repository

> **Note** Since operations in the database are carried out, the duration primarily depends on the size of the objects to be edited. Additionally, the result of the SPDD adjustment needs to be considered in this phase. If, during the adjustment, it is determined that a field needs to be deleted from a table, not only the field itself is deleted from the data dictionary, but also the associated data in the database. Since such a change—a field deletion—cannot be carried out directly from the database, a table conversion is effected, which is performed via ABAP programs. For this purpose, the remaining fields of this table are copied row by row, which can take a long time for large tables. The following section about modification adjustments shows an appropriate example.

Now that the tables for the data dictionary are consistent after these adjustments, the "TABIM_UPG" step includes the finalizing import of Customizing data, and the subsequent "XPRA" step (*Execution of Programs After Put*) adapts specific tables logically (see Figure 16.11). For example, if it makes sense to use new functions together with existing data the old data is copied from existing tables to the new tables.

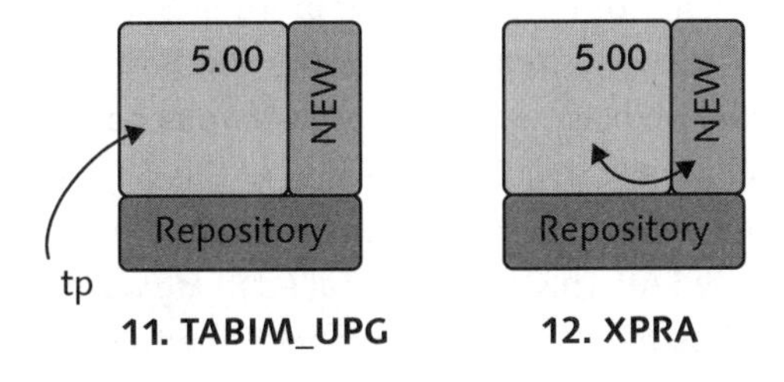


**Figure 16.11** Finalizing table import and XPRA

During the "completion" step, after all technical and application-relevant adjustments have been carried out, objects that were inactive before downtime are now copied as inactive versions as well, and a potentially necessary adjustment of repository objects not belonging to the data dictionary is naturally provided via Transaction SPAU (see Figure 16.12).

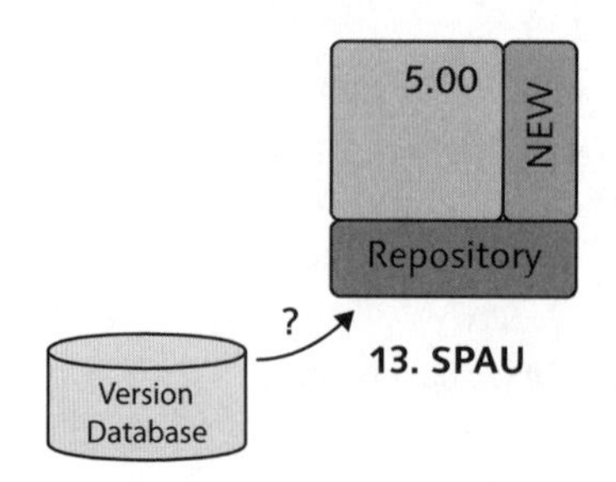


**Figure 16.12** Adjustment of repository objects via SPAU

## 16.3 Modification Adjustment

The SAP system contains several levels to adapt the standard version to an actual operational work environment:

- Customizing
- Personalization
- Business Add-Ins
- Custom development
- Modifications of the standard

In most cases, the software can be adapted to the processes without modifications. If modifications are required, however, when applying SAP notes, importing SAP Support Packages and changing releases, you will have to check your changes over and over again and adapt them, if necessary, to ensure that they still work after upgrading the SAP versions.

When changed SAP standard objects are imported either by importing Support Packages or by an SAP release change, the SAP system detects the modifications that were applied to these SAP repository objects. In other words, if you change a repository object delivered by SAP, you modify the default version of this object. Such a customer modification of the SAP standard version must be compared to the new version of the object delivered by SAP. This process is called *modification adjustment*. Therefore, a modification adjustment is necessary only if the following two facts exist:

- SAP ships an object with a Support Package or an Upgrade Package that has been changed since the last version.
- You changed this object since importing this Support Package or in the old release.

If SAP modifies an object that has not been modified by you, it is simply taken over in its new version. You can also forego a modification adjustment if you change an SAP object that is not delivered in a new version by SAP. Customer-developed objects are also unaffected by the modification adjustment.

For this adjustment, you must determine the differences between the objects and then decide which properties the objects should possess in the updated SAP system. You should adjust all objects that you changed and that are included in the new SAP delivery.

Depending on the category of the relevant object, you must use either Transaction SPDD or Transaction SPAU for the modification adjustment (see Table 16.1). Transaction SPDD is used for most ABAP Dictionary objects and must be executed before activating the new ABAP Dictionary objects. Transaction SPAU is used for most repository objects and is run after activating the new repository objects.

| Transaction | Object category |
|---|---|
| SPDD | Domains, data elements, tables |
| SPAU | Reports, menus, screens, views, lock objects, matchcodes |

**Table 16.1** Transactions for the modification adjustment of different object categories

At the appropriate stage, the Support Package Manager SPAM or the release change program `R3up` automatically ask you to perform a modification adjustment. A modification adjustment leads to one of the following results:

- Modification Adjustment denied, which means the old object will be overwritten by the new standard version. This is called "Return to the SAP standard."
- You do not revert to the SAP standard version. If you choose this option, the corresponding transaction for the modification adjustment is displayed (Transaction SPAU or Transaction SPDD). There, you can keep the modification as it is, or create a new modification by merging the new SAP version with the existing changes.

**Note** You should definitely not ignore this request for modification adjustment, because if you do, the modified objects are automatically overwritten with the new SAP repository. Even if you decide in favor of the new SAP standard object, you should use the explicit reversion procedure in Transaction SPDD and Transaction SPAU. This prevents you from being requested to per form another modification adjustment for the same modifications in subsequent release changes. Consequently, the use of the reversion procedure saves time for future release changes.

During the modification adjustment for data dictionary objects, you need to be particularly careful if you want to revert to the SAP standard version. Often, tables are modified by being extended by customized fields, like the field **E** in the example shown in Figure 16.13. If SAP now delivers a new version of this table (extended by the field **D**), you are prompted to perform a modification adjustment.

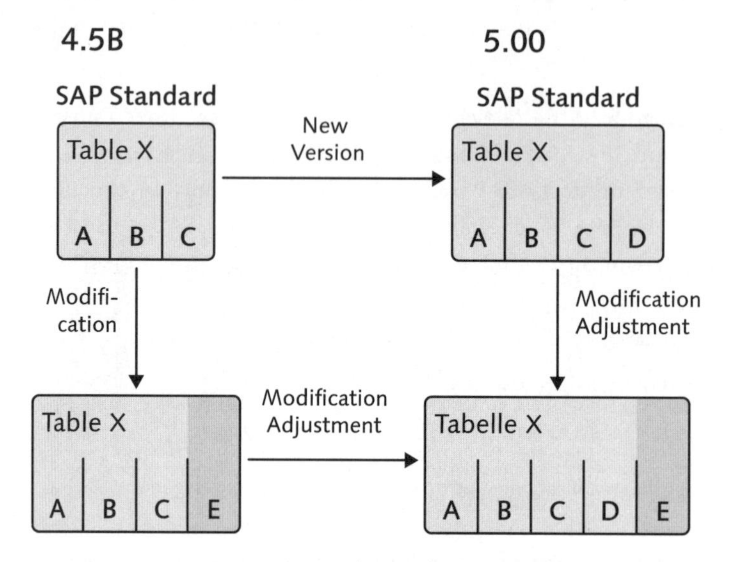


**Figure 16.13** Possibilities during the modification adjustment for tables

If you then revert to the SAP standard version during the adjustment, you not only delete the field **E** from the table description, but the values of this field are also deleted from the database using a conversion. However, if you keep your modification, errors can occur in SAP programs during the upgrade or during the subsequent operation because the expected field **D** cannot be accessed. Therefore, one aim for the adjustment could be to create a new modification using both your own modification and the SAP extension.

Apart from the modification adjustments for tables, there are also adjustments for the other repository objects like menus, text elements, dynpros, and reports.

**Example: Modification Adjustment for Programs**

Figure 16.14 shows the source text of the SAP standard object M07DRAUS. The customer added functionality to this program in the source text lines 12–14. The program is now delivered in a Support Pakkage with the additional source text lines 10 and 13 to correct a reported error.

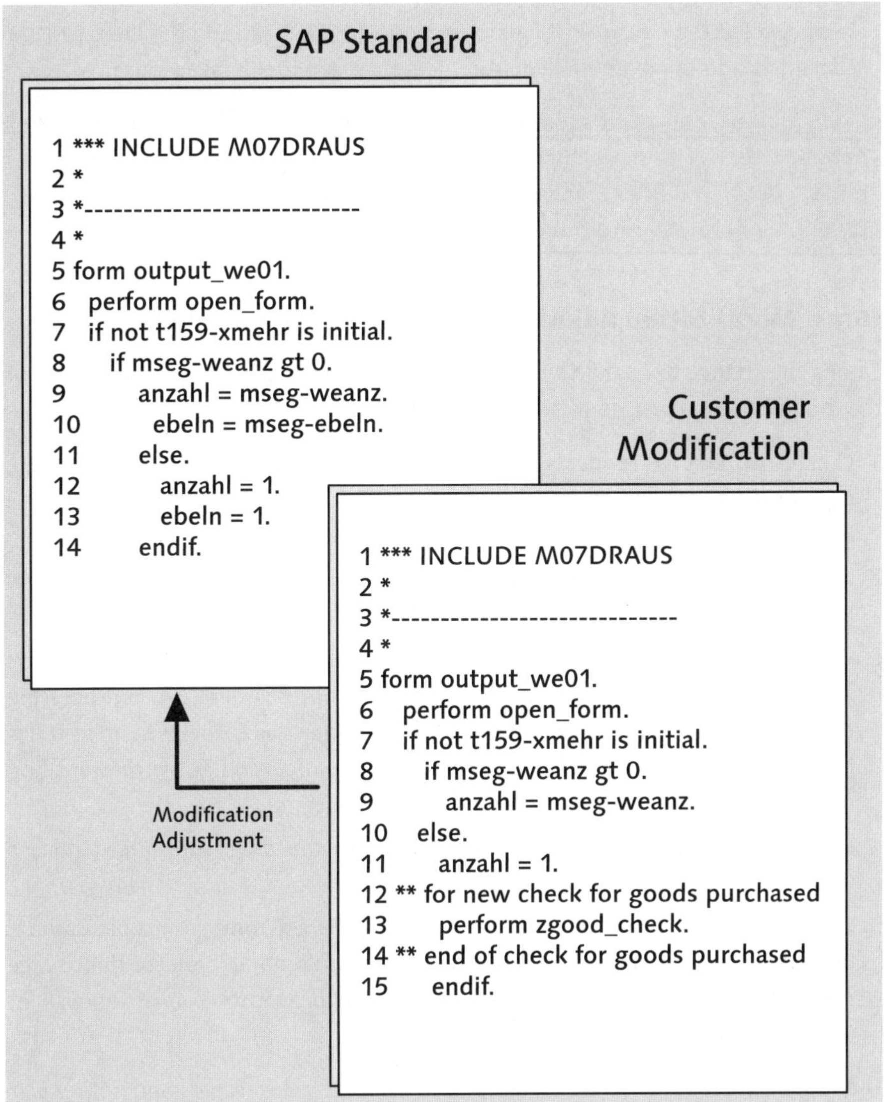

SAP Standard

```
1 *** INCLUDE M07DRAUS
2 *
3 *----------------------------
4 *
5 form output_we01.
6   perform open_form.
7   if not t159-xmehr is initial.
8     if mseg-weanz gt 0.
9        anzahl = mseg-weanz.
10        ebeln = mseg-ebeln.
11       else.
12          anzahl = 1.
13          ebeln = 1.
14       endif.
```

Customer Modification

```
1 *** INCLUDE M07DRAUS
2 *
3 *----------------------------
4 *
5 form output_we01.
6   perform open_form.
7   if not t159-xmehr is initial.
8     if mseg-weanz gt 0.
9        anzahl = mseg-weanz.
10    else.
11       anzahl = 1.
12 ** for new check for goods purchased
13       perform zgood_check.
14 ** end of check for goods purchased
15      endif.
```

Modification Adjustment

**Figure 16.14** Source texts of the new SAP standard version and the customer modification

Since the SAP standard version was modified and a new version was delivered, the adjustment is offered in Transaction SPAU. The customer has the following possibilities:

He can accept the new SAP standard and lose the functionality he implemented in the lines 12–14 of his modified version.

He can decline the new SAP standard version and forego the correction delivered in the lines 10 and 13.

He can accept the new SAP standard version and manually add the lines 12–14 so that the additional check required by the customer still takes place.

If the modification adjustment using Transaction SPAU is not carried out, the new SAP version is implemented automatically and the state of these objects remains set to **modified**. However, the adjustment can still be performed later using the information from the version database.

### 16.3.1 Modification Adjustment During Release Changes

During the change to a new SAP release, use the following standard procedure for the modification adjustment (see Figure 16.15):

1. Create two change requests in the Workbench Organizer (Transaction SE09): one for the modification adjustment using Transaction SPDD and one for the modification adjustment using Transaction SPAU.
2. Create one task for every developer who is involved in the modification adjustment.
3. Using Transaction SPDD or SPAU, respectively, the developers need to determine whether the modifications should be kept or discarded. While processing the object list, the developers should mark an object as **Done** as soon as it has been completely processed. All changes must be recorded in the relevant task respectively in the corresponding change request.
4. After completing the modification adjustment, the developers must release their tasks.
5. When all modified objects in the list are marked as **Done**, you must flag the tasks as **Release for Transport**. However, you should not yet release the change requests because `R3up` automatically releases and exports change requests at the end of the release change.

The modification adjustment should be carried out by developers and not by SAP system managers. The employees responsible for the modifications must be involved in the release change process and be present at the time. They should also review the full documentation of every modified object.

**Note** The more modifications exist and the more complex they are, the longer the change of release takes in a development system.

In subsequent release changes in the other systems of the system landscape, `R3up` detects the existence of change requests resulting from Transactions SPDD and

SPAU and prompts you to import them. When you import the change requests into these systems, you don't need to carry out the same modification adjustment in every system.

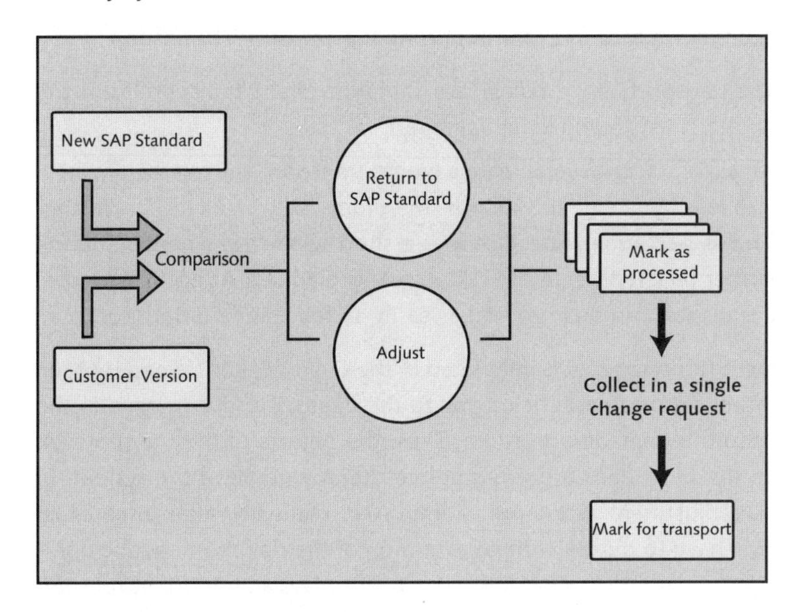


**Figure 16.15** Modification adjustment process

If you agreed to import the change requests, the modifications in the change requests are automatically compared to the corresponding objects in the target system and the results of this comparison are displayed. During the change of release, all you need to do is confirm that the changes from these change requests should be applied.

Ideally, the result of such a comparison is that all systems in the system landscape received identical modifications before the change of release. This is the case, for example, if you applied the recommended procedure, that is, if you created all modifications in the development system and then distributed them to the downstream systems before the change of release. If the comparison shows that a change request contains all modifications existing in the current system, `R3up` skips the request for modification adjustment and directly continues with activating the ABAP Dictionary. Even if not all objects can be supplied with the automatic adjustment transport, it is often useful to use it anyway in order not to have to process this part again.

One prerequisite for a change of release in the remaining systems of the system landscape is that the global changeability is set to **Changeable** (for the time of the release change).

Another benefit of using the modification adjustment transport, particularly for the SPAU adjustment, is the gain of time during the upgrade. Often, several hundreds of objects need to be adapted in such an adjustment.

Basically, there are two procedures for importing the adjustment transport:

- An automatic transport; `R3up` recognizes the adjustment transport from the systems and "attaches" them to the upgrade.
- A manual transport; for this, you create a typical transport, the release of which is not controlled by `R3up` and which therefore isn't marked for further upgrades. This is performed specifically if a short *code freeze* period (during which no further developments can take place) is planned. After the upgrade, this manual transport can be imported as easily as any standard transport.

For an adjustment transport that is integrated in the upgrade, it is treated by `R3up` as if it was another set of objects belonging to the upgrade and is merged in the correct order into the upgrade procedure. Thus, the objects of the transport are taken over into the new repository even before the downtime of the system. In case the SPAU adjustment transport is imported manually after the actual upgrade, you will have to put up with an extension of the downtime by the duration of this import. Therefore, if the downtime factor plays an important role and the SPAU adjustment takes several hours, you should try to avoid the subsequent transport. When asked for an adjustment transport, you can also proceed by providing `R3up` with another adjustment transport than the one originally exported. The corresponding procedure is described in detail in SAP Note 68678.

**Note** In any case, you should test the procedure and its result both for the automatic adjustment transport and, in particular, for the subsequent change of the automatic adjustment in a test upgrade to avoid potential errors or data inconsistencies for the productive system!

### 16.3.2 Modification Adjustment During the Import of Support Packages

When importing Support Packages, the option to integrate SPDD or SPAU requests in the Support Package queue exists only since SPAM version 0020 in the SAP Web AS 6.x releases. If you need to adjust a large number of modifications, this procedure ensures both an increase in time and security when compared to a manual adjustment. Proceed as follows:

1. Start importing the selected Support Package queue via the Support Package Manager in Transaction SPAM in the development system.

2. If you modified SAP Dictionary objects and these objects are imported together with the Support Package, the Support Package Manager stops automatically. You must then adjust these objects using Transaction SPDD.
3. Create a change request in the Workbench Organizer (Transaction SE09) for the modification adjustment using Transaction SPDD. Also create one task for every developer who is involved in the modification adjustment.
4. After the adjustment is completed, the developers must release the tasks and inform you so that you can release the request in Transaction SPDD via **Utilities • Mark for transport** and mark it for the import into subsequent systems.
5. Continue importing the Support Package queue.
6. If you modified SAP Repository objects and these objects are imported together with the Support Package, the Support Package Manager stops automatically. You must then adjust these objects using Transaction SPAU.
7. Create a change request in the Workbench Organizer (Transaction SE09) for the modification adjustment using Transaction SPAU. Also create one task for every developer who is involved in the modification adjustment.
8. After the adjustment is completed, the developers must release the tasks and inform you so that you can release the request in Transaction SPAU via **Utilities • Mark for transport** and mark it for the import into subsequent systems.
9. Finish the import of the Support Package queue by continuing the import in the Support Package Manager.

For the other systems of the landscape, the SPDD or SPAU request can then be used to import the adjustment changes into subsequent systems. Proceed as follows:

1. Start the Support Package Manager using Transaction SPAM and select the Support Package queue as you imported it into the development system.
2. After defining the Support Package queue, you're asked in Transaction SPAM whether you want to integrate modification adjustment transports (this query can be suppressed using appropriate Support Package Manager settings). As soon as you confirm the request, the existing adjustment transports are listed in a dialog box. To add the adjustment transports to the Support Package queue, select **Accept selected adjustment transports**.

   For every adjustment transport listed, the status field shows if it matches the current Support Package queue and can therefore be integrated or not. The matching adjustment transports are already selected in the table. An adjustment transport "matches" the queue if the target Support Package status of the current queue corresponds to that of the export system at the time of exporting the modification adjustment transport.

3. The selected adjustment transports are thus integrated in the queue of Support Packages.

   If a modification adjustment transport is imported as a part of a Support Package queue, it is removed from the normal transport flow for Workbench requests. An automatic forwarding to the follow-up system does not take place. For example, if you are operating the classical three-system landscape of development system (DEV), quality assurance system (QAS), and production system (PRD), the modification adjustment transport is placed into the import queue of the QAS system after being exported from the DEV system. The integration of the adjustment transport into a Support Package queue in the QAS system now leads to the removal of this transport from the QAS import queue. Since there is no transport forwarding during the import of a Support Package queue, the adjustment transport is not forwarded to the import queue of the PRD system, that is, the modification adjustment is not imported with the Transport Management System into your PRD system.

   As in the QAS system, you should then import the adjustment transport as a part of a Support Package queue into the PRD system.

4. Start importing the Support Package queue from Transaction SPAM.

   Please ensure that only dictionary objects exist in the SPDD request and only repository objects exist in the SPAU request. Otherwise, severe problems might occur because transport steps for the adjustment request would start actions for the Support Package import as well.

If you're not using Version 0020 of the Support Package Manager in SAP Web AS Release 6.x, or are generally using a lower SAP Basis release, the SPDD adjustment must be carried out manually. For this purpose, customize the objects displayed in Transaction SPDD according to your needs using Transaction SE11 and save them without directly performing an activation. For the SPAU adjustment, however, you can create a transport request in the development system in which you integrate the adjusted repository objects. These objects can be imported via the Transport Managment System (TMS) import function after the Support Package queue has been completely imported in the follow-up system; the request for adjustment by Transaction SPAU can be ignored in this case. As a precaution, however, you should review the modification browser, the version information of the adjusted objects, and the corresponding code after importing your adjustment transport to ensure that the adjusted repository objects have been properly integrated.

### 16.3.3 Modification Assistant

To achieve a simpler modification adjustment during an upgrade or a Support Package implementation, the modification assistant was introduced with Release R/3 4.5. To ensure the implementation of the modification assistant, go to a specific modification mode when calling the editors of the ABAP Workbench for modifying objects of the standard version. The original is protected in this mode and can be changed only by using additionally provided pushbuttons (see Figure 16.16). Using the modification assistant, changes are logged to enable a quick and detailed overview of modifications and to reduce the upgrade effort.

**Figure 16.16** Change options of the modification assistant

The modification assistant provides support in the following subareas of the ABAP Workbench:

- ABAP Editor
- Class Builder
- Screen Pointer
- Menu Pointer
- Text element maintenance
- Function Builder
- ABAP Dictionary
- Documentation

Modifications to objects of the ABAP Workbench that are not supported by the modification assistant are logged and displayed in the overview. During the upgrade, modifications to these objects are adjusted in the traditional way.

In general, SAP recommends that you leave the modification assistant active, even if the modification of the object is a bit more complex, because it simplifies the modification adjustment. You can obtain an overview of the modifications you carried out and can easily revert the object to its original state. Although the modification assistant can be switched off, you no longer will receive any detailed information about your modifications and must carry out the adjustment manually via version management. Because the modification logs are based on the original version that was imported with the last upgrade or Support Package and record only the differences between the original version and the modified version of the object, this information gets lost if you switch off the assistant. Therefore, the modification assistant cannot simply be switched on again later.

**Note** As you can see in Figure 16.17, line 16 was replaced with the lines 17 to 19; additionally, the lines 22–23 were inserted. Also, you can see the transport request MODK920030 in which these changes were recorded. It is therefore easy to understand that changes carried out via this assistant can be easily adjusted with newer versions.

As mentioned above, the modification assistant was introduced with Release R/3 4.5. If you carry out an upgrade from a release prior to 4.5A to a release higher than 4.5A, all objects modified by you and redelivered by SAP are displayed in Transaction SPAU in the category **Without Modification Assistant**. Additionally, objects that cannot be versioned and that have not been managed by Transaction SPAU are displayed here. The adjustment of these objects must then be done manually supported by version management only.

```
10  MODULE USER_COMMAND_0100 INPUT.
11    CASE OK_CODE.
12      WHEN 'SHOW'.
13        CLEAR OK_CODE.
14        SELECT SINGLE * FROM SPFLI WHERE CARRID = SPFLI-CARRID
15  *{   REPLACE        MODK920030                                1
16  *\                              AND   CONNID = SPFLI-CONNID.
17                                  AND   CONNID   = SPFLI-CONNID
18                                  AND   CITYFROM = SPFLI-CITYFROM
19                                  AND   CITYTO   = SPFLI-CITYTO.
20  *}   REPLACE
21  *{   INSERT         MODK920030                                2
22      WHEN 'CHNG'.
23        PERFORM CHANGE_SPFLI.
24  *}   INSERT
25      WHEN SPACE.
26      WHEN OTHERS.
27        CLEAR OK_CODE.
28        SET SCREEN 0. LEAVE SCREEN.
29    ENDCASE.
30  ENDMODULE.                 " USER_COMMAND_0100  INPUT
```

**Figure 16.17** Changes using the modification assistant

Additional information about the modification assistant and the adjustment can be found in the SAP online help.

## 16.4 Upgrade Strategies for a Transport Landscape

In a transport landscape, release changes should be performed in exactly the order defined by the transport route. The modification adjustment for a change of release is carried out in the development system and then transported along the transport route to downstream systems.

Still, not only the modification adjustment plays an important role when planning a system landscape for an upgrade. You might need to check in a preliminary study whether the target release fulfills the demands on the new functionality at all. Furthermore, you don't want to stop development in the existing development system by an upgrade. So, you would create a mock system, for example, a copy of the existing system in addition to the existing landscape. Or, there may be demands from various projects requesting a short code freeze period. This can rarely be achieved with a three-system landscape. Development and Customizing tasks for different release statuses must be performed in separate SAP environments as described in Chapters 4 and 6. Therefore, the following sections introduce the most important landscapes that are implemented during the upgrade.

### 16.4.1 Change of Release in a Three-System Landscape

In a change of release in a three-system landscape, the tasks need to be performed in the following order (see Figure 16.18):

1. Carry out the change of release and the modification adjustment in the DEV development system.
2. Carry out the change of release in the QAS quality assurance system or create a new QAS quality assurance system as a copy of the PRD production system. The latter option is preferable. Then, import the change requests with the results of the modification adjustment into the QAS and test and validate the functionality of the system.
3. Implement the change of release in the PRD production system. Import the change requests with the results of the modification adjustment into the PRD.

The three-system landscape is the standard landscape recommended by SAP for live operations. As you can tell from the modification adjustment sequence above, the processing during an upgrade follows the normal itinerary as well. However, this also shows that this landscape cannot meet all requirements. The most important aspect in this regard is the missing maintainability of the production system during the upgrade of DEV and QAS. As soon as the development system is in the upgrade phase, there is no system available to carry out potentially necessary corrections for problems in the production system, unless you make these corrections in the test or production system. Both procedures hold certain risks—on the one hand, the success of these changes poses a risk; and on the other hand, the results achieved in the upgrade of the development system can no longer be completely transferred to downstream systems. The risk is calculated from the duration of the test system upgrade, including the time reserved for testing.

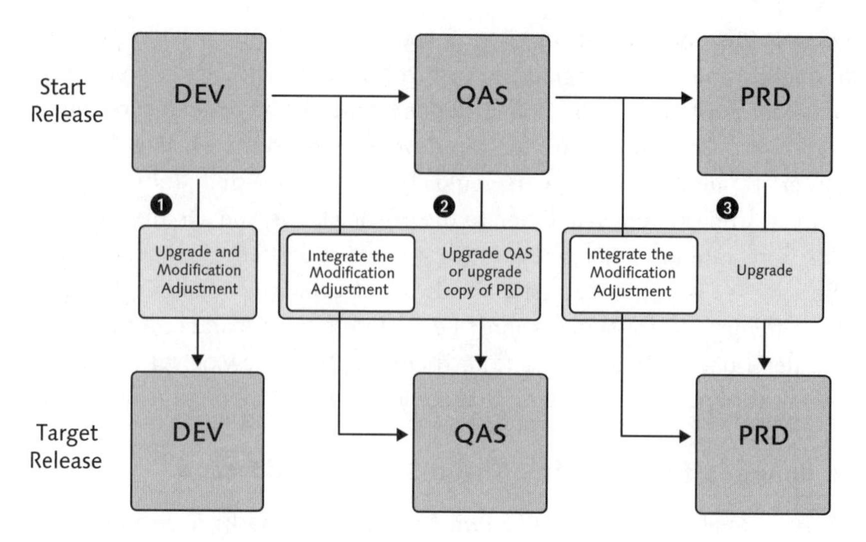


**Figure 16.18** Order of the release changes in a three-system landscape

### 16.4.2 Change of Release with Additional Development System

If you have a fourth system available, you can avoid some problems of the standard three-system landscape. In this case, you would proceed, for example, as shown in Figure 16.19.

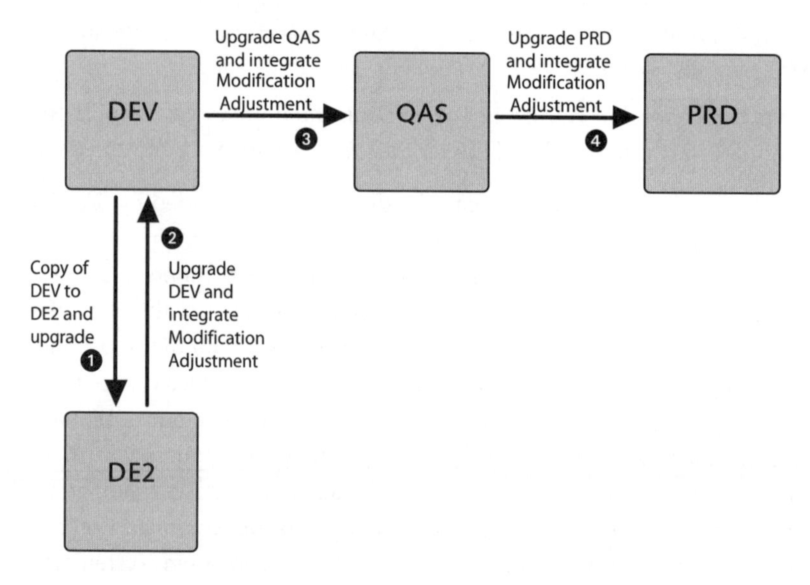


**Figure 16.19** Upgrade in the three-system landscape with additional development system

At first, a system copy of the development system is created on which the upgrade is carried out. As long as you carry out the upgrade, adjust the modifications, or validate new functions in the DE2 system, you can still perform the maintenance of the existing release in the original system landscape. When the work on the DE2 system is completed, the upgrade of the actual development system and then the upgrade of both the test and the production system are carried out as described above.

This procedure has certain benefits, but it has its drawbacks as well. Apart from the additional hardware that needs to be provided for the second development system, it is also necessary to manually recreate all developments and corrections on the new DE2 development system that were carried out on the DEV development system, after the system was copied from DEV to DE2. However, new developments after the DEV upgrade for the new release can be carried out easily via normal transports. Therefore, it is understandable that in an environment in which extensive project work is still done in the old release, the maintenance effort is accordingly high because of applying those changes twice—in the new and probably also in the old release.

However, you can also regard this system landscape in a slightly different way in that the development system does not directly produce a new development system, but a mock system in which various components such as a new Customizing or new functions are tested but not saved as transport requests. With the information gained here, the upgrade in the actual development system can often be carried out faster since unwanted actions that were carried out in the mock system don't remain in the landscape.

On the whole, this kind of system landscape still has the problem that the development work must be frozen for a certain period. The primary reason for the code freeze is that tests, which should be performed in an upgraded test system with relevant data, can often last several weeks.

### 16.4.3 Change of Release with Five Systems

In contrast to the two previous variants, we will now introduce a model with five systems. If you're planning a change of release to achieve additional functionality, such as implementing a new SAP module, for example, PP, MM, or HR, you must configure a "phase-based development environment," that is, an environment in which you can map different phases of the development process—different release statuses in this case. This helps you to avoid long development freezes. While the new release is being configured, you can still carry out supporting customizing and development works for the current release in production operation. Even for the tests in the new release, you can take more time with such a system landscape. The following example describes which actions and customizations are to be expected in detail.

**Example: Phase-Based Change of Release in a System Landscape**

An enterprise is in live mode with the R/3 application modules Financial Accounting, Logistics, and Human Resources. The current R/3 implementation consists of a standard three-system landscape with one development system (DEV), one quality assurance system (QAS), and one production system (PRD).

The enterprise plans to change from R/3 Release 4.5B to SAP ECC 5.0. To support this change of release, two additional SAP systems are installed because, on the one hand, testing and verifying the new SAP release is rather time-consuming and, on the other hand, required corrections must be imported into the production operation every two months.

In order to support the production operation with changes every other month (production support), the system PPS is created using a system copy of the development system. A system copy of the existing QAS system is used for creating another quality assurance system, PQA. The PPS and PQA systems now provide production support for the PRD production system. All employees involved in customizing and development who need to make changes in the context of production support will do so in the PPS system. Tests and validation take place in PQA. After acceptance tests done, the corrections are imported into the PRD production system. All changes are documented so that they can also be implemented in the DEV system after the change of release. The synchronization is necessary to ensure consistency among all SAP systems.

The PPS system enables the technical team to carry out the change of release to SAP ECC 5.0 in the DEV and QAS systems. When the change of release has been completed and all available Support Packages have been imported, the customizing and development team of the new implementation phase begins with the release customizing in DEV. All customizing and development changes made in PPS are also implemented in DEV. After the functional tests have been completed, the changes are released and exported to QAS for verification.

The three-system landscape is now a five-system landscape (see Figure 16.20).

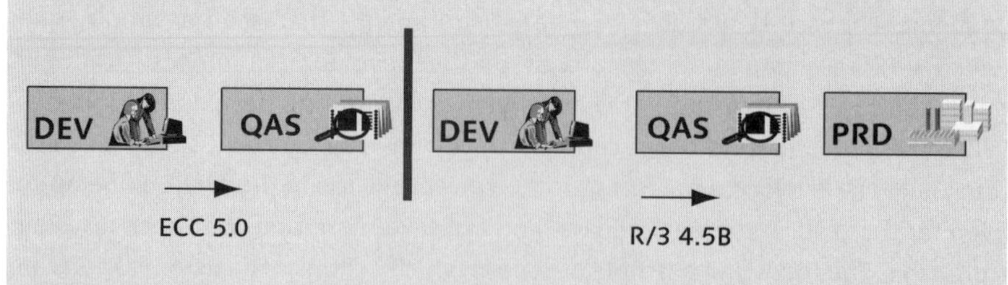


Figure 16.20 A five-system landscape consisting of different releases

The initial proposal of configuring the Transport Management System (TMS) to enable the implementation of the release change and provide production support at the same time is illustrated in Figure 16.21.

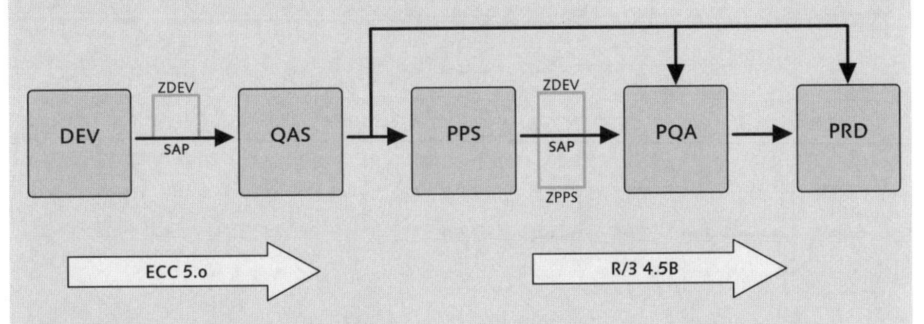


**Figure 16.21** Five systems connected through itineraries

Technically speaking, this initial proposal is feasible, however, the system managers are worried, because the import queues of PQA and PRD receive changes from both development systems, DEV and PPS. The import of change requests from DEV to PPS, PQA, and PRD before the change of release could be prevented using the `sourcesystems` transport profile parameter.

But, this solution is not completely satisfying, because the existence of change requests from R/3 Release 4.5B and from SAP ECC 5.0 in the import queues of PPS, PQA, and PRD could lead to confusion.

Another proposal is to create a second transport directory for DEV and QAS. The existing transport directory would be used for maintaining the import queues of PPS, PQA, and PRD and would receive only change requests for production support. Although this solution is feasible, it requires that nobody use the TMS for copying change requests between different transport directories, because this would automatically add change requests from ECC 5.0 to the import queues of PPS, PQA, and PRD. Using authorizations, you can restrict the TMS access and thereby reduce this risk, but not completely eliminate it.

Therefore, the TMS configuration proposal illustrated in Figure 16.22 is eventually accepted, which involves the creation of the R45 virtual system. The import queue of this virtual system receives a list of sequential change requests from ECC 5.0 that need to be imported into the PPS, PQA, and PRD systems after the release of these systems has been changed to SAP ECC 5.0.

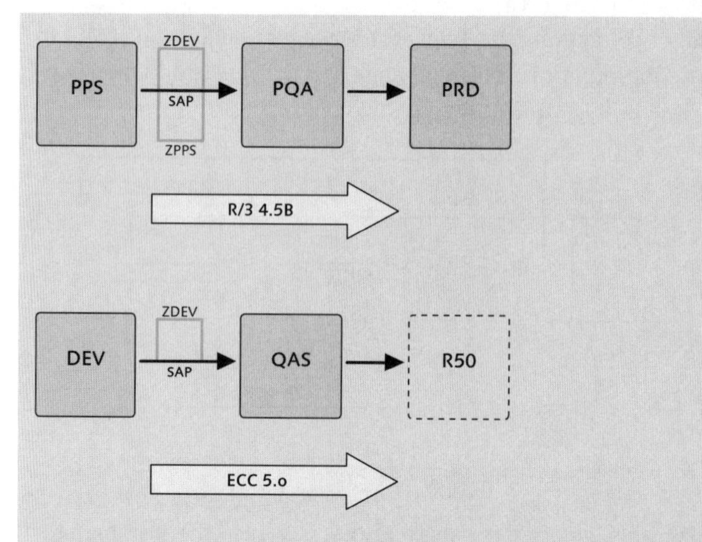


**Figure 16.22** TMS configuration with R50 virtual system

While the change of release is prepared in PRD, change requests are imported from DEV to QAS for verification and are then delivered to R50. In the next step, the import buffer is copied from R50 to create an import buffer for PQA; the change of release is carried out in PQA. Change requests are imported to ensure that the change from R/3 Release 4.5B to ECC 5.0 can be completed without problems. If the tests run successfully, the change of release is carried out in the PRD system. Then the import buffer is copied from R50 to create an import buffer for PRD, and the change requests are imported from ECC 5.0 into the PRD production system. Finally, change of release, import buffer copy, and change request import are done in PPS.

## 16.5 Further Recommendations for a Change of Release

After the rather technical descriptions of the previous chapters, this chapter introduces general recommendations for carrying out a change of release and gives you an overview of useful tools and services.

### 16.5.1 Upgrade Tools and SAP Upgrade Service Offers

As already mentioned in the introductory section about upgrades, not only technical aspects need to be considered during an upgrade project. The course for the project is set long before the upgrade program is started for the first time. Here, too, the general rule applies: An SAP upgrade project is a "real" project and should be planned carefully.

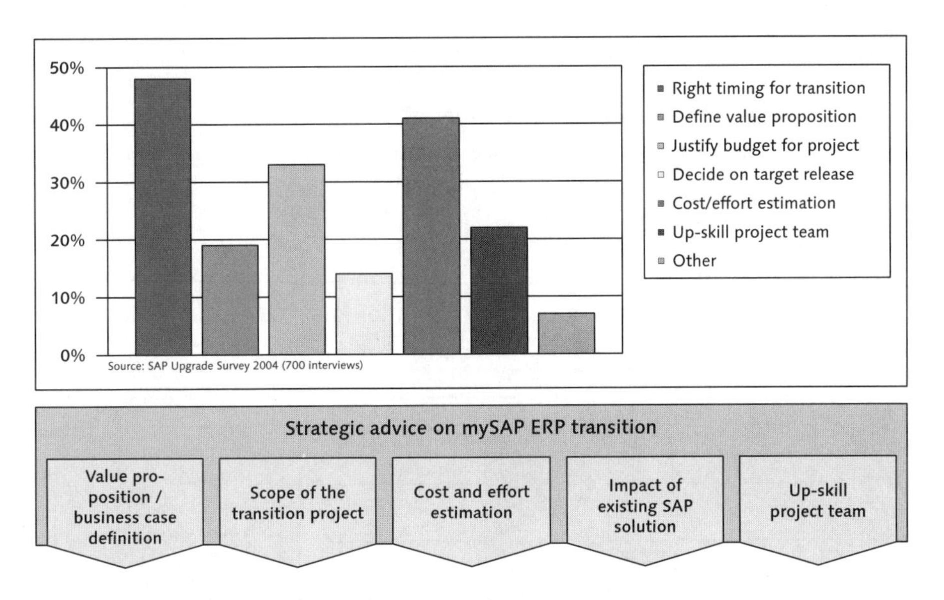


**Figure 16.23** Challenges before the start of an upgrade project

In the customer survey mentioned above (see Section 16.1.2), customers were also asked for the challenges during the planning phase of an upgrade. It turned out that customers have problems particularly when it comes to finding the right time for an upgrade. They also frequently have difficulties estimating both the effort and costs involved (see Figure 16.23). Naturally, challenges vary depending on the level of knowledge and experience. As soon as you have carried out an upgrade project for the first time and ensured that it was well documented, you can produce a good estimate for another upgrade project based on this data, even though the volume or the system landscape to be changed will not always be directly comparable. To provide the right support tailored to meet your individual requirements, SAP has extended its consulting services based on these results. For example, there is a "mySAP ERP Discovery Workshop" for the topic "Upgrade Value," which gives you an overview of the functionality of mySAP ERP. Additional benefits can then be developed per customer in a Value Assessment. The upgrade project team that should ideally be informed about the innovations, even before the start of the upgrade project, can be educated in different training courses such as the "SAP Upgrade Methodology Workshop" or in online classes.

For the areas of impact of a change of release on the current system landscape, however, there is no service offer regarding only the estimate of time and effort. An individual contemplation of the effort, direction, or effect on the existing landscape by itself does not go far enough in this respect. With a service like the "SAP Quick Upgrade Evaluation," however, all of these three factors of the upgrade project are seen in context. For example, a customer who uses only one SAP system and already disposes of some upgrade experience will face other challenges during a change of release project, and other effects on the system landscape than a customer who uses a complex landscape with several connected mySAP Business Suite components and wants to upgrade the central SAP back end system.

When all decisions have been made during the preparation for the actual upgrade project, the upgrade is carried out. The survey mentioned above also covered questions about problematic areas in the execution of the upgrade, which led to the result shown in Figure 16.24.

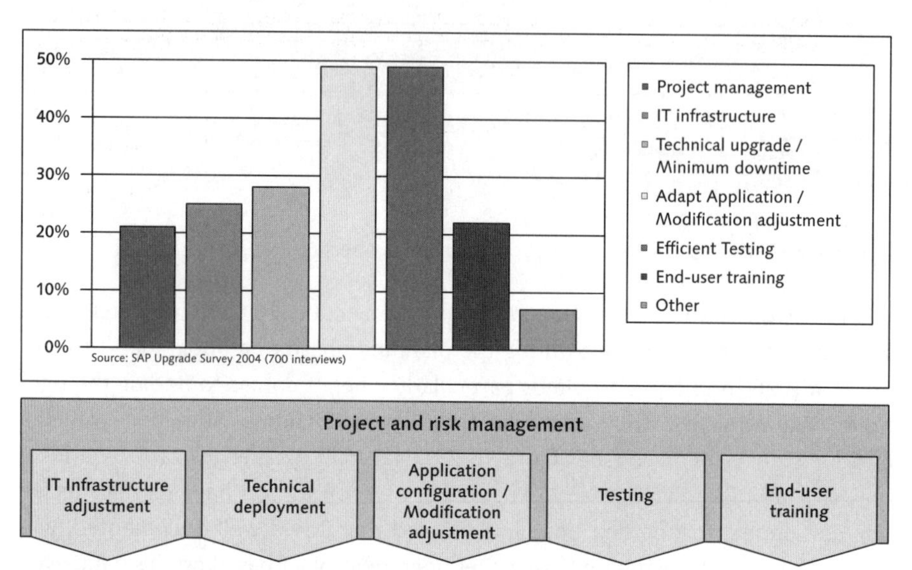


**Figure 16.24** Challenges during the execution of a change of release

You can see that the areas of testing and modification adjustment or customizing the application, respectively, demanded the greatest effort and therefore, usually, the highest costs, even exceeding the areas of end-user training and additional hardware purchases. As a result of this survey, SAP also put together appropriate tools and services to support you individually in the most required areas. We will now explain these areas in detail

It is critical that you plan an upgrade project with the utmost care. Therefore, to help you, SAP summarized its experience and the working steps necessary for a successful upgrade project in the "Upgrade Roadmap." The Upgrade Roadmap is the successor of the ASAP Roadmap for Upgrades and describes all tasks that are required for a successful upgrade of a mySAP solution. The new edition is an extension of the old roadmap. Not only does it contain information about mySAP

ERP; it also contains information about other mySAP Business Suite components. The Upgrade Roadmap is available in an HTML version, but displays its full functionality when used from the SAP Solution Manager. Due to this benefit and others as well, the mandatory use of SAP Solution Manager as a prerequisite for implementing a technical upgrade was introduced with mySAP ERP 2004, which, for the first time, includes the delivery of a comprehensive ERP software solution with different additional software components. For example, a key is required for starting the `R3up` upgrade control program, which is generated using SAP Solution Manager (see Figure 16.25).

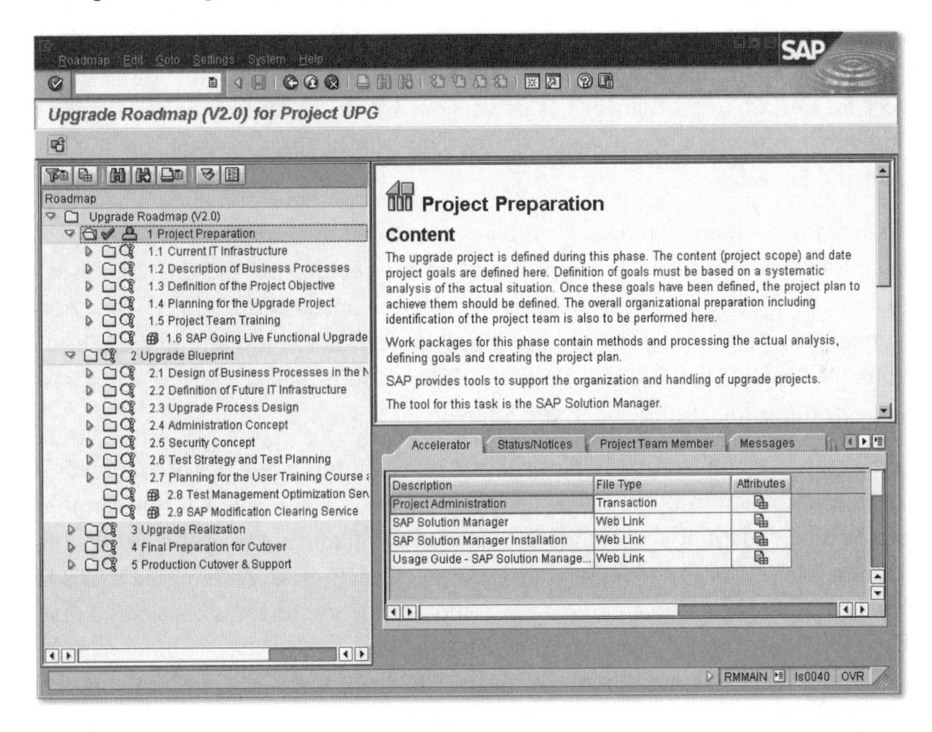


**Figure 16.25** Upgrade Roadmap in SAP Solution Manager

The Upgrade Roadmap follows the various phases of an upgrade project—preparation, concept design, implementation, preparation of the production system, and Go Live support. For each of these phases, corresponding work packages and tasks have been stored. Besides their general description, the results to be achieved, and other tasks possibly required, the task area also includes interesting notes for the execution, as well as accelerators that are often available for this purpose. The accelerators are transactions for system information or hyperlinks directly referencing Best Practices in the SAP Service Marketplace. Because both the tasks and the accelerators are supplied with attributes, you can easily filter the tasks for the project manager or the system administrator, for example, using the SAP Solution Manager filter functions. You can also centrally store your own information about the individual tasks like the current task status, project members involved, or extended documentations. In addition to further personalization options, you can export tasks to Microsoft Project from the Upgrade Roadmap of SAP Solution Manager.

If you want to get an overview of the Upgrade Roadmap contents without using SAP Solution Manager, you can load the HTML version from the SAP Service Marketplace to your PC and view it locally using a Web browser. Even there, you have the complete contents with all accelerators at hand; only the extended functions are not usable in this variant. You can load both the HTML version and the transport for SAP Solution Manager as of Version 3.1 from SAP Service Marketplace under *http://service.sap.com/upgrade*. The Upgrade Roadmap is available in German and English.

Apart from the more extensive possibilities available by using the Upgrade Roadmap, SAP Solution Manager supports you in further steps of the upgrade. Especially if you already used it for carrying out a system installation, you can now easily read the used processes from the blueprint, create appropriate upgrade tests from the test plans, and analyze the existing system landscape. We'll address some of these topics in detail in the following.

During a change of release, in particular, if several interim releases are skipped, it is often necessary to upgrade the hardware as well. When viewed from another perspective, adapting the hardware can also influence the decision on the upgrade time if, for example, specific leasing contracts exist. With regard to the IT infrastructure, the hardware of database and application server is considered first. This extension often derives from increasing the functionality of a new release. This implies an adjustment not only for the SAP software, but also for the operating system and the database software. You can obtain a first clue by carrying out a Quick Sizing project. Note that this can only be regarded as an approximation, because the QuickSizer calculates its workload in SAPS via the document volume or the user numbers to be expected. The actual usage of the system and the projection of this current data to the new release is only possible via the Analysis Session of the *SAP Going Live Functional Upgrade Check* (short: SAP GLFU). For this purpose, the system load is calculated from a download of your system and recalculated using the appropriate factors so as to enable an evaluation of both the existing and the planned servers for the coverage of the load to be expected. Therefore, the SAP GLFU should be booked well ahead—particularly if the system already shows a poor performance in its start release—to react accordingly during the project by adapting the hardware. Within the scope of the SAP standard maintenance, the GLFU is free of charge if no other remote service, for example, an Early Watch Service, has already been delivered for the same installation during the same year. The GLFU can be ordered directly from the SAP Service Marketplace under *http://service.sap.com/servicecat*.

In addition to server changes, it is often necessary to replace the front-end PCs. This is partially due to the pure demands on CPU speed or main memory in order to enable the presentation of the enhanced User Interfaces, but partially also due to the necessity to install a new operating system version on the PCs, which can result in increased hardware requirements as well. Another aspect to be considered can be the network infrastructure between application server and front-end PCs. Particularly when introducing Release R/3 4.6C and thereby enhancing the usability—keyword "Enjoy SAP"—there was also an increase in the network load. Unlike before, when parts of lists were transferred to the PC and every scroll operation in these lists required a new editing on the application server, the entire list and the scrolling itself are now on the PC itself. Additionally, numerous transactions that were executed using several dialog steps were converted to control-based transactions in which a lot of the required additional information is available right from the start. Thus, the network load of a transaction can increase from 3 to 4 KB to 6 to 9 KB on average. If instead of the SAP GUI for Windows the SAP GUI for HTML is used, for example, via the Internet Transaction Server (ITS), this value can even be higher. If the current network usage is unknown, you can carry out an estimate using a whitepaper located in the SAP Service Marketplace under *http://service.sap.com/upgrade* under **Upgrade Content**.

To keep the activities of application adjustment as low as possible, this adjustment is widely carried out by the upgrade, for example, in the form of XPRA reports. Additionally, SAP combined the other adjustments in upgrade and delta Customizing. Upgrade Customizing refers to the extensions of Customizing that are necessary due to the improved possibilities of an already existing process step for the new release. The delta Customizing is designed for those processes that were newly imported into the system during the change of release. Both Customizing activities can be filtered easily in the Customizing IMG. This filtering reduces the adjustment tasks to a minimum. Nevertheless, you should take your time and perform this adjustment in the development system after the upgrade and integrate it in the transport requests. Consequently, these supplementations can be easily transferred to the other systems of your system landscape.

Testing should be regarded as one of the main efforts in an upgrade project. The more different modules, custom developments, and interfaces are used, the more testing is required. Fortunately, there are various tools and services to help you out.

In SAP NetWeaver 04 underlying mySAP ERP 2004, for example, there is a comprehensive Test Workbench, which when compared to the SAP 4.x Basis releases was particularly improved in its support for automatic tests. Using eCATT, an enhancement of the proven CATT, you can create automatic test cases for all SAP GUI-based transactions even if these use control technologies. Additionally, the execution of test cases beyond the system boundaries was improved. Therefore, you can now create automatic tests that can verify cross-system business processes. At the same time, this tool can be integrated in the SAP Test Workbench. The Test Workbench now enables the central creation of test plans for different application cases. These test plans can be divided according to various criteria, and smaller work packages can be assigned to different users. After logging on to this Workbench, these users will find their individual work list covering both automatic and manual tests. From there, you can start the tests, read corresponding documents like test case descriptions, and store the test results as statuses like "test successful," "subsequent test required," and so on. Since the statuses are stored centrally, up to date evaluations regarding the test process can be created very easily.

Even if you could use the ECC 500 system itself we recommend that you use the Test Workbench within SAP Solution Manager, because the tests can be stored and validated centrally and the automatic extended Computer Aided Test Tool (eCATT) test cases can be run across system boundaries.

To determine the test cases for which automation is beneficial or how to set priorities in the tests for different business processes, the SAP Service "Test Management Optimization" is very useful. Within five days at your site, they compare the current state of your test processes to the industry standard using a benchmark, offer recommendations regarding the creation of test plans and test cases, and introduce you to the use of tools like eCATT and Test Workbench.

The more releases are skipped in an upgrade and the more new functions are used or modifications are replaced with the SAP standard version, the greater the need to train end users in handling the system. If the users work in many different locations, training in a traditional classroom implies extensive traveling and therefore high costs. In these cases, it is advisable to train users via the existing network infrastructure using eLearning. For this purpose, SAP provides the *SAP Tutor* program.

SAP Tutor enables the creation of training material by capturing any Windows-based screen output like SAP GUI or Web browsers. Additionally, texts and interaction fields can be stored along with the recorded screen sequences. Through the texts, for example, task descriptions or explanations can be added, which can be read aloud by the system via an integrated speech engine. Using the interaction fields, you can then edit the images displayed so that you can simulate transactions, data entries, and much more without actually being connected to an SAP system (see Figure 16.26).

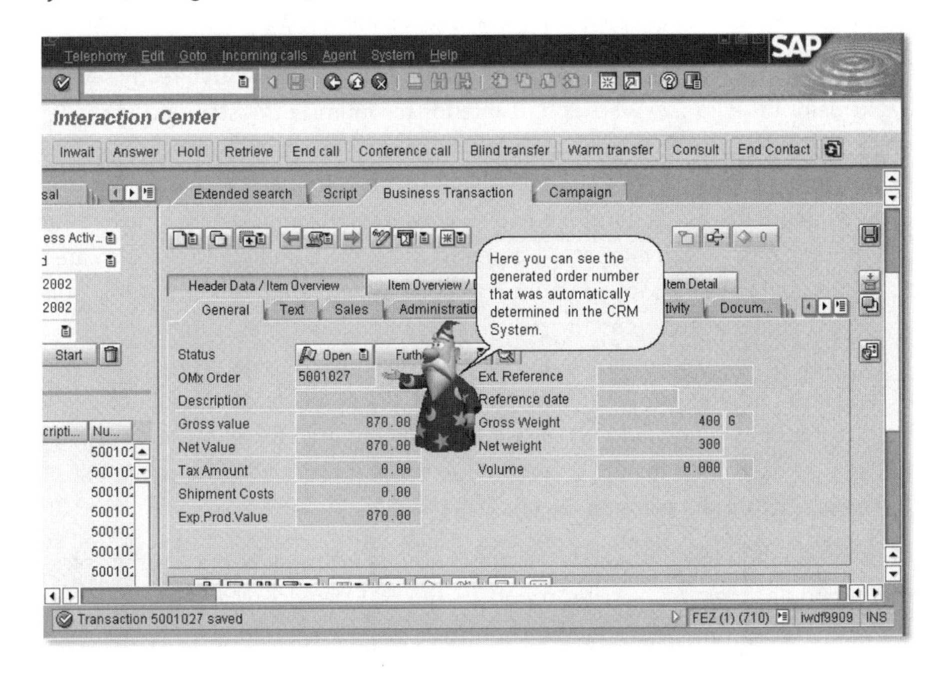


**Figure 16.26** Recorded transaction and playback using SAP Tutor

The created tutorials can also be run in different modes—in demo mode, where the entire sequence is run without user entries; in practice mode, where the end user is guided through the entries via help texts; and, in exam mode, where there is no additional help available after an initial task description and where the rate of correct user actions can even be evaluated. More information and example tutorials are available in the SAP Service Marketplace under *http://service.sap.com/saptutor*.

The technical upgrade is an expense factor both directly and indirectly. On the one hand, you need to consider the time and the resources necessary to perform the upgrade throughout the entire system landscape. On the other hand, every hour of downtime for the production system means a loss in business activity, which can also be measured in money. To minimize the risk of downtime, there are two service offers, which aim to provide better support in case of errors and, alternatively, intend to achieve a real reduction of downtime.

The *Upgrade Weekend Support* supports the most critical part of the upgrade project, that is, the weekend during which the production system is upgraded.

For this purpose, you are assigned a direct contact from the SAP Support. His or her task is to accelerate the process of handling messages and finding solutions by forwarding them directly to the right contact person and by monitoring and returning the processing results until the task is completed.

Downtime Assessment is a service offer that should be carried out already several weeks before the go-live weekend. It intends to optimize the standard upgrade, which has already been much improved by the system switch procedure, and adapt it as far as possible to your individual situation. To this end, particularly the long running database actions like conversions or XPRA reports are checked for their potential for improvement. As a prerequisite, the complete log files created during an upgrade of a copy of your production system are required for this purpose. Respective instructions for reducing downtime are then summarized in a report. Since these recommendations deviate from the standard procedure, we recommend that you run another test upgrade, for example, to be able to verify the duration. If you now add up the time usually required for all these steps, you obtain a point in time for the Downtime Assessment of eight to a minimum of four weeks before the planned Go Live.

More information like costs and ordering methods for these two and other services regarding upgrades can be found in the SAP Service Marketplace under *http://service.sap.com/upgradeservices*.

### 16.5.2 Other Recommendations

As a summary of the previous chapters, a change of release can be regarded as another project continuing the original implementation project. Therefore, an upgrade must be handled like any other project, beginning with roles and responsibilities up to a detailed project plan. The more knowledge that the individual teams retain from their working with the implementation projects—both regarding the project plan and the implementation and corresponding program adjustments—the easier it will be to carry out the upgrade. Note that you have the best chance of ensuring the success of the project in the planning phase of the release change. Apart from the usual planning like the desired organization structure or work, resource, and budget plans, the project volume should be accurate right from the beginning like the consideration of an archiving project, because a smaller database can positively affect the downtime during the upgrade. On the other hand, an archiving project would be another parallel project requiring resources and coordination. Furthermore, a new release often provides more comprehensive archiving objects that would then facilitate the task—whether only a technical upgrade should be carried out, whether new functionality should be implemented to the utmost extent, or anything in between these two options.

Contrary to other implementation projects, you have to consider other ancillary conditions during a change of release, for example, that you should build up an additional project system landscape for the change of release, particularly if the project will span several months. For this purpose, you need to check whether the existing resources in the system administration and development areas are sufficient to ensure both the maintenance of the existing system and that of the new release, or, if you need to include additional consultants in the project. In general, you should assign external resources to the maintenance tasks, because after completion of the upgrade project, the related knowledge is often lost when the consultants leave. The time of the development freeze for the upgrade project must be coordinated as thoroughly as possible with other potentially planned projects. The longer the development can be frozen, the easier the project planning for adjustments and tests will be, as well as the project planning for the required landscape.

This duration and the aforementioned planning for the project should be observed, because design changes affect the landscape and then rapidly lead to the problem that time and costs increase more if short-term adjustments need to be carried out during the implementation if a large team is occupied with the project. Therefore, it's preferable if corrections like these are incorporated during a small project after the upgrade has been completed.

This also applies to integrating additional Support Packages. Even though their most recent version is advantageous, the changes introduced by them into the system landscape can result in new adjustments and tests. Therefore, additional Support Packages should be imported into the upgrade project landscape only if the rest of the project plan (i.e., modification adjustment and tests) is matched accordingly. Overall, the upgrade project is simply easier to carry out if fewer requirements were defined and if a minimum of other parallel projects need to be coordinated. But, if these recommendations cannot be adhered to—due to comprehensive modifications that should be reverted to the SAP standard version, or due to many complex interfaces—you should plan project milestones including time buffers even more carefully and observe the critical itinerary so as not to fall behind.

Particularly if you don't upgrade on a regular basis, it is almost normal that errors will occur both in the technical execution and in the subsequent tests, or that the time required for the adjustment of previous modifications will take longer than scheduled, or that key personnel will not be available due to illness or vacation. If no time buffers exist, the schedule can easily slip. At the very beginning of the project, you should also check which steps you can take proactively, irrespective of the actual release change, like replacing front-end PCs, distributing the SAP

GUI, or making other adjustments to the hardware, since the hardware delivery itself can be delayed, too.

During the tests, you should ensure that you can work with real data, if possible. This is often not yet required for the module tests. However, the more complex the changes are to the business processes and the more critical the application is, the more you should pay attention to the quality of the test data, and to the volume and level of detail of the test cases. This applies to the tests of business processes and interfaces and, if necessary, also to the downtime test for the upgrade, since the QAS system cannot always be compared to the PRD system in a way that enables the tests to provide meaningful results. Additionally, it is advisable to prepare test cases for validation after the change of release to quickly find out whether or not the upgrade was successful. During the actual execution of the productive upgrade, you can no longer carry out extensive test series; these tests must have been completed successfully beforehand.

On the technical side, it is recommended that you read both the upgrade guide and the relevant upgrade notes; the latter should also be checked for changes on a regular basis during the project. Normally, there is a note for every SAP product, which refers to the database platform, the underlying system basis and the product itself. If other software is installed in the system, such as SAP add-ons or third-party products, you need to look for further documentation on how to proceed with these during an upgrade. Please check in the SAP Service Marketplace or with the software partners themselves. You should note, however, that these upgrade notes are often only an entry point for dependent notes, which all must be checked for their relevance to the current project.

When choosing the ideal point in time to start the upgrade, we would like to point out the following phenomenon of the system switch upgrade—the copying of data from technical tables to the "shadow tables." This is done to further reduce downtime. For data consistency reasons, a database trigger is created after the copy process, which is triggered as soon as the data is changed during normal operation after it has been copied. If a long time passes between the MODPROF_TRANS phase and the actual beginning of the downtime, the probability increases that these triggers become active and that the data needs to be copied again during the downtime. If the schedule is not observed during the test of the upgrade duration and user actions similar to those planned later are not carried out, but the upgrade is immediately resumed instead, it is possible that these effects were not detected and that the downtime might be extended accordingly. Depending on the affected table, this can be a matter of minutes or take up to several hours.

If downtime is a critical aspect, you should consider this carefully during the tests. The upgrade of the production system should be uneventful. This can be achieved with frequent upgrade tests and using an upgrade script created therein. You can base this upgrade script on the upgrade phase list delivered by SAP, for example, where relevant instructions are stored for every action required. Ideally, you should provide screenshots, detailed descriptions, and schedules so that anyone can perform the upgrade in case the person who is usually responsible for the upgrades is ill. Even for the administrator, actions to the production system are not routine, and a system query is easily confirmed inadvertently at the wrong time, or the high availability solution, which has never been implemented, does not behave as expected.

Therefore, you should also have an appropriate emergency plan in place if insurmountable difficulties arise. The "point of no return" at which the upgrade should be completed at the latest—before having to begin with the *system restore* to resume the operation on time using the old release—should become just as familiar to all involved as the telephone numbers of all relevant persons or, if necessary, the passwords of the superusers for SAP, the operating system, and the database. Even the restore should have been tested beforehand to avoid a backup error from being detected during the restore.

## 16.6 Questions

1. Which of the following statements are true of the SAP release strategy?
   A. The so-called 5-1-2 maintenance strategy applies to all of the mySAP ERP products.
   B. New products first go through the so-called ramp-up phase.
   C. During the ramp-up phase, the product is already generally available.
   D. No SAP Support Packages are delivered during the ramp-up phase.
2. Which of the following statements are true of release changes?
   A. The objects in the customer namespace are not overwritten.
   B. A repository switch replaces your current repository with the repository in the new release.
   C. All customer modifications to ABAP Dictionary objects are lost.
   D. The customer modifications to SAP objects that you want to keep must be transferred to the new release via the modification adjustment.
3. Which of the following statements are true of the modification adjustment?
   A. Transaction SPAU is used for most of the ABAP Dictionary objects.
   B. Transaction SPDD is used for most of the ABAP Dictionary objects.

C. If Transaction SPDD is not used although it is required, this can lead to data losses.

D. During the modification adjustment, you must revert to the SAP standard version.

4. Which benefits are provided by the system switch upgrade?

A. The system switch upgrade makes a modification adjustment redundant.

B. The system switch upgrade makes the creation of a backup before the upgrade redundant.

C. The system switch upgrade shortens the time during which the system cannot be used productively.

D. The SPDD adjustment can be carried out before the beginning of the downtime.

# 17 SAP Solution Manager

SAP Solution Manager is a central system for managing and documenting a complex and distributed solution landscape. It supports the entire lifecycle of a software solution—from the business blueprint through implementation projects to productive operation. SAP Solution Manager provides access to tools, methods, and preconfigured content. The individual functions of SAP Solution Manager are as follows:

- **Implementation Projects**
  - Creating the business blueprint
  - Central storage of project documentation, training documents, test cases, and so forth
  - Access to implementation roadmaps and best-practice documents
- **Customizing Distribution**
  - The Customizing Scout enables you to compare Customizing in different SAP components, for example, SAP R/3 and SAP Customer Relationship Management (SAP CRM).
  - Customizing Distribution enables you to transfer customizing settings from a source system to a target system and therefore keep the settings consistent.
- **Global Rollout**

Creating project templates that can be used in a rollout from the corporate headquarters to the subsidiaries, for example

- **Test Management**
  - Environment for organizing and performing functional tests subsequent to software changes
  - Tools to automate test procedures are also available (extended Computer Aided Test Tool, eCATT).
- **E-Learning Management**
  - Creating training materials using SAP Tutor
  - Distribution of the learning materials in learning maps (computer-aided self-paced trainings) to train end users subsequent to software changes, or after a new functionality has been implemented
- **Solution Monitoring**
  - Monitoring of all connected SAP systems from a central system

    - Business-process related monitoring
      Here, the transactions, interfaces, and protocols of a specific business process are particularly monitored.
    - Service level reporting
- **Service Delivery**
  Access to programs and services that help you to optimize your system landscape's performance and availability, and minimize the risks during system operation
- **Service Desk**
  Workflow for the creation and editing of problem notifications
- **Change Management**
  This tool provides a workflow for managing software changes. All changes are clearly documented and Transport Management System (TMS) functions are called in the background.

In this chapter, we'll describe the SAP Solution Manager functions that are specific to change management. These functions are:

- Customizing Synchronization
- Change Management

But before we begin, we must clarify some central concepts used in SAP Solution Manager.

SAP Solution Manager provides a repository for the central storage of your SAP system landscape information. In that repository, you can store all the required information such as hardware, OS and database version information, as well as details on systems, software components, and patch statuses. The data can be read from the system landscape directory (SLD), provided the SLD has been configured in your system landscape.

A properly maintained system landscape is an essential prerequisite for the other functions of SAP Solution Manager such as implementation projects and template projects, change management, customizing synchronization, solution monitoring, services, and service desk.

In SAP Solution Manager, you can maintain the system landscape in Transaction SMSY.

You can use the business process function to document those business processes of your company that you want to map in the systems. During the creation of a business blueprint for projects, you set up a project structure in which all relevant business scenarios, processes, and process steps are hierarchically structured. Moreover, you can create a project documentation that you assign to individual scenarios, processes, or process steps. Lastly, you can assign transactions to each process step and thereby determine the flow of your business processes in the SAP systems.

The business process is a central concept within SAP Solution Manager. Many other functions such as business process monitoring or testing, for example, are based on the business process concept. You can maintain business processes in Transactions SOLAR01 or SOLAR02.

In the project management component of SAP Solution Manager (Transaction SOLAR_PROJECT_ADMIN), you can create Solution Manager projects and perform all central administrative project tasks. There are several types of projects that you can manage in SAP Solution Manager:

- **Implementation project**
  Project for implementing business processes in an SAP landscape
- **Template project**
  You can use a template to make your project structure or parts of it, including the assigned objects (documentation, test cases, IMG activities) available for other projects. You can lock templates completely or partially against changes when they are used in other projects.
- **Upgrade project**
  Project for upgrading existing systems
- **Optimization project**
  Project for optimizing an existing system, for example, optimization projects can be used in combination with SAP Services
- **Safeguarding project**
  Project for eliminating a critical state during the implementation or operation of an SAP solution
- **Maintenance project**
  Project for maintaining a system or system landscape
  This project type plays an important role in change management.

## 17.1 Customizing Synchronization

If you operate several SAP components simultaneously in a solution landscape, for instance SAP R/3 and SAP CRM, it is often necessary that specific Customizing settings be identical for all systems involved. You can ensure that this is the case via Customizing Synchronization. Areas to be synchronized, among others, can be customer and product groups, sales districts, terms of payment, terms of delivery, picking groups, currencies, countries, regions, and units of measurement.

SAP provides the following two tools that support Customizing Synchronization: Customizing Distribution and the Customizing Scout.

1. *Customizing Distribution* transfers Customizing from a source system to a target system. A distinction is made between initial distribution and delta distribution. Delta distribution is used to keep the two systems in a continuous consistent state. Customizing Distribution is a tool that performs various tasks, such as:
   - Configuring training, demo, and test systems using the initial distribution of Customizing
   - Keeping SAP R/3, SAP CRM, and SAP Supply Chain Management (SAP SCM) systems in a synchronous state by using the delta distribution so that cross-component processes can run smoothly
   - Synchronizing Customizing in different SAP R/3 systems in order to prepare an Application Link Enabling (ALE) distribution of master data
2. The *Customizing Scout* is a tool that enables you to perform Customizing comparisons between different systems.

You can use several predefined synchronization objects for both Customizing Distribution and the Customizing Scout. These predefined objects are customizing objects that must be stored simultaneously in different components. Furthermore, you can select any transportable customizing object of the types *Space* (table), *V* (view), *S* (table including text table), *C* (view cluster), *T* (individual transaction), and *L* (logical transport object) for Customizing Synchronization. The customizing objects however, must meet several requirements that are described in great detail in the online help.

### 17.1.1 Customizing Distribution

Customizing Distribution transfers Customizing from a source system (e.g., SAP R/3) to a target system (e.g., SAP CRM). Customizing Distribution always takes place between development systems. When the distribution is completed, the data can be transferred via transport request into the downstream systems of the transport landscape. Customizing Distribution represents a new functionality, primarily for comparisons, distributing customizing changes, and logging options.

In a development landscape, Customizing Distribution enables you to:

- Download Customizing from a source system into a target system for the first time (initial distribution)
- Distribute Customizing in a time-controlled manner

- Distribute Customizing automatically with each transport release or customizing change (from Release 4.6C)
- Distribute Customizing manually

> **Note** There can be only one type of distribution active per Solution Manager project and source client, which means that you must decide which type of Customizing Distribution you want to use. The same applies to Customizing Distributions that do not pertain to a particular project.

Specific customizing objects that need to be synchronized frequently are already predefined in the system. These are known as the *synchronization objects*. You can edit the predefined synchronization objects and create additional customizing objects for the distribution in the editor for synchronization groups.

Customizing settings that must be changed via Customizing Distribution can be locked against manual changes in the target system. The lock may apply to the entire customizing object, or you can use filters to restrict it to individual key areas. This enables you to accept additional settings in the target system, which differ from those in the source system.

### Requirements for Customizing Distribution

Before you can configure the Customizing Distribution, you must do some preliminary work, which is illustrated in Figure 17.1.

1. First, you must maintain the involved systems in the Solution Manager system landscape (Transaction SMSY).
2. Next, you must maintain RFC connections between SAP Solution Manager and the involved systems.
3. Then, you must create a Solution Manager project of the implementation project type. The systems to be synchronized must be assigned to that project. You can do this in Solution Manager Transaction SOLAR_PROJECT_ADMIN.
4. In the development systems to be synchronized, you must generate IMGs that have the same name as the Solution Manager project.
5. Lastly, you can load the synchronization objects.

Please see the online help for detailed instructions on how to configure Customizing Distribution.

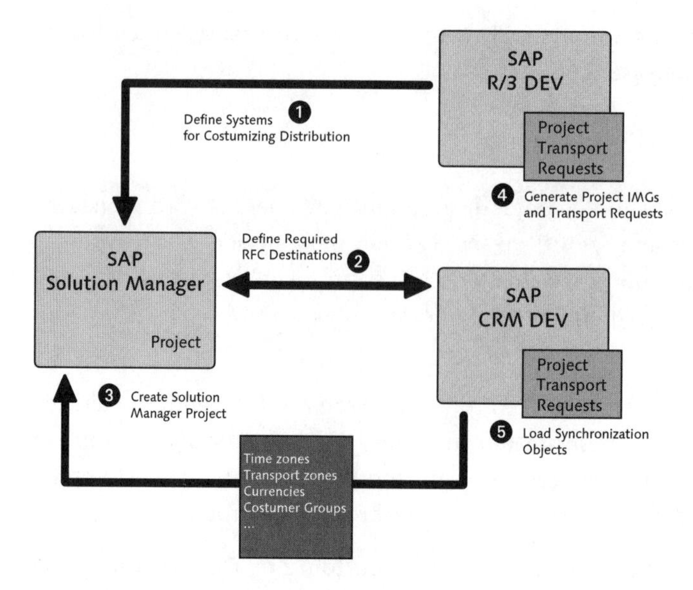


**Figure 17.1** Configuring customizing distribution

Now, you can set up the Customizing Distribution using predefined or custom synchronization groups (Transaction SCDT_SETUP):

1. Select the customizing objects or IMG activities that you want to distribute. To do that, you must create a synchronization group in the synchronization group editor. The synchronization group should contain all customizing objects you want to consider for the distribution of a source component to a target component.
2. Start the *Initial Distribution* to synchronize selected Customizing in a source system with Customizing in target systems only once. When doing that, you must specify the following:
   - Which synchronization group should be activated for the Customizing Distribution
   - From which development system do you want to distribute changes (source system)
   - To which development systems do you want to distribute changes (target systems)
3. To enable the transfer of selected Customizing changes from a source system into target systems, you must set up automatic Customizing Distribution. In this context, you can also define whether Customizing Distribution is to take place during Customizing, at the time of a transport release, or at fixed time intervals.

### Customizing Distribution Procedure

The procedure in Customizing Distribution is as follows:

1. Perform Customizing changes in the Customizing Distribution source system.
2. The source system then notifies the SAP Solution Manager system about the changes. The SAP Solution Manager system checks the following:
   - Whether the Customizing changes are part of a synchronization group for which the Customizing Distribution is active
   - To which target systems the changes are to be transferred
3. The SAP Solution Manager system converts Customizing data that must be distributed into Customizing data for the target system.
4. The SAP Solution Manager system transfers the Customizing changes to the target systems.
5. Due to the Customizing Distribution, changes are written to the transport requests in the target systems. These changes enable you to transport the new Customizing settings into the downstream systems of the transport flow.

The target systems notify the SAP Solution Manager system about possible errors during the Customizing Distribution. Then you should check the logs of the Customizing Distribution in SAP Solution Manager. After that, you can use the Customizing Scout to verify whether the Customizing was actually synchronized with the Customizing Distribution.

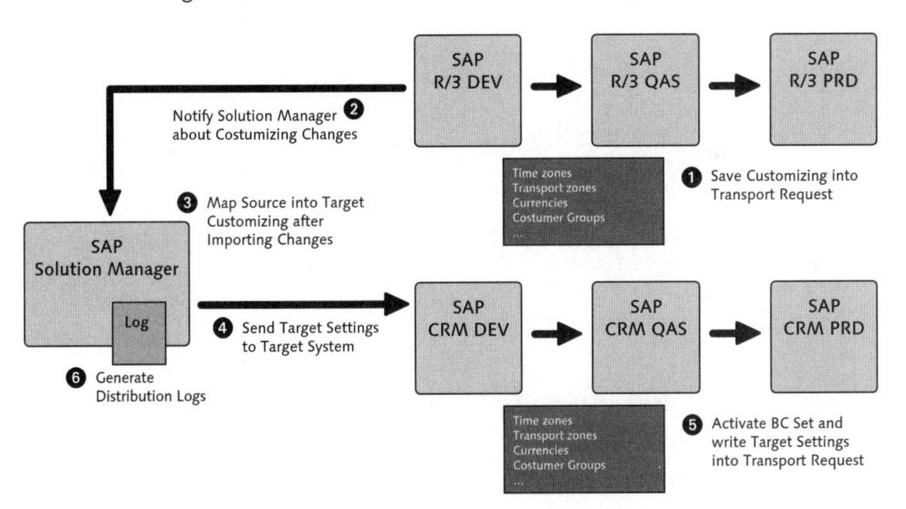


**Figure 17.2** Automatic customizing distribution flow with transport control

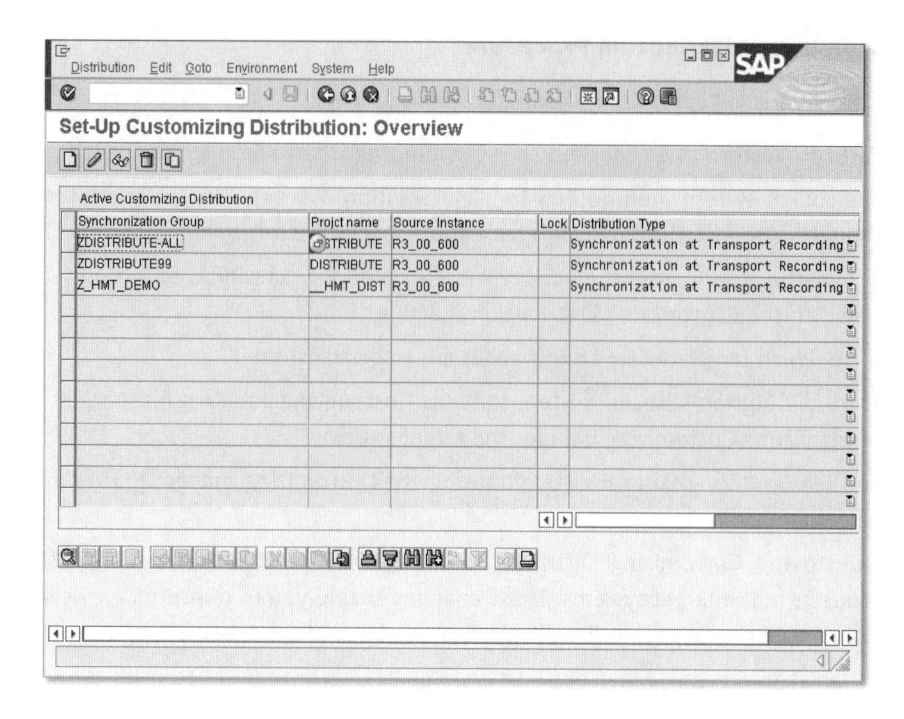


Figure 17.3 Customizing distribution, initial screen—transaction SCDT_SETUP

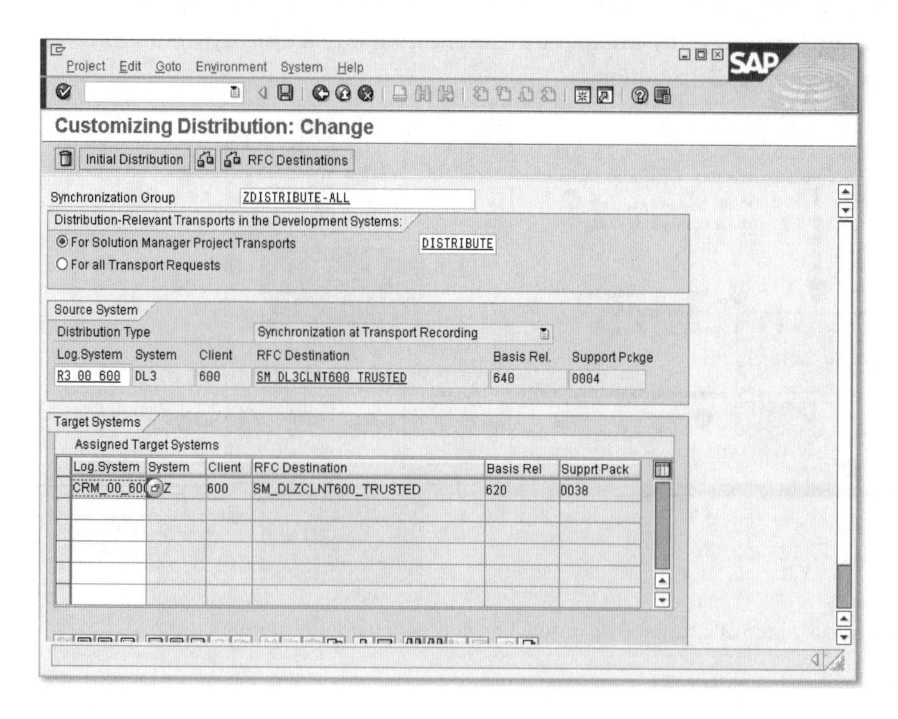


Figure 17.4 Configuring customizing distribution

Customizing Distribution always takes place in development systems. If data is to be transported to a QA system, and later on to a production system, you must release the relevant transport requests. This ensures that the Customizing settings are synchronized not only in the development system, but in all other downstream systems as well.

You can change or copy Customizing Distributions at any time via the menu. After copying, you can change the distribution option or the distribution project, for example.

### 17.1.2 Customizing Scout

To compare the Customizing settings of different SAP systems, you can use the Customizing Scout. The comparison always occurs between two SAP systems, for instance, between an SAP R/3 system and an SAP CRM system.

Customizing objects that must be frequently synchronized are predefined for selected components in the system. They are referred to as *synchronization objects*. The synchronization group editor enables you to edit existing synchronization objects and to create new ones.

**Note** In the following sections, the system that is used as a reference for a comparison is also referred to as a source system in an SAP system landscape. This will be an SAP R/3 system. All other systems in your SAP system landscape are referred to as target systems and will only be compared with the source system.

The comparison is used to synchronize the Customizing settings during an implementation or change of a system landscape. You can use the comparison as a starting point for eliminating differences in the Customizing settings of the systems, for example, by using the Implementation Guide (IMG) or the Customizing Distribution once the comparison is completed.

#### Selecting the System Landscape

Before you run a comparison, you should select the system landscape that you want to use, for example:

- A system landscape that was defined in SAP Solution Manager in the context of a specific project, or
- The entire system landscape

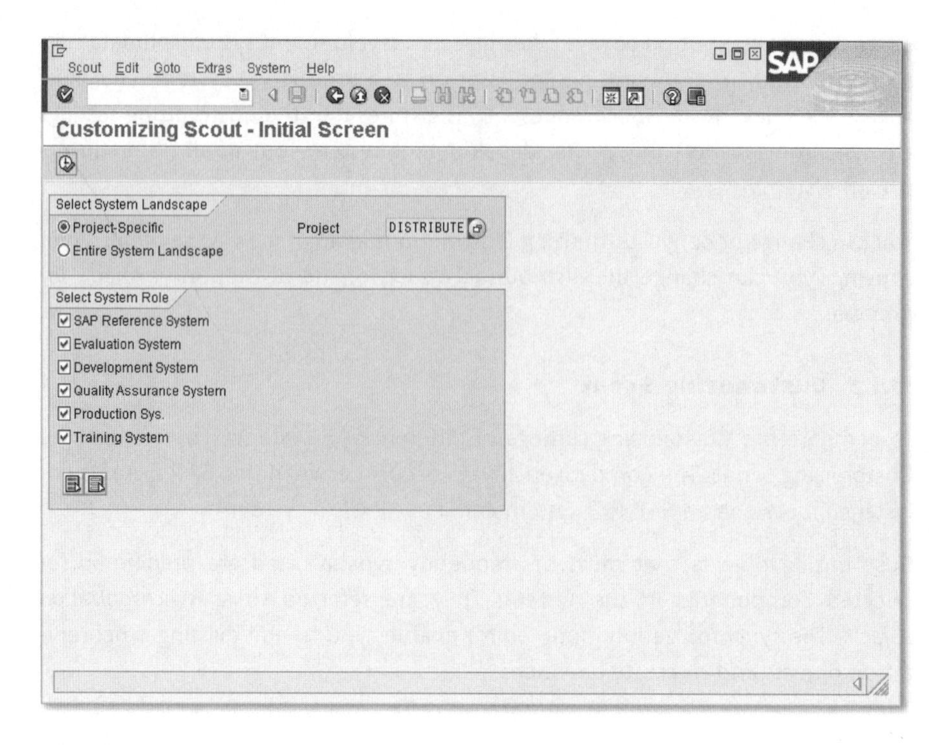


Figure 17.5 Customizing Scout, initial screen—transaction SCOUT

### Comparison Runs

All comparison runs within a Solution Manager project are always based on the same source system. The source system serves as a reference for Customizing settings. The target system can be selected from the existing system landscape.

Figure 17.6 shows an overview of available comparison runs for a specific Solution Manager project. You can display or delete existing comparison runs. New comparison runs can be performed in the dialog or in the background. Moreover, you can schedule periodic background comparison runs.

You can also create specific comparison runs for only those systems whose Customizing must be synchronized with the Customizing Distribution.

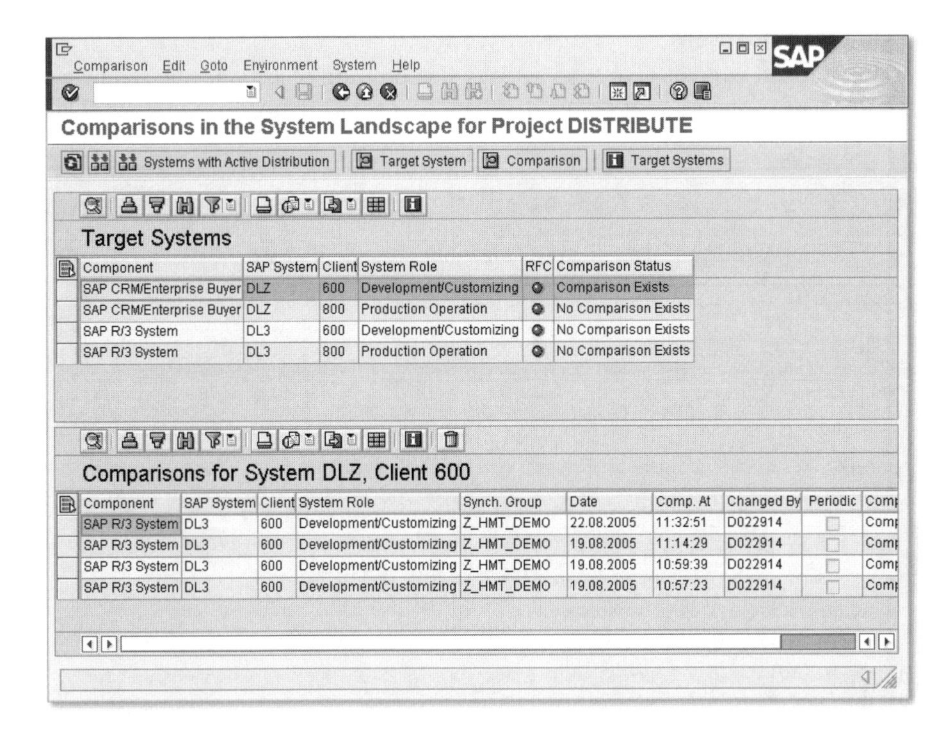


**Figure 17.6** Existing comparison runs in the Customizing Scout

## Displaying the Comparison Result

The comparison result can be displayed in levels of detail:

- **Comparison runs in the system landscape**
  You'll obtain an overview of all the systems you have selected for the comparison runs. Furthermore, you can view a list of all existing comparison runs for each system (see Figure 17.6).
- **Object overview**
  For each system, you can display a list of all compared objects including their comparison and processing statuses (see Figure 17.7). Utilities and other functions enable you to perform the following tasks in the object overview:
  - Display a comparison log for erroneous comparison runs that have been aborted
  - Change the processing status of specific objects
  - Filter the display of objects according to various criteria for the processing status, comparison status, and the object type
  - Select individual objects and go to the corresponding IMG activities in the source or target system to perform changes

▶ **Object comparison**

In the object overview, you can select a Customizing object and start and view a detailed comparison of the field entries (see Figure 17.8).

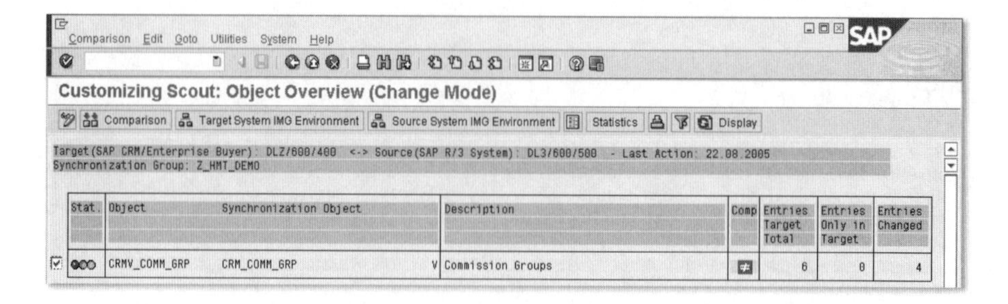


**Figure 17.7** Result of a comparison run for a synchronization object

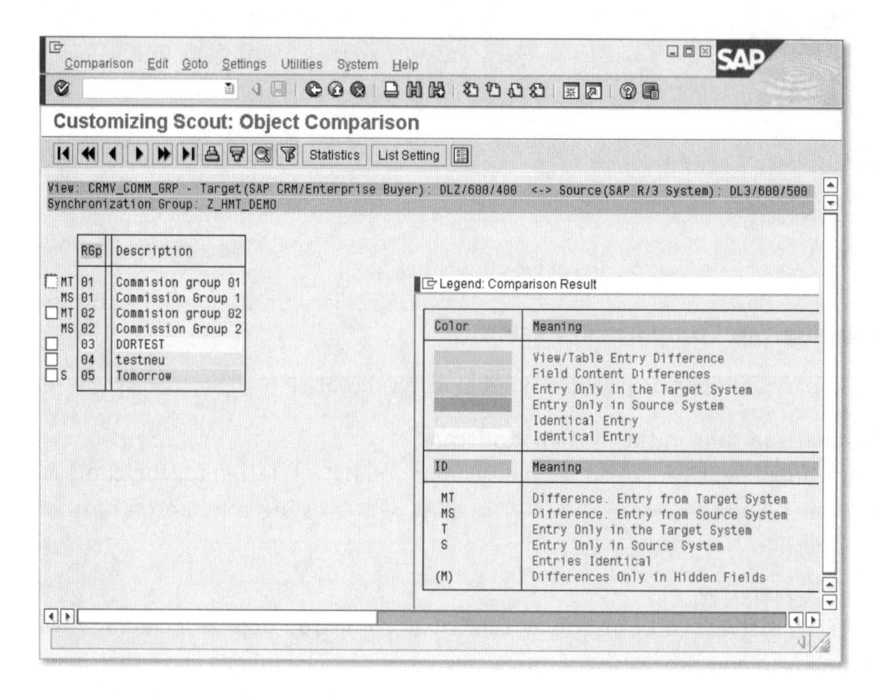


**Figure 17.8** Display of the different table contents

## Loading Object Lists

Before you can start a comparison run between an application component such as SAP CRM and an SAP R/3 system, you must provide the Customizing Scout with the list of Customizing objects that are to be synchronized in your landscape. Those object lists are contained in the standard versions of several application components. Once you have downloaded the object lists from the application component into the SAP Solution Manager system, the Customizing Scout has access to them.

1. To launch the Customizing Scout, select **Tools • Customizing • Distribution • Customizing Scout** from the SAP menu or enter Transaction SCOUT.
2. Select **Extras • Load Object Lists**.
3. Specify a system from which you want to download the object lists.

   If you have already downloaded an object list, you can set the flag **New objects only** so that only new objects are downloaded that aren't yet contained in your object lists.
4. Select **Next**.

The system downloads the respective object list and then displays an overview. In the overview you can see the systems for which object lists have been downloaded, how many objects have been added during the last download, and how many objects have been modified during that download.

### Customizing Comparison

You probably want to compare the Customizing of one or more target systems with the Customizing in a source system.

1. In the SAP menu, select **Tools • Customizing • Distribution • Customizing Scout**, or enter Transaction SCOUT.

   The system displays the initial screen of the Customizing Scout (see Figure 17.5).
2. Select a system landscape and one or more system roles.

   You can use the input help to select a project from SAP Solution Manager. The system then also involves the corresponding system landscape in the comparison run.
3. Select **Edit • Display Selection**.

   The system now displays a list of all systems that belong to the system landscape you selected or to your transport domain. You can view all existing comparison runs by double-clicking on a system (see Figure 17.6).
4. To compare the Customizing objects of one or more target systems with Customizing objects in a source system, select one or more target systems in the list displayed, and click on Compare

   The subsequent dialog then displays all selected logical systems. A check is run in the background to determine whether an RFC destination exists. In the event of an error, a log is displayed.

5. Specify a synchronization group, or select all synchronization objects for the component.
6. Enter a source system and a source client.
7. If you compare only one system with an R/3 reference system, you should now decide whether you want to run the comparison in the currently active dialog or in the background. If you want to compare more than one system with an R/3 reference system, the comparison will be run in the background in any case.
8. If you have started a background comparison, proceed as follows:
   - If necessary, specify a server in the dialog that pops up, for running the background job.
   - Specify your start date values for the background processing and save your entries.

   The system now checks whether you have the authorization to run such a comparison and whether an RFC destination exists. A log is displayed in case of an error.

If you select the option **Comparison in Dialog**, the system displays a list of objects compared. This list provides information on the processing status and the comparison result for each object.

Once the total comparison has been completed, you can select a system and click on **Refresh**. After that, you can display the last completed comparison run.

In the **Object Overview**, the system displays the technical name and the description from the target system for each Customizing object. If a synchronization object exists for a Customizing object, the technical name of that synchronization object will also be displayed.

There are two possible status indicators for each Customizing object:

- **Comparison status**
  This status indicates the existence and type of differences. It is automatically assigned.
- **Processing status**
  This status enables you to differentiate between objects that have already been processed and those that are yet to be processed.

You can assign the processing status manually. However, if you run a new comparison, the processing status of objects that no longer differ automatically changes from **Open** (red traffic light) to **Completed** (green traffic light). You can view a list of these settings via the legend (see Figure 17.9).

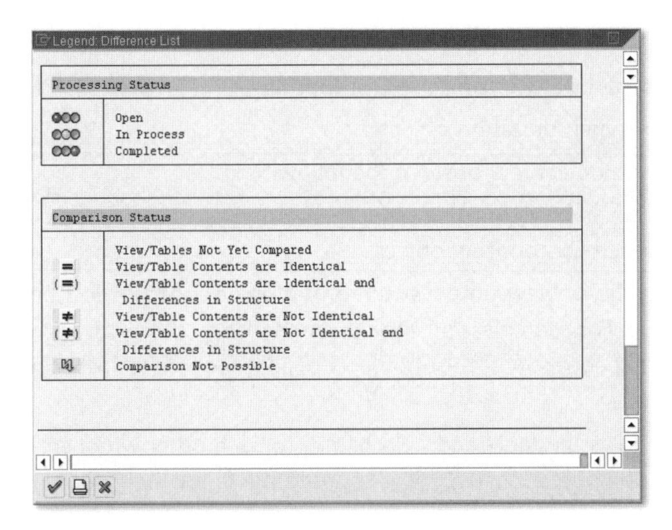


**Figure 17.9** Possible values for the comparison and processing statuses

### Changing the Processing Status of a Comparison Object

You have compared one or more systems with a source system (e.g., an R/3 system) and based on this comparison, you made some changes to Customizing objects. For that reason, you want to change the processing status of individual Customizing objects.

Search for the relevant object in the list and click on the processing status. If you click on it several times, you'll see that the status changes again.

> **Note** The processing status is recalculated after each comparison run. In particular, all processing statuses are reset to **Open** for objects that still contain differences even if you have changed the processing status in the last comparison run. If your list contains objects that show differences which aren't relevant for your Customizing, you can use the synchronization group editor to restrict the selection to relevant objects only.

## 17.1.3 Creating and Loading Synchronization Objects

The comparisons of Customizing settings and Customizing distribution are based on synchronization objects. These objects must first be created in SAP Solution Manager or loaded from the SAP systems to be synchronized. Synchronization objects are required if Customizing objects in different systems contain identical content but different structures, for example, if they contain different table and field names.

To create synchronization objects, proceed as follows:

1. Log on to the target system for Customizing Distribution.
2. Start the entry tool for synchronization objects.
3. Create a synchronization object and observe the following rules:
   - If a table is used in several Customizing objects, you must create a synchronization object for each Customizing object.
   - Summarize those tables or views into a synchronization object that must be transported together. For example, you should summarize all those tables in the target system that correspond to subobjects of a view or view cluster in the source system.
4. If necessary, you should assign table and field names to each other when creating the synchronization object. When doing so, note the following:
   - The data types of the fields don't need to be identical, just assignment-compatible.
   - The ends of fields get truncated, if they're longer in one component than in another.
   - Data fields that don't exist in one component will be ignored.
   - For the target system, all key fields of the involved tables and views must be defined for a Customizing object. For the source system, you can use any field of the tables and views involved.
   - If you use several tables or views for the source system, the system links the records of the individual tables or views with each other according to the following algorithm:
     a) One of the tables is labeled as the primary table.
     b) For secondary tables, an inner join is performed for the key fields and the fields of the same name in the primary table in order to link the two tables.
     c) Additional key fields of the secondary table may exist and be mapped to fields in the target structure.
     d) If you use a table with a text table, the text field is automatically identified as such by the system.
   - If you assign a table with a text table in a source system to a view in the target system, you must specify filtering rules for the source object. To do that, create a filter for the language field that has the value $SPRAS or $SLANGU.
   - If you assign a table or view to another table or view, without mapping all source object fields to fields of the target objects, you must specify the filtering rules for the source object. Create a filter for those key fields that haven't been considered and contain a fixed or generic value.
5. Check all created and existing synchronization objects that you want to use.

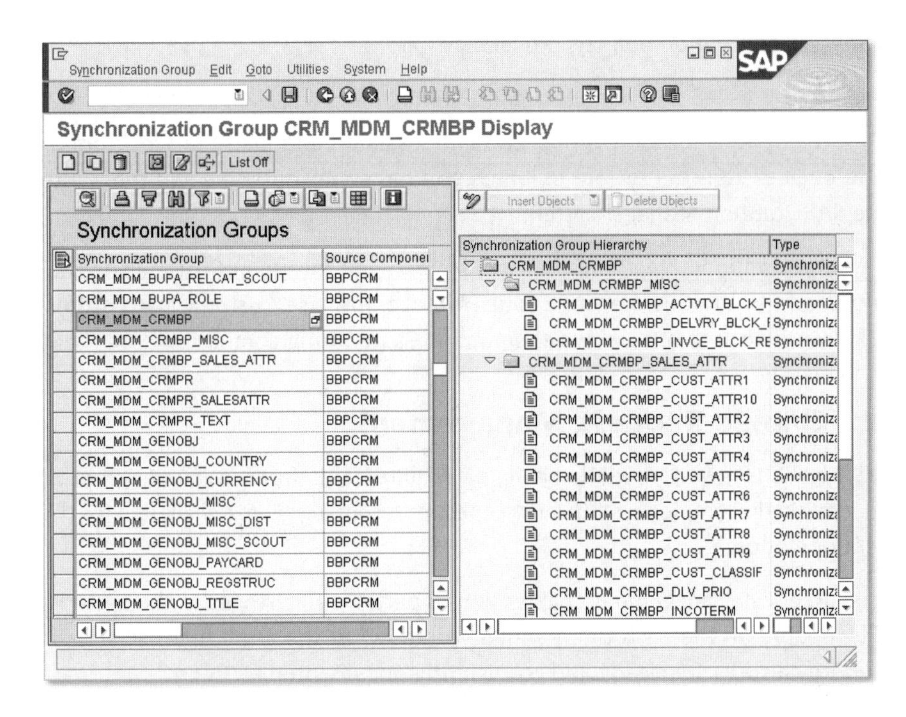


**Figure 17.10** Synchronization group editor, initial screen—transaction SCDT_GROUPS

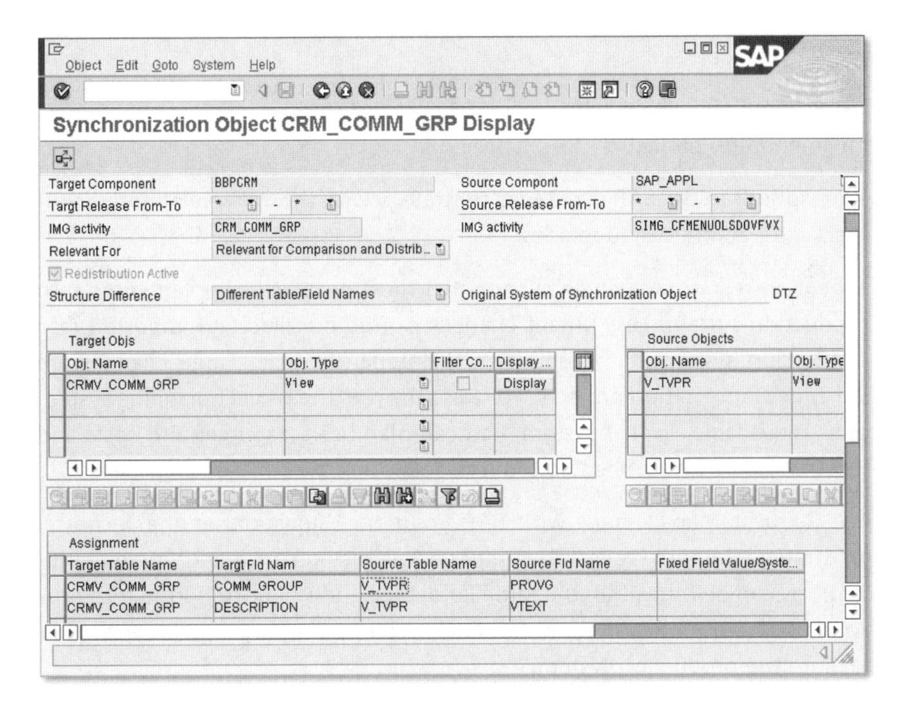


**Figure 17.11** Changing synchronization objects

To load synchronization objects, proceed as follows:

1. Log on to the SAP Solution Manager system.
2. Start the Synchronization Group Editor Transaction and load the synchronization objects from the system in which you have previously created them into the SAP Solution Manager system.

The synchronization objects are then available to you for use in Customizing Distribution and in the Customizing Scout. You can now use Customizing Distribution for your work or run a cross-component Customizing comparison.

## 17.2 Change Request Management

Continuous changes, frequently changing requirements from user departments, and increasingly complex system landscapes represent a growing challenge for the system operation.

Change Request Management enables you to perform all changes to the SAP system landscape on the basis of a defined workflow. At the same time, all actions and approval steps are clearly and consistently documented.

The change process preconfigured by SAP as a best practice comprises three types of changes:

- Urgent correction
- Regular correction as part of a maintenance cycle
- Implementation project

This corresponds to the SAP maintenance strategy with the delivery of notes, support packages, and release upgrades.

The urgent correction is a single change that must be quickly implemented into the production system. Less urgent changes can be bundled and imported into the production system at the end of a maintenance cycle. Large changes are treated as implementation projects. For this purpose, the project planning system cProjects is available. In that system, you can plan both resources and costs and transfer the values to a connected SAP system.

Change Request Management with SAP Solution Manager uses the technical import strategy, Import Project. This means that maintenance and implementation projects can be run within the same landscape and still be imported into production at different points in time. Moreover, you can import urgent corrections quickly into the production system.

The creation, release, and import of transport requests is integrated in the workflow and can be controlled via SAP Solution Manager. This is a great support for the administrator.

Change Management provides the following benefits to you:

- ▶ Software changes are carried out according to a predefined workflow.
- ▶ No untested changes are imported into the production system.
- ▶ Changes are transparent and can be traced.
- ▶ Legal regulations such as SOX or FDA are observed.
- ▶ Increased maintenance and project efficiency are ensured.

Change Management contains interfaces to the following SAP solutions:

- ▶ SAP Solution Manager for managing Customizing projects
- ▶ Service Desk for creating and managing change requests (optional)
- ▶ cProjects for managing project plannings (optional)
- ▶ The change processes preconfigured by SAP comply with the (IT Infrastructure Library) ITIL recommendations. ITIL is a product-independent description of IT service processes. The ITIL scenario for change processes is illustrated in Figure 17.12.

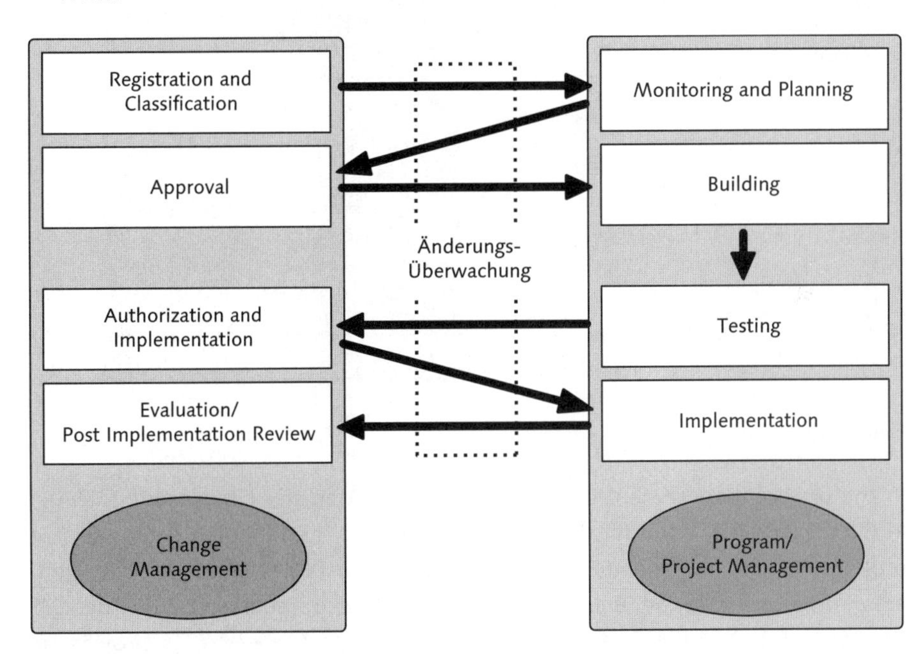


**Figure 17.12** Change management according to ITIL guidelines

### 17.2.1 Configuring and Setting Up Change Management

Change Management must first be set up in SAP Solution Manager, and then in the connected satellite systems. For detailed instructions on the setup procedure, you should refer to the online help or to the SAP Solution Manager Configuration Guide. The Implementation Guide (IMG) of SAP Solution Manager contains step-by-step instructions on how to set up this functionality. In this chapter, we simply want to provide a brief outline of the necessary steps.

The development, test, and production systems affected by the changes must be maintained in SAP Solution Manager Transaction SMSY. In addition, you must assign the systems to a logical component. This corresponds to a transport flow with development, test, and production systems. In this way, SAP Solution Manager knows which systems are involved in the change process.

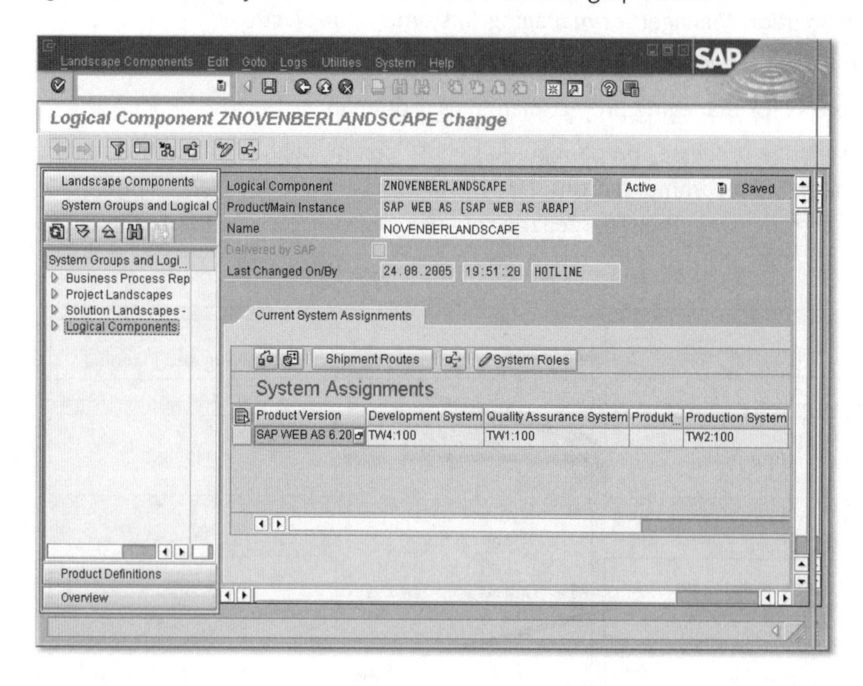


Figure 17.13 Setting up the logical component

In the project management tool of SAP Solution Manager (Transaction SOLAR_PROJECT_ADMIN) you must create maintenance and implementation type projects. When you generate an IMG project, the system will automatically generate IMG and CTS projects in the relevant development systems. The CTS projects form a container for transport requests. At the end of a project, all requests are imported collectively into the production system. This interrelationship is illustrated in Figure 17.14.

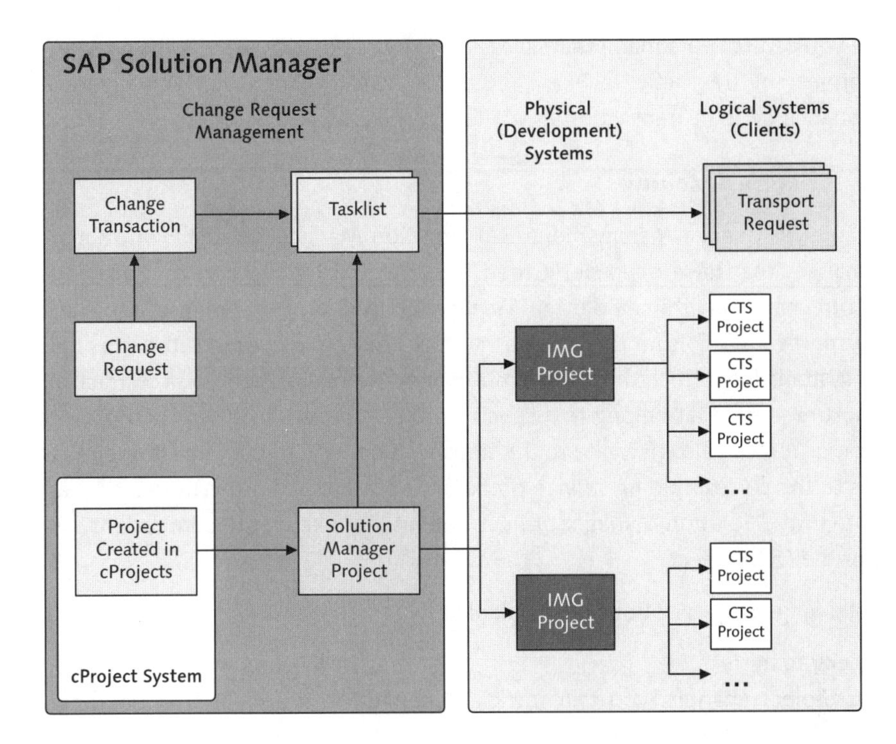


**Figure 17.14** Projects in change management

The systems in which changes are to be performed must be connected to SAP Solution Manager via a secure RFC connection. The following specific settings are considered as defaults in the Transport Management System (TMS) settings of these systems:

- Extended transport control activated
- Mandatory assignment of requests to projects
- Single import strategy
- Quality assurance procedure deactivated as the workflow is controlled by SAP Solution Manager

A maintenance cycle is a period in which you can perform corrections to an SAP system. At the end of a maintenance cycle, all corrections are imported collectively into the production system. Then, the maintenance cycle can be closed and a new one can be created.

**Note** Both urgent and regular corrections must always be assigned to a maintenance cycle. Therefore, the creation of a maintenance cycle is a prerequisite for managing change requests.

Before you can set up a maintenance cycle, you must first create a Solution Manager project in Transaction SOLAR_PROJECT_ADMIN. Then you can create a maintenance cycle in Transaction /TMWFLOW/CMSCONF.

### 17.2.2 Change Tracking

In addition to Change Management, SAP Solution Manager enables you to analyze changes that have been performed. You can track all actions that are connected to changes within a Solution Manager or IMG project. You can also track all transport requests from the system in which they have been created, through to the systems into which they were imported. Within a project, you can track all transport requests that belong to a specific project across all systems of a project landscape. You can also navigate to the transport logs and to the import queue, as well as to the corresponding service processes or task lists. Furthermore, you can navigate to the Solution Manager project, the IMG project in the component system, or the CTS project.

The following analysis options are available:

- **Project analysis**
  In a project analysis, you can track all changes to a project that has been defined in Solution Manager.
- **System analysis**
  The system analysis enables you to compare transport requests between two SAP systems. You can identify missing transport requests and differences in the processing sequence.
- **Analysis of change requests**
  This type of analysis enables you to track change requests from systems in which a request was created, through to all systems into which the transport is imported.

#### Comparing Transport Requests in Two Systems

You want to compare two systems with each other (e.g., a development system and a consolidation system) to determine which transport requests have been imported or exported (see Figure 17.15).

1. Access Transaction /TMWFLOW/CMSCONF.
2. Select the **Search** tab in the **Change Management—Change Tracking** screen.
3. Use the F4 help in the System Analysis group box to select the two systems you want to compare with each other (and optionally their clients too).

**Note** The data you enter in the **Project**, **Date**, and **Time** fields refers to both systems.

4. Use the F4 help in the **Status of Transport Request** field to select the statuses you want to compare with each other.
5. The default selection is **Exported** for the first system and Imported for the system with which you want to compare it. Note that you can also change these entries.
6. If you want to display information on the support packages and SAP notes that have been imported into the system, check the **Include Support Packages** and **Include Note Corrections** fields.
7. Click on the **Search** button.

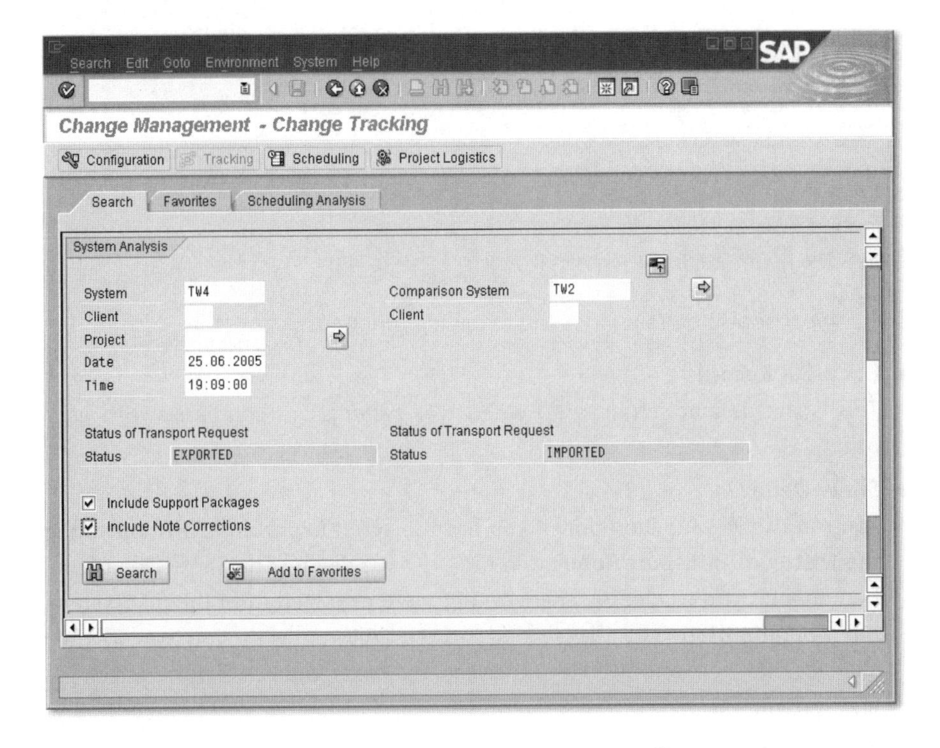


**Figure 17.15** Comparing transport requests between two systems: selection screen

A new screen, which displays all the information on the two systems, reflects the criteria you have selected (see Figure 17.16). In this screen, you can display the data used in the last run of the data collector by clicking on the Refresh Data button.

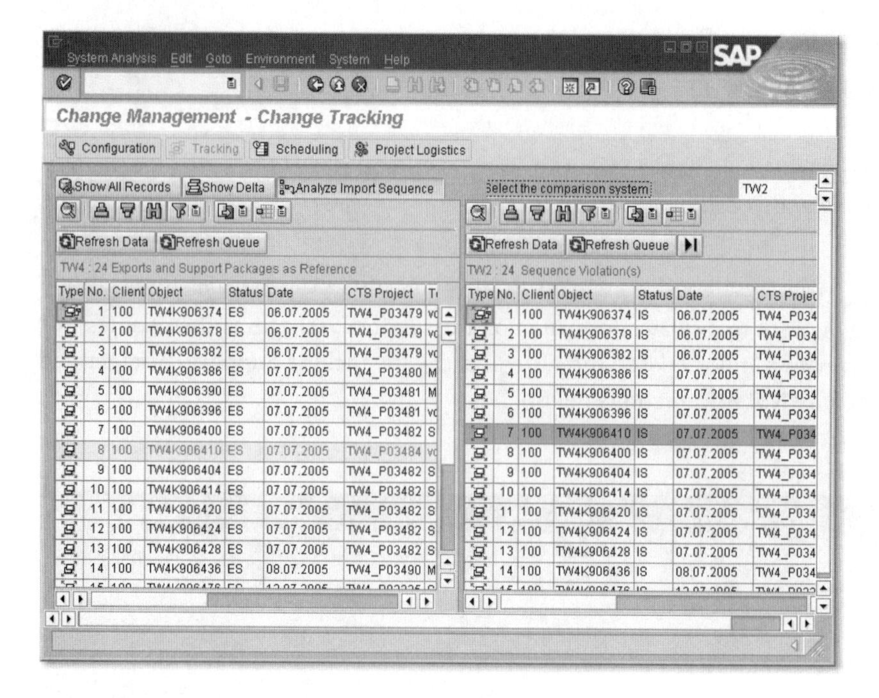


**Figure 17.16** Comparing transport requests between two systems: results list

The comparison screen provides the following functions:

- **Show All Records**
  This is the default setting used when two systems are compared with each other.
- **Show Delta**
  You can use this function only if you have selected **Exported** and **Imported** as the **Status of Transport Request** in the previous dialog. The Show Delta function enables you to identify changes that were exported from the first system, but not imported into the second system. Alternatively, you can identify changes that were imported into the second system, but not exported from the first system.
- **Analyze Import Sequence**
  Use this function to find out whether there are differences in the sequence in which the changes were exported from the first system and imported into the second one. The number of sequence violations is displayed in the top right-hand area of the screen. If violations exist, you can display them individually by clicking on the **Next Sequence Violation** icon (next to the **Refresh Queue** icon). The violations are highlighted in red. In the corresponding row, click on the **Type** icon to display the respective violation in the left-hand pane of the screen.

### 17.2.3 Change Processes

The workflow for a correction usually starts, because of an error that has occurred in the production system or because required functions aren't available. The error is first recorded in the Service Desk and checked by the responsible Service Desk employee. If a change in the system is necessary, the employee creates a change request. The change request is then checked again. If the change is approved, a change process of the type **Urgent Correction** or **Regular Correction**—depending on the change request—is created. Alternatively, the type of the change process can be an individual one, provided you have defined it in SAP Solution Manager Customizing. The change process then runs through several stages:

- Correction development
- Correction test
- Import of the correction into the production system

Several employees are involved in a change process. These employees must be maintained as business partners in SAP Solution Manager. A business partner can have different roles such as developer, tester, IT operator, or change manager. All users involved in the correction process navigate from the change process into the respective target systems in the maintenance landscape. In those systems, each user performs different tasks and then forwards the change process to the next user. The status of the change request changes accordingly each time. At the same time, transport requests are released or imported in the connected development, test, and production systems. Whenever the status of the change request changes, the technical transport processes are automatically triggered and run in the background. Thus, a manual processing of the transport activities isn't necessary. This ensures that all changes are logged in SAP Solution Manager.

SAP recommends that you collect changes for a certain period of time and then import them as bundles into the production systems, rather than import individual changes on a continual basis. These maintenance cycles are highly advisable, because you can then test all changes simultaneously and avoid incurring adverse side effects that might occur with the individual transport requests. Furthermore, you can test the potential for problems for business processes that already exist in the system (regression testing). During the testing phase, a code freeze must be ensured in the test system so that the test can be based on an exactly defined software status. In a worst-case scenario, even a single erroneous transport request can result in making all other tests, performed up until this point, obsolete.

A maintenance cycle is divided into several different phases that contain SAP's best-practice approach. The following phases are contained in a maintenance cycle:

- Created
- Development without Release
- Development with Release
- Test
- Emergency Correction
- Go Live
- Beeing Completed
- Completed

You can only import the contents of the import buffer into the production system during the production phase. This is because, during that phase, all transport requests in the buffer that have been released as part of the maintenance cycle are imported in the same sequence in which they have been exported. After that, the cycle can be confirmed or reset to an earlier phase (e.g., to **Development without Release**). During the maintenance cycle, the following steps are run through:

1. A user creates a maintenance cycle. Once the cycle has been created, its status changes to **Created**. Urgent and regular corrections can be created only as change transaction. Their status is also **Created** until the administrator activates the corresponding task list.
2. The change manager sets the maintenance cycle status to **Development without Release**. If this status is set, you can develop corrections and create transport requests and transport tasks. Exports however, are not permitted (except for urgent corrections). With the exception of the Go Live phase, urgent corrections are always permitted.
3. If the change manager changes the maintenance cycle status from **Development without Release** to **Development with Release**, you can release transport requests from a regular correction. The administrator uses the task list to import all released corrections into test systems.
4. If regular corrections exist whose status isn't yet **Tested Successfully** at the time the maintenance cycle phase changes from **Development with Release to Test**, the system returns a warning message. Those corrections are then excluded from integration testing and cannot be released.
5. During the test phase, errors are detected in the test systems, and are reported to the relevant developers by means of test messages. The developers correct these errors. If all error messages have been closed, the maintenance cycle proceeds to the **emergency correction phase**.

6. If changes have to be performed upon completion of the test phase, transport requests and jobs may be created and released during the **Emergency Correction phase**, but that's only possible via the task list of the schedule manager.
7. The Go Live phase is reserved for the import of the entire project buffer into the production system. Neither transport requests nor urgent corrections can be released during that phase.
8. If open transport requests still exist, you must return to the **Development with Release** phase and repeat the process, including the test phase, to ensure that all open requests can be released and transported.
9. If no open transport requests exist, you can close the maintenance cycle by setting the status to **Being Completed**. After that, you can create a new maintenance cycle.

> **Note** You can perform regular corrections even during the test phase of a maintenance cycle can you perform regular corrections, however, you can no longer export the corresponding transport requests.

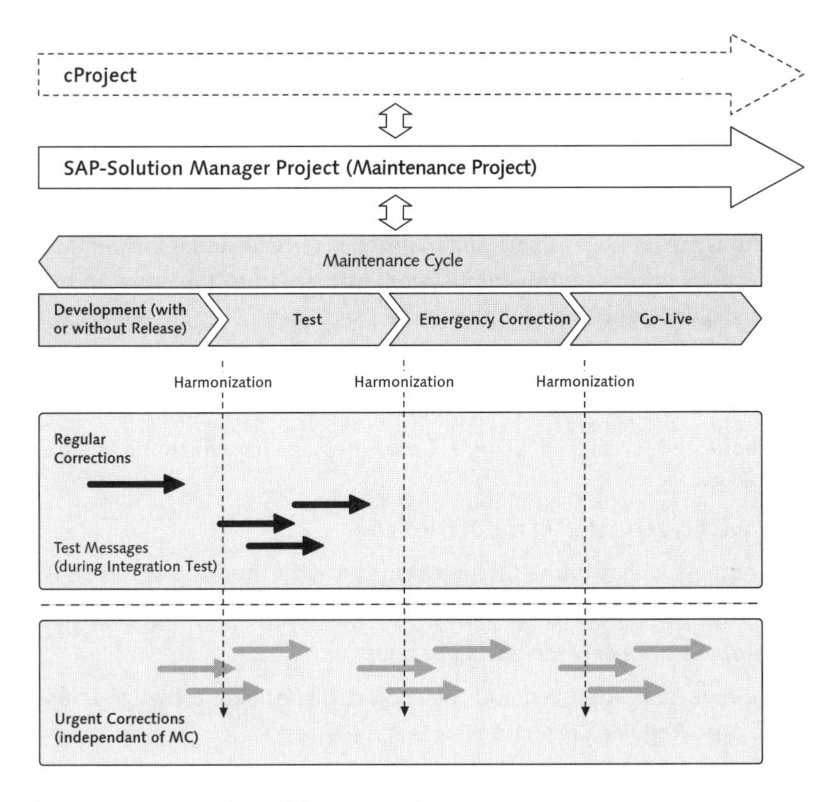


**Figure 17.17** Phases of a maintenance cycle

Extensive software changes such as the implementation of a new SAP module or a new business process cannot be mapped as individual change requests. Those projects often involve many employees and the implementation requires extensive planning. For this purpose, the project planning tool cProjects is provided. It enables you to perform comprehensive resource and cost plannings and provides an interface to SAP R/3 and its successors.

Implementation projects often have their own go-live date, irrespective of the maintenance cycles. Therefore, you can create one or more implementation projects in addition to the maintenance project in SAP Solution Manager for a system landscape.

Implementation projects run through the same phases as maintenance cycles.

If several projects with different go-live dates exist in a system landscape, you must ensure that these projects are not connected. This is especially true for each SAP object, which can only be part of one project. To ensure this, SAP Solution Manager provides various protection mechanisms. For example, during the test phase, a transport of copies is first transferred to the QA system. The actual transport request remains in the development system until the test has been successfully completed and maintains the object lock of the Transport Organizer. Moreover, a check is run to identify identical objects in different systems.

Contrary to the maintenance project, no urgent corrections can be made in an implementation project, because the project is not yet productive. Therefore, urgent corrections must always be assigned to a maintenance project.

Regular corrections are created as part of a maintenance cycle and imported as a bundle of corrections into the production system at the end of the cycle. In this way, transports are always imported in the correct sequence. The following steps must be performed:

1. A user discovers an error or missing functions in a system.
2. The user (requester) creates a Service Desk message in which he or she describes the request.
3. A change request is generated in the Service Desk.
4. The change request is sent to the Change Manager who approves or rejects it.
5. The Change Manager checks the complexity and urgency of the request. Then he or she approves or rejects the change request.
6. If the change request is approved and the subject is specified, a change transaction of the type **Regular Correction** is generated.
7. The change transaction is transferred to a developer who sets the status to **In Development**.

8. The developer creates a transport request by means of action in the change transaction.
9. Once the correction has been performed, the developer releases the transport request from within the change transaction.
10. When the change process has been successfully completed and all respective transport requests have been released, the developer sets the status to **Correction Completed**.
11. A tester or another developer sets the status of the change process to **Tested Successfully** to indicate that the new function has been tested and can be imported into the production system. This illustrates the application of the dual control principle.
12. The new function is imported into the test system during a regular import of the project buffer.
13. The new function is imported into the production system when the corresponding maintenance cycle is in the go-live phase.
14. If the regular correction has been imported into the production system, along with all the other regular corrections of this maintenance cycle, you can only set the status to **Productive**. You can set this status for all imported regular corrections at the end of a maintenance cycle by scheduling the following batch job: `CRM_SOCM_SERVICE_REPORT`.

**Note** Regular corrections that are still **In Development** trigger a warning message in the process of the respective maintenance cycle, if the status is set during the test phase. You can create regular corrections during the test phase of a maintenance cycle, but if you do, the corresponding transport requests can no longer be exported. They will be transferred to the production system with the next maintenance cycle.

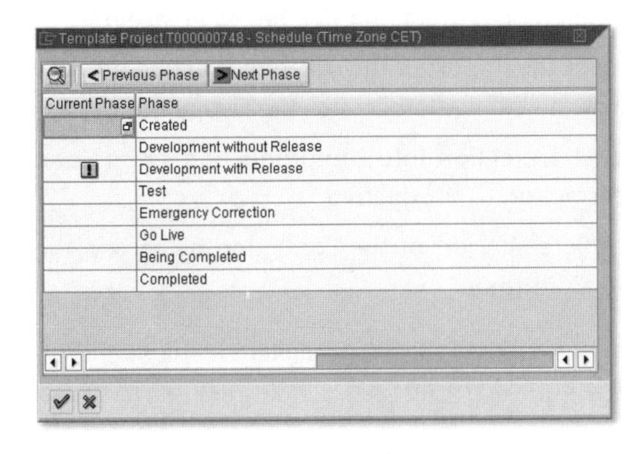


**Figure 17.18** Phases of an implementation project

Urgent corrections must always be assigned to a maintenance cycle. Initially they are imported into the production system as a preliminary transport, but they remain in the buffer of the maintenance project and are re-imported into the production system at the end of the cycle in the correct sequence. The following steps must be performed:

1. An end user discovers a problem in a system.
2. The user (requester) creates a Service Desk message in which he or she describes the problem.
3. Based on the support message, a change request is generated in the Service Desk.
4. The change request is sent to the Change Manager who approves or rejects it.
5. The Change Manager checks the complexity and urgency of the request. Then he or she approves or rejects the change request.
6. If the change request is particularly urgent, the Change Manager determines that this is an **Urgent Correction**.
7. The change request is forwarded to the developer who is supposed to implement the urgent correction. Concurrently, a specific task list for the urgent correction is generated in the Schedule Manager in the background. This list contains tasks that are necessary for implementing the urgent correction.
8. The developer implements the urgent correction in a development system and forwards the change transaction to a tester.
9. The tester logs on to a test system to check whether the urgent correction works without errors.
10. If the correction doesn't contain any errors, the tester forwards the change transaction to the Production Manager. (If errors occur during the test, the tester returns the change process to the developer who must adjust the correction accordingly. Then, the modified correction must be tested again.)
11. The Production Manager approves the import of the urgent correction into the production system and forwards the change process to the IT operator.
12. The operator imports the urgent correction into the production system and sets the status of the urgent correction to **Productive**.
13. The requester confirms the implementation of the correction by setting the status of the change request to **Confirmed**.

If no support message is created and an urgent correction must be implemented, you can manually create a change request. To do that, go to Solution Manager Transaction CRMD_ORDER.

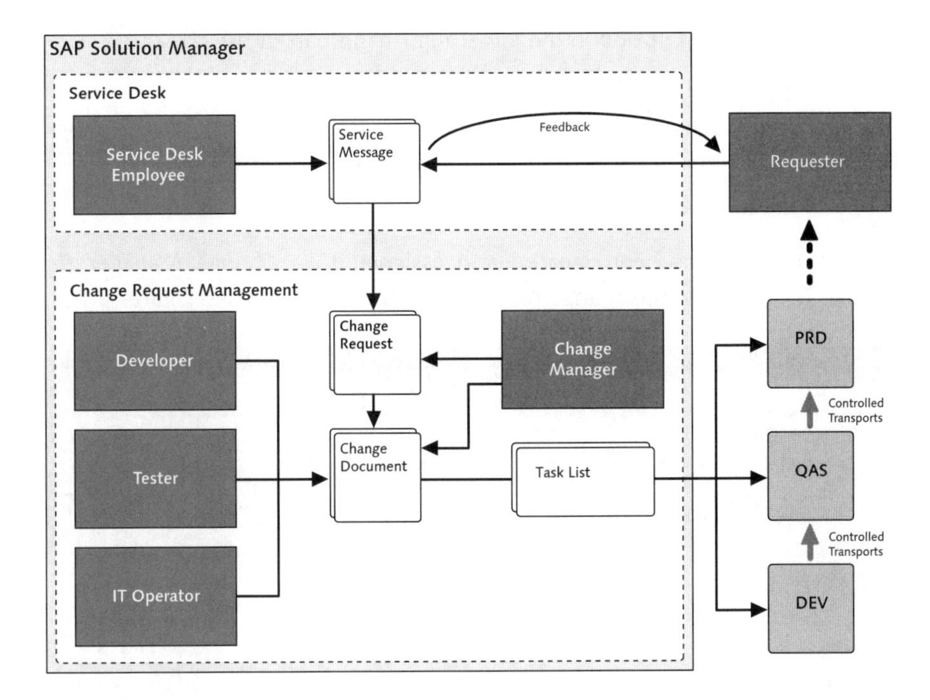


**Figure 17.19** Workflow for an urgent correction

### 17.2.4 Change Process Steps

This section describes the individual steps that are necessary to perform an urgent correction.

#### Creating a Change Request

A problem was found in the system. Although no support message has been created, you want to create a change request.

1. Call Transaction CRMD_ORDER.
2. Select **Create Change Request**.
3. Enter the corresponding data into the following fields:
   - **Description**
   - **Sold-to Party**
   - **Requester**
   - **IBase component** (which you have defined in the Implementation Guide under **SAP Solution Manager • Basic Settings • SAP Solution Manager System • Service Desk • iBase**)
4. Select the entry **Urgent Correction** in the **Subject** field.

5. Select **Change Description** in the lower right-hand part of the screen.
6. Enter a description of the change you want to implement.
7. In the **Change Manager** field, enter the business partner (user) of the Change Manager who is in charge of approving or rejecting the change request.
8. Click on the **Save** icon.

A change request has been created and assigned to a Change Manager for approval. The status of the change request is **To Be Approved** (see Figure 17.20).

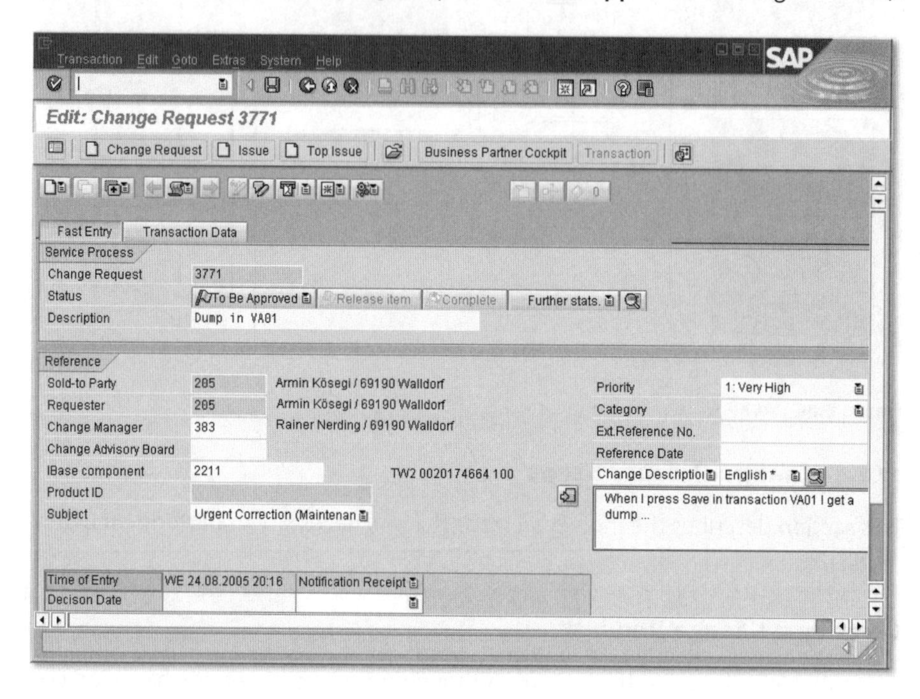


Figure 17.20 Change request in 'to be approved' status

## Approving a Change Request

If a serious problem is detected, an urgent correction must immediately be implemented into the production system. For this purpose, a change request is created. The change request must be approved by a Change Manager.

1. In the **SAP Easy Access** screen, select **Change Requests • My uncompleted Change Requests**.
2. Select the change request you want to approve by double-clicking on the entry in the **Number** column. The system opens the change request.
3. Select the entry **Urgent Correction** in the **Subject** field.

4. Select the icon with the quick info text **Actions**.
5. Select **Approve change request** from the dropdown list.
6. Click on the **Save** icon.

The status of the change request is set to **Approved**. A document of the type **Urgent Correction** has been created in the background. You can access this document by clicking on the button with the quick info text **Document flow**.

### Rejecting a Change Request

A change request has been created. As the responsible Change Manager, you have decided that the problem isn't serious enough to warrant initiating an urgent correction. Therefore, you'll reject the change request.

1. Select the relevant change request from the work list by double-clicking on it.
2. The system opens the change request.
3. Select the icon with the quick info text **Actions**.
4. Select **Reject change request** from the dropdown list.
5. Click on the **Save** icon.

The status of the change request is **Rejected**. The process is now closed. If the change request was generated because of a support message, you can navigate back to the support message by clicking on the icon with the quick info text **Document flow**.

### Performing an Urgent Correction in the Development System

Due to an approved change request, you now want to perform an urgent correction in a development system.

1. Make sure your user name is entered in the field **Current Processor**.
2. Select **Actions**.
3. Select **Set To 'In Development'**.
4. If the maintenance cycle is not unique, enter the maintenance cycle in the dialog.
5. Click on the **Save** icon. The entry in the Status field changes to **In Development**.
6. Select **Actions**.
7. Select **Log On to System**.
8. If you can't find any transport request that can be modified, select **Actions • Create Additional Transport Request**.
9. Perform the necessary correction in the development system.

10. Release the task in the corresponding transport request.
11. Select **Back**.
12. Select **Test Instructions** from the dropdown box in the lower right-hand part of the screen.
13. Enter the test instructions for the tester.
14. Enter the user name of the tester in the **Current Processor** field.
15. Select **Actions**.
16. Select **Correction passed to test**.
17. Click on the **Save** icon.

The system creates a task list in the scheduling tool of Change Management. A transport request is created for the current processor in the development system. The system releases the transport request that contains the changes. The transport request is then imported into the test system. Then the task list is included in the document flow.

The **Developer** partner function contains the business partner of the developer. The **Current Processor** partner function contains the business partner of the tester. The status of the urgent correction is **To Be Tested**.

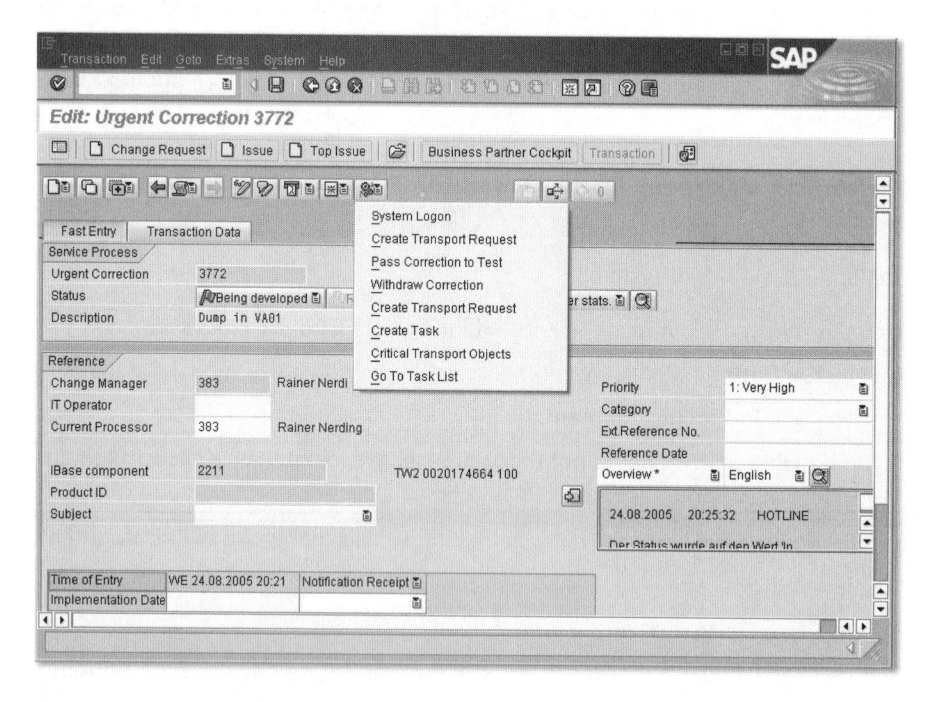


Figure 17.21 Urgent correction in 'being developed' status

### Testing an Urgent Correction

An urgent correction has been implemented in a development system and you now want to test it in a test system.

1. Make sure that your user name (business partner) is entered in the field **Current Processor**.
2. Select **Actions**.
3. Select **Log On To System**.
4. Check the correction in the test system.
5. Select **Back**.

If the test was performed successfully, proceed as follows:

1. Select **Test Report** from the dropdown box in the lower right-hand part of the screen.
2. Enter a test report.
3. If you know the name of the production manager, enter it in the field **Current Processor**.
4. Select **Actions**.
5. Select **Confirm Test Success**.
6. Click on the **Save** icon.

If the test fails, proceed as follows:

1. Select **Test Report** from the dropdown box in the lower right-hand part of the screen.
2. Enter the errors in the test report.
3. Enter the user name of the developer who developed the correction in the **Current Processor field**.
4. Select **Actions**.
5. Select **Reset to In Development**.
6. Click on the **Save** icon.

If the test was successful, the status of the urgent correction changes to **Tested Successfully** Then the production manager must approve the import into the production system.

If the test failed, the status of the urgent correction changes to **In Development**. The developer of the correction must perform the required changes after which the correction is tested again.

### Importing an Urgent Correction into a Production System

An urgent correction has been tested in a test system. The test was successful, and the urgent correction was approved for import by the Production Manager. As an IT operator, you now want to import the correction into the production system.

1. Make sure that your user name is entered in the field **Current Processor**.
2. Select **Actions**.
3. Select Import **Correction Into Production System**.
4. Click on the **Save** icon.
5. Make sure no errors are being displayed.
6. Select **Actions**.
7. Select **Go To Task List**. Check the processing status of the task list.
8. Select **Back**, and navigate back to the Service Desk.
9. Select **Actions**.
10. Select **Log On To System**.
11. Check the transport logs in the production system to see whether the import was successful.
12. Select **Back**.
13. If the import caused errors or didn't solve the original problem, reset the status of the urgent correction to In Development by selecting **Actions • Reset to 'In Development'**.

If the import caused errors, the status of the urgent correction changes to **In Development**. In that case, you must perform corrections again, and the urgent correction must be tested once more.

If the import was successful, the status of the urgent correction is **Productive**. The status of the change request is now **Realized**. The requester must now confirm the urgent correction.

### Completing an Urgent Correction

An urgent correction was imported into a production system, the status is **Confirmed**, and you now want to complete the process.

**Note** If you have completed an urgent correction, you can't make any changes to it.

1. Select **Actions**.
2. Select **Complete Correction**.
3. Click on the **Save** icon.

The status of the urgent correction is now **Completed**. The urgent correction can no longer be modified.

## 17.3 Questions

1. Which of the following statements are true of Customizing Distribution?

   A. Customizing Distribution synchronizes Customizing settings in different systems.

   B. Customizing Distribution only works for systems with identical release statuses.

   C. Customizing Distribution can also be set up without SAP Solution Manager.

   D. Customizing Distribution usually takes place between development systems. The QA and production systems are provided with transport requests.

2. Which of the following statements are true of the Customizing Scout?

   A. The Customizing Scout can only be used for systems with identical release statuses.

   B. Comparison runs can be saved and displayed at a later point in time.

   C. It is always synchronization objects that are compared.

   D. Comparison runs can't be performed in the background.

3. Which of the following statements are true of Maintenance Projects?

   A. Urgent corrections can be created even if no maintenance project exists.

   B. Regular corrections can be released in any phase of a maintenance cycle.

   C. A maintenance project is created in Transaction SOLAR_PROJECT_ADMIN.

   D. A maintenance cycle is created in Transaction /TMWFLOW/CMSCONF.

4. Which of the following statements are true of Urgent Corrections?

   A. Urgent corrections can be part of a maintenance project or implementation project.

   B. Urgent corrections can also be directly released in Transaction STMS of the corresponding development system.

   C. Urgent corrections are controlled via the Schedule Manager.

   D. Urgent corrections must be approved by the Change Manager.

# 18 SAP NetWeaver Development Infrastructure

The NetWeaver Development Infrastructure (NWDI) is the environment developed by SAP for developing software projects in Java especially for the SAP Web Application Server (SAP Web AS). The NWDI supports the development process in many ways to achieve a comfort and stability of the developed projects similar to what you know from the ABAP development environment. However, you cannot directly compare these two environments, because their architectures are clearly different. Nevertheless, the following sections compare the ABAP development environment with the NWDI environment, wherever possible, to get a better insight into the workings of the NetWeaver Development Infrastructure.

## 18.1 Structure of the SAP Web Application Server

The SAP Web AS provides the runtime environment for both the ABAP- and the Java-based applications in SAP NetWeaver. Thus, both server- and client-based web applications can be implemented. Depending on its installation, SAP Web AS can run ABAP or Java programs, or both. Thus, both ABAP-based Business Server Pages (BSPs)—ABAP programs with embedded HTML code for presenting the pages on the web—and Java-based Java Server Pages (JSPs) can be used during the creation of web applications.

During the installation, SAP Web AS Java can be installed either as a standalone version or as a so-called add-in of SAP Web AS ABAP. For that reason, the scalability known from ABAP-based systems can be easily created for Java as well by using a corresponding number of application servers. With the platform independence inherent in SAP Web AS ABAP, additional components like the User Management Engine (UME), the connection to other SAP systems via the proven RFC technology using the Java Connector (JCo), the NWDI, and many other features, SAP Web AS Java meets the operation requirements for stability, scalability and security.

The main part of SAP Web AS Java consists of the SAP J2EE Engine (Java Enterprise Edition), which enables the execution of applications that were created according to the J2EE 1.3 standard. The SAP J2EE Engine supports all those technologies that became popular with this standard, like JSPs, servlets, and Enterprise Java Beans (EJBs).

The SAP J2EE Engine is composed of three logical layers:

1. The Java Enterprise Runtime, which consists of several low-level subsystems (so-called *managers*) and provides different kinds of basic functions.

2. The J2EE Engine components, which are based on the runtime, communicate with it, and use its functions. There are three types of components: interfaces, libraries, and services.
3. The applications themselves as a third layer; the border between the applications and the J2EE Engine components are defined in the Application Programming Interfaces (APIs) of J2EE 1.3 along with several SAP-proprietary APIs.

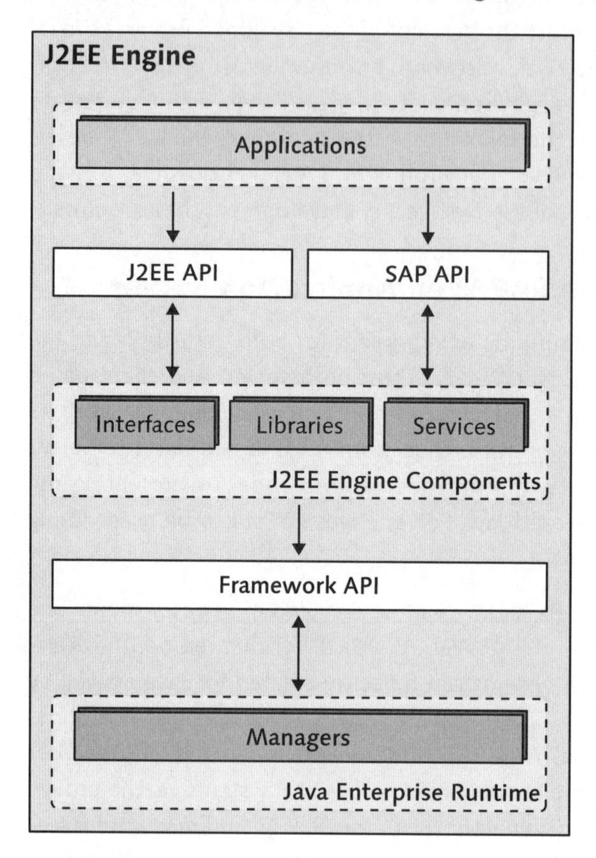


**Figure 18.1** Structure of the J2EE engine

The architecture of the J2EE Engine is based on the following general rule: Components of a higher level can use components of a lower level. However, components of the lower level do not know the interfaces of the components above them and therefore cannot use them. This rule is also reflected in the order in which the modules are started: At first, the runtime is started; then, the services and libraries; and, at the very end, the application itself.

## 18.2 Overview of the Java Development Process

In this context, we will first answer the question: What is Java?

Java was developed in 1991 by Sun Microsystems for domestic appliances. The intention was mainly to create a language that is small and fast and can be ported easily to very different hardware platforms. Thus, Java was ideally suited as a powerful language for programs to be executed online over the Internet. Java itself is an object-oriented programming language with great similarities to C or C++. The entire Java code is organized in methods of classes, and all states are represented as attributes of classes. Java disposes of a comprehensive library of classes, some of which facilitate the work with TCP/IP-based protocols like HTTP or FTP.

Furthermore, Java has moved into a different direction with its approach of platform independence for executing programs. Contrary to traditional translators of a programming language that generate machine code for a certain platform, the Java compiler produces program code for a virtual machine, a so-called *byte code*. Byte code is comparable with microprocessor code for a fictitious processor that knows statements like arithmetic operations, skips, and more. A Java compiler, which is integrated in Java similar to the one from Sun, generates this byte code.

In order for the program code of the virtual processor to run, the Java Virtual Machine (JVM) runtime environment must execute the byte code after the translation phase. Therefore, Java is both a compiled and an interpreted programming language.

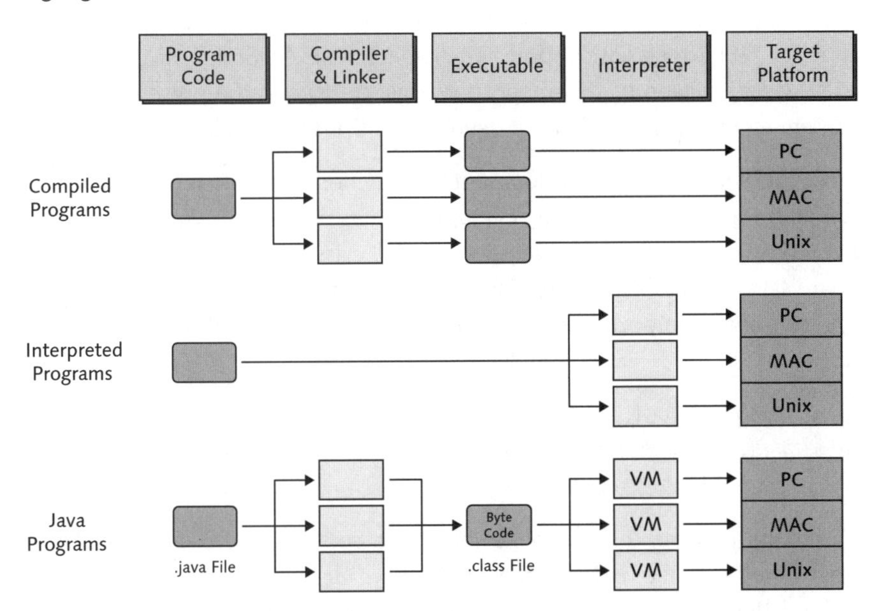


**Figure 18.2** Platform differences of programming languages

JVM must be developed individually per platform. In this respect, JVM is a standalone runtime environment that forms the interface between Java programs and the operating system. Besides Sun and IBM, there are other operating system vendors for JVM providing this virtual machine for their platforms. The SAP J2EE Engine is then executed within this JVM, and the corresponding applications run within the engine, as mentioned above.

J2EE applications consist of individual components. A J2EE component is a complete and functional software unit forming a J2EE application along with associated classes and other files (assembly), which can also communicate with other components via interfaces. The J2EE specification distinguishes between the following J2EE components:

- Java applets—presentation portions running on the client
- Java servlets and JSPs—presentation portions or J2EE web components running on the server
- EJBs—components with the business process control running on the server

The communication between the J2EE server and the user is based on the Internet standards HTML, HTTP, or XML. The J2EE server can create HTML pages or XML files via JSPs or Java servlets running in a *container* for J2EE web applications within the J2EE server. Java applets can make up parts of the HTML pages sent to the browser. These are small Java applications running on the client JVM; naturally, this requires that JVM is installed on the client computer as a part of the J2SE (Java Standard Edition, the less extensive version for PCs, for example, which, in contrast to J2EE, does not support server functions). According to the architecture of J2EE applications, the application logic (EJBs) and the presentation layer (JSPs, servlets) are separated in the development phase as well.

The activities during Java development are divided into different roles. When developing application logic, the developer creates his or her own Enterprise Java Beans. For this purpose, the developer can use classes that are contained in the standard Java libraries or in other Java classes of other developers. These classes are all included or imported, for example, by inserting the following lines in the source code:

```
import java.awt.Toolkit;
import java.awt.event.ActionEvent;
import java.io.FileInputStream;
```

The structure and the runtime behavior of the application are described in the context of an XML file, namely, the deployment descriptor. This descriptor lists the transactional behavior as well as the persistence and security settings. To a certain extent, this permits setting and reusing the applications without changing the source code.

As soon as the development is completed, the developer uses standard Java programs to merge the EJBs, the used classes, and the deployment descriptors in a Java archive (.jar). This process is then called the *build process*. When creating the presentation logic, JSPs or Java servlets and HTML pages are assembled into Web archives (.war) in the same way, thereby also creating a deployment descriptor.

At the end of the entire development process, these archives can then be bundled with new deployment descriptors into Enterprise archives (.ear). This assembly process is then carried out by the Application Assembler.

Finally, the platform-independent Enterprise archive must be installed on the individual J2EE servers. This deployment step is usually carried out by an expert of the respective operating system environment. During this step, the tools analyze the different deployment descriptors and assign the application, for example, specific database resources or security settings.

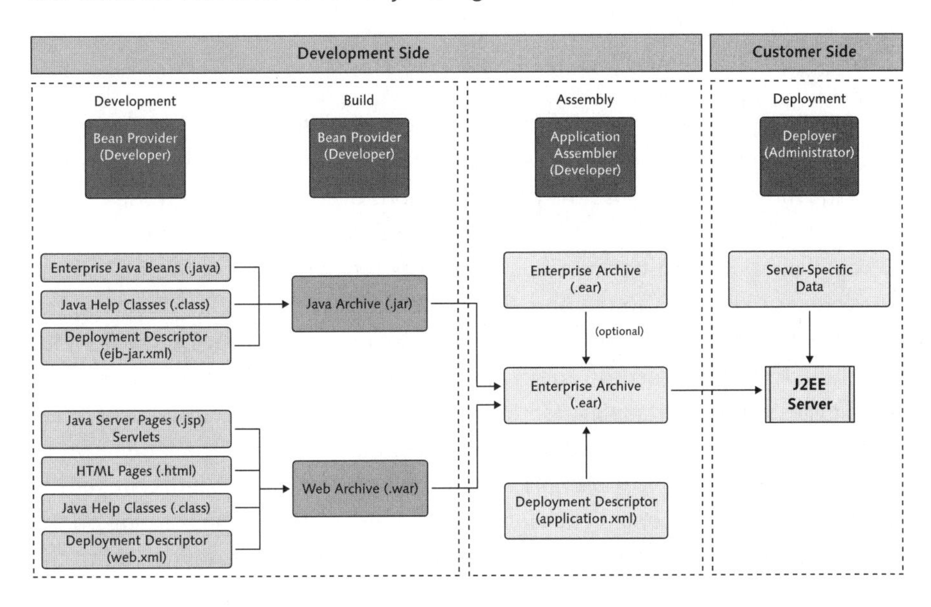


**Figure 18.3** Standard Java development process

This basically summarizes the individual steps for creating a Java application. All parts required for this process are included in the Java Software Development Kit (J2SDK). Nevertheless, this environment is not feasible for creating larger developments or for working with larger development teams. Therefore, an Integrated Development Infrastructure (IDE) is used for a more suitable development environment. But, even with an IDE, you can still encounter challenges and problems, which stem from individual developers developing locally in their own runtime environment. This localized development often results in errors due to lack of consistency between local and central system environments.

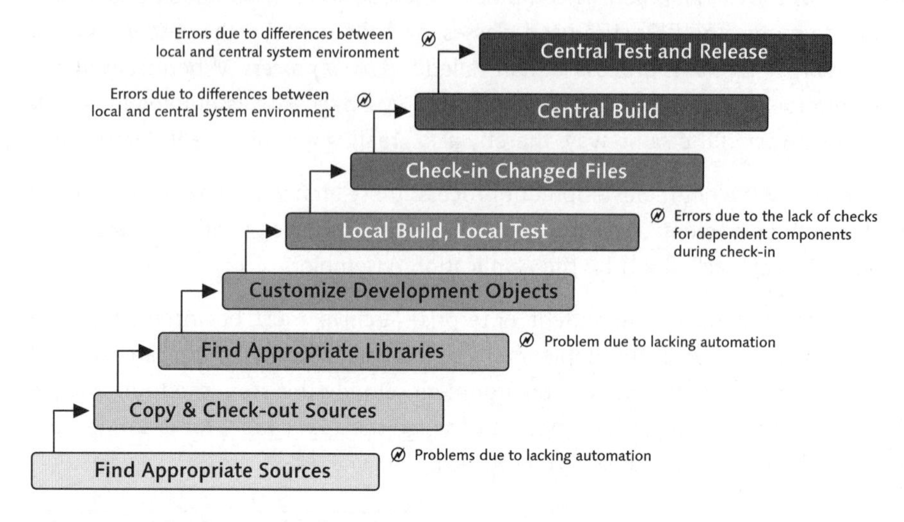


**Figure 18.4** Possible mistakes in the Java development process

Like ABAP applications, Java applications can exist in different versions. Therefore, before a developer creates a new application or changes an existing application, he or she must be sure to use the correct versions of source code and used libraries. Often, to use the different versions within different development steps, the IDE configuration must be changed. As soon as the correct versions of all necessary sources have been found and checked out of the central file directory, the local development can begin. The developer then creates his or her own builds from time to time—based on the respective operating system environment—in order to test his or her application locally. After the development is completed, the changed sources are copied back to the central directory. Errors might occur during this process if, for example, referenced objects have been changed by other developers and copied back into the central directory. When testing on the central system, this can lead to different runtime environments compared to the developer's computer.

These problems do not occur when developing in ABAP, because the development environment and the runtime environment are provided centrally on one system. The goal of the NWDI is therefore to avoid the aforementioned problems of standard Java development and to use the concepts of the ABAP world instead.

## 18.3 Parts of the SAP NetWeaver Development Infrastructure

The SAP NetWeaver Development Infrastructure (NWDI) consists of local development environments, the SAP NetWeaver Developer Studio (NWDS), as well as additional server-based software components and services, which can provide a development team with a consistent central environment and thereby support the entire lifecycle of a product.

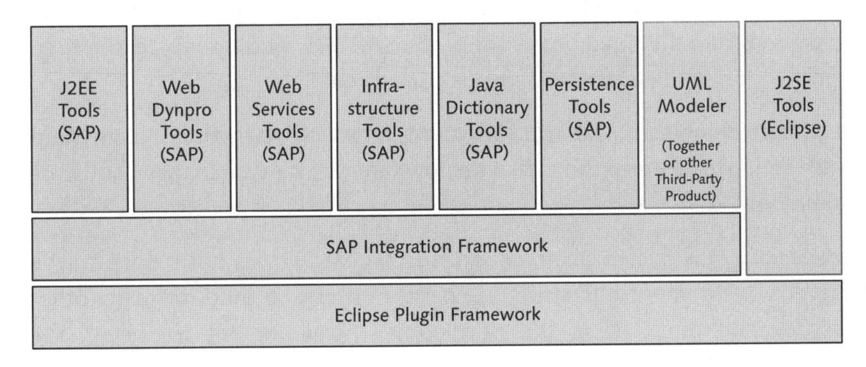


**Figure 18.5** Eclipse and the SAP NetWeaver Developer Studio

### 18.3.1 The SAP Development Environment

The SAP NetWeaver Developer Studio (NWDS) is the SAP development environment for creating all kinds of SAP J2EE applications. The NWDS is based on the Eclipse open source development platform. Using existing tools, Eclipse supports the development of Java programs in many ways. But, the integration with J2EE application servers and with other functions required for the SAP environment is missing. This is enabled by implementing plug-ins, which are included in the NWDS installation package. Both local and team-oriented development, testing, and deployment of business applications are supported through versioning. Additionally, tools for different kinds of application development are included, like WebScreen tools for creating web interfaces or J2EE tools for developing J2EE applications like Enterprise Java Beans. With the use of these tools, and by integrating them with the other components of the SAP NetWeaver development environment discussed in the following sections, it is possible to fully support the Java development process.

The central storage and versioning of the Java sources and other resources required for development is taken over by the Design Time Repository (DTR). To enable the development in a team, there is also an automated conflict detection and the corresponding conflict resolution for different versions. Together with the SAP NetWeaver Developer Studio, the DTR allows for the support of all projects, such as Web dynpros or Enterprise Java Beans.

The Component Build Service (CBS) is responsible for creating runtime objects like Java archives, which can later be deployed in the J2EE Engine. The CBS allows for incremental builds, as well as an automated rebuild of dependent software components, by reading the necessary resources from the DTR. The component builds are based on the SAP component model.

The Change Management Service (CMS) controls the transports and deployments in the development environment by carrying out the appropriate installation, distribution, or deployment in the SAP J2EE server environment for the archives which resulted from the build processes of the SAP CBS. Additionally, is the CMS is responsible for configuring the transport landscape.

The Software Deployment Manager (SDM) is the tool called by the Change Management Service to perform the actual deployment of a new or changed software component version.

Strictly speaking, the System Landscape Directory (SLD) does not belong to the NetWeaver Development Infrastructure, because it can be used for many other purposes even without using the development environment. However, the NWDI builds on the SLD as a central server application to access information about the existing system landscape, the software components contained therein, and the name range reservation (name server).

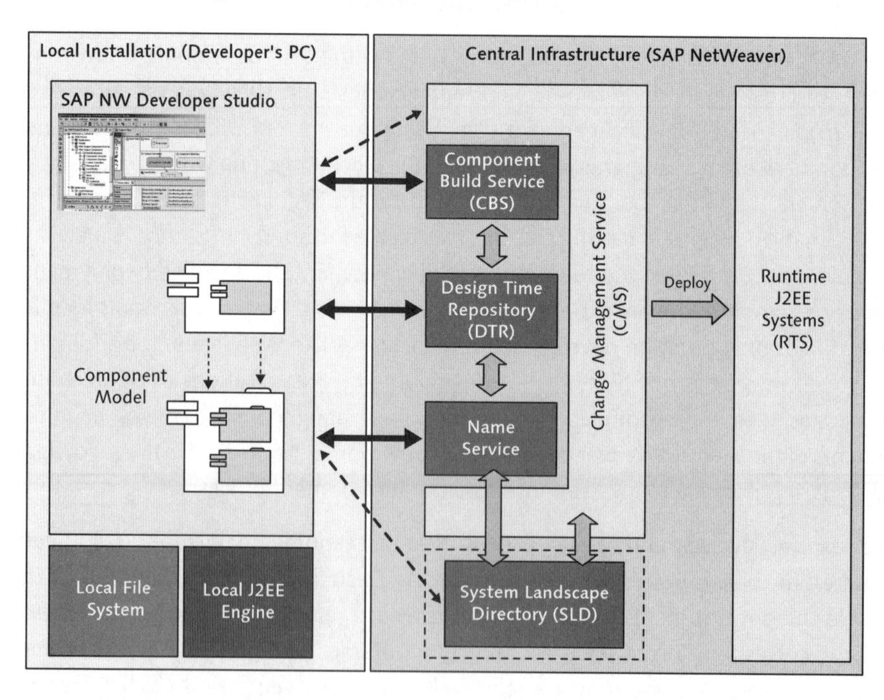


**Figure 18.6** Parts of the SAP NetWeaver Development Infrastructure

The development of Java applications in the NWDI is based on the SAP software component model. Using this model, software projects can be systematically structured, because programming units which can be maintained and reused in a more optimal way are usable from the beginning. The components themselves can use other components in a defined and controlled way by making only specific functions available via a set of public interfaces, namely, the public parts. In addition to the componentization of the development process, the usage of a name server within the SLD helps to avoid naming conflicts for software objects, even with distributed development. These conflicts would not be apparent during local development or in a local test. But, as soon as the different software objects are brought together in a common runtime environment, any error, up to the deactivation of the applications, can occur.

To protect the productive systems from premature further developments in the local or central development systems, the productive environment and the development environment must be strictly separated. Apart from that, ideally there should be a stable runtime environment reflecting the software status of the productive system so as to test new developments. To achieve these goals, SAP recommends a four-system landscape (see Figure 18.7). The four systems represent the different process states, where DEV and CONS stand for the two possible development states of the software components.

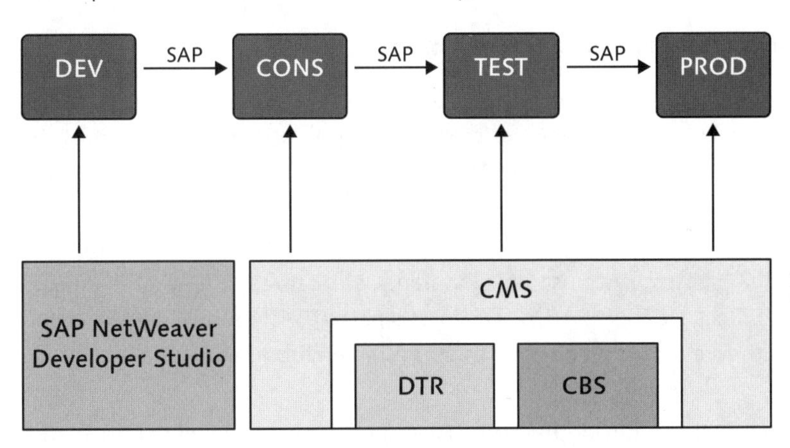


**Figure 18.7** Four-system landscape in the NWDI

The central development system DEV is used by the individual developers to test their local developments in a larger context. This means that the interaction with developments of other programmers can be tested. In the consolidation system CONS and the TEST test system, either certain fixed states of software components are consolidated or a complete test, for example, an integration test, is carried out. Only after successful testing can the new development be imported into the productive system PROD. The transports between the different systems are then started and monitored by the CMS.

**Note** As mentioned above, the NetWeaver Development Infrastructure has defined four systems per default. Still, you do not necessarily keep four runtime systems ready, even though this would make sense in view of the different tests within the Java environment. But if, for example, there is a transport landscape for parallel ABAP-based systems with only three systems, you could also adapt the runtime systems to the Java transport landscape. In that case, you would build up runtime systems for only DEV, TEST, and PROD. Irrespective of this scenario, there would still be a workspace in the DTR and a build space for the CONS system in the CBS, on the basis of which the deployments would be built.

## 18.4 Configuration of the SAP NetWeaver Development Infrastructure

Before the SAP NetWeaver Development Infrastructure can be used, it must be installed and configured. Depending on how the NWDI will be used or which types of development will be performed, there are different scenarios that are described in more detail in the following sections.

### 18.4.1 Local Development Environment

Java applications are created in the SAP NetWeaver Developer Studio. Since the NWDS is installed on a developer's PC, the applications created must be deployed on the J2EE Engine of the SAP Web AS. Thus, the J2EE Engine serves as a runtime environment.

**Note** In ABAP-based systems, developments are carried out via the ABAP Workbench. Because the ABAP Workbench is part of SAP Web AS ABAP, it can be used both as a development and as a runtime environment.

This illustrates that the development of Java applications generally consists of a combination of local development and testing, on the one hand, and central testing, deployment, and execution on the other hand.

**Note** If, apart from the development of Java applications, an ABAP development and runtime environment is required, SAP Web AS ABAP + Java needs to be installed instead of SAP Web AS Java. This is the case, for example, if the interfaces must be created in Java, but data access takes place via an ABAP-based system.

Then, the order of the installation steps is as follows:

1. Installation of SAP Web AS (Java or ABAP + Java)
2. Local installation of the SAP NetWeaver Developer Workplace, which consists of the SAP NWDS and local SAP Web AS Java
3. Optionally, the installation of further SAP NetWeaver Developer Workplaces

The recommended hardware requirements for installing the SAP NWDI can be found in SAP Note 737368, based on the applicable development scenario. The following hardware requirements are specified for a PC with SAP NWDS: 2 GB RAM, CPU with a clock rate of 2 GHz and about 3 GB available disk space; on the software side, Windows 2000 SP3 or Windows XP is required with Internet Explorer Version 5.5 or higher.

### 18.4.2 Overview of the Different Development Scenarios

The SAP NetWeaver Development Infrastucture supports several development scenarios, which are based on each other respectively:

- **Scenario 1—team-oriented development**
  Although it is possible to wholly support pure Java and J2EE projects with this scenario, you cannot carry out any Web dynpro development. If you decide to work in software components later on, there is no tool support to migrate existing developments to the component model. Because this involves manual effort, you must determine early on which scenario should be used.
- **Scenario 2—development of software components**
  Contrary to Scenario 1, this scenario allows you to develop software components. However, it still uses only the DTR and therefore must carry out the build process or the deployment manually.

  As with Scenario 1, SAP does not provide any automatic migration tools to higher scenarios for this scenario either. Therefore, this is considered to be a demo for developing in software components.
- **Scenario 2+—development of software components with a track**
  This scenario enables you to develop software components, provides you with the complete range of administration functions, and allows you to use the build environment.
- **Scenario 3—development with multiple layers**
  This scenario is necessary if different software components, which depend on one another, need to be developed in parallel. Because this scenario enables you to combine different tracks and therefore develop interdependent applications, it is considered to be an extension of the second scenario.

### Scenario 1: Team-Oriented Development

In general, this scenario is recommended for only smaller development teams that don't require any central administration. Development should be restricted to pure Java and J2EE applications. The components of the SAP NWDI used in this case are the DTR for the storing and versioning of program sources, as well as the SAP NWDS for the actual development process. Because no components are used, neither the CBS nor the CMS is required.

The order of installation and configuration steps is as follows:

1. Installation of SAP Web AS Java
2. Deployment of NWDI components on this server
3. Installation of the SAP NetWeaver Developer Workplaces (with the NWDS and, optionally, local SAP Web AS Java)
4. Configuration of the DTR servers, specifically the creation of the workspaces, the user management system, and the users and their authorizations upon which it is based on
5. Configuration of DTR client definitions for all NWDS in use
6. Selection of files for automatic storing in the DTR
7. Setup of runtime systems in the DTR
8. Setup of manual or automated processes for Software Change Management (optional)

In this scenario, developers each have their own local development environment consisting of the SAP NetWeaver Developer Studio and, optionally, local SAP Web AS Java for tests. The development takes place in the NWDS. The Design Time Repository (DTR) is used for centrally providing the program sources to all team members. In the DTR, the sources and their versions are then stored in files and directories, and a concurrent development on their basis is appropriately controlled. The developed applications are then compiled and assembled with the integrated tools of the NWDS. The deployment of the applications is performed manually from the NWDS by starting the SAP Deployment Manager.

In this scenario, it the quality manager's responsibility to maintain different states of the program sources in the DTR. To meet this requirement, different DTR workspaces should be created for development and consolidation.

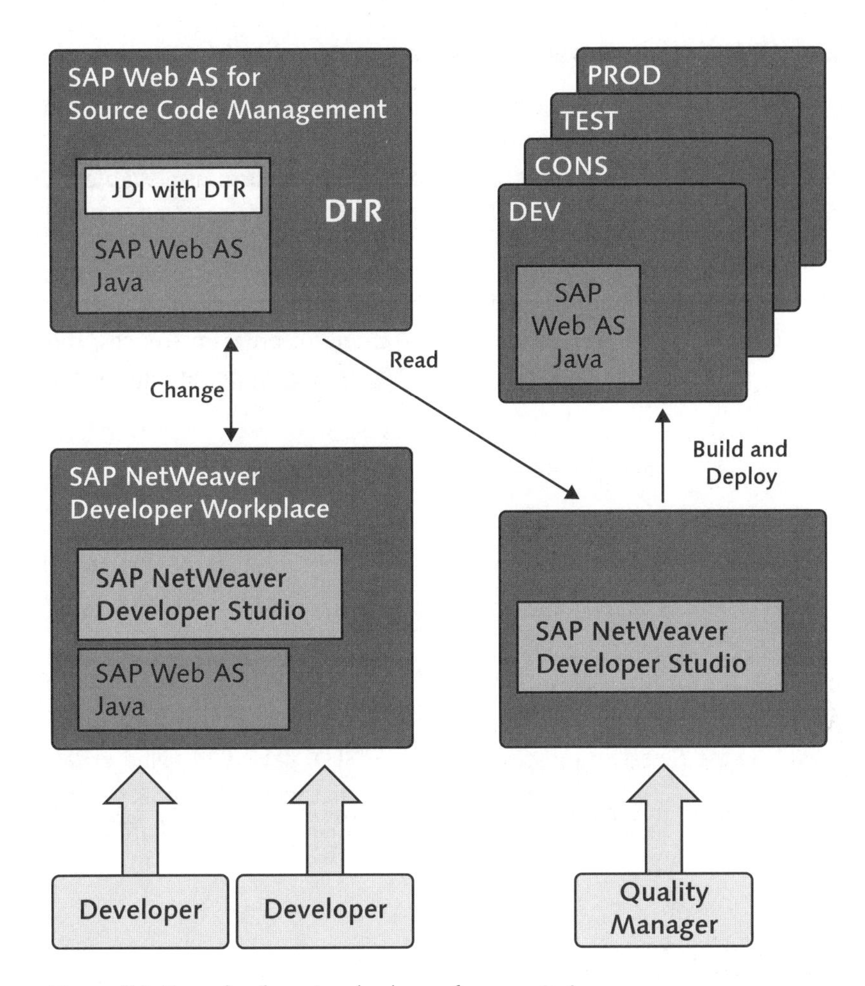


**Figure 18.8** Example of a system landscape for scenario 1

### Scenario 2: Development with Software Components

This scenario is appropriate for smaller development teams if you don't want to restrict development to pure Java and J2EE applications, or, if you want to test how to use software components in development and how to modularize programming by defining their dependencies. As with the previous scenario, the only components of the SAP NetWeaver Development Infrastructure used here are the DTR for the storing and versioning of program sources and the SAP NWDS for the actual development process.

The installation and configuration steps, and the parts and tasks of the NWDI, in this scenario are the same as those in Scenario 1, with one exception—you can use the SAP component model.

#### Scenario 2+: Development with Software Components in a Track

This scenario is ideal for customers who want to work with software components and use all the benefits of the administration and automation of the NWDI. This is the scenario that can be used, apart from Scenario 3, to customize Web dynpros for Employee Self Service (ESS) and Management Self Service (MSS) to meet special requirements.

It uses all components of the SAP NetWeaver Development Infrastructure: the Design Time Repository for the storing and versioning of program sources, the Change Management Service, and the SAP NetWeaver Developer Studio for the actual development.

The order of installation and configuration steps is as follows:

1. Installation of SAP Web AS Java
2. Setup and activation of the SLD
3. Installation of one or several SAP Web AS Java instances for the NWDI components

**Note** Although the different components of the NWDI like DTR, CBS, and CMS, as well as the System Landscape Directory (SLD) can be installed on a server, for performance reasons, SAP recommends that you install at least the DTR and the CBS on separate hosts. For basic information about hardware requirements, see SAP Note 737368.

4. Deployment of the NWDI components
5. Installation of the SAP NetWeaver Developer Workplaces (with the NWDS and, optionally, local SAP Web AS Java)
6. Installation of SAP Web AS Java as a central test system
7. Creation and setup of the user management system, and the users and their authorizations on which it is based on
8. Creation of a domain and a track in the CMS
9. Check-in and import of the required program sources
10. Customization of the authorization for the DTR workspaces
11. Import of the development configuration

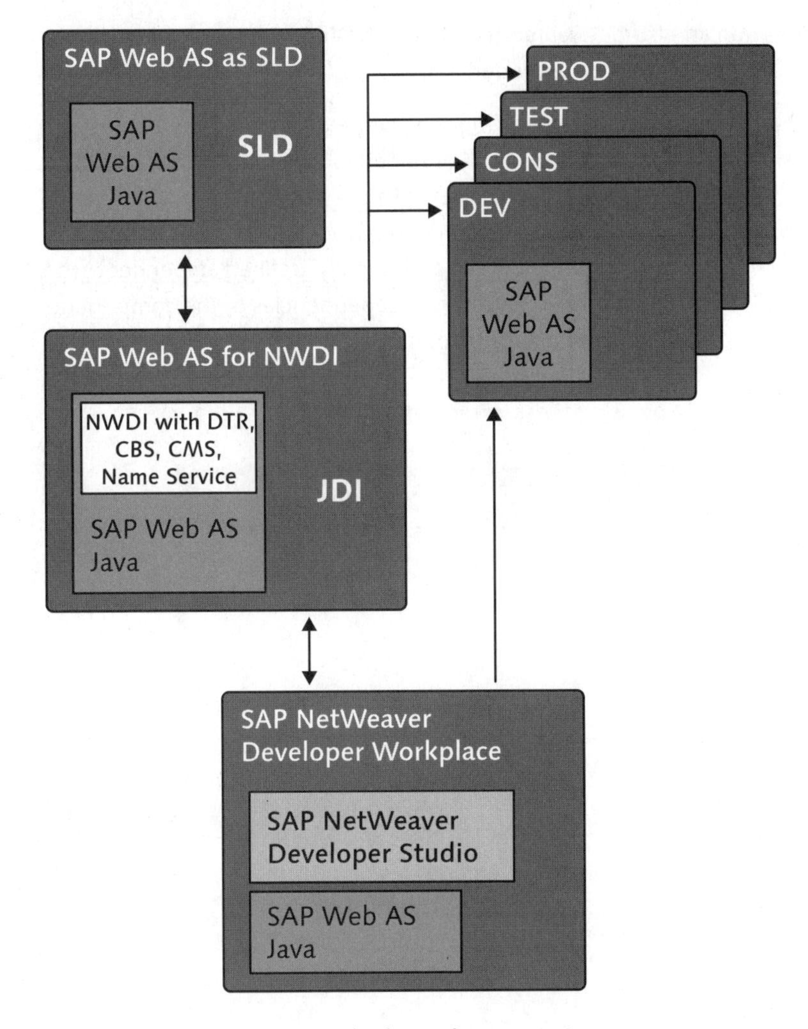


**Figure 18.9** Example of a system landscape for scenario 2+

As in the previous scenarios, every developer has locally installed his or her own SAP NetWeaver Developer Studio as well as SAP Web AS Java. The DTR is used as a central storage of the sources as well. However, by using the software components, the developers can now distribute their programs among the team members in order to create smaller, reusable, more modular units that are easier to use and maintain. This is achieved via the type of encapsulation or by sharing only certain interfaces, that is, the public parts. Additionally, by completely using the NWDI, some processes are automated; for example, in SAP NetWeaver Developer Studio, the DTR access is set up automatically by importing the configuration of the development environment (development configuration). Now a special component build can also be created in the SAP NWDS, which creates components based on their types and dependencies.

The advantage of the SAP component model as an extension of the classes and interfaces visibility concept that is already contained in Java is that—via the extension by the development and software components —each of these components is visible in one direction only and is defined exactly via public parts as an interface. For this reason, and because of the additionally defined dependency on other components, a collision due to cyclic interdependencies of the components no longer poses a possible problem. The builds are therefore always provided with the current libraries, and the creation of the aforementioned "incremental builds" is possible only by using these extensions.

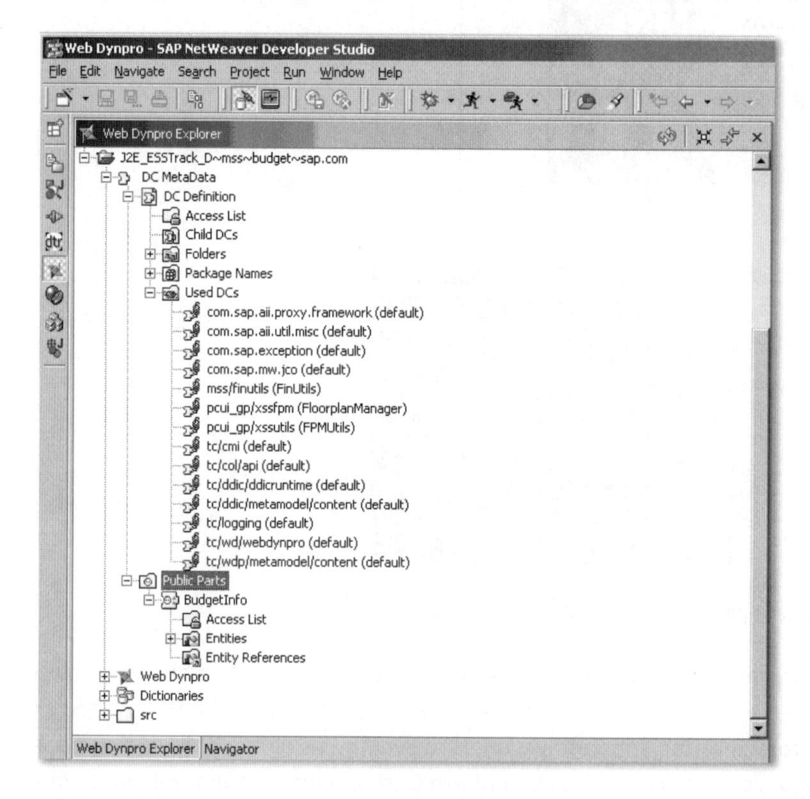


**Figure 18.10** Example of the dependencies of development components

> **Example**
>
> Figure 18.10, which shows the Web Dynpro Explorer perspective of the SAP NetWeaver Developer Studio, helps you to understand the dependencies of the individual development components and the builds.

The dependencies of com.sap.budget.mss are visible via **Used DCs** (like com.sap.aii.proxy.framework or com.sap.aii.util.misc). If, for example, an object of the development component com.sap.aii.proxy.framework was changed, a build request is automatically created in the CBS. The same applies to dependent development components—as in this case com.sap.budget.mss—which are then rebuilt via another build request. For example, if other development components use the interfaces shown under **Public Parts** (in this case only BudgetInfo), these components would be rebuilt automatically as soon as there are changes to com.sap.budget.mss, because they entered com.sap.budget.mss as Used DCs.

By using the Component Build Service (CBS), there is no longer a need to use command-line tools and individual build scripts to create a central component build. On demand, the CBS creates builds from components and their dependent objects, and also provides ready-to-use libraries and deployment tools for developers and runtime systems. The process of software distribution is now automated as well by implementing the SAP Change Management Service (CMS). The CMS is responsible for transporting the software, that is, program sources and libraries, within the landscape and supports the automatic deployment of executable programs on the relevant servers.

### Scenario 3: Layered Development

This scenario is an extension of Scenario 2+ in that several software components that are based on each other are developed in parallel. The development can be coordinated hierarchically. The requirements regarding the system landscape and the individual tasks therefore correspond to those of Scenario 2+, except that more J2EE Engines might be necessary for testing the applications. This is the scenario SAP uses for software development. Figure 18.11 shows an example of the various software layers.

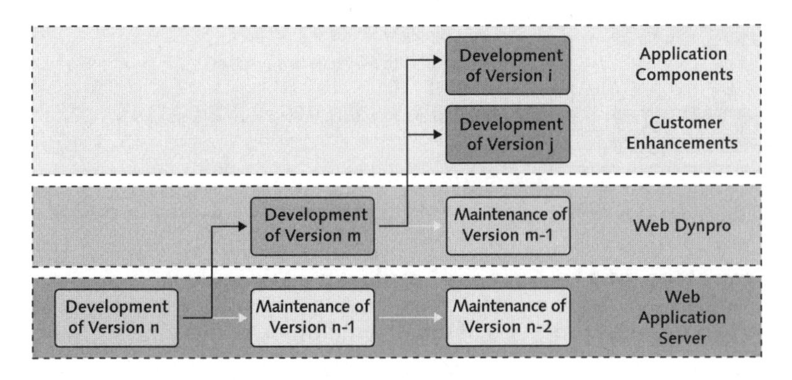


**Figure 18.11** Different layers in the Java development process

## 18.5 Configuration of the SAP NetWeaver Development Infrastructure

After the basic demands on specific services and components for using the NWDI have been introduced in the previous chapters, we will now describe the configuration of the individual parts so you can use manual or automated processes in the SAP Software Change Management. Since the individual scenarios are built on each other, we'll discuss the configuration of Scenario 2+ in particular, because it requires all parts of the NWDI and therefore also reflects the DTR configuration for Scenarios 1 and 2.

Figure 18.12 gives you an overview of all steps to be carried out during Java development; the details will be further described throughout the rest of this chapter. Before you can begin the actual development, you must determine the parts that make up the software, and in which environment the development should take place. As soon as the development has been completed, it is distributed using other parts of the NWDI.

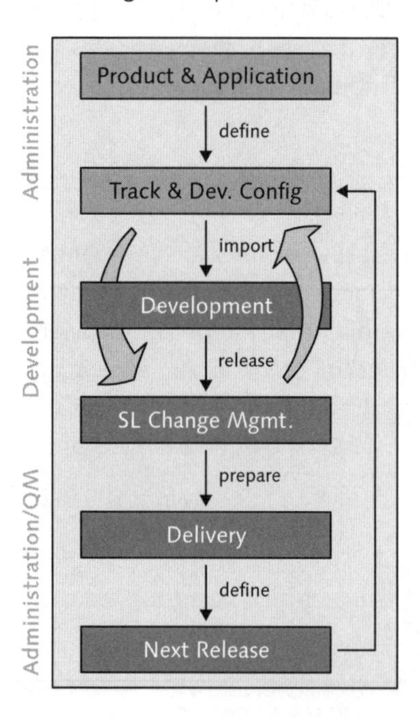


**SLD:** Structure software to be developed

- Define product
- Define one or more software components (SCs) the product is supposed to consist of

**CMS:** Define development landscape

- Define a track for each release of the SCs
- Development configurations are generated for each development status of the SCs (both DEV and CONS)

**Dev. Studio:** Change and build development objects

- Run devlopment projects using SAP NWDS and its access to the NWDI
- Release objects for further processing by administrator/QA

**CMS:** Describe further usage of SCs

- Compile transport into downstream systems by using the CMS

**CMS:** Supply with SCs and patches

- Supply with SC versions a product consists of

**CMS:** Create new track for the next release of SCs

**Figure 18.12** The lifecycle in Java development

### 18.5.1 Configuration of the System Landscape Directory

To map the complex business processes of today, a multitude of different software components are required on different hardware platforms. In part, there are dependencies between them regarding installation requirements, software updates, and the interfaces connecting them. Therefore, the administration of such a system landscape can become complex and hard to handle. In general, the System Landscape Directory (SLD) facilitates the administration of an SAP system landscape by serving as a central storage for this information. All installable and installed components of a system landscape are stored based on the standard Common Information Model (CIM), which provides a general, flexibly extensible schema for the description of such components, and has been enhanced by SAP with proprietary SAP-specific classes.

The information regarding the installable SAP software components is provided by SAP on a regular basis as a data package that can be imported into the System Landscape Directory (SLD). The SAP software components can be registered automatically and cyclically in the SLD with their current software status (e.g., version numbers, current patch levels and dependencies on other components). Furthermore, you can enter the information about software statuses of third-party products manually in the SLD. In this way, the SLD provides you with a complete picture of the system landscape in its current state.

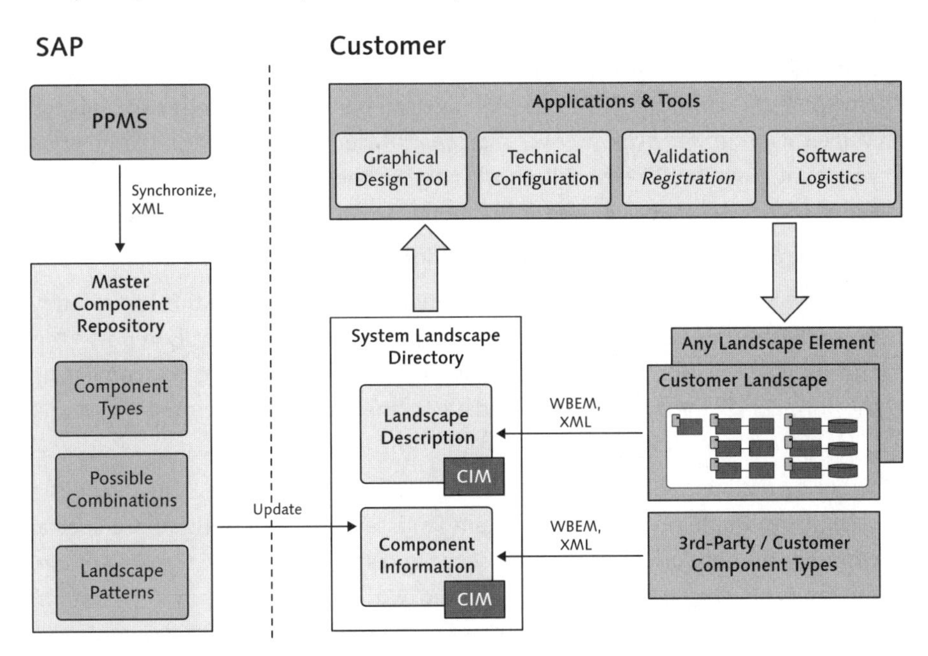


**Figure 18.13** Data flow between SLD and other components

The SLD is therefore ideal as a data source for extremely different other applications, for example, the Software Lifecycle Manager (SLM), which can be used as a planning tool for executing software changes as of NetWeaver Support Package Stack 12. Or, it can be used for Web dynpros for storing target systems of Web services, or for the SAP NetWeaver Development Infrastructure (NWDI) to manage information relevant to development.

The SLD is a server application that communicates with the clients only via Hypertext Transfer Protocol (HTTP or HTTPs). The SLD is installed automatically during the installation of SAP Web AS Java, but must be appropriately configured and activated before it can be used. Here is an overview of the individual steps that are required for this purpose:

- Adapt the virtual memory size (depending on the creator of the JRE/JDK) to at least 512 or 1024 MB using the J2EE config tool
- Create users and roles depending on the system used as User Management Engine (UME)
- Log on to the SLD with a user belonging either to the J2EE administrators group or to the SAP_SLD_ADMINISTRATOR group; this access is carried out via a browser using the address *http://SLD-Host:Port/sld*.
- Specify basic SLD settings like persistence and Object Server via **Administration · Server Settings**

  In the Object Server area, you can enter the name range known from the ABAP environment without "/". This name range can be requested in the SAP Service Marketplace under *http://service.sap.com/NAMERANGES*. If this is not what you want, you should enter the host name of the SLD. In this case, however, the SLD can no longer be used for name range reservations in the NWDI.
- Start the SLD server from the administration window
- Start the SLD bridge from the administration window as well; this is necessary only if the systems of the system landscape are to automatically report their current status to the SLD, because the SLD bridge is required for converting the formats of the various system data to the Common Information Model (CIM) format which is used by the SLD.

  It is also possible to operate several SLDs in a system landscape. This can be the case, for example, in very large system landscapes or where there are special demands on network topologies or security restrictions. Then, the SLD bridge can exchange the data of an SLD system with that of another SLD system. More detailed information can be found in the document *Planning Guide* in the SAP Service Marketplace under *http://service.sap.com/SLD · Media Library*.
- Initial data import of the SAP product and software component description via **Administration · Import**

  The file required for this can be found in the SAP Service Marketplace under *http://service.sap.com/SWDC · Entry by Application Group · Additional Components · SAP Master Data for SLD* and in the corresponding subdirectories. What is needed is the appropriate `CRContent` file. If an initial import has already occurred, only the `CRDelta` file is necessary. If an extension of the SLD CIM model is required, it is determined at the beginning of the data import. You would then have to import the appropriate `CIMSAP` file first. Additional explanations can be found in SAP Note 669669.

- Configuration of data providers

  This procedure varies depending on whether an ABAP- or a Java-based system should register with the SLD. ABAP-based systems only register per RFC; Java-based systems can also transfer their data directly per HTTP to the SLD bridge. Details can be found in the *Post-Installation Guide*, which is available in the SAP Service Marketplace under *http://service.sap.com/SLD* • *Media Library*.

  Please note that only ABAP-based systems from R/3 4.0B and higher, as well as Java-based systems from SAP Web AS J2EE 6.30 and higher, can automatically register with the SLD. For ABAP-based systems, a minimum Support Package status is required, which is listed in SAP Note 584654.

- Register the SLD itself

  This step is required for only the SLD. Via **Home • Technical Landscape • New Technical System**, you first create a system for SAP Web AS Java in which the SLD has been activated, or the system is created automatically for this SAP Web AS Java by activating the SLD registration services from the Visual Administrator. Then, via **Home • Technical Landscape • New Technical System**, a system landscape directory entry is set up based on this system.

- If the name range reservation is used in the NWDI, the SLD that fulfills the name server function must be appropriately registered in the DTR as soon as the DTR has been set up.

### 18.5.2 Setting Up Users and Authorizations

The correct setup of users, their roles, and their authorizations significantly contributes to whether the developments can be carried out in a coordinated way and, for example, whether a dual control for acceptance and tests, or a division of tasks between the actual development activity and the transportation is possible. In this context, the following users are distinguished in the NWDI area:

- Developers who work both in their SAP NetWeaver Developer Studio and in the SAP NetWeaver Development Infrastructure (NWDI) must have access to the SLD and the other NWDI components.
- An NWDI administrator who needs access to all components of the NWDI. However, for the configuration in the CMS, it is not really necessary to access the SLD; this can be carried out via an SLD's own administrator.

- Change Management Service (CMS) users who carry out a variety of activities in the SLD, the CMS, the DTR, and the CBS that are necessary for setting up the NWDI and for operating the CMS.

Ideally, the development in the NWDI is hierarchically structured and its procedure corresponds to Figure 18.14.

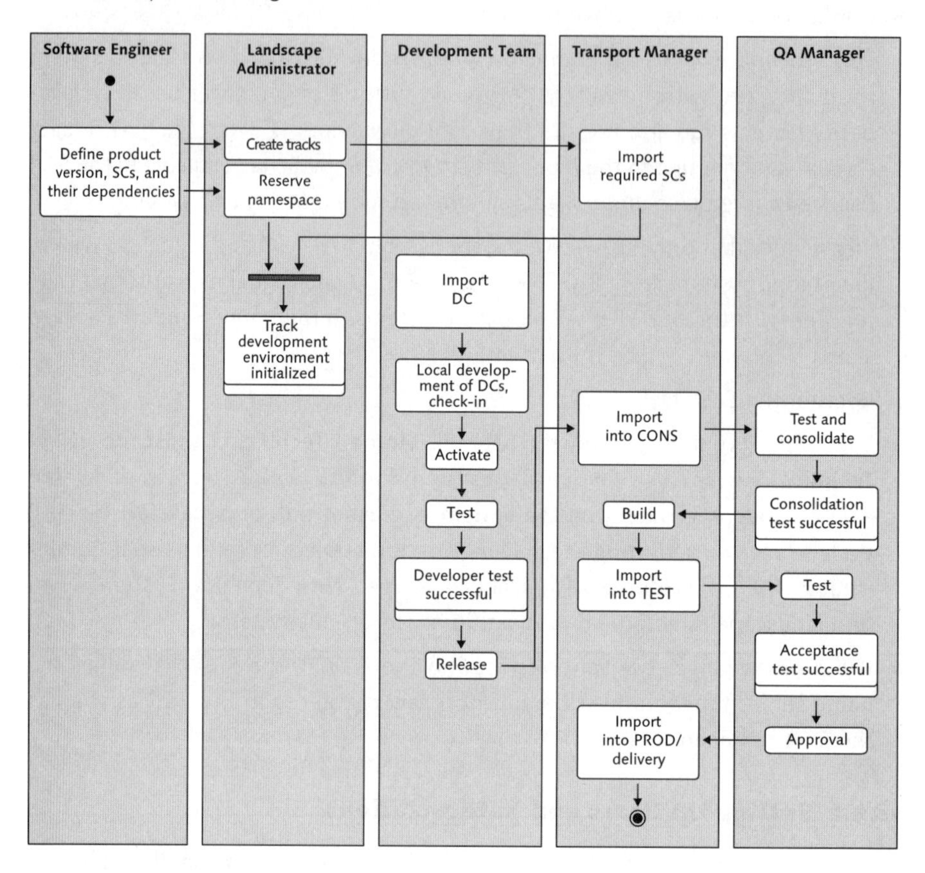


**Figure 18.14** Hierarchical structure of Java development

The following table shows how these users can be assigned to various roles and user groups:

| NWDI role | User | UME role | UME group |
|---|---|---|---|
| Member of Development Team | Developer_1<br>Developer_2<br>Developer_n | NWDI.Developer | NWDI.Developers |
| NWDI Administrator | NWDIadmin | NWDI.Adminstrator | NWDI.Adminstrators |

**Table 18.1** Assignment of users to roles and user groups

| NWDI role | User | UME role | UME group |
|---|---|---|---|
| (internal user) | CMSuser | NWDI.Adminstrator | NWDI.Adminstrators |
| Transport Manager<br>Quality Manager | NWDImanager | NWDI.Manager | NWDI.Managers |
| Software Architect<br>Landscape Administrator | Administrator | NWDI.Adminstrator | Administrators<br>NWDI.Adminstrators |

**Table 18.1** Assignment of users to roles and user groups (cont.)

Although the CMSuser needs to be created, it should not be assigned to a person but is used only internally by the CMS. This user is made known to the NWDI in the domain definition.

Excluding the authorizations of the NWDI Manager, the NWDI Administrator also possesses administrator authorizations so that he or she can carry out special restore options in case of an error, for example, which would require extended authorizations. Possible assignments of users to UME activities or security roles of the SLD are listed in the following table:

| User/role | UME activity | Java security role |
|---|---|---|
| NWDI.Developer | CBS.Developer<br>CMS.Display<br>CMS.Export | LcrInstanceWriterNR |
| NWDI.Adminstrator | CBS.Administrator<br>CMS.Administrate | LcrInstanceWriterAll |
| CMSuser | CBS.Administrator<br>CMS.Administrate | LcrInstanceWriterAll<br>LcrInstanceWriterLD |
| NWDI.Manager | CBS.Developer<br>CBS.QM<br>CMS.Administrate | LcrInstanceWriterNR<br>LcrInstanceWriterCR<br>LcrInstanceWriterLD |
| Administrator | CBS.Administrator<br>CMS.Administrate | LcrInstanceWriterAll<br>LcrAdministrator |

**Table 18.2** User assignments to UME activities and SLD roles

**Note** If no central ABAP system or LDAP is used for user management, but the users are created in the local UME and the SLD is installed on a separate J2EE Engine, users (in this example Developer_1 or CMSuser) must be created in all UMEs with the same authorizations and passwords. With respect to the SLD, the assignment needs to be done via **Visual Admin • Server • Services • Security Provider • sap.com\com.sap.lcr*sld • Security Roles**.

Additionally, the authorizations for the DTR must be assigned. The corresponding detailed description can be found in the online help under *http://help.sap.com • Documentation • SAP NetWeaver • English • Application Platform • Java Technology in SAP Web AS • Administration Manual • Administration of SAP NWDI • Configuring User Management in SAP NWDI • User Authentication and User Authorization • Configuring DTR clients*.

### 18.5.3 Setting Up the SAP NetWeaver Developer Studios

Lastly, every SAP NetWeaver Developer Studio must be set up and configured appropriately, which is usually done by the responsible developer.

Depending on the chosen scenario, the storage location for different data types is specified first. Unlike Scenarios 1 and 2, the Scenarios 2+ or 3 do not store the .project and .classpath types. This is checked in the NWDS via the **Window • Preferences • Team • Ignored Resources** menu. For Scenarios 2+ and 3, the checkboxes for the .project and .classpath types must be enabled.

If SAP Web AS Java was installed locally along with the NWDS, it must be set as a runtime environment. This is done via the **Window • Preferences • SAP J2EE Engine** menu. If no local J2EE Engine is used, another SAP Web AS Java must be entered as a remote host, which will then serve as a runtime environment for the NWDS.

To enable access to the configuration (development configuration) in the SLD, the development configuration pool must be maintained in the NWDS settings. There, the URL of the SLD is entered via the **Window • Preferences • Java Development Infrastructure • Development Configuration Pool** menu.

### 18.5.4 Creating Products and Software Components

As mentioned previously, the usage of software components allows a reasonable structuring of large projects into reusable units that are easier to handle. Figure 18.15 provides you with a better idea of how the elements of the SAP component model are related to one another.

A development component (called DC in the following) is a kind of container for development objects in Java and thus forms the smallest build unit. A DC has defined external interfaces and is otherwise known as a *black box*. DCs can use other DCs via their interfaces (public parts) and are therefore the elementary reusable units of the component model.

A development object (called DO in the following) is a part of a DC that provides parts of the DC functionality. This can be a Java class, a table definition, a JSP, or other objects.

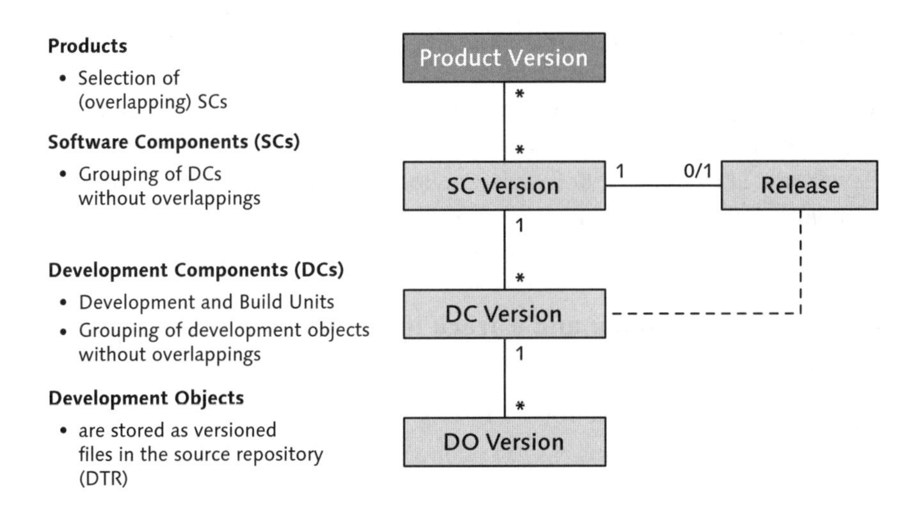


**Figure 18.15** Elements of the SAP component model

Software components (called SC in the following) connect DCs for the delivery and the deployment to larger units. Ideally, the corresponding business processes can therefore be connected.

A release identifies a bigger step in the development process that usually involves the provision of new or updated functionality.

Lastly, a product consists of one or more software components.

Products and software components are created in the SLD via **Home • Software Catalog**.

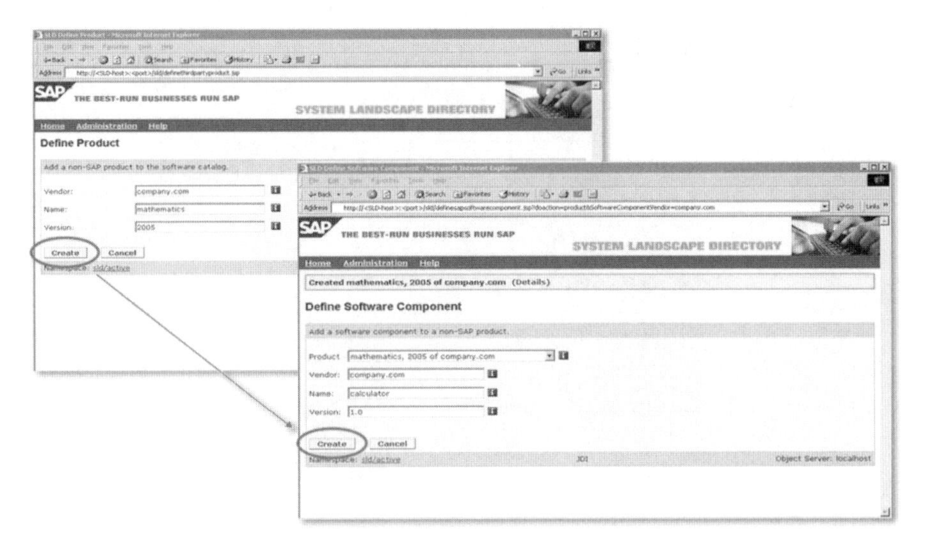


**Figure 18.16** Products and software components in the SLD

Both products and software components must be created before starting the development process if this is necessary for your own development components. In the SLD, the dependencies of this software component are specified, and this, in turn, determines the dependencies for the central build. These conditions are maintained via **SLD Home · Software Catalog · Product Version · Software Component · Usage dependency**. For the Java software component development, the dependency must be selected in the **Build Time** context.

### 18.5.5 Creating a Domain and a Track in the Change Management Service

To be able to structure the transport landscape, a Change Management Service (CMS) domain must be created. A CMS domain describes that part of the development landscape, which is administered using the Change Management Service. The CMS domain stores the following various information:

- The transport directory in which the transport information is stored
- The CMS administration user (mentioned above as CMSuser) who executes the various tools
- The SAP Web AS Java running the CMS

The individual tracks in which the software components are developed are later created within this CMS domain and connected to the transport landscape. A domain is created via the CMS user interface, which is called from a browser using the address *http://<HOST>:<Port>/devinf · Change Management Service*. For this purpose, you need to log on to this screen with a user of the NWDI.Administrators group. You can then specify the settings according to Figure 18.17.

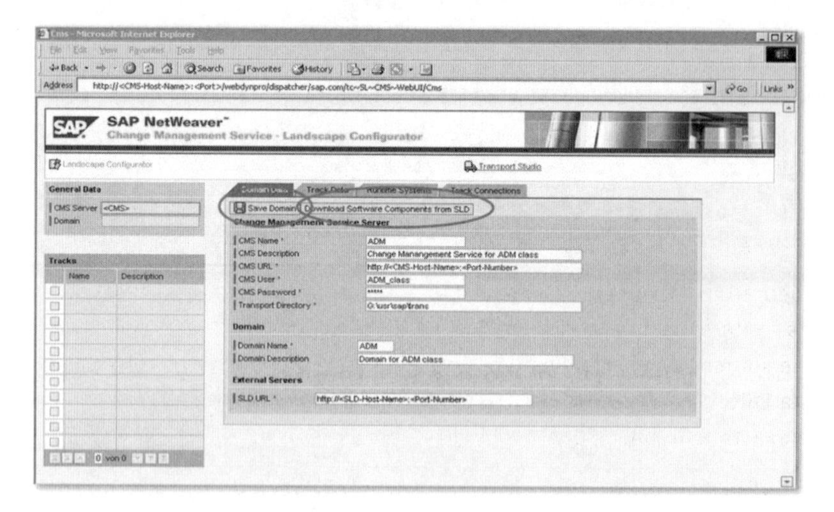


Figure 18.17 Creating a domain

**Tip** Please note that the data for **Domain Name** and **CMS Name** are stored in the SLD and can therefore be assigned only once. The domain name can consist of a maximum of three letters or digits.

After a domain for structuring the transport landscape has been created, a development track is created in the next step. Additional parts that represent a track are shown in Figure 18.18.

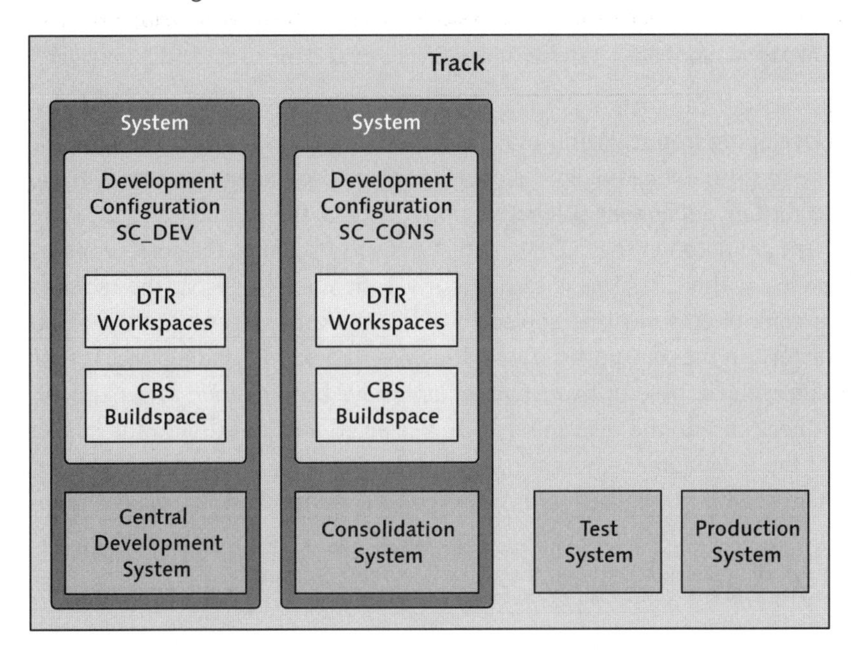


**Figure 18.18** Parts of a track

The development structure (development configuration, called configuration in the following) determines the view of the developer on the development landscape. The configuration describes the software components to be developed and thus organizes the access to the NWDI. Therefore, all developers working with the same configuration work with the same objects, which ensures consistency.

Every configuration in the Design Time Repository (DTR) is assigned up to two workspaces—one for active and one for inactive program sources. A workspace contains the sources of a certain software component status. The workspaces are accessed via URLs. Every configuration is stored in the Component Build Service (CBS) with exactly one build space.

The CMS handles the transporting software changes between the systems. In general, a system can consist of a configuration and a runtime environment; that is just a configuration, just a runtime environment, or both, depending on whether program sources or deployable archives are to be transported. A system is connected to a development status (development, consolidation, test, production).

The track contains all configurations and all runtime environments that are necessary to develop, test, and use one or several software components productively.

**Note** Contrary to transports in ABAP, a separate track is created in the NWDI for every release of a software component. In ABAP, however, developments for different applications are often transported via one and the same transport layer.

When developing in tracks, you must provide the CBS with the corresponding environment so that it can build the components appropriately. Therefore, if you specified further dependent software components in the product and software component definition in the SLD, you must transport them to the corresponding environment of the CBS. This is carried out via the check-in. First, the required software components must be copied to the CMS/Inbox directory of the transport directory. In the transport studio of the CMS, the corresponding track is then selected, for which these software components have been defined as dependent. Via the **Check-in** tab, the relevant archive is selected and placed into the import queue of the development system using **Check-in**. Finally, the software components must be imported, which is done in the CMS transport studio via **Development** by sharing the software components therein for import. This must be carried out for all systems for which the track has been created.

### 18.5.6 Creating a Development Component

Configurations (development configurations) are created and stored in the CMS. The SLD contains the information where, that is, in which CMS, the relevant configuration is stored. The configuration is then imported from the CMS into the NWDS. In this way, the development environment is available for a specific software component in the current development state. Therefore, every development process starts with the selecting of a configuration.

The configuration import is carried out from the **Development Configuration** perspective of the NWDS. However, the URL to the SLD must have been maintained beforehand. As soon as the import process is completed, a tree structure for the configuration and the software component is displayed in the **Inactive DC View** window of the NWDS. Now a new development component can be created from the **Development Configuration** perspective by right-clicking on the new software component and selecting **Create new DC** to enter the necessary data in the windows displayed. Afterwards, an activity should be created immediately.

An activity contains a set of changes that are carried out by a user and are then assigned to a workspace. In Java development, this is known as a change list.

## 18.6 Developing in the SAP NetWeaver Development Infrastructure

After the NWDI and the tracks and development configurations have been set up according to the aforementioned steps, the actual development can take place. Figure 18.19 illustrates the individual steps of the development process and how the different NWDI parts are used in this process.

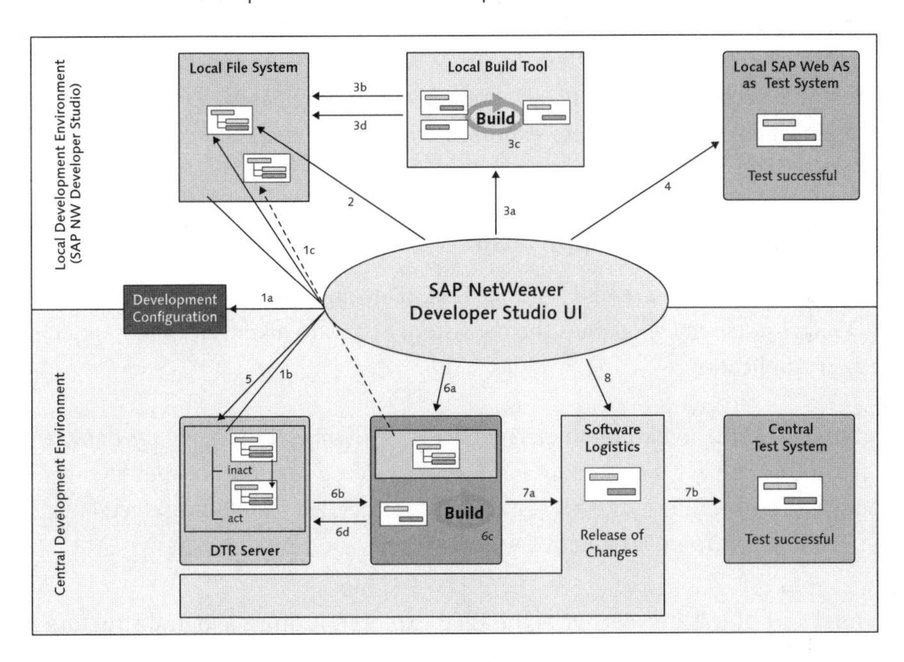


Figure 18.19 Development process using the NWDI

The development configuration is the development environment for the various software components at their current state. Therefore, every development activity starts with selecting the development configuration. Since the configuration is created and stored in the CMS, it is imported into the NWDS in Step 1a. Thus, local files are synchronized with the sources of the DTR (Step 1b) and the archives of the CBS (Step 1c). In the next step, sources are recreated or existing sources are corrected (Step 2). They can then be used for creating a local build whenever a local test is desired. This can be started from the NWDS (Step 3a). First, the sources and necessary archives are loaded (Step 3b), and then the build process is started automatically (Step 3c). The archives created during this process are then written back to the local file system (Step 3d).

The results of this local build are then used to be tested on the local test system (Step 4).

After a successful test, the sources in the DTR are updated to the current state (Step 5). After this has been completed, the central build can be started as well from the NWDS (Step 6a). For this purpose, the sources and further necessary archives are loaded into the CBS (Step 6b), after which the automatic build is started (Step 6c). As soon as the build has been successfully completed, the sources in the DTR are activated automatically (Step 6d).

The automatic deployment of the generated archives in the central test system is then started using the CMS (Steps 7a and 7b). Then, a common test can be carried out in the central test system together with other software components. If this test was completed successfully, the activities are released. With the release of the activities, the changes are exported and placed into the import queue of the consolidation system.

### 18.6.1 Creating a J2EE Application

J2EE applications are created in the **J2EE Development** perspective of the NWDS. This perspective enables the consistent access to all development objects of a J2EE application.

**Note** The **J2EE Development** perspective is shown automatically by default when a J2EE project is started. If, for example, a Web service or a Web dynpro needs to be developed, the corresponding perspective should be selected via the **Window · Open Perspective · Other** menu.

A central part of this perspective is the J2EE Explorer. It offers a logical structured composition on the local project structure, as well as a reasonable starting point for appropriate activities like creating or changing development objects. When an object is selected from the Explorer via a double-click, the appropriate editor is started by default (for example for XML, JSP, or HTML). If new objects need to be created, wizards provide corresponding support.

Usually, Java Server Pages (JSPs) are used as a part of the presentation logic, which is created in the NWDS in the context of the Web module projects. This context can easily be created from the context menu of the NWDS via an entry of the relevant development component in the J2EE DC Explorer. As soon as a JSP has been created, the JSP Editor is automatically started. This editor consists of two views—a preview that shows what the HTML program will look like in a browser, as well as a source code view in which the program can be displayed and edited in parallel.

Similar to JSPs, Enterprise Java Beans (EJBs) are built from the J2EE DC Explorer. You only need to create an appropriate development component first.

A J2EE application is created and deployed from an enterprise application project in the form of an Enterprise archive (.ear file). Further JSP or EJB modules can then be added to such an .ear file.

**Note** How the various archives are composed and assembled is shown in Figure 18.3.

### Creating a Local Build and Carrying Out the Local Tests

When a local build is started from the NWDS, an .ear archive is created from the enterprise application project. When this local build has been carried out, the created sources are compiled in the local context of the versions of the referenced objects. If necessary, .jar or .war archives are generated simultaneously for the referenced projects (Web module project or EJB module project, respectively). Besides the .jar and .war archives, the .ear archive contains the deployment descriptors as well. Optionally, other libraries can also be added to the .ear archive. As soon as the local build has been carried out successfully, the created application can be deployed and tested on the developer's local SAP Web AS Java.

### Check-in of Changes

In the SAP NWDI, the Design Time Repository (DTR) has the task of managing the versions of program sources in order to enable larger teams to work on the software development. Therefore, the DTR must be informed about the planned changes at the beginning of a development activity by creating an activity in which the change information is then stored. Afterwards, the program sources are checked out and changed in the local NWDS. As soon as the program changes have been completed, the sources are checked into the DTR again. Using the check-in mechanism of the DTR, the changes become active as soon as the activities are released and are then visible to all developers. By activating these changes in the second step, they are then rebuilt so that the sources (libraries) become visible for all other developers and additional development components that use them.

The DTR basically consists of two parts—the DTR clients and the DTR server. The main activities of the individual developers like check-in and check-out, as well as the correction of sources, take place in the NWDS. The DTR server handles file versioning. The various resources are accessed in the context of a workspace, and the versions are administered in the context of the activities. Therefore, a workspace references a set of resources, each in exactly one version. Alternatively, one resource can be referenced in several workspaces. For the Employee Self Serive (ESS) example, this means that ESS_DEV can be referenced with MSS_CONS. Since the files in a workspace form a software component, every workspace corresponds to the status of the sources for this software component.

When a versioned resource is changed or deleted, a new version is created for this resource. Every resource version created in a workspace receives a unique number. This consecutive number reflects the order in which the versions were created in the workspace. The DTR shows the relationship between the individual versions of a versioned resource as a version graphic. Changed sources are always checked into the inactive workspace of the DTR. Both the inactive and the active workspace show a version of the files which are stored in the DTR.

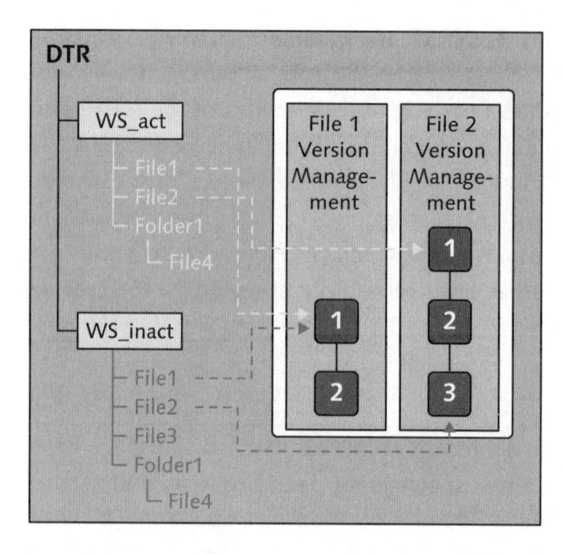


**DTR Workspace**

- Logical Development Location (Virtual Repository)
- Used for a status of a software component (e.g. different workspaces for Web AS Java 6.40 SP 9 DEV, Web AS 6.40 SP7 CONS etc.)
- Each workspace contains separate
  - current versions
  - version management
  - activities (change lists)
- Versions of a workspace can be integrated into other workspaces.

**Figure 18.20** Structure of the Design Time Repository (DTR)

**Example**

Figure 18.20 shows that File 2 has been modified several times already. After the last change, Version 3 was generated during the check-in. However, the changes were last activated with Version 1 so that the active workspace shows this version.

After the check-in, the changes carried out are available to other developers as well. When required, development components are checked out; the active versions of the development components are always transferred to the local PC when the inactive versions of a developer's own development components are checked out.

The DTR client functions are only necessary for administrative activities like sync-to-date, defining the ACLs, and deleting software components from the NWDS.

### Activation in the CBS, Central Deployment, and Central Test

After the resources have been checked into the inactive workspace, the application is activated in the next step. After a build has been completely carried out for the first time, and since the SAP NetWeaver Development Infrastructure is based on the component model, only the changes to the sources and to the dependent development components need to be carried out (incremental build), which will then be processed much faster. During the activation, which is started from the NWDS, the request for a build is sent first to the CBS. The CBS then tries to create a central build using the selected sources.

The result of this activation is that runtime objects are now available. If the activation was successful, the build space of the changed software component is filled with the generated archives, and the active workspace in the DTR shows the current file version as well. This process ensures that the active workspace in the DTR contains only sources of successful builds and that the active workspace is always synchronized with the build space. Build spaces always contain the appropriate version of the software components of a development configuration so that there is always a consistent development environment available for developments in larger groups. After a successful activation, if the system is set up accordingly, the application can be deployed automatically in the central development system of the used track. There, it can be tested in its interaction with successfully activated applications from other development teams.

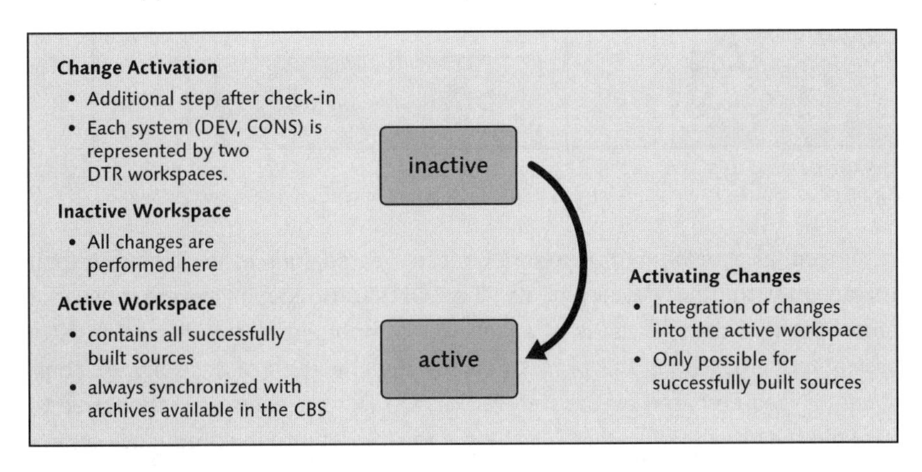


**Figure 18.21** Interaction between the Component Build Service (CBS) and the Design Time Repository (DTR)

### Release of Changes to the Consolidation System

As soon as the development is completed, and the developers involved have checked in their sources and tested them in the central development system, the changes carried out can be released for transport to the consolidation system. This is comparable to the release of change requests in the development system of an ABAP system. Contrary to ABAP, however, here, the transport requests are not written to an import buffer on the file system but are stored sequentially in the NWDI database.

## 18.7 Transporting Java Projects

After the developments have been successfully tested and released in the central development system, they are transported to the subsequent systems. This process is controlled by the CMS. A track contains the development configuration, as well as the corresponding runtime systems for the various development statuses of the software components, and, by default, consists of a four-system landscape.

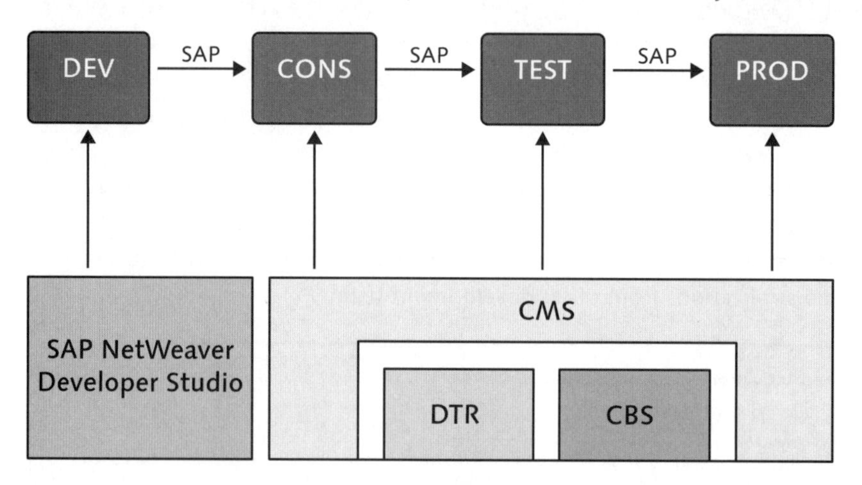


**Figure 18.22** Four-system landscape as a standard development environment for Java

In the central development system DEV, the created sources are tested in their interaction with other developments. The CONS consolidation system is used for consolidating a specific status of a software component and additional tests of this component. During this process, an additional version of this software component is created based on the status in CONS. This new version is then used to carry out the integration test in TEST before the import into the productive system PROD finally takes place.

These four system roles can be assigned to specific runtime systems into which the deployment is automatically effected during the import, and which enable testing the software component versions in their corresponding development status. Figure 18.23 illustrates this path of transport steps in a track.

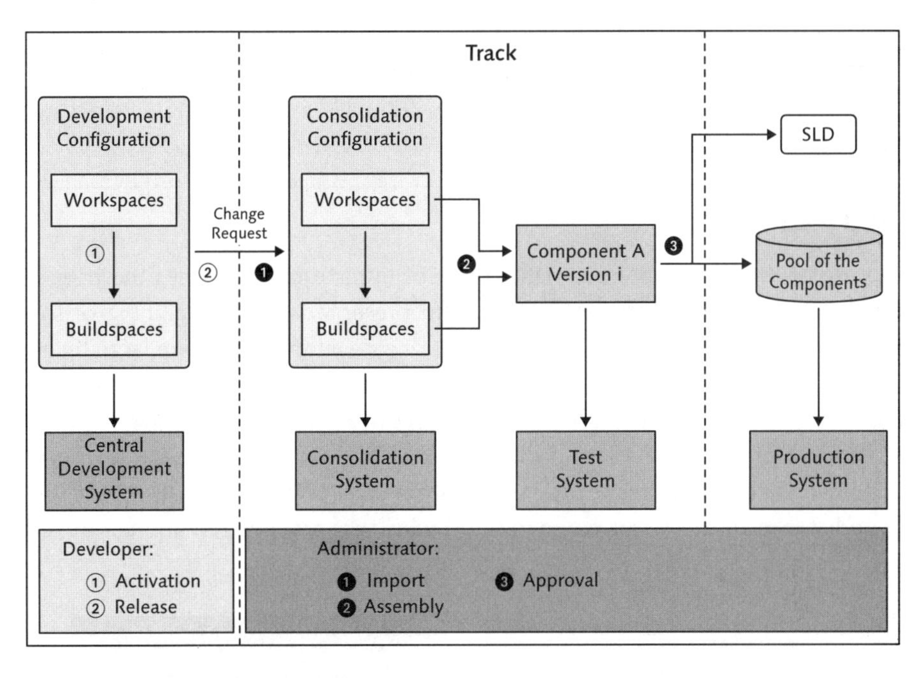


**Figure 18.23** Overview of transports within a track

**Example**

After the newly created or changed sources have been checked in, the developer can transfer the changes to the Component Build Service (Developer, Step 1). The CBS tries to reinterpret all components that are directly or indirectly affected by these changes. If this can be carried out without problems, the changes are accepted and the results of all developers of the same development configuration are made available in the form of archives or libraries. If the activation and the developer test were successful, the developers release their activities in the NWDS and transfer the changes to the CMS (Developer, Step 2). All activities selected by the developer are then summarized in a change request and placed in the import queue of the consolidation system.

With the import into the consolidation system (Administrator, Step 1), the system administrator integrates the released changes into the DTR workspace of the consolidation system and the CBS automatically compiles the changed software components. After testing the application functions, the CMS creates a new version of the application based on the status in the consolidation system (assembly) and prepares it for further transport to the test system (Administrator, Step 2). After the subsequent import into the test system and the integration test taking place therein, the quality manager can approve the transport of the software components to the productive system (Administrator, Step 3).

## 18.8 Summary

The use of the SAP NetWeaver Development Infrastructure reduces the risks of the Java development process, which were presented at the beginning of this chapter and which can occur most often during development where large teams are involved. The reason is that the operations that can lead to inconsistencies in the development process, like obsolete libraries or archives, are improved by controlling the processes centrally. With the centrally available build service, a new build can be created simply on demand from the NWDS. This can reduce the periods for resolving errors compared to builds that are initiated and controlled only centrally.

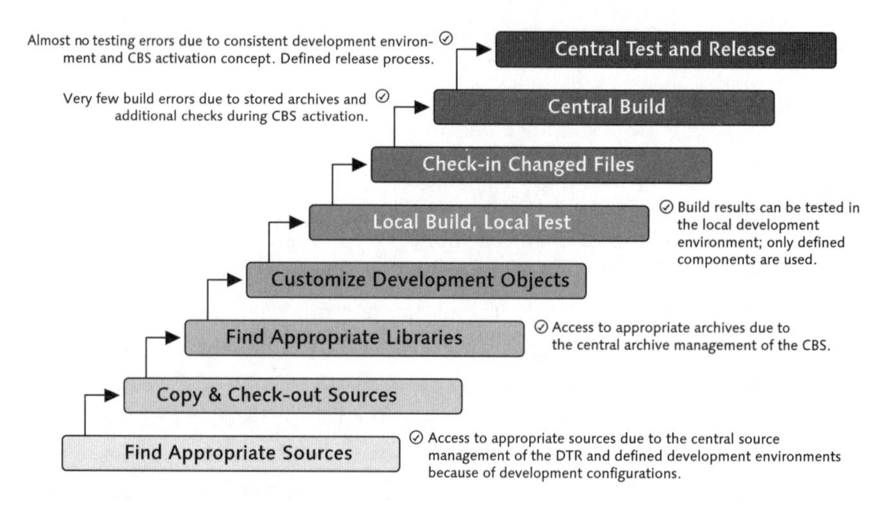


**Figure 18.24** Benefits of using the SAP NetWeaver Development Infrastructure

## 18.9 Questions

1. Which of the following statements about the NetWeaver Development Infrastructure (NWDI) are correct?
   - A. It consists of several coordinated tools for designing, developing, and testing Java programs.
   - B. It can be used both as a local and a central development environment.
   - C. It is not suitable for teams with several developers.
   - D. It is not suitable for transporting ABAP and Java components.
2. Which functions are fulfilled by the SAP Design Time Repository (DTR)?
   - A. The DTR takes care of the central storage, versioning, and management of Java sources.
   - B. The DTR provides automated conflict verifications.
   - C. The DTR can also store Word files.
   - D. The DTR manages archives that are required for software development.
3. Which functions are fulfilled by the SAP System Landscape Directory (SLD)?
   - A. It is a tool for the central user management.
   - B. It stores information about the system landscape.
   - C. It works like a central data cache.
   - D. It stores version information about the installed software components.
4. Which of the following services are required for Java transports?
   - A. Java Activation Framework (JAF)
   - B. Design Time Repository (DTR)
   - C. Component Build Service (CBS)
   - D. Change Management Service (CMS)
   - E. Enterprise Information System (EIS)

# A Creating RFC Destinations

In an SAP environment, you can use the Remote Function Call (RFC) interface system to call function modules in the same or different computer systems. RFCs allow communication between two SAP Systems—R/3, R/2, Business Information Warehouse (BW), or Advanced Planner and Optimizer (APO)—or between an SAP System and a non-SAP system.

RFCs are mentioned in this book in the following contexts:

- Remote client copies between two different clients
- Client comparisons using the Cross-System Viewer
- Communication between the Transport Management System (TMS) and the transport control program `tp`

Since the TMS is designed to communicate with the operating system level through a predefined TCP/IP connection, you do not have to manually define the RFC destination. However, to perform a remote client copy or compare two different clients, you must create the required RFC destinations. These procedures require an RFC destination originating from the target client (where you initiate the remote client copy and client comparison) and connecting to a source client.

To create an RFC destination for a remote client copy or a client comparison:

1. Log on to the target R/3 client.
2. Display existing RFC destinations by calling Transaction SM59 or, from the R/3 initial screen, by choosing **Tools · Administration · Administration · Network · RFC destinations**. A tree structure shows the different connection types, such as R/3 connections or TCP/IP connections, and all existing destinations.
3. Create a new RFC destination by choosing **Create**.
4. Provide the following information:
   - In the field **RFC destination**, enter a unique name, which should include the system ID and client number of the source R/3 client.
   - In the field **Connection type**, enter **3** to indicate a connection with an R/3 System. This type of RFC destination is called an *R/3 Connection*.
   - In the field *Description*, enter a short text that describes the RFC destination.
5. To complete the creation of the R/3 Connection, enter the following information:
   - In the field **Target host**, enter the host name of the source R/3 System.
   - In the field **System number**, enter the system number of the source R/3 System.

6. Choose **Save**.
7. Test the RFC destination:
   - From the **RFC Destination** screen, choose **Test connection**. If the connection is successful, the table on the next screen displays the required connection times for logon. If the connection is not successful, an error message will be displayed on this screen. Errors result if the source system is down or if you have entered an invalid combination of host name and system number.
   - To test your ability to log on to the source client, from the **RFC Destination** screen, choose **Remote logon**. Since you have not provided logon information for the source system, you will not access that system directly. A logon screen will be displayed—you must log on to a client in this system in the usual way.

### Automatic Logon

You can set up RFC destinations with default logon information. For example, you can provide a default language and a default client number. Additionally, you can set up an automatic logon to the source client with a default username and password. This eliminates the need for the user to log on to the source client during a remote client copy or a client comparison. Such a default user requires the correct user authorizations to perform a remote client copy. (See Chapter 9 for more information on client copy user authorizations and Chapter 11 for information on Cross-System Viewer user authorizations.)

**Tip** To execute a remote client copy or a client compare in the background, the logon data defined in the RFC destination must include the username and password.

When you create an RFC destination that provides access to a client in an R/3 System without requiring logon, limit the user authorization of the username for the RFC destination. This prevents inappropriate activities, such as viewing or copying sensitive data.

**Note** For more information on maintaining RFC destinations, see R/3 online documentation.

# B Transport Profile Parameters

This section provides information on the different transport profile parameters used to support the delivery of change requests to import buffers and the import of change requests into R/3 Systems. Chapter 7 describes the configuration of the transport profile for R/3 Release 4.5 and prior releases. This section lists useful transport parameters and provides the following information for each:

- Name of the parameter
- Possible values
- The default value
- For which R/3 Releases the parameter is valid
- A description of the parameter

### abapntfmode

**Values**: t or b
**Default Value**: t
**R/3 Release Information**: As of R/3 Release 4.5

**Description**: This parameter is meaningful only if the transport control program `tp` is running on Windows NT platforms. The value of the parameter determines whether text files are opened in Unix compatibility mode. The Unix compatibility mode is necessary if a transport directory is shared between Unix and Windows NT application servers. When `abapntfmode` is set to "t", all text files are opened in normal Windows NT text mode. When `abapntfmode` is set to "b", all text files are opened in binary mode, which is compatible with Unix file formats.

### alllog

**Value**: Text
**Default Value**: ALOG$(syear)$(yweek)
**R/3 Release Information**: All

**Description**: The name of the log file in the transport directory `log` that lists all the `tp` single steps.

### Buffreset

**Value**: Boolean
**Default Value**: TRUE
**R/3 Release Information**: All

**Description**: The transport control program `tp` and `R3trans` reset all the buffers of the R/3 System so that all the application servers can react to changes in the database. Buffer synchronization takes several seconds until all the application servers have read the request to reset all buffers. You can set the repetition period for reading the synchronization requests with profile parameters for the R/3 System (`rdisp/bufreftime`). Although this buffer reset is by default turned on, you disable the buffer reset by `tp` when setting `buffreset` to FALSE.

**bufreftime**

**Value**: Integer
**Default Value**: 180
**R/3 Release Information**: All

**Description**: The value of this parameter specifies how long the transport control program `tp` should wait in seconds until it can assume that all the buffers of the R/3 System have been synchronized. The value of this parameter should correspond to the `rdisp/bufreftime` profile parameter of the R/3 System in question.

**c_import**

**Value**: Boolean
**Default Value**: FALSE
**R/3 Release Information**: All

**Description**: Allows or disallows the import of change requests that are the result of a relocation transport (change requests of type "c"). By default, all types of change requests can be imported. However, you can disallow the import of relocation transports (created using Transaction SE01) by setting the parameter `c_import` to TRUE.

**cofilelifetime**

**Value**: Integer
**Default Value**: 365
**R/3 Release Information**: All

**Description**: The number of days since a control file has been touched. A file in the transport directory **cofiles** is considered to be not needed if the corresponding change request is not in the import buffer for any R/3 System and has a time stamp that is older than the value set by the parameter `cofilelifetime`. If the file is no longer needed based on the criteria, a combination of the commands `tp check` and `tp clearold` will delete the file. You can set the minimum age of a control file in days using this parameter. Because a data file requires a control file for import, the value set by `cofilelifetime` should correspond to the value for `olddatalifetime`.

### ctc

**Value**: Boolean
**Default Value**: FALSE
**R/3 Release Information**: As of R/3 Release 4.5

**Description**: **ctc** stands for Client Transport Control, and when set to TRUE, it activates extended transport control, allowing you to specify client and system combinations in transport routes. Extended transport control requires a new import buffer format (the transport parameter `nbufform` is set to TRUE implicitly). This new buffer format is only supported beginning with `tp` version 264. As a result, you can set the new parameter *ctc* only if all the transport control programs that work with a specific R/3 System have at least version 264. Older `tp` versions destroy this new import buffer. To protect the new import buffer from being destroyed by older `tp` versions, set the value for transport parameter `tp_version` to at least 264.

### datalifetime

**Value**: Integer
**Default Value**: 200
**R/3 Release Information**: All

**Description**: The number of days since a data file has been touched. A file in the transport directory **data** is considered to be not needed if the corresponding change request is not in the import buffer for any R/3 System and has a time stamp that is older than the value set by the parameter `datalifetime`. The file is then moved to the transport directory `olddata` during a combination of the commands `tp check` and `tp clearold`. You can set the minimum age of a data file in days using this parameter.

### dbcodepage

**Values**: american_america.us7ascii or american_america.we8dec
**Default Value**: american_america.us7ascii
**R/3 Release Information**: As of R/3 Release 4.0

**Description**: The code page of the Oracle database instance. The Oracle databases are installed with the code page american_america.we8dec. In this case, you must enter the value american_america.we8dec in the transport profile. When upgrading a Release from 3.x or later to 4.x, the code page american_america.us7ascii is retained.

### dbconfpath

**Value**: Text
**Default Value**: $transdir
**R/3 Release Information**: All

**Description**: You can use this parameter to inform the transport control program `tp` where the configuration files for Oracle SQL*NET V2 are located. The default value $transdir mirrors the fact that SAP has already stored these files centrally in the transport directory. From this parameter, `tp` derives the value of the environment variables TNS_ADMIN. However, if the transport parameter `dbswpath` is set, the parameter `dbconfpath` is ignored.

### dbhost

**Value**: Text
**Default Value**: None
**R/3 Release Information**: All (no longer required as of R/3 Release 4.0)

**Description**: This parameter specifies the host name—the computer on which the database runs or (valid for Oracle and DB2 on AIX) on which the database processes run. For an Informix database, the host name is case sensitive. For MS SQL, the TCP/IP host name on which the database runs is used.

### dblibpath

**Value**: Text
**Default Value**: /usr/sap/$(system)/SYS/exe/run/ for Unix
**R/3 Release Information**: As of R/3 Release 4.5

**Description**: The directory in which the dynamic R/3 database interface is located. In the standard system, these files are always in the executable directory of the application server. Therefore, you do not have to change the default value. From the value of this parameter, `tp` derives the value of the environment variable `dir_Library`.

Under Windows NT, you have to enter the path to the dynamic R/3 interface only if it is not located in the environment variable path set under Windows NT. Otherwise, the DLL in the default path is searched for.

As of R/3 Release 4.5, `tp` sets this variable according to the value of the transport profile parameter `dbtype`.

### dblogicalname

**Value**: Text
**Default Value**: $dbname
**R/3 Release Information**: All

**Description**: Sets the logical name that identifies the database instance in an Oracle network.

### dbname

**Value**: Text
**Default Value**: $(system)
**R/3 Release Information**: All

**Description**: The name of the database instance. The standard installation uses the name of the R/3 System for the name of the database instance or the logical name of the database.

### dbswpath

**Value**: Text
**Default Value**: None
**R/3 Release Information**: As of R/3 Release 4.0

**Description**: The value of the directory in which the Oracle client software is installed. If the parameter is set, the transport control program `tp` derives the following environment variables in a Unix environment:

- Oracle_HOME = $(dbswpath)
- TNS_ADMIN = $(dbswpath)/network/admin (on Unix)
- ORA_NLS = $(dbswpath)/ocommon/nls/admin/data (on Unix)
- ORA_NLS32 = $(dbswpath)/ocommon/nls32/admin/data (on Unix)
- ORA_NLS33 = $(dbswpath)/ocommon/nls33/admin/data (on Unix)

Note that the environment variables ORA_NLS, ORA_NLS32, and ORA_NLS33 are no longer set with R/3 Release 4.6.

### dbtype

**Values**: ora, ada, db2, db4, db6, inf, or mss
**Default Value**: The R/3 System's database type
**R/3 Release Information**: All (described here as of R/3 Release 4.5)

**Description**: Used to set the environment variable *dbms_type*. This variable has to be set correctly to be able to load the correct shared dbsl-library.

### dummy

**Value**: Boolean
**Default Value**: FALSE
**R/3 Release Information**: All

**Description**: You can use this parameter to make a dummy system, such as a virtual system, known in the transport profile. Imports are not performed for an R/3 System with the parameter `dummy` set to TRUE, but an import buffer for the system will be maintained. With R/3 Release 4.5, for example, the entry that sets the `dummy` value to TRUE is automatically added to the transport profile for all virtual systems. In releases prior to R/3 Release 4.5, if you create a virtual system—for example, the system TST—you will need to make the entry `TST/dummy=TRUE` in the file `TPPARAM`.

### informix_server

**Value**: Text
**Default Value**: $(dbhost)$(dbname)shm
**R/3 Release Information**: All

**Description**: The Informix database server name for a local connection.

### informix_serveralias

**Value**: Text
**Default Value**: $(dbhost)$(dbname)tcp
**R/3 Release Information**: All

**Description**: The Informix database server name for a remote connection.

### informixdir

**Value**: Text
**Default Value**: /informix/<SID>
**R/3 Release Information**: All

**Description**: The directory name where the Informix database software is located.

### informixsqlhost

**Value**: Text
**Default Value**: $(informixdir)/etc/sqlhosts[.tli|.soc]
**R/3 Release Information**: All

**Description**: This parameter is used to specify the complete path and name of the SQL host's file for an Informix database.

### k_import

**Value**: Boolean
**Default Value**: FALSE
**R/3 Release Information**: All

**Description**: Allows or disallows the import of Workbench change requests (change requests of type "k"). By default, all types of change requests can be imported. However, you can disallow the import of Workbench change requests by setting the parameter `k_import` to TRUE.

### language

**Value**: Text
**Default Value**: None
**R/3 Release Information**: All

**Description**: The value passed to `R3trans` to indicate what languages are to be exported. By default, this parameter is empty; therefore, `R3trans` exports language-dependent data from all the languages that it can find—in other words, all languages installed in the R/3 System. If the parameter `language` is transferred, `R3trans` tries to export the languages specified in this text. A single letter identifies each language. You can specify several languages by entering a sequence of letters. Note that the transport parameter `lsm` is used with the parameter `language` beginning with R/3 Release 3.1G.

### loglifetime

**Value**: Integer
**Default Value**: 200
**R/3 Release Information**: All

**Description**: The number of days since a log file has been touched. A file in the transport directory `log` is considered to be not needed if the corresponding change request is not in the import buffer for any R/3 System and has a time stamp that is older than the value set by the parameter `loglifetime`. If the file is no longer needed based on the criteria, a combination of the commands `tp check` and `tp clearold` will delete the log file. You can set the minimum age of a log file in days using this parameter.

### lsm

**Values**: MASTER, VECTOR, TRANSLATION, NOMASTER, or VECTORANDMASTER
**Default Value**: VECTOR
**R/3 Release Information**: As of R/3 Release 3.1G

**Description**: The language selection mode parameter. If this parameter is not set and the default value VECTOR is used, `R3trans` will export language-dependent data from the languages defined by the transport parameter `language`. If the language parameter is empty, all language-dependent data is exported. The other parameters for *lsm* behave as follows:

- MASTER:
  The "master" language for a Repository object is also known as its original language—that is, the language in which the object was created or maintained. In this mode, the language-dependent data for the master language only is exported, and all other translated texts are ignored.
- NOMASTER:
  In this mode, only translated text is exported—that is, all text maintained in languages other than the object's original language.
- TRANSLATION:
  In this mode, only translated text is exported for the languages defined by the parameter *language*.
- VECTORANDMASTER:
  In this mode, all text maintained for an object's original language and all text for the languages defined by the parameter *language* are exported.

### mssql_passwd

**Value**: Text
**Default Value**: None
**R/3 Release Information**: All

**Description**: The password for a user in the MS SQL database. This is used in conjunction with the parameter *mssql_user*.

### mssql_user

**Value**: Text
**Default Value**: None
**R/3 Release Information**: All

**Description**: The username for a connection to the MS SQL database. This information, in combination with `mssql_passwd`, allows for access to an MS SQL database using a unique user and password rather than the default user and password.

### nbufform

**Value**: Boolean
**Default Value**: FALSE
**R/3 Release Information**: As of R/3 Release 4.5

**Description**: Transport request names in newer R/3 Releases may have a length of 20 characters. However, these transport requests cannot be processed in the previous format of the import buffer. The parameter `nbufform` is set to TRUE implicitly when you set the parameter `ctc` to TRUE. As with parameter `ctc`, you have to protect this change to the import buffer format from transport control programs that use the old import buffer format. The new format of the import buffer requires at least a `tp` version of 264. Older `tp` versions destroy this new import buffer. Therefore, when parameter `nbufform` is activated, set the value for the transport profile parameter `tp_version` to at least 264.

**new_sapnames**

**Value**: Boolean
**Default Value**: FALSE
**R/3 Release Information**: All

**Description**: A file is created in the transport directory **sapnames** for each user of an R/3 System in the transport group. By default, the file corresponds to the user's name. However, usernames in the R/3 System may not be valid filenames at the operating system level. For example, a certain length of username or the use of special characters such as a space or a period may not be permissible as filenames and could cause problems. As a solution, the usernames can be modified to create filenames that are valid in all operating systems. The real username is stored in the corresponding file. Setting the parameter `new_sapnames` to TRUE activates this. Once this parameter is set to TRUE, you should not set it to FALSE (unless you also delete all the files in the transport directory *sapnames*).

**olddatalifetime**

**Value**: Integer
**Default Value**: 365
**R/3 Release Information**: All

**Description**: A combination of the commands `tp check` and `tp clearold` move data files from the transport directory **data** to the transport directory **olddata** based on the parameter `datalifetime`. These commands also delete any data files in the **olddata** transport directory whose time stamp is older than the value set by `olddatalifetime`. You can set the minimum age of a data file in days using this parameter. Note that the minimum age refers to the date the file was created and not to the date on which the file was copied to the directory **olddata**. Therefore, the value for `olddatalifetime` should be greater than the value for `datalifetime`.

### opticonnect

**Value**: Boolean
**Default Value**: FALSE
**R/3 Release Information**: All

**Description**: Required to be TRUE for a DB2 database environment when Opticonnect is installed.

### r3transpath

**Value**: Text
**Default Value**: R3trans for Unix and AS/400 and R3trans.exe for Windows NT
**R/3 Release Information**: All

**Description**: This parameter is used to pass the complete name of the program `R3trans` to the transport control program `tp`. The default value is not a complete path specification. The operating system and the settings of the operating system are used to find the correct value. If this is not case, you can provide the complete path to `R3trans`.

### recclient

**Values**: ALL, OFF, or list of client values separated by a comma
**Default Value**: OFF
**R/3 Release Information**: All

**Description**: Activates the recording of changes to Customizing settings during import for either ALL clients or the clients listed. By default, recording of imported Customizing settings does not take place. The value of this parameter should correspond to the value of the R/3 System's profile parameter `rec/client`.

### repeatonerror

**Values**: 0, 8, or 9
**Default Value**: 9
**R/3 Release Information**: All

**Description**: After successful import, a change request is typically removed from the import buffer (unless a special import option is used to keep the change request in the buffer after import). The parameter `repeatonerror` defines the criteria for a successful import. It specifies the return code up to which a change request is considered successfully processed. Return codes less than the value defined for `repeatonerror` are accepted as successful. Change requests that result in a return code greater than or equal to the value of `repeatonerror` are not removed from the import buffer because they have not been successfully processed.

### sourcesystems

**Value**: Text
**Default Value**: None
**R/3 Release Information**: All

**Description**: A list of R/3 System names separated by a common. This list defines the R/3 System from which change requests have originated that can then be imported. By default, this value is empty; therefore, change requests from any R/3 System can be imported. However, if the transport parameter has been defined, only those change requests whose source system is listed can be imported. This parameter is useful for protecting an R/3 System's import process.

### stopimmediately

**Value**: Boolean
**Default Value**: FALSE (as of R/3 Release 4.6, the default value will be TRUE)
**R/3 Release Information**: As of R/3 Release 4.5

**Description**: By default, the transport control program `tp` stops at the end of an import step if an error occurred during that import step. When this parameter is set to TRUE, `tp` reacts to errors immediately following the error rather than at the end of the import step. For example, if `stoponerror` is set to 9 and one change request gets an error 12, with `stopimmediately` set to TRUE, the import process stops immediately after the errant change request. If `stopimmediately` is set to FALSE, the main import step is completed for all change requests before *tp* reports an error from the one change request.

### stoponerror

**Values**: 0, 8, and 9
**Default Value**: 9
**R/3 Release Information**: All

**Description**: The maximum return code `tp checks` for at the completion of every transport step. If the return code is equal to or greater than the value set, the import process is stopped. For example, if the DDIC transport step results in return code 8 (indicating an error), the default value of `stoponerror` will not cause `tp` to end the import process. However, if `stoponerror` is set to the value 8, a return code of 8 will cause the import process to stop. If `stoponerror` is set to zero, `tp` is never stopped.

### syslog

**Value**: Text
**Default Value**: SLOG$(syear)$(yweek).$(system)
**R/3 Release Information**: All

**Description**: The name of the log file in the transport directory `log` that lists all the `tp` import activities for a specific R/3 System.

### t_import

**Value**: Boolean
**Default Value**: FALSE
**R/3 Release Information**: All

**Description**: Allows or disallows the import of change requests that result from a transport of copies (change requests of type "t"). By default, all types of change requests can be imported. However, you can disallow the import of the transport of copies (created using Transaction SE01) by setting the parameter `t_import` to TRUE.

### testimport

**Value**: Boolean
**Default Value**: TRUE (as of R/3 Release 4.6, the default value will be FALSE)
**R/3 Release Information**: All

**Description**: By default, after export of a change request, the transport control program `tp` performs a test import, testing whether the Repository objects in the change request may generate errors upon import into the target system. From time to time, the test import into the target system is not possible—for example, when the target system is not running R/3 or is nonexistent, as in the case of a virtual system. Setting `testimport` to FALSE for the source system can turn off the test import. For example, to turn off test imports for all change requests exported from the development system, you must set `testimport` to FALSE for the development system.

### testsystems

**Value**: Text
**Default Value**: None
**R/3 Release Information**: All

**Description**: You can define a list of R/3 System names (up to 50). Commas must separate the names. If the export of a change request is successful, the transport control program `tp` adds the change request to the import buffer for the change request's defined target system as well as any R/3 Systems defined by `testsystems` for that target system. For example, typically, all change requests released from the development system have a target system defined as the quality assurance system. Release and export of such a change request causes the change request to be added to the import buffer of QAS. If the parameter `testsystems` is set to TST, the change request is also added to the import buffer for the R/3 System TST.

### tp_version

**Value**: Integer
**Default Value**: None
**R/3 Release Information**: All

**Description**: This parameter sets the oldest version of `tp` that can be used to perform `tp` commands on an import buffer. Any `tp` version equal to or greater than this version can be used. This parameter does not usually need to be set—except when the parameter for `ctc` or `nbufform` is TRUE. In such a situation, the `tp_version` needs to be set to at least 264. This ensures that older `tp` versions do not destroy import buffers using a new import buffer format.

### transdir

**Value**: Text
**Default Value**: None
**R/3 Release Information**: All

**Description**: The path to the root of the transport directory. This parameter is required and therefore must be set. For example, `transdir` is often set to /usr/sap/trans/ for a Unix environment.

### vers_at_imp

**Values**: NEVER, C_ONLY, or ALWAYS
**Default Value**: NEVER
**R/3 Release Information**: As of R/3 Release 4.5

**Description**: Normally, versions for Repository objects exist only on the source system—that is, where the object is changed. During the transport of a new source, no version is created in the import system. However, customers often need to have a detailed storage of all versions in either their quality assurance or their production systems so that if these systems are copied or upgraded, version history can be maintained. If you set the parameter to either C_ONLY or ALWAYS, additional steps are started during the import that generate versions of the imported objects in the target system. Prior to the import of the ABAP Dictionary objects, the change request's command file is imported, and a version of all objects listed in the command file is added to the target system's version database.

Versions are created only if the current version of the object is not the same as the latest version in the database, or if a version does not yet exist for the object in the version database. Although the value ALWAYS activates versions at import for all objects, the value C_ONLY creates versions of objects only when the change request to be imported is a relocation transport (with or without development class and transport layer change). Relocation transports are created and released using the Transport Organizer (Transaction SE01).

### w_import

**Value**: Boolean
**Default Value**: FALSE
**R/3 Release Information**: All

**Description**: Allows or disallows the import of Customizing change requests (change requests of type "w"). By default, all types of change requests can be imported. However, you can disallow the import of Customizing change requests by setting the parameter `w_import` to TRUE.

# C Selected Transaction Codes

Table C.1 lists the most important R/3 Transaction codes for the support of change and transport management in the R/3 System. You can enter R/3 Transaction codes in the command field of an R/3 screen in the following ways:

- /n<Transaction code>

  Entering the Transaction code in this way exits the current R/3 screen and displays the initial screen of the Transaction.

- /o<Transaction code>

  Entering the Transaction code in this way sends the current user session to the background and creates a new user session to display the initial screen of the Transaction.

| Code | Description |
|---|---|
| AL11 | Display SAP directories |
| AL12 | Buffer Synchronization |
| BALE | ALE Administration and Monitoring |
| DB02 | Analyze tables and indexes (missing database objects and space requirements) |
| OSS1 | Log on to SAPNet—R/3 Frontend Services (formerly known as SAP's Online Service System) |
| PFCG | Profile Generator: Maintain Activity Groups |
| RZ01 | Job Scheduling Monitor |
| RZ10 | Maintain Profile Parameters |
| RZ20 | Alert Monitor |
| RZ21 | Customizing the Alert Monitor |
| S001 | ABAP Workbench |
| SADJ | Transfer Assistant |
| SALE | ALE IMG activities |
| SARA | Archive Administration |
| SB09 | Business Navigator |
| SCAT | CATT |
| SCC1 | Client Copy Per Transport Request |

**Table C.1** Transaction codes used for change and transport management

| Code | Description |
|---|---|
| SCC3 | Client Copy Logs |
| SCC4 | Client Administration |
| SCC5 | Client Delete |
| SCC7 | Client Import— post-processing |
| SCC8 | Client Export |
| SCC9 | Remote Client Copy |
| SCCL | Local Client Copy |
| SCMP | Individual View/Table Comparison |
| SCPR2 | Business Configuration Sets (R/3 Release 4.5) |
| SCU0 | Customizing Cross-System Viewer |
| SCU3 | Table History |
| SCUM | Central User Administration |
| SE01 | Transport Organizer |
| SE03 | Workbench Organizer: Tools |
| SE06 | Processing after Installation for CTO |
| SE09 | Workbench Organizer |
| SE10 | Customizing Organizer |
| SE11 | ABAP Data Dictionary Maintenance |
| SE12 | ABAP Data Dictionary Display |
| SE13 | Maintain Technical Settings for Tables |
| SE14 | Utilities for Dictionary Tables |
| SE15 | Repository Information System |
| SE16 | Display Table Content |
| SE17 | General Table Display |
| SE37 | Function Builder |
| SE38 | ABAP Editor |
| SE41 | Menu Painter |
| SE51 | Screen Painter |
| SE71 | SAPscript forms |

**Table C.1** Transaction codes used for change and transport management

| Code | Description |
| --- | --- |
| SE72 | SAPscript styles |
| SE80 | Repository Browser |
| SE93 | Maintain Transaction Codes |
| SE95 | Modification Browser |
| SLIN | ABAP Extended Program Check |
| SM02 | System Messages |
| SM04 | User Overview |
| SM12 | Display and delete R/3 enqueues |
| SM13 | Display update requests and resolve errors |
| SM21 | System Log |
| SM28 | Installation Check |
| SM30 | Table/View Maintenance |
| SM31 | Table Maintenance |
| SM35 | Batch Input Monitoring |
| SM36 | Schedule Background Jobs |
| SM37 | Background Job Overview |
| SM39 | Job Analysis |
| SM49 | Execute external operating system commands |
| SM50 | Work Process Overview |
| SM51 | Instance Overview |
| SM56 | Reset or check the number range buffer |
| SM58 | Error Log for Asynchronous RFC |
| SM59 | Display or Maintain RFC Destinations |
| SM63 | Display and Maintain Operation Modes |
| SM64 | Trigger an Event |
| SM65 | Analysis Tool for Background Processing |
| SM66 | Global Work Process Overview |
| SM69 | Maintain External Operating System Commands |
| SMLG | Maintain Assignments of Logon Groups to Instances |

**Table C.1** Transaction codes used for change and transport management

| Code | Description |
|---|---|
| SMLI | Language Import Utility |
| SMLT | Language Transport Utility |
| SMOD | SAP Enhancement Management |
| SNRO | Maintain number range objects |
| SO99 | Upgrade Information System |
| SOBJ | Attribute Maintenance Objects |
| SPAM | SAP Package Manager (SPAM) |
| SPAU | Display Modified Objects in the Runtime Environment |
| SPDD | Display Modified DDIC Objects |
| SPRO | Customizing from within the IMG |
| SPRP | Start IMG Project Administration |
| ST02 | Statistics of the R/3 Buffer |
| ST03 | Workload Monitor |
| ST04 | Database Performance Monitor |
| ST06 | Operating System Monitor |
| ST08 | Network Monitor |
| ST09 | Network Alert Monitor |
| STEM | CATT Utilities |
| STMS | Transport Management System |
| SU01 | Maintain Users |
| SU01D | Display Users |
| SU02 | Maintain Authorization Profiles |
| SU03 | Maintain Authorizations |
| SU05 | Maintain Internet Users |
| SU10 | Mass Changes to User Master Records |
| SU12 | Mass Delete of User Master Records |
| SU20 | Maintain Authorization Fields |
| SU21 | Maintain Authorization Objects |
| SU22 | Authorization Object Usage in Transactions |

**Table C.1** Transaction codes used for change and transport management

| Code | Description |
| --- | --- |
| SU26 | Adjust Authorization Checks |
| SU3 | Maintain Own User Data |
| SU30 | Full Authorization Check |
| SU56 | Analyze User Buffer |
| SUPC | Profiles for Activity Groups |
| SUPF | Integrated User Maintenance |
| SUPO | Maintain Organization Levels |

**Table C.1** Transaction codes used for change and transport management

# D Glossary

**ABAP** Advanced Business Application Programming. Programming language of the R/3 System.

**ABAP Dictionary** Central storage facility containing metadata (data about data) for all objects in the R/3 System. The ABAP Dictionary describes the logical structure of application development objects and their representation in the structures of the underlying relational database. All runtime environment components such as application programs or the database interface get information about these objects from the ABAP Dictionary. The ABAP Dictionary is an active data dictionary and is fully integrated into the ABAP Workbench.

**ABAP Editor** ABAP Workbench tool for developing and maintaining ABAP programs, function modules, screen flow logic, type groups, and logical databases. Besides normal text operations (such as insert, search, and replace), the ABAP Editor offers several special functions to support program development.

**ABAP Workbench** SAP's integrated graphical programming environment. The ABAP Workbench supports the development of and changes to R/3 client/server applications written in ABAP. You can use the tools of the ABAP Workbench to write ABAP code, design screens, create user interfaces, use predefined functions, get access to database information, control access to development objects, test applications for efficiency, and debug applications.

**activation** Process that makes a runtime object available. The effect of activation is to generate runtime objects, which are accessed by application programs and screen templates.

**activity group** Subset of actions from the set of actions that were defined in the Enterprise IMG. From the activity group, you can use the Profile Generator to generate the authorizations needed by R/3 users for these actions.

**Add-On Patch** Support Packages that are component patches for add-on software. They are specific to an add-on of a particular R/3 Release. They contain corrections for only the specific add-on.

**ADO** Application defined object.

**ALE** Application Link Enabling. ALE is a technology for building and operating distributed applications. The basic purpose of ALE is to ensure a distributed, but integrated, R/3 installation. It comprises a controlled business message exchange with consistent data storage in nonpermanently connected SAP applications. Applications are integrated not through a central database, but through synchronous and asynchronous communication.
ALE consists of three layers:

- Application services
- Distribution services
- Communication services

**ALE Customizing Distribution** Process that enables you to ensure that the Customizing settings related to ALE scenarios are identical on the different R/3 Systems in the system landscape.

**Alert Monitor** A tool that enables you to monitor all actions that have been performed with TMS and that draws your attention to critical information.

**API** Application Programming Interface. Software package used by an application program to call a service provided by the operating system—for example, to open a file.

**application data** Client-specific data that comprises master data and business transactional data.

**application server** A computer on which at least one R/3 instance runs.

**ArchiveLink** Integrated into the Basis component of the R/3 System, a communications interface between the R/3 applications and external components. ArchiveLink has the following interfaces: user interface, interface to the R/3 applications, and interface to external components (archive systems, viewer systems, and scan systems).

**archiving object** A logical object comprising related business data in the database that is read from the database using an archiving program. After it has been successfully archived, a logical object can be deleted by a specially generated deleting program.

**ASAP** AcceleratedSAP. Standardized procedural model to implement R/3.

**automatic recording of changes** Client change option that permits changes to the Customizing settings of the client and requires these changes to be automatically recorded to change requests.

**background processing** Processing that does not take place on the screen. Data is processed in the background, while other functions can be executed in parallel on the screen. Although the background processes are not visible for a user and are run without user intervention (there is no dialog), they have the same priority as online processes.

**backup domain controller** R/3 System that can assume the functions of the transport domain controller if it fails.

**BAPI** Business Application Programming Interface. Standardized programming interface that provides external access to business processes and data in the R/3 System.

**batch input** Method and tools for rapid import of data from sequential files into the R/3 database.

**Business Configuration Sets** A preserved snapshot of Customizing settings that can be used for comparison with the Customizing Cross-System Viewer. Business Configuration Sets can be created as of R/3 Release 4.5.

**business integration testing** Testing of a chain of business processes that form part of the same workflow and the relevant cross-functional boundaries. Integration testing also involves outputs, interfaces, procedures, organizational design, and security profiles, and focuses on likely business events and high-impact exceptions.

**button** Element of the graphical user interface. Click a button to execute the button's function. You can select buttons using the keyboard as well as the mouse. Place the button cursor on the button and select Enter or choose the Enter button. Buttons can contain text or graphical symbols.

**CATT** Computer Aided Test Tool. You can use this tool to generate test data, and automate and test business processes.

**CCMS** Computing Center Management System. Tools for monitoring, controlling, and configuring the R/3 System. The CCMS supports 24-hour system administration functions from within the R/3 System. You can analyze the system load and monitor the distributed resource usage of the system components.

**Change and Transport Organizers (CTO)** The Organizers in the R/3 System for managing change requests as a result of development efforts in the ABAP Workbench and Customizing activities in the IMG. It comprises the Workbench Organizer, the Customizing Organizer, and the Transport Organizer.

**Change and Transport System (CTS)** Tools used to manage changes and development in the R/3 System and their transport to other R/3 Systems. It comprises the Change and Transport Organizers, the Transport Management System, and the operating system level programs *tp* and *R3trans*.

**change management** The handling of changes to software and their distribution to various environments. These changes may be required by changes in the way an enterprise does business. From a technical perspective, change management is the process by which changes made to one R/3 System are distributed to one or more R/3 Systems in a consistent and timely manner after appropriate testing and verification to ensure a stable and predictable production environment.

**change request** Information source in the Workbench Organizer and Customizing Organizer that records and manages all changes made to R/3 Repository objects and Customizing settings during an R/3 implementation project.

**client** From a commercial law, organizational, and technical viewpoint, a closed unit within an R/3 System with separate master records within a table.

**client compare** Determining the differences in Customizing settings between two R/3 clients.

**client copy** Function that allows you to copy a client in the same R/3 System (a local client copy) or to another R/3 System (a remote client copy). Client copy profiles determine what will be copied: Customizing data, business application data, and/or user master records.

**client copy according to a transp. request** Functionality with which you can transport client-dependent objects of either a change request or a task between clients in the same R/3 System.

**client copy profile** A profile that enables you to copy certain data (e.g., Customizing data, application data, or user master records) from a client into another client. SAP provides all possible profiles and requires that you select the appropriate one for what you need to copy from one client to another.

**client settings** During client maintenance, options exist to determine whether client-dependent and client-independent changes can occur, and whether recording of those changes is automatic. You can also define the client's role, and set additional restrictions and protection for the client. The system administrator should consciously decide the appropriate client settings for all clients in the system landscape.

**client transport** Functionality with which you can copy the contents of one client to another client in a different R/3 System by performing first a client export and then a client import.

**client-dependent** Specific only to one client. Settings in client-dependent tables relate only to the client that was accessed during the logon process. Such tables contain the client number in the table's primary key.

**client-independent** Relevant for all clients in an R/3 System. Client-independent is synonymous with cross-client.

**client-specific transport route** A transport route that consolidates or delivers to an R/3 System and client combination rather than simply an R/3 System. Client-specific transport routes are available with extended transport control in R/3 Release 4.5.

**Conflict Resolution Transport (CRT)** A type of Support Package exclusively used for R/3 add-ons such as industry solutions—for example, IS-OIL. They are designed to resolve conflicts that can occur between either a Hot Package or a Legal Change Patch and the add-on.

**consolidation route** Regular transport route of an R/3 Repository object from the integration system to the consolidation system. The consolidation route is specified for each R/3 Repository object by the transport layer for the object's development class.

**consolidation system** System in the system landscape to which change requests are exported as defined by a consolidation route. The consolidation system in a three-system landscape is the quality assurance system and, in the case of a two-system landscape, the production system.

**control file** List of required import steps for each released and exported change request. All command files are saved to the transport directory **cofiles**.

**Control Panel** Central tool for monitoring the R/3 System and its instances.

**Controlled Availability (CA)** Related to phase FCP in the R/3 Release Strategy. In this phase, a new R/3 Functional Release is available. R/3 Functional Releases are available only for a limited number of customers.

**Correction R/3 Release** Corrections used primarily to support the continuous improvement of software quality rather than introduce new functionality are collected together in Correction Releases. SAP provides Support Packages for Correction Releases that correct several types of software errors. SAP recommends a Correction R/3 Release for production activities.

**CPI-C** Common Programming Interface-Communication. Programming interface—the basis for synchronous, system-to-system, program-to-program communication.

**cross-client** Relevant for all clients in an R/3 System. Cross-client is synonymous with client-independent.

**Current Settings** Allows for certain kinds of Customizing changes, known as data-only Customizing changes, to be carried out in a production client without being saved as change requests.

**customer development** Additions to the standard, delivered SAP software using the ABAP Workbench. Customer developments involve creating customer-specific objects using the customer's name range and namespace.

**Customizing** Adjusting the R/3 System to specific customer requirements by selecting variants, parameter settings, etc.

**Customizing Activity Log** The ability in R/3 Release 4.5 to analyze table logs for Customizing activities. Table logs are generated only when table logging has been activated for the client.

**Customizing change request** Change request for recording and transporting changed system settings from client-specific tables.

**Customizing Cross-System Viewer** The client comparison tool with R/3 Release 4.5. In addition to determining the differences in Customizing settings, the Customizing Cross-System Viewer provides for the correction/adjustment of differences. It is often simply referred to as the Cross-System Viewer.

**Customizing Organizer (CO)** Tool to manage change requests of all types in an R/3 System. The Customizing Organizer is part of the Change and Transport Organizer.

**Customizing Transfer Assistant** A tool in R/3 Release 4.5 for the comparison and adjustment of client-dependent changes imported into an R/3 System.

**data archiving** Removing data that is currently not needed from the R/3 database and storing it in archives (see "archiving object").

**data file** Exported R/3 Repository objects and/or table data that resides at the operating system level in the transport directory *data* for each released and exported change request.

**database** Set of data (organized, for example, in files) for permanent storage on the hard disk. Each R/3 System has only one database.

**database copy** Also known as system copy. If you create an R/3 System using a database copy, the R/3 installation is not set up with the SAP standard database, but with a database whose content is supplied by an existing R/3 System using R/3 migration tools specific to your platform and R/3 Release.

**database instance** An administrative unit that allows access to a database. A database instance consists of database processes with a common set of database buffers in shared memory. There is normally only one database instance for each database. DB2/390 and Oracle Parallel Server are database systems for which a database can be made up of multiple database instances. In an R/3 System, a database instance can either be alone on a single computer or together with one or possibly more R/3 instances.

**database server** A computer with at least one database instance.

**DBA** Database administrator.

**delivery class** Classification attribute for ABAP Dictionary tables. The delivery class determines who (SAP or the customer) is responsible for maintaining the contents of a table. It also controls how a table behaves during a client copy, a client transport, and an R/3 Release upgrade.

**delivery route** Continuation of the transport route, after the consolidation route, for developments in the ABAP Workbench and Customizing. After being imported into the consolidation system, change requests are also flagged for import into the target systems of all delivery routes.

**delivery system** R/3 System type in a system landscape. A delivery system is linked to a consolidation system. By means of this link, the delivery system continually receives copies of change requests imported into the consolidation system. A production system is an example of a delivery system in a standard three-system landscape.

**Delta Customizing** Customizing activities that the customer needs to do to be able to use new functionality in the business application components after an R/3 Release upgrade. While Upgrade Customizing is mandatory for existing functionality, Delta Customizing is only necessary to make use of new functionality.

**development class** A grouping of R/3 Repository objects belonging to a common area. Unlike the objects in a change request, the grouping is logical rather than temporal. The development class is assigned a transport layer to ensure that all objects have the same consolidation route.

**development system** System in a system landscape where development and Customizing work is performed.

**dialog box** Window that is called from a primary window and displayed in front of that window.

**dialog work process** R/3 work process to process requests from users working online.

**dispatcher** The process that coordinates the work processes of an R/3 instance.

**EDI** Electronic Data Interchange. Electronic interchange of structured data (for example, business documents) between business partners in the home country and abroad who may be using different hardware, software, and communication services.

**end mark** An end mark is a marker placed in import queues to indicate that only the requests before the marker should be imported. If you look at an import queue, an end mark is indicated with the statement "End of import queue." Only one end mark is possible per import queue. The terms *end mark* and *stopmark* are often used interchangeably.

**enhancement** Enhancements generally consist of user exits provided by SAP in the program code to call up external customer-developed programs. The source code of the SAP standard R/3 Release does not need to be changed, as the connected customer objects also lie in the customer name range. The advantage of using enhancements is that during a subsequent upgrade, you do not need to perform a modification adjustment. Enhancements are not affected by upgrading to a new R/3 Release.

**enqueue** R/3 enqueues help to ensure data consistency by prohibiting the changing of data by more than one user at a time. An R/3 enqueue is set explicitly within an ABAP program by an enqueue function module and explicitly released by a dequeue function module. R/3 enqueues can continue to be in effect over several steps within an R/3 transaction. Remaining R/3 enqueues are released at the end of the R/3 transaction.

**Enterprise IMG** Company-specific Implementation Guide.

**export** The processes by which all objects of a change request are extracted from the database of the source R/3 System. The extracted data is saved to a data file at the operating system level. In addition, a command file is created that indicates how the data should be imported into an R/3 System.

**extended transport control** Enhanced transport configuration options as of R/3 Release 4.5. With extended transport control, transport routes can include client specifications or groups of client and system combinations.

**external system** An R/3 System defined from within TMS for which no physical system exists. As with virtual systems, an import queue is maintained for them if defined as part of a transport layer. Unlike virtual systems, external systems have their own transport directory that may be explicitly defined.

**FCS Final Delta Patch** Support Package that brings FCS R/3 Systems into the final state before other types of Support Packages can be applied.

**firewall** Software to protect a local network from unauthorized access from outside.

**First Customer Shipment (FCS)** The phase between the first shipment of a new R/3 Release and going live. The customer must apply for participation in this program.

**First Production Customer (FPC)** Phase following the FCS in the R/3 Release Strategy. In this phase, the first customers are productive with a new R/3 Functional Release. This phase is also referred to as CA (controlled availability).

**forward** To deliver change requests to other R/3 Systems outside the predefined transport routes.

**Functional R/3 Release** An R/3 Release that introduces improved business processes and/or new technology into the R/3 System. Functional Releases are delivered upon request to those customers who want to test the new functionality. For Functional Releases, SAP provides Support

Packages that correct major software errors. SAP recommends not using a Functional R/3 Release for production activities.

**General Availability (GA)** A phase in the R/3 Release Strategy in which a new R/3 Correction Release is available to all customers.

**GUI** Graphical User Interface. The medium through which a user can exchange information with the computer. You use the GUI to select commands, start programs, display files, and perform other operations by selecting function keys or buttons, menu options, and icons with the mouse.

**high availability** Property of a service or a system that remains in production operation for most of the time. High availability for an R/3 System means that unplanned and planned downtimes are reduced to a minimum. Good system administration is decisive here. You can reduce unplanned downtime by using preventive hardware and software solutions that are designed to reduce single points of failure in the services that support the R/3 System. You can reduce the planned downtime by optimizing the scheduling of necessary maintenance activities.

**Hot Package** A type of Support Package that corrects errors or provides enhancements to the R/3 Repository and ABAP Dictionary for core R/3 services.

**IDoc type** Internal document in SAP format, into which the data of a business process is transferred. An IDoc is a real business process formatted in the IDoc type. An IDoc type is described by the following components:

- **A control record:**
  Its format is identical for all IDoc types.
- **One or more records:**
  A record consists of a fixed administration segment and the data segment. The number and format of the segments differ for different IDoc types.
- **Status records:**
  These records describe stages of processing that an IDoc can go through. The status records have the same format for all IDoc types.

**Implementation Guide (IMG)** A tool for making customer-specific adjustments to the R/3 System. For each application component, the Implementation Guide contains:

- All steps to implement the R/3 System
- All default settings and all activities to configure the R/3 System
- A hierarchical structure that maps the structure of the R/3 application components
- Lists of all the documentation relevant to the implementation of the R/3 System

**import** The process by which all objects of previously released and exported change requests are transported into a target R/3 System using either the TMS or the transport control program *tp*.

**import all** The import of all change requests in the import queue or import buffer that are waiting for import.

**import buffer** A file at the operating system level containing the list of change requests to be imported into a specific R/3 System. This file resides in the transport directory `buffer`. The terms *import buffer* and *import queues* are often used interchangeable.

**import options** Import options that can be assigned either from within TMS import functionality or when using the *tp* command. They are used to cause specific rules of the Change and Transport System (CTS) to be ignored. Traditionally, transport options are known as unconditional modes.

**import queue** The import queue in R/3 reflects the operating system level import buffer and contains the list of requests that will be imported during the next *import all* process. Because of end marks and nonstandard change requests, there may be more requests in the import buffer than are highlighted in the import queue. The terms *import buffer* and *import queues* are often used interchangeable.

**Industry Solution (IS)** Industry-specific applications for R/3. For example, IS-H (IS Hospital), IS-RE (IS Real Estate), or IS-PS (IS Public Sector).

**integration system** System in the system landscape where developments and Customizing are carried out and then transported to the consolidation system. Each R/3 Repository object is assigned to an integration system through its development class and transport layer.

**Internet Transaction Server (ITS)** Gateway between the R/3 System and the World Wide Web.

**LAN** Local area network.

**legacy system** Typically refers to a customer's previous system (for example, a mainframe system). The data in this system has to be reformatted before it is imported into a new system (for example, into a client/server system such as R/3).

**Legal Change Patch (LCP)** A type of Support Package that provides corrections and other adjustments required due to legal changes for the Human Resources (HR) component.

**local change request** Change request that cannot be transported to other R/3 Systems.

**local object** A Repository object assigned to a local development class such as the development class $TMP. Local objects are local to the R/3 System on which they are created and cannot be transported.

**locks** The locking of data during transaction processing and R/3 Repository objects during development work.

- If a user changes a data record with a transaction or changes a Repository object, the same record or object cannot be accessed simultaneously by a second user. The record or object is locked for the duration of processing (ENQUEUE), and only afterwards is it released or unlocked (DEQUEUE).
- Repository objects are locked in Workbench change requests until the change request is released.

**logical system** A way of representing a client in an R/3 System without having to define the R/3 System. Logical systems allow applications to run with a common data basis. In SAP terms, a logical system is a client defined in a database. Logical systems can exchange messages and can be used, for example, by ALE.

**manual transport** The recording of Customizing changes to a change request using a manual rather than an automatic method. Some IMG activities can only be transported using a manual transport option.

**master data** Master data is a type of application data that changes infrequently, but is required for the completion of most business transactions. Examples of master data include lists of customers, vendors, and materials, and even the company's chart of accounts.

**modification** Change made by a customer to SAP-owned R/3 Repository objects. During an R/3 Release upgrade, modifications may require the new SAP standard to be adjusted.

**modification adjustment** Editing of R/3 Repository objects during an R/3 Release upgrade or when applying Support Packages, based on a comparison of SAP-owned Repository objects as they were before the upgrade (old state) and the same objects as they will be after the upgrade (new state).

**Modification Assistant** Functionality designed to help manage the repair of a Repository object using the ABAP Workbench tools. The Modification Assistant guides the change process to ensure that changes are well documented, original forms of the objects are preserved, and the change request to which the changes are recorded is indicated.

**Modification Browser** Detailed documentation of all repairs made in an R/3 System.

**name range** A name range is an interval in a namespace. The name range for customer programs is the set of program names beginning with Y or Z. Customer name ranges can be reserved in view V_TRESN.

**namespace** Set of all names that satisfy the specific properties of the namespace. A namespace is defined by a prefix SAP provides to the customer or complementary software partner.

**nametab** A nametab is the runtime object of a table. The runtime object contains all the information stored in the ABAP Dictionary in a format that is optimized for the application programs.

**object checks** When activated, object checks subject Repository objects in a change request to checks, such as a syntax check for ABAP programs, prior to the release of the change request.

**Object Directory** Catalog of R/3 Repository objects that contains the following information: object type, object name, original system, person responsible, and development class.

**object list** List of R/3 Repository objects and/or Customizing objects in change requests or tasks. Whenever changes are made, objects are added to the object list of a task. When a task is released, its object list is placed in the object list of the request to which it is assigned.

**OCS** Online Correction Support. OCS is a global term comprising various tools designed to help you support your production environment by supplying Support Packages.

**original object** The original of an object is normally the version maintained in the development system. Because all changes and developments are made using the original, it may never be overwritten by a transport.

**OS** Operating system.

**performance** Measurement of the efficiency of a computer system.

**preliminary import** Import of a single change request. Preliminary imports allow you to expedite an individual request through the defined transport routes. A preliminary import imports the request and adds it to the next import queue defined by the transport route. To minimize the risks associated with preliminary imports, the request remains in the original import queue after the import and is reimported the next time the entire import queue is imported. This guarantees that the order in which groups of objects are imported is always the same as the order in which they were exported.

**presentation server** A computer providing GUI services.

**production system** System that contains an enterprise's active business processes. This is where "live" production data is entered.

**Profile Generator** Automatically generates an authorization profile based on the activities in an activity group.

**Project IMG** Subset of the Enterprise IMG, containing only the documentation for the Enterprise IMG components required in a particular Customizing project.

**Project IMG views** Subset of a Project IMG, containing, for example, all mandatory activities for the project.

**quality assurance system** System in which final testing is carried out. Tested, stable development objects and

Customizing settings are transported into the quality assurance system from the development system at times defined for final testing. After verification and sign-off, development objects and Customizing settings are delivered to the production system.

**R/3** Runtime System 3.

**R/3 instance** Group of resources such as memory and work processes, usually in support of a single application server or database server in an R/3 client/server environment. Instance processes share a common set of buffers and are controlled by the same dispatcher process. An R/3 System can consist of one or more instances.

**R/3 Notes** SAP's announcements of corrections or enhancements to R/3. Often, an R/3 Note provides solutions, or a solution will be provided in a Support Package.

**R/3 Repository** Central storage facility for all development objects in the ABAP Workbench. These development objects include ABAP programs, screens, and documentation.

**R/3 runtime environment** Set of programs that must be available for execution at runtime. The ABAP interpreters in the runtime environment do not use the original of an ABAP program. Rather, they use a copy generated once only during runtime (early binding). Runtime objects, such as programs and screens, are automatically regenerated (late binding) when a time stamp comparison between the object and the ABAP Dictionary detects a difference.

**R/3 System** Consists of a central instance offering the services DVEBMGS (dialog, update, enqueue, background processing, message, gateway, spool), a database instance, optional dialog instances offering the service D (dialog), and optional PC frontends.

**R/3 System service** Logical function required to support the R/3 System, such as the database service and the application services, which may include the services Dialog, Update, Enqueue, Batch, Message, Gateway, and Spool.

**R/3 Upgrade Assistant** Support tool for R/3 upgrades. The R/3 Upgrade Assistant provides one or more graphical user interfaces for the upgrade control program. It also permits you to execute an R/3 upgrade remotely and monitor its status.

**R3trans** A transport utility at the operating system level for the transport of data between R/3 Systems. `R3trans` is also used for the installation of new R/3 Systems, for migration to different R/3 Releases, and for logical backups. Other programs usually call `R3trans`, in particular the transport control program `tp` and the upgrade control program `R3up`.

**RDBMS** Relational Database Management System.

**RDDIMPDP** Background job that is scheduled event-periodic. It starts the background jobs that are required for transports. `RDDIMPDP` is triggered by `tp`, which uses the executable `sapevt` on the operating system level to send event `SAP_TRIGGER_RDDIMPDP`. `RDDIMPDP` is also known as transport daemon and transport dispatcher.

**release** The process by which the owner of a change request or task indicates that the contents of the change request or task have been unit tested. Release of a change request of either type Transportable or Customizing initiates the export process.

**Release Customizing** Only those IMG activities affected by a given R/3 Release upgrade in the business application components concerned are presented for processing. SAP distinguishes between Upgrade Customizing (corrected or amended functionality) and Delta Customizing (new functionality) for R/3 Release upgrades.

**relocation transports** The transport of Repository objects for the purpose of changing the ownership, development class, and/or transport layer for those objects. Relocation transports are possible using the Transport Organizer.

**repair** An R/3 Repository object that is changed in a system other than its original system is entered in a repair. All modifications of SAP standard objects are repairs, because the customer's system is not the original system for SAP objects.

**repair flag** A flag that protects an object changed in a system other than its original system from being overwritten by an import.

**Repository Browser** ABAP Workbench navigation tool for managing development objects. The user interface of the Repository Browser resembles a file manager where development objects are grouped together in object lists in a hierarchical structure.

**Repository object** Object in the R/3 Repository. Repository objects are development objects of the ABAP Workbench.

**Repository switch** A procedure during an R/3 upgrade that replaces an existing R/3 Repository with a new R/3 Repository.

**return code** Value that indicates whether a tool (either within R/3 or on the operating system level) ran successfully, with warnings, or with errors.

**RFC** Remote Function Call. RFC is an SAP interface protocol, based on CPI-C. It allows the programming of communication processes between systems to be simplified considerably. Using RFCs, predefined functions can be called and executed in a remote system or within the same system. RFCs are used for communication control, parameter passing, and error handling.

**SAP Business Warehouse Patch** Support Packages that contain a collection of corrections for the SAP Business Information Warehouse (SAP BW) component.

**SAP Patch Manager (SPAM)** SPAM is the R/3 System interface to SAPNet, SAP's support services, for the purpose of downloading Support Packages. It is also known as SAP Package Manager.

**SAP Reference IMG** Complete Implementation Guide containing all Customizing activities supplied by SAP. It is organized according to business application component.

**SAP Software Change Registration (SSCR)** A procedure for registering those users who change or create Repository objects using the tools of the ABAP Workbench and for registering changes to SAP sources and SAP Repository objects.

**SAPGUI** SAP Graphical User Interface.

**SAPNet** SAP's support and information services from which you access R/3 Notes and Support Packages. It was formerly known as SAP's Online Service System (OSS).

**SAPNet—R/3 Frontend** Access to SAP support services directly from your R/3 System using a remote connection and going through the SAProuter.

**SAPNet—Web Frontend** The communication channel with SAP support services available through the Internet.

**SAProuter** A software module that functions as part of a firewall system.

**server** The term *server* has multiple meanings in the SAP environment. It should therefore be used only if it is clear whether it means a logical unit, such as an R/3 instance, or a physical unit, such as a computer.

**session** A user session in an SAPGUI window.

**Session Manager** The tool used for central control of R/3 applications. The Session Manager is a graphical navigation interface used to manage sessions and start application transactions. It can generate both company-specific and user-specific menus. The Session Manager is available from R/3 Release 3.0C under Windows 95 and Windows NT.

**shared memory** Main memory area that can be accessed by all work processes in an instance. The term *shared memory* is also used to mean the main memory area shared by the RDBMS processes.

**SID** SAP System Identifier. Placeholder for the three-character name of an R/3 System.

**Software Component Patches** A type of Support Package available in R/3 Release 4.5. Patches of this type are generic patches for one software component—for example, Basis or Human Resources—and contain corrections for errors in the Repository and the Dictionary only in this component.

**software logistics** Procedures and tools required for the creation, documentation, and distribution of development and Customizing changes throughout the SAP-recommended system landscape.

**SPAM Update** Support Package that contains improvements and extensions to the SAP Patch Manager.

**SQL** Structured Query Language. A database language for accessing relational databases.

**standard request** A default change request automatically used to record changes without prompting for a request number. A standard request must be manually set and is valid for a specified period of time.

**standard transport layer** The default transport layer for an R/3 System and the transport layer used by all Customizing change requests released from that system.

**stopmark** A stopmark is a marker placed in the import buffer to indicate that only the requests before the marker should be imported. The terms *end mark* and *stopmark* are often used interchangeably.

**Support Package** A generic term for the different collections of general improvements and changes to the SAP standard software that SAP provides through SAPNet.

**Support Package Collection** Support Packages are grouped into Support Package Collections at regular intervals. These are stored on CD-ROMs and delivered automatically to all customers. Support Package Collections are available for Support Packages of type Hot Package and Legal Change Patches.

**system change option** Global setting to permit changes to R/3 Repository objects based on the object's namespace and type.

**system copy** Also known as database copy. If you create an R/3 System using a database copy, the R/3 installation is not set up with the SAP standard database, but with a database whose content is supplied by an existing R/3 System using R/3 migration tools specific to your platform and R/3 Release.

**system landscape** The R/3 Systems and clients required for a company's implementation and maintenance of R/3. For example, a common system landscape consists of a development system, a quality assurance system, and a production system.

**table logging** Activating the logging of all changes to SAP-selected Customizing tables for the purpose of providing an audit history as to who made what changes to the data.

**target group** A group of R/3 System and client combinations to which transport routes can consolidate or deliver. Target groups are available with extended transport control in R/3 Release 4.5.

**task** User-specific information carrier in the Change and Transport Organizers for entering and managing all changes to R/3 Repository objects and Customizing settings. When an object is changed, the changed objects are recorded to a task. Tasks are assigned to a change request.

**TCP/IP** Transmission Control Protocol/ Internet Protocol.

**transaction code** Succession of alphanumeric characters used to name a transaction—that is, a particular ABAP program in the R/3 System. For example, Transaction VA01 (*create customer order*).

**transaction data** Data collected during standard business activities/transactions and typically related to specific master data. For example, data relating to a specific sale is regarded as transaction data and can be assigned to the master data of the purchaser.

**transport** The movement (export and import) of change requests between different R/3 Systems.

**transport control program** (`tp`) An operation system level utility for controlling the transport of change requests between R/3 Systems and R/3 Release upgrades.

**transport directory** Operating system disk space that provides the management facility for all data to be transported between R/3 Systems.

**transport domain** All R/3 Systems to be administered using the Transport Management System (TMS) belong to a transport domain. In this transport domain, system settings such as the transport route settings are identical for all R/3 Systems. To have consistent settings in the transport domain, one R/3 System (the domain controller) has the reference configuration, and all the other R/3 Systems in the transport domain receive copies of this reference configuration.

**transport domain controller** An R/3 System in the transport domain, from which transport configuration activities for the entire transport domain are controlled. These activities include accepting R/3 Systems into the transport domain, creating virtual R/3 Systems, and establishing transport routes between the different R/3 Systems.

**transport group** All R/3 Systems in a transport domain that share the same transport directory.

**transport layer** Means by which the integration and consolidation system for R/3 Repository objects are determined. A transport layer is assigned to each development class and thus to all R/3 Repository objects in that development class. It determines the R/3 System in which developments or changes to R/3 Repository objects are performed, and whether objects will be transported to other systems when development work has been completed.

**transport log** Record of the transfer of the objects in a particular change request from a source system to a target system. A transport log contains:

- A summary of transport activities
- A log detailing the export of objects from a source system
- The results of the import check
- A log detailing the import of objects into a target system

**Transport Management System (TMS)** The tool in the R/3 System that enables centralized transport configuration, and the execution and monitoring of exports and imports between R/3 Systems in a single transport domain.

**Transport Organizer (TO)** Tool for preparing and managing transports that supplements the more commonly used Workbench Organizer and Customizing Organizer. The Transport Organizer is part of the Change and Transport Organizer.

**transport profile** The parameter settings for the operating system transport command program *tp*. This file resides at the operating system level in the transport directory *bin*.

**transport request** A released and exported change request. This term is often used synonymously with the term *change request*.

**transport route** Transport routes are used to define both the target system in which you want to consolidate change requests and the R/3 Systems to which change requests are delivered after verification and testing. Transport routes are of either type *consolidation* or type *delivery*.

**transportable change request** Change request that will be exported to a defined consolidation system when released.

**unit testing** Lowest level of testing where the program or transaction is tested and evaluated for faults (contrasted with business integration testing). Unit testing is the first test that is completed, normally during the Customizing and development effort, while business integration testing usually occurs in the quality assurance system. With unit testing, the focus is on the program's inner functions rather than on system integration.

**Upgrade Customizing** Customizing activities that are required if you want to continue to use the same functions as before in your business application components after a system or R/3 Release upgrade. Upgrade Customizing covers changes to functions already used in live systems.

**user master data** Logon and authorization information for R/3 users. Only users who have a user master record can log on to a client in an R/3 System and use specific transactions.

**version database** Storage location for versions of R/3 Repository objects when a change request is released.

**view** "Virtual table" simultaneously displaying data from several real tables in the ABAP Dictionary. When you create a table, you assign a key to it. However, the fields in the key may be inadequate for solving some problems, so you can generate a view from several tables or parts of tables.

**virtual system** R/3 System configured as a placeholder for an R/3 System that has not yet been set up. Transport routes can be defined for virtual systems, and the import queue can be set up and displayed.

**WAN** Wide area network.

**work process (WP)** The application services of the R/3 System have special processes—for example, for:

- Dialog administration
- Updating change documents
- Background processing
- Spool processing
- Lock management

Work processes can be assigned to dedicated application servers.

**Workbench change request** Change request for recording and transporting R/3 Repository objects and changed system settings from cross-client tables (client-independent Customizing).

**Workbench Organizer (WBO)** Tools for managing Workbench change requests required to record changes as a result of development efforts using the tools of the ABAP Workbench. The Workbench Organizer is part of the Change and Transport Organizer.

# E Further Resources

This section provides information on SAP online help, SAP training courses internet links, and a bibliography related to SAP change and transport management.

## E.1 SAP Online Help

To access the online help of a mySAP ERP system, choose **Help • SAP Library** from the initial screen. Then, choose the following paths:

- **SAP NetWeaver • Solution Lifecycle Management • Software Change Management**
  Here, you find information on the change and transport management system for ABAP. In addition, the section deals with client copy and client transport, language transport and namespaces.
- **SAP NetWeaver • Solution Lifecycle Management • Customizing**
  In this area, you find relevant information for executing Customizing changes.
- **SAP NetWeaver • Application Platform • Java Technology in SAP Web Application Server • Administration Guide • Administration of SAP NetWeaver Java Development Infrastructure**
  This chapter explains how to deal with administrative tasks related to SAP NetWeaver Java Development Infrastructure.

SAP Solution Manager provides an online help of its own. You can access this help when being logged on to an SAP Solution Manager system; from the inital screen, choose **Help • SAP Library**. The areas relevant for change management are:

- Customizing Synchronization
- Management of Change Requests

## E.2 SAP Training Courses

SAP currently offers the following training courses for change and transport management issues:

- **ADM325**
  Software Logistics
- **ADM200**
  SAP Web Application Server Java Administration

- TADMJ8
  Java Development Infrastructure Administration
- USMF55
  Management of Change Requests using SAP Solution Manager

## E.3 SAP on the Internet

SAP Service Marketplace is a Web platform separated from the public site *http://www.sap.com*. Using a special authorization, customers, partners, SAP employees, and others can access the Service Marketplace at *http://service.sap.com*. Using so-called Quick Links which have only to be attached to the Service Marketplace Web address, you can quickly access relevant information.

Important Quick Links are */customizing*, */upgrade*, */solutionmanager*, */jdi* (Java Development Infrastructure), and */swdc* (Software Distribution Center).

## E.4 Books


- Sigrid Hagemann, Liane Will: *SAP R/3 System Adminitration*. 2nd edition, SAP PRESS 2004.
- Andreas Schneider-Neureither et al.: SAP System Landscape Optimization. SAP PRESS 2004.
- Karl Kesser, Peter Tillert, Panayot Dobrikov: *Java Programming with the SAP Web Application Server*. SAP PRESS 2005.

# F Questions and Answers

## Chapter 1: R/3 Architecture and Data Components

1. Which of the following components indicate that R/3 is a client/server system?

   A. Multiple databases

   B. A database server

   C. Three separate hardware servers—a database server, an application server, and a presentation server

   D. A database service, an application service, and a presentation service

**Answer:** D

2. Which of the following is NOT contained in the R/3 database?

   A. The R/3 Repository

   B. The R/3 kernel

   C. Customer data

   D. Transaction data

   E. Customizing data

   F. The ABAP Dictionary

**Answer:** B

3. Which of the following statements is correct in regard to R/3 clients?

   A. An R/3 client has its own customer data and programs, which are not accessible to other clients within the same R/3 System.

   B. An R/3 client shares Customizing and application data with other clients in the same R/3 System.

   C. An R/3 client shares all R/3 Repository objects and client-independent Customizing with all other clients in the same R/3 System.

   D. An R/3 client enables you to separate application data from Customizing data.

**Answer:** C

4. Which of the following statements is correct in regard to SAP's client concept?

   A. All Customizing settings are client-independent.

   B. A client has a unique set of application data.

   C. A client has its own Repository objects.

   D. All Customizing settings are client-dependent.

**Answer:** B

### Chapter 2: Realizing Business Processes in R/3

1. Which of the following strategies enables R/3 customers to avoid making modifications to SAP-standard objects?

   A. Using enhancement technologies such as program exits and menu exits

   B. Modifying SAP delivered programs

   C. Changing SAP-standard functionality using the Implementation Guide (IMG)

   D. Performing Customizing to provide the required functionality

**Answer:** A, D

2. Which of the following statements are correct in regard to the Implementation Guide (IMG)?

   A. The IMG consists of a series of Customizing activities for defining a company's business processes.

   B. The IMG is an online resource providing the necessary information and steps to help you implement R/3 application modules.

   C. The IMG is client-independent.

   D. All of the above.

**Answer:** D

3. Which of the following strategies enables an enterprise to meet its business needs by changing or enhancing R/3 functionality?

   A. Maintaining application data using the various R/3 business transactions in the SAP standard

   B. Using the ABAP Workbench to create the required R/3 Repository objects

   C. Using Customizing to modify R/3 programs after obtaining an access key from SAP's Online Support Services (OSS)

   D. Using customer exits to enhance the functionality of existing SAP-standard objects

**Answer:** B, D

4. Which of the following statements are correct in regard to modifications?

   A. A modification is a change to an SAP-standard object.

   B. A modification must be registered through SAP Software Change Registration (SSCR).

   C. SAP recommends modifications only if the customer's business needs cannot be met by Customizing, enhancement technologies, or customer development.

   D. All of the above.

**Answer:** D

5. Which of the following statements is correct in regard to Customizing?
   - **A.** Customizing enables R/3 application processes to be set to reflect a company's business needs.
   - **B.** Customizing can be performed only from within a Project IMG.
   - **C.** Customizing is necessary because R/3 is delivered without business processes.
   - **D.** None of the above.

**Answer:** A

6. Which of the following statements are correct in regard to R/3 Repository objects?
   - **A.** Customers can develop new Repository objects using the tools in the ABAP Workbench.
   - **B.** Customer-developed Repository objects reside in the R/3 Repository alongside SAP-standard objects.
   - **C.** Customers can create and assign new Repository objects to a development class.
   - **D.** All of the above.

**Answer:** D

### Chapter 3: The R/3 System Landscape

1. Which of the following statements is correct in regard to critical client roles as recommended by SAP?
   - **A.** Customizing changes can be made in any client.
   - **B.** All Customizing and development changes should be made in a single R/3 client.
   - **C.** Repository objects should be created and changed in the quality assurance client.
   - **D.** Unit testing should take place in the Customizing-and-development client.

**Answer:** B

2. Which of the following activities should *not* be performed within a system landscape?
   - **A.** Customizing and development changes are promoted to a quality assurance client before being delivered to production.
   - **B.** The R/3 System is upgraded to new R/3 Releases.

C. Development changes are made directly in the production client.

D. Clients are assigned a specific role.

**Answer:** C

3. Which of the following benefits does the three-system landscape recommended by SAP have?

   A. Customizing and development, testing, and production activities take place in separate database environments and do not affect one another.

   B. Changes are tested in the quality assurance system and imported into the production system only after verification.

   C. Client-independent changes can be made in the development system without immediately affecting the production client.

   D. All of the above.

**Answer:** D

4. Which of the following statements is correct in regard to multiple R/3 clients?

   A. All clients in the same R/3 System share the same R/3 Repository and client-independent Customizing settings.

   B. No more than one client in the same R/3 System should allow changes to client-independent Customizing objects.

   C. If a client allows for changes to client-dependent Customizing, the client should also allow for changes to client-independent Customizing objects.

   D. All of the above.

**Answer:** D

5. Which of the following statements is correct in regard to the setup of a three-system landscape?

   A. There is only one R/3 database for the system landscape.

   B. One client should allow for the automatic recording of client-dependent Customizing and for client-independent changes.

   C. All R/3 Systems have the same system ID.

   D. All clients must have unique client numbers.

**Answer:** B

6. Which of the following statements is correct in regard to the CUST client?

   A. It should allow changes to client-independent Customizing, but not Repository objects.

   B. It should automatically record all changes to Customizing settings.

C. It should not allow changes to client-dependent and client-independent Customizing settings.

D. It should allow for all changes, but not require recording of changes to change requests.

**Answer:** B

7. Which of the following statements is correct in regard to a two-system landscape?

 A. It is not optimal because there is limited opportunity to test the transport of changes from the development system to the production system.

 B. It allows for changes to Customizing in the production system.

 C. It is recommended by SAP because Customizing and development do not impact quality assurance testing.

 D. All of the above.

**Answer:** A

8. Which of the following statements are correct in regard to a phased implementation?

 A. All Customizing changes made in the production support system must also be made in the development system.

 B. The system landscape requires five R/3 Systems.

 C. Changes in the production support system do not have to be made in the development environment.

 D. The system landscape needs an environment that supports the production system with any required changes.

**Answer:** A, D

9. Which of the following statements is *not* valid in regard to a global system landscape?

 A. A global template can be used for the rollout of corporate Customizing settings and development efforts.

 B. Management of different Repository objects (those developed by the corporate office versus those developed locally) can be managed using namespaces and name ranges for the Repository objects.

 C. Merging the Customizing settings delivered by the corporate office with local Customizing efforts can easily be done using change requests.

 D. SAP provides different tools to aid in the rollout of a global template.

**Answer:** C

## Chapter 4: Managing Changes and Data in an R/3 System Landscape

1. Which of the following statements is correct in regard to Customizing and development changes?

   A. All changes are recorded to tasks in Customizing change requests.

   B. The changes should be recorded to tasks in change requests for transport to other clients and systems.

   C. The changes must be manually performed in every R/3 System.

   D. The changes can easily be made simultaneously in multiple clients.

**Answer:** B

2. Which of the following statements in regard to change requests is FALSE?

   A. The Customizing Organizer and the Workbench Organizer are tools used to view, create, and manage change requests.

   B. A change request is a collection of tasks where developers and people performing Customizing record the changes they make.

   C. All changes made as a result of IMG activities are recorded to Customizing change requests.

   D. SAP recommends setting your R/3 System so that Customizing changes made in the Customizing-and-development client are automatically recorded to change requests.

**Answer:** C

3. For which of the following activities is the TMS (Transaction STMS) *not* designed?

   A. Releasing change requests

   B. Viewing import queues

   C. Viewing log files generated by both the export process and the import process

   D. Initiating the import process

**Answer:** A

4. Which of the following statements is correct after you have successfully imported change requests into the quality assurance system?

   A. The change requests must be released again to be exported to the production system.

   B. The data files containing the changed objects are deleted from the transport directory.

C. The change requests need to be manually added to the import queue of the production system.

D. The change requests are automatically added to the import queue of the production system.

**Answer:** D

5. Which of the following statements is correct in regard to the change requests in an import queue?

A. They are sequenced according to their change request number.

B. They are sequenced in the order in which they were exported from the development system.

C. They are sequenced according to the name of the user who released the requests.

D. They are not sequenced by default, but arranged in a variety of ways using the TMS.

**Answer:** B

6. Which of the following techniques can be used to transfer application data between two production systems?

A. Recording transaction data to change requests

B. Using ALE to transfer application data

C. Using the client copy tool

D. All of the above

**Answer:** B

7. Which of the following types of data transfer are possible with an appropriate use of interface technologies?

A. Transferring legacy data to an R/3 System

B. Transferring data between R/3 clients

C. Transferring data to non-SAP systems

D. Transporting change requests to multiple R/3 Systems

**Answer:** A, B, C

8. Which of the following statements is correct in regard to user master data?

A. User master data can be transported in a change request.

B. User master data is unique to each R/3 System, but is shared across clients in the same R/3 System.

C. A specific client copy option enables you to distribute user master data together with authorization profile data.

D. User master data includes all user logon information, including the definition of authorizations and profiles.

**Answer:** C

## Chapter 5: Setting Up a System Landscape

1. Which of the following clients should you copy to create new clients and ensure that all data from post-installation processing is also copied?

   A. Client 001

   B. Client 000

   C. Client 066

**Answer:** B

2. Which of the following is *not* an SAP-recommended strategy for setting up a system landscape?

   A. Using a client copy from the development system to set up your quality assurance and production systems when the change request strategy is not an option

   B. Creating the production system as a combination of a client copy from the quality assurance system and change requests from the development system

   C. Using the same setup strategy to establish both the quality assurance and production systems

   D. Setting up the quality assurance and production systems by importing change requests promoted from the development system

**Answer:** B

3. Which of the following are correct in regard to the setup of the TMS?

   A. The TMS should be set up when the development system is installed.

   B. The TMS should include all R/3 Systems in the system landscape even if the R/3 Systems do not physically exist.

   C. The TMS is critical in establishing the transport route between the development and quality assurance systems.

   D. The TMS should be set up before change requests are created in the Customizing-and-development client.

**Answer:** A, B, C, D

4. Which of the following is correct in regard to the system copy strategy?
   A. SAP recommends the system copy strategy, because all Customizing and development objects are transferred.
   B. SAP does not recommend the system copy strategy, because there is no easy way to eliminate unwanted application data.
   C. A system copy is the easiest setup strategy recommended by SAP.
   D. A system copy eliminates the need for change requests for your entire R/3 implementation.

**Answer:** B

### Chapter 6: Maintaining a System Landscape

1. Which of the following activities is NOT necessary for releasing and exporting a change request?
   A. Documenting every task in the change request
   B. Releasing every task in the change request
   C. Verification of the contents of the change request by the system administrator
   D. Unit testing the change request

**Answer:** C

2. Which of the following statements is correct in regard to the tasks used in change requests that record Customizing and development changes?
   A. Tasks belong to a change request.
   B. Tasks can be used by several R/3 users.
   C. Tasks are the direct responsibility of a project leader.
   D. Tasks record only client-specific changes.

**Answer:** A

3. Which of the following indicates that a change request has been signed off after quality assurance testing?
   A. The change request is released after unit testing.
   B. The change request is successfully imported into the quality assurance system.
   C. The change request is added to the import queue of all other R/3 Systems in the system landscape.
   D. The project leader communicates their approval of the change request.

**Answer:** D

4. Which of the following is NOT an SAP recommendation?

   A. Imports into the quality assurance and production systems should occur in the same sequence.

   B. Even if the import process is automatically scripted, a technical consultant or system administrator should review the results of the import.

   C. Project leaders should manually add change requests to the import queue of the quality assurance system.

   D. Change requests are imported in the same sequence that they were exported from the development system.

**Answer:** C

5. Which of the following is SAP's recommendation on how to rush an emergency correction into the production system?

   A. Make the change directly in the production system.

   B. Transport the change from the development system to the quality assurance system and production system using a **preliminary import**.

   C. Make the change and use a client copy with a change request to distribute the change to production.

   D. Make the change in the quality assurance system and transport the change using a **preliminary import**.

**Answer:** B

6. Which of the following transport activities is NOT typically the responsibility of the system administrator?

   A. Importing change requests into all clients within the system landscape

   B. Verifying the success of the import process

   C. Releasing change requests

   D. Assisting in solving either export or import errors

**Answer:** C

7. Which of the following does SAP provide as customer support?

   A. R/3 Release upgrades to provide new functionality

   B. Support Packages to correct identified problems in a specific R/3 Release

   C. R/3 Notes to announce errors and corrections for the reported problems

   D. All of the above

**Answer:** D

### Chapter 7: Transport Setup Activities at R/3 Installation

1. The R/3 System ID (SID):

   A. Must be unique for each system sharing the same transport directory

   B. Must be unique for each system in the system landscape

   C. Can start with a number

   D. Can consist of any three-character combination

**Answer:** A, B

2. Which of the following statements is correct in regard to the transport directory?

   A. There can be only one transport directory in a system landscape.

   B. All R/3 Systems within a transport group share a common transport directory.

   C. In system landscapes using heterogeneous platforms, it is not possible to have a common transport directory.

   D. Only the production system can contain the transport directory.

**Answer:** B

3. The transport control program `tp`:

   A. Is stored in subdirectory **bin** of the transport directory

   B. Uses program `R3trans` to access the databases when transporting changes

   C. Cannot be used directly on the operating system level

   D. Depends on the settings of the transport profile

**Answer:** B, D

4. The transport profile:

   A. Is stored in subdirectory **bin** of the transport directory

   B. Contains comments and parameter settings that configure the transport control program `tp`

   C. Is managed from within TMS as of R/3 Release 4.5, but is modified with operating system text editors in earlier releases

   D. Contains only settings that are valid for all R/3 Systems in the system landscape

**Answer:** A, B, C

5. The initialization procedure of the CTO:

   A. Is especially required after a system copy

   B. Establishes the initial value for change request IDs

C. Is not mandatory for the purpose of enabling transports

D. Is performed automatically during R/3 installation by program `R3setup`

**Answer:** A, B

6. Which of the following statements is correct in regard to the settings governing changes to Repository objects?

   A. Only the customer name range should be modifiable in production systems.

   B. Developments are possible in an R/3 System only if you have applied for a development namespace.

   C. If the global change option is set to **Not modifiable**, it is nevertheless possible to make changes in certain name spaces or clients that have their change option set to **Modifiable**.

   D. The global change option should always be set to **Not modifiable** for the quality assurance system and the production system.

**Answer:** D

### Chapter 8: Setting Up the TMS

1. Which of the following statements is correct in regard to the R/3 Systems belonging to a transport domain?

   A. They all share the same transport directory.

   B. They are managed centrally using TMS.

   C. They belong to the same transport group.

   D. They must run on the same operating system and database platform.

**Answer:** B

2. Which of the following statements is correct in regard to the domain controller?

   A. It must be the production system.

   B. It occurs once in a transport domain.

   C. It occurs in each transport group.

   D. It can only be the R/3 System that was originally designated as the transport domain controller.

   E. It should never be the production system due to the high system load that the domain controller causes.

**Answer:** B

3. Which of the following statements are correct in regard to the TMS?

   A. It needs to be initialized only on the transport domain controller.

   B. It needs to be initialized only on the transport domain controller and the backup domain controller.

   C. It must be initialized on every R/3 System.

   D. It must be set up before you can set up transport routes.

**Answer:** C, D

4. Which of the following statements are correct in regard to the RFC destinations for TMS connections?

   A. They are generated automatically when a transport route is created.

   B. They are generated between the domain controller and each R/3 System in the transport domain.

   C. They must be established manually before you can use the TMS.

   D. They are generated during the TMS initialization process.

   E. They are only needed for importing change requests.

**Answer:** B, D

5. How is the actual system landscape, including R/3 System roles and relationships, defined using the TMS?

   A. By including all R/3 Systems in the transport domain

   B. By configuring transport routes

   C. By assigning a role to each R/3 System during the TMS initialization process

   D. By designating real, virtual, and external R/3 Systems

**Answer:** B

6. Which of the following statements is correct in regard to a consolidation route?

   A. It is defined by an integration system and a consolidation system, and is associated with a transport layer.

   B. It is created in the TMS by defining only an integration system and a consolidation system.

   C. It is not necessarily required in a two-system landscape.

   D. It can be defined only once in a transport group.

**Answer:** A

7. Which of the following statements are correct in regard to client-specific transport routes?

   A. They are possible as of R/3 Release 4.0.

   B. They are possible only as of R/3 Release 4.5, and only if extended transport control is activated.

   C. They are only allowed for target groups.

   D. They may not be used in conjunction with client-independent transport routes.

**Answer:** B, D

### Chapter 9: Client Tools

1. After you create a new client entry in table T000, which of the following activities enables you to provide the client with data?

   A. A remote client copy to populate the client with data from a client in another R/3 System

   B. A client transport to import data from a client in another R/3 System

   C. A local client copy to import data from a client within the same R/3 System

   D. All of the above

**Answer:** D

2. Which of the following *cannot* be used to restrict a client from certain activities?

   A. The client role

   B. The client-dependent change option

   C. The client ID-number

   D. A client restriction

   E. The client-independent change option

**Answer:** C

3. Which of the following tasks can be performed using the client copy tools?

   A. Merging application data from one client into another client

   B. Copying only application data from one client to another client

   C. Copying only Customizing data from one client to another client

   D. All of the above

**Answer:** C

4. Which of the following tasks can be performed using the client copy profiles?
   A. Scheduling a client copy to occur at a time when system use is low
   B. Selecting the subset of application data that will be copied when a client copy is executed
   C. Providing required user authorization for the use of client tools
   D. Determining the data that will be copied when a client copy is executed

**Answer:** D

5. Which of the following statements is correct in regard to table logging?
   A. Table logging should be used instead of change requests whenever possible.
   B. Table logging provides an audit history of who made what changes and when.
   C. Table logging does not negatively impact system resources.
   D. All of the above.

**Answer:** B

### Chapter 10: Managing Development Changes

1. Which of the following statements is *false* in regard to development classes?
   A. Development classes facilitate project management by grouping similar Repository objects.
   B. All Repository objects are assigned to a development class.
   C. A development class determines the transport route that a changed Repository object will follow.
   D. A local object does not need a development class.

**Answer:** D

2. Which of the following kinds of changes are transported using Workbench change requests?
   A. Client-independent changes
   B. Modifications to SAP-delivered objects
   C. Changes made using the ABAP Editor and ABAP Dictionary
   D. Repairs to R/3 Repository objects that originated in another R/3 System
   E. All of the above

**Answer:** E

3. Which of the following data is *not* contained in the object list of a task?

   A. The actual change made to the objects listed in the task

   B. The list of changed objects recorded to the task

   C. Whether the objects recorded to the task are locked

   D. The complete Object Directory entry for the object

**Answer:** A, D

4. Which of the following statements are correct regarding repairs and modifications?

   A. Repairs are changes to SAP-delivered objects; modifications are changes to any object that originated on an R/3 System other than the current R/3 System.

   B. A repair flag protects an R/3 Repository object against being overwritten by an import.

   C. All repairs are saved to Workbench change requests.

   D. A modification is a change to an SAP-delivered object.

   E. All of the above.

**Answer:** B, C, D

### Chapter 11: Managing Customizing Changes

1. Which of the following requirements must be met before you can change both client-dependent and client-independent Customizing settings in a client?

   A. The client settings must allow for changes to client-independent Customizing objects.

   B. The client role must be **Production**.

   C. The system change option must be set to **Modifiable**.

   D. The client settings must allow for changes to client-dependent Customizing.

**Answer:** A, C, D

2. Which of the following statements are correct when project leaders and project team members receive only the recommended authorizations?

   A. Only developers can create change requests.

   B. Only project leaders can create change requests and are therefore responsible for assigning project team members to change requests.

   C. Project team members can create and release change requests.

   D. Project leaders can release change requests.

**Answer:** B, D

3. Which of the following statements are correct with regard to Project IMGs?
   - A. The Project IMG provides access to the Customizing activities defined for a particular project.
   - B. Customizing is performed in the Project IMG tree structure.
   - C. The Project IMG enables you to display project status information and document Customizing activities.
   - D. All of the above.

**Answer:** D

4. Which of the following activities are performed using the Customizing Organizer?
   - A. Viewing all Customizing change requests related to a particular user
   - B. Viewing all Workbench change requests related to a particular user
   - C. Viewing all change requests related to a particular user
   - D. Managing change requests you own or reviewing change requests in which you have assigned tasks

**Answer:** A, B, C, D

5. Which of the following statements is correct in regard to Customizing?
   - A. All Customizing activities in the IMG are client-dependent.
   - B. All changes resulting from IMG activities can be transported.
   - C. All Customizing changes are automatically recorded to a change request if the client change option is set to **Automatic recording of changes**.
   - D. A Customizing activity may involve the creation of client-independent objects and therefore requires a Workbench change request.

**Answer:** D

6. Which of the following activities are performed using client comparison tools?
   - A. Comparing the Customizing settings of two R/3 clients in the same R/3 System or in a different R/3 System
   - B. Adjusting the Customizing differences between two different R/3 clients
   - C. Transporting Customizing settings into the production client
   - D. Comparing the objects listed in the object list of a change request with an R/3 client

**Answer:** A, B, D

## Chapter 12: Promoting Change Requests

1. Which of the following is a prerequisite for copying client-dependent changes to a unit test client using a *client copy according to a transp. request* (Transaction SCC1)?

   **A.** The change request has been released.

   **B.** The tasks have been released, but the change request has not.

   **C.** The tasks have been released after successful unit testing by the owner of the task.

   **D.** The change request has not been released.

**Answer:** D

2. Which of the following are the result of releasing a task?

   **A.** A data file is created in the transport directory and contains the objects recorded in the change request.

   **B.** The object list and documentation for the task are copied to the change request.

   **C.** All objects recorded in the task are locked.

   **D.** You can no longer save changes to that task.

**Answer:** B, D

3. Which of the following are the result of releasing and exporting a change request?

   **A.** A data file is created in the transport directory to contain copies of the objects recorded in the change request.

   **B.** Versions are created in the version database for all R/3 Repository objects in the object list of the change request.

   **C.** All repairs recorded in the change request are confirmed.

   **D.** You can no longer save changes to that change request.

**Answer:** A, B, D

4. When you release a Customizing change request, you have the option to do which of the following?

   **A.** Release the change request to another Customizing change request.

   **B.** Schedule the release of the change request for a later time.

   **C.** Release the change request to a transportable change request.

   **D.** Initiate immediate release and export.

**Answer:** C, D

5. Which of the following is a prerequisite for releasing a transportable change request?
   A. There are no syntax errors in the ABAP programs recorded to the change request.
   B. You must own the tasks in the change request.
   C. All Repository objects in the change request are locked by the change request.
   D. The change request has documentation.

**Answer:** C

6. The export process initiates which of the following activities?
   A. The creation of files in the transport directory
   B. The automatic import of change requests into the target system—for example, the quality assurance system
   C. The addition of the exported change request to the import buffer of the target system.
   D. The deletion of the change request within the R/3 System.

**Answer:** A, C

7. Which of the following activities result in a version history for all Repository objects?
   A. A Repository object is recorded to a change request.
   B. Change requests are imported into an R/3 System, and the transport parameter `vers_at_imp` is activated.
   C. A task containing a Repository object is released.
   D. A change request containing a Repository object is released.

**Answer:** B, D

### Chapter 13: Importing Change Requests

1. Which of the following statements are correct in regard to import queues?
   A. Import queues are the TMS representation of the import buffer on the operating system level.
   B. You have to manipulate import queues to transport change requests.
   C. Import queues should be closed before starting an import using TMS.
   D. You can import only an entire import queue.

**Answer:** A, C

2. Which of the following statements are correct in regard to preliminary imports?

   A. SAP recommends using preliminary imports rather than imports of entire queues.

   B. Preliminary imports should be performed only in exceptional cases.

   C. Change requests imported as preliminary imports remain in the import queue.

   D. Change requests are deleted from the import queue after preliminary imports. This prevents them from being imported again with the next import of the entire import queue.

**Answer:** B, C

3. Which of the following statements is correct in regard to imports into an R/3 System?

   A. Imports can be performed only by using the **start import** functionality in the TMS.

   B. Imports can be performed only by using `tp` commands on the operating system level to prepare the import queue and then using the **start import** functionality in the TMS.

   C. Imports can be performed only by using `tp` commands at the operating system level.

   D. Imports can be performed by using either a `tp` command on the operating system level or the TMS import functionality.

**Answer:** D

4. Which of the following statements is correct in regard to transports between different transport groups?

   A. They are not possible.

   B. They can be performed only by using *tp* on the operating system level with special options.

   C. They can be performed using the TMS with special options provided by the expert mode.

   D. They require you to adjust the corresponding import queues.

**Answer:** D

5. Which of the following statements are correct in regard to transports between different transport domains?

   A. They are not possible.

   B. They require you to create a virtual system and a virtual transport directory.

   C. They require you to configure identical transport groups within the different transport domains.

D. They require you to create an external system and an external transport directory.

E. They require you to adjust the corresponding import queues.

**Answer:** D, E

### Chapter 14: Technical Insight—the Import Process

1. Which of the following statements are correct in regard to the transport control program `tp`?

   A. To perform imports, `tp` must always be used directly on the operating system level.

   B. SAP recommends that you use the TMS instead of `tp` to perform imports.

   C. `tp` is responsible for exporting and importing objects from and to R/3 Systems.

   D. `tp` does not observe the sequence of change requests in the import queue when performing imports.

**Answer:** B, C

2. Which of the following statements are correct in regard to import queues and import buffers?

   A. Import queues are the TMS representation in R/3 of the import buffer files on the operating system level.

   B. Import queues and import buffers are completely independent of each other.

   C. Import buffers have to be manipulated before imports can be performed on the operating system level.

   D. Manipulating import buffers may cause serious inconsistencies and should be performed only in exceptional cases.

**Answer:** A, D

3. Which of the following statements are correct in regard to the import options formerly known as *unconditional modes*?

   A. Import options cannot be used when imports are performed on the operating system level using `tp`.

   B. Import options are used to cause specific rules of the Change and Transport System (CTS) to be ignored.

   C. Import options must be used when importing into multiple clients using `tp`.

   D. Import options can be selected in the TMS using the expert mode.

**Answer:** B, C, D

4. Which of the following statements are correct in regard to the sequence of processing steps `tp` follows when performing imports?

   A. `tp` collectively processes each import step for all change requests in an import queue before proceeding with the next import step.

   B. `tp` processes all import steps for a single request before proceeding to the next change request.

   C. The processing sequence followed by `tp` ensures that when a change request with a faulty object is followed in the import queue by a change request with the corrected object, the faulty object will not affect the runtime environment of the target system.

   D. `tp` imports and activates ABAP Dictionary structures prior to the main import phase to ensure that the current structures are able to receive new data during the main import phase.

**Answer:** A, C, D

5. Which of the following statements are correct in regard to troubleshooting imports?

   A. In R/3, you cannot display log files that do not depend on a specific request. For example, you cannot display log files related to generic import steps, such as structure conversion.

   B. SAP recommends that you check the SLOG file and the ALOG file before checking the single step log files.

   C. By default, all return codes greater than eight cause *tp* to abort a running import.

   D. `tp` is the only transport tool that uses return codes.

**Answer:** A, B, C

6. Which of the following statements are correct in regard to buffer synchronization?

   A. Transport activities do not affect buffer synchronization.

   B. Imports affect buffer synchronization even in central R/3 Systems.

   C. `R3trans` can invalidate buffer content.

   D. Importing data into a production system can significantly impact performance, because some buffer content may be invalidated and reloaded. This causes high system load.

   E. Importing programs and ABAP Dictionary data cannot cause inconsistencies in the target system, even if the programs or data affect running programs and their environment.

**Answer:** B, C, D

7. Which of the following statements are correct in regard to the interaction between transport tools?

   A. During exports, `tp` calls `R3trans` to access the database of the source system and extract the objects to be transported.

   B. `tp` triggers the transport daemon `RDDIMPDP` in R/3 using the operating system tool `sapevt`.

   C. Using the tables TRBAT and TRJOB, `tp` communicates with ABAP programs involved in the transport process.

   D. `tp` communicates with only `RDDIMPD`.

**Answer:** A, B, C

### Chapter 15: Maintaining SAP Software

1. What are the benefits of importing SAP Support Packages?

   A. Proactive solution of known problems

   B. Functional extensions to SAP software

   C. Improved ease of maintenance and reduced time and effort for repairs and maintenance

**Answer:** A, C

2. Which of the following statements are true of the SAP Note Assistant?

   A. It simplifies the maintenance of programs in the customer namespace.

   B. It enables you to import Notes that contain code corrections.

   C. It simplifies the process of making changes to Data Dictionary objects.

   D. It identifies dependencies between SAP Notes.

   E. It can replace the process of importing Support Packages.

**Answer:** B, D

3. Which of the following statements are true of Support Packages?

   A. They change the SAP standard of your SAP system before the next release up-grade.

   B. You can import all types of Support Packages into all SAP systems, regardless of the components installed in the target system.

   C. Support Packages are available only to customers who are taking part in the ramp-up.

   D. Different types of Support Packages may be required for SAP systems with different components.

**Answer:** A, D

4. Which of the following statements are true of the SAP Patch Manager?
   A. The Patch Manager ensures that Support Packages are imported in the correct order.
   B. The SAP Patch Manager does not check whether the type of Support Package that you want to import is suitable for your SAP installation. You have to determine whether you need a particular Conflict Resolution Transport, for example.
   C. The SAP Patch Manager does not allow you to protect SAP objects that you have modified. These objects are automatically overwritten.
   D. The SAP Patch Manager automatically opens transactions SPDD and SPAU for the modification comparison process, if required.

**Answer:** A, D

5. Which of the following statements are true of Support Package stacks?
   A. Support Package stacks are combinations of Support Packages that are recommended by SAP.
   B. Support Package stacks should be imported only if an urgent problem is preventing an import from being carried out.
   C. Support Package stacks are Support Package combinations that have been particularly well tested by SAP.
   D. The SAPGUI version also must be upgraded to the latest level with every Support Package stack upgrade.

**Answer:** A, C

### Chapter 16: Change of SAP Release

1. Which of the following statements are true of the SAP release strategy?
   A. The so-called 5-1-2 maintenance strategy applies to all of the mySAP ERP products.
   B. New products first go through the so-called ramp-up phase.
   C. During the ramp-up phase, the product is already generally available.
   D. No SAP Support Packages are delivered during the ramp-up phase.

**Answer:** A, C

2. Which of the following statements are true of release changes?
   A. The objects in the customer namespace are not overwritten.
   B. A repository switch replaces your current repository with the repository in the new release.

C. All customer modifications to ABAP Dictionary objects are lost.

D. The customer modifications to SAP objects that you want to keep must be transferred to the new release via the modification adjustment.

**Answer:** A, B, D

3. Which of the following statements are true of the modification adjustment?

   A. Transaction SPAU is used for most of the ABAP Dictionary objects.

   B. Transaction SPDD is used for most of the ABAP Dictionary objects.

   C. If Transaction SPDD is not used although it is required, this can lead to data losses.

   D. During the modification adjustment, you must revert to the SAP standard version.

**Answer:** B, C

4. Which benefits are provided by the system switch upgrade?

   A. The system switch upgrade makes a modification adjustment redundant.

   B. The system switch upgrade makes the creation of a backup before the upgrade redundant.

   C. The system switch upgrade shortens the time during which the system cannot be used productively.

   D. The SPDD adjustment can be carried out before the beginning of the downtime.

**Answer:** C, D

### Chapter 17: SAP Solution Manager

1. Which of the following statements are true of Customizing Distribution?

   A. Customizing Distribution synchronizes Customizing settings in different systems.

   B. Customizing Distribution only works for systems with identical release statuses.

   C. Customizing Distribution can also be set up without SAP Solution Manager.

   D. Customizing Distribution usually takes place between development systems. The QA and production systems are provided with transport requests.

**Answer:** A, D

2. Which of the following statements are true of the Customizing Scout?
   A. The Customizing Scout can only be used for systems with identical release statuses.
   B. Comparison runs can be saved and displayed at a later point in time.
   C. It is always synchronization objects that are compared.
   D. Comparison runs can't be performed in the background.

**Answer:** B, C

3. Which of the following statements are true of Maintenance Projects?
   A. Urgent corrections can be created even if no maintenance project exists.
   B. Regular corrections can be released in any phase of a maintenance cycle.
   C. A maintenance project is created in Transaction SOLAR_PROJECT_ADMIN.
   D. A maintenance cycle is created in Transaction /TMWFLOW/CMSCONF.

**Answer:** C, D

4. Which of the following statements are true of Urgent Corrections?
   A. Urgent corrections can be part of a maintenance project or implementation project.
   B. Urgent corrections can also be directly released in Transaction STMS of the corresponding development system.
   C. Urgent corrections are controlled via the Schedule Manager.
   D. Urgent corrections must be approved by the Change Manager.

**Answer:** C

### Chapter 18: SAP NetWeaver Development Infrastructure

1. Which of the following statements about the NetWeaver Development Infrastructure (NWDI) are correct?
   A. It consists of several coordinated tools for designing, developing, and testing Java programs.
   B. It can be used both as a local and a central development environment.
   C. It is not suitable for teams with several developers.
   D. It is not suitable for transporting ABAP and Java components.

**Answer:** A, B

2. Which functions are fulfilled by the SAP Design Time Repository (DTR)?
   A. The DTR takes care of the central storage, versioning, and management of Java sources.
   B. The DTR provides automated conflict verifications.
   C. The DTR can also store Word files.
   D. The DTR manages archives that are required for software development.

**Answer:** A, B, C

3. Which functions are fulfilled by the SAP System Landscape Directory (SLD)?
   A. It is a tool for the central user management.
   B. It stores information about the system landscape.
   C. It works like a central data cache.
   D. It stores version information about the installed software components.

**Answer:** B, D

4. Which of the following services are required for Java transports?
   A. Java Activation Framework (JAF)
   B. Design Time Repository (DTR)
   C. Component Build Service (CBS)
   D. Change Management Service (CMS)
   E. Enterprise Information System (EIS)

**Answer:** B, C, D

# G The Authors

Armin Kösegi has been working in the Service & Support department of SAP AG since 1998. He specializes in the SAP NetWeaver Application Server. Besides handling problem tickets he focuses on development and delivery of support services in the area of software logistics. Furthermore, he is responsible for the various upgrade services of SAP Support.

For further questions you are welcome to contact Armin at *armin.koesegi@sap.com*.

Since 2000, Rainer Nerding has been working in the area of software change management at SAP Active Global Support. In the beginning, he was responsible for handling problem tickets. Today, he focuses on development and delivery of services and consulting offerings in the areas of software change management, upgrades, and Support Packages.

You are welcome to contact Rainer at *rainer.nerding@sap.com*.

# Index

## C

## D

## E



## F

## S

## U

## V



## W



## X



## Z

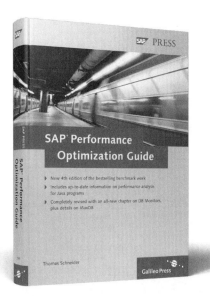

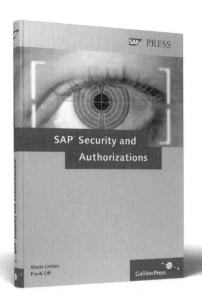

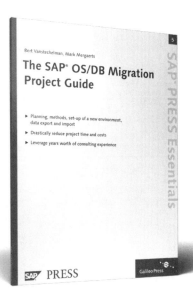

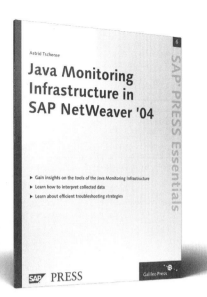

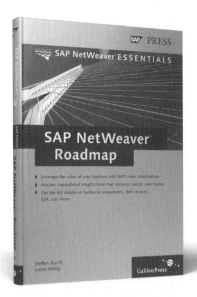